Writing & Fighting from the Army of Northern Virginia

WRITING & FIGHTING

FROM THE

ARMY OF NORTHERN VIRGINIA

Edited by WILLIAM B. STYPLE

Best Regards,
WMBStyple
Gettysburg Pa.

BELLE GROVE PUBLISHING CO.
2003

Belle Grove Publishing Co.
P. O. Box 483
Kearny, N. J. 07032
Email: bellegrove@worldnet.att.net
Website: bellegrovepublishing.com

ISBN 1-883926-20-3 (Hardcover)
ISBN 1-883926-21-1 (Softcover)

Library of Congress Control Number 2003091286

This book is the third volume in the Writing & Fighting the Civil War Series.

Volume One—Writing & Fighting the Civil War, Soldier Correspondence to the New York Sunday Mercury, ISBN 1-883926-13-0 Published September 2000.

Volume Two—Writing & Fighting the Confederate War, The Letters of Peter Wellington Alexander, Confederate War Correspondent, ISBN 1-883926-15-7 Published July 2002.

Table of Contents

Map of Virginia

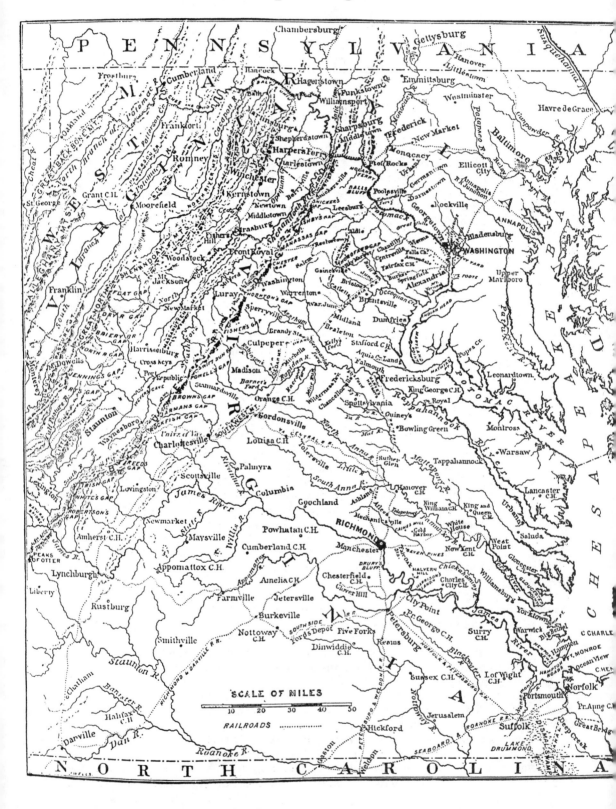

Preface

This book is the third in a series of volumes I began in 2000 with the release of *Writing & Fighting the Civil War: Soldier Correspondence to the New York Sunday Mercury*. At the outbreak of the Civil War the *Sunday Mercury* was the most popular weekly newspaper in the United States. After the firing on Fort Sumter and the interruption of communication between the North and South, the *Sunday Mercury* lost its Southern readership, a financial blow that nearly forced the paper out of business. Unable to hire professional war journalists and in desperate need of war news, publisher and editor William Cauldwell conceived the idea of asking the departing volunteers to serve as war correspondents, offering a free newspaper to every soldier who supplied a letter. This novel concept generated nearly 3,000 letters written from the battlefront during the course of the conflict, resulting in the *Sunday Mercury* becoming "the soldier's newspaper." Contrasting itself with other northern journals that had reporters following the army, observing, or interviewing General so-and-so, the *Sunday Mercury* stated that "our army of war correspondents are writing and fighting at the same time, and are, therefore, competent to describe the actions in which they bear their parts."

For me, the *Sunday Mercury* collection is the only authentic history of the Civil War; it is history written without hindsight, by those qualified to tell us what it was like. Out of this remarkable collection I selected 500 letters that best reflect the story of the Civil War as it was seen through the eyes of the common soldier. Because the *Sunday Mercury* correspondence is exclusively Union, my thoughts naturally turned to one day creating a Confederate volume— letters written on the same day, from a different trench.

In 2001, while researching at Columbia University, I discovered the Peter Wellington Alexander Letter Collection. "P. W. A." was a war correspondent for the *Savannah Republican* and several other Georgia newspapers. As the war progressed, Alexander's fame grew and his dispatches began to appear in almost every paper in the Confederacy; when the war was finished, he had written nearly 800 letters from the front and proposed writing a history of the Confederacy. Unfortunately, Alexander died before completing his project.

In 2002, in recognition of Alexander's long-forgotten contribution, I published *Writing & Fighting the Confederate War: The Letters of Peter Wellington Alexander*, a collection of 250 of his wartime letters, providing another fresh insight to the history of the Civil War.

Among the "P. W. A." archive (numbering 7,500 letters and documents), I also found a large collection of Confederate soldier correspondence that either appeared in print alongside Alexander's columns, or had been clipped by him—possibly for his proposed history. Since Alexander was a Georgian, who primarily wrote for Georgia newspapers, the majority of letters in his collection are by soldiers from that state. After reading these letters, I felt they were a perfect Confederate complement to the *Sunday Mercury* book, and the third volume in the *Writing & Fighting* series was underway.

For this volume, as letters from the western theater of operations were scarce, I decided to use letters written exclusively from the foremost fighting organization of the Confederate States—the Army of Northern Virginia.

In existence for a mere 200 weeks, the Army of Northern Virginia, led by General Robert E. Lee and his lieutenants, became no less honored and remembered than the soldiers of Alexander, Caesar or Napoleon. After Appomattox, survivors penned memoirs, poets composed verse and historians wrote countless volumes, albeit always in post-war reflection.

The purpose of this volume is to present a real-time documentary of that army—a record written by its soldiers unknowing of the outcome.

After amassing approximately 350 soldier letters for the years 1861-1863, I was disappointed to find only 50 or so for the final fifteen months of the war. Of course, this lack of communication is understandable given the hard campaigning, scarcity of writing materials, loss of territory to Federal occupation, and, above all, the increasing casualties amongst the corps of correspondents. Despite the setback, I selected 300 letters to best tell the story of the Army of Northern Virginia as it was seen through the eyes of the common soldier, basing the letter selection on historical importance, content, descriptive quality, and the ability to guide the reader through the conflict. With few exceptions, I arranged the letters in chronological order as they were written, and not as they were published (some letters, owing to the slowness of the mails, took longer to reach their destination).

I have also included many personal letters written by the soldiers. Frequently, the family of a soldier would make available for publication a "private letter," meaning a personal communication written without publication in mind. These private letters were passed along to an editor, and by appearing in a hometown newspaper, provided a very useful service for the community: these shared letters, written by soldiers away in Virginia, supplied important news to many other worried friends and families at home.

It was common practice for many soldier correspondents to add a dash of adventurous romance to their letters by using a *nom de plume* such as *Soldier Jim*, *Tout le Monde*, *Bohemia*, or *Potomac*. Soldiers more commonly signed their letters with simple initials, or perhaps an editor might utilize three asterisks (***) in place of initials for complete anonymity. For those correspondents whom I could positively identify, I have included a short biographical sketch. To provide a timeline, I have also included a brief description of the course of military events, major battles, campaigns, etc. All of my comments appear in italics.

For editing purposes, I have used brackets to identify persons, regiments, locations and dates. Immediately following each letter date is the date of publication and in which newspaper the letter appeared. All italic emphasis within the letters is as it appeared in print, done either by the paper's editor or typesetter or letter writer. I have left misspellings uncorrected and without a *sic*. Some letters contain disturbing racial epithets and other offensive terminology; however, in order to preserve the historical integrity of the letters, I have refrained from removing any such material.

It is with great pleasure that I would like to mention all those who have assisted me in the preparation of this volume. First is Sonia Krutzke, whose grammatical criticism I always welcome. Also, my sincere thanks to: Ed Bearss, John Valori, Brian Pohanka, Jack Fitzpatrick, Rob Hodge, Dr. Richard Sommers at the U. S. Army War College at Carlisle Barracks, Steve Zerbe at the Civil War Library in Philadelphia, Bernard Crystal and the librarians at the Columbia University Rare Book and Manuscript Library, Seton Hall University, University of Georgia, and the Kearny Public Library.

Extra special love and thanks to my devoted family: Nancy, Kim and Brad.

William B. Styple
February 22, 2003

Newspaper abbreviations:
AWCS—*Augusta Weekly Chronicle & Sentinel*
ASC—*Atlanta Southern Confederacy*
CS—*Columbus Sun*
MAR—*Mobile Advertiser & Register*
RDD—*Richmond Daily Dispatch*
SR—Savannah Republican

☆☆☆ Spirit of '61

After the election of Abraham Lincoln as President of the United States on November 6, 1860, decades old political tension between the Northern and Southern United States boiled over. The State of South Carolina, choosing to exercise the right of secession, left the Union on December 20, 1860. Mississippi, Florida, Alabama, Georgia, Louisiana and Texas soon followed, and a Southern Confederacy was formed in February 1861, electing Jefferson Davis as its first president. The shooting war began on April 12, in Charleston Harbor, when Federal forces at Fort Sumter refused to surrender to Confederate authorities.

On April 15, President Abraham Lincoln called for 75,000 militia from loyal northern and border states to quell the insurrection. Two days later, the State of Virginia adopted an ordinance of secession, and the State Convention instructed the Governor, John Letcher, to use the militia to protect Virginia from any Federal encroachment. Shortly thereafter, Arkansas, Tennessee and North Carolina also left the Union. On May 20, the Provisional Congress of the Confederate States of America chose the city of Richmond, Virginia, as their capital—95 miles south of the Federal capital of Washington, D. C. Spontaneously, more than a hundred thousand citizen soldiers, north and south, rushed to their capitals to settle the matter once and for all.

LETTER TO THE EDITOR
ATLANTA SOUTHERN CONFEDERACY April 15, 1861 [4-18-61ASC]

Dear Editor: Now that the scurvy, long-eared, knock-kneed, hog-backed, lantern-jawed, turkey-trodden, trumpet-bellied, cushion-footed Rail-splitter, Abe Lincoln, has turned loose his "*dogs* of war," against the true, generous, long forbearing, God-fearing, God-serving, heaven-desiring, patriotic people of the Confederate States, let us all, without distinction of party or sex, be up and doing, and give his Black Republicanship's hireling Hessian hordes, a caloric reception.

There are, within this city, mothers, wives, sisters, and, maybe, lovers, of the gallant and patriotic soldiers, who have recently buckled on their armor and departed from Atlanta for the seat of war. The question is, shall these brave representatives of the "Gate City" be neglected or forgotten? Say, never! The honor and patriotism of those left behind, forbid it! I suggest, therefore, that a meeting of the ladies of Atlanta, married and single, be at once called, and that plans be adopted by them to supply the surgeons of our troops with lint, bandages, and such other appliances as may be needed in the medical department of the army, for the comfort and cure of the disabled soldiers after the battle shall have been fought and the victory won.

Already the ladies of Charleston, furnished the soldiers, on duty, in her harbor, with an abundance of bandages, lint, and many other conveniences, calculated to soothe the sufferings of those who may fall in the conflict, or be wounded in the defense of the rights of the right, the homes and firesides, of the people of the South, in their struggle for our independence and freedom from abolition domination and free-soil subserviencey. And shall the women of Atlanta be behind their Palmetto sisters of Charleston in efforts to enhance the comfort and meliorate the sufferings of the gallant braves, who, at their country's call, have marched to the field of danger, and who are ever ready to risk their lives and sacrifice all for their protection and defense?

A bloody conflict is impending. No time is to be lost, and whatever is done in the way of carrying out the foregoing suggestions, should be promptly and immediately done.

SPIRIT OF '76.

ADVICE TO VOLUNTEERS,
HOW TO PREPARE FOR THE CAMPAIGN [5-7-61ASC]

1. Remember that in a campaign more men die from sickness than by the bullet.
2. Line your blanket with one thickness of brown drilling. This adds but four ounces in weight and doubles the warmth.

3. Buy a small India Rubber Blanket (only $1.50) to lay on the ground, or to throw over your shoulders when on duty during a rain storm. Most of the Eastern troops are provided with these. Straw to lie on is not always to be had.
4. The best military hat in use is the light-colored soft felt; the crown being sufficiently high to allow space for air over the brain. You can fasten it up as a continental in the fair weather, or turn it down when it is very wet or sunny.
5. Let your beard grow, so as to protect the throat and lungs.
6. Keep your entire person clean; this prevents fevers and bowel complaints in warm climates. Wash your body each day, if possible. Avoid strong coffee and oily meat. Gen. [Winfield] Scott said that the too free use of these (together with neglect in keeping the skin clean) cost many a soldier his life in Mexico.
7. A sudden check of perspiration by chilly weather or night air often causes fever and death. When thus exposed do not forget the blanket.

AN OLD SOLDIER.

☆☆☆To Virginia! Eager for the Fray

Throughout the newly formed Confederacy, thousands of volunteers, regulars, state troops, and local militia companies, rushed to Virginia for a chance to take part in the great battle for independence. And to keep the population of the infant nation informed of gallant deeds and Yankee treachery, letters to the editors of hometown newspapers and private letters given to the editors for publication became the exclusive means of communicating doings at the scene of strife.

THIRD REGIMENT ALABAMA VOLUNTEERS
HEADQUARTERS, LYNCHBURG, VA., May 6, 1861 [5-11-61CS]

There are said to be 5,000 volunteers now encamped near this city, equipping thoroughly for the coming campaign. Both regiments of Alabama Volunteers are here with ten full companies each. In their ranks are to be found the very flower of the young men of the various sections of the State from which they came. I doubt very much whether two thousand finer looking, or more robust men will be found in the Confederate army during the war. Our Regiment is quartered near the Fair grounds, and is being equipped as speedily as the great press upon the Quartermaster's Department will permit. The weather is cold, rainy and of course very inclement, yet the men are cheerful, and put up with the inconvenience of our present situation without murmuring.

When the weather permits, the ladies throng our encampment, and manifest their kindly feelings by generous offers of assistance in any way they can be of service to us.

The act of the convention dissolving the connection of the State with the late Union meets with universal favor. The people are alive with enthusiasm for our gallant President and the Southern Confederacy. Volunteer companies are organizing throughout the State, and "old Virginia," will give a good account of herself when Lincoln "turns loose the dogs of war," as he threatens to do.

This city has already sent three thoroughly organized companies to Richmond and three more are anxiously awaiting orders to march.

Col. [Robert E.] Lee, the gallant commander of the Virginia State troops, has inspired the greatest confidence, and the people are rallying to his standard with unwonted enthusiasm. The Confederate States flag is to be seen proudly kissing the breeze from hilltop to vale all along the railroads, while the cry of determined resistance to Republican rule reverberates from the mountains to the seaboard. The "railsplitter" may devastate and ruin this fair land, he may lay its cities and towns and beautiful cottages in ashes, but he can never conquer its spirited people and make them bow their proud necks to his abject yoke—never—never!

As opportunity offers, I will comply with your request and send you an occasional letter.

HOLMES.

FROM AN OCCASIONAL CORRESPONDENT
HARPER'S FERRY, VA., May 6, 1861 [5-13-61 SR]

Mr. Editor: The ever-gushing waters and craggy mountains which stamp this place with one of nature's patents of nobility, might seem to bid man to check his wanton passions, and be governed by the Creator of this wild beauty. But fanaticism mocks at this bidding, and here drew the blood which hurried on this crisis; while blackened embers and warped iron record the malicious destruction of what it could not use. Nor is the tragedy yet ended. The loathsome serpent of Federalism has twisted his coils around the heart of Maryland, and as soon as they are sufficiently tightened upon Baltimore, he will dart out his fangs against this point sooner or later, though Alexandria, Norfolk or Savannah may receive the first shock. But this *black* (Republican) snake will find brave defenders to every nest where he may seek his booty. Lincoln's troops (some 2,000) have possession of the Relay House, where they inspect the trains and search all baggage they deem suspicious. By Thursday night [May 9] they will have subjugated Baltimore or laid it in ashes. Now the Baltimoreans have no fancy for this latter contingency, so they will bow to the blast, and champ the cruel bit, as the people of Venice are doing now, with similar hopes of deliverance. If the presence of northern troops at Chambersburg and Gettysburg, in Pennsylvania, does not sufficiently overawe the Maryland Legislature at Frederick city, a detachment can be sent in a few hours from the Relay House to Frederick Junction, which will effectually do the business.

The weather here is horrid, but must soon brighten; the air is milder to-day, and the mountain-side is visibly assuming a greener tint. That one across the Potomac, on the Maryland shore, rises precipitously from the canal, at its base, for several hundred feet, then trends up at a sharp angle till it meets the summit ridge. It commands this point, but we shall see. Our scouts are out on the opposite shore and at Point of Rocks, and our cannon can sweep the bridges. The Virginians are doing as well as can be expected of raw troops. Six hundred Kentuckians arrived yesterday, stout and resolute looking men. They will be armed here as they brought no weapons but their knives. The rifle factory on the Shenandoah is in operation. The machinery from the musket factory on the Potomac is being slowly moved to Winchester for Richmond; 14,000 muskets were burnt here.

Col. [Thomas T.] Fauntleroy, of the United States army was arrested here to-day, in disobedience of orders, but immediately released by the gentlemanly and efficient commander here, Colonel [Thomas J.] Jackson.

There has been no demonstration against Washington by the Virginians, that I know of. Lincoln can take Alexandria whenever he pleases.

Yours truly,   STRANGER.

Col. Charles D. Dreux commanding the First Battalion of Louisiana troops arrived in Virginia in early June. Just before leaving for the front lines near Yorktown, Colonel Dreux penned the following letter to his wife.

PRIVATE LETTER, FIRST LOUISIANA BATTALION
RICHMOND, VA., June 18, 1861 [7-23-61ASC]

Dear Wife: I wrote you a long letter yesterday, and, as if Providence wished to encourage me in writing to my own dear M., I received almost at the same time a long, welcome, and long wished for letter from you. It makes my heart beat with emotions of noble patriotism, when I read the burning words of inspiration that flow from your pen. In fact, I have read a few passages of your letters to my fellow soldiers, and every one ardently wished that he had such a brave and noble hearted wife.

The days of political differences and party feuds are gone, and only one spirit animates us all. The invaders are at our gates and they must be repelled. You have, doubtless, before this, read of the glorious victory achieved by our troops a few days ago at Bethel Church. I have seen and conversed with eye witnesses of the battle. The Yankees ran away like whipped curs, leaving for over five miles all their muskets, canteens, knapsacks, etc., on the ground. It was a perfect rout, a complete defeat. The moral effect produced by that exploit on the part of the troops is not easily to be estimated. The Southern volunteers are all awake and "eager for the fray," and Richmond looks like a "champ de Mars," so many soldiers are to be seen around it.

You hear nothing here but the sound of the drums, the piercing notes of the fife and rumblings of heavy wagons loaded with heavy war baggage. Troops move every day and every hour. To tell you the truth, my dear, we also have to move. The orders have just been received by me from the Adjutant General, and the camp is now in a stir preparing to move, army and baggage. We are ordered from this place to Yorktown, within eight miles of the enemy's line, and most glorious prospects of an early and good brush. When there we shall be under command of Col. [John B.] Magruder, who succeeded so well in his *debut* at Bethel Church. The boys are delighted with the prospects before them, and we all are in the highest glee.

May the God of Battles smile upon us. Cheer up, my dear wife. I have brave hearts and strong arms to sustain and cheer me on, and I feel confident of the result. Many a noble son of Louisiana may fall by my side, and I may be the first one to bite the dust, but rest assured that they or I will always be worthy of the esteem and respect of our countrymen, and endeavor to deserve well of our country. When I reach Norfolk I shall write again, and give you full particulars. Rest assured, until you hear from me or until the telegraph gives you bad news of our expedition. Come what may, my dear, I belong to my country, and you know you belong to me. One and all, all in one, we owe our duty and lives to both. Were you as good and brave a man as you are a true and noble woman, I know I would have you by my side, fighting with all your might the base and miserable invaders.

Excuse me, dearest, for the digression. To-morrow we leave for the seat of war. What to-morrow will bring forth I know not; but through prosperity of adversity, opulence or poverty, easiness or danger, I am still your own dear C. Tell father I am ashamed to promise to write, for he may know I shall break my promise. Kiss one and all for me at home; press your sweet little darling to your heart, and tell her to love and cherish you for the sake and love of her dear papa.

Your own,   C.

This was the last letter Colonel Dreux wrote to his wife. On July 5, Colonel Dreux led 100 volunteers on an ambuscade near Newport News and during the ensuing skirmish he was shot and killed. Col. Charles Dreux was the first Confederate officer of note to be killed in action.

LETTER FROM THE ATLANTA GRAYS
[COMPANY F, EIGHTH GEORGIA INFANTRY]
PINE GROVE CAMPGROUND, RICHMOND, VA., June 1, 1861 [6-6-61ASC]

I will endeavor to give you a few dots in regard to the condition of our Company. We arrived here on Friday [May 24], A. M. at 10 o'clock—marched to the Fairfield Camp Ground—remained there until Monday evening, and then moved to the Pine Grove Camps, recently occupied by the First Regiment of North Carolina, now at Norfolk. Our members are generally healthy at present, though we have had some sickness, mostly from exposure and loss of sleep in coming from Atlanta to Richmond. We are now comfortably situated in a large and beautiful grove, with plenty of water and everything calculated to render the soldier healthy. Col. [Francis S.] Bartow is very strict, but every man expresses a willingness to do whatever he instructs, and also anxious to meet the Lincolnites. We expect orders to march from Richmond as soon as all the Regiment is formed, provided the Yankees don't make a rush to this city, which is expected.

I suppose there are fifteen thousand Confederate soldiers stationed around Richmond, besides thousands that have marched away from here. They are marching in continually from every Southern State.

Alexandria is taken by Federal troops, but from the way our men are marching in, I don't think they will hold the place long. Several of our corps that were left behind have arrived. We have at present ninety-seven men, and expecting others to-day, who will fill the ranks. We have dress parade every evening at 5 o'clock, and are visited very extensively by the patriotic ladies of Richmond. On yesterday evening I made several acquaintances among the ladies, and received several bouquets which was very cheering to soldier Jim. I expect to visit the city on the afternoon to-day.

My love to all, especially the young ladies of Atlanta.

SOLDIER JIM.

"Soldier Jim" was Cpl. James A. Adair of Company F, 8th Georgia Infantry and cousin of George W. Adair, publisher of the Atlanta Southern Confederacy.

THIRD ALABAMA VOLUNTEERS

ENTRENCHMENT CAMP, NEAR NORFOLK, VA., June 1, 1861 [6-7-61CS]

Since my last letter to you the Third Regiment Alabama Volunteers, has changed its position from the left to the right wing of the line it occupied at that date, being the third camp we have pitched since our arrival in this neighborhood. These several changes have imposed upon us no small amount of exposure, inconvenience and hard labor. To an outsider, it seems that the move, from our encampment at Lynchburg to our present quarters, would have been amply sufficient without entailing upon us the trouble and inconvenience of preparing to be comfortable in two intermediate camps, which were occupied about one week each, not to mention the expense incurred by our several changes. Of course your correspondent is not permitted to look behind the scenes and know the reasons prompting those in authority to such movements. They may have been unavoidable and necessary to the public welfare, and the safety and defense of the kind and generous people among whom our fortunes were temporarily cast. However this may be, they certainly indicate the great want of systematic arrangement and wise concert of action on the part of the departments having the control and direction of the military operations in this branch of the service.

Virginia having ratified the act of secession by a unanimity hitherto unparalleled in the history of States, by the almost unanimous voice of her people, having united her destiny with that of the Southern Confederacy, the control of military operations will now be turned over to the government of the Confederate States, and the genius of our President—the warrior statesman—will speedily bring order out of confusion, and infuse new life and vigor into all these operations.

The entrenchments in front of our camp is rapidly approaching completion, under the constant labor of some three hundred able-bodied negro fellows, collected from various quarters of the State especially for this work. When completed and mounted, as it is expected to be, it will be utterly impossible for the vandal hordes of the demoralized North to reach the city of Norfolk by land from this direction. It will be defended, beside our regiment, by one from North Carolina, and two, perhaps three, from this good old State—being in the aggregate, four or five thousand men eager to meet the cruel invader, whose hellish motto is "Beauty and Booty," and administer to him that chastisement he richly merits.

The published accounts of the actings and doings of Lincoln's army of clouts and scavengers, at Alexandria, have filled the cup of indignation to overflowing and terrible will be the vengeance dealt out to them, by an outraged people, when the day of retribution comes. That day, in the order of time, is rapidly approaching, when the blood of the martyr [James W.] Jackson, and the insults to unoffending womanhood will be abundantly avenged. It may be delayed, but it will certainly come; and when it passes away the cause of the South will stand out in bold relief before an admiring world, amply vindicated. Ten millions of people, armed with justice and fighting for their homes and firesides, for the protection of their wives and daughters, can never be subjugated by a fanatical and mercenary foe. This vandal foe has landed a large body of troops at Newport News, taken possession of the quiet town of Hampton, driven its peaceful inhabitants from their homes, and by acts of cruelty, disgraceful even to savage tribes of untutored Indians, has added largely to that awful account of wrongdoing for which ample atonement will, ere long, be demanded and exacted by an outraged people. Payment will be determined to the uttermost farthing, and the just vengeance of an insulted people amply satisfied, before our swords are returned to their scabbards, and peace smiles upon our borders.

HOLMES.

LETTER FROM VIRGINIA

RICHMOND, VA., June 2, 1861 [6-7-61ASC]

As a drop or two of heavy rain, and a slight rustle among the leafy trees, *precede* the bursting of an angry storm, so do our recent fierce skirmishes with the "Black foe" forebode that we are on the eve of important battles, *soon* to be fought and decided upon the soil of the Old Dominion.

On Saturday [June 1] there came to the city a well authenticated declaration that a fight occurred between two picket guards of the armies, near Fairfax Court House, in the vicinity of Alexandria, each numbering 25 men. The "Blacks" were stated to have been totally routed, losing seven or eight killed and others wounded. Our loss was represented to have been one or two killed and perhaps as many wounded.

Capt. [John Q.] Marr of Fauquier, a gallant officer and member of the State Convention, was reported to have been killed.

Later and more reliable intelligence says that a considerable body of United States horsemen galloped rapidly into Fairfax Court House, about day break in the morning, with the hope to surprise and cut to pieces a small body of soldiers they knew to be stationed there. Capt. Marr was instantly killed by them, and several others seriously wounded.

Our men immediately recovered from their astonishment and fought, it is said, with the ferocity of tigers—scattering the marauders, who came as thieves in the night, like chaff before the wind. Fully fifteen of their party were killed on the spot, a good many severely wounded, and an equal number of valuable horses captured by our brave little band, who, in the *defense of their homes and flag*, fought as did the heroic Jackson—each showing, like him, the unconquerable spirit of a Marco-Bozzaris.

There can be no doubt that we are now on the eve of important and bloody battles, and notes of preparation will soon give place to the clash of resounding arms. The *people are demanding* with one loud voice that the hell-born vagabonds who have invaded their sacred soil, captured their cities, murdered in cold blood their inhabitants, and outraged their shrieking women, *shall be consigned at one gigantic swoop of our brave armies*, to the everlasting overthrow and destruction they so richly deserve.

Our forces will no longer remain idle. Aggressive movements and pressing invitations to battle from the Confederate troops must now be looked for. Ten thousand soldiers are expected to pass through here on to-morrow, destined for some of the points where engagements are early contemplated.

Gen. [Milledge L.] Bonham of South Carolina, with about 10,000 men under his command, is within 20 miles of Alexandria, where, at present, he is making a stand. His men are said to be eager and panting for a fight, and are prevented with great difficulty from marching to Alexandria where are quartered Lincoln's army of invasion, who retreated from where they had formerly advanced into the city to avoid a battle with Bonham's South Carolinians, although they exceeded them at the time in numbers. Bonham may, within the next day or two, be ordered to attack the Lincolnites at Alexandria, and both armies be strengthened and swollen by reinforcements until the battle at that point shall be made terrible and decisive in its results.

About 20,000 troops guard Harper's Ferry, and the place has been so strongly fortified that the best military judgements now declare it to be perfectly impregnable. The approaches to the place are all defended by heavy and numerous pieces of artillery; and an assault by any number of men, it is believed could be easily repelled.

President Davis, in company with the Governor and Mayor, visited on Friday last, the "Camp of Instruction," situated on the border of the city, and whilst reviewing the troops there, a soldier who stood near him in the ranks, rushed franticly forward and throwing his arms about the neck of the warrior President, kissed him with tender earnestness.

After the incident, the President addressed some stirring remarks to the military, which elicited their warmest applause. On yesterday, however, an event occurred that seemed to cast a dark shade over the faces of our brave military: a large portion of a Tennessee Regiment of Volunteers refused to accept the guns, flint-lock muskets, tendered them by the State. Gov. [Henry A.] Wise, in a speech made at the Spottswood Hotel last night, declared such conduct to be cowardly and treasonable, and said if no guns could be procured, they must fight with scythe blades, pitch-forks, or pikes like those prepared by John Brown for the first invasion of the blessed old Commonwealth.

The remarks were greeted with loud applause.

OBSERVER.

LETTER FROM VIRGINIA

RICHMOND, VA., Monday, June 3, 1861 [6-8-61ASC]

The sacred inviolability of Virginia's soil is being trampled to the dust, by an infuriate mob, upon almost every portion of her border. At innumerable points is her *sovereignty insulted* by an armed and lawless foe.

Norfolk is threatening menaced, and Hampton, a village near there, is in the possession of her enemies. All the approaches and heights surrounding Alexandria are being diligently strengthened and guarded by the "Blacks," whilst the whole line of the Potomac is under the strict watch of the unprincipled marauders.

Black Republican forces from Ohio, have penetrated as far as Grafton, in North-Western Virginia, and as far as Charleston, in the county of Kanawha.

Wheeling, the *Sodom* of the *putrid North-West*, is in the hands of traitors to our cause, and Federal support is supplied freely to the disaffected people in that section.

The movement of occupation in the North-West is under the command of Gen. [George B.] McClellan, whose proclamation to the citizens is of the most flattering nature—assuring them that no interference will be made with *their slaves*, but, on the contrary, any attempt *at insurrection will be crushed with an iron hand.* His available force will, in a short time, be swollen, by additional forces from Ohio, North-Western Virginia and Pennsylvania, to 20 or 25,000 men.

His destination is believed to be Harper's Ferry, where he will arrive simultaneously with the command of Gen. [Robert] Patterson, on the Maryland side, when the attack will be made upon Harper's Ferry from different points.

No ground, however, as yet (except in the Abolition North-West), has the *foul invader* dared to venture on, where our enraged and burning soldiery can meet him in fair field and open fight.

His steamers are continually presenting themselves at Aquia Creek and other places where we have coast defenses, but are always welcomed with a salute of *iron indignation*, at which they move off to repair damages.

On yesterday, 500 shots are reported to have been exchanged between our battery at Aquia Creek and three of the enemy's vessels. The particulars are not yet known.

On last Friday and Saturday severe fighting occurred between four steamers and a company of artillery in possession of the same battery. Several of the men were killed during the first day's engagement, and two of their vessels badly injured.

On Saturday, the fight was kept up for six or seven hours, the vessels firing between six and seven hundred shots, without inflicting the slightest injury.

Our battery is reported to have fired 150 shots, many of which took almost fatal effect, carrying away the flag of the *Anacostia*, and cutting down the mast of a large propeller.

Private intelligence says the Lincoln Government are throwing regiment after regiment into Alexandria, and will soon organize the *great invading column*, which will move against Manassas Junction, a short distance above Alexandria, give battle to the Confederate forces there, and *if victorious, proceed at once to visit Jeff Davis at his head quarters in this city.*

This *grand movement* will be made by an enormous army of picked men, numbering between forty and fifty thousand.

The possession of Manassas Junction, where the battle will be fought, is indispensably essential to the protection of the rear of out army at Harper's Ferry, as in arresting the *penetration* of the invading column into the interior of the Commonwealth.

Impressed with the terrible import of this battle, and the momentous results that hang upon it, our gallant army will fight until every turf between Manassas and Richmond *shall become a soldier's sepulchre, and streams of blood and carnage ascend to heaven.*

OBSERVER.

LETTER FROM VIRGINIA

RICHMOND, VA., June 4, 1861 [6-10-61ASC]

Our city has been unusually quiet for several days past. The people have become so accustomed to the sight of soldiers that the arrival or departure of a regiment scarcely excites any attention. Nearly all the regiments which were encamped near Richmond, have gone to the "seat of the war."

Col. Bartow's regiment of Georgians is still encamped at Howard's Grove, a delightful locality beyond the eastern suburbs, but they expect marching orders at any moment.

The arrivals to-day embrace Col. [E. B. C.] Cash's regiment from South Carolina, and the celebrated Battalion of Artillery—the "Washington"—from New Orleans. It was gratifying to observe that both came well armed and equipped for service.

In Virginia there is no lack of men, but, unfortunately, we are deficient in arms. We have the consolation of knowing, however, if figures do not lie, that there are muskets and rifles enough in the Confederacy to arm 400,000 men—a larger force than will, probably, be required to convince the Yankees of the impossibility of subjugating the freemen of the South.

Every day some new rumor is put in circulation, and furnishes the staple of town talk until it is ascertained to be false, or is superceded by fresher reports. Yesterday it was currently asserted that another fight had taken place at Fairfax Court House, between Col. [Joseph B.] Kershaw's regiment from South Carolina, and a large body of the enemy, resulting in the total route of the enemy. It is sufficient to say, that the report "lacks confirmation." The rumor to-day is that five thousand Lincoln troops have arrived at Martinsburg, near Harper's Ferry. This is doubtful.

RICHMOND.

THIRD ALABAMA REGIMENT

ENTRENCHED CAMP, NEAR NORFOLK, VA., June 7, 1861 [6-15-61CS]

On the night of the 4th inst., our whole camp was thrown into great excitement by an order which was received at 8 o'clock, P. M., ordering a detail of one hundred men, with knapsacks, blankets and ammunition, to report forthwith to an officer at quarters about one mile from our encampment. The object of the detail was not known to a single man in all our camp and the inference was that the vandals had effected a landing, and the chance for a brush with them was good. The boys were all anxious to be on the detail, and have a place in our first engagement, and great was the disappointment of the nine hundred who were passed over. Six weeks of camp life passing in idly drilling have not abated the ardor of our Southern troops, or lessened their intense anxiety to meet the heartless invader, and administer the chastisement he so richly merits. Nor have the accounts of his actings and doings in Alexandria and Hampton had a tendency to ameliorate the terribleness of that punishment when their wishes are gratified in the storm and tempest of battle. Then, methinks, outraged virtue, and insulted manhood will be satisfied with the sacrifice, when slaughtered hecatombs of heartless wretches shall smoke upon the alter, the victims of that righteous vengeance which tens of thousands of the bravest and best of our proud and indignant people are carefully treasuring against them.

The night's detail proved a grand mistake, and a sore disappointment to those who were ordered out. It seems the detail was intended to make fascines for the embankment, and the order was issued at Division Head Quarters in the morning, but was not delivered until 8 at night. Our ammunition is distributed, and our arms in perfect order, and nothing would please our boys better than a trial of skill with some of the boasted regiments of the North.

Last Sunday was a bright, beautiful day. Strictly regarding the sanctity of the day no duties were attended to but the weekly company inspection, Guard Mounting and the Indispensable Dress Parade. A rustic alter had been erected beneath the shadow of some wide-spreading Mulberry and Locust trees near the centre of the encampment, and at 10¼ o'clock the drum called to the services of the sanctuary. It was a beautiful sight to see hundreds of brave men gather promptly around the rural pulpit and, as the venerable chaplain entered the stand, reverently uncover their heads and evidence by the strictest propriety of behavior, their high respect for the solemn services before them. The sermon was a most excellent practical exposition of the text. "Thy commandment is exceedingly broad," in which the preacher, with great fidelity rebuked many of those vices in which men with our surroundings are more or less liable to indulge.

For several days there has been a perfect stagnation in the way of fighting. Even Madam Rumor with her fertile imagination, has been unable to manufacture a skirmish for yesterday; however, we heard brisk cannonading for sometime, and have heard there was an engagement at Pig's Point [on June 5], on the Nansemond river, between the famous *Harriet Lane* and our batteries there; of the particulars we have, as yet, no reliable accounts, though it is said the cutter was severely damaged. The *Harriet Lane* is a great gad-about, and has a very wide range. She is occasionally seen at almost every point along the coast, and now and then approaches with great independence, near the guns. Some of these days a well-directed shot from one of our batteries will strike her between wind and water and cut short her daring career.

The young man Hunt, who killed Lieut. Storrs of the Wetumpka Light Guards, while on duty as a sentinel, was tried on last Tuesday upon the charge of murder and acquitted. A jury of his country, after an impartial investigation, has pronounced him innocent, and the unfortunate killing purely accidental.

The work upon the entrenchment is progressing bravely. Guns will shortly be mounted upon it, and then Norfolk will be impregnable to any force the vandals can bring against it.

Miss Augusta Evans, the distinguished Southern authoress, is in our camp, passing among her numerous acquaintances, and gladdening their hearts by her pleasant words and beaming smiles. It is said she aspires to be the Florence Nightengale of this most glorious revolution, and surely no one possesses higher qualifications for the mission than the author of *Beulah*.

The weather for a day or two has been disagreeably wet and unpleasant, giving us a foretaste of what we may expect in the way of mud and water when a rainy season comes. Fortunately for us our tents are generally good and well floored, and therefore quite comfortable under any circumstances.

A "box of eatables" is always very acceptable to the soldiers. A lady in North Carolina claimed the "pleasant privilege based upon long standing friendship" of sending your correspondent one well filled with such good things as only the refined Housewives of the South can prepare. To-day it arrived, and its choice contents were highly enjoyed by a circle of appreciative friends. Among other things there was a bouquet of roses pleasantly reminding him of a quiet little home, a thousand miles away, where the "Queen of flowers," in a hundred varieties, sheds her fragrance for the enjoyment of wife, children and friends.

HOLMES.

Miss Augusta Evans was the foremost female novelist of her time. Her nursing career began during a yellow fever epidemic in Mobile, and the experience inspired her novel Beulah. Later in the war she established a hospital near Mobile.

LETTER FROM VIRGINIA

RICHMOND, VA., Monday, June 10, 1861 [6-16-61ASC]

On Saturday last [June 8] there came a startling report that between three and four thousand Federal troops had landed on a portion of the Mount Vernon Estate, about twelve miles below Alexandria. The rumor has since been confirmed in all its essential features, and Federal forces to the number of 3,000 men were landed on Saturday at "White House Point," situated about twenty miles from the Aquia Creek Battery, who will begin offensive operations on land instead of the water, where our gallant Battery so often repulsed and crippled their largest war vessels.

Reliable information has also been received that 800 South Carolinians had been thrown forward, and others were to start immediately to attack the enemy.

The Federal troops now in the occupation of North-Western Virginia, are variously estimated to be between ten and twenty thousand in number. Whether they will move against Harper's Ferry or march further into Western Virginia, hoping to give predominance to the

Union feeling by their work of bloody coercion, affords a subject for conjecture. These, however, are not conjectures: the term of their tyranny is short—a killing frost will soon fall. Death's approach is terribly near. Ten days more and their odoriferous stench of their oppression and villainy will be buried with their buzzard carcasses three feet in the earth. On Saturday last, a beautiful and costly flag was presented to the Maryland Battalion, on duty here, by a Mrs. McLaughlin, the wife of a naval officer, who brought it from Baltimore, through the enemy's camp, concealed beneath the folds of her spacious crinoline.

OBSERVER.

☆☆☆Summer 1861

In early June, Confederate General P. G. T. Beauregard was given command of the Confederate military forces in northern Virginia. Officially known as the Alexandria Line, this conglomerate of troops was at times called the Department of Alexandria, the Potomac Department, and the confusing Army of the Potomac—the same title given the Union forces gathered for the protection of Washington, D. C.

LETTER FROM VIRGINIA

RICHMOND, VA., June 12, 1861 [6-19-61ASC]

The blast of war which sent its bloody echo to us yesterday, will soon blow on our ears from the direction of Harper's Ferry and Manassas Junction.

Both ends of the Baltimore & Ohio Railroad are in the possession of Lincoln—making the former place accessible to his soldiery both from the North and South.

The road from Washington to Loudoun county, is also in the possession of the United States. The [Manassas] defenses have been constructed under the immediate supervision of an able engineer—Major [W. H. C.] Whiting—who was appointed by Gen. [P. G. T.] Beauregard to conduct the fortifications in Charleston harbor for the reduction of Fort Sumter.

The provisions furnished our soldiers at Harper's Ferry by the rich valley counties of the State, are reported to be of the most superior kind, and the supply almost inexhaustable. A soldier writes that the army are growing fat off the superb beef, bacon, butter and bread furnished by the wealthy country adjacent to the great stronghold.

A battle will be fought at Manassas within the next six or eight days. The Argus-eyed officer in command of our forces—Gen. Beauregard—is firmly convinced that he will be assaulted by twenty or twenty five thousand Lincolnites within the time designated.

He has issued orders to his men to hold themselves in readiness for immediate action, and under no circumstances to be absent for a moment from the encampment. His men are reported to have unbounded confidence in him and to be confident of victory.

The regiment of Zouaves, together with the Choctaw Indian warriors near Norfolk, will be immediately ordered, it is stated, to North-Western Virginia, where, from the dense jungles with which the country abounds, they can leap upon the "babboon's" *litter* and annihilate the whole brood.

Severe complaints are being uttered against our military leaders for failing to fortify and defend, to the last extremity, Alexandria. The fault-finders proclaim that the moral effect of defending it until reduced by attack and counter-attack to even a mass of ruins, would have been worth more to our cause than a dozen such cities.

About three hundred negroes have been captured at various points along the sea board and on our peninsula, some of which have been set to hard work in the construction of fortifications; but quite a number, it is reliably stated and believed, have been sent to Cuba to be sold, in order that the proceeds may be applied to assist in defraying the expenses of the Yankee war.

The black hypocricy and devilish philanthropy of these negro pirates will not go unpunished. The press and people declare that the procedure must be met by the *enslavement* of Yankee prisoners until indemnity is wrung from their sordid souls for the robbery.

OBSERVER.

LETTER FROM "PRIVATE," SIXTH ALABAMA INFANTRY
LYNCHBURG, VA., June 14, 1861 [6-20-61CS]

We arrived here yesterday at 12m., after a journey of five days. A portion of the Regiment, 600 strong, had got within 50 miles of Richmond where we were ordered, when they were met by a dispatch from headquarters to return to this place.

Our men are well with a few exceptions and eager to go forward. I was surprised to see this so large and business a place. But the best feature about it is the kind, generous and hospitable population. I have often heard and read of their proverbial hospitality and kindness, but now I have seen and had practical demonstrations of the fact. Mr. Editor, say to our friends for us, that our reception in this State from the moment we entered its borders, has been all that our hearts could desire. At every stopping place almost, there were congregated these kind people, who had prepared for us provisions in endless quantities and of the nicest kind. Such hams, butter, cakes, coffee, cheese, (home made) apple butter and barrels of milk just from the spring house, and numerous other things too tedious to mention were given us without stint. We are treated as though we were their brothers, husbands and fathers from the treatment we received in portions of Tennessee, where [Andrew] Johnson, [Emerson] Ethridge, [William] Brownlow and other traitors have been doing their work; but thank God! their day has passed and to-day a large and overwhelming majority of the people of Tennessee are with us.

Seven companies of the Regiment leave this evening for Manassas Gap, the balance of the Regiment to-night at 2 o'clock, for the same destination. You can judge from this what sort of chance we have of meeting the enemy soon.

We are encamped here at one of the most beautiful places I ever saw, in an oak grove, with an abundance of the coldest and purest spring water my lips ever tasted, and a fine, clear, bold running stream near by where the men can bathe, all of which we hate to leave, and go we must, and I assure you we go not as sluggards in the great struggle, but with cheerfulness and alacrity.

PRIVATE.

FROM PRIVATE, SIXTH ALABAMA REGIMENT
IN CAMP, NEAR MANASSAS GAP, June 18, 1861 [6-24-61CS]

We are here within 35 miles of the Federal City, 27 of Alexandria, and 11 miles of Fairfax C. H. The camp of our regiment is two miles from Manassas Gap, which is the headquarters of Gen. Beauregard and immediately on the railroad leading from Richmond, Lynchburg, and to Washington. The bridges have been burnt beyond Fairfax Station, eight miles beyond this, by our troops, and are being repaired near Alexandria by the Lincolnites.

Col. [Maxcy] Gregg, of S. C., is in command at Fairfax C. H. Gen. Bonham at a point eight miles from this and between this and Fairfax C. H., and Gen. Beauregard is at the Gap. There are various reports here as to the number of troops here and along the road at different points for ten miles, but there are not less than 15,000 or 20,000.

The cavalry of the Confederate States scour the whole country between here and Alexandria, going frequently within sight of the enemy's lines, and occasionally picking up a sentinel or spy. One of Old Abe's birds was picked up within the lines of Manassas a few days ago with the whole of the entrenchments, &c., accurately drawn off in his pocket, and sent to Richmond.

Col. Thos. G. Bacon's regiment is with us, besides a Mississippi regiment, numbering altogether about 3,000 men.

Heavy guns were heard yesterday evening in the direction of Gen. Bonham's camp, but we have not heard anything from there since, and know not what was the cause of the firing.

A train has just passed and the engineer informs us that the South Carolinans (we suppose Col. Gregg's regiment,) had a fight yesterday. No particulars.

The Confederate troops have burned and evacuated Harper's Ferry, and fell back upon Winchester, a point thirty miles distant from us, in consequence, it is said, of Gen. Scott intending to throw a column between the troops here and those at Harper's Ferry. Gen. [Joseph E.] Johnston is in command at Winchester.

Virginia has large numbers of troops ready to take the field, and companies are forming in all directions. If Scott ever succeeds in getting an army far in Virginia he will never get it out in my opinion. Opinions here are plenty and various as to the chances of a fight, some of which are entertained by those in positions, who ought to be well posted. I would like to give you them, but do not think it prudent to do so.

There is the tattoo, and I must close, for the lights must go out now and everything get still.

PRIVATE.

LETTER FROM THE MUSCOGEE RIFLES
[COMPANY E, TWELFTH GEORGIA REGIMENT]
CAMP FAIRFIELD, NEAR RICHMOND, VA., June 22, 1861 [6-27-61CS]

As you know, we left Columbus on Tuesday, the 18th inst., and proceeded to Gordon, where we were joined by the Putnam Light Infantry, Captain [Richard T.] Davis, which company forms a part of the same regiment that the Rifles belongs to. Our journey to Augusta was very pleasant, and the boys all enjoyed themselves finely; but 'tis more than can be said for the balance of the journey. The rail roads from Augusta to Richmond are conducted in such a manner as to give general dissatisfaction to every company that has come over them. They do not prepare any way for the troops to have water, and when they stop at a station, the time is so short that it is almost impossible for the troops to get it. At Kingsville we were packed in some old box cars and had to ride in them all night; and when we got to Wilmington, we fared even worse, for then they conveyed the companies in platform cars, riding on rough planks, with nothing to protect us from the sun, dust and smoke, and when the boys arrived, 'twas hard to tell whether we were from Georgia or Africa.

At all the stations on the road, we were received with every demonstration of joy and enthusiasm. I must be allowed to particularize in regard to two places on the route—first, in Sumterville, S. C., where the ladies met us at the depot, with water, cakes, flowers, &c.; also, at Whitaker's Turnout, N. C., the same thing over again. One old lady told me she had four sons in the Confederate army, and intended to act as a volunteer herself in cooking and furnishing the soldiers with provisions as they passed along the road.

Our company seem to enjoy themselves finely. The sporting department is conducted by Private [William] Mooney, who is a genuine Irish wag. He wants to be sent to visit "Old Abe" and surround him by himself. A short time ago he bought a negro, he says, to have something to fight for. He is the idol of the camp and keeps the boys in a continuous uproar. On the road, coming up, he was put under guard for some of his mischief, but the boys would not consent to have him punished for it.

Capt. [Willis] Hawkins' company left on Thursday, for Yorktown. Captain Jones' and Strother's are both here. We are encamped about two miles from Richmond, on the Fairfield Race Course. There are a great many soldiers here. They are coming and going all the time. The Davis Rifles [Co. C, 12th Georgia Infantry] came to-day from Macon county, Ga., which forms the seventh company in the regiment. We are looking for Col. [Z. T.] Connor every day.

We had a storm last night, which was very severe. It blew down most all the tents on the encampment. The officers' marquee came down with a smash, covering up captain, lieutenants and all.

Tell our friends that we are well and in good spirits. Direct all letters to care of Capt. T. B. Scott, Muscogee Rifles, Richmond, Virginia.

MUSCOGEE RIFLES.

The Irish wag, Private William Mooney enlisted on June 15, 1861. He was reported absent without leave on November 24, 1862.

THIRD ALABAMA INFANTRY
ENTRENCHED CAMP, NEAR NORFOLK, VA., June 25, 1861 [7-2-61CS]

While you, who reside further down in the Sunny South, are needing rain and in the midst of severe and scorching drought, we, sojourners in the Old Dominion, have been favored with refreshing showers and invigorating seasons, which promise an abundant harvest to the industrious farmer. At propitious intervals the fertilizing showers descend, cooling the atmosphere, tempering the otherwise fervid heat of summer, and cheering the patriot's heart with the substantials of life and making him feel that his beloved section, favored of God, independent within itself, and strong in its own resources, can and will stand the model Republic, in spite of the malevolence and bitter hate of worse than vandal foes, who would crush the very spirit of liberty, and reduce its high-toned, chivalrous citizens to a condition of vassalage to a race of stock jobbers and large speculators in very small matters. Our troops are strong in the faith that God and the right are on our side, and while there is the absence of all fanaticism and bigotry in the strong, pervading sentiment which animates every heart, it is based upon the consciousness that they are engaged in a struggle for the maintenance of the dearest rights known to freemen. Their soil has been invaded—the rights of private property has been disregarded—patriotic blood has been shed in defense of the sanctities of home— defenseless woman has been insulted beneath the shadow of her own vine and fig tree, and the best blood of their hearts has been stirred by the heartless cry of "Beauty and Booty," with which their hireling foes are estimated to the contest. They are cheerful and buoyant, and bear themselves with the firm deportment of men whose hearts are fully determined to accomplish perfectly the work before them. Sustained by this consciousness they may be overpowered by superior numbers, but conquered never. Somewhat acquainted with the material of which our Southern armies are composed, and the settled purpose which animates them, I have no idea they will be defeated in any pitched battle during the war. Like our gallant troops at Buena Vista, though whipped they will never know it, and will fight with determined courage and undaunted bravery until victory perches upon their banners.

The other day the announcement was made at Dress Parade that the Paymaster was "abroad in the land," and having a plenty of money, would pay off the troops on the 30th inst. This announcement was received with the liveliest interest, and welcomed with many hearty expressions of satisfaction. Two months in the service without any pay or bounty, and having to furnish clothing, &c., have pretty well drained all our purses, and the prospect of being replenished, though at the seemingly insignificant rate of eleven per month, is decidingly refreshing.

While pay is not the object for which we fight, and while our rations are abundant and most excellent quality, yet it is pleasant to feel we serve a government able to meet its contracts, and so firmly grounded in the confidence of the people, that that ability will be maintained throughout this contest by their liberal loans and contributions. The substantial manifestations of this confidence developed daily in every part of the Confederate States by citizens of every grade of pecuniary ability, are not the least among the many gratifying evidences that the Southern Confederacy is a fixed fact, and has to be, of necessity, so acknowledged by all the leading powers of the world before a great while.

The preparations now being made seem to indicate that the "powers that be" anticipate an attack at an early day—in fact it is said that they have information that an attack is contemplated by Gen. [Benjamin F.] Butler shortly. The gallant (?) Bombastes Furioso will find another and a greater Bethel by the wayside should he attempt to reach Norfolk by this route. Alabama is eager to gather some of the laurels to be won in this war, and contest with North Carolina and the other Confederates the palm of gallantry.

HOLMES.

PRIVATE LETTER FROM THE ATLANTA GRAYS
[COMPANY F, EIGHTH GEORGIA INFANTRY]
CAMP HOLLINGSWORTH, NEAR WINCHESTER, VA., June 27, 1861 [7-3-61ASC]

My Dear Wife: We are quartered here—how long I cannot say. What the intentions of the enemy may be, in withdrawing from Virginia, I cannot say. If for peace, well and good; if to deceive they will be mistaken; for, in General Johnston, commander of this division of the

Confederate forces, is to be found all that it requires to make an able General. The enemy will never find him asleep at his post. Besides, let every Georgian who has a friend or relation in this division, remember that we are under the immediate command of one of Georgia's noblest and truest sons—General Francis S. Bartow. We have nothing to fear either from surprise or on the battle-field. Besides, the Atlanta Grays have advantages (allotted to few companies) in their immediate commanding officers, Capt. T. F. Lewis and Lieut. S. B. Love, who are gentlemen of the first character and every way qualified to discharge their duties. The members of the Grays are willing at all times, to place their destiny in the hands of these two officers.

While writing, I am standing sentinel under the shade of two very large and ancient willow trees, situated immediately in front of the dwelling once occupied by Gen. Washington and staff during the Revolutionary War. This house is quite ancient. It dates back to the year 1754. It is situated about three-quarters of a mile from the town of Winchester, and is built of gray and white limestone. The main building shows marks of recent improvements. Beyond this, everything shows old age. 'Tis a lovely spot, has around it all that makes life pleasant and home comfortable—a large orchard containing all kinds of fruit adapted to this climate. About fifty yards from the house is a large fish pond, containing fish in abundance for family use. In the center of the pond is a small flower garden neatly paled in. It, too, bears the marks of time. Scattered through the yard are beautiful shade trees of different kinds—the Aspen and Poplar among them. In the lot adjoining the yard and around the fish pond, is seen the common and weeping willow of tremendous size—and look as if they had been standing for centuries. On the bank of the fish pond stands a large flouring and saw mill, turned by water power. Through the yard and lot, conveyed in iron pipes, is water in abundance of the purest kind. Taken in connection with its revolutionary history, it is one of the loveliest places on earth. The building was erected by Free Masons in 1754. The inscription placed over the door, facing to the East, is so dim that it cannot be read. The room in this house occupied by Gen. Washington, is the same that is now occupied by Gen. Bartow. The flooring of the room is the same laid nearly a century ago.

The nearest the enemy have been to this place, is Martinsburg, twenty-five miles from here, except a few of them who paid us a visit a few days ago—not willingly, however. Circumstances beyond their control forced them here, and we have them to support. On yesterday the advance guard of our army crossed the Potomac, by wading, to attack Gen. [George] Cadwallader's forces stationed at Martinsburg. On the approach of our forces the enemy fled without firing a gun. They left two pieces of cannon on the field, both loaded.

The health of the Seventh and Eighth Georgia Regiments is good. A very sad accident occurred in Col. [Lucius J.] Gartrell's [Seventh] Regiment yesterday morning. A young man named Camp, from Coweta, accidently shot himself. In lifting a trunk into a wagon his pistol fell from its belt, the hammer striking the trunk and exploding, the ball entering his breast at the upper part of the breast bone, killing him almost instantly. I trust by this time our officers have had accidents enough from the wearing of small fire arms, to rigidly enforce the discontinuances of their use. They do more harm than good. The health of the Atlanta Grays is very good. Plenty to eat and little to do. I am unable to say anything as to how long hostilities will last.

I neglected to tell you, the property of which I have given a description, has remained for the last two hundred years in one family. It bears the name now it did two centuries ago. It is known as "Hollingsworth Mills." There stands near the house a cottonwood tree, which measures twenty-six feet in circumference. I and Mr. [J. B.] Wilson, of Marietta, measured it this evening.

Your husband,   Wm. C. Humphreys.

William C. Humphreys enlisted as private May 22, 1861. He was listed absent without leave from November 1, 1862 - October 31, 1864.

TWENTIETH GEORGIA INFANTRY
CAMP FAIRFIELD, NEAR RICHMOND, VA., June 28, 1861 [7-2-61CS]

You probably remember that our company [B], the Border Rangers, left Columbus, on Thursday, the 13th inst. We came directly on, with no material detention, and reached Richmond on the following Sunday morning.

Along the road there is much enthusiasm yet. One might suppose that the ardor of the people would tire from a continued strain, but it does not seem so. Such inhabitants as those along the way do not flag in expressions of patriotism.

At the depot in Richmond, we were promptly met by a Quartermaster's aid and piloted through the streets to our present encampment North of the city. Here we are surrounded by long lines of sheds, like the racehorse houses you have often seen, and innumerable tents, in which are quartered companies and regiments of our brave troops. Along and besides us, on plain and hill, the same tents and houses stretch away in the distance. On other sides of the city, in like manner, corresponding neighborhoods of soldiers rise up.

In our vicinity there is a constant drill—an incessant training for the field, from sun to sun. All day the voice of command rings out from the parade grounds, for squads, companies, or regiments. At night, a sentinel's challenge is always in the air. Everything is wrapped up in preparation for a conflict, and profound military plans.

The number of troops about the place it is impossible to estimate in close figures. They are being ordered off and changing quarters continually. At one time, our company is surrounded by numbers of others, with their merry stirring camps; at another, they are ordered off to distant points on the slightest notice, and deserted grounds only mark their former positions.

The bodies of men we are thrown with, or see from time to time are mainly very intelligent, able-bodied and well officered. I have been greatly entertained since our arrival here, in witnessing a dress parade of a battalion of Louisiana Artillery. This corps has three West Point graduates at its head, and with its brilliant uniform and fine music presents the most imposing appearance. Every man in the battalion seems an accomplished gentleman, and in surveying its ranks, I have often thought it a shame, a burning shame, that such men should have to face such foes as are before them. I saw this fine corps, a few days ago, cheerfully marching aboard the cars for Manassas. But although the disposition of troops is so varied, and to some may appear without due method and system, I believe the entire management that of a master hand. Any one who has visited the various Government Departments in Richmond, feels well convinced of the immense *working power* which sustains them. Overcrowded as they are with business, and unprepared as they must be in many cases to meet the requisitions made upon them, they are steadily laboring through. There is an immense demand for arms, but by degrees and a little delay, the requisitions are being all gradually filled.

As is reasonable to suppose, and as ought to be, every one has the fullest confidence in our President. William L. Yancey well said, in introducing him, "The man and the hour have met." Truly, a volume in a line. He is at present at his post in the city, and on almost any afternoon can be seen, superbly mounted on a fine grey charger, making his way out to the various camps. When he first visited our former neighbors, the Orleans Artillery, the sentinel on post, ignorant of his rank, unhesitatingly halted him. The President promptly waited quietly until his character was made out. The Artillery battalion and himself afterwards became best friends, and he much admired their fine equipment and splendid drill.

Our Border Rangers are making good headway. We have been mustered into service, been furnished with arms, and are progressing satisfactorily in drill. We have a fine instructor in Chas. Shorter, of our city, a recent graduate of the Kentucky Military Institute, fresh from all the right training of the schools. The Government provides us the best supplies, and our men are contented and cheerful. We have now a plan afoot to get into a regiment, and then!— away.

I wish I could give you some intelligent opinion as to the present and future operations of our Government, but sensible people unite that it is hard to form one, and indiscreet to express it. I believe, myself, that the enemy's force, when applied, will be mainly exerted in a direct attack from Washington City, with a column of at least 50,000 men, and that the brave Gen. Beauregard will be put forward to meet it. It does seem, from whatever stand-point we view the state of our country, whether as a civilian or a soldier, reason is baffled in any attempt to peer into the future. The progress of events soon outruns the speculations of the wise, and the goal of to-day becomes the starting point of the morrow.

Thus far in the war, I think, we have steadily gained ground, and the justice of our cause and the prospect of our success is every day more apparent. Here in Virginia, the determination to conquer is written on the countenances of perhaps the bravest soldiers the world has ever seen.

H. C. M.

Henry C. Mitchell was mustered in as First Lieutenant of Company B, 20th Georgia Infantry on May 23, 1861, and was elected Captain on January 16, 1862. Captain Mitchell was wounded at Gettysburg on July 2, 1863 and was reported present for duty on October 31, 1864.

LETTER FROM VIRGINIA

WINCHESTER, VA., June 29, 1861 [7-11-61ASC]

We destroyed Harper's Ferry, and evacuated it—it was a sudden movement on the part of our commander, and astonished us all. The secret of the matter was, we were too secure, and the enemy would *never* attack at that point, and to keep upwards of 20,000 men idle so long, was a costly operation. In addition to this, there seems to be no good reason why Harper's Ferry should be held. It would take a dozen pages of foolscap to explain all the particulars of the affair. Just above us, at a place called Williamsport, in Maryland, was Patterson's division of the Federal army. They had designs upon Winchester, as well as to get in our rear and cut off the supplies of Harper's Ferry. Strategy was necessary to get at them. It was supposed their number was double ours, and even more. We could not meet them, but were willing to risk it if they would advance upon us. Gen. Johnston, commander of this division of the Confederate army, wished to convey the impression that he was fearful of Patterson and had something new in view. To accomplish this, he ordered the bridge blown up and the Government buildings destroyed, and commenced to transport baggage and army equipments per railroad to Winchester, as well as, one or two regiments of men. This movement was purposely made very tardily, in order that the news might reach Patterson, and induce him to cross the river and come down upon us. We slept upon our arms two nights at the Ferry, awaiting what might transpire. It was evident that they were nonplussed and suspicious that some "dead-fall" was not for them. We set out very quietly on foot—10,000 of us—in the direction of Winchester. Our leaving the Ferry was regarded as a retreat; and Patterson supposed we had gone by railroad to Winchester, instead of which, we had taken the interior route, and were marching in the direction of Martinsburg. The *ruse* succeeded most admirably, and the news soon reached us that he was crossing the river with a force as numerous as the leaves in the forest—our scouts variously reported the number at from 20,000 to 40,000. His object was to reach Martinsburg, thence to Bunker Hill, and on to Winchester. Our object *now* was to reach Martinsburg first, and throw up fortifications, and thus give our advancing guests a hospitable reception. Then commenced that *"forced march."* We pitched out and went 21 miles the first day, on foot, in a broiling sun, over a rough, mountainous country, with gun, haversack and canteen upon our shoulders. To you, no doubt, 21 miles seems a small matter, but if ever you should try it as we did, it will seem more like a thousand, *sure.*

We reached Bunker Hill, under the impression that our Yankee friends were still advancing in ignorance of our close contiguity to them, as well as of our rapid approach. Rumors various and contradictory reached us every hour. At one time it was said they were at Matinsburg, some 10 or 12 miles ahead, coming like a whirlwind, and eager for a fight; again they were halted at the latter place behind fortifications, and awaiting our arrival. It was decided to push ahead and meet the crisis now so imminent. So we were ordered to march. Col. Bartow made a short, encouraging speech, in which he stated that in a few hours we should have an engagement—that his regiment was expected to perform a conspicuous part, and enjoined upon every man to do his duty. Ammunition was given out, 30 or 40 rounds to the man, guns examined, the Surgeon's wagon for *dead* and wounded drawn up, bandages, lint, surgical instruments, &c., ready for use, were in full view, *and off we started*. I must acknowledge, in all candor, that the prospect did not seem so pleasing. It was a new position to us all. I was cool and calm, *but not near as mad* as when I left Georgia. We experienced *all that men feel* just on the eve of a battle, and you have my word for it, the sensations are not pleasant. I can conceive of nothing more terrible than such suspense; if, *in an instant*, we could have gone into action, it would not have been so painful. Some of our boys had been enquiring all along the route at houses if there "were any Yankees ahead;" but they did not seem *now* quite so anxious to find them, though not a man faltered for an instant. We were just on the point of forming a line of battle, when the announcement was made that our enemy, on hearing of our approach, *turned and retreated across the river again!* It was afterwards ascertained that 2,000 of them had crossed the river at Williamsport, and intended crossing in full numbers (18,000 or 20,000) as fast as possible, when our unexpected movement astonished as well as dismayed them. It is said they re-crossed the river in great confusion and retreated to a position in the rear of Hagerstown, in Maryland. Thus ended our first "engagement."

The evacuation of Harper's Ferry is not generally understood properly throughout the country. You can judge for yourself that it is not a desirable position for our Yankee friends, else they would have gone in there before this. The place is now deserted. Military men regard it as of little consequence to us as a military station.

We are now encamped near Winchester—this is known as Gen. Johnston's division, consisting of Infantry, Cavalry and Artillery. I have no idea what is on foot, though something is brewing, if I am to judge from appearances. Some interest is felt by our troops to know what the Lincoln Congress, so soon to assemble, intends doing. Many sensible men give it as their opinion that overtures of peace will be made to our Government, and express some gratification at so happy a termination of our national troubles, but there is not a man here who would accept any proposition for peace unless Old Abe backs square down and acknowledges he is whipped—the settlement must be entirely honorable to us in every particular, or it must never be made.

We are having a first-rate time spending the summer here, but we wonder what the d—l we are to do when winter comes. An old gentleman resident told me that they have fine sleighing in this town all winter. If we have to face such weather as this in tents, it will prove more disastrous than Yankee guns to our-ill-clad Southern boys.

I wish you could see this Valley of Virginia—it is the loveliest country in the world. I cannot imagine anything more beautiful or luxuriant than these rich dales. The water is pure, cool, and in great abundance.

Yours very truly,   V. P. S.

LETTER FROM SOLDIER JIM

WINCHESTER, VA., July 1, 1861 [7-7-61ASC]

I write to inform you how we are getting along in the mountains of Virginia. This is a beautiful country—too good for Abraham and his tribes to occupy and if they run every time like they did from us a few days ago, it will be a long time before they posses it.

Two weeks ago to-day, after having left Harper's Ferry on Saturday previous, we formed a line of battle, within two miles of about 10,000 of Abe's boys who heard of us, after they crossed the Potomac. They at once came to the "about face," and crossed back to the "tother side of Jordon." Our force was about 6,000. We had prepared for a forced march on them, and were already moving forward, when our messenger arrived and reported that the enemy had retreated. Col. Bartow then marched us to Winchester, where we have remained ever since. The boys are all anxious for a fight before they return home, but of course we do not know whether we are to have it or not.

We are situated in a beautiful grove, near the old head quarters of Gen. Washington, where he fought the British in the Revolution. We have a fine spring of cool water.

The lands in this section are very good—producing mostly wheat and clover, which makes corn bread very scarce.

"Cousin John" is with us and looks as natural as pig-tracks. He talks as fast as he can, when he is in our camps. He says the girls in Atlanta won't notice the young men who have remained at home, and refused to go to the wars; that they expect to content themselves until the Soldier boys return home, when they can marry those who protect them. So I guess Soldier Jim will have a chance to

> Change his situation in life,
> Get him a patriotic wife,
> And be happy all his life.

I can write no more, as I must now attend a battalion drill.

SOLDIER JIM.

SECOND LOUISIANA REGIMENT
YORKTOWN, VA., July 4, 1861 [7-10-61ASC]

I have concluded, on this memorable day, to give you such a description of this post and its forces, as the space of an ordinary letter will permit.

The graphic pen of the historian has rendered unnecessary for me to say much of a place so famous in American history where the last blows for independence was struck. It is the hallowed spot where the hellish prosecutor of tyranny—Cornwallis—surrendered his sword through his aid, O'Hara, to Major General Lincoln, who was appointed by Gen. Washington to receive it, on the 19th of October, 1781.

The associations and memories that cluster around this consecrated spot, made sacred by the glorious triumph of patriots, who deemed nothing too good to be offered upon the alter of Liberty, and nothing too dear to be sacrificed when their country called, causes us to bow our heads with veneration for the spot, and inspires us with courage and patriotic pride to transmit in its unsullied purity to posterity, that independence which was proclaimed eighty-five years ago, to-day, by our forefathers, "who knew their rights, and knowing, dared maintain."

I believe, that could the illustrious dead, whose bones lie bleaching upon, or entombed within the sacred plot of earth, rise like a Phoenix, from the ashes of ages, they would bid us "battle on bravely, and preserve that sacred legacy of freedom, for which we toiled, shed our blood, and died."

Ten thousand cherished memories of this spot, and others equally as dear, crowd upon my mind and struggle for utterance, as contemplation brings to memory the heroic deeds of our fathers in days agone. But I must desist, or my intended letter will turn out to be an oration.

The soldiery composing the forces of this post consists of the 2d and 5th Louisiana Regiments, of the former of which I am a member; the 2d and 5th N. C. Regiments, Colonel [John A.] Winston's Alabama, and Col. [Alfred H.] Colquit's Georgia Regiment; a Virginia and a Louisiana Battalion; the New Orleans Zouaves; the Howitzers and other Artillery; making in all, about ten thousand hardy sons, who are stationed on this, the south side, of York River. On the opposite beach, called Gloucester Point, are stationed about three thousand soldiers. The brows of this stream on both sides, are frowning with heavy Artillery upon the bosom of the waters below.

Old Abe's vessels were seen crossing the stream below about the head of Chesapeake Bay, on yesterday, as if they were busily engaged in some movement, and now while I am penning these lines, I hear distant cannonading, some twenty miles below, roaring and muttering like distant thunder.

The blockading steamer is anchored in sight about ten miles below us. Had I the trident of Neptune to wield at my will, I would give her a watery bed, where she could no more disturb the peace and quietude of a justly indignant people.

We feel almost impregnable here, having added to our naturally strongly fortified post, many redoubts and entrenchments. It would take twenty-five or thirty thousand Hessians to dislodge us.

We have had only one engagement with the enemy thus far, and then our Louisiana Regiment was just too late to participate in the fight and share a portion of that brilliant victory, which decks the brows of the North Carolinians and Virginians with imperishable laurels. I allude to the battle at Bethel Church, the result of which is already well known to every Southron. We marched at the rate of "double quick," to assist those brave sons, who sent up their Macedonian call of *"Come and help us;"* but we were crest fallen when we learned that we were too late, by three quarters of an hour; and we had the privilege only of standing among those whose swords were flushed with recent victory, and of surveying the battle field then reeking with carnage. The only loss was a beardless North Carolina, who died like a man, thinking as did Horace, when he said, *Dulce et Decorum est pro patria mori.*

The soldiers are generally in good health and high spirits, and are celebrating the 4th of July by the rattling of spades in entrenchments, and our boards decorated with pickle pork, corn bread, etc.

Kindly yours,   J. LEE C–

VOLUNTEERING FOR TWELVE MONTHS AND FOR THE WAR, A PATRIOTIC LETTER FROM A SON TO HIS FATHER [7-12-61ASC]

Dear Father: The Lester Volunteers [Co. E, 14th Georgia Infantry] are now preparing to start for the seat of war, and I feel it to be my duty to ask your consent before I go. When I volunteered for one year, you seemed perfectly willing; but when I saw you last, you appeared dissatisfied that I had agreed to go during the war. It is needless for me to say anything in regard to the change which the Congress of the Confederate States has made. Let us suffice to say that I think it nothing but right, and if I did *not*, I would be willing to go anyhow. Nothing can be too hard, no sacrifice to great, when Liberty is at stake. But a father's love will foresee dangers, and urge a cause of fear. You point me to the toils, hardships and dangers of a soldier's life. These I know are great; but is the strong right arm of God too weak to protect, too short to defend me from the vices and crimes which surround the soldier? —the only enemies I fear. Shall I not trust in Him? "Ah! but death is almost certain," you respond. Would you teach me to fear to die in defense of right, of truth and justice? Fighting for the land of my birth, for the rights guaranteed to us by the Eternal God, for the home I love, I feel that death, in its most horrid and ghastly form, would have no terrors for me. "But perhaps you will not be needed; wait until you are called for again," you reply. I have heard this advanced often, and have as repeatedly inquired, *when will that be?* Will it be necessary only when our land is invaded and laid waste with fire and sword; our homes desolated; our loved ones butchered—when the Confederate Flag trails in the dust, our army defeated and disorganized? No, father; the first gun that boomed from Fort Sumter called in thunder tones upon me to rally to the standard of my country, and I burn to answer that call.

But I feel that I cannot go without your consent, for you are my father, and as such have the right to say whether or not I shall go. I beg you, as you love me, withhold not your consent. If you refuse, I must obey; but when it is done life will have lost all charms for me, even if the South should, by a vigorous campaign, soon end the war, by driving from our land the vandals of the North.

Oh! call me not back. Rather immure me in some loathsome dungeon; let me be the erring vassal of some heartless tyrant; bind, rivet the clanking chains of an ignoble, perpetuated slavery upon me, rather than shower on my head the blessings of a liberty bought with the blood of others. Let me pour out the gushing fountain of my own heart to secure my own rights, and I am content. I want no liberty but my own, achieved by my own exertions and purchased with my own blood. Call me not a blind enthusiast. Does love of country need a stimulant to call it into action? Must Reason be dethroned that the fires of patriotism may be aroused? No idle dream of fame, no slavish love of money, actuates me. All I ask is to fight for my country. I want no remuneration. Give me a few tattered rags to hide my nakedness, a crust to appease the gnawings of hunger, and Liberty, and I am happy.

You want me to continue my studies. Do you suppose I can forget a bleeding country and devote my time and attention to the study of the law? Impossible! I sometimes take up my books, determined to forget everything else, but soon my mind is wandering over the plains of the Old Dominion, and in my imagination I hear the thunder of cannon on our borders, and see the smoke of battle ascend in dense columns towards Heaven, and books, home, self, are forgotten, and I long for the hour of departure to arrive.

I know it will wring my heart to bid you perhaps a last farewell. Were I the only one to regret my leaving, I could go without a sigh; but to see my friends in tears is too much for me. Every day I think of that sad, sad hour, and my heart swells with grief; tears flow unrestrained. I sit down sometimes in my room, at the lone hour of the night, when all eyes save those of an All-seeing God are closed in sleep, sometimes in the depths of the forest beneath the overshadowing branches of some monarch of the woods, and give vent to the long pent up feelings of my aching heart. Do not, however, suppose that this or anything else will keep me from going. Tell mother to make what clothes she wants me to have; we expect to start in two or three weeks.

Now, father, let me entrust you with all the earnestness of my heart, to give your consent willingly, and a father's parting blessing. I cannot go without them; I cannot live and stay at home.

Your son,   W. E. Rogers.

William E. Rogers, age 19, enlisted in Company E, 14th Georgia Infantry as private on July 4, 1861. He was wounded at Seven Pines, Va., on May 31, 1862, and later discharged on account of insanity on March 10, 1863. According to his service records, Rogers was killed at Willow Creek, Cobb County, Ga., in 1864.

LETTER FROM RICHMOND

RICHMOND, VA., July 10, 1861 [7-16-61ASC]

The question universally propounded, by old and young, in this city, at every meeting with an acquaintance, is, "What's the news?" For the last forty-eight hours, the unvarying response has been: "Nothing." Indeed, there is "nothing new," either from the seat of the war, or locally; and, with such a dearth as now exists, the newspaper folks, and correspondents especially, have a hard time in keeping up their communication with the reading public. It were an easy task to write out and publish the various sensation rumors which are put in circulation by wags and designing persons, but a proper regard for the feelings of others, to say nothing of respect for the truth, should always restrain a writer for the press from giving currency to any report which is not traceable to a reliable source. Happily, such discrimination does not devolve upon me, as your extensive arrangements for obtaining the latest and most reliable intelligence from the war, through other and more direct channels, relieves me of the necessity of weighing and sifting the reports circulated in this city every day, of engagements and impending conflicts between the Sons of Liberty and the myrmidons of Black Republicanism.

Richmond continues very quiet. Regiments of troops continue to arrive and depart by every train, and, to this extent, the monotony incident to this season is relieved. It is curious to notice the diversity of opinion as to the number of Southern Confederacy soldiers now in the field. Some say that the army does not exceed 90,000, whilst others confidently assert that it numbers more than 150,000. Be this as it may, every loyal citizen believes that our army can whip any force which Lincoln may marshal against it. The Dictator may call loudly for 400,000 more men, but they will not come; and if they should, Jeff Davis can easily raise 200,000 additional troops to repel them.

In ten days the Confederate Congress will meet in Richmond, despite the silly threats of the Lincolnites to occupy our beautiful city before the 20th instant. Congress will meet, by invitation of the State Convention, in the Hall of the House of Delegates, at the Capitol. [James G.] Bennett, of the *New York Herald*, with characteristic impudence, has applied to President Davis for the privilege of sending a staff of reporters, to report the proceedings and debates. I take it for granted that the application has been promptly negatived.

The late requisition of Gov. [John] Letcher for an additional quota of 3,000 troops from Virginia, for the war, will be promptly responded to. In this city, which has already sent three Regiments to the field, several new Companies are in the course of formation. Should it become necessary to do so, the President, through the State Governors, may adopt the Napoleonic plan, of declaring every man in the Republic, not muster free, to be a soldier for the campaign. The Adjutant-General of the State published an order, this morning, calling out the militia in the counties adjacent to Manassas Junction.

The Committee appointed by Congress to provide accommodations for the President, etc., have declined to accept the tender of a residence for His Excellency from the City Council of Richmond, unless with the understanding that the Confederate Government shall be allowed to pay the interest on the outlay—amounting to some $2,800 per annum. The Council had to assent, of course, and thus the Government is relieved of any trammel in the selection of a permanent Capital, which a sense of obligation arising from this tender might have occasioned. The President will occupy the mansion purchased for him next week.

RICHMOND.

☆☆☆Battle of Manassas

At dawn on July 21, Federal forces under Brig. Gen. Irvin McDowell attacked Beauregard's scattered brigades positioned along Bull Run near Manassas Junction. Fighting raged throughout the day, and the thinly stretched Confederate line began to give way in the afternoon, until timely reinforcements from Johnston's Army of the Shenandoah arrived to turn the tide resulting in a clear victory for the Confederate forces.

LETTER FROM SOLDIER JIM
[EIGHTH GEORGIA REGIMENT, SECOND BRIGADE, ARMY OF THE SHENANDOAH]
RICHMOND, VA., July 24, 1861 [7-31-61ASC]

On Sunday morning our boys were marched up in front of the enemy. We had to fight against 30,000. It was two o'clock before relief forces came to our relief. Though we (Col. Bartow's and Col. Gartrell's Regiments) were weak, we kept the wretches at their position until we were relieved. When the shot was showering at us thick as hail, we loaded and fired at them as though we were shooting squirrels. I killed some very large Yankees, and feel as though I had discharged my duty; though I expect to be with the boys as soon as I recover. I was shot through the muscle of my arm below the elbow. I think it will soon heal.

The citizens of Richmond are rejoicing at the victory, and many have kindly asked me if they could serve me in any way.

I have been asked ten thousand questions about the battle; and I see that Mr. Prichard has given you a wrong statement about some of the boys. I see that he has the two Hammonds killed, when I informed him that I saw them wounded, and had heard they were killed. I now hear that they are not killed. Frank is not killed. I wish I could write you more, but I am fatigued and must close.

SOLDIER JIM.

PRIVATE LETTER, DAVIS INFANTRY, SEVENTH GEORGIA REGIMENT
RICHMOND, VA., July 26, 1861 [8-2-61ASC]

Dear Brother: Having an opportunity to write a letter, I hasten to make use of it.

As you see, I am in Richmond—came down yesterday, with one of my comrades, from Manassas, (Alonzo Sneed—I suppose you knew him,) who was wounded in the foot by a grape shot. I am also slightly wounded in the head, by a Minie rifle ball. It was only a *"tip,"* but the tip went to the skull, but without any fracture. I did not think it went to the bone, until about an hour ago, with two glasses [mirrors], I could, with a pair of scissors, probe to the bone without pain.

The particulars of the battle you will find in the Richmond papers, fuller than I can give them; but I will say that it was a terrible, bloody battle, and I was in it. I have seen the horrors of war, in all its blood and terror. My curiosity is satisfied; but I am as anxious to again brave its perils to defend our country and repel her invaders.

A man who has never witnessed the carnage of a battle-field, can form no idea of its terror and grandeur. It is true, that during the intense excitement of the conflict, the sight of a man being shot down by your side, or another mangled by a bomb, does not effect you; but, after all is over, and you walk over the field of strife, you have time to consider and reflect on the horrid scenes around you—here a man, perhaps your friend, with a bullet through his heart, cold in death, others torn and mangled—some dead, some dying, others wounded beyond hope of recovery—mutilated bodies and parts of bodies—it is horrid to contemplate, especially when you remember that, amid all this carnage, you was one of the actors, and only the smallest partition of bone was between you and death.

The Yankees were so badly whipped that they did not ask permission to bury their dead, nor take charge of their wounded. We did so, but many of them were in a deplorable condition before we could render any assistance. Such scenes were at first sickening, but they were so numerous that we soon got "used to it."

It was my full intention, before I ever knew what a battle was, to take charge of any of my particular friends who should get hurt and spared. I expected same from them. Sneed, I am sure, would have spent all he had and his time for me, had there been occasion. I shall do for him all in my power. I have brought him here, and have him in one of the most noble mansions I ever was in. He has a room to himself, fitted up in the most magnificent style. We are now in the care of Mr. Thomas W. Dudley, sergeant of the city of Richmond, who has offered to take charge of us both until there should not be the least sign of a wound on us, and would be happy to take charge of as many more as his house would hold, without fee or reward, except the pleasure of serving the protectors of his country. The good lady says we shall be considered as her children as long as we are under her care.

I have been pleased with the kindness and hospitality shown soldiers all through Virginia, who seem to vie with each other in doing all they can for us, except at Harper's Ferry, where I believe the people would have betrayed us, if they could.

I suppose you have heard of the death of John A. Puckett. There never was a braver man on a battle-field than he, or one with a kinder heart in camp. He was shot dead while shouting and encouraging the boys, who followed him as they would a father. His death is much lamented by the whole company. Mr. [William] Bagwell was also killed on the field. Of the Davis Infantry, two were killed, and eleven wounded. I should like to give you a detail of my past few weeks, which has been pretty rough, if hard marching, and actual starving occasionally, be considered such.

Tell everybody that I am yet alive, and expect to be in at the big battle at Alexandria before long.

Ever your brother, A. C. McPherson.

A. Campbell McPherson was mustered in Company K, 7th Georgia Infantry as First Sergeant on May 31, 1861. He was wounded in the battle of Second Manassas on August 30, 1862 and died of his wounds on October 12, 1862.

LETTER FROM RICHMOND
RICHMOND, VA., July 27, 1861 [8-2-61ASC]

Our city wears a much brighter and more cheerful aspect than it did before the glorious victory on Sunday last. Countenances which were elongated by the apprehensions and uncertainty of the future, are now radiant with smiles. The children seem to prattle and gambol more gleefully, and the aged walk with an elastic step, since they have realized the glad tidings of the triumph of right on the plains of Manassas. There has been no extravagant demonstrations of joy on the part of this community. The hearts of our citizens have been too full. They have experienced an overwhelming sense of gratitude to the noble volunteers who have saved our devoted city from the ravages of an unbridled band of mercenaries. Ask any one of our people, from the highest to the lowest, what his or her emotions were upon the conviction of the truth of the reports of the Confederate victory, and the reply will be, in substance, "I knew not whether to shout or to weep, but I gave thanks to God for the mighty deliverance."

The reception and care of the wounded have occupied the attention of the people of Richmond during the week. Hospitals have been established for the accommodation of those requiring frequent surgical attention, but the larger number of sufferers have been provided for at private residences, where all that nursing and kindness can do will be used to restore the heroic defenders of our common rights.

The public mind has enjoyed a calm for several days, but a premonition prevails that stirring events will take place within the next week or ten days. A battle is expected in the vicinity of Newport News, or Hampton, and the occupation of Washington is deemed not improbable ere the setting of to-morrow's sun.

About twelve hundred federal prisoners are confined in this city, in buildings formerly used as tobacco factories. They embrace representatives of every grade of Yankee society from the nabob to the *chiffonier*. The opinion has been expressed that the safest and most appropriate place for these disappointed plunderers and cut-throats, are the jails belonging to the negro traders. We hope that their polluting bodies will soon be removed from
RICHMOND.

PRIVATE LETTER, FROM DR. THOMAS A. MEANS

MANASSAS JUNCTION, VA., July 25, 1861 [8-6-61ASC]

Dear Father: The pressure of active professional duties, since my arrival here on the day of battle, (21st instant,) has prevented me from giving earlier attention to your claims, and even now while I write, my services are demanded.

The great victory of Sunday last, cost us many lives, while thousands of the conquered foe yet lie wounded, dying, or dead, and uncared for, upon the battle-field and the surrounding grounds, about three and a half miles distant from this place.

One hundred and ninety victims of the fight are under our charge, 123 of whom are Federalists, hailing mostly from Maine, Wisconsin and New York.

I have faithfully devoted myself night and day to their relief and comfort, with unremitting toil, while my couch is any spot, however inconvenient, which I may for a time incidentally secure.

I regret exceedingly, to find the medical department so poorly supplied with fixtures, blankets, water, wine, brandy, &c. Indeed, it may be said to be almost entirely destitute of these necessary appliances. I have been constrained, therefor, to tax my ingenuity in overcoming many obstacles which would otherwise have greatly embarrassed successful treatment. Physicians are still needed, notwithstanding that many have offered their services; while of nurses there are *none*, save one ungainly woman from Michigan, whose homely features and broad dialect, sometimes provoke a smile. She is busy, however, in the culinary department. Even her own people seem to claim but little of her sympathies or attention, as she considers them to have acted foolishly, and to have been greatly deceived. Four *Federal* physicians are in camp, serving their men; but exhibit much "don't carishness" upon their lugubrious countenances, as to render them anything but agreeable. All of us, with one heart and one accord, pay *their* wounded, as much attention as *our own*, for suffering knows no distinction of caste, kindred or condition; and Christian charity, under such circumstances, should make none.

The wild waste and general scattering of munitions of war, baggage, wagons, ambulances, cannon, &c., were almost without a parallel in the history of warfare. I counted, and have, therefor seen with my own eyes, 98 pieces of artillery. In addition to these, we have taken guns, knapsacks, cartridges, balls, &c., to outfit an army twice as large as our own.

One of the most interesting articles of the capture, was the load of hand-cuffs (several thousand, it is said,) which the thoughtful and benevolent invaders brought with them, perhaps (?) for the purpose of making the attachment of the Southern "rebels" to the Union stronger than their own Punic faithlessness have ever been able to effect. Might not a few of these specimens of Northern artizanship, sent to every town and village in the South, produce striking results upon the minds of our people?

I have just read an interesting letter found upon the field, written in pencil, over the signature of J. H. H., addressed to his sister in Milwaukie, Wis., a brief extract from which I give you. He says, "When they" (the "Grand Army") "reached Centreville, on Saturday night, (20th,) they numbered 50,000, whilst a re-inforcement of 40,000 came in from Alexandria and other places." He further says, it is "an easy matter to conquer the South; but I suspect the rebels will make a stand, as their forces are numerous, and exceedingly well armed and equipped. Three days rations were put in our haversacks, with the understanding that the fourth day should be spent in Richmond."

He gave some interesting accounts of the New York Zouaves, whom he denounces, in his own language as "a set of blood-thirsty thieves, having less of sympathy than brutes." They entered an old Virginia mansion on this side of Alexandria—the inoffensive inmates of which were about seating themselves to dine—took possession of the table, devoured the outspread meal, and then bade them "good day," some of them placing their thumbs contemptuously upon the tip of their noses and scornfully twitching their little fingers as they passed off.

I have two young men from Georgia, now by my side, belonging to the 8th Georgia Regiment, Col. Bartow—who were badly wounded. Mr. T. J. Hills, of Rome, Ga., and Mr. Yarborough, of Floyd county, cousin to Rev. John Yarborough, our excellent minister. The latter died, in great pain, last night, but was resigned to his fate, and sent many words of consolation, by members of his company, to his friends and relations. Young Hills, notwithstanding my constant attention, is, I regret to say, at this date, still in a dangerous condition. His wounds were inflicted by two Minie balls, which struck him on the left side below the fifth rib, penetrating his body. I have his effects, and will promptly turn them over to any authorized friends, should he not recover.

I have just this moment, for the first time, since my arrival seen Col. [G. T.] Anderson. He is well, and hearty; but chafing over his disappointment in not having shared in the fight—arriving, as he did, three days after the battle. This Regiment (10th) is encamped six miles North-East of this place, *en route* for Alexandria.

> Thos. A. Means,
> Assistant Surgeon 10th [11th] Regiment
> Georgia Volunteers.

ANOTHER LETTER FROM DR. MEANS
RICHMOND, VA., July 29, 1861 [8-8-61ASC]

After a sojourn of one busy and anxious week at Manassas, I returned to this city on last afternoon, only that I might complete my outfit for camp-life in the surgeon's department.

My labor on the battle-field has been arduous but profitable to my professional experience, from the vast number and variety of important surgical cases which have been thrown under my treatment, while I humbly trust my services have been, at least in some degree, useful to my country and to many a suffering soldier. I dressed, while there, 200 Federal prisoners, (besides scores of our own) whose sufferings were heart-rendering. Some were brought in shot through the head; others through the neck, arms and legs; some with thigh bones shattered, and the limbs hanging suspended by skin, muscle or ligament. The miseries of many were intensified by the want of covering, food and water for which they piteously begged. Scarcely a portion of the human body was exempt from the violence of some weapon of war.

When I moved in the midst of such a melting scene, my Southern heart grew too large for the indulgence of hatred, and I therefore dressed their wounds and nursed them in their sufferings, as willingly as though they had been our own dear people.

I have been occasionally mortified at the cold heartlessness with which *some* who boasted a Southern birth, could ridicule and abuse these suffering creatures, before their faces, even when Death was about to perform his fatal work.

We have shipped 286 to the Hospital in this city, 350 to Culpepper Court House, and some 400 to Charlottesville. Indeed, they are scattered over the country far and wide. Some of the wounded Federals are lodged in the costly and comfortable dwellings of the rich; others committed to the hospital, and hundreds and hundreds more to the cheerless enclosures of a prison.

Too much praise cannot be bestowed upon the generous inhabitants of this Queen City of the Old Dominion. They have voluntarily offered to take their private residences, as many as their rooms can accommodate and their means comfortably sustain. Woman, lovely, sympathizing woman—God bless her! is ever ready, with her heart in her hand, to relieve their sufferings.

The battle-field, when we visited it, presented a horrifying spectacle. Yet, this is the legitimate fruit of war, and Liberty must be purchased even at this high premium, as our enemies are not content that we should enjoy it at a less cost of human life.

A request was made of Gen. Beauregard, by Gen. [Irvin] McDowell, that they might be permitted to bury their dead, which, notwithstanding slanderous rumors to the contrary, was readily granted. Yet, in such hot haste was the task performed, that, perhaps, two-thirds of their number were left upon the surface with a few spades full of earth carelessly thrown over them. Numbers were traced by the bloody track along which they had crawled to the stream—Bull's Run—where they had gone to seek water and died.

The vandal barbarism and blasphemy of some of the Federal troops are characterized by the following incident: While quartered but for one day on the little village of Centreville, they destroyed a magnificent Episcopal Church, desecrated the alter with profuse inscriptions, tore up the carpets from the aisles, scattered the mutilated leaves of the Holy Bible to the four corners of the building, and wrote, in *large letters*, just over the pulpit, the following diabolical sentence: "Death to the d---d Rebels and Jeff. Davis. So saith the Lord and Abe Lincoln." Many scurrilous devices, obscene figures, vulgar caricatures, and profane denunciations, were scratched upon the walls of the gallery, and left as melancholy memorials of the infernal spirit which actuated them. Many similar scenes were witnessed by the citizens of the place, whose hands were motionless, and whose mouths were closed, for they dared not resist. They have since, however, "reaped the whirlwind" as the fearful reward of their wickedness, and are now at our feet pleading for mercy—attributing their defeat to the Government at Washington. Many Colonels, Captains and privates—all, indeed, with whom I have conversed, say that they had no idea there would be any fighting on our side, but now acknowledged that we fought well, and desperately—more like demons than men—saying that all the combined powers of the world could not subdue a people of such undying courage. Many of them had been forced to stay beyond the time for which they had volunteered, that having expired two or three days before the battle. One intelligent officer—a Lieutenant—told me that we had, *hereafter*, to contend with the *rabble*; that those whom we routed were mainly their picked men—the very flower of the North, and the idols of old "fuss, feathers and foibles," and his royal cub—Old Abe.

Manassas is now one wild waste. Farmhouses stand deserted, the green orchards parched and beaten to the earth by the tread of horses and men. Surely, never in modern days, has there been such a complete rout of confident, vainglorious hosts. Heaven will yet continue to smile upon us, and crown our efforts with Independence.

T. A. Means.

Assistant Surgeon Thomas A. Means enlisted on July 12, 1861 in the 11th Georgia Infantry. He was appointed Surgeon on February 1, 1862 and was captured at Gettysburg, Pa., on July 3, 1863. Dr. Means was paroled at Fort McHenry and sent to City Point, Va., for exchange on November 21, 1863. Muster Roll for March—April 1864, shows him "absent, exchanged and ordered to report to Medical Director in Ga."

SIXTH ALABAMA INFANTRY
[SECOND BRIGADE, ARMY OF THE POTOMAC]
UNION MILLS, VA., July 26, 1861 [8-3-61CS]

The advance of the Lincoln army upon us and the great events which recently occurred near here, and of which I suppose you have been informed by telegraph and otherwise, have prevented me from writing you sooner.

A part of our picket guard came in from their posts about 8 o'clock a. m. of the 17th inst., and reported the enemy in large numbers about three miles off, advancing by two routes upon us, by way of Burke's Station and by Reynolds', and about the same time a courier arrived from Gen. [Richard S.] Ewell, ordering us to fall back upon this place, which is about six miles from Sangster's Cross Roads, and near where the Orange and Alexandria Rail Road crosses Bull Run Creek. The tents were struck, baggage and camp equipage packed, and we quietly took up the line of march for this place. We could hear very distinctly as we left, the sound of their axes cutting the trees from the road, which we had obstructed by falling them across it, and but for which the battalion would certainly have been cut to pieces or compelled to surrender.

We encamped that night on the western [eastern] side of the creek, and on the morning of the 18th, crossed the rail road bridge, which had been floored with plank, and then burned it. We were then moved down the creek, with Col. [John J.] Seibel's regiment and a portion of a Louisiana regiment, and stationed where the wagon road crosses the creek, to prevent the passage of the Lincolnites should they attempt it. Here we lay concealed in the bushes, expecting the enemy every moment, but only a few scouts appeared within sight, one of whom was killed by our men, and two wounded.

About 12½ o'clock the booming of heavy guns and volleys of musketry was heard, a few miles above us, at McLean's [Blackburn's] Ford, where the enemy attempted to cross, but were repulsed with great slaughter. The battle lasted three hours, when the enemy retired, leaving a large number of killed and wounded on the field, our loss being trifling when the numbers of the enemy engaged are taken into consideration. Three pieces of artillery were taken from the enemy in the engagement. A New Orleans company, known here as the "Tigers," captured the artillery, throwing down their rifles and using their large knives upon the enemy, and driving them from the guns.

Early on the morning of the 21st heavy firing was again heard, and continued until night. We remaining in our position at the creek ford until about 2 p. m., when we were marched, with a Louisiana regiment and the 5th Alabama regiment, across Bull Run and towards the battle ground, for the purpose of attacking the enemy on their flank, but had not marched more than a mile before we received orders to recross the creek, and march on the west side to the scene of action, eight miles distant, which we did, making the eight miles in one hour and a half, hearing as we approached the battle ground that the enemy were totally routed and in full retreat towards Fairfax C. H. and Alexandria.

We were immediately marched back to the position we had left at the creek ford, where we remained until the evening of the 24th, when we were moved about half a mile to the east side of Bull Run, where we are now encamped. Two days of this time we were almost entirely without food, sleeping upon the ground, most of us without a coat or blanket, and entirely without tents, and one day the rain pouring down the whole day and a portion of the night, notwithstanding which we all kept in fine spirits.

Sergeant T. J. Bates, Privates John Howard, Jas. O. Perkins, W. A. Prince, A. J. Smith, Sr., and Richard Pool, were on picket guard on the 17th, 2½ miles from camp, at Reynolds, and as the enemy approached retired to a house within about a mile of camp, where they halted and awaited the approach of the enemy and when near enough fired upon them and retreated to camp and finding it evacuated they made their way to Fairfax Station, which had also been evacuated by the troops stationed there. Approaching the Station they saw about 300 men and enquired who they were? When they promptly answered that they "belonged to the Confederate army;" and were of course taken prisoners and sent to Washington.

These are the facts as we have learned them from citizens in the neighborhood where they were supposed to have been killed, until yesterday, when a scouting party was sent out and their fate ascertained, much to our relief, for they were among the best soldiers we had.

The Lincolnites have burned, stolen and destroyed a great deal of property between this place and Alexandria, taking from many of the citizens every horse they had, killing their cattle, hogs and poultry, and carrying off their negroes.

On the morning of the 23rd, I obtained permission to visit the battle grounds of the 18th and 21st, which I did in company with a friend, walking during the day between 25 and 30 miles and returning to camp by 9 o'clock at night, almost exhausted with fatigue.

I wish that I were capable of giving to your readers a just description of the field where the great battle was fought on Sunday, the 21st, as it presented itself to me on the 23rd. It seemed as if the ground was intended by nature for the maneuvering of a great army, and from the numbers of men and horses lying in every direction, a great army was maneuvered here. The ground was strewn with the dead of the enemy and their horses for miles up and down on each side of Bull Run creek, above and below the Stone Bridge, on the road leading from Manassas to Centreville and Fairfax Court House.

I stood where one of their batteries was stationed and counted within a few yards around 28 dead horses. At this place [Henry Hill] the batteries of the Lincolnites and the Confederates were only 200 yards apart, and all around on every side lay there a disabled caisson or gun, while in every direction lay shot and fragments of shell which had done the deadly work. The dead bodies of our men had been buried or removed from the field; those of the enemy lay where they fell, presenting a horrid and ghastly spectacle, and creating a stench almost intolerable. This was not the case in one place only, but for miles and miles, over fields and woods, in roads and gullies, in the fence corners, wherever you turned your eyes the same sight met your gaze, until the heart sickened. I followed the broad, macadamized turnpike road, along which the enemy fled; for miles in the direction of Alexandria and all along the road the same sad sight presented itself, of dead bodies of men and horses, while on every side, was strewn every kind of wearing apparel, guns, cartridge boxes, bayonet sheaths, provisions, canteens, havresacks, chairs, camp stools, in fact everything requisite for the equipment in the best style of a large army. The hospital immediately on this road, where the Confederates had gathered the wounded of the enemy, who had been shot down by the Confederates as they fled in terror from the battle field, presented a sad spectacle. The [Stone] house was crowded with the wounded men so that a person could scarcely move between them, while a few feet from the door lay a number who had died since they were brought in, their bodies fast decomposing.

I conversed with a number of the wounded men who seemed quite penitent, and vowed that if they ever got back to their homes they would stay there. I was told by one of the wounded men, quite an intelligent man, that they left Washington with 130,000 men, and that they had no doubts of having an easy time of marching to Richmond, or wherever they chose to.

We have any quantity of artillery of the best kind, one piece of heavy calibre, an Armstrong [30-pdr Parrott] rifle cannon, about 10 feet long. Most of the pieces are rifled cannon. There are also caissons with ammunition in abundance, besides a large quantity of small arms of every description, 36 cases of which were unopened, having been brought along for the purpose of arming the tories. We got also 300 fine horses, and 100 wagons, quite new. The ambulances taken are very fine indeed.

How many prisoners have been captured it is impossible to tell yet, for the cavalry are still scouring the country, picking them up and bringing them to Manassas, and among the balance two negroes.

I do not suppose there ever was an army more completely routed, though it cost us dearly and we have lost many brave men and gallant officers, among others, F. S. Bartow, of Savannah.

I do not suppose the number of the killed of the enemy will ever be known, as the battleground extends for ten miles up and down the creek. My opinion is, that the killed of the enemy numbers about 6 or 7 to our 1. This is my candid opinion after going over the battlefield.

PRIVATE.

OUR SPECIAL WASHINGTON CORRESPONDENCE
WASHINGTON, D.C., July 30, 1861 [8-11-61ASC]

Enclosed please find a list of Confederate prisoners now in the custody of the Lincoln Government at this place. They have been cared for by us, so far as clothing, beds, and bedding, with such other little attentions as the "rule and ruin" government here will permit. We are not allowed now to visit them in their prison, nor to get them any articles of food. They are limited to the regular army rations, of which they do not complain, though it would greatly ameliorate their solitary confinement within the walls of a prison, far away from home and friends, if they were allowed to receive the visits of friends and to receive at their hands the generous tokens of their sympathy. But both they and we must be content with such favors as Lincoln's hirelings deal out to us. At all events, you can safely say to their friends at home that they shall not suffer from want or neglect. If it were safe or even prudent, I would give you the names of some of those who are most interested in their behalf.

We are still under the reign of terror, though many of us have not refrained from fully or freely expressing our condemnation of the war policy of the Administration and the folly and madness of the Black Republican party.

This war is not one for the maintainance and perpetuity of the Union—for this is a foregone conclusion—but one for the maintianance of the Chicago Platform, the utter overthrow of the South and the extinction of slavery. To accomplish these, they are willing to sacrifice hundreds of thousands of lives and hundreds of millions of treasure, besides the overthrow of all liberty and all government. But thanks to God, who rules in Heaven and *on earth*, their pet schemes of conquests and overthrow of the South, received a glorious check in the salutary lesson taught them at Bull's Run on the ever-to-be memorable 18th and 21st of inst. I have not language to express to you the forlorn looks and universal paroxysm which seized this community of republican aiders and abettors on the night and day following that "*great* FEDERAL RUN."

Of course, we *all* shed tears, but some were more the tears of *joy* than sorrow. Not that we rejoiced at the death of any man, or a victory over the Constitution and the Union, but *because it was a glorious victory over the vile presumptiveness of a wicked and unholy sectional organization for the overthrow and utter annihilation of the people and institutions of fifteen sovereign States.* The fact is, this sanguinary defeat at Bull's Run, will defeat their entire plans for the farther prosecution of the war. They are thoroughly fortifying themselves behind their works on Arlington Heights, where they will rest for the present. They will there coax an attack; *though I am not of opinion that General Beauregard intends this to be a war of conquest*, simply one of defence(?).

If Gen. Beauregard had followed up his victory of the 21st, he could have run the entire federal army ("the grand Union army") into the Potomac, and to-day been in possession of Alexandria and its surroundings. I am confounded that he did not. It would have at once liberated the "Old Dominion," and set her captives free. But, as it is, the federal army and government is demoralized. The army is disorganized, and the government is unable to effect a loan of even $5,000,000. Treasury notes are a drug at 95 cents on the dollar. I am assured that they have placed large amounts of these in the hands of brokers and others to be converted into specie at any price, for the cry is, "they must have money." They are only *beginning* to feel the legitimate consequence of their own folly and madness. This is already opening the eyes of the better portion of the population of the North, which must, ere many months, put an end to this damnable war, and the recognition of the independence of the Confederate States. God speed the day as one of peace.

I trust that our people will practice upon the maxim, that "in concentration—and union there is strength."

***.

FROM THE SEMMES GUARD
[COMPANY C, SECOND GEORGIA REGIMENT]
RICHMOND, VA., August 1, 1861 [8-6-61CS]

According to promise, I will drop you and your readers a few dots as to the whereabouts of the "Semmes Guard." We are now in Richmond. We arrived here yesterday after traveling six days and a few hours. Our trip was very fatiguing in consequence of the means of transportation being so unpleasant. The rush of Southern soldiers is so great to Virginia, that we were necessitated to make our way to this point in baggage and box cars. There was no accident on the way even if we did lose several nights' sleep. Our noble hearted Captain did everything in his power to make our transit agreeable. Capt. [William S.] Shepherd is devotedly attached to his company and they to him, and I would assure his patriotic and public-spirited mother that her son is "every inch a soldier," and that he commands a clever and moral set of young men as ever left the city of Columbus, to grapple with the enemy.

Some forty of our company are members of some church, and we have agreed to have prayer meeting on every Sunday and Wednesday nights. We feel this to be our duty. It is true that the scenes and associations of camp life do in a great degree remove the mind from all that is devotional and religious, and from this fact we have set apart two nights in a week to acknowledge our dependence upon God, to remember in prayer for the welfare of our own souls. We know our friends at home will pray for us.

We will leave to-morrow for Manassas. It is understood that our regiment is to be placed at the post of danger, and consequently at the post of honor.

The regiment is actively engaged making preparations for leaving. The officers of the "Semmes Guard" are making every effort to have us supplied with all necessary comforts for the "tented field."

We will go from here to Manassas, and when we get settled down in regular tented style I will write you *in extense*.

All are well. In honor of our pleasant camp whilst at Columbus you may call me, your correspondent,

LINWOOD.

SIXTH ALABAMA INFANTRY

ARMY OF THE POTOMAC, UNION MILLS, VA., August 2, 1861 [8-8-61CS]

Nothing of interest in the way of military operations, which I would be at liberty to communicate has transpired since my last. The 6th Alabama regiment is still at this place. Gen. Ewell's Brigade has been reorganized and is now composed of the 5th, 6th, and 12th Alabama Regiments, 12th Mississippi Regiment, and two companies of Virginia cavalry.

The Lincolnites had opened communication by Railroad on the 21st July, between Alexandria and Fairfax Station by removing the obstacles placed on the road, and rebuilding the Bridges destroyed by the Confederates, and communication also by Telegraph to Fairfax C. H.

A large party of Federalists, among whom were members of Congress, of the Cabinet, Reporters for the Press, many distinguished citizens and a large number of ladies, followed the grand Federal Army and were at Fairfax Court House during the battle of Stone Bridge, and had come prepared with all the necessary eatables and delicacies, with any quantity of wines and liquors, to have a general jollification over their first great battle and victory, never dreaming, I suppose, from what I can learn from the Yankee prisoners, of any such thing as defeat, much less the total rout and almost perfect annihilation of General Scott's Grand Army. All these good things of course fell into the hands of our troops, who were in great need of refreshments after a hard day's fighting, and who, I am told, did them ample justice, on this, to them happy occasion.

Not a day passes but we learn of some further outrages committed by Federal troops during their march from Alexandria to Bull Run upon citizens and their property. Numbers of instances, where they killed all the stock, fowls, &c., on the place, and then took every horse to be found and packed their spoils on them and carried them off. Besides ransacking every room, cellar and garrot of the houses, seeking for money, arms and valuables, and offering insults and indignities to females, too barbarous and inhuman to relate.

I see by extracts published in the Richmond papers, from the Washington correspondence of the *Baltimore Sun*, that the most cruel outrages were committed upon the persons of our men taken prisoners by the Federalists on the 17th ult., by the soldiers in the streets of Washington City. Thanks to God, a just retribution has already overtaken these cowardly scoundrels, of Lincoln's army, and when Confederate soldiers meet them again, these indignities offered to brave men, and cruelties inflicted upon them while in the power of enemies, that ought to damn them in the eyes of all civilized nations, *will be held in remembrance*.

Many prisoners have been picked up by our cavalry since the date of my last, straggling through the country nearly starved to death, and many of them wishing to be taken prisoners to be kept from starving.

The large rifle cannon captured, has been removed to a point where it will be of great service. It was thought some difficulty would ensue of obtaining balls of the proper description for this piece, but this has all turned out right.

Captain R. A. Hardaway of your place (in command of two batteries at the Junction) believing that the Federalists must have left their ammunition for this gun somewhere on or near the battle field, mounted a horse several days after the battle and sent to the place where the gun was taken, and after searching for some time found an ample supply for it, in a piece of woods where the enemy had attempted to conceal it.

A correspondent of the *Cincinnati Times* writing from the site of Gen. [Robert S.] Garnett's disaster in North Western Virginia, speaks of the articles left by the Confederate troops on their retreat, and particularly of the number of playing cards strewn along the road for 30 miles, as he says. I am well satisfied that I saw on the Turnpike Road by which the Federalist retreated from Stone Bridge on the 21st, within a distance of two miles, twenty playing cards, for each one this correspondent says he saw in a distance of 30 miles, and as far as I went in the direction of Alexandria, the thicker they were strewn along the road and through the woods.

An interesting letter from a Yankee lady to her husband in the Federal army, was found on the Turnpike Road, in which she begged her husband to get the officers to place him in battle where he would not be hurt. God forbid that there should be a Southern wife, mother or sister in the Confederate States who would make such a request as this of her husband, so or brother; I do not believe there is one such. No they are made of far better material.

A paper purporting to be a dispatch from the *Federalists at Richmond*, was read to the soldiers, throughout the whole of the Federal army engaged in the battle of Stone Bridge, on the night before the battle, stating that Richmond had been taken by Federal troops, from Fortress Monroe &c., and they were told that all they had to do, was to cross Bull Run Sunday morning, and have a slight skirmish at Manassas, and march on to Richmond without any difficulty. The object of this false deception on the part of the Federal commanders, you will readily perceive was to infuse into their deluded followers a spirit of enthusiasm, which would carry them through the battle next day. There is no doubt that this is true, as it is corroborated by all their prisoners. They also state that any quantity of spoils were promised them.

The health of our men is better than it has been for some time, the measles having gone through the whole Regiment, but little material is now left for that disease. We have in our company a few cases of the mumps, which is about all the sickness in our company.

The weather for several days past has been very hot and sultry, as much so as I ever felt it in your latitude [Georgia]. Notwithstanding the days are so warm the nights are cool enough to make two or three blankets comfortable. We have good spring water in abundance, and a fine stream to bathe in.

Provisions which were plenty and could be had at fair prices, when we first arrived in Virginia, such as butter, milk, eggs, fowls, &c., are very scarce indeed, in fact cannot be had for love or money. The Confederate troops have consumed a great deal, and then the robbing of the farmers by Lincoln's hordes has made a clean sweep. There are no vegetables to be had at all, the gardens generally being very poor indeed. We have been getting a few small pears, within the past week, the only fruit we have had, and I have seen no such thing as a melon of any description.

The mail arrangements here are very bad indeed. We get no letters and I have not received a number of your paper in two weeks. This is a great annoyance indeed, and to me particularly, for I have been a newspaper reader for years, and have yours daily since its first issue, always looking for its arrival anxiously, expecting to find something new and interesting, which it was almost sure to contain. I can but believe that the papers are stolen by some one. They should be directed for the present to Manassas Junction.

I see that the Confederate Congress has passed an act giving soldiers the privilege of mailing letters without prepayment of postage. This is some accommodation to the soldier, as there are no stamps for postage as yet, and the postmasters here will take nothing but specie for postage, which puts us to great inconvenience; but I think the act should have gone further and made the soldier's postage free; as a large majority of them are poor men, who have left no resources behind them, which yields them anything, but have left families, in many instances, dependent upon charity for something to eat and wear, and are fighting for the trifling pittance of $11 per month out of which this high rate of postage has to be taken.

We find in the Confederate army, many old acquaintances of former days, from various parts of the Confederacy. Among others I find John L. Lewis, formerly of Columbus, in command of a company in the 12th Louisiana Regiment.

Hon. David Clopton, who joined a company from Tuskegee, Alabama, is Quartermaster of the 12th Alabama Regiment.

Col. [Egbert] Jones, of the 4th Alabama Regiment, who was reported to have been killed, and whose regiment suffered so severely in the battle of Stone bridge, is not dead, but is doing well, and will probably recover. This I learn from one of the regiment who visited our camp to-day.

We will never live long enough to cease regretting being marched almost in sight of the left wing of the enemy at Stone Bridge, on the evening of the 21st, and marched back again.

This was a hard lick upon us, though it is conceded here that this movement of our brigade towards their flank was the cause of their retreating as soon as they did, if they would have done so at all, had the movement not have been made.

I shall continue to write you occasionally, though I can't tell that my letters will ever reach you.

PRIVATE.

SIXTH ALABAMA INFANTRY
ARMY OF THE POTOMAC, UNION MILLS, VA., August 4, 1861 [8-10-61CS]

It is with great pleasure that I hasten to inform the friends and acquaintances of Sergeant Bates and others of our company, prisoners in Washington City, that they are all well, in good spirits, and are being well treated. This information I have from a Mr. Harroven, just from Washington, and has resided in Washington for six years past, being a policeman of the city for several years.

The Confederate prisoners who were abused and beaten by the mob in Washington, were captured and carried to that place, on the day after the battle of the 18th, and were not Sergeant Bates and his comrades, as we had good reasons for believing was the case. They are confined in the old Capitol building.

Senator [John C.] Breckinridge visited them the day after their capture, besides many others, the ladies not forgetting them with various niceties, in the way of eatables &c. Mr. Harroven saw a carriage driven to the prison the day before he left, containing several ladies, who brought with them a number of splendid bouquets for the prisoners.

The officer who has them in charge is said to be clever and will see that they are well treated.

What I write to you about these unfortunate men, you may rely on as reliable, for I feel a great interest in their fate, they being my comrades, and two of them my messmates, Bates and Perkins, and what I write in relation to their capture, I know to be facts, or have information from most reliable authority.

Application was made for an exchange as soon as it was definitely ascertained they were prisoners, but the Lincoln Government refuses to exchange, as by so doing they would yield the point, as they contend, that we are rebels and traitors.

Mr. Harroven says there are about 20,000 troops in Washington, but does not know how many are in Alexandria. We have many friends in the Federal City, but they are for the present powerless.

The panic was so great in Washington after the battle at Stone Bridge, and the flying cowardly Yankees came straggling in to the city, that a few Confederate Regiments, could easily have taken it.

The unfortunate mistake in the movement of Gen. Ewell's Brigade, on the 21st, I learn from the best authority, occurred in the following manner. Gen. Ewell received orders from Gen. Beauregard to cross Bull Run and attack the left flank of the enemy about two o'clock in the afternoon. The Brigade was promptly marched across Bull Run and towards the enemies left flank, about four miles distant, and when our advance was within one mile of them, a trooper galloped up to Gen. Ewell with a verbal message for the Brigade to recross Bull Run and hasten to the assistance of our forces at the Stone Bridge, that they were hard pressed by a greatly superior force, and would probably be compelled to give way, if not reinforced speedily. This verbal message was obeyed, unfortunately, and upon inquiry afterwards, it was ascertained that no such order was given by General Beauregard, or any one else. No one knew the trooper who delivered the message, nor can it be ascertained who he was. These are the true facts of this unfortunate affair, as I learn from high authority.

Gen. Ewell's Brigade is no doubt the body of troops referred to, by the *New York Times* correspondent, who was on the field as "a body of 10,000 riflemen Sharp-shooters, and a Regiment of Cavalry, approaching our (third) left flank, which created the panic."

The future movements of the army of the Potomac is the general topic in camps and what they will be is only conjecture, from what we see around us; for Gen. Beauregard keeps all his plans to himself, very wisely too. I will say there is but one opinion here about our next movement.

Gen. Beauregard's soldiers have the most unbounded confidence in his military skill and sagacity, coolness and courage, and are patiently awaiting the word from him, whatever it may be, never doubting for an instant his ability to wrestle with any or all the leaders of Lincoln's vandal hordes and defeat them again, whenever he meets them, with anything near an equal force. But few military men have ever lived in my opinion, who were more respected and esteemed by their men, than is Gen. Beauregard by the army of the Potomac. Whatever his next movement may be, it will be with them as it was at the battle of Stone Bridge, "the man and the hour have met."

The camps in the army of the Potomac are filled with visitors, some who have come to visit sick friends or relatives, others bring clothing &c., for the soldiers, to offer their services in nursing the sick, &c., while still others come as gentlemen of leisure, to gratify a morbid curiosity. This latter class the commanding General has already given his attention, and in future, persons found in camps without sufficient excuse will have to shoulder a musket and take their place in the ranks, just where they ought to be.

I must mention the conduct of a citizen of Russell county, at the risk of incurring his displeasure for mentioning his name in a public manner. Mr. W. J. Bickerstaff was here at the time of and before the battle of the 18th, to visit his sick son (who had died before his arrival,) and when he heard that the enemy had left Alexandria and were approaching us, although overwhelmed with grief at the loss of his boy, he called for his son's rifle and accoutrements, promptly took his place in the ranks, marched there and shared the hardships and fatigue we had to undergo for several days, and continued so to do while he remained here.

The Army of the Potomac, as all armies are in this country, is infested by numbers of faro dealers, many of whom have joined the army as privates for the purpose of swindling the poor soldier out of his hard-earned pittance of $11 per month. A number of these gentlemen are at Manassas Junction, and one, a well known character from your section, told Capt. H. a few days since that he would soon visit the 6th Alabama Regiment, for the purpose of opening his "institution." Col. Seibels was promptly informed of the gentleman's intentions, and is patiently awaiting his arrival. I venture he will meet with such a reception as will in future be a warning to all such cattle, to give the 6th Alabama Regiment at least a wide berth.

How do you like the little war that is going on in the "Old Wreck" between the friends of Gen. Scott and the friends of Lincoln, as to who shall shelter the responsibility of the grand failure to march to Richmond. This is altogether unnecessary and entirely out of place, as it was not in the power of any or all of them to have had it otherwise. This difficulty between "old fuss and feathers" and "honest old Abe" is quite amusing to us here, and we shall leave it to them to settle as best they can. The comments of the Abolition press as to the causes of their defeat are rich, rare and racy, but the great fact, as stated by the correspondent of the *N. Y. Times*, stares every one in the face, that they were "legitimately" defeated, but not by "superior numbers" as he states, for such is not the fact; but by a force inferior to theirs in numbers, but greatly superior in the "material" of which it composed.

We are all on tiptoe to see the report of Mr. W. H. Russell, the *London Times* correspondent, who was on the battle field, and from whom we expect a full and impartial account of the whole affair.

PRIVATE.

LETTER FROM RICHMOND
[COMPANY G, TWENTIETH GEORGIA INFANTRY]
IN CAMP NEAR RICHMOND, VA., August 5, 1861 [8-10-61CS]

Capt. Jno. R. Ivey's Company still remain at this place. We have been under marching orders since the period of which I informed you in a previous letter, but these orders have day after day been suspended. The cause is, probably, want of convenient transportation. Since the great battle of Manassas (or Stone Bridge, as it will be more properly described in history,) the utmost powers of the rail road corporation from that place to Richmond, have been tasked to transport the wounded and other prisoners of the enemy, and the large quantity of munitions of war which fell into our hands on that eventful day. Already, several companies have been supplied with arms taken from our foes. They are mostly the U. S. Springfield musket, marked 1856, and a very superior arm. They are generally in good order, a little rust being the principle damage. The largest number of those taken proved to be loaded—some with one, two, and as high as three charges. I counted over twenty thribly loaded, and myself unloaded one of the latter. *In each instance the ball had been put first in the gun, the powder being put on top!*—showing either great ignorance or excitement upon the part of the loader!

You have already learned of our immense gains in arms, munitions of war, and provisions from the enemy. There is no exaggeration of the fact as respects the last named. I have it from the most authentic source that the amount of provisions taken will prove fully sufficient to feed an army of fifty thousand men for nine months. It must be remembered by those disposed to dispute this fact, that the invading army fully expected with its columns, to penetrate Virginia, at least as far as Richmond, and was properly supplied with every requisite to feed that army and establish depots of stores for the reserve which were to follow. Many of the officers' personal stores were marked, "Manassas" and "Richmond, Va." The wounded of the enemy that are in the hospital here, are being kindly cared for, as well as the sound prisoners, who are confined in a warehouse. Some of the officers are on parole. The men are generally a fine, able-bodied set. Some appear, even yet, entirely ignorant of the result of the conflict in which they were engaged, and lament the personal misfortune to themselves, that they are prisoners, when their army won the battle! Others acknowledge their defeat, and regret the errand upon which they entered, while others, again, assume a bold, defiant, and even insolent tone, saying that if released they "would do the same thing over again." This number is small.

The anxiety of our company has been so great to leave this place for the scene of active operations that, we were on eve yesterday, of being sent to Fredericksburg, by railroad, to march from thence forty odd miles to Manassas. It was concluded, however, for us to remain, as the prospect brightened of a chance for a direct travel in a day or two. "A few days! just a few days!"

Capt. Ivey and his command are doing finely, so far as health and condition are concerned. There is not a single absence from drill predicated upon serious illness, and the five hours a day of martial exercise appears to be relished and enjoyed.

***.

PRIVATE LETTER FROM MANASSAS [8-14-61CS]

I have sent you a valise or bag with a sample of the captured property. I suppose it arrived safely. I sent also one of the shells of the celebrated siege guns, styled the "Armstrong," but it was a Parrott gun. This shell had been "*drowned*"—that is the men who brought it in had wet the fuse and charge with water to keep it from exploding. I have two others, one a twelve and the other a six pounder shell now by my tent, both charged. I would like to send them to you, so you might see all about war.

As dangerous as the shells look they did very little damage.

Dr. Bozeman told me the second day after the fight, he had treated only one gun (cannon) shot wound. Most of the wounds were from Minie balls. I saw a musket barrel cut through by a Minie ball and yet enough of the metal left on each side to hold the barrel together.

The stock was bloody and I suppose the soldier was killed.

The cannon of several batteries of the Lincolnites were marked with splotches of blood as large as this paper, showing that the spongers and loaders had been shot at their pieces by our cannon.

I saw one caisson (ammunition wagon) which had received a full charge of canister shot. Every spoke in the wheels seemed shot through and many of the shot went through the ammunition chests and yet strange to say, the caisson is serviceable.

It is only part of a great lie when the Northern papers say that their batteries were short of ammunition, and in carrying their wagons to the rear for another supply, the teamsters became alarmed and the panic spread, making a regular stampede.

I examined every caisson and took an inventory of its contents. Not more than one chest (there are three to each caisson) out of the *whole lot* was exhausted and we took several extra caissons on the field. The chest which was exhausted belonged to [James B.] Ricketts' (called Sherman's) battery; and there was any quantity of the same kind of ammunition left.

It is amusing to see how many different regiments captured the celebrated Sherman's battery, and still more amusing to think that Sherman's battery was not in the battle at all. Ricketts who is wounded and captured is very indignant when his battery is called Sherman's. Sherman is now Colonel of a regiment and was not in the fight. This battery was styled Sherman's by the Northern papers and in the account of the battle of the 18th, it was mentioned as Sherman's. But it is certain that the battery consisted of six 3 inch rifle guns, marked on the trunnion, R. P. P., W. P. F., 1861, that is Robert P. Parrott, West Point Foundry, 1861.

I saw one of the regulars of Company I, First Artillery, who gave me full particulars of the fight and of their different positions.

An incident after the battle will bear relating in this connection. Gen. Samuel Jones of Virginia, late Chief of Artillery, called at the Lewis House in the battle field to see Capt. Ricketts who was wounded and is a prisoner. Ricketts and he were classmates and friends. He found Mrs. Ricketts attending her wounded husband, and offered her the use of his house and servant, and told her that he could not be with them as duty called him elsewhere, but that Mrs. Jones would be happy to have them with her. Mrs. R. without accepting the invitation, turned towards the cot of Col. [Orlando B.] Willcox, formerly of the U. S. A., but in the battle, commanded one of the Michigan Volunteer Regiments, and pointedly remarked, "Col. Willcox is also of our party." Gen. Jones' immediate reply was, "Madam, I can appreciate the position of your husband, a Northern man and officer of the Regular Army, who is here simply in the discharge of the duty which a soldier owes to his government. But I cannot appreciate the spirit that makes a man volunteer to invade my State and desolate my home, because I assume to act as a freeman." She declined the invitation and is silly enough to say that this is the only act of discourtesy which has been displayed since she has been in our lines.

Col. Wm. Pendleton, the present Commander of the Artillery battalion, graduated at the West Point Military Academy in 1830. I think he was a short time, one of the Professors in the Academy. For many years he has been the beloved pastor of a church in Lexington, in this State. When the invader came to lay waste her fields and apply the brand to the home of his native State, his flock called him to lead them in battle. He took the battery of toy guns from Lexington Academy, mounted boxes on the hind and front hounds of plantation wagons, and with the boys he went to meet the best appointed artillery that Europe or America could furnish. Officers, men and horses were all trained by years of service on one side. Every thing that ingenuity could suggest, or art supply in guns, projectiles, extra wheels, Jack screws, carpenters, harness makers, and smith's appliances were exhausted in the armament for the artillery of the Northern army. Racks for carrying small arms for the gunners were attached to the caissons and filled with polished weapons. And a goodly sight it was to see this splendid army with banners, as it passed out of Washington to march through Richmond and the South. "But Bull Run saw another sight," when Gen. Johnston at 12 M. ordered up the Parson with his uncurried farm horses to make five miles in thirty minutes, which they accomplished across the hills and hollows jolting the boxes and extra-gunners full 18 inches high across the ruts of the old fields. And at 12½ P. M., 12 guns of Pendleton's [Rockbridge Artillery], [E. G.] Alburtis' and [P. B.] Stanard's batteries under Pendleton's command, belched forth a sheet of solid flame upon Rickett's and Sprague's [Capt. Charles Griffin's] batteries which never ceased until the enemy retreated. When the infantry charged upon the Northern batteries, they found fifty dead horses and the gunners piled around the guns.

As a matter of history the first Confederate flag which waved over the Rickett's or Sherman's battery, was the Regimental flag of the Seventh Georgia Volunteers. It was placed upon the gun by a Virginian who begged the color bearer to allow him this honor. The color bearer advanced side by side with him. In a minute after these colors were planted, more than a thousand Southerners closed around the battery.

This stand of colors exhibited to me by the Lieut. Col. James Cooper, has 14 bullet holes through it.

It will be a matter of much pleasure to the many friends of Col. Cooper, the first Chief Engineer of the Mobile and Girard Railroad, to hear that he bore himself gallantly in the fight, and with his unusual modesty does not claim to have killed his man, to have taken Sherman's battery individually, or to have a severe wound.

[John D.] Imboden's, [H. G.] Latham's and the Washington Artillery all did good service during the day. I think it is settled for now that Latham's battery opened the fight and the last shots were fired by the Washington Artillery with their rifled cannon, when the enemy were retreating and were out of range of the six pounders of the other batteries.

It is settled here now that Gen. [Nathan G. "Shanks"] Evans opened the fight on the left of our army—that Gen. [Barnard E.] Bee and Gen. [Philip St. George] Cocke supported him, and Bartow advanced across the Turnpike to support them. And it is equally certain that Kirby Smith and [Arnold] Elzey with their four [two] regiments [and one battalion], come as opportunity as Blucher at Waterloo. Elzey passed out near my battery, stopped his men and told them all to drop their knapsacks and double quick. He is repaid now for his surrender (of the Arsenal) at Augusta.

You can't appreciate the great physical and mental labor of watching a battle in full view, for eight hours. I saw the enemy advance upon us, and our front change from North to Northwest; and I then saw our caisson blow up, and soon after a caisson of the enemy. Then I saw columns of dust in the rear of our line, and I thought here came our forces upon the entrenchments and the enemy will come in pell mell with our own men and we cannot fire because our forces will be at the muzzles of our guns. But I determined in my own mind to wait until the most of our troops were in and the enemy comes in force and I will fire thro' the last of our ranks upon the head of their column, and of our own men, "devil take the hindmost." We had our 32's loaded with double charges of canister, equal to about a nail keg of musket balls at each fire—though the canister for the 32's are, some of them about a pound in weight. But soon I saw the line of musketry fire come back to a point opposite two little trees near my battery and then pass to the right or east of this point, and then before our men on the field knew, I saw the column of dust rising in their rear and I knew the Confederate States was one of the nations of the earth.

Our men fought like devils. I heard the wounded when brought in about 3 p. m., when it was said the enemy would overrun us, say, "lean us against the breastworks and give us your guns; we can fight yet." There is no doubt of one fact, Johnston's army of the Shenandoah by luck of position fought the battle.

***.

PRIVATE LETTER, CAMP BARTOW
NEAR MANASSAS JUNCTION, VA., August 12, 1861 [9-12-61ASC]

Dear Doctor: We who are in the centre of the operations of the Army of the Potomac, really know less of what is going on here in the aggregate than you who are seven or eight hundred miles away. Looking out from our camp, we see, on every side, a wilderness of tents whitening the green hills as far as the eye can reach. Immediately around us are the 7th, 8th, and 9th Georgia Regiments, and a Kentucky Battalion, which all belong to our brigade. Nearly a mile away, and in plain view, is the camp of the Georgia Regulars and the Georgia 13th; on the other side are the North Carolinians. The entire army, numbering not less than ———— men, according to the best information I can get, is now stationed in an extent of country equaling Hall county in area. In going about over the country, one is always surrounded by camps, never losing sight of them. The troops are moving about every day; but we only know what we see, and have no idea what are the general movements of the army. We seldom see any newspapers; and, perplexed with continual camp rumors, we know nothing at all.

After mustering into the service of the Confederate States, at Atlanta, on the 3d of July, we took the cars for Richmond by the Northern route, where we arrived about the 10th, having been detained a few days at Lynchburg. We remained a week in Richmond, during which time, we were reviewed by President Davis and staff. At that time, Gen. Patterson, with a large force, was maneuvering before the army of the Shenandoah, commanded by Gen. Johnston; and an attack being anticipated, we were hurried off from Richmond on the 15th of July, for the supposed point of action. Without leaving the cars, we went for 36 hours, as fast as steam could carry us. Passing Manassas Junction, where Gen. Beauregard was strongly entrenched, during the night of the 16th, we arrived at Strasburg, and encamped, without pitching the tents, in the midst of a field; and, after cooking the scanty rations furnished by the Quartermaster at this point, we lay down to rest, with the blue, star-gemmed canopy of Heaven for a covering, and the cold ground for a bed.

The scenery along the route from Manassas to Strasburg is very pretty. Crossing the mountains, into the celebrated valley of Virginia, and at Strasburg, the mountains rise picturesquely on every side. The next morning early we set out for Winchester, along a lonesome and hot turnpike road, on each side of which was an unending stone fence, and the richest lands in the world; but no shade. The water throughout this whole section of country is so strongly impregnated with limestone as to be almost undrinkable by those accustomed to good freestone water. The day was hot, and the men drank every time they could get water. To me it tasted exactly like epsom salts, and had the same effect; and I believe it was the same with all of our men. We marched about 20 miles, and arrived at Winchester. After marching through the village, we encamped on a bleak hill, on the opposite side, where we again cooked and ate a scanty supper, and slept without tents. In the meantime, it had been discovered that Gen. Patterson's operations were only a *ruse de guere*, the real point of attack being at Manassas Junction. We knew nothing of this, however, when, on the next morning, an order came for us to cook all the provisions we had, and to be in readiness for marching by 11 o'clock. Having been informed that our regiment been attached to a brigade commanded (by seniority of commission) by Col. Bartow—three companies of which were encamped on the opposite side of the village, about three or four miles distant—I very naturally concluded that we were going to move our camp to the vicinity of theirs; but, upon arriving in the village, we found the streets crowded with a dense column of soldiery—the entire army of the Shenandoah, numbering many thousand men, were pressing forward with a rapid step. As we passed thro' the streets, women with tears in their eyes upbraided us for leaving them to the mercy of the foe; all of which was incomprehensible to us. We fell into line of march at our place in Bartow's brigade, which brought up the rear; and, after leaving the village some distance, Col. Bartow and his staff halted and communicated to the regiments, that Gen. Beauregard was sorely pressed by an overwhelming Northern army, and that everything depended upon our speeding to assistance. The news was received with enthusiastic shouts, and the serried columns pressed forward at almost double-quick time. The men of our regiment, worn out by the want of food and loss of sleep, and exhausted by the toilsome march of the preceding day, marched on with a step as light as the lightest. The Gainesville Light Infantry (being Company A) was in front of the regiment; and well might Hall county have been proud on that day to see her sons, determined not to be outdone in the generous rivalry to go to the assistance of our General—their brave spirits striving with the weakness of the flesh, and determined to keep up with the older and fresher troops in advance of them. But this could not last long. Nature asserted her sway, and the restless spirit that would annihilate distance, was compelled to measure with slower and more unsteady steps the weary furlongs that seemed like miles. At one o'clock at night, we waded the Shenandoah, which was about as wide, and deep as the Chattahoochee at Shallow' Ford. By this time, thousands even of the fresh and experienced troops before us had sunk exhausted by the roadside. Two only of our companions had fallen off, and they had been sick. By daylight, we reached a small town called Paris, where we halted for the first time, and remained about an hour. Two more of our company had fallen off—making four in all—while some of the companies of our regiment could not muster more than ten or fifteen men, out of 80 or 90.

Before reaching Paris, while some wagoners were watering their horses, we halted for two or three minutes. The men were so weary, that upon the command to rest, they lay flat down in the road, and, in a moment, they were all fast asleep. On each side of the road were large piles of limestone rocks, which had been thrown out to render the roadside passable. The men had scarcely lain for a moment, when the alarm was given, and suddenly a party came thundering down the hills. Thus suddenly awakened, the men scrampled out of the road as quickly as possible. The cavalry, without stopping or slacking their speed, kept on, and run over the legs of some of the men who had not awakened. Fortunately, none were hurt. But one of our company, in trying to get out of the way, strained his ankle. Soon after daylight, we left Paris, and, after marching seven or eight miles, we arrived at a small railroad station, in the midst of the mountains, called Piedmont, which we had passed three days before on our way from Manassas to Strasburg. This forced march brought to my mind, very forcibly, the celebrated retreat of Napoleon from Moscow; and more than once I was satisfied that we were retreating before Gen. Patterson; and what encouraged the belief was the fact that, after night, fires were built at intervals along the route, in the shape of camp fires, and left burning, as if to confuse and perplex a pursuing enemy. Our brigade was in the rear, and I momentarily expected an attack. Although I was mistaken in the main, it was only a chance that we did not have a collision, for I have since been informed that, during the same night, Gen. Patterson crossed the Shenandoah, within three miles of where we crossed it, with an army of 40,000 men. About 8,000 men left Piedmont daily, crowded into every train, day and night, yet our time did not come until Monday morning, 22d July. A part of our brigade, the 7th and 8th regiments arrived at Manassas, in time to participate in the battle of the 21st, and were badly cut to pieces, as you will learn more fully by the newspapers. It was raining hard on the morning of the 22d, when we arrived at Manassas.

After arriving at Manassas, and during the time that Col. [George T.] Anderson was gone to Gen. Johnston for orders, I had the opportunity of seeing some of the captured Yankee officers, cannons, and other trophies of the fight. Several hundred privates, who had been taken, were kept in a pen close by, but I did not go to see them. I also saw a great number of our own men who had been killed and wounded in the battle. Nearly all of our own wounded had been brought to the Junction. I also had an opportunity of looking over the wilderness of tents, surrounded on every side by strong sand batteries, with heavy guns of every calibre frowning from the embrasures, and bidding defiance to attack. Beauregard says that the camp at the Junction is impregnable, and expresses regret that the Yankees did not come within reach of his fortifications, where they would doubtless have been mowed down like grass. After waiting a short time, we were marched from the Junction towards the battle-field; the way led through an old field; but a holiday being given in honor of the victory, the whole earth had been trodden to mortar by the thousands whom curiosity or booty had lured to the battle-field, notwithstanding the inclemency of the weather. Soon after leaving the Junction, we began to meet the returning soldiers loaded with Yankee blankets, overcoats, knapsacks, canteens, rifles, pistols, and in fact, every kind of equipment that could be conceived of. The further we went the denser became the crowd, and we met hundreds of wagons returning with captured arms, &c. Some wagons that had been sent with us to carry our provisions (all our blankets, knapsacks, tents, &c., had been left at Winchester) were forcibly pressed into the service by those who were sent to pick up arms, &c., and every vehicle, regardless of ownership, was taken in the same way. It was still raining hard when we stopped in a sort of swampy place, about a mile from the point where Sherman's battery was taken.

We took up camp without tents, or blankets, or any sort of covering or convenience. Having had fires built, there being no provisions to cook, and, indeed, nothing to do but to take the rain, Anderson, [A. G.] Dorsey and myself took a stroll over the battle-field. The first dead Yankee I saw had his head shot off by a grape shot, while kneeling behind a fence. After leaving him, we went but a short distance before we came to another and another, thicker and thicker, till the ground was literally strewn with them and their dead horses. All of the wounded of whom there was any hope of their recovery, had been removed, but I saw several who showed signs that life was not extinct. It was a sad sight to see them laying there in the cold rain, with their gay uniforms disfigured with mud and blood. Once I paused to look at a handsome young man, clad in the gaudy uniform of the New York Zouaves—blue cloth jacket, trimmed with lace, and red trousers. His youthful and expressive countenance seemed to bear vestiges of the death struggle; but although the blue lines began to appear around his eyes, there was a sweet, generous expression about them that arrested my attention. He was lying on his back; his hand withered by long saturation in the rain, resting on his breast, which had been pierced by a bullet. I had looked but a moment, when there came a convulsive shudder over his whole frame; his breast heaved tremulously, and with that momentary struggle the thick clotted blood burst from his mouth and nostrils, covering his whole face. From this horrid spectacle I turned away, but similar ones met the eye on every side. At the point where Sherman's battery was taken, the slaughter was tremendous. From one stand-point I counted the dead bodies of fifty splendid horses; and the men so numerous that I did not think of counting them. In a house about fifty yards from this point, occupied by a Mrs. [Judith] Henry, (said to have been of the family of Patrick Henry,) the Yankees took refuge, and in a moment it was riddled by the Southern Artillery. Mrs. Henry, who is said to have been 90 years of age, was unfortunately killed. She was buried in her own garden.

After seeing more than enough to satisfy our curiosity, we returned to the camp, where we arrived near night, and where a cheerless prospect awaited us. The men had built large fires, but it was no protection from the cold rain, which fell incessantly throughout the dreary night. Some sat up all night, and others, overcome by fatigue, lay down in the mud and rain, and slept as composedly as if they had been in their comfortable homes. Towards morning the rain slackened, and by sunrise the clouds had dispersed. The warm sun now shone out, and as the water evaporated from the ground, there was an almost suffocating smell of *fresh fish*—that sickening smell peculiar to a butcher's pen. We remained at that same point till the wet weather springs and mud holes (our sole dependence for water) dried up. We suffered mostly from the scarcity of provisions, resulting from the sudden and unexpected concentration of so large a body of troops. We have moved several times, and are now only a few miles above Manassas, on the eastern side of the railroad, and about six miles from the battle-field. The last time I passed through the battle-field, it presented a horrible spectacle; the blackening and unburied bodies of the dead Yankees, covered the ground, tainting the air with a stench that can only be imagined. The Yankees did not offer to bury their dead, and the weather favoring rapid decomposition, it soon became impossible to bury them all. Many were buried by our troops.

I have seen and talked with many of the prisoners taken in the battle. They speak highly of the Southern soldiers, saying that such fighting was never seen before, as was done on the 21st. There was a Mississippi Company which, after firing away all their cartridges, threw down their guns, and pitched in with their Bowie knives. I heard one of the prisoners say, that they had the Bowies knives fastened with a string to their arms, and threw it after the manner of the sling shot. He said nothing could resist such troops; every man fought on his own hook, and they did not know when they were whipped. Near one of the dead Yankees I found a letter, written the day before the battle, addressed to his sweet heart, and telling her that he was about to start for Richmond—that there would be a slight battle at Manassas, where they would gain the victory, and in two more days would breakfast in Richmond. Poor girl! if she loved him, it will grieve her heart to hear how his high hopes melted away, when Southern prowess turned the tide of invasion at Manassas. Some the Yankees, however, were pretty saucy, and said that we had done no thing great in killing a few men and taking a few cannon—that there was plenty of the same sort left where they came from.

Notwithstanding the want of water and provisions, and the exposure of our men, little or no sickness has prevailed till within the past week, except occasional cases of diarrhea. At this time we have many cases of measles, mumps, and some typhoid fever. Out of 760 men composing our Regiment, not more than 250 men are fit for duty. Some of our Regiment have died—none of my company as yet. The sickness and mortality is not confined to our own Regiment; scarcely an hour passes without hearing a volley discharged over the grave of some deceased soldier. I trust, but it seems almost beyond hope, that our men may pass through the ordeal without a single death.

A few days ago, Col. Anderson told me he wished to adopt, as a regimental uniform, a suit of brown Jeans, and wished the Captains to make the arrangement. I find, upon the receipt of letters by some of the company, that the suit has been anticipated by the citizens of Hall County. They have truly been kind and liberal to my company, and I am sure they will feel satisfied when they know what our boys have undergone, and how much they have suffered without complaint, every trial and vexation incident to a soldier's life. They have won the good will and esteem of all, and I am proud to say they have received in public an especial compliment from the regimental Chaplain.

I have now written you a long letter, and have in some sort given you a succinct history of the Gainesville Light Infantry, up to the present time, and I ask in return that you will give me a similar account of Gainesville.

    Sincerely and truly yours,   W. H. Mitchell,

Captain William H. Mitchell, Company A, 11th Georgia Infantry was mustered in on July 3, 1861. He was wounded at the battle of Second Manassas, August 30, 1862, and killed in action at Funkstown, Maryland on July 10, 1863.

THIRD BATTALION, GEORGIA VOLUNTEER INFANTRY

CAMP DAVIS, LYNCHBURG, VA., August 18, 1861 [8-25-61ASC]

As I write you, a thousand lights from our different camps illuminate the hill tops and plains, and the merry songs and ludicrous jests are heard on every side, while the pleasant breeze, blowing pure and fresh from the mountains, revives the spirits and invigorates the frames of our men. Around rude pine tables the soldiers are enjoying their rations of beef, ham, bread, &c., besides discussing the war with a vim. "I tell you, boys," says one, "the 7th and 8th pitched into them, and so will all the Georgians." "The S. C. Legion," says another, "is my favorite; for they went at double quick right over them, and next to them the Tigers." "Give me the death of Bartow," says a third. "I had rather be a dead Bartow than a live Yankee," says a Colonel. This talk, and a great deal more is said all over camp. Nothing is thought of or talked of but fight, fight, fight; and verily the spirit animates them, and the flesh is not weak. The cry is, when shall we move? where to? and the wish is, that we may be placed where the bullets fly the thickest, and where death claims us fastest. Our hearts are nerved for the fray, and with a firm reliance on Providence, a determination to "conquer or die," we await our onward march. I feel more and more convinced every day that this conflict cannot last—that we are becoming more and more invincible. In truth, as the Virginians say, we will burn every bale of cotton, tumble our sugar into the Mississippi, and our tobacco into the Potomac, yet the spirit of our people is not overcome. If we are rebels, we will always be rebels.

Our encampment is this evening unusually active in consequence of the advance of the 11th Virginia Regiment on to Fairfax C. H. This regiment is one of the finest in the service, and the State is proud of this well-drilled corps. They drill entirely by the bugle, and by this means their orders cannot be understood by the enemy, when, by the ordinary method, might counteract the movement.

We conclude the bombardment of Washington City a certainty, and in the event of its capture, we predict that from thence to Baltimore will be one continued battle-field, rivaling in its grandeur any of the great campaigns of ancient or modern history. Then we will see our little sister, Maryland, rising as a little star above the horizon of her future destiny, and shaking the dew drops of tyranny from off her down-trodden children, proclaim her magnitude, and move within her prescribed orbit beside her twelve sister planets. What an upheaving of the masses there will then be! What joy over the lost, but now found, prodigal! Every bush will become a musket, every house a fortress, and *every inhabitant a freeman!* 'Tis worth the fight to gain for her this liberty; and the sword that shall sever the last tie that binds her to the old Union, is now poised, waiting for the same hand that led us at Manassas to strike the blow. I weary you in this digression, but I do feel for the goodly people of Maryland, and long to see them free.

The health of all in the camp, so far, is very good, though I am sorry to see so much sickness at other places. Typhoid Fever is getting to be quite as formidable an antagonist as the Lincolnites. Our boys at Stanton, Monterey and Manassas are suffering badly with this epidemic, though the measles is raging more at Manassas than anywhere else. The people of the cities and towns are doing all they can to alleviate their sufferings. A good many will never see the dear familiar faces of the loved ones at home again, and yet it is but the fortunes of war, a great lottery, where Death secures all the prizes. Severe colds are prevalent among us here, in consequence of our change of latitude, but as the winter approaches, we hope to be free from all diseases; we have assurance from the Virginians who know this to be the fact.

Col. Boyd has been quite sick, but now convalescent. He is being entertained at a private house, and is very comfortable. And here I must speak once more of the hospitality of these Virginians. It appears to be on the advance every day, and verily it is unbounded. When it became known that the officers of our company could not draw rations from the Government as long as we were near a place where we could purchase them, several gentlemen of this city kindly offered to furnish them with the best their tables afforded at their own houses. Behold us, then, dear *Confederacy*, ensconced at every meal beside a pure specimen of the Virginia gentleman and Virginia lady! See with what care they lavish every attention upon us, and are entirely too fearful of their inability to please! I eat, and eat, yet I must take more, for I am pressed so kindly. First the gentleman insists, then the lady, and last though equally pressing, comes the invitation from the daughters. The fact is, we are getting spoiled, fairing too well; and as an instance, I cite you to our Lieutenant, J. D. Gilbert, who has actually grown so large and weighty, that when we go to roust him for *reveille*, we do not know where to find his head, being equally as thick as long; and the Surgeon is getting sorely puzzled at this extraordinary case.

The name of the kind family with whom we fare so well is JOHNS, and no matter in what part of this continent I may be thrown, whether as soldier or civilian, I can never forget their hospitality; and coming, as it does, to entire strangers, I appreciate it the more.

There are some of the "Tigers" in the city, and inconsequence of leaving Manassas without leave, they were all ordered to be arrested. One of our Corporals went into the city, and having a red shirt and Zouave cap, was forthwith halted and commanded to go to the *Bars*. On inquiring the reason, the reply was, that they had orders to arrest all "Tigers," and our Corporal protested that he was no Tiger, never saw a Tiger, didn't resemble one in the least, in short, hadn't the remotest idea what a Tiger was. It was no go—a scuffle ensued, and in the scuffle our Corporal proved a real live *Tiger*, for he gained his liberty, and, I am happy to state, is now quite tame, and is still of the opinion that he never fought a Tiger but once, and then *"lost every red."* More incidents in my next.

Yours,   T. D. W.

Thomas D. Wright enlisted as Junior Second Lieutenant on June 11, 1861. He later transferred to Company I, 37th Georgia Infantry, and later served in the Western Theater.

ELEVENTH GEORGIA REGIMENT
CAMP BARTOW, 3½ MILES NORTH-EAST OF
MANASSAS JUNCTION, August 20, 1861 [9-4-61ASC]

The present condition of our regiment, the 11th—not the 10th as formerly numbered— its wants, comforts and sanitary condition, so much concern for me, that I cannot longer refrain from laying before you our condition and wants—hoping thereby to awaken a new interest at home in behalf of those whose health and bodily comforts I have pledged myself to look after and sustain as far as possible, whether on the battle-field or these green slopes of the Old Dominion.

Misfortunes seem to have been with and constantly in advance of us since leaving Richmond; for no sooner had we reached there, than a hurried movement to Winchester was ordered. Within five hours after reaching the latter place, we were again ordered on a forced march to reinforce Gen. Beauregard at Manassas, leaving tents, knapsacks and baggage behind to be transported at a convenient time. After plodding our weary way through rain, mud, swollen streams and over spurs of the Blue Ridge, we arrived twelve hours too late to have our names recorded on the battle list or share the honors of the fight. Wet to the skin and fatigued, we were thrown or rather *planted* in a meadow on the banks of the famous Bull Run, without tents, rations or comforts—having no water save that afforded by the muddy stream, then highly flavored with the dead bodies of the Yankees. Through necessity, our brave fellows partook of the *distillation* as though unmindful of its condition. For nine days we were thus bivouacked. At length our superiors had compassion on us and changed our location. Within ten hours thereafter, we were ordered to Camp Bartow where we now are. We here, have more comforts, such as good water, wood and provisions.

Tents have been furnished which, added to the remnant forwarded us from Winchester, together with a few pressed into our service and given us, render our hill-side home less desolate than before. The hygiene of the regiment is my daily study; for upon this depends, in a great measure, the efficiency of the men. Yet all this can effect but little so long as they are forced to sleep in their miserable wedges of tents furnished us by the Governor before leaving Georgia. They are low, narrow, pinned tightly to the ground, without flies and made of ordinary osnaburgs. Under such bolting cloths, who can expect to keep dry? The heavy dews we are now having penetrate them like a sieve; indeed, moisture seems to have been woven in their very texture—in a word, they are unfit to shelter half a dozen ordinary cabbages from an October frost. Straw, ditching, daily airing, everything devised and furnished cannot improve them, and so long as men are forced to *burrow* in such *kennels*, disease and death will be constantly with us. Notwithstanding all this, with other pests, such as incessant rains, &c., general good cheer prevails. Scarce a murmur escapes the lips of most of them. There are some, however, who are *tenderlings*, in body and spirit, who crave a respite from camp life and piteously ask to be discharged, lest the approaching winter or another forced march should prostrate them beyond recovery. Boys, for such they are, should have remained home in the care of the nurse until they had reached manhood's years. I would suggest that all applicants for enlistment should first be thoroughly examined by a physician appointed either by the company or county. We have had too much of these overzealous specimens of the nursery and school room.

A few suggestions to citizens of counties from which companies have been formed, and I am done. The winters in Northern Virginia are exceedingly severe, sudden in approach and of long duration. I would urge the necessity of refitting each company with all their wants, such as clothing, caps, woolen under shirts, shoes, socks, &c., and above all, a new supply of tents—large, with wall and fly, so as to make the men *at least* comfortable. Let each county, then, call a meeting, raise the funds, make the article, pack and ship them to Quartermaster-General Foster in Atlanta, and they will be *transported free of charge.*

I would remark just here, that whilst at Bull Run, exposed to constant rain, and bad water, without tents, 48 was the highest number reported on the morning sick list; but whilst here, blessed (?) with the comforts of Dutch oven tents, the number has reached a much higher figure. The French bivouac is decidedly more healthy than the American *wedge*, whose base is close to the damp ground and no ventilation. Let us have, then, ample tents sufficiently large to accommodate six men, and I guarantee better health and fewer applications for discharge.

Measles and its sequences alone troubles us in the way of disease—the latter now, being our especial pest. Otherwise, our *appetites* are our greatest annoyance, since the "going out" of the measles. A few days of such appetites as we are now blessed with will place all on their feet and bring back the ruddy hue of health and vigor.

MORE ANON.

PRIVATE LETTER, FROM TOM COBB'S LEGION

RICHMOND, Va., August 22, 1861 [8-28-61ASC]

Dearest Uncle: There is not much news—no great battles, or anything of the sort, to write about; so I will have to confine myself principally to local subjects.

As to our Legion, all the infantry companies are here, and two of the cavalry. The Atlanta and Augusta horse companies are at Petersburg, and will be here, I suppose, to-morrow, if not sooner. Our company, the Stephens Rifles, will, I understand, be the Banner Company—our flag being the most beautiful and chaste in the Legion. It is generally admired for its proportions, &c.

There is considerable sickness in the Legion, though none of a serious nature. The sick list to-day numbered over forty, mostly summer complaints, etc. Dr. Marshall, in our Company, has the measles.

I went up in town to preaching last Sunday, and heard a splendid sermon from Rev. Moses D. Hoge, a Presbyterian of considerable celerity—probably the most noted in Virginia.

I went around, also, to see the prisoners. We have some 3,000 of the rascals in our possession—exclusive of the late Missouri capture; while they have succeeded in securing only 300 of ours—one tenth less. The prisoners looked well satisfied, and most say they will fight no more against the South. The wounded ones look sad, and a shade of melancholy broods over their faces. Doubtless, they are thinking of pleasant homes and happy firesides far away. I saw some not more that 14 years of age; also, some of the New York Fire Zouaves. I visited, also, St. John's churchyard and church. This church has some peculiar, hallowed, historical associations connected with it. It is the identical church in which Patrick Henry, in the magnitude of his emotions, with the gigantic eloquence of patriotic enthusiasm struggling in his breast, made his famous ever-to-be-remembered Liberty Speech, which closed with those remarkable words: *"Give me Liberty, or give me death!"* I could almost conjure up the person of that statesman, and imagine myself to be a listener to his magic words, in thus surveying the edifice in which those flaming sentences were uttered. The church has been recently repaired, and presents a handsome appearance. There are some graves, or tombstones, in the churchyard 120 years old. I send a blade of grass, which I gathered near the church. It is an Episcopal church.

I then went on Church Hill, where I had the most splendid view of the city that I had yet seen. When I got back to camps, I was rather tired.

My duties have been changed in the last day or two. By request of Surgeon S. G. White, of Milledgeville, (Surgeon of the Legion,) and the interposition of Dr. Tidwell, and other friends, I am now the Surgeon's steward. I have dispensed with all camp duty, in the way of drilling, &c., and, instead of that, my province now lies in the medical line. I have not been fully initiated into the routine of duty yet; but my principal business will be to assist the Surgeon generally in mixing up, dividing out, and dispensing the medicine—pretty much the same as an apothecary's shop—only more so. All on the sick list (who are able) come to the medical tent every morning at 6, where their present wants are relieved. The doctor then visits those unable to come to the tent, and I have to go around with him. He writes down the prescriptions, and when the round is complete, I go back, fill out the prescription, carry them around to the patients, see that they are taken, &c.

I consider this a fortunate streak. I will have opportunities to witness all manner of diseases, besides seeing, and assisting probably, in performing all manner of surgical operations. I will try and notice everything as much as possible; and if I can ever get home again, I can probably be of some real assistance to you.

Yours as ever,　　　　　　　　　　　　John M. Hardman.

FROM CAPTAIN IVEY'S COMPANY
[COMPANY G, TWENTIETH GEORGIA INFANTRY]
NEAR FAIRFAX COURT HOUSE, VA., August 25, 1861 [9-3-61CS]

After I wrote you from Manassas, we received sudden orders to break up camp and leave at 2 o'clock, a. m., the next morning. It brought our Colonel (Wm. D. Smith) immediately to his saddle, although he was very low with typhoid fever, with the remark that one of two things had cured him, "the orders for the frontier, or a magnificent blister which was nursing him." Shortly after our arrival at Fairfax Station, and while the quartermaster's wagons were being loaded, a messenger arrived with tidings that fighting was going on near this place. Ammunition was instantly distributed to the amount of forty rounds to each man, and with bayonets fixed, the entire regiment doubled quicked to this place, a distance of fully four miles. The road was of clay, made very heavy by recent heavy rains, and somewhat hilly. Our company performed the whole distance carrying knapsacks and haversacks with provisions, canteens, &c., and only left one man in the rear.

Some of the companies threw off their knapsacks, &c., for the wagon masters to gather, but the regiment itself arrived in splendid condition, having expended an immensity of breath in enthusiastic cheers along the route. High and loud amid them all could be constantly heard the ringing company cheer of our gallant Captain and his command, —"One, two, three, four: hip, hip hurrah," as he and his men leaped ankle deep through the heavy clinging clay. Upon reaching here we found that the engagement had consisted in a firing and killing of some of the enemy's pickets near Fall's Church, and shortly after our arrival Gen. Wm. L. Jackson's brigade of Virginians, Col. [James] Longstreet's regiment from South Carolina, and the celebrated Washington Light Artillery, of New Orleans, who had gone out in anticipation of a battle, returned. They came back in good humor, and with loud shouts, notwithstanding their disappointment in having been unable to meet the enemy and cope with him. One thing is very marked in this campaign, as well on the battle-field as in the quiet camp. I mean the terrific enthusiasm of our forces. Such vim and energy in well-appointed forces must prove resistless.

We made our bivouac on an old field on wet ground, and with the heavens for a canopy. To-day we have taken possession of an elegant encampment about two miles from town, with a beautiful country surrounding it. A park of artillery is stationed on our right. No one knows how long we are to remain here. We are satisfied, that at least, we are in the advance.

Ivey's command continues generally healthy, only a few cases of chills and slight fevers, a little aggravated by the fast tramp of yesterday. I should do injustice to the company, should I fail to remark that while it was passing the Colonel's quarters to-day for the first time, it gave him three rousing cheers, upon which he remarked, "a fine company, a very fine company indeed," as they double quicked to their ground.

***.

FROM CAPTAIN IVEY'S COMPANY

NEAR FAIRFAX C. H., VA., August 26, 1861 [9-4-61CS]

At about 3 o'clock yesterday afternoon, while the men of the regiment were enjoying by sleep the little leisure now afforded in camp, they were aroused by the beating of the "long roll" the call for immediate arming and preparation for battle. The call was obeyed with such celerity that in less than 15 minutes the entire force was en route with the quick step towards Falls Church. We went about four miles before the order was given to return. The march was not as fatiguing as the one to this place, as on two occasions we were stopped to allow the artillery and dragoons to pass us. Our regiment constituted the right of the infantry, and the "long roll" was first beat at our camp.

The necessity for an immediate force grew out of a slight skirmish between our own and the enemy's pickets.

Prompt action is now the standing order. Each man sleeps with his arms and ammunition by his side, and his knapsack packed. One day's rations is also prepared, and the canteens filled, ready for an immediate march.

Our pickets extend some distance all around this place, and nearly every night they and the enemy come within gun shot of each other. You will remember that this place was in the possession of the enemy up to the battle of Manassas. Our company go on picket to-morrow.

Possessing but little information here as to the movements of our own or the enemy's troops, there is much and varied speculations as to the future of the war. My judgement is that no general battle will take place this side of the Potomac, unless it be at Arlington Heights. The enemy will doubtless remain where he is in considerable force until attacked, in the meantime subjecting us to annoyance by frequent feints, and make his grand stand at Washington. His late disasters as well as the summer solstice will incline him to this.

The weather here, in the daytime, is very warm, much warmer than we had experienced it in Georgia, up to the time of leaving, while the nights, from our elevated situation, are quite cold. We have a very heavy dew—a species of juvenile rain—and we only escaped a white frost last night by a degree in the thermometer. I am fearful that this kind of weather is to breed much sickness among the troops, forced as we are to rest on the cold hard ground with only one blanket as a protection, added to the sudden change from heat to cold.

Although I have slept upon as hard a bed, and roughed a climate to which this is a Paradise, I must own that it is not without some little prompting of indignation, that I cast my eyes over the town which we are protecting, and the surrounding country thickly dotted with large mansions, enclosed by substantial plantations, with huge stacks of hay and wheat-straw within convenient distance, and remember not a solitary article for a soldier's comfort has been offered by a mother's son of Virginia, and that in the matter of "luxuries" (I write what I heard an officer of one of the companies say, for such things are interdicted to privates,) one dollar and a half is charged for a pint of "rifle whiskey," sure to kill at even four hundred yards. Yet the great boast of Virginia, is, that she has as many troops in the field as Georgia!

***.

SIXTH ALABAMA INFANTRY

SANGSTER'S CROSS ROADS, VA., August 30, 1861 [9-5-61CS]

Gen. Ewell's Brigade has been held in readiness since Sunday last, to march within a moments warning, without tents, baggage or camp equipage and we are now expecting to move every moment. This evening, we learn that our troops occupy all important points between Fairfax C. H. and Arlington Heights. One point, said to be the strongest position between Bull Run and Arlington Heights, Munson's Hill, (I think it is called) and not more than two miles distant from the Heights, it is thought there will soon be a struggle for. It is now held by our troops.

A Federal picket on Friday last [Aug. 23], seeing a scouting party of the 12th Mississippi Regiment, threw down his arms and ran to them, glad he said to have the opportunity of doing so, and declaring he had determined not to fight the South. This man, who seems to be intelligent and well informed, states that there are several Regiments who have been forced into the Federal service, who will, in the first engagement with our troops, throw down their arms and surrender, rather than fight the Southern people.

The Confederates have communication now as far as Fairfax Station, on the railroad, having rebuilt five bridges between Bull Run and Fairfax Station, destroyed by them on the 17th July.

The friends of the soldiers at home could send them many things in the way of provisions, which they really need and which are actually necessary for their health, if they could be sent by Express, to reach here speedily and without delay, so as not to spoil on the way, which they are sure to do if sent by freight trains. But the charges of the Express are so high, that persons of moderate means are debarred from sending these necessaries to their friends here.

It is really a pity to see the condition of the boxes and trunks of niceties prepared by friends at home, anxious to contribute to our health and comfort, and sent to us. The cooked meats, bread, cakes, most kinds of preserves, &c., reach here entirely ruined and unfit for use. Such articles may probably reach here in better condition, after the weather becomes cold, but now it is a waste to send them, besides being quite expensive.

We have had several days of rainy disagreeable weather, and the roads are becoming much cut to pieces by the continued travel over them of heavy laden baggage and provisions wagons, besides artillery, caissons, &c.

PRIVATE.

SEVENTH GEORGIA REGIMENT
CAMP BARTOW, August 31, 1861 [9-6-61-ASC]

The weather, that them of such moment to bashful *beaux* and blushing *belles*, and oft of no little interest to the anxious farmer, is a subject of prime considerations with the Southern soldiery. For three weeks it has been raining almost incessantly. The light lime soil upon which we are encamped very soon becomes muddy. Hence, it may be easily imagined that it has been some time since we have been able to "kick up a dust." For some time we were expecting to move daily; therefore, we took but little pains to guard against mud. But we have recently ditched out our entire encampment and cleaned up generally. Things now wear a dryer, healthier aspect. The sickness in our regiment has been truly fearful. Though we number near one thousand men, we could only produce about three hundred on dress parade, and about one hundred of that number were unfit for active duty. This made it rather hard on the few well ones; for they had to stand guard very often, in the rain at that. But our noble, brave boys, worthy the soil that gave them birth, do all things cheerily. Notwithstanding the continued rain, the health of the regiment is improving. The result of this good treatment is evident, for most every day they return much improved and in high spirits. There have been very few deaths considering the number sick and *the scarcity of proper medicines*.

We have plenty of good fresh beef to eat, but many would much prefer the flesh of the swine; for we are by no means *Israelites*.

We have a sutler, but the exorbitant prices very much curtail his usefulness. With what we can buy, and what our good friends send us, we live very well. We miss, more than anything else, the good peaches and melons that grow so abundantly in Georgia. A small melon sells here for $1.25, and ordinary peaches, such as we would throw to the pigs, at 25 cents per dozen; good peaches at five cents a-piece; and it is very difficult to get them at these rates. But with all the rain, hard fare, want of luxuries, and sickness, the men still keep in fine spirits, and are eager to get a chance at the Yankees. If you could hear the jokes they "crack" around the camp-fires and the hearty, merry peals of laughter, you would be almost tempted to envy the soldier his happy lot.

Many of our boys are making excellent cooks, and if the young ladies, at home, don't visit the kitchens more frequently than has been customary of late years, the boys will make them blush when they return and make biscuit for them. We have desert occasionally in the shape of green apple and blackberry pies.

We were honored recently with a visit from Gen. Robert Toombs and Vice President [Alexander H.] Stephens. Our boys were delighted to get a peep at these two honored sons of Georgia.

There is some great uncertainty in the mails somewhere near this place, and many of our letters and papers never reach us. We hope this will soon be remedied. We prize a newspaper very much. I would suggest to all persons visiting the camps to remember this and try to procure as many late papers as possible. And those friends who send packages might place many late papers in the spare crevices or wrap them around the articles sent. We prize Georgia papers especially. Remember that a paper old at home would be new in camp.

> Officers and men, we're on rising ground,
> And ever in duty's path will be found.
> The Seventh has fought and gained a name,
> And still will fight to maintain the same.
>
> J. B. H.

FIFTEENTH ALABAMA INFANTRY
"CAMP SHORTER," VA., August 31, 1861 [9-8-61CS]

I have concluded to write you a short letter, as it may be of some interest to your many readers and subscribers about Midway, Ala., the majority of whom so generously afforded means for the equipment of the company which left there in July last. To the shame of some, however, it may be said, though "rich in this world's goods," they not only refused to render in their "mite" but consulted an attorney as to the propriety of arresting soldiers who, on their departure, were so unfortunate as to be indebted to them. I say God save all such country (or rather money) loving patriots!

We remained at our encampment near Richmond about two weeks, and it can be truly said, it was no Elysium unless such a place is composed of stones, undulations and mud; but the "boys" did not seem to mind it, and had learned the important truth that vigilance and obedience are the first duties of a soldier.

I made but one or two visits to the city and being on business saw but little of the "elephant" or other curiosities.

Through the kindness of one of the surgeons (a prisoner, and classmate of mine while in New York,) I was permitted to visit the prison and converse with the inmates. I had the honor, if it was an honor, of being introduced to Hon. Mr. [Alfred] Ely, and the sum and substance of his conversation was that he was not as strong a Republican as the world gave him credit for, that the only speech he had ever made in the Federal Congress was in opposition to the war. His fellow prisoners state that he is an arrant hypocrite and do not like the association. I was also introduced to Col. [Michael] Corcoran, of the 69th New York Regiment. He is doubtless a brave man and fought on the memorable 21st, for what he deemed principle and the respect he owed "the stars and stripes." Misguided being! it is a pity that his talent and courage had not been exerted in a better cause.

We left Richmond on the 23rd instant. Nothing of interest occurred en route to Manassas. We are now encamped about two miles from the battle field of Manassas. The majority of the regiment have visited it and brought some little relic to send to their friends at home. Owing to the sickness in camp, I have not yet had an opportunity of going over, but hope to do so in a few days.

The health of the regiment (if we except the measles, of which we have six or eight cases,) is very good. We left two or three in Richmond, and are satisfied of the fact that they will receive every attention. Never were people kinder, and many a wearied soldier, with grateful heart, as he reclines upon his couch of straw, offers up his nightly orison for their protection. Many of them have children in the army, and have often been heard to remark, "such favors as I show to the sons of others may mine receive."

Tattoo has sounded, and the cry of "lights out" compels me to stop. More anon.
                                                                MIDWAY.

☆☆☆Autumn 1861

The Union and Confederate Armies of the Potomac spent the autumn and winter months organizing, drilling, and occasionally skirmishing. Perhaps the most serious threat to each army was the deadly disease that plagued the camps.

FROM CAPTAIN IVEY'S COMPANY
[COMPANY G, TWENTIETH GEORGIA INFANTY]
NEAR FAIRFAX COURT HOUSE, VA., September 1, 1861 [9-10-61CS]

I wrote you the other day detailing our trip to Mason's Hill and return. The company which relieved ours on picket duty, on Thursday [August 30], it is reported had a smart skirmish with the pickets of the enemy, in which we lost ten, and the enemy fourteen men. The pickets have been actively engaged every day since, and yesterday, the enemy appeared in some force, but did not venture a general attack. Frequent skirmishes are also had on the road leading beyond Falls Church, which place is in the possession of our forces. Col. Smith keeps his regiment actively engaged in drill, and as we occupy an advance position, we expect to be called upon at any moment for service where danger lurks, and credit is to be won.

I was in town yesterday, and had an opportunity of viewing the place. It is an old settlement, small and wearing in every respect, a dilapidated appearance not the first sign of thrift or late improvements being visible. The people seem very indifferent as to what is going on, and appear to take the military occupation of the place, as a matter of course the same as they did, I suppose, when the "Yankees" were here. The latter have left their mark in an occasional injury to small dwellings, and painted prominently upon a fence near the Court House is to be seen, "79th Regiment N. Y. S. M.," and other regimental numbers. By the way I should mention that the Maryland troops who were with us at Mason's Hill, were in possession of fine army overcoats left by the enemy in their flight from Manassas, as are many of the Virginia troops; also, many army trappings. It is quite unusual to see officers and men with belts, the buckle to which have "U. S." marked upon them. These are worn with the figures inverted. Many of the horses and baggage wagons which are used were captured, and have "U. S." marked upon them. An old negro gave me an amusing description of the difference between the entrance of the Federal troops into this country site, and their exit from it after the battle. When they arrived advancing they were very anxious to inquire of the negroes, and all whom they met, whether there were any "Seceshes" about, and being told that they were farther down the road, seemed to despair, and would say to one another, "Well, its mighty hard to catch up with these fellows, they run so, but we'll chase them a little more." When returning they stopped for no inquiries, but on, on, in one hurried and disordered flight, Officers and men, mules and horses drawing wagons, and loose, camp followers, all in one huddled mass. I was offered a book to-day to read, called "Donesbury House," by Mrs. Henry Wood. Within is written, "To Warren Cox, Co. B, 3rd Regiment Maine, from Arabella, Augusta, June 30th, 1861," Poor Arabella! in all probability, Warren received attention but little expected when she presented him with this token of her affection or remembrance.

*** .

Sgt. Warren Cox, age 28, of Co. B, 3rd Maine Infantry, was captured at First Manassas and confined in Richmond until September 6, 1862. He was exchanged and returned to his regiment in October 1862, and was commissioned First Lieutenant on December 21, 1862. Lieutenant Cox was killed in action at Chancellorsville on May 3, 1863.

SIXTH ALABAMA INFANTRY
SANGSTER'S CROSSROADS, VA., September 2, 1861 [9-12-61CS]

There have been some skirmishes within a few days past between our advance forces and those of the enemy, between Falls Church and the Potomac. A decisive battle is looked for here hourly, and we have received orders almost every day and night for eight days past, to be in readiness to march at a moments warning, consequently we have been kept in great suspense, during this time. Every one here is tired of inactivity and anxious to go forward.

What the intentions of our Generals are is all speculation and guesswork, but from the movements at present, there is little doubt of demonstration at an early day of great importance, upon one side or the other, for the contending forces cannot possibly remain as they are at present, and avoid it many days longer.

Persons who have arrived within our lines lately from Baltimore and Washington represent the prospects of the Lincolnites as any thing but flattering, in many places, and giving it as their opinion, that revolution and civil war will occur among themselves soon.

Recruits arrive here daily in numbers more than sufficient, in most instances, to fill the places of those who have fallen in battle, been discharged or died. This is as it should be, and presents quite a contrast, when we look at the difficulties the Lincolnites labor under, in filling their thinned and broken ranks. This fact alone is sufficient to show the spirit that animates the people of the Confederate States.

And here let me say a word to those who are coming to join the army, in relation to what they should bring with them. There are but few who come into the army, that do not bring superfluous arms, clothing, &c., and the consequence is, the government being deficient in baggage wagons, and the men having more than they can carry upon their backs, are compelled to throw them away.

In the first place bring no side arms, infantry particularly, as they are totally useless and money expended for them is thrown away. A soldier who will do full justice in using a musket or rifle in battle has no earthly use for side arms, as the instances are very rare, where opposing forces cross bayonets, or are near enough to use effectually small arms, besides the weight of repeating pistols of size sufficient to do execution any distance, and a large bowie knife, is an item of no inconsiderable importance I assure you, when a man has to foot it and carry besides his gun, pistol and knife, a knapsack, wearing apparel, blankets, canteen and provisions sometimes for several days, to say nothing of the difficulties men are liable to get into, particularly those who are young and inexperienced, when they have side arms convenient to use upon each other on the slightest provocation. I have seen enough of these things in the army to authorize me in advising all young men coming here to leave pistols and bowie knives at home. A good substantial pocket knife, is all the weapon an infantry soldier needs, besides his rifle or musket.

A man has no use for clothing, but that of the most durable and substantial kind, and just as little of that as is actually necessary. He will need two pair of pants, one coat, two heavy flannel shirts, two hickory shirts, two pair drawers, two pair woolen socks, and a good substantial hat or cap. These, with his blankets and an oil cloth to protect him from rain, will be about as much as any one will be able and willing to carry upon his back.

And here I would advise those purchasing Oil Cloths, to purchase no more from G. H. Peabody & Co., of Columbus, Ga., unless they have made great improvements lately, upon those that have been used by persons here, as they fail entirely to protect them from rain. I regret to have this to say, but candor and a desire to protect soldiers from impositions of kinds, come from what quarter they may, compels me to say this much. I would be glad were it otherwise, but after a trial of them here it is the opinion of those who have used them that they will not do. Another article I would advise our friends at home against purchasing, is a Map of Virginia, published at Richmond, by J. W. Randolph, it being a perfect humbug, and entirely unreliable, so considered here by every one who has seen and examined it.

Persons engaged in raising companies and getting recruits, should be very particular as the health of those they enlist and their physical ability to endure in camp life, what the stern and unbending rules and regulations of military discipline demand of them. This is no place for a man who is not stout and strong and able to undergo hardships I do assure you, for I have seen enough to fully satisfy the most skeptical upon this point, and no one need enter the army with a weak constitution and in feeble health, flattering himself that camp life in the army will benefit him; if he does he will be very apt to find himself sadly mistaken, besides there is no necessity for persons of this description entering the army, when there are so many stout and able-bodied young men who are able and I hope and believe, willing to endure hardships and privations, in numbers sufficient to drive back all the armies Lincoln will ever be able to bring against us.

The War Tax Act has been received here in the Richmond papers and meets with the approbation of every one who has read it. Its provisions are just and equal, bearing alike upon property holders of every description, and being liberal to the poor.

There are many in the Confederate States who have contributed largely and liberally of their means towards the support of the war, and seem willing, if necessary, to give all they have, while there are others who have not given of their *abundance* as they should, and what they have given has been contributed grudgingly and sparingly and in sums contemptible when compared with the interests they have at stake. I am truly glad this act reaches these men who have their thousands hoarded around them, who have failed to respond liberally with their means, voluntarily, in support of the Government in the hour of its need.

PRIVATE.

THIRD BATTALION GEORGIA INFANTRY
CAMP DAVIS, LYNCHBURG, VA., September 9, 1861 [9-14-61ASC]

The soldiers have all gone to offer up their devotions at the alters of the Most High at the various churches in the city. This manifestation of reverence for the deity, on their part, is universally commented upon by the citizens of Lynchburg—especially in references to the Georgia troops. If I see a man, regularly as the Sabbath comes, going to church, and eagerly devouring each word of the discourse as it is uttered by the divine with prayerful attention, and the eye speaking praise to God, I cannot but think his dear parents are Christians, God-loving people, and be a true patriot and soldier. As I now write you, our camp is almost deserted, the soldiers, in squads, under charge of an officer, have marched in good order to the houses of worship, whilst, on our right, the Mississippians are having a sermon preached them, and hither and thither they are scattered, seated on camp stools, whilst the beauties of the gospel is being unfolded to them. Truly, I can exclaim: "Glory to God in the highest on earth; peace and good will towards men." What a sight for the parents of those brave men, could they but behold it! What depths of emotion would arise in the fountains of their hearts at such a scene. They know, by this, that the bringing up of their children "in the nurture and admonition of the Lord" is not lost upon them, even in the tented field.

How earnestly the good man strives to impress upon them the divine precept, "Honor thy father and thy mother, that thy days may be long in the land;" and the attentive ear, the tearful eye, and the convulsive throb of a soldier's heart, bespeak that the lesson is not forgotten. The mothers of Georgia's soldiers can congratulate themselves that the once prattling babes, now in the vigor of manhood, and arrayed in the panoply of warriors, are daily calling down blessings on their heads for the counsels given them in youth. The fathers of these noble boys, who have placed the musket in their hands, may feel assured that their stout arms and brave hearts are nerved for the conflict by the cheering words, "Trust in God, I give you up for your country." If you could see with what willingness and cheerfulness they perform every laborious duty assigned them, and the proud look of consciousness they give when they know that it has been done well, you would be doubly proud of them. Such soldiers the world has never furnished before for the defense of a nation's liberty. But often our hearts are almost rent by the ravages of a foe we cannot conquer. Many who have periled their lives in the thickest of the fight, and escaped one death, have fallen by the unseen shaft of disease. We were called to witness just such a scene on Friday last, in the death of Lieut. Wm. Goggins, of Virginia. A young man of noble daring, brave and chivalrous, the pride of his parents, and the favorite of the Lynchburg community, was suddenly snatched from them by this unseen power. He was at the engagement at Bull's Run on the 18th, and also at Manassas on the 21st, in both of which he gallantly led on his comrades, and, though death was all around and about him, and men falling by the scores, yet he escaped unhurt. Immediately after, he had an attack of typhoid fever, which ended his life. He died in the bosom of his family, but no human art can give the father back his son, the mother her darling boy, the brother his dear associate, or the sister her protector.

A detachment of 50 men and six Lieutenants, by order of our Colonel, were detailed to pay the last, sad tribute to a stranger, but a brother soldier. We proceeded to the residence of the deceased, taking open order in front; and I never did experience such feelings as I entered the room where the deceased lay. A beautiful metalic case, all wreathed in flowers, hung entwined around it in beautiful festoons, interspersed with evergreens, first met my gaze. As we carefully raised it to bear him hence, convulsive sobs from relatives were heard, and I involuntarily, with greater care, proceeded with our sad task. I trod lightly the ground, for every noise was an arrow to loving hearts. They knew we had come to take their boy away, and we could but bespeak our sympathies with scalding tears. We reached the cemetery—a beautiful spot near the James River; and, as the report of our fire-arms broke the stillness of the hour, I felt deeply for the parents of such a boy. Would that our country had many such sons to give in her cause.

The health of the different regiments and battalions is excellent. In our company we have but one or two cases, and they are slight. The good health of our troops is owing to the fact, that the police duty is rigidly enforced, and the camps are thoroughly swept and cleaned every day; and the good water and regular diet we have.

I chronicle the arrival to the rifle and cavalry Legion, (Col. [William] Phillips,) of a splendid Irish company from Macon. They came last week, and such brawny arms, big men, brave looking and determined, are seldom found. Dear old Erin is well represented now in our army, and, my word for it, they "know they're right, and will go ahead." They are already vastly popular, and are generally the favorites in our army, and we hope for many more such from Georgia.

Georgia troops still keep pouring in, and I verily believe that every third man you meet is from the "Empire State." To say you are from Georgia, is a sufficient passport to the hearts of these people, and so with Alabamians and Mississippians. The hospitalities of the citizens continue on the increase to all the soldiers, and they will (I may say) starve themselves to feed a man with a musket and stripes down his pants.

Your excellent sheet is eagerly inquired for by the few who take it here, and almost every soldier in our Battalion says he either takes it for his family or intends subscribing. You may, therefore, look out for a larger subscription list than you bargained for, and I do not wonder at it; for they all acknowledge its superiority over any other for reliability and general information in Georgia. They also admire the *independent* stand you have taken in regard to your paper, and the perseverance and indefatigable exertions you make to give it a higher tone than is generally found in newspaperdom. We say, then "Go ahead," and no danger will happen that will knock you into *pi*. The paper comes regularly every morning, and strange, that others who take dailies generally get one or two a week, whilst the *Confederacy* is found on our table every day.

We hear every day important news from the seat of war. It is now reduced to a certainty as I predicted before, that Washington City will be ours, for our cannon are in easy range, and our flag floating on one side of the Potomac, and the Stars and Stripes on the other. I read a letter yesterday written in plain view of the city, from an officer in our army, and the troops are eager for the commencement of the bombardment. We expect to be present at its beginning, unless we are doomed to remain here. We only live in hope. You may, therefore, look for startling and grand movements before I write you again, and your patrons may rest assured that I will give you nothing but facts—reliable facts.

T. D. W.

LETTER FROM SOLDIER JIM

CAMP BARTOW, MANASSAS, VA., September 9, 1861 [9-19-61ASC]

We arrived here last Saturday night about 9 o'clock, in good health, and found the boys doing much better than I expected. A few who have had measles are not well enough for service, but are improving rapidly. Those who were wounded, and who had left sick, are now coming in nearly every day, though some are also being carried away.

Our gallant and brave-hearted boys are more anxious for a fight than ever before. I don't think they can be stopped when they get after old Abe's *pet lambs* again. We will make them believe we are all "Tigers."

Our camp is on Bull Run Creek, in a very awkward position—though surrounded by springs of good water as any in Georgia. A cornfield is close by, where our boys are allowed to get plenty of green corn for "roasting-ears," which, by-the-way, is very agreeable to Soldier Jim. Our mess is composed of stout, hearty fellows, and we ate 15 ears to-day for dinner.

We have orders to hold ourselves in readiness to march. We expect to move in a few days—to what place, I cannot tell, though I suppose it will be nearer the Potomac. Our boys who occupy Munson's Hill are in sight of Washington City, where the Federals can take their glasses and make discoveries, but they are too cowardly to come out and fight the rebels, as they call us.

Everything about camp is as "natural as pig tracks" (there, I've said it again)—though not quite so pleasant as in Atlanta, where I could see the fair ones in all their beauty and loveliness.

> Yes, they are the sweetest flower
> That ever drank the amber shower;
> And could I see them now,
> I'd make a pretty bow.

> Though the Atlanta Grays
> Must fight a few more days
> Before they reach Washington dome
> And return to their lovely home.

> SOLDIER JIM.

TRIBUTE TO JAMES S. GEORGE OF THE ATLANTA GRAYS [9-15-61ASC]

The unnatural and unnecessary war which is entailing sorrow, and suffering, and bereavement throughout the Southern Confederacy, is marked by many revolting facts. Among these, and by no means the least revolting, is the difference in social position, family influence and moral and intellectual worth of those composing the two armies arrayed against each other. As a general fact, the Black Republican army consists of mercenary hirelings, unprincipled blackguards, whose high ambition is plunder and the destruction of domestic happiness, and whose most animating watchword is *"Booty and Beauty."* In the army of the Confederate States are to be found in large proportion, men of property, education, talent, private worth and commanding influence. Hundreds of these men occupied positions of usefulness and honorable distinction. All of them, with but little exception, comparatively, are beloved and cherished at home, as sons, brothers, relatives and friends, *of the best families in the land.* Among them are no *hirelings*—not even a *drafted* soldier answers his name when the roll is called. Prompted by no sordid considerations, and unaffected by unworthy motives of any sort, they constitute an army of self-sacrificing and devoted men, presenting a bulwark of defense against the vile invaders of their common country—a noble band of *volunteers*, whose highest ambition is their country's *independence*, and whose most inspiring watchword is *"Liberty or Death."*

An illustration of the truth of these remarks is to be found in the subject of this article—Serg't James S. George, who left his native State, Georgia, on the 22d of May, as a member of the Atlanta Grays.

Serg't George was quite young, being only twenty years old on the 22d of December preceding the memorable battle in which, as a soldier and patriot, he offered his life a willing sacrifice upon the alter of his country. He had just entered upon the arena of public life as a competitor for distinction in the profession of his choice. Having received a respectable elementary education, he commenced the study of law under Col. [Daniel] Printup, of Rome, and concluded his legal course at the Law School in Athens. During the few months of his residence and practice in the city of Atlanta, he had many valuable friends, and had given flattering indications of his future success. In the bloom of youth, surrounded by relatives and friends who loved him, the cherished son of an aged father, with talents above the ordinary standard, and professional prospects growing brighter every day, he heard the call of his country for her young men to repair to her borders and repel the invasion of an insolent and disappointed despot. Prompt and cheerful to respond with others like himself of our noble State, he obeyed the call, and was among the first who went forth to meet the dangers and liabilities of the camp and battle-field on the soil of Virginia. At Harper's Ferry, and Winchester, and Darkesville, he was always at his post; and in the hour of threatened attack, was ever found ready to act his part in the expected struggle. He contributed his full share, bravely and nobly, in giving enviable distinction to the gallant 8th Georgia Regiment, and side by side with the dauntless Bartow, on the Plains of Manassas, poured out his heart's blood in defense of his country's rights. As a messmate he was beloved by his comrades for his mild, generous and manly bearing. As a private, and afterwards a subaltern, he enjoyed the confidence and respect of his superior officers, and the friendship and esteem of his companions in arms. He was one of those who made the almost unparalleled forced march from Winchester to Piedmont—who waded the Shenandoah in the night—who hastened with noble, generous impulses to the scene of strife, and who, weary and faint from hunger and continuous exertion, boldly dashed into the thickest of the fight, and gloriously "illustrated their native State," by a stern, unflinching courage that claimed and received from the magnanimous Beauregard the high compliment—*"8th Georgia, I salute you."* Poor George! he heard not that proud recognition of his valor and self-devotion, for he lay upon the battle-field, stricken to the earth by the death wounds he had received. The battle of Manassas Plains will occupy its page in the record of great and triumphant achievements, and when the names of its *heroes* are registered, let not the name of James S. George be forgotten.

A. T. HOLMES.

SIXTH ALABAMA INFANTRY
SANGSTER'S CROSS ROADS, VA., September 15, 1861 [9-23-61CS]

There has been no movement of importance made by our forces here, within several days. We still hold all the strong points in front of Arlington Heights, to wit: Munson's Hill, Mason's Hill and Hall's Hill, upon each of which fortifications have been thrown up and artillery planted. Munson's Hill is 3½ miles from Arlington House and 4½ miles from the Long Bridge, due West, and is considered a position of great importance to the Confederates. General Longstreet, who is in command of our forces in that neighborhood, has endeavored for several days past to draw the enemy out from their fortifications, but with little success.

A few days since [on Sept. 11] they ventured out some distance from Chain Bridge with 2,500 men and 6 pieces of artillery and drove in our pickets. Gen. Longstreet immediately sent forward *four companies*, who attacked their force of 2,500, killed 14 of them, captured several, and took several horses, and drove them back within their lines. They are evidently tender-footed about giving us battle, at this time anywhere in that neighborhood, whether from fear of the risk of a general engagement with our forces at present, or because of a change of schedule in their plans. I am inclined to think that their forces are not sufficiently reorganized since their rout at Bull Run to give battle to our troops here, and at the same time guard against our crossing the Potomac above and below Washington, of which they no doubt have great fears, but whether well grounded or not I am unable to say. They evidently have their hands full just now.

From a gentleman in Gen. Longstreet's Brigade, whose company is stationed on Munson's Hill, I learn that persons who have left Washington within ten days past and come within our lines, bring information that their Hospitals in Washington, Georgetown and Alexandria are filled and crowded with their sick. Typhoid fever and chills and fever are the prevailing diseases.

Col. [Micah] Jenkins, of South Carolina, on the evening of the 4th inst., reconnoitered some distance above Arlington Heights, and discovered at Big [Great] Falls, on the east side of the Potomac, where the water works which supply Washington City with water are situated, an encampment of the enemy, and that the houses belonging to the works were occupied as barracks by the troops, and concluded to dislodge them.

That night about 10 o'clock, Col. Jenkins, with his regiment and four companies of artillery, quietly moved down and took his position without the enemy knowing anything about it, until he opened upon the houses with his artillery the next morning quite early, when they poured forth like hornets disturbed in their nests to see what the matter was. Perceiving what the difficulty was very readily, they ran out two pieces of artillery from some bushes where they had it concealed, and made preparations as if they intended returning fire, but did not do so. About this time a white flag was displayed from one of the windows of a house, and Colonel Jenkins paying no attention to it they then hung out a yellow rag of some description (the signal for a hospital) and thinking the houses might be occupied by the sick, the Colonel changed his fire to the tents beyond, when they immediately struck them, packed up and moved off without ever firing a gun, the place being made rather too hot, to be comfortable. They lost about 30 killed outside of the houses, that could be seen by our troops. The river at this point is supposed to be 400 yards wide.

The enemy has their balloon up ever day, and sometimes oftener, endeavoring to get the position and number of our troops. They have made one ascension in the night, throwing out signal lights and rockets during their elevation.

A large balloon was carried to Munson's Hill yesterday, to be used by the Confederates, in case it is thought it can be used advantageously.

Lieut. Col. Baker, who was officer of the picket at Springfield several days since, sent out four of his men on a scout, and succeeded in capturing three Yankees at a house six miles below Alexandria, on the road leading to Accotinck. They were well armed, but our men were too quick for them, they had no chance to use their arms. They were from Maine, and quite respectable looking men. These men had a good many complaints to make of matters in their army, and represent that there is a good deal of dissatisfaction existing among their troops.

Mr. Robert Mason, the independent scout, who has been of so much service to the Confederate army, has received the appointment of Brigade Quartermaster of Gen. Ewell's Brigade, with the rank of Major. This is a well-merited appointment, and one of which every man here is truly glad who knows Mr. Mason, though the loss of his services as a guide are much to be regretted. He is a brave and gallant man and as modest as he is brave.

PRIVATE.

LETTER FROM SOLDIER JIM

MUNSON'S HILL, VA., September 17, 1861 [9-29-61ASC]

Last Sabbath morning we marched from Camp Bartow, near Manassas, to this place—distance about twelve miles. The march was warm and fatiguing. We arrived here about 5 P. M. Although the boys were tired, they were ready to pitch into a fight.

Mason's Hill is just below Munson's Hill opposite Alexandria and the Heights of Arlington, with several other elevated points occupied by the Federals are in plain view. The U. S. flag waves in the breeze where we can see it at any time. We have a fine view of the Potomac, where we can see the vessels that pass up and down.

We are well fortified here—having sufficient force to keep back all of Abe's minions, if they make an attack on us. We expect to remain here four days, and then go back to our encampment.

Our regiment is nearly as full as it was in the last fight. The boys are hearty and eat like log rollers. "Soldier Jim" don't like the cooking business, but he knows he has it to do; he therefore takes hold, and gets up a meal as soon as any old cook you could pick up. Our beef is very tender and nice. We boil it very done, and let it get cold. We then make *hash*, which is first rate. Very often I chop it, and make the best *steak* imaginable. The worst I hate about cooking is the smoke getting in my eyes and burning of my fingers; but there is one consolation to "Soldier Jim:" our soldiering will come to an end one of these days—let that day be long or short—and then if we survive we can get somebody to *cook for us* the balance of the time.

The Federals call our regiment the Georgia Gray Devils. I guess if the gallant Eighth gets after them again, we will make them quake and howl.

SOLDIER JIM.

FIFTEENTH GEORGIA REGIMENT
[TOOMBS' BRIGADE, SECOND CORPS]
FAIRFAX COURT HOUSE, VA., September 24, 1861 [10-3-61ASC]

The Fifteenth Georgia Regiment suffered severely from measles, and still more from its sequel, while at Camp Walker. The same trouble has been experienced in every camp so far as my observation has extended. This is a matter worth the special consideration of those who may yet bring soldiers into camp; because it is from mismanagement of measles that most of the sickness of a dangerous character has arisen.

Six men with measles are generally crowded into one small tent, which is closed in front and pinned down closely to the ground on every side. In ten minutes' time there will not be a cubic inch of atmosphere in the tent which has not been, in great measure, exhausted of its vitalizing principles. The peculiar exhalations of the body in this disease, not only mingle with the air, which, already deoxogenized, must continue to feed the blood; but saturates every particle of matter in the tent, in such a concentrated degree, that a week's sunshine will not remove it. In this situation they are kept a week or two, and then allowed to indulge an abnormal appetite in eating and drinking. A low, and frequently malignant, form of fever, which is more troublesome and far more dangerous than measles, is generally the result. That from this character of disease, more of Georgia's soldiers have gone to the grave, than fell in the battle of Manassas Plains, I have not a doubt.

Soldiers who die in their desolate little tents, far away from home or relations, certainly realize the greatest degree of anguish that the "king of terrors" can inflict on mortals. Bright hopes of the greatest achievements all vanish; the anticipated pleasure of returning to the enjoyment of home and independence is lost, and even the privilege of dying gloriously in battle is denied them.

Strange as it may seem, an enemy more dangerous than Lincoln's army is lurking in our camps, and through stealth is picking off our men; and only inefficient measures are used to rout him.

A very small part of the expense and attention that is required to nurse these soldiers through their fever, and to consign hundreds of them to their mother earth, would, if properly applied, restore them to usefulness in their respective positions without going through a long and terrible course of suffering.

The remedy in this particular class of cases is simple: Let a hospital for measles be obtained at once on the appearance of the disease in a regiment. Any building which can be ventilated at will, and has been decently kept, will answer for a hospital. Then, as fast as cases occur, let them be carried into the proper apartment of the house. Here good nurses with proper dieting and ventilation will be sufficient to carry nearly every case safely though to a good recovery.

Measles has now gone through this regiment—Col. [Thomas] Thomas being the last case. The sick have been sent to the hospital at Richmond, and the camp again has a lively appearance. The Brigade is now near enough to the enemy for the various regiments to take their turn in serving on picket. This regiment will probably go out next Friday.

A church in this place is now used for a hospital. At one door lies a man wounded in the left leg, as he says, by a cannon ball, in the battle of Manassas Plains. Yesterday, with some friends, I visited him. We asked what State he was from. He replied, "from the United States." In speaking of his condition, he only regretted that he was not killed instead of being wounded. We told him that he would soon be well and could get an opportunity of having his desires accomplished. He replied that between his wound and imprisonment he should never be released.

With the exception of an embarrassed look of the eye, he had a very pleasant countenance, and conversed intelligently; but when the war was the subject, he displayed a good share of the non-committal policy peculiar to Yankees. We had the pleasure of seeing two South Carolina ladies approach him. They spoke kindly and said he was a fine looking Yankee—really too good a looking man to be engaged in such a bad a cause. They told him they were South Carolinians, and of course were death on Yankees. He replied that he was a German and belonged to the Regulars; that Yankees would not fight—they would put others forward, or would argue a man out of anything, but would not fight while there was any other chance of accomplishing their designs. In taking their leave, the ladies shook his hand and expressed a hope that he would soon recover and take up arms in a better cause than the one in which he had been engaged. He promptly replied that the Government was owing him a considerable sum of money—four months wages were due him when he came off here. Evidently, here was the cord which bound him to his country. If he should abandon the cause in which he was engaged, he would *lose his wages* which had already accumulated. He was evidently looking back to the fleshpots.

And can it be that the infatuated Northern leaders expect to subjugate the chivalrous South through such instruments? Will the treasure of the North, and the promise of plunder be sufficient to pay her men to fight her battles? So far they have been sufficient; but with every struggle, both treasure at home and hope for plunder abroad have diminished, and none can see it more clearly than the calculating Yankee. It really seems that the princi*pal* and *interest*, too, for which the Northern soldiers are fighting, will soon be at a discount.

ELBERT.

LETTER FROM THE MUSCOGEE RIFLES
[COMPANY E, TWELFTH GEORGIA INFANTRY]
CAMP BARTOW, GREENBRIER CREEK, VA., October 3, 1861 [10-12-61CS]

The opportunity so long and anxiously waited for by us has at length arrived. We have had a brush with the Yankees. This morning at about 5 o'clock the enemy advanced and fired on our pickets. The Arkansas and Virginia Regiments took charge of the breastworks, while our regiment formed in line of battle in the open field, so that the enemy could have a fair fight with us. They opened their batteries upon us about 9 o'clock, which we returned with will. Col. [J. N.] Ramsey was ordered to our right and Col. [Albert] Rust to our left, to prevent the enemy from flanking us, while the Macon City Blues with another company, were dispatched to the top of the mountain before the enemy came in sight. We had not been formed more than an hour when the firing commenced. At first their range was entirely too high, as the bombs and balls passed over us, hitting the tops of the trees 300 yards behind us. The enemy had formed in a field some 8 or 900 yards from us. Our battery was too hot for them where they stood, so they marched to the road and took the mountainside, endeavoring to flank us, but before getting to the road, however, one of our shells burst in their ranks killing several of them. We then moved forward in regular order to meet them, when our brass cannon opened on them, which broke their ranks and made them take up the mountain. We continued to advance, as well as they. While advancing to our position our boys did not seem to notice the advancing foe, but to watch the execution of our cannon which were playing on the enemy's ranks as we were marching to our position.

After we had reached our position we had to get on our knees in the mud, and there remain for three long hours. One man of our company, John Dean was wounded in the arm while taking his position, though it is not severe however. Some five or six horses were killed, and one sick man in our hospital had both legs shot off by a cannon ball, and two others lost one each. So far as I can learn we lost only three or four men in the engagement. At one time fears were entertained for Col. Ramsey, as his horse was found with blood on him, but late in the afternoon he made his appearance. He stated that during the fight he was cut off and had to remain on the top of the mountain, from where he could see the enemy carrying off their dead in wagons for hours. After the fight, we found three of their dead, there may be more yet left on the field. The fight lasted from 9 a. m. to 1 or 2 p. m. We found numbers of their balls and shells, the latter of was some for rifle guns measuring 9 inches. We are sleeping on our arms expecting an attack hourly.

G. W. Cooper.

George W. Cooper was mustered in as Fourth Corporal in the 12th Georgia Infantry on June 15, 1861. He was captured at Spotsylvania Court House on May 8, 1864 and sent to Elmira Prison, and was released on May 15, 1865.

A TOUR OF PICKET DUTY

CAMP JONES, S. E. OF FAIRFAX STATION, VA., October 5, 1861 [10-15-61ASC]

Picket duty, all things considered, is not unpleasant—especially if one needs an appetite, for it soon creates a huge one. The grunt, the cripple, the big lazy and the brave, set out with us regardless of surgeon's certificates of disability, or captain's vetoes, in this outdoor exercise.

Our orders were first to report to Gen. Longstreet at Fall's Church; but when we came in sight of this town of ancient Barons (Fairfax) some half dozen of both sexes, who were *en route* hence to some place of safety, informed us that the enemy had taken possession of Munson's Hill, one and a half miles distant and were advancing in large numbers to attack us; that Gen. Longstreet had ordered the immediate retreat of all wagons belonging to the transport service, of all private citizens, and of the beef cattle fenced in for our rations.

Caring but a fig for this startling (?) announcement, we pushed on and drew up to rest in front of Headquarters. Soon, the General in person informed us that Col. [J. E. B.] Stuart's pickets had come in and reported the advance of the Federals towards us from two points—Lewinsville and Alexandria—intending to cut off our supplies and take us captive. Two pieces of the Washington Artillery and 300 men were dispatched to Lewinsville, and we commanded to post ourselves, throw out skirmishing parties, fall back under cover of a few young peach trees, and bare our arms for the conflict. The calmness and self-possession of the 11th [Georgia] was truly commendable. Not a man shrank from the brush which seemed at hand, which was to establish the bravery or prove the cowardice of each one.

Soon, brisk cannonading was heard in the direction of Lewinsville. Excitement now became intense, and as I looked down the lines every ear seemed to reach itself out like a bugle mouth towards the music of arms, whilst thrown all eyes were out on the road which swept in a gentle curve up the hill to our right.

Couriers brought news that the federals 500 strong had thrown a shell into the yard of a house owned and occupied by a sister of the brave Jackson, of Alexandria, who killed [Elmer] Ellsworth at the sacrifice of his life, for the honor of his house, his country and his flag, and that our forces had driven them back a mile and a half beyond the town.

The heroic courage of Miss Jackson on this occasion is worthy of record, and of being handed down to future generations. When the sound of the first shot had passed away, and the fragments of shell were buried in her door and the trees in her yard, and scattered on the grassy plat, she threw herself in front, in full view of the enemy, and exclaimed, "Kill me, and be revenged; for in my veins courses the blood of a Jackson; but *you* shall taste death for the deed."

She then returned to her house, buried her face in her garments and hands and wept because she was unable to destroy the vandal wretches who have invaded our country, laying it waste, and planting sorrow in almost every home. At this moment our forces came up, and with a few shots put the rascals to flight. This was the firing we heard. The news gladdened our boys, who now fell back on their arms. They took the rich hay from a well-filled Yankee barn, and made for themselves comfortable couches in the midst of rank weeds, beneath the low spreading branches of young peach trees—there to dream of their Nancies and Janes, with snow white sleepless eyes to fret and grow nervous over a fail to get a fright.

Col. A. and myself, proud as sprigs of royalty, made headquarters of a neat little cottage. Here we luxuriated on fine potatoes, juicy pumpkins, rich beans, &c.—caring but little just then for such elegancies as rich tapestry, fine linens, soft beds, or such delicacies as are served up for sated appetites.

At 8 o'clock that night a slip of paper from the hand of a bearer of dispatches warned us of danger; to have the wagons hurried back—the men drawn up in order of battle—all the lights extinguished, and keep as still as the tomb. It was cold, wet and windy; but the boys braved it all. After a two hours' stand, we were ordered to retreat slowly, and take position at Mills' Cross Roads, three miles distant, where two regiments awaited us—the 15th Ga., and the 17th Va. Here we bivouacked—no fires allowed, and but a "smile" or two having been granted us through the whole day.

Our Q. M. and myself went back next morning to look over the modern deserted village. A solitary picket posted on two exposed points were the only living creatures to be seen. No army had yet possessed it, but before we got back to camp, a runner came by announcing the grand entry of the grand army on a grand scale, which, would in all probability attack us before night. During the day multiplied rumors kept us on the *qui vive.* Now a gun could be heard in the direction of our outposts—then orders to flint our guns and eat but two meals—thus passed our day.

Privates Seaborn Jackson and Henry W. Mann, of the Houston Volunteers, were shot on picket duty by the pickets of the 15th Regiment—the former through the forearm and in the shoulder—the latter slightly bullet scorched on the left side just above the hip—neither dangerously. Such accidents are of too frequent occurrence to be excused every time. Scarce a day passes without similar errors. In some cases it arises from the incompetency of the officers commanding. Such men should be put back into the ranks.

I made a tour of observations alone to Mason's and Upton's Hills, in order to satisfy as to their position, extent, their fortifications, and to look at that modern Sodom, known as the city of Washington. These Hills lie almost on a line facing Georgetown Heights, the Potomac, and overlooking the rich, green pastures of the valley beneath. The extensive breastworks, ponderous cannon and immense force of our men said to have occupied these points existed only in imagination. The Washington Artillery, with four pieces, remained for a day or two on Upton's Hill—just in the rear of Munson's—simply to play scarecrow to the enemy. No heavy ordnance was there, save that monster gun, mounted on cart wheels and made of four joints of an ordinary stove pipe. Occasionally the boys would take the tongue of the cart and swing it around, pointing it in the direction of the federal pickets but half a mile distant, simply to amuse themselves during their weary hours by seeing the Hessians scamper to their hiding places in the houses and barns on Mason's Hill. A like ponderous Parrott gun, made of a 10 inch *pine tree*, blackened and mounted on cart wheels, also plays the frightful to these Northern Vandals.

Some incidents in camp life are amusing. Whilst on duty, a night or two since, the Col. [M. D. Corse] of the 17th Va.—senior officer in command—instructed us to have every spark of fire put out; that the enemy was close by, and the utmost vigilance must be exercised. Guards were stationed among the thick pines, instructed to keep a sharp look and report as secretly as possible the first approach of the enemy. About 12 o'clock a sentinel crept up to Col. A. trembling from head to heels, and said in a whisper—"Colonel! Colonel!! the *h*enemy's 'proachin' jest in thar; I heard a bush or two crack near unto my beat!" "Keep your eye skinned," said the Colonel in a bass voice; "much depends on the vigilance of the men on guard." Could that sentinel's scalp speak, what a story it would tell!

All surplus baggage was to-day ordered to Fairfax Station, and all the sick to the general hospital, and each man to hold himself in readiness to strike tents at a moment's warning. This means something; but what? is the question. A fight is expected, but will it come?

MORE ANON.

SIXTH ALABAMA INFANTRY

SANGSTER'S CROSS ROADS, VA., October 8, 1861 [10-18-61CS]

Considerable activity prevails in every department of the army here. The sick have all been removed to the rear, to different places where hospitals are located, and extra baggage sent back to places of safety, in case of emergency; in fact every precaution adopted usually by wise and skillful commanders, preceding a great military movement or engagement has been taken by our Generals.

President Davis, had a grand review of the troops on the 3rd, and left that evening on his return to Richmond. His departure was witnessed by a large number of the troops who flocked to see the "great Rebel Chief," they love and respect so much. The President being called upon for a speech, remarked that the day for speaking had passed; we must wait until Lincoln's minions were whipped out and then we could sit and have a chat over the matter.

Gen. Earl Van Dorn, who captured the U. S. troops in the western part of Texas, last spring, together with a large amount of military stores and equipments, and afterwards succeeded in taking a steamer belonging to the old Government, near the mouth of the Rio Grande, has arrived here and been assigned to the command of the 2nd and 3rd Brigades, (Gen. Ewell's and Gen. [Jubal] Early's) and has entered upon the discharge of his duties.

His appointment gives great satisfaction to those under his command. He looks more like a *fighting man* than any General who has been seen here, and is said to be a man who always seeks the post of danger as the post of honor, and at the same time sagacious, skillful and prudent.

The weather has been quite hot and sultry for this latitude and the season of the year, for several days past.

Heavy cannonading has been heard to-day, from 8 a. m. to 1 p. m., in the direction of Falls Church. We have no particulars yet.

PRIVATE.

SIXTH ALABAMA INFANTRY
SANGSTER'S CROSS ROADS, VA., October 13, 1861 [10-21-61CS]

The heaviest fall of rain we have seen in Virginia fell here on Monday [October 7] night last, commencing to pour down through the night with little intermission, ceasing about daybreak Tuesday morning. The creeks have been very high and some damage done to the Rail Road bridges between Manassas and Fairfax Station, so as to interfere with the passage of trains, for several days, but the damages have been repaired and the trains are again running regularly. Again on Friday night last we had a very heavy rain, but have heard of no damage resulting from it.

Two deserters from the Yankee army reached Gen. Ewell's headquarters on the night of the 8th inst., having left an Artillery company stationed near Alexandria, during the rain of Monday night. They are from Maryland. The only news they bring is that 30,000 troops have been sent from Washington to the relief of [John C.] Fremont in Missouri, and to endeavor to retrieve their disasters in that State, and that the Yankees do not at present contemplate an advance upon our forces here, but are looking for us to attack them in their entrenchments or cross the Potomac into Maryland.

Tuesday night [Oct. 8], at 2 o'clock, the long roll was beat, and we were in a few minutes ready to march. The cause of the alarm was said to be that the enemy were advancing on the Pohick road, numbers unknown. One half of our regiment was marched in the direction of Occoquan. We were accompanied by cavalry scouts, who reconnoitered the country for several miles in advance, who soon ascertained the alarm was false, and we returned to camps. The alarm was general through the entire army, signal rockets were seen in the direction of Fairfax Court House, and the whole line seemed to be in motion or preparing for it. So you will see we are on the alert and not likely to be caught napping.

PRIVATE.

FROM COBB'S LEGION
CAMP WASHINGTON, YORKTOWN, VA., October 9, 1861 [10-19-61ASC]

We left Richmond on the 15th of September. Our march was over grounds rendered sacred by the tread of the sires of the Revolution. We slept, the first night, upon one of their old camping grounds, and drank from a spring that had slaked the thirst of many a weary soldier. We passed an old church [St. Peter's], in which, it is said, Gen. Washington was married—quite a dilapidated looking building. We also encamped at a church said to have been his *headquarters* for a short time. It was built in 1775, of brick imported from England. I there saw a tombstone dated 1748. I have since seen one, a mile below here, on the river, dated 1655. We spent a day in Williamsburg, where stands the celebrated William and Mary College, now converted into a hospital for our sick soldiers, under the superintendence of Dr. John G. Westmoreland.

We are now encamped on the battle-field of Yorktown. Within a few hundred yards, and in full view of our camp, stands a monument where Lord Cornwallis surrendered his sword; still nearer, is the [Moore] house in which the terms of his capitulation were signed. It is a staunch looking building—might stand the shock of another battle or revolution, and witness the capitulation of another invading General. Our camp is on the bank of York River. It is a beautiful plain. Have a fine view of the blockading fleet, which lies off ten miles below. The river here is about two miles wide.

There was a little incident, the other night, which, though not of much importance, created some excitement at the time. About one o'clock, Thursday night last [Oct. 3], we were aroused from a deep sleep by the shrill notes of the bugle and the heavy roll of the drum. "To arms, to arms," was the cry; "the enemy are landing in great numbers below here." We donned our arms, saddled our horses, and put off at triple-quick time, and sped down the river nine miles, expecting every moment to come face to face with the enemy. We were, however, most sadly disappointed, to learn that none of the enemy had landed or attempted to.

It seems that the two pickets stationed there were either drunk or fools; for they mistook a small fishing smack, with three or four men in it, for five or six large war steamers, with as many thousand men in them. The fishing smack, on coming near the shore was hailed by the pickets, who, receiving no reply, fired off their guns, mounted their horses, put out up here at full speed. They aroused the whole brigade at this place; none, however, were sent but the cavalry.

On our way down, four or five miles below here, the battalion was thrown into some excitement, occasioned by the firing of two guns in the rear. Ten or twelve men were sent back to find out the cause of the firing, who soon returned and reported "nobody hurt," and we went on without any further disturbance.

We returned to camp about ten o'clock A. M., Friday, sadly disappointed and tolerably mad. I think if some of our men were allowed to handle those pickets for a little while, they would learn to inform themselves better hereafter before reporting. To have such a heavy ride and no fight was too bad.

Gen. [John B.] Magruder, as you know, is in command of this division of the army. He has subdivided it into three divisions. [T. R. R.] Cobb's Legion goes to Cockletown, in the first division, under command of Gen. [Gabriel J.] Rains, there to be held in reserve. Cockletown is six miles below here. We go there to-morrow. It is a general impression that we will have a fight here soon.

As "taps" have sounded, I must extinguish my light.

Yours very respectfully,　　　　　　　　　　J. R. G.

☆☆☆Battle of Leesburg

On October 21, a Federal reconnaissance-in-force crossed the Potomac at Harrison's Island and climbed the precipitously steep and heavily wooded Ball's Bluff and advanced towards Leesburg. A swift Confederate counterattack resulted in another military disaster for the Union. Official losses: Federals, 49 killed, 158 wounded and 714 missing—many presumed drowned in the retreat for 921 casualties; Confederates, 36 killed, 117 wounded, 2 missing for 155 casualties.

EIGHTEENTH MISSISSIPPI REGIMENT
IN CAMP AT CARTER'S MILLS,
SIX MILES SOUTH OF LEESBURG, VA., November 12, 1861

Monday morning, the 21st October, musket firing was heard at an early hour in the direction of Harrison's Island on the Potomac, and it was soon after ascertained that Capt. [William] Duff, of the 17th Mississippi, who had been picketing in that direction with his company, had encountered and driven back the advance guard of the enemy. But as it was known that they had only fallen back to a stronger position, and most likely on a stronger force, two companies of the 18th—the College Rifles, Capt. [Johnson W.] Wilborn, and the Burt Rifles, [Adj. Martin] Campbell—were promptly dispatched to the scene of action. Capt. [Lowell] Fletcher, of the 13th, with his company, took part in this affair. About 10 o'clock the firing became more general, and it was apparent that a sharp conflict was to progress. The enemy, for the first time at that point, opened an artillery fire, and the 8th Virginia, Col. [Eppa] Hunton, was ordered up. He reaches the field, I should think, after 1 o'clock P. M., and before 2, the vollies on both sides were general—the enemy using their artillery only. I may mention here that we had no artillery engaged in the fight, and did not fire a cannon all day. We had a small battalion of cavalry, but I cannot learn that it took any part in the fight—the ground, probably, not admitting of their movements.

While the forces just mentioned were engaging the enemy at Harrison's Island, General [Nathan G.] Evans was deploying what was left of the 13th, 17th, and 18th Mississippi regiments on the hilltops and in the plains near Edwards' Ferry, two or three miles farther down the Potomac. It was here that he made so much of us. My company, with two others— Capts. [Walter] Kearney and [W. H.] Luse—were so posted as to make the enemy, if they saw us, believe we were an entire regiment. I have no doubt all the others were posted to like advantage. From a promontory near my station, we could plainly see the Yankees with our naked eyes passing their reinforcements within a few hundred yards of where the fight was going on. Of course we caused Gen. Evans to be informed of this fact. But he held us to our position. The enemy was crossing below us, at Edwards' Ferry, in still greater force, protecting their advance and keeping us at bay by a formidable battery, so planted as to rake the entire country for at least two miles around.

All day we had not fired a gun, except a single shot early in the morning, discharged by our company at a squad of Yankee cavalry that dashed in among us, and then dashed out again. It was now near 3 o'clock; suddenly, and as if by magic, the different companies and squads were called together, and the whole force marched forward, as if we meant to attack without regard to the consequences. The fight at this moment was waxing hotter and hotter at Harrison's Island, and we were marching right away from it. You may imagine how the souls of the brave but uninitiated privates and subordinate officers chafed under such treatment. Suddenly again we were halted, and ordered to countermarch. Slowly we retraced our steps. After marching half a mile as if we were going to a funeral, the enemy looking on and doubting, I suppose, whether we were falling back to a stronger position, or to get some other way to advance on them, we suddenly found ourselves covered from the country in our rear, by a hill and skirts of wood; instantly the order "double-quick" was given, and off we plunged, at a long trot, for the fighting ground, now about two miles in our front, leaving the Yankees wondering what had become of us. In less than [?] minutes the 17th and 18th Mississippi, in all their force, were in the hottest of the fight.

The 13th, Col. [William] Barksdale, was left behind to watch the enemy we were now leaving in our rear, and, if possible, prevent their advancing. Here the 13th had the post of honor, because it was eminently the post of danger; and right well did they maintain it. Col. Barksdale, at this point and at this hour, with his single regiment, kept back a column powerfully reinforced, which Gen. Evans had not dared to engage with his whole army in the morning, before it was reinforced. If this was not a prodigy of valor, there has been no such thing on our side since the war commenced. Barksdale boldly sallied back and forth, and impudently (excuse the expression) attacked the force. Of course, if they had known his real strength they would have walked right over him. He had about 800 men of all arms, and they about 4,500, according to their own account. Instead of advancing in all their force, they kept feeling about to find out what become of us, until Barksdale went out and gave them a spat, killing 42 of their men and wounding their General, with little or no loss to himself; and then, thinking he was trying to withdraw them into an ambuscade of *infuriate* rebels and masked batteries, they fell back under shelter of their cannon, planted on the opposite side of the river. Here they began throwing up breastworks and rifle pits, at which delighted work they toiled incessantly all night long. Poor devils! with powerful batteries in their rear and breastworks in their front, and no enemy attacking, they took flight, and sneaked back in the night, across the river, into Maryland, to meet their disconcerted and discomfitted friends from Harrison's Island. What frightened them?

The answer to this question leads me back to the 17th and 18th Regiments. On they went, right into the fight—the 18th in front, and the 17th close behind. As we neared the field, the firing on our side became perceptibly weaker. Just as we were filing down a small ridge, through a wood, and some five hundred yards from the enemy, we met Capt. Wilborn's "College Rifles," who had been beaten back. They called out, "hurry up, the Virginians are out of ammunition, and can't hold out much longer!" At this critical moment, James Small, a private in my company, sung out, "give 'em a cheer, boys!" The whole line caught the inspiration, and such an unearthly yell as went up has not been heard since Pandemonium was inaugurated. The Yankees from that moment felt whipped. They knew that howl, for they had heard it at Bull Run. On we went, plunging down a deep declivity and up a hill, and then we stood in less than one hundred and fifty yards of the almost victorious Yankees.

Col. [E. R.] Burt, of the 18th, impetuously leading the van, swept forward, and in less than one minute was engaged, leading Captains [Joseph] Jayne's, [Clarance] Hamer's and two other companies in an almost hand to hand fight with the enemy. The other companies, of which mine was one, were brought up almost at the same moment, by Lieut. Col. Griffin. Burt's command swung around to the right, and was thus thrown directly in Griffin's front. We could not for the moment fire, Col. Burt and his men being directly between us and the enemy. I called to my men at this instant, standing in the edge of an open field, to fall. They did so, and simultaneously a terrific shower of bullets swept over our heads, killing Sergeant [James] Dier, and wounding private J. E. Lewis severely in the head. We lost nothing after this. In an instant Col. Burt's horse came dashing furiously, without a rider, through our lines. There was something akin to a shock manifested among the men, and I said, "steady, men! steady!" Then came another volley of musketry, and the artillery, right in front, belched forth its fiery missiles of death, distant from us 150 steps. The men were firm.

While this was going on, the rear of our (18th) regiment was getting into line, and Colonel [W. S.] Featherston was rapidly bringing the 17th into position. In less than three minutes the whole line of battle was complete. The Virginia 8th on the left, the 17th Mississippi in the centre, and the 18th on the right. Col. Burt, at this instant, was borne from the field, mortally wounded. He passed through my company, and fearing the effect on the men, I said, "There goes our Colonel, let us avenge his wrongs!" The boys replied, "we will, sir!" and the Colonel, game to the last, said, "Go on my brave fellows; don't mind me; you can whip them!"

I had formed my company on the extreme left of the 18th, and consequently on the extreme right of the 17th. Featherston, being senior Colonel, and General Evans not being personally present, took the command. His speech, in ordering us forward, ought to immortalize him.

He said: "Soldiers, the Yankees are before you. You must drive them across the Potomac or into eternity—Forward, march!" At the word march, the whole line stepped off as if it had been on parade. Advancing a few steps, the order was given, "ready, aim, fire!" when the whole Brigade poured a volley into the woods in front, from which the enemy had been firing. It was returned by random shooting, and it became apparent the Yankees were falling back. Again the order was, "forward, march," and the whole line, in the same good order, moved up—reaching the point where the enemy stood. When we reached the field we found they had moved back perhaps one hundred yards—their line through the woods presenting an uneven zig-zag appearance. We again poured in a terrific volley and pressed on. The enemy fled; and after this the shots on our side were aimed at such of them as our men chanced to see as they fled through the woods, or as they attempted to rally in broken squads. We pressed on to the high bluff, overhanging the river, just as the terror-stricken Yankees were leaping pell-mell down the deep declivity, and again our whole line poured forth a hurricane of shots.

Night was now gathering in, and in the dense forest on the brink of the river, it was soon measurably hidden from our view by the darkness, was being enacted in the little vale at the water's edge. The Yankees, driven like so many frightened sheep, were huddled together. Hundreds crowding the light transports, sunk or upset them. Other hundreds, frantic with fright, plunged head-long into the river, to find only a watery grave. Some doubtless made their way in safety to the island shore; but we know that many hundreds perished. How many were killed or drowned will never be known. A thousand, I am satisfied, will not cover the list. In five minutes we should have slaughtered five hundred more, if they had not begged for quarters. As it was, our officers had great difficulty in restraining the men. I had myself to threaten some of my own men with death before I could stop them from firing.

The field, after the battle, presented a fearful picture—a picture of war—of civil war. All along our line of march lay the dead and the dying; and as we returned the bodies of the slain lay like swine in a slaughter pen, while the groans of the wounded pierced the air, and made the night hideous. It was strange to contemplate the twinkling stars and clear, bright moon riding in the Heavens at that hour, and wonder if they were not mocking the distress of these poor victims of a sad but wicked delusion.

I have said nothing, you will observe, to indicate to whom I think the greatest credit is due for this most signal and remarkable victory. I have not, because all did their duty, and all had to do it to make success certain and signal. It is due to the Virginians to say they made one bold and desperate charge after we reached the field. What they did before that I cannot say. The 17th came up to their work like veterans. They could not have been better commanded, and no troops ever behaved better. Of the 18th it hardly becomes me to speak, and yet I feel that eulogy might exhaust itself and hardly do it justice. Burt will live in history as Mississippi's first great martyr to Southern liberty. After he fell Lieut. Col. [Thomas] Griffin commanded with an intrepidity and coolness that at once marked him as a soldier, while Major [Eli] Henry was always in the right place at the right time. The captains and their officers behaved as became Mississippians. If I mention one or two by name no unfriendly inference is to be drawn as to the rest. Capt. Jayne was with Col. Burt when he fell, and being the senior officer in that part of the field for the moment, took the command. He fought like a tiger, and led his men from the field literally dripping with blood. Capt. Harner fought with equal courage. Captains [Albert] Hill, Kearney, Luse—all of them, indeed, plunged into the fight, regardless of danger, apparently resolved to conquer or die. For myself, I shall be abundantly satisfied if it be the judgement of my countrymen that I did my duty. My company has the credit of killing twelve Yankees at one fire, and of having at every fire done more or less execution. How all this may be I will not pretend to say. But this I know: all along the line of our march the ground was well strewn with dead bodies. We walked over a rifled cannon, but I do not pretend that we took it. That honor belongs to the entire brigade. It lay in the line of our march, and we were the first to lay hands on it. We deserve that much credit, and no more.

I am conscious of having given you a very imperfect sketch of a very brilliant battle. My object has been truthful and fair, and not to mislead by over coloring at one point and not coloring enough at another. If you get no other than correct ideas from my letter, my regret will be less that I have been able to give you every incident, both of a public and private nature, calculated to enlighten you in regard to the fight, and those of every grade engaged in it.

A. G. B.

Captain Albert G. Brown of Company H, 18th Mississippi Infantry, resigned shortly after the battle of Leesburg and was twice elected to serve in the Confederate Senate.

How 54 Men Captured 320
LEESBURG, VA., October 31, 1861 [11-20-61CS]
The following incident in connection with the battle of Leesburg I deem it worthy of especial mention, and shall therefore give the names of both officers and privates who were concerned in it. After night had dropped her mantle over the field of battle, and the Virginia 8th had been ordered to the breastworks known as Fort Evans, Lieut. Charles F. Berkeley, who had command of the picket stationed on the field, and Corporal Elijah White, (a better than whom never drew a trigger,) discovered a large body of the enemy, which they estimated at between six and seven hundred, on the bank of the river crossing in boats to the opposite shore. It was quickly agreed by them that Corporal White should endeavor to raise a force to capture them, and Lieut. Berkeley should watch them with his picket of six men until he returned. The remnant of the Virginia 8th, numbering not more than 150 men, (the rest being in Leesburg, inquiring after their wounded comrades,) had just finished their late dinner and were lying down on the ground when the corporal rode up and demanded one hundred or one hundred and fifty men to endeavor to capture the body of the enemy at the river, which he estimated at some six or seven hundred.

Fifty-four men all told, under command of Capt. Wm. N. Berkeley, started for the river at the best pace they were capable of. When some two-thirds of the distance to the river had been passed, we passed a picket of Mississippians under an officer whose name I did not learn, who also fell in behind us. Upon nearing the river the groans of the wounded on the banks, and their supplications for water were truly distressing. Our force was here divided and a part of it left on the top of the bluff. About thirty men, including the two captains and lieutenants, descended to the bank of the river, and crept silently through the darkness toward the enemy. Upon the command being given, we fired our pieces and charged into the midst of the enemy, calling upon them to surrender, which they immediately did, and to the number of three hundred and twenty, including some commissioned officers, were marched into Leesburg and delivered to General Evans. Lieut. Berkeley employed some of his men the greater portion of the night in carrying hundreds of fine rifles and muskets from the river banks to the top of the bluff, and brought in the morning five additional prisoners. In justice to some others of our officers and men, I would state that whilst returning with our prisoners, we met a party coming to our assistance, but who arrived too late to participate in the capture. Adjutant Evans counted the prisoners and will vouch for the correctness of the number taken. Believing this to have been the best haul of the season, I take pleasure in sending you the above statement of it. While upon this subject I will mention an anecdote of our Colonel Eppa Hunton, who was always to be found where the bullets were flying thickest. Wishing to obtain accurate information of the position of the enemy, he dismounted and crept on his hands and knees 150 yards, getting sufficiently near to obtain the desired information and returned unharmed, to the great relief of his men, who are greatly attached to him.

*** .

LETTER FROM SOLDIER JIM

CENTREVILLE, VA., October 22, 1861 [11-1-61ASC]

Since I last wrote you, we have made a backward move to this place. We are now encamped in sufficient force and strength of position to whip four times as many Yankees.

On Wednesday night last [Oct. 16], after we had eaten our supper, retired to our tents and laid ourselves in the arms of sleep for the night, the long roll of the drum was heard, a courier came dashing through the camps street for us to strike tents and get ready to leave there. Our companies had not a wagon apiece, and our baggage had to be curtailed. Many trunks, camp chests, tents, cooking utensils, &c., were thrown into a heap and burned. It looked like destruction was among us doing its worst work, and that we would soon be stripped of everything we had, though it could not be avoided. We have full confidence in our commanding Generals, and the necessity and propriety of whatever they order, and are prepared to endure all such mishaps as best can.

During our march in the night, many of our men fell by the way. The night was damp and cold, and the march through the mud was wearisome and fatiguing. When we reached this place next morning, our men formed in line, stacked arms, and fell down on the grass to sleep.

Since then, nothing much has been done but cook and eat. Many of our men are unfit for duty—in their tents with sickness. The weather has been damp and cold, and very bad for the soldier. I have been confined to my tent for near a week with severe cold; but hope to be out in a few days and able to go where the old drum calls me.

We have just heard from the Leesburg fight. I hope a few more good brushes will cause the wretches to find out that they are a whipped and demoralized race, never to conquer and always to be conquered. Thank Heaven; I am on the right side in this fight. Though I may soon be slain by the hand of the enemy, I shall die in a good cause, if I breathe my last in the rage of a fierce battle.

The time is near when we must prepare a refuge for winter. I know not where it will be; but in a short time we can rear up small cabins and daub them tight with mud, and keep as warm and comfortable in them as squirrels during the winter. Then we will need something to read to keep our minds from tainting with idleness. Continue to send us your paper. I am always happy to hear from Atlanta—especially the *ladies* of the city. When I get a paper and see in it that the patriotic ladies are daily working for the soldier, it cheers my heart and inspires me with courage and resolution.

> Yours truly,
> SOLDIER JIM
> A sitting in his tent,
> A writing on his knee.

SIXTH ALABAMA INFANTRY
UNION MILLS, VA., October 26, 1861 [11-2-61CS]

Since the battle of Leesburg on the 21st inst., matters have been remarkably quiet here. You have doubtless learned the main particulars of this glorious achievement of our troops, from other sources before this time. For three days past we have had fine, cold, bracing weather. We were visited on the morning of the 24th with a slight frost and yesterday morning with a heavy frost. Ice was plenty.

The troops were busily engaged making all needful preparations for the reception of the grand army the 2nd, should it come this way. The prisoners captured at Leesburg say that McClellan will certainly advance upon us soon in very strong force.

The wearing apparel of many of the guard who brought the prisoners from Leesburg to Manassas was in rather a seedy condition, and after their arrival at the latter place one of our troops approached a very finely dressed Federal officer, and smiling, asked him if he did not feel cheap to be brought there a prisoner by those ragged rebels. The officer replied, "you may laugh now, but our men will laugh next week." (alluding to the approach of McClellan's overwhelming forces.) The Confederate rejoined, "I shall laugh at you anyhow now, and *take the chances* of getting whipped next week."

Major John B. Gordon, of the 6th Alabama Regiment, has resigned and returns to his home in Jackson county, Alabama. There are several aspirants for the position vacated by Major Gordon, among them Lieut. [A. M.] Gordon, Lieut. [M. L.] Kirkpatrick and Capt. James F. Moddell. I think I am safe in saying that the latter will be elected.

Col. [Robert E.] Rodes, of the 5th Alabama Regiment, has received the appointment of Brigadier General.

PRIVATE.

NINETEENTH GEORGIA VOLUNTEERS
CAMP PRYOR, NEAR MANASSAS, VA., October 27, 1861 [11-7-61ASC]

Our regiment is located very near to Manassas Junction. On Tuesday last [Oct. 22], we had reports all day that a fight had taken place at Leesburg, and 500 prisoners were captured. I was on guard all day, and all our soldiers mostly within their lines; so we had but little opportunity to know the truth of it. About midnight on Tuesday night, a courier passed me, with orders for Maj. Blair, the Commissary at this post, to have breakfast prepared for 525 Yankee gentlemen.

Next morning, the vicinity of the Grand Guard house at Manassas was thronged with anxious spectators from the neighboring regiments, who had managed, with *water-buckets* for passes, to get out of their respective lines; and curiosity ran high with them to look upon the Yankess—notwithstanding Manassas is the muddiest place I ever saw.

About 10 o'clock they came by the camp of our regiment, marching four abreast, between files of Confederate soldiers with bristling bayonets.

There was a striking contrast between the dress of the captives and captors, and their appearance brought vividly to our minds the days of the first revolution, when our forefathers, in rustic, tattered suits, led captive the sleek, well-fed British soldier, arrayed in gay uniforms. Then, as now, the tax-gathering invading tyrant prided himself upon his good looks, good fare and elegant clothing, and counted considerably on the potency of these for the victory he came to win over the sons of Freedom; and now, as then, captivity, defeat and disgrace is their just reward. These Yankees had heavy cloth and cassimere uniforms, and many of them heavy army overcoats—everything, in fact, necessary to their comfort—while their victorious *escort* were clothed in coarse homespun, with wool hats on their heads. It was a striking illustration of that great truth that fine clothes do not make men honest, moral, wise or great; if it were so, these Yankees would never had been found in arms against us.

As they marched along the guard lines, all had an opportunity to see them; and I am happy to say that not a soldier in our ranks showed the slightest disposition to insult the conquered and captive foe. The commissioned officers, and some who had lost their shoes in endeavoring to swim the Potomac, were allowed to ride in a wagon. On their arrival, the officers were quartered at one of the public buildings, and the privates at the Guard-house, and all refreshed and fed with the best the place afforded.

At 6 o'clock in the evening, thirty of our regiment being detailed as an escort, under the command of Lieut. [William N.] Tumlin and Lieut. Colonel [Thomas C.] Johnson, commenced putting the prisoners on the cars, and by 10 o'clock started to Richmond. The commissioned officers were allowed a passenger car, while the privates were put in freight cars. Each car carried thirty-five prisoners and five guards. We were considerably crowded; and the Yankees, being fatigued, piled one upon another and slept like pigs in a cold night, growling on top of the heap, when the bottom would become unbearable from the weight of numbers. The night was extremely cold for this season, and the Yankees though far better clothed than we, shivered like they had agues upon them, while our boys did not seem to suffer much. It seems to me that they cannot stand the cold so well as we, and that their hope to conquer us by the assistance of the cold weather during this winter will be vain.

Some of them were very communicative, and tried to impress upon our minds that they were not Abolitionists; that they detested abolitionism as much as the Southern people possibly could; and that the abolition of slavery would injure the North as much as the South, and that a great revolution in northern public sentiment had taken place, in favor of slavery, and against abolitionism, since the war commenced. They said that, if the two sections could understand each other, the war would cease, and the Government be restored. They say they never suffer the idea of two governments to exist within the original bounds of the United States to find a lodgment in their minds, and that both must sink forever, or again be united. They thought they would be able to conquer us and establish peace by next spring.

Those under our charge were mostly from Massachusetts and Pennsylvania, and were men of fair intelligence.

Nothing of importance happened on our route to Richmond. We were met there by thousands of speculators of all colors, anxious to get a look at the Yankees, but no one offered any indignities, save some small boys, who cheered a little.

Yours, &c.,   A VILLA RICA GOLD DIGGER.

SIXTH ALABAMA VOLUNTEERS
UNION MILLS, VA., November 7, 1861 [11-12-61CS]

We were visited with a furious storm of wind and rain during the night of the 1st inst., which continued until noon the next day. The rain began about 9 o'clock in the night and the wind from the South East; about 1 o'clock, blowing a perfect gale, prostrating and tearing in pieces many tents, leaving the inmates shelterless and exposed to the storm. Bull Run rose rapidly and very high, the water carrying away the Orange and Alexandria Railroad Bridge, near here, besides a large quantity of Bridge timbers, which had been collected at various points above here, for the purpose of building bridges across the creek. The troops suffered no little during the storm, I assure you.

A soldier belonging to the 12th Mississippi regiment, was drowned Sunday morning, in attempting to cross Bull Run during its highest stage, and he in a state of intoxication. His body was recovered yesterday morning a short distance below where he was drowned.

Gen. Rodes has been assigned to the command of the 2nd brigade (Gen. Ewell's) and entered upon the discharge of his duties yesterday.

We have not learned where Gen. Ewell will go. His command parts with him with deep regret, and go where he may, he carries with him the best wishes for his welfare, and success, of both officers and men who were under him.

In a synopsis of Gen. Beauregard's report of the battle of Manassas, given by a correspondent at Manassas, of the *Richmond Dispatch*, I see it is stated that the courier sent by Gen. B. with an order for Gen. Ewell to make an attack with his brigade upon the left wing of the enemy, was killed, and the order consequently did not reach Gen. Ewell; hence the non-action of that General with his brigade.

The Sixth Alabama was paid off last week in South Carolina funds; the privates receiving $22, the amount due them for their services during July and August. This makes three and a half months pay we have received altogether, besides $21 for clothing, &c.

There are no tidings of any approach of the enemy any nearer our lines.

PRIVATE.

SIXTH ALABAMA INFANTRY

UNION MILLS, VA., November 14, 1861 [11-20-61CS]

The camps are full of rumors to-day, of an advance by the enemy, but it seems next to impossible to ascertain the truth. This much I can say, we hope it is true. We are ready and waiting for them.

A small scouting party, numbering 11 men from the 12th Mississippi, left their camp here last Tuesday morning and proceeded by way of Burke's station towards the lines of the enemy, and when near the Bone Mill on Accotinck creek, seven miles below Alexandria, came across a marauding party of Lincoln's cavalry numbering about 20 men, and succeeded in capturing a Captain, an orderly sergeant and one private, together with their horses, arms, &c., bringing them into camp before night. The horses were very fine ones. The Yankees had been out upon a regular thieving expedition, and were loaded with various articles of household furniture. Among other things were pillows, bolsters, carpets, looking glasses, tumblers, &c., besides a quantity of cooked provisions. They deny any advance by their forces. Their company numbering 108 men are stationed between Alexandria and the residence of Mrs. Brodus, and are from the city of New York and vicinity.

It is truly gratifying to those here, who have left families behind them particularly, to notice that the Executives of the different States, City Councils, Vigilance Committees and the press generally, are noticing the Shylocks, who are traveling through the Confederate States, buying up articles of prime necessity, for speculation. If public opinion cannot stay these mean sordid wretches in their course, the strong arm of the law should be made to reach them. Let the representatives of the people immediately by legislative enactment, put a stop to this disgraceful business. Shame upon these men who stay at home speculating upon their less fortunate fellow citizens and preying upon the necessities of the Confederate Government in the hour of its need. They are to be worse dreaded than all the hosts of Lincolndom. "Oh for a lash in the hand of every honest man, to lash these rascals naked through the land!"

The health of the regiment improves steadily. We have been here one month, and have not lost a man. Several have been discharged. The Regiment numbers between 1,200 and 1,300 men.

The policy lately adopted by the Government in relation to Army Surgeons, I think a very wise and judicious one. As I understand it, a board of competent Surgeons have been appointed, whose duty it is to go through the army and examine thoroughly all of the Army Surgeons and Assistants, and those who cannot stand this test and prove to be disqualified will be removed and competent ones appointed in their stead. This seems to me proper and just, and a step in the proper direction by the Government in the Medical Department of the army. If the Government will only continue in its good work thus begun and send competent military men to examine Field and Commissioned officers of the army, they will find many who could not stand the test of a proper examination, such a one as they should undergo, before the lives of men are placed in their hands.

It is a notorious fact, and I regret to have it to say, that there are officers in the Confederate Army, and a good many of them who know precious little about the business they are engaged in. Some who do not earn the salt that goes in their bread for the Confederate States, but draw high salaries.

The private soldiers as far as I know, are perfectly satisfied with their pay, for they do not fight for money, being stimulated by a far different and nobler motive than gain, but they do think that the pay of privates and officers entirely disproportionate.

The Confederate Army can boast of many fine officers, men who would honor any army in the world, but it has many in its ranks who would do better some where else, in a different occupation. As I predicted in your columns months since, the Lincolnites, Brownlow's and Johnson's followers in East Tennessee, are giving us trouble. The Government has pursued a policy entirely too lenient towards these men, and if it had made examples of a few of them some time since, it would probably have deterred these villains who are at work now, from their present course and saved us a deal of trouble.

PRIVATE.

SIXTH ALABAMA INFANTRY

UNION MILLS, VA., December 3, 1861 [12-10-61CS]

The reported advance upon our lines which I wrote you in my last, turns out to be large bodies of the troops of the enemy thrown forward in advance of their lines, for the purpose of protecting their laboring forces engaged in cutting and carrying to Washington and Alexandria large quantities of wood, and the prospect which we thought so promising at that time for a battle has vanished and matters have relapsed into their former quietness.

Gen. Van Dorn's Division was reviewed on yesterday, near Blackburn's Ford, on the road leading from Manassas to Centreville, by Gens. Johnston and Beauregard. After the review of the troops, each of the regiments present, ten in number, through their commanders were presented by General Beauregard with a battle flag, the one lately adopted for this army. An address from Prince [Camille A. J. M.] Polignac was delivered on the occasion, brief but to the point. The day was bitter cold and the wind piercing, the men suffering no little.

Gen. Rodes' brigade has received orders to remove to the west side of Bull Run, and consequently we shall pull up stakes in a few days leaving our partially completed winter quarters at this place, upon which we have expended so much hard labor, for the benefit of others. But we are told by our kind Colonel, that go where may we shall have houses to stay in this winter.

An election was held in our regiment on the 30th inst. for Lieutenant Colonel, to fill the vacancy occasioned by the resignation of B. H. Baker, resulting in no choice, there being several candidates and no one receiving a majority of the votes cast, since which an order has been received from Gen. Beauregard, prohibiting an election being held until further orders, as there seems to be a good deal of doubt in the minds of many, as to whether volunteers have the right under the existing law to elect officers to fill vacancies. Many are of opinion that vacancies should be filled by promotion and in regular succession. John T. Morgan of the 5th Alabama, in whose regiment a similar case is existing, has gone to the proper authorities for the purpose of arguing the question in favor of promotion in succession by rank. This gentleman was elected Lieutenant Colonel of his regiment, after the promotion of Gen. Rodes but will not accept under an election, claiming the office by promotion.

Maj. Gordon, of the 6th Alabama, has been ordered to return to his regiment and resume his duties, his resignation not having been received, consequently the election ordered to be held to fill his vacancy will not come off.

Our company has been again called upon to mourn the death of one of its most youthful but best, soldiers, in the person of W. Thurston Waddell. The deceased was attacked with a severe case of Rheumatism, several weeks since and after much persuasion, by his friends before he would ask for it obtained a discharge and was on his way home to his parents, under charge of Dr. John Norwood, when he was seized with Typhoid fever and died at the residence of Mr. Norwood, at Hillsboro', North Carolina, where he received every attention during his short illness, that could be bestowed upon him by kind and tender friends. The deceased was about sixteen years of age. He was one of the first last Spring, to step forth and offer his services to his country. The Confederate States had no better a soldier of his age. It seems difficult to realize that he is gone forever, and that we shall see him on earth no more. But it is too true, he has been summoned by the Great Commander above, and snatched from aged and tender parents, affectionate brothers and sisters, and comrades who loved him. May the sod rest lightly upon his breast.

PRIVATE.

LETTER FROM SOLDIER JIM, CAMP SCENES AND CAMP LIFE

ARMY OF THE POTOMAC, CENTREVILLE, VA., December 3, 1861 [12-13-61ASC]

I am tolerably well myself, though some sickness prevails in the camps. Brother D. has been sick for ten days with camp fever, but is better.

No movements of importance on hand at this time either by us or the enemy. We have been at a stand still for some time. The weather is freezing cold, and the mountains are covered with snow.

Some are daily being detailed to cut and haul wood, while others are bringing up rocks and grass turf to build chimneys to their tents—all of which proves successful—renders the soldier comfortable and more content in his little home.

We are ordered out on the lines for picketing, where we are stationed for four days in the woods; and while there, our beds are oak leaves, underneath the brush, with log-heap fires, watching for the approach of Mr. Yank, and listening for the long roll. Four days expire, but Mr. Yank does not come. We are relieved and return to camp, while others take our place and watch and listen four days more.

We have no certainty when we shall go in winter quarters, in consequence of the exported attack of the enemy. McClellan has made many excuses for not giving us a fight. Now I suppose it is cold weather. Ah! yes; Mr. Yank is accustomed to quartering in warm houses in the winter and can't expose himself to snow, though he ventures out occasionally to search for food for his starved horses, when our bold cavalry then dart out, pounce on him, and bring him to Centreville; thence he is sent to Richmond where he has been desiring to go, lo these many days; but not exactly in that style.

I feel proud of your interesting paper. The smiling face of the *Confederacy* sheds forth a blaze of light and cheerfulness whenever it makes its appearance in camp.

Since writing the foregoing, Generals Johnston and [Gustavus W.] Smith have reviewed the left wing of Gen. Smith's Division of the army. The turn out was a grand one, consisting of three brigades; and while in line, an order was read to each regiment, notifying us that the Federals were advancing towards us. We are ready to receive them night or day. Look out for a big fight.

SOLDIER JIM.

SIXTH ALABAMA INFANTRY

DAVIS' FORD, VA., December 14, 1861 [12-20-61CS]

General Rodes' Brigade arrived here on the 7th inst., and it is now said that we are permanently located for the remainder of the winter season. We received orders to build winter quarters a few days after our arrival, and they are now rapidly progressing towards completion.

The men, from the orders we received the night before our march here, were in high spirits at the prospect of a fight but it has all vanished and matters in camp have relapsed into usual dullness and inactivity.

The weather for ten or twelve days past has been delightful indeed for the season, being almost like an Indian summer. As Gen. McClellan has not availed himself of this opportunity, afforded him by the weather for offensive military operations there is no one here now who entertains the idea that McClellan will make a general advance this winter. He may attack our batteries, as they are a thorn in the side of the Yankees.

The Confederate Congress has passed an Act giving twelve months men the privilege of returning home now, and staying there two months, provided at the end of that time, they will re-enlist for two years.

I am inclined to think there will be but few, who will avail themselves of the provisions of the act, the twelve months generally preferring to remain the balance of their time and then be left free to enlist again or not as they choose.

We are encamped at Davis' Ford, six miles from Manassas, and upon the road leading from Manassas to Dumfries and Occoquan. We are distant ten miles from the village of Occoquan and fourteen from Dumfries. Col. Wade Hampton's Legion has been stationed until a few days past, at Bacon Race Church, three miles from here, but has been removed, and is now not far from Evansport, on Occoquan Bay.

Capt. James F. Waddell, of company H., (Opelika True Volunteers) has tendered his resignation to take effect on the 1st January next. His reasons for resigning are, that he is tired of inactivity and desires to enter a different and more active arm of the service. He designs raising an artillery company, and if he returns to Russell county for that purpose, I would advise any one who wishes to enlist in defense of their country to go with him, for they cannot find one more cool, courageous and efficient; besides he treats those under his command, as all here will testify, with the greatest kindness.

I would dislike very much to be looked upon as a grumbler, but do think there is one imposition by the Government upon soldiers, which should be remedied in some way. We are paid off with any kind of Bank bills the Government chooses to offer us, but they will receive nothing for postage but coin or Confederate bills, and for Confederate bills, will not sell you less than $5.00 worth of stamps. A man cannot buy here with a $5.00 Confederate note, fifty cents or $1.00 worth of stamps. This is unjust, it does seem to me. The Government ought certainly to be willing to receive the money from soldiers that they pay out to them for their services.

Our mail matter now reaches us with more promptness and regularity than it has since we left home.

PRIVATE.

PRIVATE LETTER FROM THE PENINSULA

NORFOLK, VA. December 19, 1861 [12-27-61ASC]

Norfolk was thrown into a perfect fever of excitement last evening by the announcement that England would demand of the "Old Wreck," the surrender of Messrs. [James] Mason and [John] Slidell, and an ample apology for the insult on the British flag. The city was illuminated, in a blaze with fireworks, and all the bells ringing. The excitement was intense and beyond description.

I visited the Gosport Navy Yard this morning and saw the old *Merrimack*, which is being rapidly completed in her repairs. It will be ready for sea in three or four months. Then you may look out for some fun, and "a heap of it." Lincoln blockaders will be hoisted, when it gets ready to give them a lift. It will mount eight large guns, and the sides and top will be perfectly bomb-proof. There are, besides *Merrimack*, three gunboats being built, which will be ready for sea in about two months. They will each mount eight guns—so the master-workman informed me. They are as busy as bees in the Navy Yard.

The Third Georgia Regiment arrived here last Monday from Roanoke Island. They had their winter quarters all ready to go into, when they received orders to march to Norfolk. They are now in camp about two miles above the Navy Yard.

Our Battalion have fared better, I dare say, than any other troops in the field. We get plenty to eat, and of the best kind; and our quarters are *very* comfortable. The "blockade" is never closed on us, we being allowed to go where we please, except to town. In fact, we could be but very little better provided for were we at home. Maj. [Thomas] Hardeman is everything that a true soldier could wish; and, not only Maj. Hardeman, but *all* of our commissioned officers are very kind and obliging, always studying the interests of the men.

An order was issued the other day, forbidding the granting of any more furloughs until further orders. What can be the meaning of the order no one seems to know, unless a fight is expected here. There is "something out," which time alone will reveal. If the Yankees should attack this place, they will have some of the *tallest* fighting to do that you ever heard of before they accomplish anything. The Confederacy has a great deal at stake here; consequently, our Generals have not been idle here since the commencement of the war, in fortifying the city. It is the opinion of learned men that two hundred thousand Yankees could not take this place. It is *utterly impossible* for any kind of a war steamer to approach Norfolk, as the channel is thoroughly obstructed.

A great many of our boys will re-enlist when their present term of service expires—I think over two-thirds, after they go home and stay a month or two.

Very Respectfully,   T. P. Holland.

THE FIGHT AT ALLEGHANY MOUNTAIN

CAMP ALLEGHANY, VA., December 21, 1861 [1-14-62ASC]

The monotony of our camp, or rather cabin-life was disturbed on the morning of the 13th inst., by some very stirring events. About 4 o'clock we were aroused from our slumbers by the intelligence that the Yankees were given to "fall in," preparatory to their reception. The morning was bitterly cold, and the cutting air and frozen ground contrasted most pinchingly with the comfort of our "bunks" and blankets. Three companies of the 12th Georgia Regiment, the 31st Virginia Regiment, and two Virginia Battalions, commanded respectively by Lieut. Col. [G. W.] Hansborough and Maj. [Albert G.] Reger, were ordered to the right of our camp to protect an approach in that direction, while the remainder of our forces were stationed in entrenchments that commanded another road coming on our left. Our whole force, embracing also two artillery companies, did not exceed fourteen hundred, of whom about one thousand were in the entrenchments, the remainder, four hundred, being stationed as already stated, on the right. We awaited in the cold two or three hours before the enemy came.

About daybreak, they were seen advancing. They came in two columns, by the two roads referred to, the one by the road on our right, coming a little first. The attack from this column commenced about sunrise, and opened with a fierce, terrific fire. The 31st Virginia Regiment received the first fire, and responded very promptly. Immediately the three companies of the 12th Georgia, rallied to the scene of the conflict, and took their places with the foremost, and for about three hours the contest raged with unceasing, and unabated fierceness. Many of the Virginians fought with unsurpassed courage, but to the Georgians belongs the honor of having been foremost in the fight, and leading every charge. Three times were the enemy repulsed before they finally yielded and then not until they had been severely punished by our gallant soldiers.

The other column made their attack a little after this began. But they were so protected by felled timber and brush, that our shots could not reach them with much effect, and as our men were also protected by their intrenchments, the shots from neither side did much damage. They continued to exchange shots for several hours before the Yankees retired.

This, I apprehend, was one of the hardest fought battles of the war, and must reflect honor on those who fought it. This victory was complete, and a glorious one considering the disparity of numbers, the Federals having about five thousand, while our force did not exceed fourteen hundred. It was dearly fought however, and cost the life of many a gallant man. The 12th Georgia sustained a severe loss in the death of Lieut. [Henry] Moore, commanding the "Lowndes Volunteers." He was a true and gallant soldier and officer, and fell while leading his men in the hottest of the fight. The total casualties on our side were twenty-two killed, ninety-four wounded and twenty-eight missing, of these the 12th Georgia, which suffered most, lost six killed, thirty-seven wounded and four missing. We do not know the extent of damage done to the enemy, though they suffered worse than we. We have buried thirty-four, have captured fourteen wounded prisoners, and four others. They had ambulances running during the whole fight, and we saw them haul off six wagon loads of dead and wounded. If we had had force enough to pursue them, we could have captured many more of them. We have done considerable work on our defences, since the fight, and if they return they will find that we have not retreated to Staunton, as they falsely reported, but that we are prepared to "welcome them with bloody hands to hospitable graves," on the summit of the Alleghany.

We are still hopeful that our regiment may be removed from this cheerless section, to a more comfortable and congenial climate for the winter. If any regiment in the service is entitled to respite from labor and service, or needs recruiting, it is certainly ours, as the history of our campaign in these mountains, and the comparison of the strength of the regiment to-day, with what it was when it entered the service, will abundantly testify. And yet, we see other regiments going into comfortable winter quarters, and into the South—even Virginia regiments being ordered to the Southern coast—while we are still here, subjected to a most rigorous and (to us) almost intolerable climate, doing heavier picket duty even in these freezing nights, than we have ever done heretofore. I think we, and our friends have a right to complain, that the Government has neglected us, and treated us unjustly, especially when it is remembered that we are the only Georgia, or Southern Regiment now left in Northwest Virginia. Yet, we will do our duty here, if it is so ordered, as efficiently and cheerfully as we may.

ANSELM.

THE SKIRMISH AT DRANESVILLE,
EXPERIENCE OF AN ARTILLERIST
SUMTER FLYING ARTILLERY [1-23-62CS]

On the night [Dec. 19] previous to the fight we left our camp at about 3 o'clock, a. m., and arrived at the headquarters of Gen. Stuart, of cavalry notoriety, who was to command the expedition. On our arrival there we found four regiments, and in a few moments the entire body was in motion towards Dranesville, a place 14 miles distant. We traveled pretty rapidly until we reached our destination, arriving at 12 o'clock, m. We were preceded by two regiments, being in the centre, and two followed in the rear.

When within half a mile of Dranesville the command halted. Skirmishers were thrown to the right and left, and in a few moments we, with four pieces, were ordered to "double quick" to the place assigned to us, and bring our battery into action. We were not slow by any means in executing our order. We brought our pieces to "action front," within 500 yards of the place, and opened fire on the Yanks, who we could plainly see, and in a round or two they scampered off, and waited for their reinforcements of artillery. While this was going on, our infantry was driven back on our left by greatly superior numbers, through the woods, and it was then that I lost all hope. I thought our battery was gone, and we turned our two pieces to play on the Yanks, so soon as our men should uncover us, and two up the road to clear it, and I cried loudly for canister. My fears were not realized, for just in the nick of time, and not a moment too soon, Gen. S. rallied them and turned them "right about face."

By this time we were the recipients of a heavy cross fire from two batteries. The officers had dismounted some time previous, but I had not, nor did I until one of my detachment was wounded and fell on the road side, carrying with him tubes and lanyard. I proceeded to him immediately, taking the articles from him and assigning some one else to his post. Their shot and shell went over us, but by this time they were getting our range very accurately, and our men began to fall rapidly. The road being narrow we could man only three pieces, and by this time two only were manned. We fired rapidly and accurately. My gunner had left his gun and stepped to gun No. 3—mine was No. 2—so had several of my detachment.

We had loaded but a round or so when Luke Hames, my No. 1, or the person who rams the cartridges, was hit—not wounded—and fell on the road side; when Lieut. [Samuel] Hays stepped up and proposed to act gunner, and he filled L. H.'s post.

Many had been wounded and fell nearby; but the worst sight of all—the most heart-rendering scene was soon to occur. Standing within a pace of the unfortunate, but brave boys, I saw the deadly effect of the shots too plainly. My gunner, John McGarrah, acting No. 1, and [Washington F.] Williams [age 16], acting No. 3; No. 3 being just in the rear of No. 1, were standing the galling fire like men, when in an instant a solid shot had severed their heads from their bodies, and the two lifeless corpses lay on the ground—their brains bespattering all who were near.

It devolved on me, as chief of the piece, to have the posts filled immediately. I looked round for men, but saw none. With the staff gory with blood and brains I went to work ramming. Only three men were at the gun. I called on my men to give me a shot and shell, when Sergeant [William] Fletcher said he would, and did so until he was wounded. Then came my most critical time. With shot falling as thick as hail and shells bursting, my second and all [were] wounded or rendered insensible by the great concussion—about the time Sergeant F. was wounded, Mr. Sims, acting No. 4, was noddled by the bursting of a shell.

Two then remained at the gun, Lieut. Hays and myself. I asked in the name of Heaven for some one of my detachment to bring me cartridges, when [Pvt. Reston] Burke, a good and brave boy, fearless of all danger, brought them to me. Two of us loaded several rounds, when, after the second order to retire from Gen. S., we ceased. I cannot think of naming all who acted like men, nor those who worked the guns of Capt. C. [Allen Cutts] I may at some future time.

B.

SIXTH ALABAMA INFANTRY

DAVIS' FORD, VA., December 25, 1861 [1-1-62CS]

The 10th Alabama suffered more than any other Regiment in the engagement near Dranesville [Dec. 20]. After Col. [John H.] Forney was wounded and Lieut. Col. [James B.] Martin killed, the command of this Regiment devolved upon Major J. J. Woodward, formerly Circuit Judge in Alabama, and Solicitor in the 9th Judicial Circuit, of that State.

Gen. Stuart had four pieces of artillery, which were pulled from the field by hand, after the horses were all shot down. The caissons belonging to the guns were taken from the enemy. The loss of the enemy is unknown. The enemy were greatly superior in numbers at the commencement of the action, and were re-enforced largely, when our forces retired from the field in good order. The Federals had eight pieces of artillery in the action. A portion of Gen. Longstreet's division was sent out later in the day, but the enemy could not be found, and from the fact of Gen. Longstreet's pickets, being placed some distance beyond Dranesville that night, is evidence that the Yankees must have retired hastily to a safe distance. Gen. Stuart is much censured here for his management in this affair. The gallant conduct of the 10th Alabama is spoken in the highest terms.

Capt. Waddell received yesterday from Secretary [of War Judah] Benjamin, authority to raise an artillery company. A battery fully equipped is now ready for him. His resignation of Captaincy in this regiment will be received only on condition of his raising an artillery company.

Private Spralding, of the 12th Mississippi Regiment, court martialed for stealing and an attempt to desert, was drummed out of the Regiment on the 16th, after having one half of his head shaved. He presented a pitiable spectacle, as he was marched through the Regiment in open ranks to the tune of the Rogue's March, and then turned adrift, amidst the shouts of his former comrades, to go where inclination might chance to carry him.

Capt. [J. T.] Montgomery, of the Jeff. Davis artillery, has been court martialed and dismissed from the service. Several charges were preferred against him, among others, drunkeness and incapacity, false mustering of men, &c.

The men in our Regiment are having a good time to-day, Col. Seibels being good enough to let them "take a little Christmas."

PRIVATE.

SIXTH ALABAMA INFANTRY

DAVIS' FORD, VA., January 1, 1862 [1-8-62CS]

Times are extremely dull here. Nothing of an exciting or important character, occurring since the fight at Dranesville, where, according to the published official report of Gen. Stuart, our loss in killed, wounded and missing, amounts to 194, which satisfied me that we got the worst of the fight.

Persons passing here from the batteries report all quiet there. A Federal vessel occasionally attempting to run the [Potomac] blockade under cover of the night, is fired upon by the batteries, with varied success. A schooner was sunk last week.

A most terrific cannonade was heard here on the evening of the 28th ult., in the direction of the left wing of the enemy's lines, and supposed to have been near Alexandria, which turns out as we expected, to be a trial of artillery by the enemy, to test the efficiency of their artillerists—and the rapidity of firing. They must have had a large number of pieces engaged, for although the distance from us was four or five times greater than that at the battle of Manassas, the incessant thunder and roar of the guns was several times greater than at any time during that bloody struggle.

General orders have been issued from headquarters, revoking all furloughs. What has caused this sudden change of policy I am unable to tell. The consequence I know is that many a poor fellow, who a few days since was high in hopes of soon seeing once more their wives and little ones, from whom they have been so long absent, is bitterly disappointed.

General Van Dorn's Division has lately been increased to 33 regiments, making it the largest in the army of the Potomac.

Col. Wade Hampton has had an additional regiment or two added to his command and is now acting Brig. General.

We had a Brigade review on yesterday, after which Col. Seibels addressed his Regiment, and made his men a proposition for reenlisting, or rather informed them of a proposition he had made to the Secretary of War, which is as follows: Col. Seibels designs raising from twelve months men now in service, or whose terms of enlistment will expire in the coming Spring, an independent self-sustaining corps, as he calls it, to be composed of from three to five Regiments of infantry, a squadron of cavalry and three batteries of artillery. The men to return to their homes on 30 days furlough, as soon as they can be spared from here, and at the expiration of the thirty days, to return and enlist for twelve months. His proposition he asked his men to consider, by the time he heard from the War Department. In conclusion, he remarked, that a number of his men had been to him and expressed perfect willingness to return to the wars again, as soon as they could have an opportunity of returning to their homes for a short time, provided he would command them as Colonel. This had touched his heart tenderly. He did not know whether this was the wish of a majority of the Regiment or not, but if it was, come weal, come woe, their destiny should be his destiny, and promotion or no promotion, he should stay with them and share their fate.

Gens. Beauregard and Johnston confidently look for an attack, by the 5th inst. This information as I give it to you has reached Centreville, there is no doubt.

Major Gordon has been elected Lieut. Colonel of the 6th Alabama Regiment—he had no opposition.

A happy new year to you Messrs. Editors and each of your numerous readers.

PRIVATE.

☆☆☆Winter 1862 Centreville

At this time the first Confederate battle-flags made their appearance. They were created in Baltimore by sisters Hetty and Jennie Cary, and their cousin Constance. The flags were squares of red, crossed with blue, and edged with white; inside the cross were stars representing the number of seceded States. Three flags were presented to the Confederate high command at Centreville, Virginia: Generals Van Dorn, Johnston and Beauregard.

GEN. BEAUREGARD AND THE FAIR BALTIMOREANS
—AN EPISODE OF LIFE AT CENTREVILLE. [1-8-62ASC]

Some negroes, at work on the roads and fortifications, took it into their heads one night to serenade Gen. Beauregard. Pleased with their performance, he went to the window and asked them to sing "My Maryland," the sweetest and most touching song the war has yet produced. They were unable to sing it. The next day Col. [Thomas] Jordan, Beauregard's Adjutant, who has a printing press in his department, caused several copies of "My Maryland" to be struck off and sent to the members of the 1st Maryland Regiment, many of whom are vocalists of the highest order.

The hint was taken, and that night Gen. Beauregard heard "My Maryland" sung with the power and pathos which exiles alone can give it. At its close, he stepped forward, and, in his modest, gentle way, said: "Gentlemen, I thank you warmly for the very agreeable serenade you have given me." The Marylanders, knowing his quiet habits, and thinking he had said all he intended to say, responded with "three cheers for Beauregard," and were about to return to their camp. What was their surprise when he called them to stay, and unfurling a flag, said: "Gentlemen, I present to you a Confederate battle flag, made in Baltimore by the most beautiful woman in that city."

Without waiting to hear more, an enthusiastic young officer called for "three cheers for Miss Hettie Cary," which were given with a will. "Not so fast," said the Major of the 1st Maryland, as the cheering ceased, "not so fast," said he, putting his hand on the shoulder of the excited Lieutenant, "it was not Miss Hettie, but her sister." "Three cheers, then, for Miss Jennie Cary," cried the Lieutenant. Of course they were heartily given. When the sound died away into perfect silence; and the audience, now comprising most of the regiment, awaited Gen. Beauregard's further remarks with rapt attention, he continued: "Yes it was made by Miss Jennie Cary, and when she presented it to me, I promised her on the honor of a gentleman that I would, with my own hands, plant it upon the Washington monument in Baltimore."

This assurance of a triumphal return to their city, coming from the lips of the Commanding General, and while their hearts were still softened by the tender strains of their chosen song of love and lamentation, produced an effect on the Marylanders which it is impossible to describe. They were literally transported with joy and enthusiasm.

Beauregard would not be able to keep his promise to Miss Cary; on January 26 he was ordered from the Potomac District to the West, where he would serve under Gen. Albert Sidney Johnston. The Department of Northern Virginia was now under the full command of Gen. Joseph E. Johnston.

SEVENTEENTH GEORGIA REGIMENT

CAMP GEORGIA, NEAR MANASSAS, VA., January 6, 1862 [1-15-62SR]

I promised to give you any incidents worthy of record in camp life, battles, marches, skirmishes, &c., which might fall under my observation, or come to my knowledge through a reliable source.

The "Sixth Brigade," indeed, has had very little experience in all of the above heads, except the first, "camp life." It has had no long marches to perform, has never seen a "live Yankee," in his belligerent character, only when he was unfortunate enough to be taken prisoner by Gen. Stuart's cavalry. The only experience the Sixth Brigade has had in *skirmishing* was within our lines, and under our drill masters. Our battles have all been imaginary—*our side* being the only visible contestants! But this is not our fault. We have been anxious, in common with the whole army, to be led against a foe we detest as the ignoble would-be masters of a chivalrous people, whom they have not the courage to conquer, nor the magnanimity to acknowledge their superiors in combat.

We have had experience in camp life—experience bitter without mixture. I speak of the "Seventeenth Georgia" in particular. The 15th have suffered terribly from disease; and perhaps the 1st Georgia Regulars and 2nd Georgia Volunteers have not been freer from prevailing epidemics. The 17th, when we reached Manassas in September, had an aggregate of about 750. The aggregate now is not exceeding 650! Our reports do not show more than two fifty to three hundred.

I regret to say it, but the regiment will bear me out in the statement that most of the noble fellows who have fallen by disease, were *victims of neglect.* They died for the want of proper and *punctual medical attention.* The disease had already done its work before the remedy was applied.

We are now building winter quarters, six miles southward of Centreville, and three from Manassas. We are progressing rather slowly. The "Bloody Seventeenth" (this unenviable *sobriquet* was gained for our Regiment by the *hog-killing* propensities of a few bad men,) is rather deficient in the matter of overcoats, but with good quarters, and plenty of wood hard by, we hope to keep comfortable through the rigors of a Virginia winter. We are in our tents, and the ground is covered with snow. The soldiers have not suffered much yet, and I believe will brave the winter through.

V. A. S. P.

Virgil A. S. Parks enlisted as First Lieutenant of Company D, Seventeenth Georgia Infantry, on August 13, 1861. Upon arriving in Virginia he began corresponding with the Savannah Republican, *promising to keep them informed on the upcoming campaign.*

A FEW NOTES OF THE YANKEE NAPOLEON, GENERAL GEORGE B. McCLELLAN

To the Editor of the Richmond Examiner:

I wish to give you some notes about this young Napoleon without a victory, that possibly may interest your readers. I call him a Napoleon without a victory, for, in the eyes of the Yankees, he is certainly a first class military chieftain, and yet he has never fought a battle of importance, and, in all probability, never will. Certainly the crushing of the gallant [Robert S.] Garnett's small command of two thousand men, with a vastly superior force, cannot entitle him to any high position as a warrior.

Alas for his military reputation, he is now, and has been for five months, confronting, on the banks of the Potomac, with his immense army, three men whom he knows well to be vastly his superior—Johnston, Beauregard, and [Gustavus W.] Smith. Smith was his captain in the Mexican war, and with both Smith and Johnston he has been for years past on terms of the closest intimacy. There are not probably two men in the world who know George B. McClellan, his character, capacity and defects, better than Generals Johnston and Smith. Even in his particular forte, *administrative ability,* of which he has certainly displayed a great deal in the *organization and disciplining of his army,* he is inferior to either. As an engineer, no one in the old army ever looked upon him as the equal of Beauregard. And yet these are the men whom, if he fight, he has to meet; against whom he has to try his skill at *handling and directing in the field vast bodies of troops.* No wonder he dreads to stake his reputation, his lofty position, in such a contest. He knows he will meet his masters in the art of war. He fears the downfall of his ambitious hopes, and has the spectre of a successor constantly before him. He may drill with ever so much assiduity his Grand (?) Army—he may exercise them constantly in sham fights—he may even learn the Yankee cavalry how to ride—but he dare not fight Johnston, Smith and Beauregard. He may have *sham* battles by the score safe behind his entrenchments, but, before a *real* battle comes off, some more foolhardy man than George B. McClellan will have to lead the Yankee hosts. He will keep his army at Washington as a sort of camp of instruction, a depot from which to send off troops to other points. It is not for the Confederate generals to advance. It is the enemy, who have undertaken to crush this "little rebellion," who must attack. As long as we have them in their capital and defy them before their entrenchments to come out and give battle, we are gaining, not losing anything. And all Europe sees the amusing and hitherto unheard of spectacle in the history of war, of an immense army, boasting their capacity to crush their opponents, remaining quietly in their camps and doing actually nothing, save holding their capital. Shades of Caesar, of Alexander, of Wellington, of Napoleon, of all the great warriors of ancient or modern times we invoke you to witness this extraordinary and absurd event in military annals, their latest improvement in the art of war. Look down upon George B. McClellan, the Yankee Napoleon, and pity his tremour, his caution, his perplexity.

But aside from the fact that McClellan dreads to meet Johnston and Smith, whose abilities he is so aware of, there is another reason for his dislike to a battle or an advance. Though his *ambition* and his head are engaged in this contest, I do not really believe his heart is. The truth is, few of the old United States army officers, aside from such miserable abolitionists as [Nathaniel] Lyon, [John] Pope, [Israel] Vogdes and [James] Ricketts, ever have entered into this vindictive and brutal crusade against the South with any heart. Scores of them are now disloyal to the North, and are not trusted by the officials. Were it not too late, many would have come over to the Southern Confederacy. As for McClellan, when the troubles first begun between the North and the South, he wrote to a high officer, now in the Confederate army, expressing his sympathy with the South, and saying that if war came he would be with the South. Afterwards when the war came, he was made a Major General of the Ohio forces, it was too much for his ambition to withstand. He then wrote again to the same officer, asking him to join him and offering him a position. It is needless to say that he rejected his proposition for a share of his infamy, and quoting his former letter to him, gave George B. McClellan, Maj. Gen. of the Ohio forces, his opinion of his course. But ambition was the sin by which the angels fell, and McClellan is certainly no angel, though fond of spirits. He now occupies the undesirable position of the idol of a people who, oppressed with the weight of their extreme freedom in former days, and tired of liberty, now love the chains which bind them and kiss the rod of the oppressor.

I am, sir, &c., CURTIUS.

LETTER FROM SOLDIER JIM

CAMP CENTREVILLE, VA., January 13, 1862 [1-21-62ASC]

In consequence of the great thaw and extent of mud, I have excused myself from any outdoor duty to-day, and so you have an opportunity to hear from "Soldier Jim" and the old Eighth Regiment once more.

We have had the most disagreeable weather I ever experienced.

Our Regiment is now in very good health, and our hospital is almost vacant. Everything in camp glides smoothly along. There is no prospect of a fight here this winter— though some attempts may be made to open the blockade of the Potomac.

Christmas passed off quietly. A part of the time our regiment was out on picket duty, during which time we picked up some very nice fat turkeys, which were soon welcomed by the dish and admirably devoured. Turkeys, chickens, eggs, butter, &c., are very plentiful here; but corn, meal, salt and potatoes are scarce. Beef and flour are principally "the go" with us; and very soon after the vessels pass Old Abe's sham blockade, we get a part of the coffee cargo they bring, which is not bad to take in the morning.

We have been building winter quarters about two weeks, and will soon be in them. They are very nice log cabins, lined, and daubed with clay. The chimneys are mostly of rock; and some have stone floors. The location is near a creek so that we have plenty of water, and we are surrounded by plenty of wood.

During the last three or four days, the snow has been three or four inches deep, which is very delightful to the soldier boys. We have had the grandest snow-balling you ever saw. The mountains are yet covered with snow, but we have a loblolly of mud, which makes it almost impossible for us to get about.

SOLDIER JIM.

SIXTH ALABAMA INFANTRY

DAVIS' FORD, VA., January 16, 1862 [1-22-62CS]

The camps in the army of the Potomac are again flooded with rumors of a general advance by the enemy, but we have heard them so often that they now fail to create any sensation whatever, and the men plod on the even tenor of their way quietly awaiting and hoping something "may turn up."

The following endorsement by General Beauregard upon an application for furlough, will give you some idea of his views as to an attack. "No applications for furloughs will be *considered* (unless in cases of sickness) so long as a battle is imminent."

Gen. Van Dorn has gone to Missouri to take command of the department of Missouri and Arkansas. This does not take his friends by surprise here at all, for he has often expressed his dissatisfaction with the defensive policy adopted by the government in this army, and his great desire to be in a field of active service. It is said here, that a perfect good understanding exists between Gen. Van Dorn and Gen. [Sterling] Price, in fact, that it is the desire of the latter, and at his instance and request that the former has been placed in command of that important department. You may look for stirring times in the far west, before many months roll round.

Since the date of my last we have had rough unpleasant weather, ice and snow being abundant. Those who were fortunate enough to obtain a pair of skates, have had fine sport skating upon the Occoquon, it being entirely frozen over. The ground is now covered with snow and ice, and has been for three days, rendering travel exceedingly difficult.

The grading upon the Railroad being built from Manassas to Centreville is about completed, a large number of the cross-ties are ready, and the road will soon be completed. A large force is at work upon it. This road is only six miles in length, but is one of great importance to the Army of the Potomac, in conveying supplies during the winter season, as the dirt roads are almost impassible during the winter.

Re-enlistments among the twelve months men, so far, progresses rather slowly. A great many of them think that they are now doing the work that others ought to have done who are lagging at home, and that the Government ought to *force* them into the army, and *make* them share its labors and perils. There is no kind of doubt but there are many men here who ought to be here, but will never be seen here unless forced to come. Yes, there is no kind of doubt but what there are able bodied, healthy young men, without families, sufficient left behind to fill the places of every twelve months man in the service, and then leave a sufficient number at home to speculate upon pork, bacon, salt, and other prime articles of necessity needed by the poor women and children.

I would be glad to hear the opinions of the old men (and women too) upon this matter. Can they spare these young men to serve their country, in the Confederate army. And I would be exceedingly glad to hear the opinion, also, of the young ladies. Can they not spare the services of these young men?

PRIVATE.

THIRTY-FIFTH GEORGIA REGIMENT

CAMP FRENCH, NEAR EVANSPORT, VA., January 16, 1862 [1-26-62ASC]

A short communication from the Stephens (35th) Regiment Georgia Volunteers, may not be unacceptable to you, notwithstanding the many letters you have received and are still receiving from the camps of the Georgia boys in Virginia.

The *Southern Confederacy* is a favorite [newspaper] with many of our relatives and friends who are deeply interested in us, and no doubt your readers generally love to get intelligence of any Georgians through our columns.

We have been assigned the right wing of the army of the Potomac, and form a part of General [S. G.] French's brigade. Our camp is about one mile from the Evansport batteries, on the side of a steep hill, from the summit of which we can have a fair view of all the movements on a very important part of the old Potomac. Our position relieves us of much of the anxiety experienced by other Regiments, farther off, on all exciting occasions, and will enable us, in case of a fight, to be among the first to take a hand. We are subjected to many inconveniences by being encamped on a steep hill-side, especially when the ground is covered with sleet and snow as it has been several times since our arrival here. Such slipping, sliding and falling, I have never seen before in any crowd.

Unpleasant as it is, however, there is fun in it, for our boys. When the snow gets deep enough for snow-balling, every man has to look out for himself; and he has to look out well if he keeps the snow-balls out of his face, and from going down his back. It is amusing in the extreme to witness their snow frolics, and listen to these old hills as they ring with the music of their merry laughter.

Our anticipation of an early attack at this point has kept us from going into winter quarters up to this time; but it will not be long before we will have comfortable log cabins to shield us from the piercing winds, the drenching rains, and heavy sleet and snow so common is this section of the "Old Dominion" at this season. Thus far the winter has been astonishingly pleasant here. A few nights since, I could not endure fire in my tent.

God is with us, not only in the trying hour of conflict, but rides upon the elements and tempers them to our situation.

The shafts of death have flown thick thro' our Regiment, and several of our noble spirits sleep under the clod, who left home but a few weeks since, fired at heart and nerved in arm for valiant deeds in the service of the country they loved. *The have died for their country.*

Our sick are improving, and the Regiment will be upon a sound and active footing in time to meet the invader when he comes. Most of them are in the hospitals and at private houses near here, where they are as well provided for as they possibly can be under the circumstances.

I feel proud of our officers, and you must pardon an expression of this feeling in regard to them. Col. E. L. Thomas is a high-toned gentleman, and a gallant officer. The deadening influences of the camp to which so many in his position become victims, have not affected him sufficiently to make him forget that his Regiment is composed of *men.* He associates with them, in health, to the last boundary line of prudence, and visits them in sickness. Delicacies often leave his table for the sick in camp, and his concern for the sick that are taken from camp to other accommodations, does not die out because they are in the hands of others. His soul is big enough to hold every soldier in the regiment, and they are all in there.

If the big fight, about which there has been so much talk ever comes off here, I predict for him an enviable addition to the laurels he won in Mexico.

POTOMAC.

PRIVATE LETTER, FIRST GEORGIA REGIMENT
CAMP NEAR ROMNEY, January 20, 1862 [2-16-62ASC]

I received your welcome letter yesterday. I see you have heard of my sickness. I had the jaundice, and from that took the camp fever at Greenbrier River. I left Greenbrier before the regiment for Stribbling Springs Hospital, in company with John H. Wiley, a brother of Lieut. [H. M.] Wiley, of our company [F]. He had the pneumonia, and died the second day after we arrived there. I was very sick for a week, but soon began to mend, and joined the regiment on their march to Winchester as they passed the Springs. We had a very pleasant trip to Mount Jackson, where we took the Manassas Gap railroad to Strasburg—twenty-five miles, and from thence we marched to Winchester—eighteen miles—traveling through the valley of Virginia. We were encamped 2½ miles from Winchester, the best camping place we ever had. We had a chance at the market in W. and the country people brought a great many things in camp to sell, so we lived finely—had a fine egg-nogg and two large roast turkeys on Christmas.

On the first of January we were ordered to strike tents and prepare for a march—we did not know where. We had Col. [William B.] Talliaferro's brigade, to which our regiment belongs. We were joined by Gens. Jackson, [William W.] Loring, and [Samuel R.] Anderson, Col. Mim's [Gilbert Meem's Militia] brigade, Col. [Turner] Ashby's cavalry, twenty-two pieces of artillery—an army of ten thousand strong—quite a long string of us; so we made very slow traveling. The second day the army marched about ten miles, and stopped to wait for the wagon train, but they did not come up that night, so we had no blankets and nothing to eat, and it snowing all the time. Next morning we had to leave for Bath (as the Federals were there) without anything to eat, and six inches of snow on the ground.

As we approached within two miles of Bath we met about fifty of the enemy on a scouting expedition. We captured nine and killed two. When we came within a mile, they opened a battery on us from the top of a high hill on the other side of town. We were halted and formed in line of battle; Gen. Anderson's brigade of Tennesseans to the right, Gen. Loring in the center, and ours on the left. The cavalry were sent out to watch the movements of the enemy. They soon reported them leaving. We were ordered to charge the town in double quick time, but when we got there nobody was to be found but two sick soldiers. From here we double quicked to Hancock, six miles; a little town on the Potomac, in Maryland. Here we stayed three days, the Federals shelling us all the time. Gen. Jackson's object in staying here so long, was to give a part of the command time to burn a railroad bridge, tear up the track, and tear down a dam on the canal, which they did and then returned, losing two men killed and seven wounded at the bridge by the Federals. We were then ordered to Romney, leaving one brigade at Bath or Bath Springs as it is now called.

We have suffered more on this trip than we did on the Laurel Hill retreat. We were out 7 days, without tents or blankets and scarcely anything to eat, and were nine days coming from Bath to Romney, about 50 miles. When we left Winchester, we had about seven hundred men on duty in our regiment; now about one hundred and fifty. This is the worst camping place we ever had; on a side of a mountain and raining nearly all the time. We have just received orders to clean our guns and send all extra baggage to town. I expect we will leave here soon. I think we will go back to Winchester in two weeks and stay there the rest of the Winter.

Yours affectionately,   David Young.

SIXTH ALABAMA INFANTRY
DAVIS' FORD, VA., January 27, 1862 [2-4-62CS]

The weather a great portion of the time for fifteen days past, has been very disagreeable indeed. Six days in succession, during this time, we have not seen the sun. We have had a storm of sleet and snow, followed by several days' rain, which has left the roads in almost impassible condition, rendering the transportation of supplies, for even a few miles, exceedingly difficult, and for any considerable distance almost impossible. Some of the regiments below us have abandoned wagon transportation, and have resorted to packing their supplies upon horses. As the winter so far has been mild for this latitude, it is reasonable to expect much bad weather during the remainder of the season, and consequently a worse condition of the roads and increased difficulties in transportation.

Several companies have been organized from this brigade, under the recent act of Congress, and enlisted for the war, and have left for their homes on 30 days furlough. Several other companies are being formed.

Capt. Waddell has returned from Richmond, having completed his arrangements for his artillery corps. He has authority from Secretary Benjamin to enlist and detach immediately from this regiment (6th Alabama) as many men as he wishes for his artillery, the only restriction being that he does not disorganize any company in the regiment. He can get from the regiment, under this restriction, between 200 and 300 men, though he does not wish to take more than 150 from the regiment.

Those who enlist under him will have 60 days furlough, and go for two years or the war. I am authorized to say that Capt. W. will receive a few able-bodied young men of character, after he reaches Alabama. Unless some obstacle intervenes to interrupt his arrangements, which cannot be foreseen, he will be at home with his men in two weeks.

He will have eight guns and at least 200 men. A better opportunity will not be offered soon, for those desirous of serving their country in the field, under a good officer.

Gen. Ewell has been appointed Major General, in place of Gen. Van Dorn. His appointment gives great satisfaction indeed, particularly to this brigade.

The 4th Alabama has been ordered to take the place of the 12th Mississippi, in Rodes' brigade, which has been placed in a Mississippi brigade. The 4th Alabama is in supporting distance of the Potomac batteries. They earnestly protest against being removed from their present position, and have sent an officer to Richmond to see Secretary Benjamin, and endeavor to get the order of removal countermanded.

The health of our regiment is not so good at present as it has been for some weeks past. Diarrhea is prevailing to a considerable extent, though but one or two deaths have resulted from it so far. The deaths in our regiment since leaving home have been 53, and the discharges 72. This is quite a small percentage, when compared with the deaths and discharges in other regiments during the same time, which do not number more than two-thirds as many men as does our regiment, but who have lost, during the same time, double as many men. The 6th Alabama numbered, when mustered into service, over 1,300 rank and file.

PRIVATE.

On February 14, the editors of the Columbus Sun *notified their readers that "PRIVATE" went home to Alabama with Capt. James F. Waddell and joined the artillery.*

CAMP MASON
NEAR WINCHESTER, VA., February 10, 1862 [2-20-62ASC]

Three weeks have elapsed since the date of my last letter, but this long delay in writing to you could not be prevented, as all my time was consumed to performing the military duties assigned me. When you and your readers remember that a private soldier in an active campaign has but little opportunity to collect facts and incidents, and but little time to pen them, you will pardon me if my communications do not come regularly once a week, and are not replete with news of interest.

It is stated, in high official circles, that General "Stone Wall" Jackson had the consent of the War Department to prolong the recent campaign in this section of Virginia so long as it would require him to accomplish the objects of routing the enemy from Bath, of destroying two bridges on the Baltimore and Ohio R. R., and of effectually breaking lock [Dam] No. 5, in the Chesapeake & Ohio canal, after accomplishing which we had orders to return to the vicinity of Winchester. But Gen. Jackson not satisfied with simply achieving these objects, and, no doubt, thinking there was a good opportunity for him to bag the whole of Gen. [Frederick W.] Lander's force then stationed at Romney, determined to prolong the campaign on his own responsibility and put his army in motion to carry out, if possible, the plan he conceived for the annihilation of Lander's army. But because of the deep snows, heavy rains and sleets, and the almost impassible roads consequent upon them, Gen. Jackson was foiled in his attempt to cut off the retreat and completely hem in the enemy.

Having heard of the rapid flight of the enemy from Romney several days prior to his arrival there, Gen. Jackson resolved to move on his column to that point and occupy it during the remainder of the Winter. But thinking his whole force more than sufficient to hold the position, and knowing the great difficulty of provisioning a large army there, he marched the First Virginia, or "Stone Wall" Brigade back to the vicinity of Winchester, leaving Gen. Loring's division, now considerably reduced in numbers of men, in consequence of sickness caused by the great exposure to which the troops were subject in the recent campaign, to brave the howling blasts of old Boreas in that frigid mountainous region, and to repel the assaults of the enemy, who, no doubt would have come against us in greatly superior numbers. I learn that Gen. Loring and all the rest of Gen. Jackson's subordinate officers protested against the move he made on his own responsibility, and in due time informed the War Department of the condition of the army, and of the impossibility of getting supplies to it during the winter. Upon the reception of this intelligence, the War Department immediately ordered that Gen. Jackson's forces should evacuate Romney, and concentrate in the vicinity of Winchester. Gen. Jackson thinking this order a slur upon his character as a General, forthwith tendered to the War Department his resignation, but that office refused to accept it.

Our evacuation of Romney was well conducted. The wagon train was loaded and started on its journey Sunday night, 2nd instant, with a detail of men sufficient to assist the train in getting along. The rest of the troops remained in camp till 12 M. next day, when we set out on our march hither.

Early Monday morning [Feb. 3], a heavy snow commenced falling and the storm raged thro'-out the whole day. We braved the fury of the storm, waded through the snow 6 or

8 inches deep, and marched to Hanging Rock, a distance of 16 miles, by 10 o'clock Monday night. During this march, notwithstanding the intensely cold weather, we waded one river and two creeks, over which there were no other means of crossing. The remainder of the journey was performed with but little difficulty. Gen. Jackson's forces are now quartered in the vicinity of this place.

I noticed in your telegraphic column of the 4th instant, a dispatch from Richmond, to the effect, that the *Winchester Republican* had stated that the reports concerning the many deaths and vast amount of sickness resulting from the hardships and exposure of the recent campaign in this section, have been "grossly exaggerated." With due deference to the Editor of that journal, I would state, that he was wrongly informed, and that in stead of these reports being "grossly exagerated," the *half* was never told. But this letter is growing too lengthy.

NESTOR.

THIRTY-FIFTH GEORGIA REGIMENT
CAMP FRENCH, EVANSPORT, VA., February 6, 1862 [2-21-62ASC]

The 35th Regiment Georgia Volunteers are stationed at Evansport, Va., midway between the mouths of Aquia and Occoquan Creeks. Our camp is near a mile from the banks of the Potomac, surrounded by several large hills which hide us from the view of the enemy, stationed in large numbers we presume, on the Maryland side of the river. From the summit of the hills we can see the "stars and stripes" floating in the breeze, and hear the shrill notes of the fifes of the enemy playing to the tunes of "Yankee Doodle" and "Hail Columbia!" But then as we turn in another direction, from every hill and valley, where Southern troops are encamped, the soul stirring strains of "Dixie" greet the ear.

Three miles North of us is Dumfries, a dilapidated cluster of old houses, the ruins of a once populous city. Near its center stands an ancient building now used as a Commissary Store, which the inhabitants say was the Academy in which George Washington acquired the rudiments of an English education. Every one of those old ruins that can be made to stand at all, is crowded with goods of some description, which are sold by these petty merchants to the soldiers at four times their actual worth; but the better part of Dumfries consists in the hospitals for the accommodation of the sick, which are neatly kept, provided with good nurses, and under the direction of first class physicians

But the greatest difficulty with which we have to contend, is in getting the sick from camps to the hospitals—the great quantity of rain and snow that has fallen during the last two months, and then the amount of transportation necessary for the use of the army combined, have rendered the roads almost impassable, though I trust ere long we will have no further use for hospitals, as the health of the Regiment is rapidly improving. Certainly we have had our proportionate share of sickness; for to-day as I look out from my tent, my heart is sad, when I behold upon a neighboring hill, those rude pens marking the graves of so many departed Georgians. Yet every comrade who falls from disease or by the missiles of the enemy I trust will animate our spirits and cause us to be more determined to avenge their noble sacrifice.

It is truly gratifying and encouraging to see the spirit of harmony and contentment which pervades the camps of Southern soldiers, and with what alacrity they re-enlist as their term of service expires. Surely none intend quitting the service till the flag of the Confederacy can wave without a rival over every Southern State.

H. H. R.

Hope H. Roberts was mustered in as First Lieutenant of Company C, 35th Georgia Infantry on September 17, 1861, and was killed in action at the Battle of Mechanicsville, Va., on June 26, 1862.

INAUGURATION OF THE PRESIDENT
RICHMOND, VA., February 22, 1862 [3-4-62AWCS]

The clock has just struck one and the inauguration is over. On a platform erected at the base of the Equestrian Statue of the Father of his country, Jefferson Davis and Alexander H. Stephens have just taken the oath of office and we are revolutionists no longer, but living now under a loyal government, established and put into operation according to legal usages of nations. The day is dark, dismal, and dreary; but the ceremony was witnessed by many thousands of people, who stood out on the cold, damp ground, while big drops of rain descended upon them thick and fast, for over an hour, only to become spectators of this scene. Solomon, it was, I believe, who said, "there is a time for all things," and I am distinctly of the impression that he was right and that this is no time for the pomp of pageantry, the mockery of ceremony, or the debauchery of revelry, however refined it may be, and however high may be the position of the revelers.

The oath of office could have both administered in a quiet, retired chamber, with just as binding an effect as it could in the presence of myriads of spectators; and when the clouds of war which are piling with such terrific grandeur upon the horizon of our frontiers are hourly threatening to burst with desolating fury over this and over that Southern city, I do not think "shows" are not in good taste. The city is thronged almost to suffocation. The hotels, boarding houses and private residences seem to be literally instinct with humanity, and talking bipeds block up the side walks and thoroughfares in every direction, and cotillion parties are the rage. Is it not in despicable taste to exhibit to the world such levity when thousands upon thousands of our brave and beloved countrymen are enduring more or less hunger, thirst, the privations and hardships incident to the Soldier's lot at the post of duty, when they are not languishing and dying on the pallet of straw, of their wounds or of fevers? While they are evacuating Nashville, they are dancing in Richmond. Reader, comment is free, and I hope you can and will do justice to the occasion.

A. H. H.

LETTER FROM SOLDIER JIM
CAMP SAM JONES, February 23, 1862 [3-15-62ASC]

I am very happy to inform you, that Soldier Jim is well, still a kicking, and all right on the war feeling. Ever since we have been in Winter quarters, we have been as comfortable as could be expected in our log pens. Our employment has been to read every old book and newspaper that could be obtained, as we are confined the most of our time in doors on account of mud and snow, so we are deprived of taking much exercise. Our men would sooner be on a march, and will, I have no doubt, rejoice to see the day when we are moved from this place. If we were to receive orders to-day to march into a battle, it would be cheering news to the boys. Loud shouts would go up from many thousand impatient soldiers, if McClellan would undertake to force the "rats" from their "holes" at Manassas.

We heard very heavy cannonading about two hours this morning in the direction of Evansport, but nobody hurt on our side I suppose.

Haloo! in comes the *Confederacy*! Now for the news! Sure enough the war spirit is again aroused in the old Empire State! Better now than later—when the enemy is thundering at our doors; and I think it is due time for all who love their homes, mothers, wives, children and sweethearts, to shoulder their arms and hasten to the battle field to check the invading foe, who is making a desperate effort to drive us from our homes. I hope we'll be victorious, trusting in God, and keeping our powder dry.

SOLDIER JIM.

In early March, Gen. Johnston abandoned the Manassas and Centreville camps and began pulling his army back to a defensive position along the Rappahannock River.

THE EVACUATION OF MANASSAS—LETTER FROM AN OFFICER [4-5-62CS]

Leaving our winter quarters was reluctantly acquiesced by our soldiers. There was nothing inviting in the country. It was a position decidedly menacing to the Federal capital, and we have held it so long in attitude of inviting an advance of McClellan that very many of our gallant fellows turned their back, upon the works so laboriously accomplished with sullen hearts and disappointment. The move was wise from various potential considerations, and ere long the country will acknowledge the skillful strategist in the hand that conceived it.

For months it has been known to be the design of McClellan to advance cautiously with the immense army at his command to overpower us. We were so near his sources of supply and munitions, that we might have beaten him twice or thrice a week, and yet failed of decided results. We were too far from our own supplies, and eight months with an army have completely exhausted the country. The Sabastepol works at Washington afforded the enemy a safe retreat in case of discomfiture. We had no such place to fall back upon, at any such relative distance. Herein was a strong succor to the moral effect of the enemy operating in diametrical ratio badly upon our own men.

It was unpleasant and indeed discouraging to think that if successful we might have to beat the sanguine Hessians every few days at heavy sacrifice, and yet have him in condition to come upon us with fresh troops from his reserve to renew the conflict, in which we might have grown wearied. We have, I presume, never dreamed of an attack upon the Union capital—if so, our chances of success were lost after the inaction that followed the great victory of 21st of July. So then we were at great hazard simply maintaining a menacing attitude. Again we had a line of immense length and being so near the enemy he could precipitate a heavy column upon any one point while he made feints elsewhere; and if we could in time concentrate we necessarily jeopardized the places from which our troops were withdrawn.

We now occupy in every way, a line of defensive works along the Rappadam [Rappahannock] river, from the foot of Blue Ridge to Fredericksburg, much less accessible to the large army of McClellan, and easy of defence with fewer men. It yields us a better region for necessary supplies. It disconcerted the matured plans of McClellan, who it was known was slowly advancing, cutting his own road as he threatened our centre.

We are now in a loyal region. It was by no means so in Fairfax and Prince William. McDowell's headquarters are said to be at Centreville, and McClellan's seven miles in his rear at Fairfax C. H. Our pickets extend very nearly to Manassas.

As I have said in my previous letters this is the finest region I have seen in Virginia. The women are as full of zeal as they are at home, and the Piedmontese loyal and many of their young men of the best families in the army. I rather like the Virginians—those of them who are with us are as true as loyalty can make men.

***.

☆☆☆Jackson in the Valley

In an effort to keep Federal troops from converging upon his retreating army, Johnston ordered Gen. Thomas J. "Stonewall" Jackson to keep the Union forces distracted and occupied. On March 23, near the village of Kernstown, Va., four miles south of Winchester, Jackson with 3,500 men attacked a Federal force of about 9,000 under Gen. James Shields. The Battle of Kernstown began what would become Jackson's Valley Campaign. Official casualties: Federals, 118 killed, 450 wounded and 22 missing for 590; Confederates, 80 killed, 375 wounded and 263 missing for 718.

PRIVATE LETTER FROM JACKSON'S COMMAND
[ROCKBRIDGE ARTILLERY]
CAMP BUCHANAN, March 26, 1862 [4-8-62ACWS]
This is the first opportunity I have had for more than a week to write to you a single line, and now I am compelled to be brief and hurried in what I have to tell you about our battle at Kernstown, on Sunday last [March 23]. It was a terrific fight, and all our men behaved like heroes. No one left his post until ordered off the ground. The loss in our battery was comparatively slight, being less than a dozen. Henry and Charlie are safe, as is George B., &c.; and it is wonderful how we all got off so well. A round shot killed one of our men not far from me, and another cut a spoke out of a wheel by which I was standing with my foot on the hub. Shell burst all around us. One struck a driver on the leg and cut it off, then passing through one horse and entering the body of another, burst inside of it and mortally wounded its rider.

The Second [Virginia] Regiment (our own glorious regiment) behaved magnificently, and Colonel [James W.] Allen proved himself worthy of his gallant command. Amongst many instances of gallantry which characterized the conduct of our men, I must tell you one or two. The banner-bearer of the 2nd was shot down, killed; whereupon Lieut. Richard Henry Lee caught up the fallen flag and bore it onward in front of the line until he fell wounded in the thigh. Then Lieut. [George] Davis seized it, when he too was shot, and as he fell another man caught it before it touched the ground, when he also was mortally wounded, Col. Allen then sprang from his horse, took up the tattered standard from the ground, and gallantly charged at the head of his regiment, with the consecrated colors in his hand. The flag staff was shot in two and bears, besides, the marks of fourteen bullet holes.

Harris Towner was killed, and John Feaman also, of Shepardstown. Poor Selby Hamtramock was wounded in the hip and left on the field.

Bushrod Washington was wounded, and when asked to leave the field and go to the rear, replied that "not so long as he had a drop of blood left in his body would he cease fighting for Virginia." His brother stood by him and assisted him in loading his gun, when the enemy's reinforcements came up and both the poor boys were killed.

Our battery lost one gun and two caissons; but the execution we did upon the enemy greatly exceeded the loss we sustained. A regiment of infantry, charging on us, came up to within a hundred yards of our battery, when our canister scattered them like scared sheep, and made them run, all that were left of them, like so many ---- Yankees.

The minie balls of the sharp-shooters rattled like hail around us, killing five of our horses, and wounding some of our men. But, as I said before, our battery escaped wonderfully well. We retired in good order, at our leisure, and regard the result as by no means discouraging; for with less than 3,000 we fought from three to five times our number of fresh troops until night put a stop to the engagement. Our loss was 400, all told; that of the enemy from 1,200 to 1,500.

On the evening after the battle my gun, with Chew's and Blakely's, were ordered to check the enemy's advance, and cover the retreat of our men, when a full battery opened upon us, and did some very good firing. One shell struck immediately in front of me. I threw myself on my face, and the fragments flying over me killed a horse from under a Sergeant who was directing behind me. Another came rushing over our heads, and bursting behind us, killed five and wounded ten of the infantry who were supporting us. We then let loose upon a column of cavalry which was cautiously approaching us, and cut them up considerably.

Yesterday morning my gun was again ordered down to picket with Col. [Turner] Ashby, and we gave the enemy a few rounds. So you see how busily we are kept at our work. Within the last five days we have marched 100 miles and have been in three engagements.

A. R. B., Jr.

Alexander R. Boteler, Jr., age 18, was born in Jefferson County, Virginia, and enlisted on June 10, 1861 at Camp Jackson on Bolivar Heights near Harpers Ferry in Company B, 2nd Virginia Infantry. Discharged from the regiment in October he joined the Rockbridge Artillery and later served as Ordnance Officer in Hoke's Brigade, Early's Division.

☆☆☆The Peninsula

In an effort to bypass Johnston's Army of the Potomac positioned along the Rappahannock line, Union General George B. McClellan embarked his 100,000 strong Army of the Potomac and boating it to Fort Monroe and Newport News on the tip of the Virginia Peninsula between the York and James rivers. McClellan's plan to capture Richmond from the lightly defended southeast stalled when confronted with a small Confederate force under General "Prince John" Magruder along the Warwick River line near Yorktown.

FROM THE ARMY OF THE PENINSULA
[TOOMBS' BRIGADE, JONES' DIVISION]
NEAR YORKTOWN, VA., April 25, 1862 [5-7-62SR]

I am so sleepy at present, my letter can be worth but little, I fear, to you. Our Brigade—Toombs'—together with Jones', have been "the outer trenches guarding," now, for ten days without any aid—one night on, and the next night off, but on our arms, expecting the onset continually. By this incessant watching, oft-times in the rain and mud, we have become fairly worn out. Our lines and the enemy's only lie a few hundred yards apart, separated by a small river which the maps do not name, but is here known as the Warwick river. It scarcely supports a volume of water worthy of this name. Along either shore the forces occupying them have raised strong entrenchments. Our breastworks consist of parallel lines of earthworks only a few hundred yards apart, from which overpowered forces can fall back and meet reinforcements. Occasional batteries along the rearmost line are raised, into which our artillery is placed, raking every direction to the front. So scanty was the body of water between us and the enemy, Gen. Magruder deemed it advisable to increase it, that the crossing might be rendered more difficult to the foe. Accordingly, large dams have been erected across, and now the back water is, on an average, 200 yards wide. This may be called the division between our forces. Our sharp shooters lie down by the water edge on this side, and the enemy's to the water edge on his side. From their post a death messenger is hurled at every head or body that shows itself above the rifle pits, which skirt the ponds. Not unfrequently a careless "rebel" gets a hole in his corporeal substance from these hidden rifles. These dams above mentioned are successively called Dam No. 1, No. 2 &c., as they go on down.

On the 16th ult., a sharp fight occurred at Dam No. 1, of which, no doubt, you have heard already. It lasted perhaps three hours, and is called by the victorious "rebels," "*a dam No. 1 fight.*" The 15th North Carolina Volunteers were surprised by the enemy, who drove in our pickets from the water's edge, and whose firing was mistaken for the usual *popping* of the sharpshooters. The North Carolinians were at work on some breastworks a short distance from the place where their guns were stacked, but so complete was their surprise they fled in much confusion and were not rallied until several were killed and wounded. However, the enemy were kept at bay until the Seventh Georgia, supported by the glorious Eighth—our lamented Bartow's command—formed and charged with fix bayonets. The enemy, then strongly posted, saw the impetuous charge in its beginning, heard the terrific shouts of the rebels plunging down upon them, but such a strange *lusus nature* took possession of their legs, at the moment they could not await the denouement, and fled most precipitously to their own lines. Such a dividing of the waters has hardly occurred since the flight of the Israelites from bondage. Our Georgia forces formed in their rifle pits and awaited the enemy's further aggression. They were reinforced by the 1st Kentucky, and, I think, the 10th Louisiana, at this juncture. On the opposite side, being supported by a brigade held in reserve, the "Yanks" again formed and were persuaded to make a second assault.

Now all this occurred just below Dam No. 1, in a body of wood. They advanced in tolerably good order, but the moment our fire from the pits was opened on them they fled to the opposite shore. They could not be persuaded to come again. Our battery from this end of the dam, which did not bear at all on the enemy, received a most tremendous cannonading, from a clearing opposite. The noise of their guns and of ours replying was deafening.

The 1st Georgia Regulars, and the 2nd Georgia Volunteers, were formed as reserves, immediately in the rear of our battery, to support it in case of an assault, and I can testify, the flight of shells in that region was most terrific. The trees were torn to pieces and crashed about us, and the bursting of shells scattering fragments, it would seem, everywhere, rendered the effort to feel comfortable and *brave* very laborious. There it seemed fit for the General to keep us the longest hour I ever timed. The close of it was near sundown. The roll of musketry died away, and the bellowing cannon hushed—the battle had ended.

All that the enemy gained was a thrashing. They left dead on our side of the river, thirty-two, and two or three wounded. Four or five prisoners were also taken; but how many sleep beneath the waters between, is not known to us, nor to them, nor how many wounded they bore away. They acknowledge a whipping and a heavy loss. We had killed, sixteen, and sixty will cover the number of our wounded. The Colonel [Robert M. McKinney] of the North Carolina troops was killed.

The next day our Regiment—2nd Georgia—was detailed to guard the trenches exactly where the battle was fought. The dead still lay about the ground, just outside the trenches, and the enemy's sharp shooters, from the opposite shore, forbade any meddling with them; accordingly, they were left unburied. One poor wretch, shot through the loin, had lain there over twelve hours, in the most excruciating agony. I gave him some water from my canteen, for which he had suffered very greatly, and talked with him a little. He belonged to the 3rd Vermont Regiment, and said he enlisted because it was most profitable to be in the army, where he was paid $20 per month. He also stated that the forces that assailed that point were paid extra to lead the attack.

We kept our watch all night, most diligently, and a more ghastly sight than the pale faces of the dead lying there silently in the moonlight, has seldom been seen.

The two armies are ready, but one awaits the other, and there the difficulty lies. If we attack the enemy, he has the advantage; if he attacks us, we have the advantage. Will this ever get up a fight? Some big game is to be played before the fight comes off—some grand strategic movement, before the dreaded collision of these two armies occurs.

H. H. P.

LETTER FROM V. A. S. P.
[TOOMBS' BRIGADE, JONES DIVISION]
CAMP OF THE SEVENTEENTH GEORGIA REGIMENT,
NEAR YORKTOWN, VA., May 3, 1862 [5-12-62SR]

Lying in suspense, and expecting hourly orders to pack up and move to the rear, I thought I could not occupy an hour more pleasantly and profitably than by giving your readers the few items of interest which have fallen under my observation, or come to my knowledge through reliable sources.

I will leave everybody to draw his own conclusions, and simply state facts. The entire army of the Peninsula, excepting Gen. Toombs' brigade, and three or four others, have fallen back to Williamsburg, twelve miles distant, or perhaps further. The remaining troops will probably leave tonight. We were in the trenches last night and ready formed to bid our line of breastworks a final adieu, when the order came to remain for further orders. We again occupied the pits until eleven o'clock, when we were relieved by the Eleventh Georgia.

I am unable to give a reason for this precipitate retreat; but it is evidently for the best, because Gen. Johnston ordered it. We have unlimited confidences in his ability.

Night before last (May 1st) the enemy kept up a noise in their camps all night—rumbling of heavy wagons, braying of mules, and occasional shouts—which made us believe they were evacuating their works. Their breastworks extend like ours, entirely across the Peninsula, and frequently within four or five hundred yards of us. The pickets keep up an incessant firing at each other, and very frequently, serious damage and loss of life, are the result. The First Georgia Regulars have been particularly unfortunate. On Wednesday, 1st May, Second Lieutenant James T. Armstrong, of Augusta, I believe, was posted with his company in the "Water Battery," at Dam No. 1, the closest point on our line to the enemy. Raising to stretch himself, a Minie ball entered his left side, and pierced his body, coming out on the left. He lived fifteen minutes. He was a noble young officer—a man of sterling worth; was promoted from Sergeant, and many who knew his worth will mourn his early fall. A Lieutenant of the Regulars informed me that they had lost four privates by the enemy's sharp shooters.

It is due to the gallant Seventh and Eighth Georgia to give the particulars of the fight of April 16th. The Fifteenth North Carolina Regiment was in the trenches at Dam No. 1, and were driven from them by the Yankees. The Seventh Georgia being in close proximity, was ordered to the support of the North Carolinians, and met them retiring before the enemy, in somewhat of an irregular manner. The enemy had possessed the trenches, and the gallant Seventh charged them, and ran them out in less time than I am writing it. The Eighth came up and occupied the right, and the two regiments united in a second and more determined attack, and repulsed the enemy with considerable loss. The Eighth did not even have a man wounded.

I thought it but just to these gallant Georgians, renowned upon the plains of Manassas, to make this statement, as some correspondents had given the North Carolinians praise that belongs to others. For proof of what I say, I refer your readers to Gen. Anderson's report.

The 17th Georgia, in fact all the regiments originally composing Gen. Toombs' brigade, are beginning to learn what it is to "soldier." The retreat from Manassas has thinned our regiments fearfully, hundreds being now in the hospital. We have been without tents sufficient to protect us from the weather, since the 10th March. We are now bivouacking, sleeping upon the damp ground, with about two blankets to the man. We are now upon half rations, and my mess have had nothing since breakfast. Many cases of pneumonia occur, but notwithstanding these hardships, and sickness, the men seem to be in high spirits. Their confidence in Gen. Johnston is undiminished, and they will suffer almost everything to follow him against the enemy. What may a General not accomplish with such an army? We may be confident of success with Johnston at the head.

I have seen a portion of the elephant since my return to camps. As the little schooner, with a hundred men aboard, neared the wharf at Yorktown, the enemy's battery a mile and a half distant begun to throw shell at us, which went beyond or fell short two or three hundred yards. These futile effects "to shell us out" of the schooner excited the jest and merriment of all on board. But as we rose the bluff, and the missiles began to fall within ten to twenty feet, the tune was changed, and tracks were made to get beyond the limits of the town. You would have been amused to see us, or perhaps, imitating our example at dodging. It is so perfectly natural.

The enemy have thrown perhaps thousands of shells into Yorktown; but one man as yet has been killed. What a waste of ammunition!

As soon as I learn our destination, and the meaning of this strange, sudden and grand movement, I will report particulars.

V. A. S. P.

LETTER FROM V. A. S. P.
SEVENTEENTH GEORGIA REGIMENT
CAMP NEAR RICHMOND, VA., May 18, 1862 [5-24-62SR]

Wonderful events have transpired since the 11th, when we were drawn up in line ready to receive the enemy if he chose to make an attack. But, it seems, nothing was further from his intention. While we rested in bivouac, hardly knowing whether to expect an attack, or look for a grand movement in another direction, the enemy was slowly and cautiously advancing in his terrible iron-clad engines of war, upon the devoted city. The distance can be easily run in six hours; but so slow and cautious were his movements, that he was several days in reaching our river batteries. You have full particulars of the attack and repulse [on Drewery's Bluff]. It seems that their iron boats are not invulnerable. A good battery of columbiads, well manned, and with plenty of ammunition, is now thought able to resist them. The people are fully aroused. Although hundreds of families are leaving the city, yet the people—the authorities— have an unshaken faith in their confidence of our ability to hold the capital against a force of 200,000 mercenaries. The river obstructions are now thought sufficient to prevent their passage up the river, nearer than ten miles of the city. To reach it then, they must approach by land and leave their gun boats; in which event they are whipped so sure as they attempt it. We *can* whip them on land.

McClellan will be loath to attack Richmond without the aid of his gunboats. He knows our superiority on land, and fears the result of pitched battle.

There has already been much said relative to the late masterly retreat from Yorktown, and I hope a recurrence to it by me will not be improper. The journals on both sides of our northern boundary were loud in their laudations of Gen. Johnston's skill in the management and execution of what was considered the most masterly conducted retreat on record— American, at least. But few Generals of the Old World ever achieved such a feat. It was generally conceded that McClellan was outwitted. But what may be said of the "Yorktown Retreat?" At Manassas the opposing armies were from fifteen to twenty miles apart. Even if the enemy became aware of General Johnston's intentions the day they were put in motion, he was more than a day's march ahead, and could keep that distance. But on the Peninsula we were in four hundred yards of the enemy. We were in speaking distance, and every day added to the list of "killed, wounded and missing." There was the immense wagon train sufficient to carry the baggage, provisions, ammunition, &c., of a vast army—probably ----thousands. There were ----pieces of field artillery—all to be moved from under the guns and vigilant watch of the enemy.

The wagons moved off in the daytime, and could have been seen from an eminence, stretching out for miles towards Williamsburg, like the slow winding movement of the feebled serpent. At 8 o'clock, with camp fires burning brightly, the vast army moved off, and the rear guard, by meridian the next day, reached Williamsburg. Not until broad daylight did the enemy discover, certainly, that our works were abandoned. They then took possession of our "ramparts," but were ill at ease in their coveted possession, for occasionally an adventurous Yankee would step upon a torpedo, and to his utter amazement and the discomfiture of his comrades, would find himself bound heavenward (skyward at least); with a velocity little suited to his liking.

The question has been asked, "If we whipped the Yankees so badly at Williamsburg, why did we leave our sick, dead and wounded in the hands of the enemy?" Well, that was rather bad—very unfortunate; but it must be borne in mind that it was not the policy of General Johnston to make a stand and give McClellan battle at Williamsburg. It would have been absolutely suicidal; for the enemy having possession of York river, could, and *did* in ten hours or twenty, at farthest, land a large force at West Point, ready to cut us off. It was his policy to get above West Point before the enemy could cut us off. Hence the necessity of leaving the sick, &c.

We did not have ample transportation for those who were unable to walk in consequence of wounds or sickness, and such only were left as could not be hauled. The dead were necessarily left, and, we hope, buried by the enemy. I trust this view of the case will relieve our favorite and famous General from all blame. He did the best he could. If General Johnston had nothing else in the course of his illustrious life, this retreat would be enough to immortalize him. He is THE GENERAL of the day—not detracting from the lustre surrounding the names of any of his illustrious coadjutors, Beauregard, Price, the lamented Albert Sydney Johnston, Robert E. Lee, Magruder, &c. History will bear me out in this declaration.

As I before said, we will hardly have a fight here, unless, indeed, the enemy's gunboats force the river obstructions and pass the batteries. If they do, they will capture Richmond in ashes. The city will certainly be destroyed before abandoned. Let our people take heart. What if Richmond does fall? The Confederacy is broad enough to meet the hireling hordes upon a thousand fields more glorious than Manassas or Shiloh. What if they take every principal city? The invader will be defeated at every attempt to penetrate the interior. We will get him from his gunboat, we will run them like sheep, and strike such a terror into their craven hearts that they will not renew the experience. "God save our country!"

V. A. S. P.

SECOND GEORGIA REGIMENT
[TOOMBS' BRIGADE, JONES' DIVISION]
BIVOUAC NEAR RICHMOND, May 22, 1862 [5-27-62 SR]

Here, almost on the suburbs of the capitol, our troops are dozing in the general sunshine of spring, waiting the advent of the "pressure" which was boasted should "drive" them to the wall. So slow is it to approach, this expression is frequently heard from some yawning backwoods specimen lolling on the green grass about the encampment: "boys, I believe fights is played out." Yes, the strong arm of this army now encompasses and swears to defend the cherished seat of the Confederate government against the beleaguered hordes of the North. The citizens protest against evacuating it, the soldiers against moving back another step from a foe they are compelled to despise as cowards and hirelings, and the commanders, so rumor goes, have determined to consummate our destiny here, if the enemy are so dispersed. It is difficult to conjecture what will transpire, for McClellan, poor fellow, does not, as he pretends, confide implicitly in his Hessian forces. Therefore, if it be allowed him, by that pressure at the North, which is driving *him* to the wall, he will continue to practice legerdemain; if not he will cast the die here and read his fate, be it weal of success or certain damnation of failure.

His scouts hung closely on our heels, dogging every foot-step of our movements; his gunboats daringly ascended the river, as near as safety, would allow, to learn our strength there; indeed, he has made every effort to know our defenses and exact vulnerability, in order to hasten to destroy this tremendous stumbling block to his fame. The reporters and spies of his camp have not satisfied his mind or convinced his credulity of the fact that the rebel army were "completely disorganized" by the "rout" from Yorktown. His Yankee sagacity was too keen for such marine narrations as they whispered knowingly in his ears, and he chooses to look a little way into the state of affairs with his own identical eyes and senses. If anything had been decomposing in the Dutch province no nasal function are surer to catch the tainted breeze than the "*Young Napoleon*" of Yankeedom. None of the feline favorites ever come in the neighborhood of his olfactory nerves and go away without the contiguity being detected; in short, he *has*, doubtlessly, smelt a rat.

No, sir, the sanguinary field of Williamsburg taught him that he must tread his way cautiously, or sure destruction hangs upon ill-advised haste. Therefore, he comes very *feelingly* to the wall and *pusses* the case as gently as possible. But this may not reach you before a bloody battle will be fought, for, as I've said, the poor fellow has the keen eyed Yankee nation—who have made great promises to the half-gulled European powers,—turned upon him. Some things go to indicate a hasty conflict, and others the delay of an immediate onset, and the predictions hazarded now are as apt to be untrue as realized. Yesterday evening an old man drove by our place of bivouac, but halted a moment to say that his son had been that morning captured by the enemy's scouts while absent a short distance from home. He lives only seven miles away, which shows that they are at least this side of the Chickahominy. What news the scouts bring to headquarters is not known in relation to the enemy's movements; but occasionally the rumor flies around that he is advancing slowly. Then, again, it seems improbable that he will push the conflict here until McDowell is ordered up to encompass the western, and [Ambrose] Burnside begins operations on the southern side of our devoted army. If however, a cool determination and absolute confidence in our ability to thrash out Yankeedom, seems to pervade the army, let them approach as they may, or where they please. Nothing appears to give any uneasiness so long as full rations are received.

For the last few days, that is, since the army has been in the immediate vicinity of the capitol, the strictest martial laws have been proclaimed, to prevent the stragglers from overrunning the city, as well as to have the full force constantly at their arms, should any sudden attack be made. Officers as high as Brigadier Generals were halted at the picket posts on the limits of the corporation, and required to produce passports from General Johnston, or report back to their commands. But the chain around the city is not connected so closely that *running the blockade* was entirely prevented. However, if left to the will of the men, the larger portion of the army, careless about the danger impending, would straggle off to the city, crowd the thoroughfare, become an absolute nuisance to the citizens, and tend to completely undiscipline and disorganize any forces. But this salutary regulation, very few are *sharp* enough to steal their way into the desired and tempting spot; and if fortunate enough to pick through unmolested, some very sly dodging has to be practiced to avoid the guards that infest every corner and block. Yet go into the streets, and one is surprised to observe the number of men in uniform, sauntering about as contentedly as if soldiers' apparel only indicated the prevailing fashion, and not the fact that our devoted country was now plunged in a terrible war. Inquire who these fair faces are, and, if you "know the ropes," you may learn that they are mostly "hospital birds," allowed to pass in this garb because they bear certificates of disability—not able to do the duty of a soldier—signed by some surgeon in charge of a hospital; able to lounge about the streets, throng the theatres at night, steal into holes after contraband whiskey, and sport fine uniforms on government pay, but not able to go into camp and share the arduous labors of their brave comrades, who do their own duty and that of these trifling vagabonds.

In spite of all laws, in spite of every effort of the commanders in the field, these dishonest *cowards* escape mostly through the instrumentality of surgeons as ignorant as they are dishonest. Many sport uniforms and escape, God knows how, that were never in the army, but who infest the dens—gambling hells—of the city into which many a poor fly is enticed and sucked to desperation. Conscript acts that can force the brave twelve months volunteers, who first rushed to their country's defence and protection, into a service *not of their selection*, pass harmlessly over these villains, who are only fit to raise breastworks to shield the truly brave and patriotic men of our army. A very mortifying picture in this city, in noticing these would-be soldiers, but who have not the courage in their hearts to make them men, is the fact that most of them are in officer's uniform. These men, some of them, were intended to control troops, and set salutary examples, but are found here taking every advantage of an officer's position, and literally deserting their comrades in the most disgraceful and sneaking ways. The privates in the ranks are subjected often to the severest rules, and officers allowed to have the advantage of every little finger ache by which they betake themselves to the pleasant streets of Richmond. Thus another source of dissatisfaction is bred, that would surely try any other army than ours.

Just now, orders have come to have everything in readiness to move as soon as it may be required. Our pickets, it is said, have been driven in from the direction of Bottom's bridge, due east of this place. It is feared the crisis is near at hand, which must tell the fate of so many brave and valuable men. I've not time to write more at present.

H. H. P.

P. S. We have been under arms now since four this evening, and are still required to remain in arms. We will, in all probability move at day light.

LETTER FROM TOUT LE MONDE

CAMP OF THE SECOND GEORGIA REGIMENT,
NEAR RICHMOND, VA., May 23, 1862 [5-28-62SR]

Our camp hitherto about four miles northeast of the capitol, has been moved about one mile east of the last position, and nearer the line of the enemy's advanced guards. Since my last, the Confederate forces have slept on their arms and incessantly required to be vigilant. No doubt of large forces of McClellan being now within five miles of us steadily reconnoitering and continually advancing by gradual steps. Whether he intends to attack our forces drawn up to oppose his "onward to Richmond," in a short time, is known only to himself. Notwithstanding indications of that nature, it is not believed he will, without preparation by which he can in some measures assure his soldiers of safety, risk a general engagement. Adequate breastworks are to be raised as a place of refuge for his Hessians, and points of protection where his forces may rally in case of defeat. With him this matter is one of serious importance, on which much time will be spent in order to obtain entire satisfaction.

There is little doubt in his mind about the fact that his soldiers fight better when convinced breastworks are ready to receive them if the fire gets too hot elsewhere. This may assure them, but if their dependence is placed in batteries and earthworks behind, to which each Yankee may flee when his cowardly heels prompt, it seems that a contusion might be got up in their ranks and closely followed that would produce favorable results to our arms. It is hoped, however, that they may not be permitted to fortify and consume their time while our troops are inspirited and in good health. If the foe is far enough from successful escape now is the time to strike, and *on d t*; if it is left to Johnston a battle will be hazarded. To-day just as we moved into a bivouac and got fairly undercover at a thick wood, a balloon majestically arose in the east, about five miles distant away. Its bright exterior glistened in the morning's sun as it ascended dancing to and fro with a breeze, and went up apparently 300 feet high. After a fifteen minutes survey of our lines, and, no doubt, a covetous glance at our Capital, it descended, but came up again in a few minutes to take a more satisfactory inspection. It looked very like the one that took a bird's eye view of us from Washington when our lines reached to Munson's Hill. One day there, they ventured up in it to some considerable height, and seemed to be very busily marking out the different positions of forces, upon which a fine rifle piece belonging to the Washington Artillery of N. O. was turned and fired. The whizzing shot fled through the air, passing with its peculiar shriek somewhere in the neighborhood of the hostile aeronauts, and only a few seconds elapsed before balloon and contents were gone from our view. After that the Confederate movements were not subjected to any more bird's eye scrutenizing. To-morrow the same minute inspection will be made again, and I believe a trick, is on foot to run a rifle piece in as near as possible to-night in order to take a shot at it. I hope to see a hole made through the "concern."

This seems to be a favorite mode of reconnoitering, which could be practiced advantageously by our side, and why it is not used more frequently is hard to understand. We had a balloon in operation at Yorktown, with good effect, exposing many of the enemy's works and encampments.   It seems to me one might be kept constantly in the clouds watching every movement of his forces, conveying the intelligence by telegraph to headquarters, and facilitating the process of giving information.

The panic, which at first threatened to take place in Richmond, when the army fell back and the forces of McClellan were known to be advancing both by land and water, has, to a great extent, subsided.   The great dread seemed to be of the gunboats, which have been heretofore unsuccessfully resisted everywhere, but those that came up to the batteries below the city, having been repulsed, the fears of the citizens have been greatly allayed.   Another thing tending to restore confidence is the careless indifference of our soldiery to the enemy's approach, presenting, as they do, that daring front which assures the people of a perfect willingness to try the wager of battle in this question of right.   A few days ago the prospects were promising to have the city materially depopulated.   Many wagons, drays, &c., loaded with furniture, bestraddled with men, women and children, with an occasional sprinkle of darkies could be seen taking the way that leads westward.   The class that were so ready to leave were mostly those strictly loyal to the South.   I am sorry to believe, many a traitor and spy has his abiding place in the very heart of our Confederacy, and at this hour and perilous moment, are aiding the enemy with their nefarious purposes of subjugation.   This class remain to receive the gracious thanks of an enemy, who is of the right stamp to appreciate and foster such cowardly villains—the only nation, making pretences to national honor, that would take Arnolds to its bosom and nurture them with distinctions.   Unfortunately, Benedict only reaped the just scorn of his debased and contemptible deed, but the surest mark of honor among those who would enslave us, is to know that one is a traitor to his home—the murderer of his own fireside.   The old gray haired wretch—the imbecile and demented [Gen. Winfield] Scott, is yet an object of veneration among those who threw him away on account of his imbecility, but still can bow at the shrine of meanness, because of hearts that flow with congenial villainy.

Just at this period in the progress of my letter some heavy firing of field pieces, discharge following after discharge in very close succession, was heard towards the north east of our position.   Remember, we are now always in line of battle.   Going to the edge of the wood and looking across a wide field over towards some hills about three miles distant in the direction named, the smoke of each gun could be plainly seen, and that of the shells which in due time were followed by reports.   I've not heard whether any pieces on our side were engaged or not, but it seemed that large volumes of white smoke rose from a valley between us and the first, and this may have been our guns replying.   Probably the enemy was shelling a piece of wood into which he designs throwing pickets to-night, or it may have been an artillery duel got up for the purpose of drawing our men from the cover of the wood that he might learn their exact locality.   In this he was foiled, although the balloon was seen cautiously and slyly peering above the tree tops while the firing was in progress, for our Colonel issued orders for every man to remain under cover of the wood.   Now this little skirmish may, and it may not, portend a fight to-morrow.   It may be the object of the enemy to come as close as possible before attempting to build entrenchments.   I shall not venture an opinion now, but wait until further developments warrant the propriety of hazarding one; at which time, if all intermediate contingencies are survived, I may have something of more importance to write than has been recorded in this letter.

TOUT LE MONDE.

LETTER FROM TOUT LE MONDE

NEAR RICHMOND, May 29, 1862 [6-8-62SR]

I may be able to send you a hasty scroll to-day, but I shall not promise; for no one can tell now what a moment may bring forth.

Still the opposing forces of the South and North are face to face, growling defiantly at each other here—the Southern army, like the sullen lioness, who has retreated doggedly to her den, and intimates "I shall go no further"—while the Northern hordes, like a pack of yelping curs, stand off from further pursuit, to growl and bark as if they would, if they could have her. The lioness seems fretful, the fire of impatience is beginning to glare frightfully from her eyes, and every moment it seems that she will turn upon her pursuers with rage enough to consume them.   We are looking for it, and care not now in anticipation to inquire of anything that is progressing about the lines. Occasional skirmishing takes place, and one is not allowed to die with *ennui*. All look for the fight, hoping for the fortunate contingency that will precipitate it. The *Supreme Heads* are delectably cool about matters—much more so than the chaffing soldier—keeping their counsel well, whiskey too, and cultivating the society of procrastination to the fullest extent.

"Stonewall" [Jackson] is spreading terror in the Federal capitol, and McClellan is permitted to return the compliment upon the women and children of our seat of government. How we could make the *Scotch plaid suit* [Lincoln] dance out of Washington now if a fatal blow was struck here, and our rapidest forces sent toward that dulcorated elysium of Yankee fancy! The men are fairly mad with impatience to accomplish it, and anxious to emulate the fame of this modern "Hickory."

Day before yesterday [May 27] the report of cannon was heard frequently from the direction of Hanover Junction, sometimes heavier than at others, and towards evening musketry could be distinguished at intervals which lasted until sundown. Reports have come in slowly; even now the casualties are uncertain. It is pretty well authenticated, however, that our forces got very well thrashed out, on account of the usual stupidity of sending four or five regiments to contend against a whole Yankee army. Fifty-eight or sixty Yankee prisoners were captured, but the killed is not known. A regiment of North Carolinians, (28th) it is said, lost two-thirds in killed, wounded and prisoners; and the enemy now, in all probability, are possessed of the railroad at that point. There were five N. Carolina regiments engaged, and one (45th) Georgia, but only three actually in the fight. Our loss is very great, if the reports are true; all probably North Carolina troops. Three regiments were left to bear the brunt, and I suppose we may acknowledge ourselves out-generaled completely. However, it is best to abstain from censure until further details are furnished on which to ground conclusions. It may not be the fault of the General [Lawrence O. Branch] commanding at that point; he may have made the best disposition of the troops in his power in the emergencies. During the entire fight the balloons of the enemy, two in number, were in the skies watching narrowly our movements.

If any reinforcements had been sent to the assistance of our men, the point from which they were sent no doubt would have been attacked, deeming it the weakest point and most accessible. The enemy is certainly on the alert for even the smallest advantage.

Yesterday everything was remarkably calm, not a gun fired in hearing, but just at night orders to have the wagons in readiness to move immediately; also, the troops in arms, and to await orders. Pulses began to beat quicker, and every one said "to-morrow the great battle will be—surely it will." So everything was got ready instantly, and with an absolute fever heat coursing through every vein, the men talked over and over the coming events, waiting and watching for the expected orders. They came not, and tired out at last, lay down in disappointment on the soldier's couch—mother earth—and dreamed of deeds of valor which their hearts burned to have done. The sun breaks on the world to-day and finds us in *statu quo*. When the fight will occur one dares not conjecture. Who will have the hardihood to make a prophecy that is seeking honor in his own country? The matter is resolved into this: "Things are *very* uncertain." The sameness in the general aspect of affairs naturally curtails my letter of to-day. I hope I shall survive a huge "smash up" of the Yankee hordes, and be able to chronicle the scene in my next.

TOUT LE MONDE.

☆☆☆Jackson in the Valley

On May 23, "Stonewall" Jackson defeated the Federals under Col. John R. Kenly at Front Royal, fueling fear among the officials at Washington of an impending attack on the Federal capital. Two days later Jackson routed the Federals under Gen. Nathaniel Banks at Winchester. These victories added to the growing legend of "Stonewall" and, more importantly, relieved pressure on Richmond by depriving McClellan of men and material.

FROM JACKSON'S COMMAND,
THE BATTLES OF FRONT ROYAL AND WINCHESTER

CAMP SIX MILES NORTH OF WINCHESTER, Sunday, May 25, 1862 [6-5-62SR]

We met the enemy at Front Royal, Warren county, Va., on Friday evening [May 23]. He made but a short stand. The first Maryland Volunteers on the Yankee side, was charged by the first regiment of Maryland rebels who put their old acquaintances to flight in short time, capturing a stand of colors, killing several and taking a number of prisoners, who were recognized by many old acquaintances.

We took the enemy by surprise and put them to flight before one-fourth of our forces had entered the town. The [6th Virginia] cavalry, among which were the Wise Troop and Jack Anderson's company, charged upon the Yankees in the retreat, killing many and capturing a large number of prisoners. Ashby's and [George H.] Steuart's cavalry did good work by taking two railroad trains, which were loaded with provisions, and bringing in prisoners all day Friday.

The number of prisoners captured, as well as I could learn and see, amounted to about eleven hundred, most of whom are Marylanders.

We also captured a large amount of stores and arms. Among the latter are about 500 improved cavalry six-shooters, an article very much needed.

I am told that the stores captured amount to $300,000 to $400,000. We also took three pieces of artillery.

When we entered Front Royal, the women and children met us with shouts of the liveliest joy. As we passed through the place in double quick, we could not stop to partake of the hospitality so generously and profusely tendered on all hands.

On Saturday, at early dawn, we were again on the march to pay Gen. [N. P.] Banks a visit, who was encamped at Strasburg, twelve miles distant. After reconnoitering for several hours, Col. Ashby's cavalry marched down the road leading to Middletown, which is six miles in the rear of Strasburg, and General Ewell's command down the road to Newtown, twelve miles in the rear of Strasburg. At 2 o'clock a courier reported that Banks was on the retreat, and had passed Middletown, but that two regiments of cavalry were still left behind at Strasburg and Middletown as a baggage guard.

Gen. Ed Johnson's division, under the command of Brigadier General [Arnold] Elzey, was at once ordered down the road to Middletown, to pursue the enemy. On our march we met detachment after detachment of Ashby's men with prisoners and horses. Among one of the squads of prisoners, about twenty in number, was a woman mounted. When we came to the Valley turnpike we found hosts of prisoners, and the road blockaded with dead and live horses, and wagons heavy laden with subsistence, &c, together with dead and wounded Yankees.

We pushed on our column for about eleven miles, when we halted for a few hours. We then learned that Banks had passed the road leading into the Valley pike near Newtown, where Ewell's command had entered the road. Skirmishing was then kept up until a late hour of the night, and at about 3 o'clock in the morning we halted within three miles of Winchester.

We found along the road about 100 wagons loaded with baggage, together with a number of boats (not of the gunboat order) on wheels, which Banks had destroyed for fear of their falling into our hands.

At early dawn this (Sunday) morning, we advanced and attacked the mighty Banks in front of Winchester. After fighting about one hour, distributing shell and minie balls profusely, our boys made a charge when the Yankees left at double quick, after setting fire to the town and burning their commissary stores.

The Lee [Raine's] Battery of Lynchburg, and two others were ordered to pursue in a gallop, and the command was obeyed, they shelling the enemy for five miles.

When the army passed through the town, men, women, and children were shouting, "thank God we are free—thank God we are free once more!" Confederate flags and white handkerchiefs were waved from every window, and the happy smiles of lovely women on all sides met the wearied soldier and cheered him as he hurriedly passed through the place in pursuit of the flying foe.

After pursuing the enemy for six miles we were brought to a halt, and left the finishing stroke to the cavalry, who have captured a large number of prisoners who have been sent in through the day. The final result of the achievements are yet unknown.

Prisoners tell me that Gen. Banks has said that he was afraid that he would have to surrender his whole command, and to be relieved of the painful necessity and to save his own bacon, left before day on an extra car.

The fire in the town was extinguished by our boys after the commissary stores were destroyed, but we succeeded in saving all of the medical stores and ammunition, both of which were very large. We also secured the depot and a train of cars, both of which were well filled with provisions.

The Yankees left behind all their knapsacks, a large quantity of arms which they threw away, and lots of trinkets, which the boys have been examining all day.

Having been on the march for 22 days, and all of the previous night, our General "Stonewall" allowed us to go into camp to rest, but I guess we will be off again in the morning in pursuit of the Yankees.

In neither of the engagements we have not had one-fourth, no, not one sixth of forces engaged, and I cannot see why the enemy have fled in such confusion after so short a stand.

We recaptured a large number of stolen negroes. The Yankees had married a number of the women and were taking them home with them. I have seen some that refused to go, and others that had been forced off at other times that had returned.

At Front Royal we captured 1,470 prisoners, and eight or nine hundred at Winchester, and numbers from points north are being hourly brought in.

At Strasburg we took six pieces of artillery.

W. W. H.

TAYLOR'S HOTEL,
WINCHESTER, VA., May 28, 1862.

This beautiful inland town has assumed quite a lively appearance since we drove the detested Yankees from its vicinity, and the people are once more breathing the air of freemen and not of slaves. To-day I heard a lady say that she was once more free, and the niggers were niggers again.

Up to this time we have captured, and have in this place, between 3,000 and 4,000 prisoners, and I am told that 1,100 more of the Hessians have been captured near Harper's Ferry and Martinsburg.

We have now in this place 8,000 stand of arms, taken since we entered Front Royal, besides a number of pieces of artillery, together with the largest quantity of the best ammunition of all grades that I have ever beheld.

The medical stores captured are estimated by the druggists of this place to be worth at least $200,000. Among them are articles very scarce in the Confederacy and much needed by the government. We captured 500 pounds of opium and 200 gallons castor oil, both of which are greatly needed, and have been shipped to the hospital in Lynchburg.

To-day news was received that the Yankees had burnt the depot at Charlestown, together with all the stores.

A portion of the army moved this evening, and it is reported that the balance will follow in the morning. Their destination is unknown, but the impression prevails that they will not stop until the State of Maryland is free. God grant that it may be so.

During the sojourn of the Yankees in this place, the people were not allowed to communicate with any one, either North or South, without the letters being first scrutinized by the Provost Marshal, and no Virginian who would not take the oath of allegiance was allowed to purchase goods from the North or elsewhere; but Yankee importers did all the business, and upon our approach on Sunday morning, left at double quick, leaving behind all the stock of goods. Some few Jews were permitted to traffic who had the audacity to refuse our money for merchandize, but old Stonewall has had them all arrested, and their goods, like those of their Northern friends, have been confiscated, and their dens closed.

W. W. H.

Union casualties for the battle of Winchester: 62 killed, 243 wounded and 1,714 missing or captured; Confederates lost 68 killed, 329 wounded and 3 missing.

☆☆☆ Battle of Seven Pines

The two day battle, called Seven Pines by the Confederates and Fair Oaks by the Federals, began at about 1 P. M. on May 31 when Gen. D. H. Hill's division attacked and routed a Union division commanded by Gen. Silas Casey. In the fighting, Gen. Johnston was severely wounded and was succeeded for a few hours by Gen. G. W. Smith. The following afternoon, the army had a new commander: General Robert E. Lee.

Official casualties at the battle of Seven Pines: Union, 790 killed, 3,594 wounded and 647 missing for 5,031; Confederates, 980 killed, 4,749 wounded and 405 missing for 6,134.

LETTER FROM V. A. S. P.

RICHMOND, VA., May 31, 1862 [6-7-62SR]

Truly no man can tell what a day may bring forth. Two days ago this city was beleagured by an army of one hundred and eighty thousand Yankees. Now they are in full retreat to their gunboats at West Point, and if our information is correct, McClellan is shipping his troops by tens of thousands to Washington, which is now threatened by the invincible Jackson. It is marvelous what a change may be effected in a very few hours. The *Dispatch* of yesterday had a long article on the "Approaching Battle," in which it urged the people of Richmond and the soldiers around the city, to put forth every effort to defend it, appealing to their patriotism, their fears of subjugation, their hatred of the Yankee oppressor, to their love of home, wives, mothers and sisters, in the most touching and pathetic manner; and in the next page was an equally well written article upon the retreat of the foe, the glorious career of "Old Stonewall," and all fears of a battle in the vicinity of the capital were dispelled! The enemy's movement was very quiet, but seems to have been known to the authorities at an early hour, as General Smith's Division started in pursuit by 3 A. M., yesterday. Unless *we make the attack*, we will *not* have a fight *here*. So I have thought all along. Now my opinion is confirmed.

The glorious cheering intelligence of Stonewall Jackson's brilliant feat, and successful entrance into oppressed Maryland, by way of Williamsport, seems to be confirmed in every particular. Thus the Federal capitol is in imminent danger of destruction or capture. Seventy thousand Marylanders, panting for so many weary months for an opportunity to assert their freedom, are said to have flocked to Old Stonewall's standard, and have swelled his army into an incredibly large host. Before these, under the blessings of the God of "our Israel," the hireling horde under the "Young Napoleon" cannot stand. They *must* be victorious.

The great Southern heart was thrilled almost to frenzy over the Manassas victory, but that cannot compare with the joy that will swell every bosom sympathizing with our distressed country, whether at home, at the North, or across the waters, when this glorious intelligence reaches them. God grant it may be true! God grant our arms in Maryland a successful campaign against the despots who have so long trodden down her people! *Amen!* is the response of every patriot.

Last night was the stormiest we have been called to pass through in Virginia. The rain began about three in the evening, the sky became very dark, the clouds hanging over us like a thick mantle, as though all Nature had donned her mourning gown. Or, her grim visage would more appropriately denote her displeasure at the sins of men in thus congregating in hundreds of thousands to take each others blood, when if they would follow her precepts— learn of her simplicity and truth, all their differences might be settled without a drop of blood being shed. The red livid lightnings played from cloud to cloud, and lit up their hoary crests in lurid flame. The whole artillery of heaven seemed to be turned loose upon this field of wicked contestants, rending the very vault of the skies by their tremendous peals, and shook the earth, till it reeled "like a giant drunk." The rain poured in torrents, and the hollow between our camps, (we are upon the sides of two opposing hills) was completely flooded. We were thoroughly drenched, for our shelter—flies, and bunks made of blankets—gave us but poor protection.

This rain, I verily believe, was providential. God had some great object to accomplish by it. What is that object, is a subject which engaged my thoughts no little while the storm raged. Jackson is in Maryland, bearing down upon the Federal Capital. The enemy, panic-stricken at the prospects of their capital falling into our hands, precipitately leave their siege works, and hurry to the rescue. They have creeks and rivers to cross, and these, by the powerful rain, have doubtless been swollen out of their banks—thus preventing their march, and, perhaps, cutting off considerable bodies of troops, which, being unable to get either supplies or reinforcements, may fall into our hands. I trust this may be so. I cannot tell.

Since I began this letter, an order has been received from headquarters to be ready to "fall in," with nothing but guns and cartridge boxes, and a large body of cavalry, I have just heard, are drawn up in line of battle near New Bridge. This would seem again to change matters materially. Surely a large force are still in front of the city, while the main force have gone to Washington. (While writing this last paragraph, we are ordered to pack up everything for an immediate movement—what it is, I cannot say.) all is bustle and confusion—drums beating, and cries of "fall in, fall in!" running along the whole line.

The "Last Day," of the "prophetic dream" is at hand. Who can tell what may be done to-day! The great decisive battle *may* be fought to-day! Beauregard, or Jackson, or, mayhap, Johnston, may this day end the war. Still, I do not look for so glorious a result. Such a thing is *possible*, but not, in human wisdom, *probable*. Troops in good health and fine spirits.

V. A. S. P.

FROM THE COLUMBUS GUARDS
[COMPANY G, SECOND GEORGIA INFANTRY]
CAMP ON JNO. EDMUNDS' FARM, NEAR RICHMOND, VA., May 31, 1862 [6-9-62CS]

I reckon an account of what we have passed through during the last two months, would be readable by you all, so I will endeavor to relate it to the best of my ability.

About the 10th of April, we were ordered to Richmond from Orange C. H., all expecting to be mustered out of service when we got there, but alas! not only were we disappointed, but also destined to see the hardest service. After staying in Richmond two or three days, we were ordered to the Peninsula to help Magruder, who was about to be attacked by McClellan and his whole force. Accordingly, our regiment and about half the regulars were put on a boat the size of the *Wave*, and down the river we went. Arrived on the Peninsula and having marched and countermarched nearly all over it, we were at last startled by the continuous rattle of musketry and roar of artillery down at the trenches, about two miles from our camps; then came the stirring long roll, and off we went at a double quick. This was about 3 o'clock in the afternoon [of April 16]; when we got near the enemy, we were drawn up in line of battle within range of their cannon, and as the shell and shot came crashing through the trees just above our heads, I felt a little "queer." 'Twas no use to get behind trees, as the cannon balls go right through at that distance. (Here I must stop, as we are ordered to pack up and be ready to leave in five minutes.) I left off about an hour and a half ago, thinking to have been on the road by this time, but as it happened, our company did not go with the regiment.

Perhaps I had better explain our present situation, that you may understand it. The Guards are off from the regiment at Mr. Edmonds' farm on picket; we have been here eight days and have had quite a good time, as there has been a good deal of rain from which we were sheltered. There is a fight going on now about five miles from here, and the roar and rattle of the guns can be distinctly heard—I don't think we will get into it just yet.

To resume my story—after remaining in line of battle until eight or nine o'clock, we marched back to camp, where we staid until next day, when we were marched into the trenches. There I learned the cause of the previous day's firing [at Dam No. 1], which was this: Two companies of the Yankees were offered a canteen of whiskey and 50 dollars to each man, if they would cross the lagoon [Warwick River] and whip our men who were digging a trench on the edge of the pond for us to stay in; but in this, they were disappointed, for many of them were killed, and the rest driven back. I went into the trench just where the fight occurred, and the dead Yankees remaining on the ground for three or four days, the stench was unbearable. At last, the Yankees raised a flag of truce and the bodies were taken away. When the dead were carried over, one poor fellow recognized his brother and fell to weeping and lamenting most piteously. The first day we got on the battleground, I had an opportunity of conversing with one of the wounded who had been left there. He said he was an Englishman and had no interest in the war at all, "but," he said, "work was dull, and they told me the best thing I could do was to enlist in the army; so accordingly they got me drunk and enlisted me." He asked me for a drink of water which I gave him. The poor fellow died of his wounds a day or two afterwards. Ah! those trenches were *gay* places, there was a ditch which ran all along on edge of a pond. Into this ditch we would crouch, so that we could shoot down the Yankees as they were crossing the pond. We relieved each other in the night, in order to prevent the enemy from firing on us. The first day we relieved in the day time, but that tempted them to fire on us many times. One shot passed near me wounding a man just behind me, another came within two inches of my head, striking the bank and throwing the dirt in my face, pretty close, I thought, as I tucked my head a little lower. The Yankees had some splendid marksmen there; they would get up in the trees where we would not see them and fire away at us.

I presume it is needless to "bore you" with an account of our march to Richmond; suffice it to say that it was one of the hardest jobs I ever undertook. Very few thought of carrying their knapsacks or clothes, all those things being thrown away. Being in the pioneer squad I managed to get them through, it being the privilege of the pioneers to have their baggage hauled. Here we are, the whole army, within five miles of Richmond, waiting for the great fight which is daily expected. While I have been writing, the firing on our right has continued pretty heavy. A moment ago, a report came that the firing was caused by our men attacking a division of Federals who were hemmed in by the great rise in the Chickahominy, it having rained all yesterday afternoon and night, thus cutting them off from reinforcements.

J. D. BETHUNE.

PRIVATE LETTER, TWENTY-EIGHTH GEORGIA INFANTRY
[FOURTH BRIGADE, D. H. HILL'S DIVISION]
BATTLE-FIELD, June 1, 1862 [6-14-62ASC]

Dear Father: Hurriedly I write you a few lines on Yankee paper. We are now resting on a hard-fought and dearly-won battle-field.

According to orders, we yesterday afternoon led off the attack against the enemy. Our brigade, under Gen. [Samuel G.] Garland's command, was the first to drive them from their positions. We entered the field immediately after the first guns fired. Our regiment carried into the fight only about 250 men. We were reduced to this by our hardships and sufferings. We had only one field officer present—Col. [T. J.] Warthen being sick in Richmond, and Lieut. Col. [George A.] Hall dead. We were under fire of the enemy's guns till dark. We lost 130 men and officers, killed and wounded.

Men fell on every side of me, but by an unaccountable provision of Providence I remained untouched. Every horse except one, belonging to our Field and Staff was shot down. I went over the field this morning. The ground is strewn with the dead bodies of men and horses, still unburied. I counted ten dead horses in the space of thirty yards.

The Yankees fought well. Our brigade suffered terribly. The bodies of dead Yankees lie all over the ground. Some of the prisoners taken say they got along finely till that regiment of sharpshooters (meaning ours) drove them from their entrenchments; so from their own accounts, our regiment did terrible execution.

I was with the regiment all through the action. We left the battlefield to-night, and have resumed our previous position—for what purpose I cannot say. I can give no further particulars now. I only write to let you know that I am so far safe. Goodbye.

Your son,   Edgar Thompson.

Pvt. John Edgar Thompson enlisted on September 10, 1861 and later served as Sergeant Major from March 1, 1862 to March 31, 1863. Service records indicate that he was in an Augusta, Georgia, hospital from December 1864 to the close of the war.

PRIVATE LETTER,
SIXTH ALABAMA IN THE BATTLE OF THE CHICKAHOMINY

[FIRST BRIGADE, D. H. HILL'S DIVISION]
IN CAMP, June 2, 1862 [6-17-62CS]

Day before yesterday we met the enemy. Our regiment was deployed as skirmishers in front of the brigade, our left resting on the Williamsburg road. We marched through the woods for about one and a half miles, when we encountered the enemy formed in line of battle in front of a series of breastworks and batteries, from which position they retired on our approach into the works and into a line of woods on their left, parallel with the line of works. On this last line our regiment advanced through a field (still deployed as skirmishers); but partially protected by undergrowth and a few logs. My portion of the line advanced to within 75 or 100 yards of the enemy's line of battle, where we were received by a shower of bullets, which mowed down the vegetation to a considerable extent; but our men lying down at the word of command were not hurt by the first volley. The firing was now kept up briskly for an hour, our men acting with the greatest coolness and making every shot tell. The enemy outnumbering us some five to one, and their fire was heavy and well directed, killing and wounding a number of our gallant boys; but *wounds* did not in every instance stop our fire. Joe Duncan being shot through the arm, showed me his wound and asked what to do. I told him to go back to his post and continue firing, which he did with as much coolness as if he was shooting beef. At this place J. M. Baker and [J. T.] Barker, and J. R. Simmons, were wounded and had to be taken off the field. Barker's wound I fear is mortal. He had fired many a shot and I think had killed more than "his man."

At about one p. m., the enemy retreated and the 6th assembled its skirmishers and moved after them in line of battle on the right of the brigade. We drove them through the woods and through their camps, taking a stand of colors, when they again made a stand in a swamp, where being protected, their sharpshooters subjected us to a very annoying fire, balls firing thickly and the men dropping around us. Just then, we looked around and saw our flag floating over the batteries [at the Twin Houses Redoubt] and breastworks of the enemy, and we were ordered forward on the scoundrels in the swamp, whom we drove before us. When we gained their position we were halted to await reinforcements on our left, for the enemy outnumbering us, extended at least two or three hundred yards beyond our right, we were subjected to a murderous cross fire which raked our whole line. Here J. H. Harris, Charley Trawick, T. E. Sherman, Wm. Dudley, A. Blassinggame, Berry Crow and Sergeant J. P. Slappy and others, of my company were wounded, while gallantly doing their duty; but I thank God they were not shot down until the enemy had felt the weight of many of their balls. Here a man from some other regiment joined my company formally and asked for orders. I pointed out the enemy and told him to fire. As he raised his gun up to fire, a ball struck him in the head, spattering some of his blood in my face. He asked me to take care of him. I told him I could do nothing for him, but I thought God would, and as I said this, he fell over dead.

Near night we were ordered to retreat, the enemy having pressed entirely around our right, and in effecting this retreat the 6th Alabama lost most of her men. The men were at first slow about it, not liking the name of the thing, and they fell in heaps. All the Captains were killed and wounded except three, and most of the other officers, shot down which created great confusion, and men could not find their companies. On arriving at the Yankee breastworks [Twin Houses Redoubt] we rallied to receive the enemy, and the 11th Virginia coming up fired a volley into us. Among the officers killed were Lieut. Colonel [James J.] Willingham, Major Le Smith and my friend Capt. [Augustus] Flournoy. They acted a gallant part, exposing themselves continually and encouraging the men. Each was shot in the discharge of his duty.

I cannot avoid giving my 1st Sergeant [John D.] Madden the praise that is due to him for the coolness and daring with which he did his duty. I never saw or heard of a man who acted any better. But if I gave praise to each one to whom it is due in that bloody fight it would lengthen my letter too much and I have not time now to do it.

Of my company, out of the thirty-six men whom I carried into the fight I had only twelve together on the night of the 31st. Three others came up next morning. The loss of the Regiment is 388, including some prisoners and 20 missing.

Capt. George W. Hooper.

LETTER FROM V. A. S. P.
IN LINE-OF-BATTLE,
NEAR THE CHICKAHOMINY, YORK RIVER R. R., June 4, 1862 [6-12-62SR]

Were it not for the fact that we are in "Line-of-Battle," (and have been for three days) separated from our wagons, which are four miles in the rear, I would apologize for the paper upon which I write you this letter. I am compelled to tear the leaves from my "Diary," or "Pocket Journal," to write what few letters I can send my friends.

In less than a half hour after my letter of the 31st was sealed for the "mail man" to carry to Richmond, we were marched some little distance to the right. The whole army on that and previous day, moved further to the right, as the main point of attack seemed to be in that direction—the roads leading to the capital south of the Chickahominy.

We were in easy hearing of the desperate fight of Saturday and Sunday. Gen. Toombs' brigade marched to the battle field to take a hand in the general engagement which was expected to come off, but our Yankee "brethren" were too cautious to hazard another pitched battle in the open field. And so we were disappointed again, although the enemy were within a mile or mile and a half. We kept our position upon the ground where the ball opened on Saturday, until dark, when we started for camps, the new one selected that morning. That night's march will be ever remembered by the brigade, as second only to the one performed on Monday, May 5th, in the memorable retreat from Yorktown. The mud in many places was absolutely *leg deep!* We had no alternative but to pitch right through, or take to the woods, which half of our regiment did. So dark, inexpressibly dark, were these woods that half of them were lost, and many did not find the regiment until the next day. At 12 o'clock we halted, yet three miles from our wagons, having marched *three miles!* Three miles in five hours! This will give you some idea of the roads over which we had to march.

It is useless for me to give to you an extended account of the actions of Saturday and Sunday. I shall confine myself to individual particulars, obtained from those in whom I have implicit confidence—persons who either participated in, or witnessed the engagements. On Sunday, you are informed, there was very little fighting—nothing like a distinct battle, but rather a continuation of the battle of the day before.

Gen. Longstreet's, Gen. [Benjamin] Huger's, and Gen. [W. H. C.] Whiting's divisions were engaged, but received reinforcements. The fighting was desperate beyond comparison, except with Jackson's defeat of Banks. Not a man, or at least, not a regiment swerved during the day. Georgia's glorious Sixth, Seventh, Twenty-seventh, and Twenty-eighth covered themselves with glory. The Twenty-eighth suffered terribly, and the Sixth heavily. Among the killed in the Sixth was George Felix Lewis, a private in the "Sydney Brown Infantry," from Hancock county. In his death, Hancock has lost one of her brightest intellects. He was a member of the bar, and widely known to the members of the bar as the most promising young lawyer. His genius was of the brightest order, his intellect most brilliant. A large circle of admiring friends, affectionate relatives are left to mourn his early death. His reverend father will, ere this reaches his eye, have said—"Lord, thy will be done!"

Lieut. James Reid, of the same company, was seriously wounded, but it is hoped not mortally. Little Gus. Pardue was also wounded in the right breast, but will, perhaps, recover. There are other casualties of the "Sidney Browns," but I do not now remember them.

As we went into the battleground on Sunday we passed the ambulance train loaded with the wounded. The sight was touching—the first I had ever witnessed. Some poor fellows were pierced through and through by minie balls, some with broken arms, legs, ankles, &c. It was, truly, a sad sight. Lieut. Wick Rains, of the 28th Georgia, from Talbotton, was among the wounded, and the only one I knew. His leg was broken by a minie, just below the knee. Amputation, I fear, will be necessary. He is a young lawyer of Talbotton, and is extensively known in his section. His fortune is now made, even if he does lose a portion of his leg! The people will reward his bravery. His young wife will not be less proud of him either. Wick is a noble fellow, a brave, kind-hearted officer, and his example is well worthy of emulation. But you have ere this received fuller particulars than I am able to furnish you. If the 17th get into a fight, then I can give full particulars.

The pickets in front had a little brush yesterday evening, and while I write they are pitching in pretty heavily on our right. We have had a fight in front of Richmond, sure enough, but McClellan did not attack us. It was a mistake about his army being in full retreat, although it is believed he sent off a considerable force to protect Washington.

The storm of last Friday night *did* prove to be a special providence. A Yankee force of 40,000 were cut off by the rapid rise of the Chickahominy, and could not have received reinforcements but for their pontoon bridges. In this I see the hand of God. That force was attacked and badly whipped, driven from their entrenchments, and lost much ammunition, arms and equipage. God be praised for the victory!

V. A. S. P.

LETTER FROM V. A. S. P.
SEVENTEENTH GEORGIA REGIMENT
ADVANCE PICKET POST, BIVOUAC, June 14, 1862 [6-19-62SR]

The horrid shells have been amongst us again, and did prove as "harmless," as formerly. On Tuesday, 10 inst., about 6 p. m., the enemy began to shell our camp, the range of which they seemed to have pretty accurately. It was a cold, dreary, rainy day, and the men had, in considerable numbers, been conveying planks, straw, &c., from a neighboring house, (of Dr. John R. Garnett's) across a hill, in full view of the Yankees over the [Chickahominy] river. By this means they had obtained our range and whereabouts. In company with quite a number of officers of my regiment, I had taken refuge in Dr. Garnett's dwelling, against the inclement rain, having neither tents nor flies to protect us—no, not so much as blankets to keep us dry, for the wagons were in the rear. The Yankees first opened upon this house, and their shells exploded all around it, showing considerable skill in their artillerists. Their shells were loaded with musket-balls, one of which penetrated the room we occupied, which I secured as a *souvenir* of the war. The first shell that bursted over the regiment did considerable damage, killing no one, however, one of these musket balls broke the leg of 1st Sergeant Fields, of Capt. A. C. Jones' Company, G.

Several fragments and balls penetrated the blanket bunks of the men. (They had their knapsacks and blankets). Two holes were made through the sides of the Colonel's fly, and Lieut. Col. W. C. Hodges was struck by a fragment of shell which gave him considerable pain, without, however, doing him any serious harm. Amid this shower of fragments and balls, and the appalling rain of exploding bombs, we came to the conclusion that shells were not such "harmless creatures" after all! But we are astonished that we sustained so little injury. Since then we have been introduced to the minie—the terrible minie—which, after all, is the effective agent of death and mangled limbs.

On the next (Wednesday) morning [June 11] before light, we took our present position, four hundred yards in front of the enemy. We occupy a narrow strip of oak woods, lining both sides of a deep hollow running at right angles with the river. It is a mile and a half long, and runs out into extensive wheat and clover fields. In front of this strip of timber, and separated by a wheat field, are the enemy's pickets. A little further on is a large camp of the vandals—of infantry, cavalry, and artillery. There is an almost constant firing between the pickets. Thus far only one man has been hit in our regiment. He imprudently ascended a ladder in full view of their pickets, in order to get a good shot, when he received a slight wound in the cheek as a reward for his temerity. A member of the 2d Georgia had his leg broken by a minie ball. I did not learn his name.

One fellow was so imprudent in coming out and firing at our boys, that I could not restrain my desire to teach him a lesson of prudence. Procuring a good rifle, and getting a good opportunity, I leveled away at him. The effect was to provoke him the more, and for my two shots I received three, which came as near as was pleasant I assure you. Several of their men have been seen to fall, whether killed or wounded, is not known.

On Thursday evening a cavalry man, riding a grey horse, came to within twenty-five paces of our line of pickets, actually passing those in the pits out in the wheat field. It seems he did not know our whereabouts, and might have been captured, if he had been halted. Discovering his situation, as it were, all at once, he suddenly wheeled and retreated, when nine shots were fired at him. He was seen to cling to his horse's neck, and it was evident he was mortally wounded, as we afterwards learned. He had papers in his side pocket, a very large envelope, and was, perhaps, a courier. His papers might have been of great importance and it is very much regretted that he was not captured. To say the least of it, he was a bold adventurer, and his curiosity, if curiosity it was, proved fatal.

A truce party came over yesterday with sealed papers from Gen. McClellan to Gen. Lee, the purport of which has not yet transpired. The answer was returned by Gen. Johnston [Brig. Gen. D. R. Jones]. While these negotiations were progressing, a party of Yankees at the "old chimney and pen," two hundred and fifty yards from the end of the strip of timber in which the right of our regiment rested, made some friendly demonstrations by waiving hats, handkerchiefs, &c. I met them a hundred yards from their post, and exchanged friendly salutations, and had quite an interesting conversation with them. Three officers afterwards came up, but the Yankees took good care to have the largest party present. They were a little timid, would not venture half way between the posts, and were quite anxious to return. Lieut. [Patrick] Herbert, of the 2d New York State Militia, was on duty at this post, and talked quite intelligently. He admitted we got the best of the fight on the 31st of May. [Silas] Casey's and part of [John] Sedgwick's Divisions were engaged in that memorable fight. Lieut. Herbert said he did not know the object of the Federal soldier above mentioned, in running into our lines, and that he died very soon after receiving the wounds. Failing to get the *Herald*, our conference closed, and we returned to our respective armies, parting with expressions of mutual esteem, &c. They expressed a strong desire for a speedy termination of the war. A few minutes after this another party of three blue coats made their appearance immediately in front of the regiment, whom I also met, in company with Lieut. O'Keefe. From these I procured a copy of the *New York Herald*—the "great thunderer of America"—rather the *Liar* of America! The party was even more timid than the first, not venturing more than forty of fifty yards from their lines. We called to them to meet us half way, but seeing they would not do it, said, "Well, if you are afraid to meet us half way, we will come to you." After the usual civilities, the first thing they said was, "What makes you fellows shoot at us so?" I replied, "O, it's only some of our boys trying their guns!" They didn't like such fun, and expressed themselves eager for this sort of sport to cease. Before we could ask them anything scarcely, they insisted strenuously upon returning to their posts—the cover of the huge pine tree and thick brush wood.

The presence of the *Herald* in the regiment created quite a sensation. Everybody flocked around me to hear what [Editor James G.] Bennett had to say. It was indeed a treat to read him. Banks reports his *entire* loss in the late battle and retreat at nine hundred and five, and fifty wagons. The *Herald* says, in speaking of the that affair, that "the whole number of prisoners in their possession does not exceed eighteen hundred men."

Bennett is fighting [Editor Horace] Greeley [of the *New York Tribune*]—"poor Greeley"—as usual, and in their family quarrel reveals an important fact, to wit: that Greeley and his party, by bringing on this war, have cost the United States the round sum of *two billions, five hundred millions of dollars!* Lincoln's Government will never pay that debt.

Bennett claims glorious victories and great achievements for the "Young Napoleon." "The rebellion is in its last throes, and will soon be crushed." "Richmond will fall in twenty or thirty days," and so forth. The Yankees must whistle to keep their courage up. But I cannot give you a synopsis of *his* news. You will see it all before this reaches you.

The enemy are in Winchester and Front Royal again. As to the fall of Memphis, I will say nothing. We must patiently await events, do our duty, and trust the result to God.

V. A. S. P.

The Federal officer V. A. S. Parks spoke with was thirty-one–year-old Lieutenant Patrick W. Herbert of Company I, 82nd New York Infantry—also known as the 2nd New York State Militia. Herbert was wounded and captured at Antietam, and later paroled. He was promoted to Captain on April 9, 1864, and was mustered out on June 26, 1864. The identity of Lieutenant O'Keefe is uncertain; he may have been Adj. William McKee of the 82nd N. Y.

PRIVATE LETTER, EIGHTH GEORGIA REGIMENT
[G.T. ANDERSON'S BRIGADE, JONES' DIVISION, MAGRUDER'S COMMAND]
WOODSTOCK, VA., June 18, 1862.

This is the first time I have had the pleasure of addressing you from the quarters of the "bloody Eighth" since early in May. Woodstock is no village, but merely the beautiful former residence of Mrs. Price on a high bluff on the South side, and about a mile distant from the Chickahominy River. It is all open ground between this house and that stream, and for some distance beyond, in some places, while in others, the woods on the other side skirt its banks. This river, that is already famous, and is likely soon to be swollen with the "crimson tide" from two immense armies, here makes a large curve—nearly a half circle—and we are in the "horse-shoe."

This is the twelfth day our Regiment has done picket duty at this post, but as only two companies are out on the advance posts at a time, while the balance are held as a reserve, the duties are considered quite light. It is a healthy place, we get plenty of rations, and the consequence is a greatly improved state of health among the men. Companies that a month since reported only twenty-five or thirty men for duty, now report from fifty to sixty, and nearly all have a robust and hearty look.

Nearly every day the Yanks shell us for an hour or two, but as yet only one man has been hurt on our side, a member of the Stephens Light Guards, wounded last Sunday. Mrs. Price's residence has been completely riddled, three cannon balls having passed through the roof, one through the parlor. She had fortunately moved away in time to save most of her furniture. We have a battery just to the west of the house, and are now throwing up a redoubt on the north and east side, utterly ruining the very elegant and tastily ornamented yard. The house is about the centre of our regimental line, and probably the enemy throw more shot at it and the battery than at other places, yet they give us a sort of miscellaneous shelling once a day. To-day six or eight of their shells burst within twenty or thirty yards of companies A and B, whose position is in a narrow ravine, the banks of which are about twenty feet high. This makes a very complete protection, and as long as we remain in this "hall" there is but little danger.

There has been considerable firing between the pickets on our right to-day, and much moving noticed among the enemy, and it is thought by many that the great fight may commence to-morrow. If the enemy advance on our forces we will have, in this immediate vicinity, at least, greatly the advantage. Our great danger lies in the possibility that the enemy may, with large force, drive back our forces above or below, and then, by a flank movement, cut us off.

On our Brigade line there is no firing now, between the pickets on the outposts, and the feds show great anxiety to hold friendly intercourse with our men. They occasionally exchange papers, coffee for tobacco, &c., but all this is contrary to strict orders. The weather is now fine and has been for the past three days. The Chickahominy, here at least, is within its banks, and the time seems propitious for the great fight.

M. D.

LETTER FROM V. A. S. P.
CAMP NEAR THE CHICKAHOMINY, June 21, 1862 [6-26-62 SR]

To-day is the "General Review and Inspection." We are but poorly prepared for such an imposing event. Our guns and side arms are in good order, and will pass a creditable inspection; but our uniforms! There are not a hundred men in the brigade who have hats or caps alike; the greatest variety imaginable, of every style, shape, quantity and description, that can be found in or out of the most extensive combination of *hatteries* in the world, may be seen in our brigade upon this auspicious "Review Day." There is scarcely less variety in the matter of coats, pants, &c. This owing, in great measure, to the constant and laborious duties to which General Toombs' brigade has been subjected for the past three or four months. But what matters all this? If we do not make a great show upon the review, and carry off the palm as the best looking brigade in the service, we can shoot as fast, yell as loud, and charge the Yankees with as much impetuosity as the finest dressed troops in the Confederate army. I am not certain but that our in-*different* uniforms will make us fight harder, for it won't make much difference if we do get them soiled, bloody or torn.

The inspiring strains of a first-rate band wafted by the "balmy breeze of early morn," tell us that the "Review" has begun, and we must don the "paraphernalia of war," and be ready to undergo the scrutiny of a strict inspecting officer. *Review over*—a very credible affair, all things considered.

Our regiment was on picket again yesterday. The Yankees are remarkably civil—as much so, indeed, that there has not been a gun fired on that part of the line for more than ten days. They walk about carelessly, in groups, and wave their caps, handkerchiefs or papers at us; and very frequently (not withstanding very positive orders against having any intercourse with them whatever) exchange New York papers for southern. One of our boys went out on the brow of a little hill to see what they were doing beyond, and stood gazing at them for some time. Quite a party of them had and were cutting and tying the ripe wheat. One of them, very much to the amusement of the Yankees and Southrons, picked up a chunk and threw it at "Jessie." Being too far off (one hundred and fifty yards), he did not betray any signs of uneasiness; but, after he had satisfied his curiosity, he very deliberately walked back to his post. At this point the opposing pickets occupy the woods skirting parallel ravines, distant from each other from two to four hundred yards. Between these ravines is a wheat field. Here it is that the pickets are so friendly. Further to the left, however, nearer the Chickahominy, they keep up a constant war upon each other. A man shows his head at the peril of his life.

You have seen full particulars of General Stuart's unrivaled feat in the rear of McClellan's army. [Beginning on June 12 and ending 72 hours later, Jeb Stuart with 1,200 Confederate horse soldiers rode around McClellan's army.] The city papers are full of detailed accounts, and heroic incidents. The whole thing seems fabulous; but the reality of Gen. Stuart's having been among their wagon trains, commissary and quartermaster's stores, and sutler's shops, is too plainly felt by the enemy to ignore.

"McClellan the Great," with the best appointed army in the world, the best artillery and scores of gunboats, with all the Greeley element at the north to urge him on, will not attack us. Impositions have been made during the past week to give him battle, but he won't accept the gauge further than to engage in heavy skirmishing. He cannot be induced to leave the swamps and intrenchments; and I do not believe he will attack our forces as long as there is a chance to avoid it. His army will be beaten, driven back, routed, and totally demoralized. This he knows, and he will be content with maintaining a menacing position without actually attacking. If there is a battle fought here, the attack will be made by the Confederates.

V. A. S. P.

☆☆☆The Seven Days' Battles

Since taking command, Lee quickly reorganized the 60,000 strong Army of Northern Virginia, now including Jackson's forces summoned from the Valley. On June 25, a small engagement at Oak Grove, six miles from Richmond, launched a week-long series of battles called the Seven Days, where Lee repeatedly attacked McClellan at Mechanicsville, Gaines's Mill, Savage's Station, Glendale, and Malvern Hill. Although suffering greater losses, Lee successfully pushed the Federals farther away from Richmond.

LETTER FROM AN OFFICER ON THE BATTLEFIELD NEAR RICHMOND
17 MILES BELOW RICHMOND, July 2, 1862 [7-16-62ASC]

The grand army of McClellan is now on the bank of the James river [at Harrison's Landing]. One of the hardest battles of the enemy's retreat was fought here yesterday [at Malvern Hill] and last night. It is one of the best natural positions I ever saw, for the defense of a retreating army. McClellan has conducted his retreat admirably, or else our Generals have committed many blunders in following him. The enemy was attacked by Jackson and cut off in the rear on the York River rail-road, and at the same time they were attacked by our left wing. They commenced retreating from Huger's division on the right, early on Sunday morning. We have been following them up, through the swamps ever since.

It is now raining, and has been since two o'clock this morning. Our artillery can go no farther, and our troops are worn out and scattered from the battle of yesterday. We were not able to take their batteries yesterday, and this morning they are gone. This place is within two miles of the river, and their gunboats shelled us all the evening.

Up to this time, McClellan has lost, at the lowest calculation, between forty and fifty thousand, in killed, wounded and prisoners. His army is completely disorganized and dispirited, and will not be able to make an advance for a long time. Our army is victorious, ready for anything, all in fine spirits, but our loss is heavy—though not one-half that of the enemy.

I am sick and tired; have had diarrhea for a month; and when our company double-quicked in pursuit of the enemy, I could not keep up. I found them, when they made a stand. Being in the rear I took several prisoners. They hoisted a white handkerchief and I went to them, and brought off their guns. I was on the battle field during the whole engagement, had my havresack shot off, but my weakness prevented my taking an active part. I consider the fighting all over for the present. McClellan got off most of his guns, but lost $25,000,000 worth of stores and property. I send you two Yankee newspapers, and some letters picked up on the battle-field.

***.

HARDAWAY'S RIFLE BATTERY
[SECOND BRIGADE, D. H. HILL'S DIVISION] [7-14-62CS]

On Thursday, June 26th, Gen. A. P. Hill's division led the attack upon the right wing of the enemy at Mechanicsville. [Roswell S.] Ripley's brigade advanced at Meadow [Mechanicsville] bridge, and [G. B.] Anderson's brigade led the main column in front of the enemy's lines at Mechanicsville. [Capt. Robert A.] Hardaway's battery was the first to cross. The *tete du point* was shelled by the enemy's batteries located on the high grounds above the meadow. A solid shot struck a squad of the infirmaries just before the first gun, killing two or three and carrying a drum twenty feet in the air. The battery advanced in a gallop under fire up the hill and came into action in front of two batteries of the enemy, which had well nigh disabled the Purcell battery. This battery had crossed above and suffered severely.

The first shell of the Hardaway battery exploded in the enemy's ranks and relieved the Purcell battery from fire. One of the Federal batteries was engaged by Rhett's S. C. battery and a section of the Jeff. Davis' artillery.

The battery opposing Hardaway's, after twenty minutes fire, retired to another position. The duel was continued until 9 p. m., at which time, General A. P. Hill sent orders for Capt. Hardaway to cease firing, as he had driven the battery out of range. The fire of the enemy was very accurate, but the 12 months drill of the company as artillerists and the practice of three weeks at Yorktown made them equal to the regulars.

Friday, June 27th—D. H. Hill's division was now under Jackson's command, and was sent to the extreme left, to turn the enemy's right. Here 25,000 regulars, infantry and artillery were posted, and McClellan told this army, if the secesh were repulsed here, he would be in Richmond by 12, p. m.

The Jeff. Davis artillery was ordered up to open fire, but a ten gun battery of the 5th Artillery had its guns trained on the position, supposing it would be taken by us, and before our battery could come fairly into action, horses, men and guns were shot down.

The Hardaway battery was then ordered up, and the Captain ordered to select a position. The Captain on foot passed the pickets, examined [Stephen H.] Weed's [5th] U. S. battery, estimated the distance, and marked the direction by tall pines in the rear. In retiring, Gen. Hill came up and being discovered, the battery shelled them. The battery was brought up under cover of a pine thicket, and the first intimation the enemy had was the explosion of the shells in their midst.

The wounded prisoners reported that the third shell cut down the men at one gun, and that the fire was most accurate. Another ten gun battery on the right cross-fired on Hardaway's battery, and but for the cover of a small hill in front, the company would have been demolished in ten minutes. Here the second rifle gun of this battery bursted, the first having bursted at Mechanicsville. A spherical case shot soon after, struck the axle of No. 4, a steel rifle gun, knocking down the entire detachment. The only very severe wound was that of private Sam. Langley, right arm shot off.

The battery was then left with two (2) guns to fight a regular battery of ten guns.

Weed's regulars worked their pieces beautifully. A hail-storm of shell, shrapnel, and solid shot were poured upon the battery. Spokes were shot out of the wheels, horses legs were cut off, the caissons were shot through while ammunition was being served, but providentially none of the men were killed and few seriously wounded. The shot from Hardaway's battery disabled many of the artillery, men and horses, and enfiladed many of the infantry supports, consisting of the 4th and 12th regulars.

In the meantime the infantry had engaged to the right of Coal [Cold] Harbor road, and three times with cheers our men had charged the right batteries, and as often been driven back. So close did the enemy push Jackson that all of the left with only a small cavalry support of Cobb's Legion; and about half an hour by sun the Yankees with cheers advanced so near, our men being between the artillery and enemy on the right, Jackson ordered the battery to retire about 100 yards, across a ravine, when it again opened fire to the front. Just at sundown the other batteries of the divisions were ordered to advance with this battery to the first position, when fire was opened upon the entire front. At nine o'clock, orders came for the artillery to cease firing, that the infantry might charge. Twenty minutes, a heavy volley of musketry, three hearty cheers, and we held the enemy's camps, baggage, and thirty-one pieces of artillery, after the hardest fight of the week. McClellan was here in person; his right wing was turned from the rear, and he was between us and Richmond. D. H. Hill's division, under Jackson, had made a detour around our army and McClellan's right, and nothing but success, saved it from annihilation. Sleep was never sweeter than that night by our cannon wheels.

Sixteen men were wounded and many horses struck with fragments of shell; fortunately no bones were broken of the men, and most held on for another fight, with their wounds.

The next morning (Saturday) two beautiful rifle guns of Weed's battery were found by Capt. H., about one mile from the battlefield, dismounted. He had them slung under a limber and mounted to replace those bursted. A beautiful brass piece was given the battery by Gen. Hill.

Saturday and Sunday were days of rest to the army, except those engaged in burying the dead and building bridges.

Monday, June 30th—The two Yankee rifle pieces of Hardaway's battery were ordered to pass the other troops for the purpose of shelling the enemy's cavalry at White Oak Swamp, on the west side of the Chickahominy. Jackson had crossed the river at the grape-vine bridge, a fine military work of McClellan's, and was now pursuing the enemy down James river, while the other corps of the army were following McClellan, but were nearer the banks of James river. Captain Hardaway went forward to reconnoitre, and returning, reported the enemy in large force, and the cavalry reported on the hill tops to be teams of artillery covering the crest of the ridge. Gen. Jackson immediately ordered up forty pieces of artillery, but only twenty-two could be brought up in time—some of them light six-pounders and howitzers. The enemy had sixteen Parrott and Napoleon (the latter a beautiful twelve-pounder brass gun.) In weight of metal the enemy had a great advantage. Fire was opened just behind the crest of a ridge, taking the enemy by surprise. Mott's celebrated [Third New York] battery was soon cut up; three pieces and many caissons left on the field.

The fire was then directed to the right, behind a point of woods, where the Federal batteries of the 2nd Artillery were firing uncomfortably near. From 12 m., until dark, the duel lasted. Hardaway's battery being placed by order of the Chief of Artillery, in the centre of the line of battle.

While the artillery fight was pending here, Longstreet was engaged about two miles to the right.

The next morning (Tuesday, July 1st,) the enemy had retired. Our pioneers had replaced the burnt bridge over White Oak Swamp, and Jackson advanced. The scene of the artillery duel was the east bank of White Oak, about twelve hundred yards from the batteries of one to the other, and near the residences of Britton, on the left, and Thomas Binford on the right. Five ladies were left alone at the house of Binford. A Federal battery was placed near it, though the officers had promised they would not draw our fire on the family. The barns and stables not forty yards from the mansion had more than one thousand holes through them, while only one shot went through the mansion. The family sought safety in the cellar. The brass twelve-pounder of Hardaway's battery fired more than 100 rounds of shrapnel (shells loaded with canister shot,) at this battery. Of course it was not known then that the ladies were occupying the house. Seventeen of this regular battery, besides many infantry, were killed; probably more in Mott's New York battery. Hardaway's battery has twenty-five wounded; only two, Jas. Upton, and Sam Langley are dangerously wounded. Twenty-three others, including Lieut. Hurt, received cuts and contusions from fragments of shell.

All of Hill's artillery had exhausted their ammunition and the reserve artillery camp up to replace them at the last battle of Malvern Hill, fought on Tuesday, the 1st July. It was unfortunate for us that the new companies had to sustain this last battle. Many of the companies had never fired a shot, and the Yankee artillery was dispersed on Malvern Hill in a lunette shape, for three-fourths of a mile, and had several thirty pounder rifles in battery. Oaks three feet in diameter were shot through and men killed behind them, at a distance of one mile.

Hardaway's battery is attached to [G. B.] Anderson's (N. C.) brigade, formerly commanded by [Winfield S.] Featherston.

Col. Alfred Iverson, of the 20th North Carolina, acted very gallantly; the only men lying up to the guns of the Federal battery at Cold Harbor belonged to his regiment. I saw them identified and buried. Col. Iverson was wounded in the hip.

***

PRIVATE LETTER, EIGHTH GEORGIA REGIMENT

RICHMOND, VA., [7-12-62ASC]

Saturday forenoon, our brigade, Col. [G. T.] Anderson in command, was brought up into line of battle in front of a large battery of the enemy, and the Eighth Regiment was ordered to charge it, and the 7th Regiment to support us. We made the charge in fine order and repulsed the enemy in their first intrenchments with great slaughter, but they were so heavily supported in their second rifle pits, and their battery played so fiercely upon us, that we were compelled to give back with the loss of many of our gallant boys. Our noble Col. [Lucius] Lamar was wounded and taken prisoner. Lieut. Col. [John R.] Towers was taken prisoner. Privates J. Johnson and W. Vestill were taken prisoners—Vestill being wounded. He and Col. Lamar were carried back to the Yankee hospital, and were recaptured the next day by our pursuing army. Our killed and wounded in the 8th is estimated to be about 85. Our company [F] had only one—Jimmy Ogletree—killed on the field. He was a brave and gallant young man. Jack Bowen was taken from the battle ground, but died that night. The wounded are, Sergeant [D. W.] Croft, in the arm; R. Ragsdale, in the side; J. Hulsey, in the mouth; J. Edwards, in the shoulder; G. Irby, in the side; [A.] Langly, in the arm; [Fred] Kroagg, in the side; [John] McGuire, in the side.

We stood a galling fire until we were ordered to retreat.

Another battle took place on the 1st of July, which was one of the hardest ever fought. The enemy had picked his position on an elevated point, and their force was very great. I never saw such a sight before. The field was nearly covered with dead men and horses. Our loss was very heavy, but from the appearance the enemy's loss was much heavier than ours. We had only one killed—Elon Smith; one wounded—Will Cooley. Soldier Jim is "right side up with care."

Your affectionate cousin,   M. D. Adair.

M. D. Adair of Company F, 8th Georgia Infantry was the younger brother of "Soldier Jim."

LETTER FROM V. A. S. P.

IN THE FIELD, July 2, 1862 [7-17-62 SR]

Amid the fatigue of marching and the thunder of battle, it has been impossible for me to write sooner. Our wagons, knapsacks, portfolios, are all in the rear, and had it not been for our boy, who found this in a Yankee knapsack, I would even now be without paper upon which to write an account of the stirring events, a description of the thrilling scenes of the past week.

It would require a volume to narrate on the interesting events of this glorious campaign, the history of which is full of thrilling adventures and instances of individual heroism. The Yankee czar and his Premier—the high priest of abolition and all villainy—stand aghast at the prodigious results of a few days hard, well directed fighting by the Confederates. The world looks on in amusement, and the South is run wild with joy and exultation.

Gen. "Stonewall" Jackson crossed the Pamunkey [Totopotomoy], and cut off the enemy's retreat. The two Hills and Longstreet crossed to the north bank of the Chickahominy, attacked the enemy, routed him from every breastwork, took 10,000 prisoners, large quantities of arms and ammunition, 26 pieces of artillery, and drove him south of the Chickahominy. The battles were immortal—the fields well contested, but the Yankees could not stand before the advancing columns of invincible Southrons.

At this time a general advance of all our lines was made—Jackson in his rear, Hill on the north, and Longstreet on the east—"a circle of fire" closing rapidly, invincibly, around the hauty McClellan, the "Young Napoleon" of the fanatical, man-worshiping North. The whole army was in high expectancy, and although they knew the enemy would now fight desperately, being hemmed, they all exhibited a burning desire to be led against him.

On Friday, 27th ult., Gen. Toombs received written orders to "feel" the enemy on Garnett's Farm, where we had been on hard duty for three weeks. The Gen. obeyed his orders strictly, and we were willing to conclude that it was a pretty rough "feel." The right and left companies of the Seventeenth, and two companies from the Fifteenth Georgia, were ordered to cross the ravine and drive their pickets from the field, the Second Georgia acting as support. In ten minutes we were startled by volley after volley of musketry, the balls falling thick as hail around us. We were ordered to lie down, or protect ourselves as best we could. The enemy were in strong force—three brigades—already drawn up in line, and fired before our skirmishers could get into position. Maj. [Jesse H.] Pickett commanded the skirmishers.

In a few minutes the 21st Georgia double-quicked to the scene of the conflict, yelling like Indians, and poured volley after volley into the Hessian horde, which it held back on the right during the entire engagement. The suspense was terrible. Leaden hail darkened the air. One man was killed and seven or eight wounded while lying there.

Presently the air rung with shouts and yells on our right. I knew that yell. The Fifteenth came dashing by through the storm of bullets, and in five minutes I heard their vollies, and the hail grew thicker around us. Presently the order came for the Seventeenth to advance and take position on the left to prevent a flank movement. Strange and wonderful as it may seem, not one man was hit after they rose to their feet, while perhaps eight were wounded and one killed when lying down. At one time we began to think the day was lost, but the gallant Second and Fifteenth stood their ground and repulsed the vandals. My regiment did not fire a gun—except, of course, the two rifle companies, which were engaged all the time and did good work. A battalion of a New York regiment advanced upon Major Pickett with such perfect order, and fired with such regularity, it appeared the Major's little band would be annihilated; but with characteristic coolness he put his men into position, gave the command "Fire and load kneeling." The boys obeyed the order with alacrity, and firing *low* soon drove them back beyond the crest of the hill. Their shots for the most part were too high. Maj. Pickett lost two men killed and five wounded. Night closed the contest.

Col. [W. M.] McIntosh [of the 15th Georgia] lost a leg while gallantly leading his regiment into the fight. Capt. Birch, of Elbert county, was killed while encouraging his men. "Fire more briskly, boys," were his last words. He was shot near the heart and died instantly. But a few minutes before he had made his graceful salute to us, for which he was distinguished, the usual good natured smile played over his features. He was a good Captain, a brave soldier, and his untimely fall will not be regretted at home by those who best knew his worth, more than by the soldiers who knew him. Peace to his ashes.

Not satisfied with what was done the evening before, and desiring to try the enemy's real strength at this point, Col. Anderson's and Gen. Toombs' brigades were ordered to renew the attack next morning. The "glorious" Seventh and Eighth Georgia led the way, charging across the field and into the opposite wood before discharging a gun. In a few seconds they were in possession of the enemy's first breastworks.

Here the noble regiments suffered severely, being exposed to the grapeshot of the enemy on the right, which fairly cut lanes through their ranks. Two hundred yards beyond this was the most formidable breastwork of logs and earth on the Peninsula, from which the enemy's sharpshooters played terrible havoc with our men, compelling them to retire. The work was too short to shelter both regiments, and was only intended as a snare.

Col. Lamar, severely wounded, was captured. Also, Lieutenant-Colonel Tower of the same (Eighth) regiment. I have been unable to obtain lists of casualties, but they are heavy enough. Col. Lamar was recovered on the following day, being too ill to be removed from their General Hospital, which fell into our hands.

Long before daylight Sunday morning [June 29], Gen. Magruder's corps (in which we are,) was in motion. The "First Brigade"—Gen. Toombs'—formed on the Garnett Farm. Daylight revealed the fact that the enemy was in full retreat, and we began the pursuit in good earnest. The first camp we entered (in sight of our picket lines), was strewn with commissary, ammunition, clothing, and other stores valuable to the Government. As we advanced, the signs of a precipitate retreat became more evident. Blankets, knapsacks, fine India rubber and blue overcoats, tents, beef, bacon, flour, sugar, crackers, soap, vinegar, &c., and new Enfield, Minie, Sharps, Maynard, Mississippi and Derrenger rifles, (and Belgian also,) were found along the road and through the woods. A grave, neatly shaped, with head and foot boards, was opened, and found to contain fifteen thousand rounds of cartridges and a half bushel of musket caps of the best quality. Large quantity of bombs, &c., were also found.

About noon, Col. [J. B.] Cumming's boy "Tom" brought in a Yankee prisoner! The fellow complained of indisposition—*to follow McClellan any further*—and on seeing the negro, came out and surrendered. Tom took his gun, and marched Mr. Nathan Bivins to Gen. Toombs. He said he preferred being our *prisoner*, to being McClellan's prisoner. Col. [Henry L.] Benning also found two, (one a Lieutenant,) who were wounded the day before, and put them under the treatment of our Surgeon.

At 3 P.M. we learned we were near the enemy, and formed to give him battle. Not showing himself, we advanced through woods, over felled trees, hills, and through marshes, for a couple of miles. By 6 o'clock [A. H.] Colquitt's Brigade and Hampton's Legion were engaged with the enemy. We took position on the left, but the enemy was not disposed to extend his line. He was badly whipped, losing a fine battery and the battle-field. The Sixth and Twenty-seventh Georgia (the only regiments in the brigade which heard the order) charged a brigade of United States Regulars, and ran them five hundred yards, across an open field. Having no supports, they were forced to retire, which was done in good order. A stubborn contest then ensued. The brigade of old regulars met one of nearly equal force. They wavered. The Georgians followed up the advantage. They retreated. The Southerners charged, and the enemy were completely routed. As they fled, they bayoneted the wounded left by the Sixth and Twenty-seventh in their charge and retreat! This fact is asserted to be true by those who participated in the glorious battle. Our loss was heavy, some companies coming out of the contest with only five men! Capt. [J. W.] Arnold of the "Sydney Browns," entered the fight with forty, and came out with five men unhurt. He had seven killed, sixteen wounded seriously, and the rest slightly.

Lieut. W. F. Jordan was wounded seriously, perhaps mortally, in the lungs. A brave officer does not reflect honor on the line, or battle for the liberties of "Secessia." John Bedgood was wounded, and started to the rear, but finding he could walk, refused to go, and deliberately loaded and fired. Unfortunately, the Sixth was taken for a Yankee regiment, and was fired into by the Sixty-first Georgia. A ball from a friend's gun pierced the brain of Bedgood, and he fell without a struggle. How sad! So patriotic and brave as to remain in the field when wounded, and then to be killed by a friend!

On the following day our division (Maj. Gen. D. R. Jones), composed of Toombs' and Anderson's brigades, moved toward the James, and reached the battle-field of the 30th June about 1 o'clock at night. What a scene met our eyes when day succeeded night! Upon the field that was occupied, and immediately in front of our lines, lay scores of dead "blue coats." They had conveyed their wounded off the field during the fight. It was a terrible conflict. The Yankees stood their ground stubbornly [at Glendale], but were driven from the field and their batteries taken by the impetuous charges of our troops with great loss.

I have utterly failed to obtain particulars of this battle, and must refer you to the Richmond press. It was a decided victory—a signal triumph of our arm; but I must hasten on to the *great battle of July 1st*; on Stuart's Farm, 15 miles from Richmond, in which the 1st Brigade took a part.

At an early hour the Brigade was ordered to advance south through the woods to the attack. As we moved forward I saw many dead Yankees, guns, &c., and a few wounded. Not finding the enemy, we rested awhile, then moved to the right. While resting, a large number of Yankees, perhaps 200, who seem to have been lost in a swamp, voluntarily surrendered, and appeared to fancy the idea of a trip to Richmond. We took up a line of march to Stuart's Farm a mile south. We had scarcely taken position (in support of Anderson's gallant brigade) when the battle [of Malvern Hill] opened. At quick time we filed to the left, through a storm of grape and shell, and in ten minutes we stood upon the edge of the battle-field. Oh, what a sight! What sounds! What confusion and mad rushing into the flood of death, with terrible yells of defiance! A thousand yards distant was the enemy's batteries, some say *twenty*, some *sixty* guns, belching forth grape and canister, mowing lanes (at times) through the columns of our troops as they advanced with unfaltering tread to the charge.

On either side, in commanding positions, were the columns of the enemy, forming a V. The battle raged, their columns poured deadly crossfires into our division, so that it seemed not a man would escape. The huge shells bursted over and around us, and tore to pieces large trees. It was a perfect hurricane of leaden hail and iron. Presently—in less time than it takes to write it—some one announced that the battery was taken, and we were ordered forward to make the rout more complete by a hot pursuit. At a double quick the 17th (the right of the Brigade) entered with a shout that made the welkin ring above the din and roar of battle, and passed through the *currents* of lead and iron balls, but not a man faltered. By some mistake or other we entered too soon, and without orders. We reached the brow of a hill 200 yards distant on the extreme right, but no enemy was there! "Down boys, lie down!" cried our gallant Colonel, "and protect against their grape shot." At this moment, with shame facedness, I write it, hundreds came rushing back in most disgraceful confusion and disorder. Nearly an entire regiment was here being rallied to charge again. They had taken the battery, but overwhelmed by numbers, and cut to pieces by crossfires, they first retired, then ran. Thinking he saw the enemy flanking our left, the Colonel ordered us to double quick by the left flank across the field, 300 hundred yards, through one of the most terrible storms of leaden hail on record. Providentially, but few of our men fell here, as the enemy overshot us. I saw one poor fellow of Co. K fall just before me, pierced through the temple. The rest of the brigade followed our movement to the left. When we reached the skirt of a woods we halted until our Colonel advanced to find a place in the smokey drama for us. Fifty yards distant was a fence and road running parallel with one of the enemy's lines, and perpendicular to the other, at the right end of which, on a hill, was his main battery. In this road, behind the fence, the Colonel determined to place his regiment. (In mean time the 2nd and 20th had passed us, going a little to the right—the 20th led by General [D. R.] Jones in person). While executing the movement the 15th came rushing up, passed through our lines, and cut off the right wing, threw us into such inextricable confusion, that we never formed again as a regiment. Platoons, sections, squads, and individuals, mixed up with the 2nd South Carolina, took position behind the embankment, and awaited any movement of the enemy, who we could not see for the clouds of smoke which darkened the sky and veiled the sun. The scene was grand and gloomy, enlivened only (or rather illuminated) by the long streams of fire from the roaring muskets, and the enemy's cannon, belching forth flame and smoke, and awful missiles of death, and great huge, terrible bombs, which seemed to rend the very vault of heaven, and set the skies on fire. Kershaw's brigade was engaging the enemy in our front, but this was not known to those occupying the road; who fired several volleys into it. Fearing something was wrong a few of us finally stopped the firing, but enough had been done to make Kershaw's men think they were flanked, and they began to retire rapidly. I saw *then* what mischief had been done. The firing was not fifty yards distant. Our South Carolina friends fired rapid volleys *at the noise*, the rest took it up, and the whole retreated in Bull Run style to the woods.

An unaccountable panic seized the whole line in the road. I could see nothing to retreat from, and failed in every effort to rally more than twenty men. In a similar way several regiments, among the rest the First Georgia Regulars, Seventh and Eighth Georgia, and some

North and South Carolina regiments, were thrown into confusion. The confusion was sublimely ridiculous, but the troops were not to blame. They were brave enough. They entered the field like veterans, but the whole thing lacked *plan*. The enemy held a formidable position, the brow or crest of a hill, and the nature of the ground was such that their lines described an angle of about 115 degrees, or an arc of a circle. Under these circumstances our only, or main object, should have been to flank them, in which event they would have been routed more completely. But instead of this, brigade after brigade were rushed into this vortex, and those coming last, not knowing who were in front, fired with deadly effect into our friends, very naturally causing a panic in the front brigades, who of course thought they were flanked. While we were occupying the road above described, a regiment came up and fired into us until they saw our battle flag. No, the soldiers were not to blame. They should have been held in reserve until they were needed, and then marched in front of the *enemy*, not in rear of their friends. The battle opened between three and four o'clock and ended at dark. We held the field, but it was dearly bought. Our loss was heavy, but the enemy's heavier.

I cannot give our total loss. The Second Georgia lost 9 killed, 54 wounded, and 8 missing. The Seventeenth lost 6 killed, 34 wounded, and five missing. The Fifteenth lost 2 killed, 30 wounded, and 4 missing. The Twentieth Georgia lost 4 killed, 59 wounded, and 29 missing. Total loss of the Brigade: 21 killed, 174 wounded, and 46 missing, making in all 241. My company had 5 wounded slightly. A majority of the wounds received in this battle are not dangerous. The enemy left about 800 dead on the field. Most of their wounded were conveyed to the rear during the engagement.

After the Regulars and another (formerly) gallant regiment were thrown into the confusion, many instances of true gallantry were displayed. Capt. H. D. D. Twiggs rallied two or three bodies of men at different times, and gallantly led them to the charge. He was at the head of one of the parties that helped to take the battery, but were unable to hold it. He is flatteringly reported at headquarters for gallantry.

V. A. S. P.

Confederate casualties for the Seven Days' battles are estimated at around 20,000; Federal casualties reached 16,000. Above all, McClellan's plan to capture Richmond from the southeast had failed despite his greatly superior numbers.

LETTER FROM V. A. S. P.
CAMP NEAR RICHMOND, July 11, 1862 [7-18-62 SR]

We are once more encamped near the capital city of the Southern Confederacy. Things are not, however, as they were. The city is not beleaguered by a bigoted, haughty invader. The "Young Napoleon" no longer threatens the sacred city with immediate destruction, and our devoted army with utter ruin and total rout or capture. "How have the mighty fallen!"

For several days the lying journals of Yankeedom made McClellan's defeat nothing more than "a grand strategic movement," into which the Confederates were unwillingly drawn. In nearly every battle they claimed a victory. Every letter to the New York press bore the lie upon the face of it. They are a nation of liars—unblushing, God-forsaken liars—and every effort to conceal the disaster to McClellan's army only stamps them as liars. It is amusing to read their correspondence and editorials. They all laud McClellan to the skies as a great strategist, and his troops as the best and bravest men in the world, and describe their feats of bravery as surpassing anything in ancient or modern times, charging batteries and breastworks, defeating the Confederates at *every point*; and yet, *mirabile dictu*, the grand army "retired" to a "better position" on the James!

After the battle of Tuesday, 1st inst., we steadily pursued the retreating enemy to Shirley on the James, about 30 miles below Richmond. Friday we rested in line of battle on the Charles City road, confidently expecting a general engagement the following morning, but were disappointed. Early next morning, we fell back a mile to Phillips' Farm, and rested until Sunday morning, when we were again thrown forward, as we thought, to engage the enemy, but really, as it turned out, to act as a rear guard to our retiring columns. At sundown Tuesday, we took up the line of march for Richmond, by the river road, and marched twenty miles by sunrise. The men were thoroughly exhausted, and could not proceed much further. Three or four miles further we were halted near a good spring to rest for a day, and yesterday were marched to our present position, which will likely be a permanent encampment—at least until McClellan's broken columns are re-organized so as to enable him to make some further demonstrations.

About daylight Wednesday [July 2] we passed the battle-field of the 30th ult. I hope we shall never have to pass through another. Hundreds of men were made deathly sick by the stench of decayed horses which lay thickly strewn upon the field.

Although you were promised lists of casualties in the different regiments, I have failed to obtain them. I have given you the aggregate loss of the 1st Brigade. I would like to furnish you the names of the noble men who fell killed and wounded.

Lieut. Williams of the Regulars, (Col. [J. T.] Anderson's Brigade,) was severely wounded; and Capt. [Tomlinson] Fort, of the same regiment, was struck in the breast by a piece of shell which stunned him. His sword was bent double by a grape shot. Partially recovering from the blow he rushed forward far in advance of his regiment, waving his crooked sword, and calling upon his men to follow. Fortunately, his wound is not dangerous. Two Orderly Sergeants were dangerously wounded—one having both legs broken, and the other losing one leg—Sergt. Brown, I believe.

Lieut. [Parham] Booker, of company H, 17th Ga., was shot through the brain, and Capt. [H. L.] French, and Lieuts. T. H. Pickett and Jones were slightly wounded. Lieut. Col. W. C. Hodges was severely wounded in the leg, but is doing well. Adjt. John R. Mott was struck on the foot by a spent ball, which disabled him for a few days. He returned to duty yesterday, and relieved your humble correspondent of an arduous task, which was imposed upon him as soon as Adjt. Mott was injured. This short connection with that office enables me to report "present for duty" 350 men. Our aggregate present and absent is about 557.

I regret to learn the death of Lieut. W. F. Jordan, of the "Sidney Browns," from Hancock, wounded on the 29th ult. Dr. Jordan, or "Bee," as he was familiarly known, was a citizen of Sparta, and leaves an aged father and affectionate mother and sister, and two or three brothers to mourn his death. He was a noble specimen of a Southern soldier. He was patriotic and brave; and few noble young men have fallen during this cruel war who have left a larger circle of friends to mourn their loss. He was an accomplished scholar and physician, and bid fair to take a high stand in his profession. If our liberties are to be gained by the sacrifice of such noble young men, how much should we appreciate and guard them when gained.

Captain [W. M.] Arnold, of the Sixth Georgia, was struck on the head by a partially spent grapeshot—a glancing lick—which cut a considerable gash, and completely stunned him. It is said that when he began to recover, he first got upon his "all-fours"—hands and knees—and said, "Steady, boys! steady!" Raising to his feet, the effort starting the circulation, he soon recovered his senses and found his regiment a hundred yards ahead, where he soon joined his company and led throughout the engagement without further injury.

I was wrong in stating that the Twentieth Georgia was led into the engagement by Gen. Jones. It was a mistake, giving him credit to which he was not entitled.

Gen. Magruder is very generally, and justly, blamed with the mismanagement of the battle of Tuesday, 1st July. He was not upon the field, and an officer on Acting Brigadier General [J. T.] Anderson's staff, says that Gen. Magruder was under a hill behind a big walnut tree twenty feet in circumference! Other officers of high standing say he acted more like a madman than a General commanding in a great battle. One thing is certain, he did not understand the nature of the ground, or the strength and position of the enemy. His only idea seemed to be to take the battery; and his only command was "Forward! Charge the Battery!" As before stated, brigade after brigade was ordered in without any more definite object than that a battery was to be taken. In this way troops were massed, and hundreds were mown down and the advanced columns were repeatedly thrown into confusion by the fire of those in the rear. I hear it, on very high authority, that Gen. Magruder was the next morning "relieved" of his command; whether for inability, or to go west, I will not say positively. One thing, however, I will say, though, and that is, I hope the brigade to which I belong may never go into battle again under his leadership.

The enemy's loss in killed on Tuesday, will not fall short of 1,200. Besides the dead upon the field, there were about 800 in the wood to the rear of their battery, conveyed there during the battle. He was beaten, but had he seen our confusion, he could have routed us.

V. A. S. P.

LETTER FROM V. A. S. P.

CAMP NEAR RICHMOND, VA., July 14, 1862 [7-19-62 SR]

Never before have I experienced as fully the tyranny of military rule as now. For weeks we have been on the most active duty, performing long, fatiguing marches, fighting battles, sleeping wherever night found us, on the damp ground, without tent, fly, or blankets; eating hard bread and bacon, broiled upon the coals—sometimes without anything at all to eat. We have suffered every conceivable privation and hardship incident to a soldier's life, and without a word of complaint. We suffered and toiled for our beloved South; for southern independence; for the "loved ones at home"; and we suffered joyfully. We thought ourselves happy men to be privileged to suffer in such a glorious cause.

During the campaign there was of course no chance to get changes of clothes. We were scarcely recognizable by our best friends by reason of the dust, tattered garments, and almost *bootless* feet. I venture the assertion many of us would have taken our image in a looking glass for some other person—perhaps an Arab—from the long, uncombed hair and shaggy beards. In the battle of "Malvern Hill" (Tuesday, 1st July), I lost my sword scabbard. On the 4th of July, some thievish soldier stole my pistol—Colt's Army Revolver, model U. S. M. R. No. 14,877—and sword-belt. My feet rebelled against "the powers that be" and burst their prison bonds; my long worn fatigue suit showed signs of giving way; and the broiling sun threatened to crisp my little glazed cap into the size and shape of a tin dipper, leaving my brain to *fry* in the merciless heat of the sun.

These facts were all stated in respectful language, and leave of absences for two days to visit the city asked, only three miles distant, for the purpose of re-equipping myself. While this application is on file at "Division Headquarters," an order arrives from Gen. Lee forbidding any leaves of absence, under any circumstances, "during the near proximity of the enemy to Richmond." Now, doesn't any reasonable man know I could come from Richmond before the enemy could get from behind his James river earth works and abatis of fallen trees, thirty miles below Richmond to save his neck? Even if Prof. [Thaddeus] Lowe were to furnish each man of the "Grand Army" with a *balloon* with a strong wind to assist their "On to Richmond" flight, they could not get in gunboat range—a distance they prefer—before I could be at camps, "habilimented" for the struggle.

Now this I call *tyranny*. Notwithstanding all the reasons why I should be allowed the short leave of absence, the absolute necessity for clothes, unless Gen. Lee would, by another "general order," declare clothes unnecessary, and establish a universal, instead of a partial, *nudity*. I am compelled to smelter through long, hot, sultry days in clothes that are entitled to "an honorable discharge from the service," and hopple about in boots that ought to be "dismissed the service" on the ground of "inability or other incapacity." Well, I can console myself with the reflection that "what can't be helped should be borne." And further, that my forefathers left the stain of blood from their shoeless, bleeding feet, upon the frozen ground, while following the immortal Washington, battling for a cause like ours.

The announcement in the Richmond papers of this morning, that "Old Stonewall" has been commissioned a full General, the highest military rank that can be conferred under the laws of the Confederacy, will be hailed with joy by the whole country. He has eclipsed even "Old Hickory" of a former glorious day. He bids fair to eclipse all generals of this war. The name "Stonewall" Jackson terrifies the vandals and Yankee hirelings, and even the baboon at Washington, more than half the army of the Confederacy. They dream of his sudden dashes and attacks, and even if they know he is a hundred miles off, they are in constant dread lest he should, by some "flank movement," institute another season of Bull Run races, in which they are so well schooled; and of which, we naturally presume, from their frequent recurrence, they are particularly fond.

Gen. Lee has proven himself the master of the art of war. It was he whose service Gen. Scott advised Lincoln to secure, by all means, for he considered Gen. Lee the ablest, most accomplished military man of America, himself excepted, of course. He has proven himself more than a match for all the martial intelligence of the North, Scott included.

The question of "promotion" by "seniority" is not yet settled. There is an unpleasant state of feeling in this regiment. Elections to fill vacancies have been held, and the elected parties commissioned by Gov. [Joseph E.] Brown, since the passage of the Conscription law. This clause is evidently unconstitutional, and is so held by some of the ablest men in the army. Colonels, in open violation of the law, order elections as fast as vacancies occur. No longer than Saturday there were five or six vacancies filled by election in this regiment. This, I think, is done with the belief that the next Congress, soon to assemble, will sustain the elective franchise in war regiments organized by Governors of States and accepted into the service prior to the passage of the Conscript Act.

A First Lieutenant, whose name I am not at liberty to use, who was "jumped" in a late election by a Second Lieutenant, took the matter before the War Department, which decided that he was entitled to the Captaincy of his company by reason of his seniority, and I believe commissioned him as Captain. The Captain elect holds a commission from Governor Brown. How is the matter to be settled? is a question of considerable interest and moment. I might make further statements of the unpleasant feelings engendered by this difference, but withhold them for prudential reasons.

McClellan's army seems to be completely demoralized. The thousands of wounded and prisoners who fell into our hands during the recent campaign, all concur, almost to a man, in the statement that the soldiers, and even the officers of inferior grade, are heartily sick of the war. Many of them are deserters; many more surrendered voluntarily to get out of the war, and beg to be *paroled never to bear arms again during the war against the Confederate States*. They do not want to be exchanged, or paroled until exchanged, for then they would have to enter the army again.

A Captain of this regiment visited, a few days since; a hospital established for wounded Yankees, and talked with a great many of them. They were mostly New Yorkers. They all deprecated the war, and wished a speedy termination, whatever might be the result upon the "glorious Yankee nation." They openly disavowed a belief in their ability to conquer the South, and said they were forced into the war against their inclinations and convictions of right. Some of them were of [George A.] McCall's Pennsylvania Reserves, and were enlisted with the express understanding that they were to defend home, and in no case to go beyond the limits of the District of Columbia. They say they were deceived. Scarcely before they were in the meshes of the deceiver's net, they were ordered to Virginia—an army of invasion. The Captain asked them what their politics were. "Democratic," was their universal reply. He asked them how many Abolitionists or Republicans they knew in the army. They mentioned a few prominent Generals. "But," said the Captain, "how many can you count in the ranks, or line?" "*Not one!*" was the reply. "Well," continued the Captain, "I want you to go home and tell the truth to the people. The Democrats are in the ranks fighting this war, a war of invasion, if not of extermination, against a people who have never injured them, while the guilty parties—the Abolitionists—the men who inaugurated this unholy war, are getting all the fat offices and Government contracts." This little speech had its desired effect. "We will do as you say. All we ask is to be paroled never to bear arms. We are sick and tired of this war. We have been deceived by our leaders!" With this he left them to their thoughts.

After the brilliant successes of our armies before Richmond, what have those moody, grumbling croakers to say? Mr. Editor, I may see things differently from a different stand point; but I think you people down South who sympathize with those who are fighting the war, ought to establish courts for the trial of croakers; and every time a *man* (?) is convicted of abusing our noble chief, or charging him with incompetency or imbecility, you ought to treat him as our early English fathers treated witches—tie him to a sweep and *duck* him three times in a mill pond or some other body of water deep enough to ensure a thorough drenching! We of the army, who are the real sufferers, who have the hardships of rain, cold, and hunger, and fight the battles about which croakers and fault-finders blow and puff so much (saying when the battle is won, "*we did it!*") are perfectly satisfied with President Jefferson Davis, and his noble circle of Generals—the most brilliant as well as solid assemblage of military genius the world ever saw. Let our noble chief ride through our camps, and as soon as he is recognized, a shout is raised throughout the vast encampment which makes the welkin ring, and shows the high esteem and affection entertained for him by the army. Croakers, (poor, pitiful, sneaking, cowardly, scarecrow wretches!) say he has accomplished nothing. *Nothing!* He begun the war without a cannon, without a ship, without a gun, without a soldier, in short, without a thing! Has he done nothing? Let history answer. In twelve months he organized and equipped the best army of any age. He has fought scores of the greatest battles, held in check, and repeatedly repulsed and routed the "grand armies" of the North. He took the reins of government without means or form, and in a very short time offered to his chivalrous, Southern constituency as a heritage for their latest posterity the *best*, emphatically the *best* government of the world. Of course he has had assistance. Then has he been an "imbecile."

The army, with a rare exception, here and there, of some dissatisfied spirit, is indignant at the uncalled for abuse of their greatest leader, in whom they have unbounded confidence, and by whom they almost swear. Those crack-brained grumblers are fertile in expedients, remedies and amendments, and tell what *they* could do if they only had the power. Poor, deluded fools! It is their shallowness which forbids them seeing the terrible weight of responsibility resting upon those who are now safely and proudly steering the ship of State through the breakers and storm of an unexampled revolution—a tempestuous commotion of all the raging passions of a blinded people, attempting to subjugate those who have a right, and are determined to be free. The South ought to be a unit—a solid phalanx, like the noble army in the field; and the good people of the South should stop the mouths of those *fellows* who imagine evil without cause, and find fault with ablest administration—military at least—of which history gives any account. Take them up and send them to the army, and they will get a *ducking*, and a *bumping* too!

V. A. S. P.

LETTER FROM SOLDIER JIM
NEAR RICHMOND, July 20, 1862 [7-26-62ASC]

Through all the protracted fighting that has taken place, brother and myself have escaped unhurt. At many times we were in the midst of showers of shot and shell, from which escape seemed almost impossible. I tried to put my trust in God and Gen. Lee. The former had the power to protect us from the shafts of death hurled at us by the enemy, while the latter led us through Yankee camps, driving back, capturing thousands of Yankees and their "baggage." Their courage was contrary to that laid down in their "on to Richmond" programme. The fighting was terrific—the scene horrible; but on we pushed after them, till they reached their gunboats, badly cut up. I guess they have entirely abandoned the idea of celebrating the 4th of July in Richmond. We are now quiet in camps, relieved from the roar of musketry and the thunder of cannon, which have fallen on our ears day and night for nearly five weeks.

Now we hear of the defeat of the enemy at Vicksburg and of our victories at other points in the South and West. Glory be to our flourishing little nation! May God grant us victory, till we are acknowledged an independent nation.

SOLDIER JIM.

LETTER FROM V. A. S. P.
CAMP NEAR RICHMOND, VA., July 25, 1862 [7-31-62 SR]

A perfect calm has reigned for more than two weeks where once all was storm and tempest. Scarcely a breeze ruffles the surface of the public mind. Daily we hear of "raids" in different quarters; but if there is any grand movement of troops, it is properly kept a profound secret. Yankee papers speak of Jackson in the Valley, but their imaginations, and a wholesome dread of this inimitable, invincible, ubiquitous Rebel Chief, would lead them to expect him there, or before Washington, or anywhere else.

There is no news at all. Yes, I did hear that our cavalry pickets had a little skirmish with the enemy beyond Malvern Hill on yesterday, but know nothing of its reliability. I met some people moving into Richmond to-day, who said they heard the enemy were advancing. I think they were mistaken. It took McClellan months to organize the army which was completely *disorganized* in the seven days' battle of the Chickahominy; it does not look reasonable that he could in two or three weeks prepare it for another advance towards Richmond. It is believed that he has not been reinforced by Burnside who is said to be at or near Fortress Monroe, ready to move to the relief of Washington or McClellan, as the fortunes of war, or the movements of the Confederates, may render necessary. But as I cannot speak advisedly, I will leave this question to the decision of time.

We have just done some of the richest picketing on record since the commencement of the war. The brigade was marched out near the "Timberlake Estate," about ten miles below Richmond, Tuesday morning, and returned Thursday. The only incidents worthy of note were the slaughter of a few swine by the boys, who declared they "would kill anybody's hog that would bite them!" The commissary had been derelict in the performance of his duty, and the boys were on short allowance for two days. This was their excuse. I have ever opposed the wanton destruction of private property so much practiced and countenanced among some of our troops; but there are times when I think the soldier justifiable in taking hogs or anything else to eat, when the owner will not accept a fair remunerative price for it. Another fact worthy of mention is, that the "Yanks" were not nearer than fifteen miles. They are busy at Berkeley [Harrison's Landing] digging ditches and constructing abattes. They think we are going to attack them every day! Perhaps by this time they have found out that our only force there is a few cavalry pickets. It may have been improper in me to state, in a former letter, that we had fallen back.

But another item: It was the good sweet milk, hot corn bread, eggs, and chickens which we got from the neighboring houses. These interested me more than all else. It was so different from our former picketing, that I could hardly realize it as such. Hitherto we were compelled to dodge from tree to tree and keep closely concealed (except when the pickets became so friendly at Garnett's farm); but here we laughed and hallooed, and strolled all over the country foraging and picking "huckleberries," and of the largest size. It was no trouble to pick a quart in a few minutes.

To-day I had the pleasure of meeting in camps my old friend and former townsman, Mr. Fraley, of Sparta. He brought good news—in the shape of a letter from a friend. With him I visited my friends in the Sixth Georgia. The gallant Captain Arnold related many interesting incidents of the recent battles before Richmond. The heroic Lieut. Jordan, of whom I made mention in a former letter, had just examined a mortal wound received in the breast by William Powell, and returned to his post, when he was mortally wounded in the left lung. He calmly turned to Captain Arnold and said: "Captain, I am wounded—mortally wounded!" pointing to the place just under the heart where the murderous ball had entered. "I trust not," replied the Captain, "the shock to your nerves is sufficient to make you think the wound more dangerous than it really is. I think it will not prove fatal." But Lieut. Jordan was an accomplished physician, and knew from its locality that it must prove fatal. He said, "It is useless for you to try to give me hope—it is useless," and his features were as calm as if nothing had happened. After sitting sometime he remarked that he would like to leave the field; but the air was almost darkened by the enemy's flying balls, the Captain dissuaded him; told him that it was certain death, and there would soon be a lull to the storm, when he could pass out with safety. He sat some ten minutes longer, when he was again struck, but fortunately by a spent ball. This determined him to leave the field, remarking that he might as well go then, as it was a matter of life and death any way. He gained the hospital without further injury. He was a genuine hero. Always at his post, particularly in the hour of danger he gained the confidence of his superior officers. His many good qualities, and his uniform attention to the sick, endeared him to his company. When the "Sidney Browns" speak of "Bee" Jordan, the big tear springs to their eyes, and their breasts heave a sigh which show how keenly they feel their loss.

I heard to-day, with the deepest sorrow, that Lieut. James M. Reid, of the same company, was dead—died from the wound received in the battle of "Seven Pines." Rather, he was seized with an attack of fever, consequent upon his fatigue and wound, (a flesh wound in the thigh) which killed him. He was the son of Rev. Mr. Reid, of Woodstock; a young lawyer of promise, a graduate of the "Lumpkin Law School," of Athens.

At the Law School he gained the reputation of being the best, most systematic student there. At home he very soon gained the confidence of the community, and did a good business, which increased up to the time he entered the service as First Lieutenant of the "Sidney Browns." His heroism and daring on the battle field were conspicuous.

While home in January last (I believe it was) on furlough, he married the lovely Miss Emma, oldest daughter of W. W. Simpson, of Sparta. What a severe blow to his aged father, who had good reasons for the highest hopes of his son's brilliant success in the profession of his choice! All his fond hopes for his son's future career of distinction and usefulness were snipped in the bud.

Who can measure the grief, or appreciate the sorrow which wrung the breast and snapped the heartstrings of his young wife? They were most devoted to each other, and his death was most sudden and unexpected. He was a truly noble young man—noble in every respect. A ripe scholar, a practical philosopher, systematic as a Franklin, sociable, generous, scrupulously honest and rigidly moral, he was as perfect a man as one in ten thousand. Few men possessed all his virtues; and the better he was known, the better he was loved. I knew him intimately, and can therefore, speak advisedly. Georgia has lost in him one of her most solid intellects—one that was destined, had he lived, to have an impress of depth, solidity and HONESTY upon her legal escutcheon which would have done honor to any State or age. But he is slain! The cruel ravages of war have robbed loving friends, relatives and a devoted wife of a prize they could not too highly value. The wicked vandals, the cruel, heartless invaders of a people who have never harmed them, will have to answer for the death of another noble Southron—Lieutenant James M. Reid.

At Malvern Hill, Tuesday, July 1st, Colquitt's brigade were supporting some other brigade which, by too precipitate a movement, was thrown into confusion, and completely blocked the way. Gen. D. H. Hill rode up and ordered Colquitt's brigade forward, but it could not move. He then ordered Col. [James] Newton to move the Sixth Georgia forward. It numbered but little over a hundred men, but gallantly moved far in advance of any other troops, right in the jaws of death, and there, without a support, received the terrible fire of the enemy, until ordered to retire. Col. Newton said he had always *thought*, but now *knew*, his regiment would go anywhere it was ordered.

I intended to have related several other incidents of the late battles, but have already wearied your patience. As they are matters of history, it will not be too late to give them in my next. By the-by, I had the exquisite pleasure of seeing a copy of the *Republican* a few days ago. I wish the P. O. Department would so arrange it that we could get papers.

V. A. S. P.

LETTER FROM TOUT LE MONDE

CAMP NEAR RICHMOND, July 28, 1862 [8-4-62SR]

If a telegram directed to you through a friend, reached you, the explanation of "Tout le Monde's" long absence from your columns has already been made. To-day the hand is very weak that directs the pen, and it is not certain that a long or very interesting letter will be issued.

In this it was only intended to speak of the army as it is, and the prospect of another engagement soon from the enemy, who has so recently been whipped and cowed into his cuddy-hole at Harrison's Landing. But in glancing over an account of the engagement at Garnett's farm, I was so struck with the flagrant injustice done to the 2nd Ga. Regiment, and the many culpable inaccuracies, it is impossible to avoid reverting to this single instance, by way of setting the fame of the neglected regiment aright. It is impossible to see how facts can be so perverted by correspondents, unless they write from the road side in time of action, "gigging" the stray reports of every straggler as he comes along loaded with more lies than valor by a great deal.

On Friday, June 27th, it was thought expedient, while our forces were hotly pressing the enemy [at Gaines' Mill] on the opposite side of the Chickahominy, and the terrific thunder of battle was in our ears, to make a feint on the enemy's right on this side, in order to prevent his throwing any fresh troops across to the assistance of his men. Gen. Toombs was ordered forward to make the attack, and selecting *the 2nd Georgia Regiment*, he ordered it to the picket line, at which point it was to open fire on the enemy and draw them out. A part of the regiment was on picket duty at the time, and three companies were so far distant on another part of the line, they did not become engaged. Seven companies alone stood the brunt of the fight for one hour. The two companies sent out from the 17th Ga. to open the fight is all mythical; not a man advanced except from the Second Georgia. The five companies of that regiment in reserve for the five on the line, were formed just a little before sundown, and moved steadily up to the front, forming along a skirt of timber within two hundred yards of the enemy. The enemy seemed apprised of the movement, for scarcely had the men taken post when a tremendous volley of small arms opened, and a perfect shower of minie balls cut the trees and bushes overhead. It was immediately answered, and then commenced the heaviest firing of small arms it has been our lot to hear since the beginning of the war. The brigade [Winfield S. Hancock's] first opening fire on us was quickly reinforced by another [William T. H. Brooks'], pouring in the deadliest rain of lead into our ranks, and at every moment cutting down some valuable soldier. It is no exaggeration to say that at every moment some one was falling. This was all, too, from the four right companies whose lot was to occupy a rise, and were unprotected from a single point. The other companies were screened by a small hill in front, both from the direct shots and those that enfiladed the whole line. This unequal contest was continued, without any orders to give way, for three quarters of an hour, and although man after man fell before the eyes of the rest, and the ranks were constantly getting thinner, not a man shrunk from his place, choosing death rather than leave the post assigned to him without orders. A dispatch was sent to Gen. Toombs for reinforcements, and the Fifteenth at last came, when it was quite dark and almost useless. In fact, it was no aid to the shattered Second Georgia, for they did not take it from the front, and yet were sufficiently exposed to suffer severely in a very short time themselves. Still the enemy continued to pour in the leaden rain, and at every instant the dull "chuck" of a flying missile could be heard to strike the body of some comrade in the darkness around—for by this time it had grown quite dark—and he either fell dead or lay bleeding. Yet no orders came to withdraw.

After a while, as the combatants stood firing through the darkness at the flashing of each other's guns, our Colonel impatient for the orders to cease firing, ordered it himself, and the regiment withdrew beneath the hill far enough for protection, and formed. But the enemy ceased as soon as we, and in a few moments everything was quiet except the groans of the wounded and dying.

Now, this is as near the facts in the case as an eye-witness can write them. The 15th Georgia, when ordered, came promptly to the assistance of the 2nd, but could do little good at the time. Yet they fought some, and lost seventy killed and wounded. The 2nd Georgia lost one hundred and twenty killed and wounded, and all from five companies, and stood the fire for one hour or more. Where the two companies of sharpshooters from the 17th were doing the execution spoken of by a correspondent, I must learn. What other errors are detected in this correspondent's account, I do not intend to mention; suffice it to say, I shall follow up any one who attempts and fails to give the due meed of merit which has been so hard earned by our regiment. If we leave our fame to correspondents, we shall be compelled to look to our laurels, and where so many are justly emulous of their country's good, will let them guard well their own fame.

Well, I cannot tell you of any new warlike movements on foot; if I could, it would not be judicious to write of it.

"Where's Old Stonewall," is a question constantly asked, but no one knows. The Yankees are *non plussed*, for they hope he is dead, and yet are afraid to cherish the delusion. I expect soon, while [John Hunt] Morgan has them thoroughly stirred up in Kentucky, to hear of "Stonewall" striking them in some strange place, in some region no one dreams of, and when the "enemy" are the least aware of it.

During the battles before Richmond, he was constantly before the troops and all had a chance to see him. He looks hard, his nose Roman, his eyes grey, (perhaps couldn't see them plainly) and looks all over one at a glance, his lips thin and close together, expressive of the most rigid firmness, his forehead broad and capacious, and all is carried along by a frame slender but stalwart enough and enduring above the ordinary capacity of men. He appears to be restless and active, always with his men, day and night, never off hunting comfortable places to stay like a great many of our *parvenu* Brigadiers, and his troops are always moving, devoted to Jackson and healthful. Give him plenty of men and *no orders*, and he'll do more in six months to conquer a peace, than the rest of our Generals, put together, will in a year.

Gen. Lee has set the various ramifications of the army in order once more, and while everything is lying idle from warlike service, the most active operations of drilling and discipline are being carried on throughout the camps. No officer can rise now without a thorough examination before a competent board, and then much of the incompetent trash that has so long impeded the proper organization and discipline of the army will be removed and competent men fill their places. These are wise steps on the part of the General, and it is not to be doubted the efficiency of the army will be increased a hundred fold from these very salutary measures.

Day before yesterday the advance cavalry scouts of the enemy had a sharp skirmish with a body of our cavalry. The enemy were repulsed, but we lost one killed and six wounded. It seems that the enemy's position begins to cramp him, and the melodious songs of frogs, mosquitoes, &c., by the majestic James, commences to get wearisome to his ears. He feels around occasionally to know where we are and finds the Confederates every where ready to confront him. He would probably give a mint to occupy Malvern Hill again, and it is believed if the worst comes to the worst, he will ditch himself there. His capacity for digging never had anything like a parallel. It would astonish the living world to see what herculean labors he had performed in building roads and fortifications extending for miles and miles of the lines he had laid out will be lasting monuments of useless labor.

TOUT LE MONDE.

LETTER FROM RICHMOND
RICHMOND, VA., July 30, 1862 [8-6-62ASC]

Since the crushing defeat of the Federal armies in the series of battle before Richmond, the Lincoln government has become furious and has become more tyrannical and reckless than it ever was before. For months past there has been a formidable peace party in the North, but it has been unable to speak out. A terrorism kept it under. Recent events have strengthened the peace party very greatly, and new forms of tyranny are employed to prevent it from breaking forth.

But the anti-Lincoln elements are actively at work in the free States. A terrorism yet rules the large cities—Philadelphia and New York, but elsewhere people are beginning to speak out with boldness and independence. Information reaches here regularly from the North through various channels. It is an easy thing for a person in Richmond to keep well posted as to the condition of things in Abe's dominions. All accounts represent that the United States Government is really in a bad way. Its financial embarrassments will break it down after a while, if it is not sooner overthrown by the upheaving of the anti-abolition party of the non-slaveholding States. Indeed, the brutal tyranny now employed by Lincoln, both in his war upon us, and in his efforts to smother the discontent of his people at home, is nothing but a desperate expedient to save the Federal Government from destruction. It is in eminent peril of dissolution, and will certainly go to pieces very soon, unless the Federals speedily achieve some signal success upon the battle field.

Heretofore Lincoln has managed to secure the support of both the conservatives and radicals of the North. He professed to have some regard for the lives and property of the people he was trying to subjugate, and this satisfied those who pretended to be guided by the restraints of the constitution. On the other hand, he satisfied the great bulk of the abolitionists by permitting his agents to kidnap slaves by the wholesale. Thus he has been a professed conservative, while, practically, he has been an utter abolitionist. Now, however, he has thrown off all disguise. He no longer even pretends to respect the lives or the property of anybody in the South. He issues a proclamation which, in effect, commands officers of the army to seize whatever they want, and destroy everything they can't use. This is done to stimulate the passions of the Northern rabble. The war upon us was commenced in malignant hatred, and has been prosecuted accordingly. Malice was the highest motive which actuated the raving mad mobs which rushed to arms in response to Lincoln's call for soldiers.

But even this malice, strong as it was, has begun to lose its power as an animus for enlistment. Lincoln seeks to revive the flagging malignity by proclaiming to the world that the South is now to be made a desolate waste. All this is highly gratifying to the fiendish brutality of the Yankee rabble. It suits them hugely. Now that niggers are to be armed, and all other kind of property indescriminately destroyed, they say, that at last "a vigorous war policy has been adopted."

The "rebellion" is not to be speedily "crushed out." The white men of the Yankee nation have failed to conquer us; but the work is not to be done in "double quick time," by the few lazy niggers which the Yankee thieves may be able to entice into the Yankee lines.

We must do the Yankees credit to say that they are acting in perfect consistency with this assumption. Professing entire confidence that the South is certainly to be subdued, now that a new class of soldiers is to be thrown into the field, they quietly remain at home themselves. For once they are consistent. If niggers can end the war, why need they bother themselves about it? It is true the force of this reasoning is not at all appreciated by Lincoln. He announced his purpose to employ said soldiers in hope that the Northern friends of the "poor nigger," would hasten to his assistance, and fight side by side with him in defense of the common cause. But in this old Abe has been mistaken. The people rally with enthusiasm to the public meetings. They shout lustily when the speakers tell them about Lincoln's new war policy. But they don't enlist. Neither the glorious privilege of fighting in the ranks with Sambo, nor the allurement of bounty offered by the U. S. Government, nor the tempting plumbs added by the States and corporations in the shape of additional bounties, will secure volunteers. Lincoln, therefore, finds the stubborn fact staring him in the face, that he will have to resort to a draft. He will have to force men into the field in order to execute his free nigger programme.

Altogether, Mr. Lincoln is in a bad way. He is massing a large army under [John] Pope, at some point near Manassas, either to prevent us from going to Washington, or to make one more desperate effort to come to Richmond. Should that army be attacked and whipped— and whipped it will be if attacked—then it will be all up with Lincoln. Another defeat in a large battle would destroy the U. S. Government. The anti-Lincoln party is well nigh ready to rise up now. It could not be kept down after another great reverse to the Federal arms.

The truth is, that the North is in a terrible condition. The prostration of the government would be followed by the wildest anarchy. As for the downfall of the government, that is a mere question of time. It will be ruined and overthrown before the expiration of the term for which Lincoln was elected. This ruin will be brought about by the Northern people themselves. The madmen and spouting demagogues who have ruled the government since the war commenced, have generated a virulent demoralization which will soon bring forth its legitimate fruits. The Northern people will soon have to re-enact the bloody scenes of the first French revolution. Mark the prediction.

                                                                    D. L. D.

LETTER FROM TOUT LE MONDE
NEAR RICHMOND, VA., July 31, 1862 [8-7-62SR]

Great moves are being made on the chess board of war, but the import just now is beyond our comprehension. McClellan appears restive, and every now and then assails our picket line from his cooped up hole at Harrison's Landing. He makes appearance of a desire to repossess Malvern Hill, which he is well assured is a very strong place, but this is supposed to be only sham; for it is well known that he is constantly sending away his troops to Pope, and that the "onward to Richmond," from this point, is now considered an utter impossibility—the term a reproach which would gladly be forgotten. It is believed that McClellan will resign, being made unable to endure the chagrin of having [Henry] Halleck placed above him, in the face of the great military feat he just performed of "changing his base of operations." Halleck promises the nation great things, and actually sets out to convince the Northern dupes of his wonderful military acquirements by a learned dissertation on the sciences of war. We poor rebels had better look sharp now, Halleck the Great has succeeded and superseded the "Young Napoleon." Woe be unto the rebellious. The Southern monster is now to be "crushed out before you can say *Halleck the Great*, if your mouth was already open. "What shall we do to be saved?" But in reality, the old military ass—the hoary-headed villain—Winfield Scott, being still an incumbrance, Halleck put in a high place, which the veriest little fool of a negro in the South would condemn if he knew him, and McClellan, a second non-entity, is all a subject for congratulation in the South. There is no doubt McClellan is the ablest man they can put in the field. No one has labored so hard to organize and thoroughly discipline his army, and whenever we have fought him it was no child's play to defeat his veteran soldiers. The battle of Williamsburg, Seven Pines and all the last battles before Richmond are still records before us how sanguinary every inch of ground was disputed. In many instances these fights were man for man, and always before we found ourselves able to cope with the vandals two or even three to one of our soldiers. Let us rejoice that the "Young Napoleon" has found his Waterloo, and hope some less competent Yankee fool will take his place. It is believed that Pope is a "soft" chap, and before long a crowd of his hordes will be left to enrich some spot in the "Old Dominion." However, it is best always not to underrate an enemy, and then every energy will be employed to meet him. Rather overrate than underrate him.

It is impossible to tell you where Jackson is, but the Yankees are terribly exercised about him, and have got wind that [A. P.] Hill and others have been sent to swell his ranks. There is a dream too in the Dictator's head that of course our forces have been materially weakened here before the capital, and it would not surprise us if a force was precipitated down this way to make *another easy* march into Richmond. I believe our government has determined not to be lethargic any more, and at present it seems to be wide awake. We are whole footed and can put just as many men into the field as the Yankees. This tremendous call for 300,000 more men scares nobody; for any one can see it will take at least three months to get them together, and eight months to discipline and make anything like soldiers of them. Let the fools send that horde of militia down here before they go through the regular course of camp instruction, and I tell you, as you well know, there will be more food for buzzards than those disgusting but *useful* birds can destroy in a short time after they arrive.

It will require so much of this new force to go to Kentucky and Tennessee; so much to come to Virginia to take this provoking capital, and when a large amount of sick is deducted, the great bugbear will have dwindled into nothing scarcely beyond a scarecrow.

The work of recruiting goes on very slowly there, so their papers say, and the whole "kit and bilin" of the Yanks are wearing long, dolorous faces, and stock is falling in Wall street amazingly. The timorous wretches are now looking anxiously towards Europe waiting for an expression of foreign sentiment on their woeful disaster before Richmond. They know or expect that the huge boasting of the whole North, and the vacant promises of an "onward to Richmond" will begin to recoil with wonderful force against them when the news reaches there, and notwithstanding the early advice of some branch of the Press to resist to the utmost any attempt at intervention from Europe, the trembling cowards would quail at the first onset of European intervention as they did in their pusillanimous surrender of Mason and Slidell.

Steadily the thorough discipline of our army goes on and the expurgating of incompetency from the ranks is a most valuable and salutary step towards its perfection. Brave, competent officers control men and on the battle field render them solid and staunch before any sort of fire. Without officers who can control and direct them no soldiers are fit to carry on a dangerous field. Almost everything depends upon the efficiency of the officers, and the first consideration in organizing an army is, be assured of the entire capability of this post. Every promotion is made now after a thorough examination by a competent board. 'Tis the wisest step yet made to insure the invincibility of our troops. But I close with the fond hope that our Confederacy may not sleep in the darkest nor the brightest periods until our freedom is proclaimed.

TOUT LE MONDE.

"WHEN WILL PEACE BE MADE?"
LETTER FROM V. A. S. P.
CAMP NEAR NEW MARKET, VA., July 31, 1862 [8-7-62SR]

No question is oftener asked than this: "When will peace be made?" is uttered with an earnestness of tone which shows how deeply sensible the country is of the burden and calamity of this war. While it shows an intelligent appreciation of the magnitude of the interests at stake, and the sufferings they endure, it does not betray a want of confidence in the justice of our holy cause—the cause of home, liberty, life, and the honor of our wives, mothers and sisters. An idea of *independence* is always connected with a desire for peace. The latter, without the former, is no peace at all. It is tyranny, slavery, degradation, insufferable woe, and the destruction of all that is held dear and sacred by a chivalrous people. Peace without independence is not wanted. War interminable, "war to the knife," war to the extermination of our race is preferred to subjugation. But I degress.

"When will peace be made?" Who can answer? While there are no prophets, no divinely inspired men, who, moved by a spirit of prophesy, are enabled to look down the turbulent streets of time, through a long vista of ages, or only a few circles of the seasons, and foretell coming events, predict with unerring certainty the councils of God, concerning men, yet, the lights which cast a ray into that dark future, revealing some of its hidden mysteries, though complicated and confused, should not be wholly neglected. Have we any such lights, such reflections which cast back a shadow with a likeness of future unfinished events or realities? I will not presume to answer positively that we have.

But, "when will peace be made?" The Northern Press, with the rarest exception, declare that the "beginning of the end is not yet." McClellan's defeat will cause a reorganization, which will require months. The war, they say, is just where it began; and they say they are determined to whip us before they quit. If so, the war, indeed, has just begun, for whip us they cannot, exterminate us they may.

Some English journals take this view of the question: That the war is not near its termination; but the *Times* and other most popular journals, think the war must, of necessity, end very soon. I am of this opinion. Why? The war begun a year and a half ago, by the call of 75,000 troops, which were to "crush the rebellion in three months." To this number it soon became necessary to add a hundred and fifty thousand. Lieutenant General Winfield Scott, "the greatest Captain of the age," was made Commander-in-chief of the armies of the Union. Beauregard and Johnston soon out-generaled and whipped his grand army at Manassas.

Because Scott did not whip us, he was very suddenly considered an imbecile, an old fogy in his second childhood, and George B. McClellan was called to be General-in-chief of the armies of the Union. This "young Napoleon" was soon stripped of part (the greater part) of his authority, and his "grand" army divided into four divisions. He, too, was outgeneraled by Johnston, and failing in his plan, was whipped. He is then sent to the Peninsula with 158,000 troops, to whip the rebel army. Here their grand army of invasion buried itself in the hill-sides and trenches, fed upon the miasmas of the Chickahominy swamp, and was just ready to march into Richmond and "throttle" the "atrocious" rebellion in its very den, when the "young Napoleon" suddenly concluded that his position was not the best one to secure a successful entrance into the rebel capital, and "in a most masterly manner *changed his base*" to a point thirty miles below the doomed city! His plan of changing his base of operations will doubtless be adopted by the United States Government as a part of the course to be studied by West Point students! It presents many new points of interest, and will beyond question give his name a place in military history.

But what use are these facts to prove that peace is near at hand? They prove that a united people, in a good cause, cannot be conquered. They prove to the intelligent of the North that their efforts to subjugate us are futile. We are better able to defend ourselves than we were a year ago.

Already one or two prominent men dared to denounce the war as insane. Already have a few papers taken the same stand, and advised their government to let the South go.

There will doubtless be two parties in the coming Fall elections—a peace and a war party. If the question is fully discussed, the peace party will prevail; for the people of the North have two good reasons prompting them to support this ticket: First, a repugnance to becoming soldiers, and secondly, to end their present sufferings, to relieve their commercial and financial embarrassment, and to save their country from utter ruin and bankruptcy, which they see will inevitably follow, if the mad career of Lincoln and the abolitionists is not checked.

Their enormous war debt hangs like a cloud over their nation, threatening to burst in ruin upon them. It weighs like an incubus upon their energies from which the really conservative would save their country. To accomplish this, and free their posterity for generations from a tyranny more dreadful than the iron rule of a despot—heavy taxation—they will vote for peace.

But another and better reason why we may confidently look for a speedy and, of course, honorable termination of this unholy war: It has been the known policy of England and France, and all the powerful governments of Europe, to let the breach become so wide between the two sections of a great power of which they were jealous, that reconciliation or reconstruction would become impossible. To accomplish this they have encouraged rebellion, favored Southern independence; and at the same time called upon the North to wage a vigorous war to save the giant young Republic.

The war has brought suffering upon the manufacturing interests of Europe to an extent that cannot be much longer borne. The Powers of Europe will first recognize the Confederate States, and then intervene to save themselves. They would have mediated months ago if they had been positively assured of an eternal separation of the two belligerent sections. That we are two distinct peoples, in feelings, interests and tastes, is evident now, and they will certainly take steps to end a war which can only result in ruin to the parties engaged if continued, and bring still greater distress upon themselves.

From all of these lights, I am led to believe that peace, an honorable peace, bringing upon its opening snowing wings the blessings of liberty and prosperity, cannot be postponed longer than Spring, if not by white frost. God grant it! is the prayer of ten millions of hearts, longing to be free from a worse than Austrian despotism. But "I am no prophet, nor son of a prophet."

V. A. S. P.

FIFTIETH GEORGIA REGIMENT
CAMP SEVEN MILES BELOW RICHMOND, VA., July 30, 1862 [8-12-62AWCS]

I write you to urge upon the people of the up-country, through your paper the necessity of entering at once upon distillation of their peach and apple crop. The immediate use of spirits in some instances have done an injury to the service no doubt, but the great want, the absolute necessity for stimulants, with the common fare that we have in camps, is no longer a question. The soldiers cannot do without it. I am connected with the medical department of the service, and know what I say. We must have some life imparting principle other than what we have, or scores upon scores will go down that might otherwise stand the service. My whole life has been devoted to habits of temperance. In fact, it never entered my mind, up to the last few months, that I would ever pen a line to any one upon the subject of this sort. The medical department should control the use of spirits in the camps alone. The use of it would not then be likely to so many abuses. Some of our bountiful corn crops can be made into whiskey also.

Richmond is one vast hospital. All is being done that can be for the relief of the suffering. A large force [A. P. Hill's Light Division] left here a day or two since—18,000 or 20,000—to reinforce Jackson, it is said. Jackson is the man of the war. It is said here that when he was about to leave for the valley, he wrote to the editors and told them that if his name was mentioned during his absence, he would hang the man that did it on his return. This may or may not be true. At any rate, the editors say nothing of him.

A few good strong articles on the whiskey question, and you will do a God's service to suffering humanity, I have no doubt. I have been here a little over a week; my confidence in our ability to defend our beloved South is stronger than ever before. The troops are in good spirits.

D. W. BRANDON,
SURGEON, 50TH GA. VOLS.

LETTER FROM PHILLIPS' LEGION
CAMP FLOYD, ON CHAFFIN'S FARM, VA., August 7, 1862 [8-16-62ASC]

We are encamped now south of Richmond, on the north side of the James river. The enemy are below us. We are here, at least, for once in our lives, "in clover," for a luxuriant clover field is all around our camp.

You have no idea how cramped I am, as every correspondent from the division, of the great army must be. In the first place, we are in a good degree confined to regimental lines, being allowed to go nowhere out of the sound of the drum; and when we learn anything, ten chances to one that its divulgement is forbidden.

I have, however, made an inspection of all the river defences, and can assure you that if our batteries are handled with skill and pluck, [Adm. David] Porter's mortar fleet will retire—if it can—for its reception will not be the most gentle.

Malvern Hill, of which you have heard so much, was re-possessed yesterday by the Yankees. They advanced with a force of two brigades [Hooker's Division], including ten guns, and a regiment of cavalry, and gave battle to our little force, which comprised only 200 infantry and a light battery. The battery resisted their advance gallantly, and continued its fire until the ammunition was exhausted, when it limbered up and left the hill, leaving behind one caisson, which had the tongue broken out. General Toomb's brigade was in supporting distance, but did not support the battery, from which we judge it was not intended to hold the hill. This I learned from a member of the 17th Ga., who was on the hill. This regiment, indeed, was the picket force which supported the battery. We lost 28 men of the 17th regiment, and 3 of the battery. A cavalry force of the enemy charged them as they were retiring, but a well directed shot put them to rout. They went back in a hurry, leaving behind at least the saddle, bridle, pistols and sabre of one of their bravest officers. Gen. Longstreet's division moved down and awaited the advance of the enemy, but they made no further advance. Yesterday our men moved forward to the hill, which they found evacuated. So ends the late skirmish at Malvern Hill.

The whereabouts of Jackson and his army is a mystery, though he will spring up somewhere before long. How would it do to change his sobriquet from Stonewall to *Locomotion* Jackson.

Richmond is crowded and prosperous, and is a striking instance of the evil influences of prosperity. It is almost impossible to get a civil answer to a civil question in the city. Go into a store to buy an article, and you will be treated with a condescension and perhaps a contempt which would illy become a king. Go into a hotel, and your chance of receiving rude and uncourteous treatment is reduced to a certainty.

The condition of our field hospitals excites much comment just now. It seems to me poor economy to pay the price we do for men and then let them die because every form of the circumlocution office is not complied with. I intend to visit these hospitals soon and let you know of my observation.

S.

LETTER FROM SOLDIER JIM, THE MALVERN HILL AFFAIR
CAMP HOLLY GROVE, VA., August 8, 1862 [8-16-62ASC]

I have just returned to camp from a Yankee chase. On Tuesday last [August 5] our regiment started by daylight for Malvern Hill to relieve the regiment which was on picket there. By the time we got half way—about five miles—we heard the guns of the enemy engaged with one of our batteries. We pushed on down the river road till we were halted by a courier. Several shots were fired at us from three gunboats in the river, doing no damage.

One of their batteries [under Capt. G. A. De Russey] had slipped in and occupied the Hill in the rear of our picketing post. As soon as this was discovered, our battery engaged them, while our pickets came out.

The Yankee cavalry came dashing after us. When they got within 100 yards they halted, planted their battery, and shelled us for 15 minutes—no one hurt on our side. We let them have the Hill for one night. Next morning they discovered we had them almost surrounded by a heavy force—so they at once double quicked away down the river. The only sign of them that was visible, when our large columns marched out on the Hill, was the smoke of one of their gunboats, eight or ten miles below. I suppose they had a council of war day before yesterday, at which some one of their generals said we had whipped them three times, and were about to do it again; and they had better "git out o' the way," while they could do so safely. We captured about twenty prisoners. The Yankee army is suffering and dying immensely from the hot weather. I believe it is an advantage to ours to give them a march. We have marched three days, and I really feel much better than when I left on Tuesday morning. D—is well, but got his heel skinned on the march.

Some of the Yankees are pretty good looking, but they will "On to Richmond" only as prisoners of war. I believe they are pleased when they are taken.

I learn the Yankees expect soon to make an attack on Drewry's Bluff. I hope when they come they will be buried in the waters of the James, as they are so fond of water.

We are encamped in a field, and it is excessively hot. We plant bushes around our tents to make shade. We have good water. We can get Irish potatoes at $12 per bushel. Berries are plentiful and cost nothing. Would that I had the pleasure of whacking into one of those fine Georgia watermelons—but no fruit for the soldier; he must fight, take what is given to him, and hope for better times when peace returns.

SOLDIER JIM.

☆☆☆Battle of Cedar Mountain

As both armies began to shift operations away from Richmond, the first battle of the new campaign flared on August 9 when Confederate forces under Stonewall Jackson attacked Nathaniel Banks' corps south of Culpeper. Badly mismanaged on both sides, the battle cost the Federals 314 killed, 1,445 wounded and 622 missing for 2,381 out of approximately 8,000 engaged. The Confederates with 16,800 men suffered 1,341 casualties.

FOURTEENTH GEORGIA INFANTRY IN THE BATTLE OF CEDAR RUN
[THOMAS' BRIGADE, A. P. HILL'S DIVISION] [8-26-62ASC]

There are few regiments from Georgia that have seen harder service than the 14th. The campaign of last summer in Northwestern Virginia was one of long hard marching, suffering, disease and death. The latter part of the fall and winter was spent in tents about Manassas Junction, at work on fortifications and ditches. At the opening of the spring campaign, it was marched from thence to Yorktown, and thence to Richmond, where it was kept constantly on picket duty in the swamps of Chickahominy until the battle of Seven Pines. Since that time it has been in *six general engagements*, in each of which it has acquitted itself with honor to the State from which it hails—in some of the battles losing as high as twenty-five per cent of the number carried into action.

But the proudest day for the 14th—as it was for many others—was the 9th of this month, at the battle of Cedar Run [Mountain], between Orange and Culpeper Court Houses. The regiment is in A. P. Hill's division, and composes a part of the third brigade, consisting of the 14th, 35th, 45th and 49th Georgia Regiments, commanded by Acting Brigadier E. L. Thomas, Colonel of the 35th.

The day was one of the hottest ever felt, and the troops were marched from daybreak until 3 P. M., when the third brigade filed off from the road to some woods on a high hill commanding a view of the valley beyond for several miles. This position had been selected by Gen. Jackson as his temporary headquarters. In the distance could be seen a Yankee force of cavalry on picket, and still further on were visible moving bodies of men, and wagons rolling up dense clouds of dust. Our artillery were winding along the base of the mountains, through thickets and along the little ravines, for the purpose of getting into position. Long lines of slow marching infantry were following different directions, their bright muskets gleaming in the light of the evening's sun, while now and then a solitary horseman might be seen dashing along the valley now so quiet and peaceful, but soon to be the scene of fearful noise, confusion, pain and death.

Meanwhile Old Stonewall sat quietly studying a map spread out before him. At length a signal flag near him gave a single wave down, an instant after the boom of a cannon away down the valley reverberated through the mountains and along the valley. The ball struck in the midst of the Yankee cavalry, and those hitherto statue like looking beings suddenly became wonderfully animated. They put into exercise their powers of locomotion, and went scampering away at the top of their speed. Cannon was answered by cannon and battery by battery. Clouds of smoke and dust went rolling up and spreading out over the valley. It was now about 4 o'clock P. M. Col. Thomas (35th Ga.) was ordered to the field near the centre of the line, and in supporting distance of Purcell's Battery. Col. [Felix] Price, of the 14th, was wounded in the hand, and retired before the regiment was brought actively into the engagement. The command then devolved upon Lieut. Col. [R. W.] Folsom.

Emerging from the woods near the road by which the brigade had approached the field, it was met by Gen. [William B.] Taliaferro's brigade, Jackson's [Winder's] division, falling back before the advancing enemy. The 14th was cut off from the brigade by Taliaferro's retreating men. Some of the men of the 14th faltered for a moment. The danger of a panic was imminent. The enemy, encouraged by the retreat of General Taliaferro's brigade, and confident of victory, were advancing, and about reaching a point at which their line would have prolonged our battle line, and within a stone's throw of, and on the flank of Purcell's Battery. This was a critical and trying time. But it lasted only a moment. Colonel Folsom caught the colors of the 14th, and bearing them forward, called upon his officers and men to follow. Nobly and gallantly did they respond to the call. Without flinching the 14th advanced to meet the confident foe, and by their well directed volleys soon brought them to a stand. The ground was not hardly contested; but the deadly aim of the Georgia boys was too destructive for Yankee ideas of personal safety, and their lines began to waver, and then gave way. They were closely followed up for nearly a mile to where the route of the 14th crossed a [the Culpeper] road. Beyond this road was a small stream, and beyond that a wheat field in which was drawn up a strong infantry force of the enemy. The road afforded our men an excellent position, from which they poured a most destructive fire into the lines of the enemy. Seeing the advantage and dreading the effects of our deadly fire, one squadron of Cavalry [1st Pa. Cavalry] was sent out to drive us from the road. The 14th seeing the cavalry advancing, without changing position, coolly awaited their approach. When within seventy-five or eighty yards Col. Folsom gave the order to fire, and down went horses and men by the score. Again the valiant Yanks sought safety in hasty retreat, and fled precipitately to the woods behind the wheat field, closely followed by Georgia's daring sons.

The Regiment had advanced but a short distance when Col. Folsom fell from utter exhaustion. It was now nearly dark, the troops were completely exhausted from the long march, hard fighting and excessive heat. Gen. Jackson thought, under the circumstances, it would be better to close the action for that night, and accordingly the pursuit of the flying enemy was given up, having been driven from the field and left hundreds of their dead and wounded behind. It was said by one of the Generals who examined the field, that the 14th killed and wounded *more men than it carried into the field.*

But it is not pretended that the 14th was the only Regiment in Col. Thomas' Brigade that acted gallantly. All did well. The 49th fired until they had shot away their last cartridge. They then took what they could find on the Yankees they had killed, and afterwards charged the enemy with empty guns. The conduct of the 35th and 45th is spoken of in the most flattering terms. It is said that this battle made the *twenty-fourth* time that Colonel Thomas has been under fire. His conduct in action is characterized by great Coolness and unflinching bravery. It is understood that he has received the appointment of Brigadier General. The appointment is a good one.

The loss of the enemy is estimated at 1,700 killed and wounded, and 800 prisoners. Our total loss was 550. Our force engaged was about 14,000, that of the enemy near 30,000. The Yankees had one regiment busy all day burying their dead, and it is thought they did not get through.

If our men had not been so exhausted, and had been able to follow up the enemy, there is no doubt the battle would have resulted in a complete rout. As it was, however, the victory was a decided one, and has added fresh laurels to the battle worn heroes who so gallantly won it.

DIXIE.

NINETEENTH GEORGIA REGIMENT
[ARCHER'S BRIGADE, A. P. HILL'S DIVISION]
IN CAMP, NEAR GORDONSVILLE, VA., August 15, 1862 [8-21-62ASC]

It would be impossible for any participant to give you an adequate idea of the whole fight, as ever one who has ever been in a battle knows a regiment—or even a brigade—occupies but a small space on a large field of battle. But of that portion of the engagement as transpired in the immediate vicinity of our Regiment, we can give some particulars.

On the evening of the 8th we reached Orange Court House, having left Gordonsville two days previously. Here we bivouacked for the night, and started about 8 o'clock on the 9th for Culpepper. The day was very sultry and the sun poured down with greater fury, than any of we Georgians ever felt in the old "empire." The march being a forced one, many fell fainting by the way side, and large numbers fell out to hunt a shady spot to cool their parching brain. We all had a faint idea some extraordinary move was going on, but none expected we would be engaged that evening, after the fatigue of such a march; hence, many who could have exerted themselves desperately and came up in time, did not do so.

We arrived in the vicinity of the battle-field about half past four o'clock, and was ordered to load and prepare for immediate action. Our brigade was carried into a wood on the left of the Culpepper road, formed in line of battle, and ordered to advance. We had advanced steadily for three or four hundred yards thro' the copse, when we came to a wheat field immediately in our front, out of which two brigades of the enemy had just outnumbered and driven two noble [27th Va. & 10th Va. Bn.] Virginia regiments. This field had the wheat still upon it, stacked in large shocks; behind these the Yankees hid and awaited our coming. When we reached the fence, they poured a volley into us with no effect, and many tried to make their escape to the opposite side of the field in another cluster of woods; but the well directed fire of the boys of the "Bloody 19th," the [1st, 7th, 14th] Tennessee regiments and the [5th] Alabama battalion, brought down every one who attempted to make his escape.

We then were ordered to charge the woods on the opposite side of the field, which was swarming with Yankees. With a yell our boys crossed the fence and advanced like veterans through the field—about the middle of which they gave us a cross fire, knocking down our colors twice. But they were immediately raised by our brave boys, and borne aloft and forward. Here we lost one third of the number we carried into the fight, but kept on, undaunted by the terrible shower of balls, until we reached the opposite side of the field and put the enemy to flight. We pursued them about two miles further, but could not overtake them again.

We then moved out of the field into a wood on our left, where the enemy had been camping before the engagement. They had moved every thing except two ordnance wagons. These we lost the next day by the cowardice of two teamsters sent for them. In this wood the enemy shelled us for several hours with little effect. Our batteries soon put a stop to theirs, and we were permitted to lay down and rest our exhausted frames upon the damp ground, without blankets or covering save the deep blue vault of heaven.

Considering the enemy had three to one against us, it was one of the most signal victories of the war. Language cannot express the brave daring of our men, and only those who saw can appreciate the daring charges into the very jaws of death, as it were, of the brave men of [James J.] Archer's Brigade of the Light Division, commanded by A. P. Hill.

A PARTICIPANT.

TWELFTH GEORGIA INFANTRY IN THE BATTLE OF CEDAR RUN
[EARLY'S BRIGADE, EWELL'S DIVISION]
HEADQUARTERS, ARMY OF THE VALLEY,
JACKSON'S DIVISION, NEAR GORDONSVILLE, VA., August 14, 1862 [8-21-62 SR]

My short letter at this time is only to give the true particulars of our last battle, at Mitchell's Station, near Gordonsville, Saturday last.

We left our camp at Gordonsville, on the 7th inst., with two days' rations and orders to march for Culpepper Court House, some 15 miles distant, in company with Gens. Ewell's, A. P. Hill's and Jackson's [Winder's] commands. We had heard that the enemy were forty miles distant. After we had passed over the Rapidan river the noble old "Stonewall" passed us, for the head of his command. As Jackson passed, for the front, we all knew that a fight was near at hand.

After marching some six miles we fell in with the Yankee pickets, drove them in, killed three and captured four. None on our side injured. Here we were camped for the night, while our cavalry could scout over the country, to try to find out the position of the enemy. At early dawn we were called up to prepare for the day's march; all ready, we marched off, Gen. Early's brigade in advance, the 12th Georgia in front. We marched all day, without news from the enemy, nor did we hear of their whereabouts until the morning of the 9th, when we were drawn up in line of battle across the vast plains of Mitchell's Station. In a few moments a bomb came whistling over, which we readily understood. Some mile and a half off the Yankee cavalry could be seen drawn up in line, about a mile long. No sooner had we discovered the blue coats than one of our twelve pounders sent off a round shot to tell them that Jackson was near at hand. No reply was made, and both armies went to work preparing for the great battle which must evidently soon commence. The enemy made great preparations, and we remained in our line until three o'clock in the afternoon.

Our brigade was then ordered to move up under the immediate eye of Gen. Jackson to give them battle. On our side all was joyful; the boys were chatting about home and their sweethearts, &c. We pressed on, passing over fences, through corn fields, over ditches and rocks. Soon we saw confusion in the Yankee ranks, for we looked too determined for them. When in about three hundred yards of their lines Gen. Early advanced a few paces, fired his piece and fell back, which was enough for us, and without orders we "let drive" at them, which caused a grand skedaddle among the blue coats. They fired but one gun and left as hard as U. S. horses could bear their cowardly riders off. We pressed on over the dead bodies of the Yankee "braves," the Thirteenth Virginia regiment was ordered to move on the right flank, the Twelfth Georgia in the front, Jackson, Ewell, and Early in the lead to cheer us on, to see if Pope was the man he was said to be. Their front was soon made their rear guard, for their horses were too hard to hold to see us any longer. We pressed on for about one mile, when, passing over a small hill, we soon discovered their batteries. We were ordered to halt and lay down. Soon their guns opened on us to drive us back, but we were there, and never to leave until an opportunity was given to go forward. Old Stonewall left us and darted off in a near wood. If it had been any one else we would have said—coward!—but no; he is only gone to be heard from again. Our batteries were soon brought up and opened on them. Bomb after bomb came whistling over us, to which our artillery replied admirably. The cannonading lasted forty-five minutes, while Jackson could see if he could not play a better game for them. During the cannonading several of our regiment (12th Georgia) were killed and wounded. We lay there as if dead until firing commenced on the left flank by Gen. A. P. Hill's [Winder's] division, under command of Gen. Jackson, who had flanked them and had nearly got in their rear. We were ordered to charge them, which we gladly obeyed, and drove them off before us under a heavy shower of rifle balls and under a cross fire of Hill's [Winder's] command led by our Chief. After they got their artillery away the cannonading ceased, and the 12th Ga., and the 13th Va. opened on them with small arms, which was all the *go*. When we were first in sight of the Yankees we saw nothing but cavalry and artillery, but now these had passed away, and on their side all was anew. Brigade of infantry after brigade was seen to fall in and march forward to meet the "rebel intruders." I never saw so many formed and on the march in so short a time as were then seen over in the Yankee lines. Seeing there were too many for us, the 48th Regt. Va. Vols. complained to Gen. Early, and his only reply was: "Go on boys; you are safe." We gave one shout and pressed on to meet that unmovable looking line, which was only three hundred yards in advance. Just then we were ordered to cease firing, fix bayonets, and prepare for the charge. Our attention was called by our General; said he, "Boys, you are not alone, only look back," which we all did and discovered a field of grey rebels in our rear advancing at the double quick. We opened fire and in slow time pressed on to close quarters. We fired deadly vollies after vollies into them, to which they bravely replied; but in a short time great confusion was seen in their lines, and we ceased firing and came to the charge, sweeping the fields and mowing down the Yankees before us as if they were only black birds before the sportsman. They had been strongly reinforced, and our reinforcements had just arrived. We followed up their retreat over the dead and dying, and gained a complete victory over Pope. Our artillery followed us up close in the rear, and as the half starved blue coated cowards scampered off before us, Gen. Ewell commanded us to halt, and said to a captain of artillery: "A little more grape, Captain, if you please, for they travel too fast for our boys." No sooner had this order been given than it was obeyed, and load after load of grape was sent after them which carried many a Yankee to his long home. The Yankees finally halted, drew up a line of cavalry which made a daring charge on us to no effect; they were soon driven back, and the victory was ours for that day.

The Federals fell back to their fortifications, and "Old Stonewall" camped his command on the battle-field. The next day was Sunday, and all was silent on both sides. Both armies took positions, and Jackson spent the day in trying to draw them out again, but he failed. Monday was spent in burying the dead of both sides under flags of truce. The engagement resulted in the loss of about 300 killed and wounded on our side; the loss of the enemy is known to be over 2,000. Among our men who fell was the noble Charles S. Winder, General commanding the First Brigade [Stonewall Division]. His loss is greatly regretted by all who knew him.

We captured several pieces of artillery and 500 prisoners, including 30 commissioned officers, among whom is General [Henry] Prince. We are looking for a renewal of the engagement every day. We never will be satisfied until Pope is driven over the Potomac.

Respectfully yours, C. W. A.

C. W. Anderson enlisted as private in the 12th Georgia Regiment on June 6, 1861; he was promoted to Third Corporal on October 7, 1861 and Fourth Sergeant on June 18, 1862. According to the regimental historian of the 12th Georgia, Anderson was wounded at Second Manassas, and went West after the war.

THIRTEENTH GEORGIA INFANTRY
[LAWTON'S BRIGADE, EWELL'S DIVISION]
CAMP AT LIBERTY MILLS, ORANGE COUNTY, VA., August 13, 1862 [8-21-62SR]

As I commenced writing you principally on account of the doings of the 13th Georgia, I think it best to continue in the same way, adding other facts that may come to my knowledge as we pass along.

I last wrote you from Richmond, after the battle of the 1st July, and as you must excuse me from giving dates, it being difficult for me to keep them, I will try, in my own way, to let you know where we have been and what we have done since my last writing.

The day after I last wrote you, sending a list of the killed and wounded in the 13th, we started for Richmond, and that same evening took the Fredericksburg [Charlottesville] train and came to Louisa Court House. We passed Beaver Dam Station the evening before the Yankee scouts burnt the depot. One of the scoundrels was taken prisoner and brought to Louisa. I heard him interrogated, but he seemed to belong to the know-nothing party, for there could be very little got from him in the way of information. After staying at Louisa Court House a few days, we marched on to Gordonsville, and stopped there several days, and were then ordered to Magruder's Mills, four miles above there, where we encamped about a week, and were then ordered back to Gordonsville and thence to Mechanicsburg, on the road between Louisa Court House and Charlottsville. We stopped there some ten days, and then went back to Magruder's Mills, where we remained until last Friday, when we were ordered to advance into the country that was in possession of the enemy.

Before proceeding, I wish you to understand when I use the word *we*, I mean the whole of General Jackson's army. On Friday evening [Aug. 8] we got about four and a half miles beyond Orange Court House, on the direct road to Washington. We crossed the Rapidan and encamped for the night about 9 o'clock. The Yankee cavalry made an attempt to cut off part of the train. The 13th were sent out to picket, and succeeded in capturing four of them. The next morning five of them were brought in and sent "On to Richmond." On Saturday the army moved on toward Culpepper Court House. On the way we heard the booming of cannon, and felt sure that Jackson had attacked the enemy, who had fallen back towards that place. Gen. A. P. Hill's [Ewell's] division, which had gone on in advance, had come up with them about six miles from the Court House, and, as usual, whipped them out, killing and wounding about five hundred, and taking four or five hundred prisoners, including Brigadier General Prince, and thirty or forty other officers. I understood we lost on our side between two hundred and fifty and three hundred. I am sorry to say that Gen. Winder was killed in the fight. The fight was severely continued for some time, and the opposing armies got into close quarters, our men using the butt of their muskets, and rocks at the Yanks. Our brigade did not get there in time to take part in the fight, but arrived in the evening, and with the rest lay on the battle field all night.

On Sunday the army stopped about the battle-ground, and on Monday [Aug. 11] fell back to Liberty Mills, seven miles above Gordonsville, for the purpose, as I understand, of drawing the enemy out. I think you may look out for stirring times here shortly, as Jackson is being considerably reinforced though everything is kept very close.

I understand from a gentleman from Richmond, that the officers taken in the last fight were ironed, in accordance with the orders of the President, though they deny that there ever was such an order read to them as is attributed to General Pope.

The weather has been very warm for the last ten days, and I have felt it as much as I ever did in Georgia. A number of the men were sun struck, and on the way to Orange Court House I saw one man (named Delor, I believe,) of the 60th Georgia, down with a sun-stroke. He was picked up, put into a wagon, and in less than two hours was dead and buried. Last evening we had a refreshing shower, which has made the weather cooler, and I hope it may continue so.

Yours, &c.   U. T.

LETTER FROM V. A. S. P.

RICHMOND, VA., August 16, 1862 [8-21-62SR]

Since I have sufficiently recovered my strength the "Confederate Reading Room" have been my favorite resort, in the cool of the morning and evening. It is a rich treat to a soldier long subjected to the tedious routine of camp life, to enjoy the privileges of the Reading Rooms. Amusement for hours is offered in looking over Frank Leslie's pictures of the war; or in perusing the large files of newspapers from every portion of the Confederacy.

In reading the interesting letters of "Tout-le-Monde," your correspondent of the 2nd Georgia, I discovered a mistake—an erroneous statement relative to the "Battle of Garnett's Farm," in his letter of July 28th. I do not think his misstatement is intentional, but arose from his misinformation by some one who was not posted, or had not the means of knowing what was done on that memorable evening. His statement of the part the gallant Second took in that affair, is correct. If "Tout-le-Monde" will trouble himself by referring to my communication which he pronounced erroneous, he will see that I speak of his gallant little regiment as acting most nobly, sustaining the fire of a vastly superior force, during the entire engagement, and without flinching. I also state that I had utterly failed to obtain a list of casualties of his regiment.

But the following bold, sweeping assertion astonished me no little: "The two companies thrown out from the 17th Georgia to open the fight, is all mythical; not a man advanced except from the Second Georgia." If "Tout-le-Monde" will put himself to the trouble to ask Gen. Toombs, or any of his staff, he will correct this misstatement in his next letter.

I know what I stated to be true; for I was standing [within] five steps of the General when he gave the order and saw the companies file by. I heard Gen. Toombs' directions to them to drive in their pickets. "*Feel* them, boys! Feel them heavy!" The companies had hardly got out of sight before the Second Georgia started to the scene of action. In less than five minutes our ears were startled by the heaviest volley of musketry I ever heard, and the balls fell like hail around us. These two companies certainly received the first fire of the enemy; or so at least I was informed by Major Pickett, who commanded them. The fire, however, was nearly simultaneous on the right and left of the line.

Again he says: "Where the two companies of sharpshooters from the Seventeenth were doing the execution spoken of by a correspondent, I must learn." I can inform him. So can the Adjutant General of our brigade. They took position on the left, fought until most of them had no cartridges left, had two men killed, and from six to ten wounded. They were upon their knees, and were overshot by the enemy. They remained upon the field until the firing ceased; and at one time by their position, (being on the slant below the enemy) their steady, unflinching courage, and deliberate firing repulsed five companies of the enemy who had advanced to the crest of the hill.

I hope "Tout le Monde" will do me the justice to look into this matter. If I have made any misstatements during any part of my correspondence, they were based upon the best information I could gather from eye-witnesses or participants, in whose statements, I thought,

I could place implicit confidence. *Truth* has been my aim; and I would not, for any consideration, knowingly make a false statement.

Everything in the way of news is dull. The city is as quiet as if universal peace reigned. Scarcely a rumor is afloat; and the only thing to amuse a stranger or render the news dearth tolerable, is the continued, deafening roar of drays, hacks, wagons, and carriages rumbling over the paved streets of the Confederate Capital. These soon tire you beyond endurance. Traders are, as usual, busy upon the streets, and in their shops, selling goods, or soliciting trade at very *moderate* prices. Out of curiosity, I asked the price of various kinds of sizes of pipes. A neat wood pipe, nicely varnished, with a horn mouth-piece, and perhaps a brass band around the stem for ornament, is selling for the reasonable sum of *six dollars!* An imitation Merschaum, (or at least, second rate,) is worth *forty dollars!* What is surprising is that there is no scarcity in that article.

There is no news from "Stonewall." Everybody feels satisfied that he is in the right place, and will pounce upon Pope when and where he least expects an attack. A few prisoners occasionally arrive, and if officers, they receive an undue amount of public attention. They are to answer for the infamous crimes of General Pope.

The recent call of Abraham the First, excites a good deal of conjectures as to what will be the course pursued by our Congress, which meets next Monday. It is the prevailing opinion that the Conscript law will be amended so as to include all between the ages of sixteen and forty-five. I agree with our venerable Chief Justice Judge Henry Lumpkin, that it will yet be necessary to call into the field *all able bodied men*, without regard to age, to drive back the dark wave of Northern Vandals, which threatens to overwhelm us. Old men of the South! if the war but last the year—which God forbid!—*you* will have to fight the last, great decisive battle. If Northern madness drives them, in their wild desperation, to hurl another million of ruthless, vindictive men against us, the middle aged, the old men, the boys, will have to don the habiliments of terrible war, and rush like Spartans to the rescue. If it comes to this pass, America—the Confederate States—will boast a hundred Marathons and Thermopyleas; and will embalm in sacred memory a thousand noble chiefs like Leonidas!

Ladies of the South! You can, you must, you will gain half the victory. Mothers, sisters, wives, to you a bleeding country looks for succor! How can we render service? you naturally ask. *How!* Why, let not an able-bodied man remain behind! Place his gun upon his shoulder, and, pointing to the dark war cloud skirting the whole horizon, say, "go, strike one manly blow! We will manage the farms, and take your places in business. Go, and rescue our sunny land from the pollution of the foul invaders."

Such a spirit, my country-women, will ensure our liberty against three times the force that can be mustered by the North. But if the crisis *does* come—(has it not already come?)—you must act promptly, *desperately*, as though every home in our lovely South were in flames, and you were struggling to save them.

V. A. S. P.

☆☆☆ Battle of Second Manassas

In late August, Lee marched his Army of Northern Virginia north from Richmond to oppose Gen. John Pope's Union Army of Virginia. A confident Lee gambled by dividing his force in the face of Pope's army and after Jackson captured and destroyed a huge supply depot at Manassas Junction, the Confederates fought the Federals near the old Manassas battleground. Jackson held his ground until Longstreet arrived to help deliver a crushing blow to Pope, who retreated towards the defenses of Washington. Federal casualties: 1,724 killed, 8,372 wounded and 5,958 missing for a total of 16,054; Confederates: 1,481 killed, 7,627 wounded and 89 missing for a total of 9,197.

PRIVATE LETTER, SEVENTEENTH GEORGIA REGIMENT
August 31, 1862 [9-8-62CS]

Dearest Mother: As you well know, there has been severe fighting going on for several days, mostly Jackson's forces. Yesterday is the first time Longstreet has participated.

Toomb's brigade opened the fight on the right, on the edge of the old battlefield of the 21st July, 1861. Our regiment was exposed to the hottest fire, from 4 o'clock, p. m., until dark. We maintained our position against four regiments for more than two hours, not giving back a foot. The loss of our regiment is 99, only 11 of whom were killed outright, two of whom being from my company. Maj. Pickett is mortally wounded; Capt. Jones, of Albany, killed. Banks Shaw was wounded in the first of the engagement, and was persuaded to go to the rear, but he soon returned and was shot through the head and killed instantly. I was knocked down by a spent grape shot, which struck me on the neck, and now have rather a stiff neck from it; had it been an inch higher it would have fractured my skull, or had it been with more force it would have taken my head off. I was also struck by a spent minie ball on the ankle, which stung considerably for a time; but is all right now.

Elbert Wells had a ball to pass through his sleeve, but not hurt. Some of the men fired 60 rounds, some used two guns, as one would get so hot that they could not hold it. They showed as much bravery as is ever shown on the field. I passed over the field this morning, and find that our shots told well, for the enemy lay promiscuously in front. The 2nd was under heavy fire, but their loss was slight. None of the Guards were killed. The Texas brigade fought like heroes. I have not learned their loss.

The enemy were driven back beyond Stone bridge, where we have just stopped as a resting place. I hear heaving firing occasionally in the direction of Centreville, also on the left. I suppose that is G. W. Smith coming up with his forces; if so, fighting will be renewed again pretty soon, and I suppose that we will again play a conspicuous part. The 20th Georgia captured a battery of six guns. Their loss is pretty heavy. Lt. [T. S.] Fontaine was wounded. I intended to mention our passage of Thoroughfare Gap on the 28th. Our regiment did not fire a gun, but lay under the heaviest shelling we ever experienced—our loss was 9—none killed. They had the position on us, but we soon drove them from their stronghold by charging up the mountains that we could scarcely climb. The 2nd and 20th both did excellent service on that occasion.

J. B. Moore.

LETTER FROM THE EIGHTH GEORGIA
CAMP NEAR BULL RUN, August 31, 1862 [9-14-62ASC]

The 8th Georgia Regiment left Richmond on the 15th of this month, en route, via rail-road, for Gordonsville; arrived there late in the evening; then took up the line of march for Orange Court House, which was in possession of the enemy. Our army drove them from their position and have been pursuing ever since. The Regiment has been engaged in three battles since we left Orange Court House. On the 23rd at Rappahannock Station, we lost, in killed and wounded, twenty-six men; on the 28th, at Thoroughfare Gap, we lost, in killed and wounded, eight men; and on the 30th, our army fought the great battle of the war. The losses on either side have not been ascertained. Our loss was considerable, but the loss of the enemy much greater—at least ten to one. The army has been fighting for four days, and will continue until we drive the last Federal across the Potomac.

I have just heard a portion of our baggage train has been ordered to Leesburg. Our army across the Potomac, Washington is ours, and Maryland redeemed.

J. F. C.

LETTER FROM SOLDIER JIM
TURNPIKE, September 2, 1862 [9-16-62ASC]

I would not now attempt to write, but I have an opportunity to send you a letter by hand all the way through. I am so near worn out, that I feel but little like writing. Our campaign has been the most active in the world. Since we left Richmond, we have jumped up the enemy and whipped him all the way from Cedar Run past Centreville. Our old gallant regiment has been engaged four times lately. The hardest fight was day before yesterday [actually Aug. 30], near, and partly on the same old Manassas battle-field—rather a singular occurrence.

I think we killed about four to one. We fought them till night, when they threw down their guns and fled. Prisoners come in from every side. All of them seem to be sick of the war and glad when they were taken. We have had a hard old time to keep up with the Yankees.

Captain [Jennings M. C.] Hulsey and Henry Forsyth, of our company (the Atlanta Greys), were wounded, and have since died. Henry Bell and W. A. Thomas were slightly wounded. Our true hearted, gallant Captain received his death-wound near the same spot of ground on which he was wounded before. He was always at his post, and fell gallantly battling for the rights and liberties of his country; but victory crowned the field and hovers over his grave. Henry Forsyth was a hero—never missing, always at his post, ready for duty, and bravely faced the foe whenever the company was placed in line of battle. Myself and brother D have so far escaped in the late fight.

We expect some hard fighting again soon. It has become an every day business to fight Yankees—though they are now running every way from the rebels. I am told they have torn up the Chain Bridge to keep us from crossing the Potomac after them, but I do not know how true the report is. We have whipped them nearly back into Washington, and now we are on our old picket ground. But I must close.

SOLDIER JIM.

Soldier Jim—James A. Adair—was elected Second Lieutenant of Company F on August 15, 1862. His Captain, Jennings Marion Clarke Hulsey was born on June 14, 1834 in De Kalb County, Georgia. He graduated from Dickinson College in Carlisle, Pa., in 1858, and was a member of Phi Kappa Sigma, and the literary society Belle Lettres. After college he studied law in Atlanta and was admitted to the Bar. He enlisted as First Sergeant, May 22, 1861; elected Second Lieutenant, July 4, 1861; First Lieutenant, July 26, 1861; Captain, August 10, 1862 and was killed in action at Second Manassas, Va., August 30, 1862. He is buried at St. Paul's Protestant Episcopal Church in Haymarket, Va.

THE TWENTY-SIXTH GEORGIA AT MANASSAS
[LAWTON'S BRIGADE, EWELL'S DIVISION]
LOUDOUN COUNTY, VA., September 4, 1862.

I suppose you have before this received news of the various battles that have been fought within the past three or four weeks, and the constant success of our arms. Our Brigade has been engaged and under fire six or seven times, and has each time proven itself worthy of the State it came from.

On Tuesday night, the 26th of August, we captured two of the enemy's trains at Bristow, on the Manassas Road, having marched over fifty miles in two days, in order to get in rear of the enemy. I look upon this movement of old "Stonewall" as being the boldest of the war; with three divisions he marched in rear of Pope's Army of 150,000 or 200,000 [70,000] men. At Bristow, sixteen of my boys were sent to capture some Yankees who had escaped from the trains; they captured 14 Yankee soldiers. On Wednesday, Gen. Ewell's division was left at Bristow to cover the retreat of our forces to Manassas.

In the evening the Yankees advanced in overwhelming force. The 26th Georgia, under the command of Lieut. Col. [E. S.] Griffin and myself, were ordered with the 31st Georgia, to support the 1st Maryland Battery, and nobly did they perform their duty. We were under fire all the evening, and were the last to leave the field. There was a constant shower of shell over and around us the whole evening. The 26th lost two men.

Again has the battle of Manassas been enacted and in point of destruction to human life, the battles of Richmond are not to be compared to this. The fight commenced just before dark on Thursday, the 28th of Aug. [Alexander] Lawton's Brigade was formed in a skirt of woods a short distance from the field of battle. We were ordered in just after dark; we marched steadily across an open field for about four hundred yards, over which the balls were flying by the thousands. Occasionally a man would drop from the ranks, yet not one faltered. When we reached the fence, the men were ordered to lie down and commence firing; we poured volley after volley into the ranks of the enemy, who were drawn up in line of battle in the field beyond. Lt. Col. Griffin and Adj. [Andrew] Lyles were both wounded at the fence. After firing several rounds Gen. Lawton ordered the brigade to charge. I led the 26th into the charge, and I do not think there has been a bloodier one since the war. At the command every man went over the fence; the Yankees did fearful execution, men fell from the ranks by the dozens. Still the gallant 26th wavered not. Our color bearer was shot down, but the colors were immediately seized by a willing hand and borne to the front. One volley from the few regiments engaged, sent the enemy flying over the hills to the woods. The night was so dark no pursuit was attempted.

When I formed the regiment after the engagement, the scene was heart rendering, only about 30 or 40 of the 173 gallant boys that entered the fight with me were left. Nearly all were killed or wounded. I have not yet been able to prepare a list of the killed and wounded for publication, but will do so as soon as all the wounded can be carried to one place. Thirty-two were killed on the field, and over one hundred wounded. The Brunswick Rifles went in under the command of Lieutenant N. Dixon, with 17 men; of these Lieut. Dixon and 12 men were wounded.

Lieut. N. Dixon, wounded in shoulder; Serg't. W. Dart, in the arm; J. J. Spears, lower part of the abdomen; John Nibbs, in abdomen; George Holmes, in both legs; Joseph G. W. Harris, through the thigh; J. Pacetty, in the breast; D. Cronan, through the arm; P. Burney, one finger shot off; T. Cumming, in the heel.

Joseph Lassere and Moore Clarke were both hit but not injured. I was knocked down by a spent ball, but not injured. You can say to the relatives of the wounded, that they need not be at all uneasy. I have seen all the wounded—none of them are mortal, nor will any of the boys lose a limb. None were killed. Nothing but the hand of Providence preserved us through the shower of balls through which we passed.

J. S. BLAIN.

James Simeon Blain, age 24, was captain of Company A, and also a doctor by profession. Captain Blain was the first to tend to seriously wounded Gen. Richard S. Ewell, whose right knee was shattered by a minie ball. Later, Corps Surgeon Dr. Hunter H. McGuire amputated the General's leg. Blain was promoted to Lieutenant Colonel and was severely wounded during Early's 1864 Maryland Campaign, and spent the final months of the war recovering. Blain died on December 24, 1886.

TWENTY-FIRST GEORGIA REGIMENT
[TRIMBLE'S BRIGADE, EWELL'S DIVISION]
FREDERICK CITY, MD., September 9, 1862 [9-25-62ASC]

The numerous friends of the 21st Georgia Regiment are doubtless anxious to know something of its engagements and losses in the recent battles, and I propose to supply this information to some extent.

We moved with our brigade ([Isaac R.] Trimble's, of Ewell's division) from the Rapidan river, when our army under Lee commenced its forward movement, and arrived at Freeman's Ford on the Hazel [Rappahannock] river. Here, on the 22nd of August, we had a heavy skirmish with the enemy, who, in considerable force, had crossed and were about to attack some portions of the army train. They had several brigades and a battery in position. Our brigade consisting of the 15th Alabama, 21st North Carolina, and our regiment, under our gallant General, deployed skirmishers, and, advancing in line of battle, drove them over the river, killing and wounding a large number, and causing them to fire their own trains on the other side. We killed, according to their newspaper accounts, the General commanding [Henry Bohlen]; and but for the river, would have carried their battery. Having accomplished our purpose, and having no artillery, we fell back to our original position. Whilst their loss was heavy (their account), ours was slight.

Next day we commenced the great flank movement through Thoroughfare Gap, and on the night of the 26th, after a toilsome march, arrived at Bristow Station, seven miles below (south of) Manassas Junction, where our division captured two trains of cars and many prisoners. Already we had marched that day 20 miles, but about 11 o'clock, P. M., we commenced a forced march to Manassas Junction, in company with the 21st North Carolina, (two regiments), under General Trimble. Arriving at Manassas about 12½ o'clock that night, without cavalry or artillery support, and finding that the enemy were expecting us, as their pickets fired into us, we formed in line and advanced into the village. We had a short and quick engagement, the enemy opening on us with musketry and artillery. Fortunately the darkness favored us, and on we pushed—the 21st North Carolina on the right, and ours on the left. Becoming separated by a long line of cars, our movements were somewhat independent of each other. The conflict was short and decisive, our regiment taking in the charge 3 pieces of artillery and some 50 prisoners, including a Lieut. Colonel, three Captains, an Adjutant, and three Lieutenants.

We stood sleepless all night as the camp fires of the enemy were close around us; and we learned from our prisoners that they were in large force, and much nearer us than our own friends. The sound of their artillery moving near us during the night, also apprised us of our danger. It is attributable to darkness and their utter surprise at our achievement, that we were not attacked. Early next morning, they were already advancing on us and shelling us, when our division and other troops arrived. We stood at rest in one of the old nooks and saw the battle of that day and saw the magnificent cavalry fight between Stuart and the enemy's cavalry.

I forgot to say that the 21st North Carolina gallantly took two pieces of artillery in their charge. An immense amount of stores, long trains loaded with goods of all kinds, and supplies for Pope's army, besides Sutler's goods, fell into our hands.

This achievement will ever be regarded by the 21st Georgia, as one of its proudest. Our loss was very slight, considering the enemy had artillery in position besides their infantry.

The next day, by crossing Bull Run at the [railroad] bridge, and again at the Stone Bridge, we arrived near Groveton, on the identical ground where we drilled one year ago, and at nightfall became engaged with [Brig. Gen. John Gibbon's] forces. We carried 240 men into the engagement, and advancing with our Brigade, soon became hotly engaged. Onward we went to a fence, the enemy falling back before us. Whilst fighting here, under a heavy cross fire, our regiment and the 21st North Carolina, suffered unusually. Owing to some mistake, the 15th Alabama and the 12th Georgia, to our left, were kept from firing, and the enemy's whole force became directed at us. Reinforced by the 26th and 61st Georgia, of Lawton's brigade, we charged across the fence, driving the enemy before us, under appalling losses to ourselves. Here Captain [J. F.] Buck Waddail fell dead, and Lieut. [Thomas] Attaway, of Company B, fell mortally wounded. Amongst the foremost slain was Lieut. [G. W.] Adderhold, of Company A.

The enemy having retired to the woods, and complete darkness prevailing, we fell back to the fence, when, after a few volleys, the firing ceased on both sides. Our loss on the memorable night of the 28th of August, was very heavy, as will be seen from the list of killed and wounded. We carried 240 men into the engagement, and our wounded were so numerous that not more than a sixth of the whole regiment escaped unscathed.

On the 29th, Major [Thomas] Glover, with the fragments of the regiment, fell into line, and in the skirmish of the morning, where General Trimble was wounded, was present. Detailing in the afternoon to bury our dead, we were unengaged any more that day.

On the 30th we rejoined our brigade. Not numbering more than 40 men, we took part in the brilliant success of that day, and with our brigade sustained and repelled the shock of three lines of battle thrown on our position with great energy and determination by the enemy. The dead on all the fields in which we had been engaged, illustrates our fighting. At the close of the fight, the enemy were in full retreat. Our losses had been very heavy, and most of the regiment were scattered in all direction, wounded and suffering for medical attention. Maj. Glover was detailed by Gen. Lawton as a physician to attend them temporarily; and leaving the command with Captain [William M.] Butt, of company A.

The little command again moved with the division to intercept the enemy between Centreville and Fairfax. Near Chantilly we were engaged again on the evening of Sept. 1st. Our loss was not many, but the lamented Capt. Butt fell here.

Since then, we have not been engaged, but have crossed the Potomac, and are now at Frederick, Md., a good deal recruited in numbers, and ready for more fighting should it be necessary. Maj. Glover rejoined us at Leesburg.

Yours,

***.

THE EIGHTEENTH GEORGIA AND THE TEXAS BRIGADE IN THE BATTLE OF SECOND MANASSAS
[HOOD'S BRIGADE, HOOD'S/EVANS' DIVISION]
September 23, 1862 [10-11-61ASC]

For the last month there has been scarcely any communication between the army and their friends at home. For the relief of those having friends in the Texas brigade, and more particularly in the 18th Ga. regiment, I attempt a short sketch of the operation of that brigade, confining myself however, more particularly to the 18th Ga. This brigade was formerly commanded by Gen. J. B. Hood, but on his taking command of this Division, the command of the brigade fell to Col. W. T. Wofford. It is composed of the 1st, 4th, and 5th Texas, the 18th Ga. and Hampton's S. C. Legion.

The brigade left Richmond on 7th August, and on the 16th, joined Gen. Longstreet's forces near the Rapidan, having marched to the North fork of the Rappahannock, and found the enemy strongly posted at all the fords, to dispute crossing. Seeing this, Gen. Lee very dexterously held them there by threatening to force his way across at several points, while Gen. Jackson passed round their right flank and captured Manassas Junction, in their rear, cutting off their communication with Washington. As soon as this was discovered, the enemy destroyed all the cars and stores not transportable, and sent a strong force to hold Thoroughfare Gap to prevent reinforcements from reaching Jackson, while they concentrated their main army upon him and endeavored to crush him. In this, however, they failed. Gen. Longstreet reached the Gap and forced his way through before a sufficient number of the enemy had reached it to seriously dispute his passage.

On the morning of the 29th, Gen. Longstreet reached Manassas, about 10 o'clock, A. M., and found Gen. Jackson already engaged with the enemy. Forming on Jackson's right, with the Texas brigade near the centre, he pushed forward for a mile, but not finding any enemy the whole line was halted for the remainder of the day. In the evening a heavy fight took place between the enemy and Ewell's division, immediately on our left, which resulted in the repulse of the Yankees with heavy loss. At dark the order came for the centre to advance upon the enemy. In a moment the old 3rd and Texas brigade were under arms and off at double quick. At the distance of three-quarters of mile they came upon a brigade [John Hatch's division] of the enemy posted in a ravine, in an open field. The night was so dark that they were not discovered till they opened fire, which they did at the distance of about ten paces. The Texans returned it with fine effect and with a yell they closed upon them with the bayonet. How shall I describe the scene which followed? A hand to hand conflict is awful enough in day time, but amid pitch darkness it is absolutely diabolical. Bayonets, butts of muskets, and even fists were used freely. The yells of the victors, the shrieks of the wounded, and the groans of the dying, together with the rattle and flash of musketry in the darkness, and the unusual confusion of men running to and fro, made up a scene which beggars all description.

The Yankees stood for a few minutes but finally left with all haste leaving three stand of colors, one of which (24th N. Y.) was taken by the 18th. Our men followed them as long as they could tell which way they went, leaving the ground strewn with dead and wounded. The loss of the Brigade was trifling—only two being wounded in the 18th. while that of the enemy was very heavy both in the killed, wounded and prisoners. The Brigade lay upon the field that night, and early the next morning retook their original position.

This little affair which is entirely absorbed in the great battle of Manassas, and is consequently scarcely heard of, is certainly one of the most daring and brilliant of the series of fights which resulted in the great victory for our arms on the 30th inst.

The morning of the day which was to close with such a glorious victory to the South, was unusually calm and beautiful. Not a gun was heard, and all were led to believe that the Yankees had decamped and fallen back on his fortifications at Centreville. But about noon we were undeceived by the heavy firing on the left. The enemy, with a strong force, attacked Gen. Jackson's position to the left of the road and for several hours a furious fight continued. At about 2½ o'clock. P. M., Gen. Jackson repulsed the enemy and drove them before him a considerable distance. At that moment Gen. Longstreet ordered the right and centre to advance, which they did in handsome style, the Texas Brigade, as usual, leading the way. One would have thought they considered fighting the chiefest of delights. Now running, now walking at quick step, they rushed forward at a charge from the word go, all the time keeping up an unearthly yell. The enemy's pickets retired rapidly on their main body, while on rushed the Texans.

At about a mile they came upon the 10th N. Y. in the woods which fired only one volley and fled closely pursued. Suddenly they charged thro' the 5th N. Y. (Duryea's Zouaves) who awaited in fine order the attack, as soon as their front was cleared they poured a most destructive fire into the ranks of the 18th Ga., then a little in advance. At this first fire at least forty Georgians fell, but the remainder returned the fire with equal effect, and with a wild yell rushed on the foe with the bayonet, literally pushing them back and forcing them to retire down the hill. In their retreat the Zouaves suffered tremendously. One hundred and forty-four of them were counted the next day shot dead in the space of two hundred yards; besides, three or four times that number were wounded and fell into our hands. The colors of both these regiments fell into the hands of the Brigade; the 18th got that of the 10th N. Y.

After demolishing these two regiments, the brigade advanced upon a battery [Capt. Mark Kerns'] which was posted on the next hill and supported by a brigade [Col. Martin Hardin's] of the enemy. In this advance they had to pass through a furious cross fire of grape from two batteries besides the one in front, which told terribly upon their ranks. But nothing daunted, they rushed forward and took the battery, driving back its supports with great slaughter. At this point they saw they were in direct range with another battery of the enemy on the next hill, which was also supported by a large body of the enemy. Upon this they started to advance, but after firing a few rounds they found the enemy too strong for them, their ranks having already been reduced by about half their number; and supports not coming up in time, they were obliged to leave the work, and retired with their shattered ranks to the rear. In this last charge the battle flag of the 18th was shot down three times, within as many minutes, but was each time snatched up by the nearest man and daringly reared in the face of the foe. Nothing could exceed the gallantry with which the color-bearer, Sergeant Weems, bore his flag to the front, until he fell with two painful wounds, the colors being pierced by 17 balls and the staff by one.

The brigade drove the enemy about a mile, broke three lines of battle, and put them to flight, took one battery, and left the ground, for a considerable distance, literally red with Yankee uniforms. But they did not escape unharmed. The 18th alone, lost 128 in killed and wounded. Among the former we regret to record the names of Capt. Jarrett, mortally wounded, and Capt. S. V. Smith and Lt. E. T. Brown, killed. Braver men never drew a sword in defence of liberty.

POTOMAC.

NOT A STRAGGLER [5-22-63ASC]

On the morning after the great battle of Manassas Plains, Sergeant ——, Co. A, 16th Mississippi regiment, being bare-footed, straggled off from his command, traversing the battlefield in pursuit of a pair of shoes which some frightened Yankee might have thrown away in his fright. After looking for a time in vain, he at last saw a pretty good pair on the pedal extremities of a dead Yankee. He sat down at the feet of the dead Yankee, pulled off his shoes and put them on his own feet. Admiring the fit, and complimenting himself upon this addition to his searching abilities, he arose, and with knapsack on his back, and gun in hand, was about starting to overtake his regiment, when he observed coming towards him a small squadron of cavalry, all of whom, as it was drizzling rain, were wrapped in their large rubber or oil-cloth overcoats. It will be remembered that cavalry are frequently assigned to the duty of picking up the stragglers, and hence there is not good feeling between the infantry and the cavalry. As they approached Sergeant ——, the foremost one asked:

"What are you doing here, sir, away from your command?"

"That's none of your business," answered the Sergeant.

"You are a straggler, sir, and deserve the severest punishment."

"It's a lie, sir, I am not a straggler—I only left my regiment a few minutes ago, to hunt me a pair of shoes. I went all through the fight yesterday, and that's more than you say—for where were you yesterday when Gen. Stuart wanted your cavalry to charge the Yankees after we put 'em running? You were lying back in the pine thickets and couldn't be found; but to-day, when there is no danger, you can come out and charge other men with straggling.

The cavalry man, instead of getting mad, seemed to enjoy his raking over from the plucky little Sergeant, and as he rode on, laughed heartily at it. As the squadron was filing nearly past the Sergeant, one of them remarked: "Do you know who you are talking to?"

"Yes—to a cowardly Virginia cavalryman."

"No, sir—that's General Lee."

"What?"

"And his staff."

"Thunderation!"   With this exclamation the Sergeant pulled off his hat, and readjusted it over his eyes, struck a *double quick* on the straightest line for his regiment.

SPECIAL CORRESPONDENCE FROM PHILLIPS' LEGION
[DRAYTON'S BRIGADE, JONES'S DIVISION]
NEAR LEESBURG, VA., September 4, 1862 [9-21-62ASC]

To give you a full succinct account of our glorious campaign up to this hour, is more than I can attempt. No doubt the telegraph keeps you posted as to the outline of events.

The design of our Generals to transfer the campaign from near Richmond to the shores of the Potomac, and it may be to the territory of another State, was formed, I think, previous to the evacuation of Westover [Harrison's Landing] by McClellan. That event followed as effect followed cause; for when McClellan discovered that a large portion of the Richmond army was gone, and Richmond effectually defended from an attack by water, he was forced *ex necessitate*, to "change his base" again.

Upon the arrival of Longstreet with his army at Gordonsville, Jackson moved forward and crossed the Rapidan river near Orange C. H. Longstreet at the same time crossed near Raccoon Ford, and the two columns moved on simultaneously—the one to attack Pope, and the other to attack Burnside, if they would give battle. This they would not do. Burnside moved down the Rappahannock to Fredericksburg. Pope, the windy chevalier, author of the never-to-be-forgotten proclamation, skedaddled in the direction of Warrenton. Longstreet followed in Burnside's [Jesse Reno's] wake as though he intended to attack him at Fredericksburg, and encamped the night after he crossed the Rapidan, near the banks of the Rappahannock. Here he remained till the next morning, when his troops marched to the right about, and were soon far away.

As I am writing more to give you authentic details than any thing else, I will give you incidents as they occur to me in order of time.

Longstreet, while at the Rappahannock, sent a Captain of one of the Virginia Regiments to reconniotre the river, and discover where it was fordable. The courier who was to return with the dispatch, was young Witherspoon of the Kirkwood Rangers, from S. C. A diagram of the river and accompanying explanations, were given to him, and he dispatched to Gen. Longstreet. The Captain afterwards returned, and on his way to camp, found the courier lying in his blood near the road. He was still able to speak and told the Captain the following story: As he was riding along the road, a man, mounted and dressed in a Confederate uniform, came near to him, and while he was off his guard presented a pistol to his heart. He surrendered, was robbed of the diagram, and then shot and left by the bold spy.

Next morning the pickets of the 20th Georgia Regiment arrested a man who answered to the description given to the Virginia Captain, of this spy. He was searched and the papers found upon his person, which fully identified him. Among them was a dispatch purporting to be from Gen. Jackson to Longstreet, (a forgery). The evidence was so overwhelming and conclusive, that he was at once ordered to be hung, and in a little while he was in eternity. He said his name was Mason, and that he belonged to Pennsylvania.

The army moved rapidly forward, and on Friday [Aug. 23] was on the banks of the Rappahannock, much nearer its source. The enemy were on the other side of the river prepared to resist our passage across. All day Friday we could hear the cannonading, and on Saturday was fought the battle of Rappahannock.

At this point where we were, there were two fords. It seems to have been the object of our Generals to convey to the enemy the idea that we intended to cross here; consequently, an attack upon their batteries was determined on.

Early Sunday [Aug. 25] morning, ere the day had dawned, Gen. [T. F.] Drayton's brigade, Gen. Toombs, Col. Anderson's, and Gen. Evans', moved down to the two fords [Waterloo Bridge and Warrenton Sulphur Springs]. Drayton and Toombs supported the 4th Company of Washington Artillery, who attacked the lower battery, while Evans and Anderson supported the other companies of the same corps, lower down at the next ford. Col. [J. B.] Walton, who was in command of the Artillery, with the battery intended to attack the upper batteries of the enemy, moved down and ordered the guns unlimbered at about 600 yards from the enemy's. We lay in the woods behind him. As soon as the fog cleared away, our guns opened, and the enemy replied with spirit. The battery on our side fought against heavy odds, as there were four opposed to it, and two of its rifled guns without ammunition; but it fought nobly, firing 360 times to the minute, 90 rounds to each gun.

We suffered some in the fight from the enemy's shelling—our Legion losing two men in killed, and Slaughter's 51st regiment about six, with perhaps three times as many wounded. The battery suffered much more, losing 5 men killed, 15 wounded, one gun disabled, and 20 horses killed and wounded. I have heard from prisoners taken by us, that the Yankees suffered much more. Gen. Evans was opposed to them lower down the stream, and was unfortunately taken in by a decoy. The enemy had planted a battery on this side of the river, and then removed it. They may have kept two guns in it till next morning, when, after firing a few shots, they retired, with the supporting infantry. It was done; and when our men reached the works, the enemy opened upon them from so many guns that they found it impossible to retire even. Here they lay, however, and received a terrific shelling, in which many were killed and wounded. Our artillery, however, did brave work, dismounting several of the enemy's guns, two of which in one battery were disabled, and in killing many infantry. Had Gen. Evans detected the snare, we would have escaped without much damage.

Here Col. Tom Anderson distinguished himself, and he has done the same everywhere he has been in an engagement. He had a fine horse killed beside him. Were it not that he is a *Georgian*, I would predict his promotion; but such is the apparent prejudice of the Secretary of War against Georgia, and two other States that I wrote of, that I hardly dare to hope for his receiving his deserts.

While we were bombarding the enemy, Jackson was threatening him at Warrenton Springs, where there was a heavy firing all day Sunday [Aug. 25]. The next morning (Sunday), we were again on the march, of which you shall hear hereafter.

    Yours, &c.,   G. G. S.

P.S. Sept. 8th—The day after the battle of Saturday, there was heavy cannonading at Warrenton Springs, but no infantry engaged, till the battle at Thoroughfare Gap on Wednesday [Aug. 28]. The enemy came down upon this point with a division, to prevent our passing the Gap. Fortunately we were in time for them, and before they could get their batteries planted, the brave Georgians of Jones' Division were upon them. They eventually retreated, leaving 40 dead on the field, and at least four times that number wounded.

☆☆☆Maryland Campaign

After the success of the Second Manassas Campaign, Lee believed that the time was right for an invasion of Maryland, thinking that a similar victory on Northern soil might encourage foreign intervention on behalf of the Confederacy. Although much weakened by battle casualties and straggling, the Army of Northern Virginia crossed the Potomac River on September 4 and headed north. Dividing his forces, Lee sent Jackson to capture the 12,000 Federals garrisoned at Harper's Ferry, while Longstreet proceeded toward Hagerstown.

LETTER FROM V. A. S. P.

NEAR FREDERICK, MD., September 7, 1862 [9-20-62 SR]

At 3 p. m. Friday, we resumed our march towards Leesburg, through a most beautiful country. Either side of the verdant valley through which our hosts moved slowly along like a huge anaconda, was lined by blue hills and lofty peaks. The extensive corn fields, and vast plains of waving clover and grass bespeak the opulence and industry of the people. It is emphatically as pretty a country as I ever saw in the wild West, where Nature's beauty, unmarred by human industry, shines resplendent; or even among the hills and valleys and winding streams of Tennessee.

Our approach was welcomed by the fair daughters of those beautiful hills and dales, with waving handkerchiefs and every demonstration by which they could show their gratitude and joy on being freed from the tyranny of a military despotism they hate.

Leesburg is an ancient and pretty town of considerable size, numbering, perhaps, five thousand souls. Many of the buildings are stone, and comparatively few are wood. Every balcony on the main street, as we passed through, was crowded with beautiful women, smiling upon their deliverers and waving their white handkerchiefs, cheering us on. I have rarely seen more beautiful women. The sombre weeds of mourning were laid aside, and all appeared gay and joyous.

Here all our sick and barefooted men were left. When they were marched in they looked as large as a brigade. Many of them will doubtless join their companies soon.

Yesterday morning we crossed the Potomac. I imagine that to the ancient Israelite the crossing of the Jordan was not fraught with more interest than was the crossing of the Potomac to the conquering Southron. The first sight of its broad surface was hailed by a shout from the whole column that made the hills echo for miles around, and told how rejoiced were their hearts.

Here I witnessed a novel sight. Preparatory to wading the stream, (at this ford four hundred yards wide and two and a half feet deep,) the army, officers and all, bared their legs and waded over! While every variety, color and style of coat could be seen, there was perfect uniformity in the lower dress! At a distance it was an amusing sight. (I would advise my lady friends to shut their eyes while they read this paragraph!)

Many persons on the Maryland side hailed our approach with demonstrations of unfeigned joy. The young men say they had already been enrolled by Lincoln's officers, and were to have been drafted on the 16th of this month. All the people, however, are not Southern. Some in the little village of "Buckettown," [Buckeystown] (I believe this is the name,) refused to take Confederate money. Many ladies, however, gave us a cheering welcome. There are avowed Lincolnites in the neighborhood, whom we leave to the quiet enjoyment of their opinions. We are determined to show our superiority over the Federals in every respect, by not imitating their nefarious example. Their property, by a very strict order recently issued by Gen. Lee, is to be scrupulously respected. We are not allowed to burn a rail or pull a roasting ear. How different was the conduct of the vandals towards our people! How different, in fact, was the conduct of our own soldiers! Between the two armies, the country from Gordonsville or Orange C. H. to within a few miles of Leesburg, is a batten waste, an Arabian desolation. Scarcely a fence remains to mark the boundaries of once splendid estates—and in many instances the mansions of the wealthy sympathizer with the "rebellion" are stripped of everything valuable, and then laid in ruins. The clover and corn fields are worn smooth by being encamped upon. Such is not the case with Maryland. The Federals, to win over all of doubtful loyalty, have scrupulously respected private property—in this section, at least—and for the same reason Gen. Lee has issued stricter orders.

The country so far, is unsurpassed in beauty. The distant mountains, the blue fringed hills, and the vast green fields, stretching out like an ocean on either side, presenting a prospect, in my notion, unparalleled in beauty. It is a modern Eden, favored by Nature in every material respect.

Rumors are afloat in camp to the effect that Jackson met the Yankees near Frederick, yesterday, and captured several hundred prisoners. This needs confirmation, and I only give it as I received it. I heard heavy firing in the direction of Harper's Ferry late yesterday evening. Rumor says it was a battle between Gen. [William W.] Loring and the Federals. Nothing definite is known.

We will march from this point to Frederick, four miles distant. We will perhaps rest there a day or so, cook rations and prepare for some important onward movement. I do not understand the programme determined upon by Gen. Lee, but guess we will first clear Maryland of our hated tyrants, and then "carry the war into Africa." The Yankees should be made to taste some of the "bitter sweets" of their cherished scheme of hostile invasion. I believe we can disorganize their present demoralized army. If we press them hard, they cannot before cold weather organize another force. Everything points to a speedy and honorable peace. We hear that our forces have been victorious in the West—Tennessee and a portion of Kentucky are now in our possession. God grant it may be true!

Crossing those streams yesterday, made our feet extremely sore, in consequence of which, many, very many, gave out. I suffered the keenest agonies from my swollen and blistered feet; but my pride kept me from falling out. I did not want to set my boys such a bad example.

My townsman, Lieut. Iverson Butts, gave me some interesting details of the battle of Bristow Station, and the burning of the trains at Manassas Junction. At the Station the enemy were held in check for several hours, by a very small force. Jackson captured two or three long trains loaded with supplies for Pope's army. After filling their haversacks of everything they wanted, the trains were fired.

There was enough to have fed Gen. Jackson's army three months, but having very few wagons, he destroyed it all. Lt. Butts describes the scene as one of peculiar grander. The flames lit up the country for many miles around, and excited a good deal of apprehension in Washington.

You may expect to hear of wonders performed by the consolidated, veteran armies of Longstreet and Jackson.

V. A. S. P.

LETTER FROM SOLDIER JIM
[G. T. ANDERSON'S BRIGADE, JONES'S DIVISION]
FREDERICK CITY, MD., September 8, 1862 [9-21-62ASC]

Brother and myself are very well indeed, though we have been marching very hard in dust and warm weather. We are a good piece into Maryland, with an army not easy to be subdued. We have been marching one week to-day, seeking the enemy, but he is hard to find—though we are now invaders.

The boys are in fine spirits, and ready to go anywhere. We have possession of the Baltimore & Ohio Railroad. I find the country to be beautiful—magnificent. Many *secesh* are here, who show their gladness for our arrival. Many are volunteering and flocking to our army about here. We have halted a few days to recruit, wash our clothes, &c.

Corn crops are good—wheat in abundance—provisions much cheaper than in Virginia, and soldiers living pretty high.

We waded the Potomac, and all other streams. We had a hard time for provisions on the march; but the soldiers made the apples fly when passing orchards. Many times we were turned loose upon cornfields, where the cobs were left in heaps. The boys called themselves Jeff Davis' foot cavalry. Some few would straggle out, but knowing they were in an enemy's country, would soon straggle in again.

I expect hard fighting to do soon; but there has been so much of it recently, it is almost like eating a meals victuals.

I would be delighted to hear from Atlanta, though I know it is almost out of the question to get a letter from you. Give my love to all.

SOLDIER JIM.

P. S.—The ladies are very pretty here, especially those who show secession signals, which is the waving of their handkerchiefs.

On the morning of September 13, three Union soldiers near Frederick spotted some cigars wrapped in a piece of paper—the paper was a copy of Lee's orders for the Maryland Campaign, carelessly dropped by a staff officer. Gen. George McClellan, once again in command of the Army of the Potomac, now knew Lee's plans and quickly moved to destroy the scattered divisions of the Army of Northern Virginia.

PRIVATE LETTER,
COBB'S BRIGADE AND TOM COBB'S LEGION IN THE LATE BATTLES, CRAMPTON'S GAP AND THE CAPTURE OF HARPERS FERRY.

CHARLESTOWN, VA., September 16, 1862 [10-3-62ASC]

Dear Uncle: I write a few lines in great haste. I wrote to Uncle Tom from near Frederick City, Maryland, the day before we left there. We marched next day before we left there. We marched next day [Sept. 10] to Middletown, eight miles. In both places considerable "Secesh" sentiment was exhibited, though *too many* are Union. A citizen shot at Gen. [Col. Daniel H.] Hamilton going through the city. Everything was cheap—butter 10 cents a pound—but very few would take our money.

The next day we crossed over a part of the Blue Ridge and came into the valley leading down to the Potomac and Harper's Ferry. Here we remained two days. On Saturday, the 13th, Kershaw's brigade in our division, stormed Maryland Heights, overlooking Harper's Ferry, while our brigade, (Gen. Cobb's) was exposed to a terrible shelling, as usual.

But on Sunday evening, Sept. 14, we had a serious engagement. The enemy attempted to come into the Valley through a gap in the mountain, and two regiments of Mahone's brigade, on our side, brought on the action. They were pressed back by superior numbers, and reinforcements were sent for. Gen. Cobb sent the Legion and the 15th N. C., immediately, and the 16th and 24th Ga. soon afterwards. They commenced fighting on top of the ridge. Gen. Burnside [W. B. Franklin] commanded the Yankees. His greatly superior force drove our men back—it is supposed they had ten to one. They flanked our position; the centre gave way before overwhelming forces. The words of Gen. Cobb were that he left the Legion, 16th Ga., and 15th N. C., *surrounded by the enemy, but still fighting them gallantly, hand to hand.* Our forces fell back half a mile or a mile. The result as to casualties, so far as known, is as follows: The Legion (Cobb's) mustered only 22 men after the fight. Only 3 commissioned officers escaped, and two of those were wounded. All that was left of the infantry of Cobb's Legion, was under command of a 3rd Lieutenant, the only commissioned officer who escaped. Those supposed or at most known to be killed, are Lt. Col. [J. M.] Lamar, Capt. [Thomas B.] Cox, Capt. [J. B.] Lamar, 1st Lieut. [T. W.] Sims, Company A; Lieut. [Cadmus] Amoss, in our Company, (Stephens Rifles, Capt. L. J. Glenn,) and many wounded. Capt. Liddell was shot through the face severely, when last seen; Lieut. [Aaron] Grier was taken prisoner, supposed to be wounded; Lieut. Amoss killed.

In our company, Norman Adams and Private McKee, were shot dead, as seen. Doc. Marshall escaped, but died of his wounds in a few hours. Only five who went into the battle escaped; these were W. W. Berry, D. Bunt, J. D. Eckles, J. W. Wesley, and Serg't Mark Brown. The wounded who escaped were M. Davis, E. Mason, J. L. Philips, A. W. Weaver, J. H. Steward, F. M. Leverett, W. D. Reagin, G. W. Pierce, W. A. Ragsdale, H. Jones, and D. B. Chupp. Of course, as the enemy held the battle-field, we know not who else was killed or wounded. Very probably Abb Chewning went in the fight and is probably a prisoner. I was somewhat exposed, but did not get hurt. We were engaged all that night and next day dressing the wounded.

The whole brigade suffered severely. Capt. [Nathaniel] Reader of the Flint Hill Greys, was killed; Gen. Cobb and Staff escaped. It was a *terrible fight.*

The next day (yesterday), our forces had surrounded Harper's Ferry, and after a few hours bombardment, the Yankees surrendered. Col. [Dixon] Miles, commanding them was killed. The prisoners taken are estimated from 10 to 15,000, and no mistake, besides 60 fine large guns, near 2,000 fine horses, 3,000 negroes, and large quantities of Commissary stores. Our division passed through Harper's Ferry last night. It is now camped in a league of this place. I came on here last night and have been here since. Charlestown is eight miles from the Ferry, and the C. H. of Jefferson county, remarkable as the place where John Brown was hung. The citizens are all "secesh." Our wounded have been brought here. I was treated to some nice breakfast this morning gratis.

I forgot to mention that two pieces of Cobb's Legion (Artillery), assisted in reducing Harper's Ferry, and that one howitzer was lost in the action of Sunday [at Crampton's Gap], by the horses running away and breaking a wheel. Our cavalry was in a fight a day or two ago, and Colonel [P. M. B.] Young was wounded; Lt. Marshall from Albany, killed, and other casualties. No one killed in the Fulton Dragoons, I was informed.

But oh! what a terrible sacrifice! Dr. Herron is left behind with sick, and may be a prisoner. I must close now.

Yours as ever,   J. Hardman.

☆ ☆ ☆ Battle of Sharpsburg

After the Federals broke through the mountain passes on September 14, Lee considered retreating to Virginia. But after the capitulation of the Harper's Ferry garrison on September 15, he decided to stay in Maryland and fight. The following day, Lee took up a defensive position along Antietam Creek near Sharpsburg. The next day, Wednesday, September 17, 1862, was the bloodiest single day of the war.

PRIVATE LETTER, ELEVENTH GEORGIA REGIMENT
[ANDERSON'S BRIGADE, JONES'S DIVISION]
NEAR MARTINSBURG, VA., September 23, 1862 [10-14-62AWCS]

Since I last wrote you I have waded the Potomac three different times, marched for nearly a week without drawing a thing from the Commissary—in fact I have almost lived on apples, corn and a few Irish potatoes. Besides this, I have taken an active part in one of the bloodiest battles ever known.

Our Captain being absent I have to command our Company. We had been on a detail for several days previous to the fight.

The day of the fight we crossed the Potomac and endeavored to join our command, but meeting an aid of Gen. Jones, we were carried over to Gen. Toombs and placed in line of battle under him. The enemy advanced on us in this position. By throwing out skirmishers and reinforcing them, we drove them back by killing some of them. They then changed their movement by a flank, and came upon the centre of the line; our line in this part of the line fled, some of them Georgians too, and left our cannon (the First South Carolina battery) entirely undefended. We, five companies of the 11th, the 17th and 15th regiments, Georgians, were run (not double-quicked) to meet the enemy powerful in numbers and just victorious. The enemy run in line with the battery they had taken, and stood bidding us defiance. As soon as we got in line, we opened fire upon them. They stood and fought us very bravely for a while. We were sheltered by a fence and embankment, so much so that we mowed them down, and they scarcely harmed us. At length some of the boys killed their flagbearer, another seized it and shared the same fate—and another who fell the same way. The enemy then planted their colors and stood on each side of it, leaving an opening in their lines. Their lines were broken so badly that they ran and we after them, with such yelling you never heard—I with the rest.

This incident was the happiest or rather the proudest of my life. We drove them from their position, retaking our cannon and occupying their position. They reinforced but were repulsed—they reinforced again, but met the same fate; our loss very small, theirs truly great, because we had a position that saved us. Our Regiment lost none killed, ten wounded. The other two regiments lost some few; several prisoners were captured. We gained a glorious victory. To tell the truth we saved the whole of the right wing of our army—we were in the centre. You will see in some of the papers an account of the fight at Sharpsburg, Maryland.

Our campaign has been the most active ever known. For not two weeks have I been at any time out of the hearing of cannon since Spring, still the war seems not to be nearer its close than when it began. Let us, however, hope for the best. I do not like Maryland.

J. W. M.

LETTER FROM SOLDIER JIM
CAMP NEAR MARTINSBURG, VA., September 22, 1862 [10-5-62ASC]

After several weeks hard marching and fighting, we are again quiet on the Virginia side of the Potomac. Brother D. and myself are well. We were in two hard fought battles in Maryland, and came through safe, though many of our boys were slain.

The people in that portion of Maryland through which we marched, were principally Union, though we found some good secessionists; but I tell you, the women looked too sour for me to stay on that side of the branch, and I was glad when we were ordered back to old Virginia—the good old "Mother of States;" and when I got back on this side I felt more like I was at home.

In the battle of Sharpsburg we fought all day long. We fell back once and gave the enemy part of the battle-field, but drove them back again and retook our position. They fought us hard, but we whipped them every time. The fight lasted till one hour after-night, and we drove them nearly off the mountain. The next morning they came with a flag of truce to bury their dead—but the Confederate Army was not there. We had left and came towards Williamsport [Shepardstown].

When we crossed to this side Jackson fixed his traps, and the enemy came on and crossed about four brigades, when he closed in on both sides. I learn that he captured about 500 of them, but killed and drowned the greater portion. The four brigades were completely destroyed.

I cannot give the casualties in our regiment in the late battle—though they are not numerous. The wounded in the Atlanta Grays were Joseph Yarboro and James Kirksey, slightly. It appears that the Old 8th is the most fortunate in the service. Our brigade commanded by Col. G. T. Anderson, did some of the prettiest fighting on the field—such at least is said to be the case by several of our commanding Generals. We met the enemy first and completely routed them, running them for a mile, when Gen. Stuart followed after and ordered us back as the Yankees were in large force on both sides of us.

I hope the time will come when I shall be relieved of this kind of life, though fighting has become almost as common as eating.

SOLDIER JIM.

LETTER FROM V. A. S. P.
BIVOUAC IN THE FIELD, VA., September 22, 1862 [10-1-62SR]

If I had paper and time I could occupy one side of your journal in detailing exciting incidents of this most extraordinary campaign, battles, marches, &c., but must content myself with giving your readers the most prominent and interesting facts connected with my brigade. Other correspondents must take thought for their respective regiments.

As we passed through the beautiful city of Hagerstown on Monday night, the clock told the hour of twelve. Daylight found us near Sharpsburg, the scene of the last bloody battle between the Federals and Confederates. We were assigned a position on a creek a mile east of the town, and were proceeding thither when the Fifteenth and Seventeenth were ordered back several miles to take the Williamsport road, to protect wagon trains. Thirty or forty wagons were captured early in the morning [of Sept. 15] by Yankee cavalry [commanded by Col. Grimes Davis as they escaped the Harper's Ferry debacle]. Our Quartermaster, Captain [B. H.] Mathis, and several of his teamsters, were captured, but the Captain and one or two of the men made their escape. Joe Swain, of my company, is still in their hands.

We reached Williamsport and crossed the river by sunset, without incident, though we were once drawn up in line of battle to repulse an attack of cavalry, which proved to be a portion of Gen. Stuart's. Tuesday we marched down the river to Shepardstown, which we found full of our wounded and sick. The ladies greeted us by every demonstration of welcome, which showed them to be the best Secessionists.

By 9 a. m. Wednesday we were once more in Maryland and within sound of battle, to which we hurried as fast as our sore feet and worn out condition would allow us. We soon saw evidences of the bloody work of death progressing, for the road was lined by the wounded in ambulances, on litters, and limping along, some supported by friends, and others leaning on sticks.

By eleven we entered the field. As we filed through an open place, the enemy hurled his terrible shells at us, one of them bursting in a neighboring barn, which was soon in flames. While we lay concealed in a corn field, waiting for Gen. Toombs to give us a place, a shell exploded in the Fifteenth Georgia, killing the color-bearer, tearing the colors to pieces, and wounding three or four.

Gen. Toombs posted us—the Seventeenth, Fifteenth and Eleventh regiments—behind a stone wall, upon a hill, with high ground in our rear, where the Washington Artillery, (Captain Rosser's old company,) took position. Upon our right and left were large corn fields, and ground much higher than that which we occupied, while all was open in front. About four hundred yards in front was a creek, and on our right (in front) was a considerable body of timber lining deep ravines.

Here I will leave the regiment for a time, while I tell you what the Second—the glorious "Little Second"—and the Twentieth did, under the leadership of our heroic Colonel. Early in the morning, Col. Benning was ordered to hold a bridge, which he did against fearful odds, for five hours. The enemy advanced in heavy columns against this little force, not numbering more than two hundred, or two fifty. The steady courage and accurate firing of the men successfully repulsed every onset, until their ammunition was expended. Impatiently they waited for reinforcements, but none came. Lieut. Col. [William R.] Holmes, who had showed conspicuous courage throughout the affair, mounted his horse to go for reinforcements, when he was killed. Col. Benning then determined to retire, which he did in good order, with slight loss. The enemy seemed satisfied with gaining the bridge, for which they had so long contended, and did not pursue. Benning retired to a good position, further back than ours, then took command where Gen. Toombs placed us. I have not obtained any further particulars as to loss &c.

About 1 p. m., we discovered three large columns advancing beyond the creek—one into the cornfield on our left, one against our position, and one on our right. They made a very handsome display. For some time there was some apprehension for our right and left flanks, which we feared were not sufficiently strong. On they came in solid phalanxes, threatening to carry everything before them by the weight and discipline of their columns. When the first column had reached the *right* place, a battery upon our left having the range accurately, and the "Washington Artillery" on the hills to our rear, let them have a few discharges of grape and shell, which broke their solid body, and caused a panic. I never witnessed such a sight. The centre first gave way, then fled, communicating the panic to the whole column. The hills for hundreds of yards were black with the flying Federals, not in platoons, companies or regiments, but in a confused mass. Those on our right were in a like manner broken and repulsed. Those in our immediate front, who had driven in our skirmishers, also retired, and everything on the vast fields overlooked by our position, became as quiet as a Quaker village on a Sabbath day. Occasionally, however, this reign of quiet was broken by artillery practice across the hills.

At 4 o'clock Gen. [Maxey] Gregg's S. C. Brigade relieved us, and we were ordered to the rear to rest. At this juncture, I witnessed even a grander sight than the one I have just attempted to describe. The hills east of the town, on both sides of the creek, are in cultivation. The west side of the creek was occupied by [James L.] Kemper's Brigade (of Virginians). The ground was high, and mostly level east of the town for several hundred yards, where it makes a rapid or steep decent into a beautiful valley of the creek. Towards this position four large solid columns of the enemy advanced in most splendid style. Shells from our batteries bursted in their lines, broke them, leaving dead and wounded on the ground, and covering the line in dust and smoke; but still, on they came.

They attacked and drove Kemper's Brigade from the field, with a slight loss, however, to the Virginians. We were ordered forward at a double-quick, and reached the point occupied by a battery before the enemy had gained the road. What a sight! A large, splendidly equipped brigade of Yankees in undisputed possession of the field, and our battery deserted! Colonel Benning posted us in the road behind a plank fence facing the enemy, and the ball opened. The 15th and a portion of the 50th [Georgia], met a large force a little to our right, advancing through a corn field.

The first few shots were too low, but very soon the boys got the exact range, when they did a fearful work with the Yanks. Their colors fell three times, and their lines melted away alarmingly fast. They stood our fire about ten minutes, when they began to retire in a pretty good order, then to run. We charged and drove them about six hundred yards. Here they rallied behind a stone fence, and we stopped the pursuit. Our rifles were ordered forward to a good position and picked off those that exposed themselves, until the enemy were finally routed. Our force numbered not more than 300 or 400.

Col. William T. Millican led on the Fifteenth in a manner which will make his name live in the hearts and memories of our people. With sword drawn, he advanced ten paces before the colors, and told his men to follow. Without haste or confusion, he led them to a stone fence within two hundred yards of the enemy, and contributed very largely to the final rout of the enemy. He was shot through the breast, and died in a short time after. For coolness and daring, he had not a superior in our army. Few Colonels has fully possessed the love and confidence of their men.

I must remark the perfect indifference of every man to danger. While the battle raged, the boys were seen to pick up canteens, blankets, swords, pistols, etc.; while those who were bare-footed, supplied themselves with boots and shoes. I am wearing the best boots I have yet seen, which I bought from one of the boys half hour after he had pulled them off a dead Yankee. This looks wrong, to allow the dead to be robbed of boots or shoes; but, my good Georgia friends, don't shudder at such a barbarian practice. Our noble boys were bare-footed, in a rocky country, and the dead had no use for shoes. It would be a waste to allow good shoes, so much needed, to be buried with the dead, even if they are Confederates.

Yesterday I passed the grave of Col. Marcellus Douglass, of the 13th Georgia, acting Brigadier when killed. He received the fatal wound in the battle of Sharpsburg, Wednesday, Sept. 17th, while gallantly and skillfully managing Lawton's Brigade. Col. Douglass was gaining an enviable position in the army, and had for some time been accounted a superior military man. In his death Georgia has lost one of her bright military representatives. He is properly called our "second Bartow."

I am told that Capt. Arnold, of whom I have frequently spoken, was mortally wounded in the same great battle. I have been unable to find the 6th Georgia, or any one belonging to it, to ascertain the truth of it. One of his men told me, before we reached the battle field, that he saw Capt. Arnold fall, and believed him mortally wounded. I yet hoped he was mistaken, and that one so truly gallant and skillful—one so talented and beloved by his command and all who knew him, yet lives to bless and honor the old State for whom he has fought so bravely. If Arnold was killed, Hancock county will be shrouded in mourning for years to come—in the hearts of her citizens will a trio of the noblest of young men hold a place: and proud monuments will be erected to perpetuate their names to future generations. Nay, a fourth will be added. It will be their pride to recount the deeds of bravery and patriotism; and cite the names of Capt. Arnold, Lieuts. Reid and Jordan, and Geo. F. Lewis, as worthy of imitation.

Capt. Robert A. Waller, commanding the 8th Florida Regiment, was killed. Capt. Waller is a citizen of Decatur county. He led the regiment into the fight in a brave and skillful manner. [Roger A.] Pryor's brigade fought well, while the Yankees, as a general thing, were easily repulsed.

During the engagement Gen. Toombs was in the hottest part of the field, and displayed, besides courage, consummate skill in choosing positions for his division [brigade]. Colonel Benning's heroic bearing throughout cannot be excelled.

On Thursday night Gen. Lee fell back across the river. The movement was effected in perfect order, and with trifling loss. The enemy had been engaged all day in changing his position, which rendered a similar movement necessary on our part. I hear some firing this morning but cannot give any idea of what is next on docket.

V. A. S. P.

THE EIGHTEENTH GEORGIA AND THE TEXAS BRIGADE
IN THE BATTLE OF SHARPSBURG
[WOFFORD'S BRIGADE, HOOD'S DIVISION]
CAMP NEAR MARTINSBURG, VA., September 23, 1862 [10-11-62ASC]

The summer campaign of the Army of the Potomac may now be regarded as at an end, and a more active one can scarcely be found in the history of wars.

The army, which in the late spring lay besieged around the city of Richmond, now encamps upon the banks of the Potomac, having seen the last remnant of an invading army across the river, and Virginia once more free from the hostile tread of the foe. During this campaign two attempts upon the city of Richmond have been defeated. This grand army of McClellan, said to be the best appointed and best equipped in the world, has been driven from its trenches and strong fortifications to a shelter under the guns of the Yankee fleet, in James river. The forces of Pope and McClellan have been beaten at Manassas, and driven back to their strong fortifications around Washington. And lastly, the combined forces of McClellan, Pope, and Burnside, have suffered a serious defeat at Sharpsburg, Maryland. The whole of the Western Virginia army has been captured at Harper's Ferry; some thirteen thousand prisoners, three thousand negroes, and an immense amount of arms and army stores fell into our hands at that place, besides vast quantities captured at other places, or destroyed by the enemy to prevent capture. Besides all this, communication between Washington and Ohio has been effectually cut off by the destruction of numerous bridges, and canal locks and dams, on the Baltimore & Ohio R. R., and the Chesapeake & Ohio canal.

Early on the morning of the 14th Gen. Longstreet took up his line of march from Hagerstown towards the Potomac, which he aimed to cross at Shepardstown. On the same morning Gen. D. H. Hill, whose small division had been left to hold the gap through the Blue Ridge, was attacked by an immensely superior force of the enemy. Fighting continued all day, our men disputing most manfully every inch of ground, but in the evening it became apparent that Hill would not be able to hold the gaps [Turner's and Fox's], and a part of Longstreet's forces, the Texas brigade among them, was sent to his support. They arrived at the top of the mountain at dark and took a position so near the enemy's lines that they could be heard talking, expecting to have a hot time on the return of daylight. But our trains having passed, the troops were ordered to follow, and before daylight the whole army was again en route for the Shepherdstown ford.

The enemy pursued closely, hoping to overtake and beat our forces before they could be concentrated in a body strong enough to meet. The next morning Gen. Lee halted at Sharpsburg and took up position between the town and the Antietam river, to await the arrival of the enemy. An hour afterwards, sharp picket firing announced the arrival of their advance guard at the bridge.

The whole of that day and the next was spent in skirmishing and cannonading at long range. Late the next evening it was ascertained that the enemy was moving large bodies of troops to our left, endeavoring to turn that flank. Quickly the old 3rd [Evander Law's] and Texas Brigades were wheeled into line to receive them. Just at dark a sharp skirmish occurred, which lasted till considerably in the night, when both parties ceased firing by mutual consent, to renew it again on the return of daylight. During the night the Texas Brigade was withdrawn to an adjacent woods to cook rations, having been out for some days, a Tennessee Brigade [James J. Archer's] taking its place. At daylight the next morning the battle opened in earnest and raged with fury till 7 A. M., when the enemy, having been reinforced, began to drive the Louisianians [and Virginians] before them slowly. Seeing this, Gen. Hood brought forward his division and sent the Texans in on their old ground. They drove the Yankees back most gallantly for a considerable distance, leaving the ground darkened with their carcasses. The enemy fell back through a cornfield, the Texans following—then thro' an open field into the woods. Here their retreating line suddenly unmasked a fresh line of troops and several batteries, both of which immediately opened their already thin ranks with minie and grape. Unfortunately, in their advance, the different regiments had been compelled to leave wide intervals between each other, in order to cover the enemy's front. This greatly weakened their line and disconcerted the movements of the Brigade. With this broken line, however, they drove the enemy till they retired behind a continuous line of much greater length of fresh troops, which immediately commenced flanking our Brigade on both sides. Seeing this, each Colonel with one consent began to fall back slowly.

The 18th had advanced to within a few yards of the enemy's battery which had been playing on its ranks with terrible effect, and had silenced the guns, when the long dark line of the enemy was seen sweeping round to its left, threatening to cut it off. Two-thirds of its men had already fallen, but the rest undaunted still continued to advance and pour a deadly fire into the enemy in their front. When ordered to retire they did so, continuing to fire upon the line that was sweeping round to outflank them. The shattered remnant of the Brigade was reformed in the woods, but for want of support, the enemy outnumbering them by at least ten to one, they were ordered to retire further. The enemy gained ground for a short time, but fresh troops coming up, they were driven back again to their original position, leaving hundreds of their dead and wounded in our hands. The Texas Brigade, much shattered, reformed and took its original position, ready to renew the conflict.

Thus ended the fight in the hardest contested part of the field. The enemy fought his best troops, (Porter's regulars) [actually Hooker's First and J. F. K. Mansfield's Twelfth Corps] and outnumbered us by at least four or five to one. At night both sides slept on their original ground, and the next day exchanged flags of truce to bury their dead, and recover their wounded. The 18th carried into the fight 176 men and lost 101 in killed, wounded and missing. Most of the missing were killed, or wounded and left behind the enemy's lines. Lieuts. T. C. Underwood, and J. M. D. Cleveland, while gallantly leading Company K on to the battery, fell, supposed to be killed dead. Capts. J. A. Crawford, and G. W. Maddox, received serious wounds.

Col. W. T. Wofford commanded the brigade during the fight, and acted with great coolness and decision. Lieut.-Col. H. G. Ruff commanded the 18th, and as usual behaved himself well. Every officer and man acted with the most distinguished coolness and bravery.

As to the general result of the bloody battle of Sharpsburg, I would add that to the right and left of the point where the Texas and Louisiana brigades fought, our forces drove the enemy back a considerable distance. The enemy claim a drawn battle, but they clearly suffered a defeat, since they were the attacking party and were repulsed at every point.

POTOMAC.

PRIVATE LETTER,
FIFTEENTH ALABAMA AT SHARPSBURG—DESPERATE FIGHTING
[WALKER'S BRIGADE, LAWTON'S DIVISION]
WINCHESTER, VA., September 25, 1862 [10-6-61CS]

As it was, we flogged them and left upon the battle field multitudes of their dead. It was worse than Manassas in slaughter to them. The bodies were lying across one another and piled up in groups of from five or six, and behind some trees twelve and fourteen bodies laid in a pile together. It was the hardest, most terrific and stubbornly contested battle of this war. The Yankees fought like devils. Our brigade was the first to fire a shot. We were placed in position the night before, and laid all night in line of battle, and at daylight next morning were attacked. We drove back three brigades of them, and fired away all of our ammunition and all we could get from the wounded. We were separated from our old beloved commander, Jackson, that day and placed in the centre under D. H. Hill; Jackson with another portion of his corps was on our extreme left, where he drove the enemy under McClellan in person two miles with great slaughter. After using up all our ammunition, we asked to retire and fill our cartridge boxes, but Gen. Hill would not let us do so; ordered us to hold the position, without a single cartridge, and to fight them with rocks! We were in an open field, exposed to a cross-fire of artillery and a front fire of small arms, and had to like and take it. At Manassas I got the prize of a Yankee sword and pistol. We whipped the three, McClellan, Pope and Burnside, combined, at Sharpsburg on the 17th.

We entered Maryland in the strongest Union part, and met a cold reception, of course. We met some secessionists, but very few, except the *ladies*, God bless them, who are for us largely in the majority. When we reached Frederick City they met our ragged, dirty boys in the streets and carried them to their houses and fed them with nice things, and even carried fruit into the streets to every Southern soldier they could find.

Our baggage wagons ever since we left the Rapidan have been left in the rear—can get no clothes. This place is cleaned out. I had to pay five cents a sheet for this paper, and scarce at that. The country around Fairfax, Centreville and Manassas, has been completely devastated. One can get on a high hill and see for miles around bare fields, with not a tree or any sign of civilization; the farm houses are all deserted, and everything as silent as the grave.

At Manassas we passed our winter quarters. The Yankees had destroyed nearly all the houses, turning them into firewood, which was cut and neatly piled up.

***.

LETTER FROM TOUT LE MONDE

NEAR MARTINSBURG, VA., September 26, 1862 [10-5-62SR]

On last Monday week, at 12½ A.M., our brigade marched from the city of Hagerstown, where I wrote you last, down to Sharpsburg, to take its place in line of battle. Arriving at the bridge over the Antietam river, a mile below the town, were the 20th and 2d Georgia—stationed to guard the passage there, anticipating an attack to force that point, in order to turn our right flank, which rested there, and which guarded our retreat across the Potomac, at Sheperdstown ford, three miles westward. A few pickets were thrown across the river from the Twentieth Georgia, to act in conjunction with the vidette.

Nothing happened that day. Some little sharp shooting occurred next day [Sept. 16] between the pickets and the enemy's scouts reconnoitering our position. Fresh orders were sent to hold the point at all hazards, should an attack be made along the whole line. Neither our regiment nor the Twentieth were relieved, and we prepared the place the best way possible to hold it, by throwing up a very inferior breastwork of rails, hardly to be relied upon against minie balls and nothing against shells.

In the evening considerable cannonading occurred along the whole line. At our point we could plainly see the enemy maneuvering across the stream, from the top of a tall oak. A battery from a high hill behind us annoyed them very much, and kept the blue coats scudding and dodging about considerably, but they did not venture to advance that day. Our little band kept steadily and cool, watching the first evidence of an assault, but they did not choose to approach.

The Second Georgia number, officers and all, 105, the Twentieth, probably 250 men. The Second Georgia was on the right, at a bend of the creek, where the bluff rose steep and high on our side. Still further to the right was Drayton's brigade, holding a much more favorable position for defense, being screened by a dense wood on the side of a steep hill. In the night some picket firing occurred, and early on Wednesday morning, the heavy boom of Jackson's guns were heard away to the extreme left. It grew heavier and heavier, sometimes seeming to approach and then to recede. Finally, the heavy roll of musketry set in, and the battle din became furious and terrible. Still our little band stood firm in the face of Burnside's host, preparing to advance at that point.

Large bodies of Yankees were seen moving in brigades directly in front of this bridge, and it was quickly seen that it was their aim to turn our right at this point. Jackson had begun to make them give way on the left, and to retrieve the ill fortune something must be done. This was our weak point, and the enemy seemed to discover it. About 10 A. M. our pickets came in and the skirmishers of the enemy were seen advancing over a hill in front, and a long line in battle array stretched out further right, partly confronting Gen. Drayton's command. It was thought a furious attack would be made all along, but the advance continued only from the forces in our front near the bridge. On they came, occasionally pouring a volley into the trees and rails behind which our men were screened, but not a gun fired from our side. Having approached to the water's edge one hundred paces distant on the opposite side of the river, the order to fire was given. Every man took deliberate aim, and it seemed a foe fell to every gun. The enemy faltered, but stood. A second fire and he broke in disorder across the hill. In a few moments a steady line of new troops came on to the same spot, and the same terrible fire, and they gave way in confusion. The plan seemed impracticable. A battery was moved up to enfilade this point, and at the same time that new forces were sent up in front, five guns opened with a most earnest and terrible fire upon this unswerving band, who, in spite of the rain of shot and shell, not *one* quivered. Some were struck down, others hobbled away through the hail storm wounded, but what remained of them stood as firm as rocks. I do not believe the world ever witnessed more carnage.

Under the heavy fire from the battery the enemy continued to advance, pouring in volley after volley of minie balls. Colonel Holmes, amidst the fire, passed back and forth cheering the men in hopes that he might hold out till reinforcements should arrive. Vain hope! None ever came. A part of Drayton's brigade had given way on the right under a fire of grape directed against them, leaving the point clear for our little band to be flanked. But to the last they stood until every cartridge was gone. Three hours the point had been held against 5,000 assailants. Col. Holmes seeing that no reinforcements would come, and he could hold it no longer without a round of ammunition, started to send for them. At this point he fell, shot dead instantly, and never breathed a word again. The regiment then moved out in good order under the command of Maj. [Skidmore] Harris. A hail storm of grape was poured into them with little damage. So few were the numbers seen by the enemy to move out, he could not believe the number had kept him at bay so long, and for a half hour afterwards continued to pour grape, cannon shot and minie balls into the place. Not a soldier was sent to our aid, and until we had gone back a mile none was seen. Here the 15th and 17th Georgia, the remainder of Gen. Toombs' brigade, came up to shelter our retreat. Forty-four of the 2nd Georgia had fallen, among them seven officers, out of eighteen. If the cowardly enemy had come immediately across, the right might have been turned and our army lost. At least the egress for retreat would have been cut off. At their first appearance one of our batteries, which in all probability had been useless when we needed them at the bridge to engage the enemy's guns, now opened on the advancing lines. The fire was a good one and the blue coats scattered like partridges over the ploughed ground. At this point the enemy advanced cautiously again, but directed a body, consisting of two brigades, to flank this battery. Approaching under the cover of some hills this force [Brig. Gen. Isaac Peace Rodman's] approached so near the guns that ere the pieces could be turned upon them the gunners were forced to fly. Happily for us, A. P. Hill's whole force came up on the right. The 15th and 17th Georgia were sent towards the centre to take position, then unaware that the enemy had captured our guns. Col. Benning, in command of the brigade, (Gen. Toombs' division) having learned this, ordered the two regiments forward, and charging boldly up the hill under a heavy fire compelled the enemy to give way in disorder. He fell back behind a stone fence and rallied, but closely pursued by our Georgians, was quickly dislodged with great loss. Many of them were cut down in their attempt to get away, for I afterwards saw this field dotted with the infernal Hessians.

The battle was a random one from then until darkness closed the scene, but the enemy was not forced back across the river. On Thursday nothing but sharpshooting occurred. We took many of the Yankee wounded prisoners, who told us that Burnside had a strong force there. So powerful were the enemy found to be that our generals deemed it advisable to re-cross the Potomac. At night we prepared to go. The enemy must have expected it; for almost on the eve of starting, while Gen. Toombs was awaiting orders to move, he was approached by several men. He asked who they were. They answered, "Massachusetts men," and fired on him. They fled immediately, but left the Gen. wounded badly in the hand. We crossed the Potomac safely, losing only a few wagons, and thus ended our *pop call* in Maryland. The enemy may truly claim a victory; at least I am willing to accede it, but it was a most ruinous one. 8,700 prisoners besides 63 pieces of artillery, ordnance stores, and provisions in abundance were the fruits of our trip. What the enemy made by claiming the battle field after a drawn fight will hardly pay them. I hate, myself, more the effect of having to fall back, and think the attempt at an invasion was premature. Our friends then will lose confidence in us, but if they examine the battle-field they cannot doubt our capacity to fight Yankees when not overpowered. In attempting too, to follow us they were defeated again, and now everything is at a stand still, one watching the other. What further is on the tapis the future alone can disclose. The nights are getting airy, very airy, and if haste is not made the campaign must close without further struggle. The mandates of winter are imperative. The Fall weather is very beautiful, but that season has not yet began to throw the wreath of summer to gold upon the trees.

TOUT LE MONDE.

P. S. I leave others to give details of the fight, on the left of which I have learned but little.

M.

Official casualties for the battle of Sharpsburg or Antietam were: Federals, 2,010 killed, 9,416 wounded, and 1,043 missing for a total of 12,469; Confederates estimated at 2,700 killed, 9,024 wounded, and 2,000 missing for a total of 13,724.

LETTER FROM COBB'S LEGION,
ONE CHAPTER IN A SOLDIER'S PRISON EXPERIENCE [10-28-62AWCS]

Since writing last, I have marched 200 miles—forded five different rivers; one of which, was several hundred yards wide, and almost swimming. On this long march, over 2,000 prisoners were taken from the stragglers that had lagged behind their respective regiments. I was unwell but kept up with my brigade, (Cobb's) and was in the battle of South Mountain, where we suffered a total defeat.

We had marched twelve or fifteen days across rivers and over mountains and were nearly exhausted, when we were ordered to "double-quick" five miles to the battle ground. And here Cobb's brigade, *minus* stragglers, had to meet a whole division [corps] of the enemy strongly posted behind trees and rocks, with their right and left wing extending around our right and left flank; enabling them to fight us in front and enfilade both our wings at the same time! In our position, trees and rocks were no protection. All at once the enemy turned loose upon us a terrific storm of shot, shell, and grape from every quarter; the air was filled with bursting shells, grape and whizzing minies, while every mountain crag was enveloped in smoke, fire and thunder; nothing mortal could stand the shock. In thirty minutes Cobb's noble brigade was cut to pieces. My company [E] officers from the Captain down to the lowest Corporal, were all killed or wounded.

I was so completely exhausted when the battle ended, that I could scarcely walk; but I made an effort to get up the mountain, while they were shooting at me from three different directions; but fortunately, they did not kill me, though my haversack was shot from off my back, and balls grazed a hand and leg. After walking some fifty yards I surrendered.

My foes treated me well; divided their provisions with me to the last crumb, and allowed me to talk as saucily as I pleased. My good fortune, however, soon turned; I was taken to Fort Delaware, where I fell into the hands of a pack of scoundrel Dutch—the *meanest* of the mean of our enemies. I was here kept confined in a lot for three weeks, and got for my breakfast, when lucky in grabbing a cold cup of coffee and three crackers! For supper, a small piece of bread and a wretched cup of soup. There were over 2,000 of us here, and only 300 or 400 could eat at once! We were divided into squads of one hundred each, and only a certain number allowed to go into the eating house at once. At the door it was rush, shove, push, from morn till night; and though I had my name enrolled in fourteen different squads, came near starving. Water too was scarce, and sometimes sold at five dollars per drink!

Man never forgets the almighty dollar till his eyes are closed in death. A great speculation was kept up among the prisoners. If I could have commanded five dollars in silver, I would have made a little Confederate fortune; but I only had two dollars Confederate, which I exchanged for a quarter in silver, and with this small capital in specie, made fourteen dollars with but little effort. For meanness, some of our Southern soldiers can match the Yankee Dutch. I was almost afraid to shut my eyes, for fear that I might awake, minus the rags that covered me; for we had many thieves among us. Almost every hour in the day, some one was rode on a rail for pilfering; and one fellow was actually stabbed and killed while in the act of hooking the property of his neighbor, who was playing possum slumber. Some friend (?) stole a blanket and shirt the Yanks gave me, and after a close search I found the rogue sitting upon them with as serene an air of content, as if he had just said his prayers. But let it be remembered that some were in a very destitute condition, and wanted to show off their beauty in the best possible manner to the pretty secesh gals.

Our trip into Maryland cost us a good deal. There are but *few secesh* in the region through which we passed; and screaming bombshells made much more noise, than the shouts or hurrahs of sympathizing friends. The doors and hearts of the people seemed inveterately closed against us. I saw more Southern signs in Baltimore than any where else in Maryland. While passing that city, the people gave us baskets of cheese, peaches, apples, also cloth—and in order to test fully their loyalty to the "stars and bars," we hurrahed for old Stonewall, which seemed to please them well; now it is fully known that a bare mention of the name of this old patriot and hero, makes a genuine, full-blooded, blue-bellied Yankee, turn white about the *gills* and shake like an aspen leaf.

I have been paroled—am now in Richmond awaiting exchange—after which, I shall again join the remnant of my Company, and go forth once more, to meet the duck-legged Yankee Dutch.

MARCUS OLIPHANT
CO. E, POYTHRESS VOLS.

PRIVATE LETTER, ANOTHER SOLDIER'S PRISON EXPERIENCE

RICHMOND, VA., October 11, 1862 [10-31-62ASC]

Dear Brother: After writing a few hasty lines to my mother and my wife to let them know the cause of my long silence, and that I was still living, I take my seat to write you a long letter but I hope you will bear with me as I have a great many thrilling adventures to relate if my paper will only hold out.

On our march toward Maryland in he early part of Sept., I took sick between Louisa Court House and Leesburg, Va., accordingly I procured a written permit from the Brigade Surgeon to march at will in the rear of our army. My sickness was a spinal affection, my back got so weak I could hardly walk, so I fell clear in the rear of our whole command. After our army had passed clear beyond Salem and I had got in a mile and a half of the place, the Yankee cavalry [led by Brig. Gen. John Buford on Aug. 27] dashed in behind, between them and Salem, galloped into the town, and captured a few sick men. Our army had left there. The citizens gave me the alarm, so I cut across by the left flank and still kept Salem a mile and a half to my right. I stopped at the house of Mr. E. J. Smith, whom the Yankees had robbed of all his negroes, 24 in number. No one was there except Mr. Smith and his little boy Philip. My object in stopping was to get a night's rest and purchase some bread. Mr. Smith seeing my condition, however, persuaded me to stop with him a few days and recruit my health, before attempting to pursue the army. You may be sure I very readily consented, for I was not only sick but I was completely worn down by fatigue and hunger. He promised to visit the village twice a day and keep me advised as to the enemy's movements as far as possible, and in case they approached his farm he would give me the alarm time enough for me to seek concealment behind the Blue Ridge mountains which lay in four or five miles of the place.

I staid with him four days, however, without being molested. After bidding an affectionate adieu to Mr. Smith and little Philip who cried when I told him good-bye, I took up my line of march and overtook my regiment at Leesburg. We forded the Potomac near by, where the water is about three hundred yards wide. We marched into Maryland about 40 or 50 miles near Frederick city. We did not stay there long until we got orders to march back. We marched on very quietly till we came to Boonsboro; there we heard the war dogs howling a distance of three miles off at what is called South Mountain [Turner's] Gap. D. H. Hill's division who had preceded our march was hotly engaging the enemy at this Gap. We hurried on in the direction of the fight. I had on a pair of old boots which were bursted to pieces. A rock got into the toe of one of them and hurt me so badly I had to stop to get it out. I had not more than got fixed to start again till a cannon ball passed in a few inches of my head and struck the middle of the road. (I was now a half mile from the fight.) Although the ball did not touch me it knocked me down and filled my eyes with dirt and gravel. I lay on the ground senseless for a few minutes and rose to my feet with a ringing in my ears I shall never forget. That is as far as I went into the fight, this was on Sunday evening, and Sunday night I had spasms nearly all night. Our army retreated that night.

I found a man who had a greater load than he could carry. He offered to give me a pair of blankets and an oil cloth. I had a splendid blanket, but I happened to think probably Ben. would need one, so I accepted the pair of blankets and immediately sought Ben. When I found the poor boy I could not refrain from tears, though I concealed my emotion from him. He was perfectly barefoot, without a blanket, and I gave him one. I looked into the noble boy's face as I took his hand to tell him good-night and was both gratified and amazed to see the holy patience with which he bore the privations and the hardships of that trying time. I have not seen or heard from him since but I do hope and trust he is safe.

As I told you that night I had spasms nearly all night. The next morning (being Monday [Sept. 15]) our infantry all having fallen back, I roused and found myself in the midst of our cavalry, who had come to cover our retreat, they told me the Yankees would soon be upon me; so, sick, hungry, and almost barefoot, as my boots were too badly worn to shield my feet from the stones, I went back in the direction of Boonsboro'. When I got to the village, I was so exhausted I had to rest. I had not stopped long till I heard the roar of horses' feet and the clanging of the cavalryman's sabres. Our cavalry dashed through Boonsboro' and took a stand in the far edge of town. I began to think I was getting into a close place. I went to where our cavalry was and asked one of the officers if I could do him any service with my rifle. He said I could not unless I was mounted; "for," said he, "we are not aiming to make a stand; it is only a feint to hold the enemy in check till our infantry can take a position somewhere in the direction of Williamsport or Harper's Ferry. When the enemy's cavalry come on us we aim to discharge our carbines at them and fall farther back; and the best thing you can do, is to leave the main road and conceal yourself in the woods till their cavalry passes; and when their infantry approaches step out to the road again and surrender."

I took a little by-path leading triangularly from the main road, and followed it about a quarter of a mile into a dense thicket, where I spread my blanket behind a big rock. I heard the Yankee cavalry advance upon ours. They exchanged a few shots. Our cavalry then right-about-faced and retreated at a rapid speed—not, however, till they had lain several Yankees bleeding on the ground.

In about three quarters or an hour I heard the Yankee Infantry advancing up the main road. Presently their skirmishers who were deployed through the woods on one side of me, and in a corn field on the other side, commenced firing all round me, yet I could not bear the idea of surrendering to them. So I kept close until a squad of eight or ten privates and a Lieutenant came upon me in my rear. Finding myself surrounded on both sides and rear, the only chance for escape was in the front, and to leave my place of concealment was almost certain death. So I made up my mind to keep my position until my adversaries in the rear came in speaking distance. When they came up in about ten steps of me, I called out for quarters, upon which the Lieutenant commanded me to step into the path, and I done so.

They carried me up the Williamsport road about three miles, now and then taking a prisoner, till they had 27 of us—mostly sick and bare-footed men. Then they faced about and started toward Boonsboro' with us. On our way we met McClellan's army, who treated us very kindly. A great many of them asked me if I wanted some beef and crackers, and coffee water, &c. Had I accepted all their proffered rations, I might have stuffed my haversack, but I only accepted enough to meet my immediate necessities. McClellan's army is the largest crowd of men I ever saw at once.

They carried us back to Boonsboro'. There our number was increased to nearly six hundred. We stayed there a day or two, and were carried on three miles beyond Frederick City to a point on the Baltimore and Ohio Railroad. There we were joined by three hundred more prisoners, swelling our number to nine hundred. We were put aboard the cars and sent to Baltimore, where the citizens, and especially the ladies, treated us with great kindness, notwithstanding the threats and imprecations of the Yankee soldiers and the city police. The ladies were strictly forbidden to administer to our wants, but those glorious women, nothing daunted at the disgraceful order, broke the Yankees guard line and gave us cakes, tobacco, pipes, cigars, apples, peaches, and numerous other little delicacies to which we had long been strangers. A lady gave a bare-footed boy who marched in front of me, a pound-cake and whispered to him not to let the Yankees see him break the cake; accordingly, when he got a sly chance, he broke the cake, and to his astonishment, found two United States five dollar notes in it.

At Baltimore we took the boats for Fort Delaware. This fort is situated on a small island in the Delaware Bay.

Here we were placed in charge of a set of the most brutal, inhuman demons that ever blacked the pages of history. They did not give us as much to eat in two days' time, as we could eat at one meal, and gave us scarcely any water to drink, except salt water out of the bay, when, instead of quenching our thirst, made it worse and fevered our brain almost to a frenzy. They brought tubs of fresh water in to us frequently, but not one-fourth enough to quench our thirst. They excused themselves on the ground that fresh water was so scarce on the island that they had to bring it in boats across the Bay. I told them they had no right to carry us to a place where they could not get water to us.

I forgot to mention that when we got to Fort Delaware we found 1,500 other prisoners, who proceeded us by three or four days. Altogether, we numbered 2,400. A hundred and fifty or two hundred took the oath of allegiance to the United States Government. All who took the oath got two new suits of clothing and fifty dollars in gold, and were exempt from military duty six months, after which time they are required to take up arms against the Confederate Government. As soon as a man would report himself ready to take the oath he was carried out of the prison barracks, and set at liberty, I suppose. We would see no more of them.

One day, in consequence of the men crowding about the dining room door, I failed getting my allowance of grub. I was very hungry. I asked a Yank if he wished to buy a knife. He looked at my knife and inquired what I asked for it. I told him I would take a piece of bread for it. He asked me if I had nothing to eat that day. I told him I had not. Said he, "you are a liar; the prisoners have all been fed and that better than they deserve; and you are a fool. Why don't you take the oath, throw aside those dirty, filthy rags, put on a decent suit, and come under the glorious old stars and stripes?" I replied, "every star has been blotted out, and every stripe turned into a serpent; moreover, I owe no allegiance to any infernal government that will deny a prisoner food and water; and furthermore, I will perish before I will forsake our glorious little Confederacy, the land of my father and my mother." Upon this he drew his sabre and said if I did not leave his presence immediately, he would run it through me—a damned impudent rebel. I retired to my bunk and went to sleep supperless, and was visited by the sweet dream which gave rise to my last poem, "The Prisoner's Dream."

To better illustrate the manner in which the prisoners are treated at Fort Delaware, I will mention a few instances. One of the prisoners lost a small sum of money and told one of the Yankee Corporals he believed "that man stole it," pointing to another prisoner who occupied the bunk next to him, upon which his corporal-ship stepped up to the accused and ordered him to draw his shirt which he refused to do, asserting his innocence. The Yankee drew his pistol, cocked it and presented it in the trembling victims face, compelled him to draw his shirt, when he received on his bare back twenty-five or thirty strokes with the flat side of the Corporal's sabre, which drew the blood at almost every stroke.

The prison is built in the form of a hollow square and the prisoners were allowed to occupy the yard in the centre at will, from daylight in the morning, till nine o'clock at night. One day I was standing in the yard talking with an old gentleman from South Carolina, by the name of Parker, (who afterwards told me he was fifty-six years old.) Presently this same Corporal came up to us and asked Mr. Parker what he was doing, and commenced whaling him across the legs with his sabre. He gave him ten or twelve strokes with the flat side of his sabre, all the time asking him why he did not get out of his way.

It was not an uncommon thing for a Yankee Sergeant to come into the yard, single out a man, follow him all round the yard kicking him at every step.

Thus were we treated by those who say they wish us to unite our destiny with theirs under one common flag. Does not the idea of Union seem insane when every feeling of unity has given way to one of inexpressible hatred? Instead of its being extinguished by ill treatment of our prisoners, it is fanned into a flame of intensity till the lowest depths of unutterable loathing and contempt for Lincoln's government and his Satanic sceptre, are fathomed.

After staying in their custody about three weeks, we were paroled and sent under flag of truce to Aken's Landing on the James river, where we were greeted by our friends with acclamations of joy. I arrived at Richmond the day after we landed, very sick with a bowel disease. Going in search of a Georgia Hospital, I lay down on the side walk very sick, and in the most excruciating pain, when a Louisiana Lieutenant assisted me to the 2d Georgia Hospital, where I have been stopping ever since. My strength is coming to me very fast. I have not been exchanged yet, but I suppose I will be in a short time or else they would give me permission to go home.

Give my love to your family and accept the same yourself.

R. A. Gains.

R. A. Gaines enlisted as a private on April 30, 1861 in Company B, 18th Georgia Infantry. On October 12, 1863 he was transferred from the Clothing Bureau at Richmond, Va., to the Clothing Bureau at Atlanta, Ga., and discharged on April 30, 1864.

LETTER FROM TOUT LE MONDE

RAPIDAN RIVER, VA., November 18, 1862 [12-2-62SR]

Longstreet's corps has come back on this side of the Blue Ridge since I last wrote you, as no doubt you have learned from various sources before now. There in the beautiful, romantic valley of Virginia, we had a happy time, for the weather was clear and fine, and it was, upon the whole, a very good *"fowl* country." The people were our friends, made strong in their attachments by the villainy of the vandals who had committed many ravages among them in the absence of Jackson. On the 29th of October, early in the morning, we turned our backs on them quite sorrowfully and took up the lines of march south. Many cherished the delusive hope that we were on our way to Georgia, believing that we would be transferred there to show our fighting capacity on the soil of our native land. Subsequent events have murdered the bright anticipations, while we have seen other comrades get aboard cars with wild shouts of joy, as they turned after so long a while towards their homes, and bid us farewell. We passed through the delicate little town of Strasburg with its lonely houses quietly lying by the foot of the big North [Massanutten] Mountain, which raises there very abruptly its great tall head to the skies. A few forlorn looking old ladies appeared at the doors as we passed through, some with smiles of encouragement, and others with tears that spoke the desolation which gathered about their hearts as they saw the army of the Confederacy going away. Our hearts were touched for them, but we could not stay the hand of fate. On a high hill a few hundred yards north of the town the *soft-footed* Banks had built a very strong square redoubt, whose empty embrasures read us a lesson of usefulness with a hint of Yankee cowardice. A mile beyond the troops plunged into the icy water of the north fork of the Shenandoah. Then we pursued the circuitous route round the base of the rugged steep, and slept that night 22 miles from our old encampment, vacated that morning. What a memorable march to many a poor barefoot soldier! 'Twas too far the first day, when a long march lay before them; but our Generals seem to forget this at times. All day the Blue Ridge was before us in the next march, and not until the night of the 31st did we reach it. At night of that day we coiled in our blankets—'twas a frosty night—at the foot of those ever-slumbering peaks. In the calm moonlight we saw them, summit reclining upon summit, resting away in their eternal and everlasting slumbers—where storm after storm have rustled about them through numberless ages, and still they slept.

November 1st we crossed. The way, called Millam's Pass, over which we marched, rose very gradually to the top, winding around the sides of the mountains, and the distance across was twelve miles. The beauty of the natural scene from the highest point cannot be described. The day was bright and clear, and it seemed that autumn had arrayed herself in state for this occasion, participating in the "pomp and circumstance of glorious war," uniforming her drowsy soldiers in the customary butter-nut hue of the real Confederate. East and west from this lofty eminence the country stretched away in its beautiful plains and undulations until we could almost see Georgia. Everywhere numerous farm-houses, quietly sending up their little volume of smoke in the still morning air, lay quietly among the hills and vales. Shout after shout echoed among the mountains as each successive file passed before the splendid panorama. At night the sun went down behind the Blue Ridge, and we felt that the region of apple butter and chickens had gone from our reach.

November 3rd, put us at Gordonsville: *i. e.*, Toombs' and Anderson's brigades, with the remnant of shoes left by a march of 95 miles, over stoney turnpikes, and the last hope of our transfer to Georgia "gone in its silent beauty." Here we tarried a day, and departed for this locality, which lies between the swift rolling Rapidan and Cedar Run mountain, the place where Pope got the first touch, which eventually finished him up "in the neatest style." Here we continue to be unmolested, but the quietude does not promise to last very long. The prospect for stirring times becomes more and more immanent, if there is any signs in orders from headquarters. Day before yesterday the commanders of regiments were required to hold the troops "ready to move at a moment's notice into battle, officers to keep perfectly cool, the men to fire steady and with deliberation, and the Generals would hold themselves responsible for results." Where the enemy is expected to turn up no one can conjecture, who is confined to quarters (as most all are, from Brigadiers down); but evidently something is on foot, for such orders do not come in fun. The papers are teeming with extracts from late northern dates about the downfall of McClellan, which can hardly be doubted now. This is certainly a God-send for us, for he is the only Northern General who has yet been able, with anything like equal numbers, to make the thing interesting to our boys. He would fabricate wonderful dispatches, but he was a gentleman in feeling, and did the best that could be done with that army of foreign vagabonds and cowards. Who and what is Burnside, who takes his place? We only hope he has the "Young Napoleon's" refinement, and will treat our stragglers as well, if he should have the fortune to get any of them. The wonderful accomplishment of the Roanoke Island affair may yet turn his head and fill it with dreams that the army of the Potomac will fly before his terrible name; but there comes just here a smoky idea that he will land in a *soft place* not unlike the *superb* general Pope. This may have prompted our generals to expect an early advance from Burnside, whose time has just about arrived to cut his caper and retire in the usual way, and the order for preparation was issued in accordance. Poor McClellan saw his doom, and did not attempt to avert it. No sort of peremptory orders could induce him to advance on our forces, after falling back from Maryland, although his dispatches spoke of "rout and disorganization among the Rebels," and the *Herald* said, "yes, the rebellion was crushed out," in its usual mendacious style. He was crippled badly—whip'd we must say—at Sharpsburg, but the poor fellow hated so badly to acknowledge it, he lied about the reports. He could not follow Gen. Lee—dared not do it, and so he fell. He has learned, like Cardinal Woolsey, that "If I had served my God with half the zeal I have my King, he would not desert me now." We do not know, nor would it be discreet to tell if we know, the designs of our commanders, who no doubt are well posted as regards the movements of the enemy, and are ever on the alert for our advantage.

The troops are becoming better clad, and every day, as fast as they are received, shoes is issued to the most needy. The army never was in better fighting condition nor in better health. These are veteran men that compose the army, strong in the belief that they are invincible and confident we have the best generals known to modern history. The thunder of cannon, the scream of shot and shell, and the horrors of battle-fields do not unnerve them, nor affect the steadiness of that terrible aim for which they have become proverbial. Therefore Burnside's nor-innumerable hordes of Yankees need never shake the confidence of friends at home, as to the final result.

We look with anxious solicitude for the descent of fleets upon our southern cities; but the hope is everything is ready, sustains us. Vicksburg is a prominent example to emulate, and it would be a burning shame for one of our large cities to fall now, after such a glorious defense there.

The subject of foreign intervention has perhaps passed out of mind among the sensible of our people. It should be no longer cherished—it is shameful to cherish it. We did not ask Great Britain to let us secede, and let us believe, if we can, that we do not belong to her one way nor the other. We have made a nation, and let us maintain it with our own strong arm.

TOUT LE MONDE.

FROM THE SECOND GEORGIA BATTALION
CAMP NEAR FREDERICKSBURG, VA., November 26, 1862 [12-1-62CS]

Our battalion arrived here yesterday evening, from Madison C. H., after a hard and fatiguing march of five days, over one of the muddiest roads I ever saw; and through the rain, all the time. The men stood up remarkably well under the circumstances. Yesterday evening, we passed several divisions of the army, all bound this way, as appearances indicate a brush somewhere about here.

Longstreet's corps is here, and that ought to be sufficient proof that the fight, should it come off here, will be in our favor; for his corps is composed of the veteran troops of the army, and has several brigades of Georgians in it. The citizens of Fredericksburg are moving all their effects out of town, and the women and children have all left, as the Yankees yesterday demanded the surrender of the town, with a threat to shell it, in case of refusal. I hear that it was left to the citizens to decide, and they determined to hold it. Up to the present, they have not opened fire on it. Yesterday morning they fired two shots at the railroad train, neither of which took effect.

Our brigade is now under command of Brig. Gen. Jno. R. Cooke, formerly Colonel of the 27th N. C., a gallant young officer. The division is under command of Gen. [Robert] Ransom, acting Major General.

The company has about 40 men along for duty and they appear in good spirits, notwithstanding they have done some pretty tall marching, and are considerably worn out.

If anything of consequence turns up, I will let you know.

FURNITURE.

LETTER FROM V. A. S. P.

CAMP NEAR FREDERICKSBURG, VA., December 1, 1862 [12-10-62SR]

You are doubtless aware that an opinion has obtained, to some extent, among a class of our citizens and soldiers, too, that the Union will be finally reconstructed. Some even argue that this alone can terminate the war; the matter will be compromised by the Northern States adopting slavery, or in some satisfactory way guaranteeing to the South her rights.

Some do not stop here. Their speculations are extremely unfavorable to the cherished scheme of the true Southerner—eternal separation from the fanatics and Abolitionists of the North. They argue that the Confederate authorities, for the sake of peace, will finally accept no better guarantees than the Crittenden Resolutions, or something like the old Compromise which lulled the Abolition storm just long enough for it to gain sufficient strength to overwhelm the country. I fear there lurks a secret desire for reconstruction in the breast of those who entertain such an opinion. I am grieved that anyone, and especially the patriot soldier, should think reconstruction even *possible*, whereas a few (and, thank God, they are few,) think it quite *probable*.

We have shown our ability to contend single handed, and successfully, with our enemies. We are better able to meet and repulse them now than we were twelve months ago. If this be true, we will be able to dictate terms, or at least reject terms which we may consider unfavorable.

If we are again to unite with them, what have we gained? What will become of all our fondly cherished hopes of national greatness? What assurance have we that the perfidious Northmen will respect a compact with those they have ever wronged, and against whom they are now waging an aimless war, except for the gratification of the worst of human passions? If they do not hesitate to trample under foot the most sacred of human instruments—the Constitution of our ancient fathers—what assurance have we that they will respect the bond which shall re-unite it upon terms of equality? They cannot be *true* to us, while they are *false* to themselves. They erect statues and sing praise to the Goddess of "Liberty," whose alters they desecrate, whose temple they profane, and proclaim freedom of speech of conscience, and of the press! They eulogize theirs as the "best government the world ever saw," while their rulers, with or without a reason assigned, suspend the *habeas corpus*, proclaim martial law all over the land, arrest and imprison those who dare to differ with the Administration, pass sweeping confiscation bills, and make emancipation proclamations, freeing millions of happy beings over whom they have no constitutional control, and whom they can never reach even with an army "like the stars for number"! They repudiate, without the least compunction of their most tender and *elastic* consciences, all the doctrines of States Rights, and their rulers wield to-day the most despotic sceptre in the world. From such a people can we expect to receive our just rights? Can they do us justice?

Should we consent to go back under the old flag, *once* the pride of every American's heart, *now* the hated ensign of tyranny, and with all the amendments to the Constitution which we could ask; should the North even adopt our Constitution, and make it high treason to agitate the slavery question, what assurance have we that they would respect the new compact more than they would the old? What is the political history of the country prior to secession? A large and influential party—those who claimed to be the schoolmasters and religious instructors of the whole country—declared the Constitution to be a "league with hell," and taught its provisions were not binding upon the people. They declared a higher law; and not satisfied to leave us alone in the enjoyment of our constitutional rights, they stole our property, canonized the midnight assassin and martyrized the murderer! After innumerable acts of aggression, when we could endure no longer their insults and injuries, we had declared ourselves a free and separate people, they waged a war of subjugation and extermination! In order to unite all classes against us in the prosecution of the most iniquitous war on record, they declared their object to be the maintenance of their national integrity—the honor of the flag; and they openly proclaimed it a war against slavery—a war which is to liberate four or five millions of the happiest and most helpless people on earth, whose bitterest curse has been free volition—a war for the subjugation of a free born, high spirited, chivalrous people to whom death is preferable to vassalage—a war, finally, for the *extermination* of a people whose bravery has baffled their numberless hosts, whose virtues have made them jealous! These are their objects—these what we may expect from a puritanical, hypocritical, perfidious nation whose pride and avarice are their chief virtues.

What will we gain by re-union? We must pay an unequal share of the expenses; for in the event of reconstruction, we will have to pay our own, and a part of their debts, which are three times as large as ours. As we did under the old government, we will have to pay an unequal share of the national taxes. We must submit to Morrill Tariffs in order to foster New England factories and fisheries. We must buy of the North all the goods and Yankee notions we will consume. We must sell our cotton to Yankee merchants. We must, as hitherto, smother all our natural resources and manufacturing interests—must let our lead, iron, copper, and coal, gold and silver mines lay buried in the earth—in a word, we must be the tributaries of the avaricious North.

"But," says one, "we will have 'direct trade,' and manufactories, and work our mines and develop our internal wealth, in spite of northern competition and monopoly." But, my friend, how can you compete behind a New England tariff? You cannot live in peace with him without giving him high protective tariffs. Deny him this, and we would soon have another war!

Aside from these pecuniary disadvantages, we would suffer much from "evil communications." Very soon their noxious works, their isms, their "free-love" doctines, and their infidelity, would find their way into our families, our churches, and our social atmosphere would soon be poisoned by their "yellow back" literature, and their politico-religious heresies.

As we will gain nothing, but lose all, in *principle*, at least, by a re-union with our bitterest, social, moral, and political enemies, we must gain *everything* in moral and political principle, as well as in a pecuniary point of view, by a separation from them. It is an established fact that "Cotton is King," though his monarchy may be a limited one. The manufacturing interests and trade of the commercial world are controlled by him. England and other cotton monopolies have tried to supply their wants from other countries than the Southern States, but have signally failed. The requisite supply can be had only in the South. This fact gives to us, at once, a commercial importance possessed by few nations of the earth. Aside from cotton, our soil is adapted to the culture of every article of food or apparel—minerals abound; and there is no product, no natural resource which contributes to the wealth and power of nations, which does not abound in our favored land. Our borders, as compared with the first powers of the old world are boundless. We have some of the best harbors in the world, and the means and the *inducements* to adventurous men, of building a powerful navy.

In a very short period after our ports are opened, every sea-port will be white with the sails of Confederate merchantmen. The "Stars and Bars," renowned as the banner of victorious Southrons upon more than a hundred bloody fields, will soon become as familiar to the inhabitants of China, Australia and the most distant islands as the flags of England or France. Our trade will be limited alone by the constantly increasing wants of the world. Our territory is broad enough to make us a truly great and formidable power. We have already gained the admiration of the world, and wrung from our scornful enemies the meed of praise for bravery, for devotion to our cause, and for unexampled feat of arms. We will be respected, and need not fear unprovoked war from any sister nation or combination of powers.

Another, perhaps greater, blessing will attend our independence. Our literature will be purely Southern—uncontaminated by the vulgar trash and the profane, but polite, effusions which emanate in the putrid atmosphere of Northern society. This remark does not apply, of course, to *all* their literature, some of which is good. Our religion will be pure, as taught by the Bible, and not perverted and warped by the prejudices and fanaticism of New England.

These are some of the blessings to be gained by a perpetual separation from the North. Who, then, that has his country's good at heart, can wish for one moment to re-unite with the fanatics, free-lovers, the infidels, the *Abolitionists* of that hated tyranny—the United States? Who can think of the sacrifice of Bartow, Bee, of A. S. Johnston, and thousands of noble Southrons, and wish to affiliate with their murderers? Who would be willing to meet Beast Butler as a citizen of the same free country? Southerners! You have fought for nothing if you would re-unite with the perfidious Northmen upon any terms! The blood of our dead heroes cries out against such humiliation! Fight them forever—fight them till the South has not a man left—fight them until every hill is a cemetery of the dead, and every plain a vast burying ground; but for the love of freedom, for the love of your posterity, do not re-unite with the Abolitionists upon any, not even the most favorable terms.

V. A. S. P.

☆☆☆ Battle of Fredericksburg

In mid-November, the Army of the Potomac (now under the command of General Ambrose Burnside) advanced toward the city of Fredericksburg. On December 11, they crossed the Rappahannock River and prepared to launch an attack on Lee's strong defensive positions along the heights west and south of the city. On December 13, the Federals achieved some success against Jackson's position on the right, but the attacks against Lee's center were doomed to failure. Confederates from Georgia and South and North Carolina posted in a sunken road behind a stone wall repulsed thousands of the attacking Federals with great slaughter. It was Lee's most one-sided victory of the war.

LETTER FROM "TIVOLI,"
EIGHTH GEORGIA REGIMENT
[G.T. ANDERSON'S BRIGADE, HOOD'S DIVISION]
CAMP NEAR FREDERICKSBURG, VA., December 8, 1862 [12-16-62ASC]

For some days past we have been on the South bank of the Rappahannock, waiting with great expectancy the coming of the foe. As yet no signs announce his presence, save here and there on the opposite side of the river, can be seen at any one time a straggler or two from the Abolition army. Our army remains in the best of spirits, and thanks to the good folks at home, our condition in the way of clothing, &c., is daily improving. Large numbers of supplies in the past few days have been received by the 8th and 9th Georgia regiments, and more are expected. God will certainly remember those who remember the poor soldier.

The weather is very cold. It requires the largest sized camp-fires to keep us comfortable, and our pickets on the outposts suffer severely. However picket duty does not last long, the labor being well divided among the different regiments.

Whilst the 8th Ga., was on picket the other day a pleasing incident occurred. Several officers of the Yankee army during the day appeared on the opposite shore and surveyed our position at their leisure. They were in full sight, and the river being narrow at that point, they would have been easily shot by our men—but as picket firing has been discontinued by both armies they remained unmolested, though many a pulse throbbed and many a heart beat with the desire to bring them down. At their leisure they came, at their leisure they retired. Scarcely had they left the bank when quietly slipping down the shallow of a hill, came one of Virginia's noble children. Placing a paper under a huge stone the child retired, casting a glance around in search of a concealed foe. At night Capt. [Sydney] Hall of the 8th, adventurously crossed over in a boat, secured the paper and forwarded it to General Lee. The spirit in the heart of that child burns in the soul of all the rising generation, and even if we were conquered by the Abolition army, the generations of the future would renew the fight, and Southern nationality at some time or other would receive its vindication.

We have but few amusements in camp at present, cards are but little used and gambling does not prevail as a vice among us. The recent advice of Gen. Lee to the officers of his army restrains them and the soldier with his sister's testament in his pocket and his mother's precepts in his heart cannot stoop to a vice so low and so degrading. Without wishing to be puritanic permit me to say, (from some experience in armies,) that there never was an army of such a number of men collected preserving so strict a morality and so high a Christian tone as ours. To be sure you hear often the ill-timed jest, the foul language and profanity, yet as a counterbalance there is not an hour time there swells an anthem of praise on high from the many camp fires that surround me. Religious meetings are also regularly held in most of the Regiments.

The health of the Georgia troops at present is very good. The small pox in Anderson's and Toomb's brigades has entirely disappeared and the disease of the season, Pneumonia, Typhoid and Camp Fevers have as yet not made their appearance.

The weather is very cold, on the 6th we had a severe snow storm and the ground is now covered with snow to the depth of several inches.

Our food is good—it might be more plentiful—but we are satisfied that our government, exerting itself like a young giant, is doing the best it can for us in this respect.

I can say without fear of contradiction that the army of Virginia was never in better spirits or better prepared to meet the enemy or the winter blows; for blows with the former we are prepared to return with interest and us for the blows of winter, it is very cold and I must nestle myself up in my blankets.

TIVOLI.

THE BATTLE OF FREDERICKSBURG
December 13, 1862 [12-23-62AWCS]

We are here, near the great line of battle, and will briefly recapitulate what we have seen and heard. The enemy attempted the passage of the Rappahannock by laying down their pontoons at one o'clock on Thursday [Dec. 11] morning. They were permitted to get their bridges half finished before our men fired upon them. About dawn, however, the 17th and 18th Mississippi, a part of Barksdale's Brigade opened fire upon them, killing and wounding a large number. These regiments were armed with Springfield rifles, and for a while, drove the pontooners from their work. Then it was that the Yankees opened upon the town with shot, shell, and grape, to the destruction of the houses and the terror of its panic-stricken inhabitants, two thirds of which were women; but doing little harm to the gallant band of Mississippians [reinforced by the 8th Florida], who were there to dispute their entrance. The firing upon the town was not responded to by our batteries. And here the magnificent spectacle was witnessed of the Yankees firing four mortal hours upon the town of Fredericksburg, with batteries placed close together, over a space of nearly two miles, and ranged in three tiers. As a result of their fiendish work, the two squares on the North side of Main street, on which was situated the Virginia Bank and Post Office, were entirely destroyed—the enemy throwing what is called "liquid fire." The sight is represented by those who witnessed it as one of terrible grandeur. The inhabitants who were caught inside can tell of many hair-breath escapes. In one instance twenty-seven shells went through a frame house, in which were some eight persons, without killing any of them. Some who sought shelter from the shells in their cellars were compelled to vacate because of the houses catching on fire over their heads.

The house so long the residence of Mary, the mother of Washington, was shelled and nearly destroyed.

While in the town they held high carnival, breaking, destroying and plundering all that lay in their way.

The deeds of gallantry performed by our men thus far challenge our admiration, and secure us that when this great struggle comes, every man will fearlessly do his duty. The army is in fine health and excellent spirits; only three sick were reported on the rolls of one of the largest brigades of the army on the 13th.

A Georgian, on picket in town on Thursday night, killed one man and brought out six prisoners. All of them thus caught were drunk; and it is said that rations of whiskey are freely supplied the men. It is also reported that the first brigade which came across, had to be forced at the point of the bayonet.

The fighting Dec. 12th, was mainly artillery dueling across the river and pickets fighting.

The Yankees tried to force citizens who remained to go across the river.

The Yankees have as many as five [six] pontoon bridges. Three just opposite the town and two [three] just below it. The gallant Mississippians [and Floridians] under Barksdale kept back the pontooners for nearly twenty-four hours, notwithstanding their exposure during the entire time to shot and shell.

The amount of suffering inflicted on the noncombatants of Fredericksburg by the unprincipled foe, is heart-rendering. The picture which meets the eye at every farm house, cabin and hut—fugitives from burning homes and desolated hearthstones, clustered in melancholy groups in the houses and about the yards watching the clouds hovering over the ill-fated city and listening to the steady roar of the artillery whose every volley adds to the already terrible scene of destruction—is enough to affect the stoutest heart, and from the most charitable call out curses on the infamous authors of so much misery. The continued inaction of the enemy gave assurance to a number of families who had for many weeks been suffering within sight of their homes that the danger of bombardment had passed, and within the past few days they returned to the city. They were startled from their dream of security by the hissing shell through the bed chamber, the rattling of grape in the street, and the solid shot opening its way through roof and floor, even of churches and ploughing up the very bones of their ancestors in the churchyards. The shrieks of women with their infants in their arms snatched hastily from peaceful sleep, as they ran in frantic amazement and terror through the streets, was enough to appall any but a Yankee heart. Some sought refuge in their cellars, blazing rafters and steaming timbers overhead drove them again into the street. How any escaped is a problem whose solution must come within the catalogue of miracles. There are rumors of women and children having been killed, or perishing amid the flames, but amid the confusion of conflicting reports, we can confirm nothing definite.

Between the present terminus of the railroad and Hamilton's crossing, about two miles, we encountered numerous fugitives from the burning city. An old man, accompanied by his wife and four or five children, was seeking a roof to shelter them. They saved nothing but the clothes on their persons, the results of long years of toil remaining in ashes behind them. A most affecting sight was a widow with four little children, some barefoot, and others in their night clothes, following her weary steps. An infant in her arms was crowing busily, unconscious of the tears coarsing silently down the mother's cheeks. This scene, however, forms only part of the sad picture on every hand presented. Let us hope that every exertion will be made by the benevolent to mitigate the sufferings of these poor refugees.

—NEAR BATTLE GROUND AT HAMILTON'S CROSSING, December 14, 1862.

Since the close of my letter on yesterday the battle has been raging fiercely and furiously along a line of 6 miles, reaching from a point just above Falmouth along the river as far down as Pratt's. The ball opened on our left with artillery about 9½ a. m., and was carried on with heavy guns until about half past one when the infantry first went into action on our right. Then it was that, for hours, the combat raged with an intensity at least equal to, if not greater, than anything that has occurred during the war.

The Yankees fought well, but were repeatedly driven back. At one time, it was said, they had been forced back to the extent of one and a half miles. Our line of battle extended along the railroad track, whilst that of the enemy was formed on the country road running parallel with the river. Here they have the benefit, in case of being forced back, of the natural fortifications which the ditching, for the purpose of draining, on either side of the road will give them. It may be asked why were they allowed this advantage? The answer must be that the enemy's guns commanded this position, and the position chosen by our Generals was for defensive operations, far superior, being all along a rise of gentle slopes skirted by woods.

The troops of the enemy on this wing were mostly old ones, being [George G.] Meade's Pennsylvania Reserves and [George] Stoneman's corps under the immediate command of Gen. Reynolds [William B. Franklin]. The prisoners seemed by no means dissatisfied at being taken.

***.

FROM THE SECOND GEORGIA BATTALION
NEAR FREDERICKSBURG, VA., December 13, 1862 [12-23-62CS]

Our battalion has just now (8 o'clock p. m.,) come off picket duty. We went on at the canal, near the city, last night, and had to lay flat on the ground in a barn yard all day in order to avoid the shells from the enemy's batteries which fell thick and fast around us. It was a most terrific cannonading. While in the barn yard, a shell passed along one side of a large stack of wheat where our boys and some of the 41st Virginia Reg't (who were on picket with us) were laying, and killed three of the 41st, and killed Private John R. O'Neal of our company (City Light Guards,) being the first man that has fallen in our battalion, by the hands of the enemy. He was a splendid soldier, a firm friend, and a high-minded whole-souled man.

From what I can learn, Jackson and Hill repulsed the enemy every time they advanced, (and they advanced seven times,) bringing up reinforcements after reinforcements, but to no effect. They could not resist the ardor of our invincible troops. We took a battery from them in the streets of Fredericksburg. The fighting was principally on our right to-day, but I expect there will be a general engagement to-morrow. I will try to write further.

FURNITURE.

LETTER FROM DR. J. N. SIMMONS
RICHMOND, VA., December 20, 1862 [12-27-62ASC]

Having visited the battlefield at Fredericksburg where the Yankees met with such a disastrous defeat on Saturday last, I propose to furnish you with a brief account of my observations there. Being called to Richmond, on business, I chanced to be here at the time of the fierce engagement; and although I had relinquished the duties of my former profession. I apprehend that I might be able to render some assistance to the wounded and therefore took the cars at an early hour on Monday morning in company with others on similar missions, to a point in the vicinity of the battlefield. The object of our visit was realized for we found an abundance of work to engage our hands and our hearts. The ambulances were busily employed in conveying those whose wounds were such as to require them, to a point beyond danger. Such attention was rendered the suffering as their conditions demanded and then they were placed on the cars bound for Richmond. Several trains were running day and night until the work was accomplished. A number were severely wounded and expired on the ground before we could transfer them to the cars. I discovered a Georgian who received a ball in one temple which made its exit at the other and as I placed my arm under his body to assist him upon the train, I addressed him. His responses indicated that he was conscious of what was then transpiring. Another poor fellow prostrated upon the ground and whose paroxysms of pain attracted my notice, had his body entirely pierced by a ball, implanting in its course one lobe of his lungs, and still another whose sensibilities were deadened by a fragment of shell, that had not only lacerated the integument, but had carried away so much of the parietal bones as to render his chances for life hopeless, his brain being much exposed.

My programme led me to the quarters of my young friend Dr. T. A. Means, the skillful surgeon of the 11th Georgia Regiment. His instruments had been brought into requisition, the large number of patients that were subjected to his treatment and that were doing well under the operations of his knife, fully attested that he was entitled to the positions he holds. A large number of wounded Yankees fell into our hands and a majority of his operations were successfully performed upon them. In one instance he amputated the thigh—the upper third— also the left arm near the shoulder joint on the same individual, who still survived the operation.

The battlefield and the slain thereon, was the next object of grave concern. Accompanied by a relation and an officer we walked over the ground that had been so recently the theatre of a far more terrible and bloody conflict than information previously received and warranted the most credulous in believing. The lines of the respective armies extended a distance of some five or six miles. The enemy formed his line of battle upon the South bank of the Rappahannock, whilst the Confederate troops occupied a ridge which extended several miles towards the East from Fredericksburg. This ridge opposite the city is about half a mile from the river and gradually recedes from it as it stretches to the Eastward, which leaves a plain from two and a half to three miles in extent from the ground occupied by our forces on the extreme right and the Rappahannock. It is conceded, I apprehend, by all acquainted with the topography of the country where previous battles have been fought during the present war, that it is the strongest position that we have ever held in an engagement, and the unanimous regret seems to be of both officers and men that Burnside did not exercise temerity enough to renew the attack on Sunday morning. Our brave soldiers, (it may be unfortunately) administered too severe a rebuke the day previous to allow even this vain-glorious chieftain longer to attempt the execution of the purpose he had formed and communicated to his superior at Washington of "carrying the crest," the next day. But if Madam Rumor is not at fault, Burnside's soldiers were content with one day's experience in the "pride, pomp and circumstance of glorious war" and more thoroughly appreciated the prowess and invincibility of their adversaries on the "crest," than their ill-fated leader, as they refused to risk the fate of their dead comrades.

You perceive that Gen. Lee, in his report, estimates our loss at 1,800; that of the enemy is much greater—generally thought to be 13,000 to 15,000 and perhaps in excess of these figures; and it is said we captured some 7,000 to 8,000 small arms. Although the enemy succeeded in removing from the field many of their slain, yet as late as Tuesday I counted as many as 75 dead bodies lying together, in another portion of the field 40, 15 in another, and others scattered promiscuously over the extensive plains.

On Wednesday [Dec. 17], near four days subsequent to the battle, I entered the city of Fredericksburg, and to my utter astonishment, my eyes greeted hundreds of lifeless Yankee bodies. I had supposed their comrades had long before buried them out of view. This was near the spot where Gen. [T. R. R.] Cobb received the shock that terminated his brilliant and honorable career. The slain in front of his gallant brigade were more numerous than I had witnessed at any other point, and which fact attested his merits as a commander, and the valor of his men. The scene gave me some idea of the greatness of our victory. An officer who had participated in a number of battles, including those of the 1st and 2nd Manassas and Sharpsburg, informed me that the exhibition of carcasses exceeded anything that had fallen under his eye. Several hundred Federals were detailed from Burnside's army during my sojourn in the city, for the purpose of burying their dead, and were so engaged when I took my departure.

I wandered through the city down to the memorable banks of the Rappahannock and decried across the stream, some 476 of our men who had fallen into the hands of the Yankees as the fight was progressing, their variegated costumes contrasted strangely with the bright and uniform blue of the foul invaders. An armistice being agreed upon, flags of truce waved on the opposite shores and the soldiers were mutually paroled and then delivered. We only had 276 Federals on hand at the time, the remainder, 1,350, had been forwarded to Richmond. The Confederates evinced much delight in being returned to their friends. They report their rations to have been two crackers per day during their brief sojourn among their enemies. They also unite in the statement that our assailants unreservedly confess to a decent drubbing. Some fifty members of the 19th Ga. Regiment were among the prisoners, they were flanked by the enemy and captured.

It has never before been my fortune to witness so many striking evidences of the vandalism of our unprincipled foes as is furnished by the city of Fredericksburg. It is certainly entitled to that appellation which the ravages of grim-visaged war has so often rendered appropriate, "*A sacked city.*" Several female refugees had temporarily returned to their homes, to ascertain the condition in which the Yankees had left their houses and contents. I ventured to interrogate several of those ladies in regard to the depredations upon their homes, and they related but one story, a most dismal one indeed. They found their homes polluted, chairs demolished, fine French bedsteads mutilated, ruined and wantonly cut into fragments, and all descriptions of furniture bearing evidence that the destroyer had effectually accomplished his fell work.

As I passed the door of an aged gentleman and lady, they politely invited me in, that I might be furnished with evidence that they had not been overlooked by the vandals. They directed my attention to a large gilt frame, which had been the receptacle of an elegant painting executed by their son, and for which they had refused the sum of $250. The picture had been removed by the intruders, together with a large number of others. The furniture in the house had been thoroughly upset; the bedtickings had been ripped open and their contents scattered about the premises. Some of the beds had been dragged through the streets and were then saturated with mud and the *debris* of a thoroughfare. The white walls of the various rooms were defaced by the names of the parties and the regiments and States from which they hailed being inscribed in bold, black characters.

They destroyed, I was informed, the Methodist Episcopal Church, discharged five shells or solid shot through the spire of the Baptist church, and nine through that of the Episcopal church. They converted the former into a hospital and the elegant cushions into mattresses for their wounded, and left them saturated with blood, and a number of dead bodies just outside the edifice. I ascended the steeple of the church, from which point I was favored with a prospect of the "Grand Army" that was respectable for all this mischief, and discovered long trains of wagons moving down the river, in search, perhaps, of another flogging or winter quarter; and I presume that we have had the last grand view of them until the opening of spring, unless we decide to visit Washington.

Our adversaries at Fredericksburg, as usual violated all the usages of civilized warfare, and from a personal observation of the damage inflicted at Vicksburg, I am persuaded that their terrible engines of destruction has left the city of Fredericksburg in a more deplorable condition.

J. N. S.

PRIVATE LETTER,
HEADQUARTERS, McLAWS' DIVISION
NEAR FREDERICKSBURG, VA., December 15, 1862 [12-31-62ASC]

Dear P. F. Hoyle: I take advantage at an interim in attending the wounded of our brigade, to give a few items in regard to the late action in this vicinity up to date, especially concerning Gen. Cobb's command. Up to the night of the 10th instant everything had been quiet, and no anxiety was felt for the morrow. But at 9:30 on the morning of the 11th an order came to Gen. Cobb from Gen. [Lafayette] McLaws, to the effect, "Fire your signal guns; the enemy is endeavoring to cross the river." One of the howitzers of our battery soon fired the signals agreed upon, awakening us from our sweet slumbers. Some still thought it was a false alarm, but the rapid cannonading which commenced an hour afterwards, dispelled such thoughts, and all were constrained to believe that the ball had opened—that Burnside would risk his all in order to appease the clamors for advance made by the Northern fanatics. Every preparation being made, our infantry sheltered themselves from the enemy's batteries by taking positions behind the hills. The 17th and 21st Mississippi Regiments, of Barksdale's Brigade, being on picket, it devolved upon them to hold the enemy in check and prevent them from building their pontoon bridges. This they did in gallant style. I saw a 32 pounder, drawn by twelve horses, and the famous "Long Tom," pass by and take position near our camp, and I knew then the Yankees had bloody work before them. But they seemed intent on shelling the town, which they did with great assiduity, destroying several houses &c. There are some lady-refugees at our hospitals who were in town when the shelling commenced, and fortunately made their escape. About 8 o'clock the 16th Ga. was sent down to occupy a position near the river, below the town. It was in gaining this position that the severe shelling of the Yankees killed two and wounded forty of that regiment. The firing continued all day. The result you know.

Our artillery was yet silent.

By a pre-conceived plan, the enemy were allowed to cross, that their overthrow might be the more certain.

On the second day, there was skirmishing on our left, and an artillery duel throughout the entire day. Saturday the 13th inst., so far as the battle has progressed, has been the great day with us. On this day Georgia mourns the loss of one of her noblest sons, and in the death of GEN. THOMAS R. R. COBB, has sustained a blow so heavy that it will be long ere she recovers from it.

Skirmishing and cannonading commenced early in the morning. Our Brigade took a well-chosen position behind a stone fence, and awaited the onset of the enemy, who came bearing down upon us in more than quadruple our numbers. At 10 A. M. the heavy musketry begun, and the field in our front was a complete slaughter pen. Protected both from shell and small arms, we only had to watch their approach in unbroken column, until within range, when a perfect sheet of flame issued forth from behind that stone wall, as the deadly missile sped on its mission. Three times they reformed and came on its mission. Three times they reformed and came on unbroken as before; but each time a deadly shower of bullets thinned their ranks, and in confusion they broke and fled the fourth time, to return no more to the charge. As yet, Gen. Cobb was in the midst of it, inciting and encouraging the brave troops under his command to deeds of heroes. About 12 M, while fearlessly exposing himself, he received the fatal wound which terminated in his death four hours afterwards. It is remarkable that the same ball that shattered his limb, produced a like mortal wound upon Capt. W. S. Brewster, 24th Ga., who was in command of the floating-battery at the battle of Fort Sumter. Gen. Cobb was removed to the hospital as soon as possible, where every attention by the ablest Surgeons was afforded him. I was by his side from the time he arrived at the hospital till he breathed his last. He spoke but few words, and these were in regard to the pain he suffered, making simple requests of the Surgeons, first for some stimulant and then for something to ease his pain. Rev. R. R. Porter, his intimate friend and constant companion, was with him from the first. He bore his sufferings unmmurringly, uttering no complaint. Every effort was made to prolong his life, but no! exhausted nature could no longer withstand the blighting effects of hemorhage and a severe nervous shock. The pale messenger claimed him for a victim, and human effort was no avail. Surrounded by weeping friends and relatives he quietly—almost unconsciously—gave up the ghost! And thus he died! In his death Georgia may well drape herself in mourning! He was a pure statesman, a noble Christian—a brave and skillful General—and half is not yet told. It is useless to say how deeply his comrades in arms lament his loss.

Col. [Robert] McMillan now commands the brigade. As to the fighting on our right, where Jackson's invincible followers beat back the tide of battle with fearful results to the enemy, you are doubtless already informed. It is sufficient to say that at the time of this writing, our troops hold every position, are in good spirits, awaiting a fresh attack from the foe, whose dead, outstretched upon the plain, are numbered by thousands, ready at any time to increase the heaps to mountain height, confident all the while of our ability to repel any attack the enemy may make. It may be proper to add that our Legion was supporting [H. H.] Carlton's battery, and were not in the musketry engagement on the 13th. However, they are on picket to-night, and may soon become prominent actors in another great battle yet to be fought. My particular sphere has been in attending to the wounded. These are sent to Richmond as fast as disposed of by the surgeons. I have had opportunities of witnessing many acts of kindness from the ladies of Virginia, which, indeed, should be household words in every family in the Confederacy.

There was heavy skirmishing and some cannonading yesterday, the 14th, but no general fight resulted from it. The same can be said of to-day. I hear it reported the enemy's loss in killed is estimated at 1,000, while our own is only 100. I also hear it reported that General [Franz] Sigel has reinforced Burnside, neither of which reports I can vouch for. I don't think the fighting here is done with yet.

I forgot to mention that the remains of Gen. Cobb are now far on their way to Georgia, to be interred in the land of his nativity. Mr. Porter, Capt. [John C.] Rutherford, and others, perform the sad duty of accompanying them home.

As ever yours,
JNO. L. M. HARDMAN,
Hospital Steward, Cobb's Ga. Legion

NINETEENTH GEORGIA REGIMENT AT FREDERICKSBURG
HEAD QUARTERS, 19TH GA., REGT., December 16, 1862 [12-30-62ASC]

About dawn of the morning of the 13th, the brigade [Archer's], our regiment on the left, took its position in a ditch at the edge of a wood. On our left the wood extended several hundred yards further down into the open field. Here, for some reason, I know not what, no troops were placed. In front of us extended an open plain, gradually sloping to the banks of the river. Very soon after we were posted the enemy began to show themselves, marching down along the bank of the river. About 10 A. M., they began a most terrific shelling of the wood in which we were stationed. This was replied to by our batteries on the right. In this artillery fight, judging from the "smashed up" caisson and wheels and from the dead and crippled horses lying around the next day, our batteries suffered greatly. The loss among the infantry was very slight.

About 12 M the cannonading subsided, and a dark line extending above and below as far as the eye could reach was soon advancing. Orders were given for every one to hold his fire until they had crossed the Railroad, which was about a hundred fifty yards in our front. Then came a dead silence for several minutes, broken only by the low cautions of officers to their companies, to "hold your fire, boys, until the command is given, be sure you make every shot count," &c. On they came, steadily advancing in three heavy columns, confident of carrying everything before them. It was the most terribly beautiful picture I ever beheld. The stars and stripes were floating proudly over them, officers were riding up and down their lines and their noises might be heard urging the men "on to victory and to glory." Rapidly they moved the fatal lines. As the foremost column crossed the Railroad a deadly volley was poured into their ranks, which made them reel and stagger. A constant fire was kept up until the 2nd or 3rd column advanced and were welcomed in the same manner as the first. Up to this time our loss had been comparatively insignificant; while the enemy were falling like hay before the mower's blast, and already had began to give way. About this time Lieut. Simms came to me reporting that we were being flanked on the left. I immediately went to Lt. Col. [Andrew] Hutchins reporting the fact. He ordered me to go to Gen. Archer asking for support. The General had sent for Gregg, anticipating the very thing which had occurred. But this gallant officer was probably ere this sleeping the sleep of death. When I returned our regiment had been compelled to fall back and the enemy, who had come up under cover of the wood on our left, had succeeded in getting completely in our rear. Whose fault it was that this gap was left I am unable to say, but I do know that men never fought more bravely. We had succeeded in repulsing three columns, either one of which numbered thrice ours. As we were going into our position, Gen. [A. P.] Hill remarked to Col. [Peter] Turney, then commanding the brigade, that we must hold our position "until hell froze over," that he knew we could do it, he had seen our brigade fight. And we would have come as near doing this as possible, but for the unfortunate error of our left being unprotected. General Archer said to us next day that he had no complaint to make of our regiment, that we had fought as bravely as men could fight, and that he was well pleased with our actions. We deeply regret that anything should have occurred to leave the least ground for the shadow of a suspicion to rest upon our hitherto fair and unblemished escutcheon, yet we feel consciousness of having performed our whole duty to the utmost extent of human ability. Out of twenty-five officers, who went into the fight, fifteen were wounded and four taken prisoners. All of our missing have returned, having been paroled, except Lieut. [Samuel M.] Payne, who is wounded, though not dangerously.

W. H. JOHNSON, Lt. & Act. Adj't.

William H. Johnson enlisted as First Lieutenant of Co. C, 19th Georgia Infantry on June 11, 1861. He was killed in action at Ocean Pond, Florida on February 20, 1864.

PRIVATE LETTER—FROM AN OFFICER OF McLAWS' DIVISION
CAMP NEAR FREDERICKSBURG, VA., December 14, 1862 [12-30-62AWCS]

Yesterday was our hardest fight. The enemy attacked Jackson's corps on our right. It was a most splendid sight, to see the enemy's masses advancing across the plain, first their skirmishers, then their line of battle, then their Artillery, then their second line of infantry and behind their immense reserves, increasing by never ending dark streams that continued to pour across the river in full view. Their batteries opened and the shells burst over the woods where our men lay concealed. Our batteries swept through their ranks, but on they came never faltering, firing as they advanced, our men held the railroad, but on the approach of this terrible array, they retreated and gave the enemy position. They sent up loud cheers and pressed forward. Their triumph was of short duration. A. P. Hill's men came from the left and right and poured in their volleys, driving back the enemy beyond the railroad. Again they rallied and advanced, again and for the last time retired in disorder across the plain. Their ambulance corps came forward and withdrew with their wounded to a deserted cabin half mile in the plain. Their reserves came forward but to join the retreating bodies, as they hurried across the plain. Their columns moved still lower down the river, and three times advanced against D. H. Hill; 'twas too far from my stand point for any of the particulars. But Jackson captured a good many prisoners; our loss was not heavy. On A. P. Hill's left I witnessed late in the evening a charge of our men; I could not see what Brigade, they came across the field in splendid order upon the enemy. We thought at one time they would stand and give our men an opportunity to test their skill at bayonet exercise, but they retired, our men driving them to their artillery. The Yankee skirmishers in front of [John B.] Hood's position commenced falling back, next to a wooded ravine where our men were advancing, I saw their officer gallop around him and shoot him [?] down. This stopped the panic. On our left at the edge of the town are fine eminences, one is called Marye's Hill; upon this was placed the Washington Artillery of New Orleans, at the base of the hill was Cobb and Kershaw's brigade of McLaws' Division, on their left Ransom's Division. Here the enemy made their chief attack, they came forty thousand strong, the artillery crashing through their ranks with most terrible effect. On they came, formed in the valley behind the last eminence and advanced; Cobb's skirmishers retired to their position. He ordered his men to remain concealed and hold their fire until he gave the command, when about 100 yards distant.

The shell from the Louisiana batteries slaying them by scores, their officers cheering and animating their men, Cobb's men, the 18th Geo., 24th Geo., and Phillips' Legion opened their fire—again they opened, and again. The dead lay before them, dotting the plain. Ransom's men poured in their volleys on the left. Again for seven different times did they advance; their troops in continuous lines, from two different points as far as the eye could reach, came down the hills from the opposite side, and joined the fighting columns—not less than 40,000 men tried their valor. Kershaw, the Carolina gamecock, advanced to Cobb's support, and his men increased the slaughter. During the seven hours that this engagement lasted, the fire from the batteries was incessant. Side by side our two [three] brigades stood, never a man faltering. They exhausted their cartridge boxes, replenished and again replenished. At nightfall they made their last attempt to drive these brigades away. They had planted batteries in the streets of Fredericksburg; their long range guns on the opposite side sent their whistling missiles, but the same deadly fire awaited their advancing columns. They were repulsed at every point. Not a success to reward their valor and cheer them for to-day's conflict. But whilst we did not have many, the dead from our ranks were the best of the South. Georgia must mourn throughout her territory, for her best son, Tom. Cobb, was killed by a shell shattering his thigh. In the prime of manhood, talented, cultivated, experienced, brave, a good soldier, unblemished moral character, of sincere piety, he benefited his people as much as any man, by the wisdom of his counsel, and more by the pure example of practical religion. He died before the dwelling of his fathers [mother's family]. On earth a bright future awaited him, in Heaven is now his home. Col. [Robert T.] Cook, of Phillips' Legion, was also killed; and Capt. [Lord] King, of Gen. McLaws' staff, is missing, we supposed killed.

Gens. Lee, Longstreet and McLaws, were all day at a battery overlooking the fight, and commanding a view of the plain, apparently undisturbed by the shells which whistled and burst around them. The long range gun, 30 pound Parrott, near which they were standing, burst, but strange to say did not even slightly wound a single person. 'Tis 9½ a. m. There has been some cannonading, but the engagement has not yet commenced.
—15th Dec. 1862, 9 o'clock A. M.

There was no engagement yesterday except with skirmishers.

The loss of this Division in the engagement of the 13th was 581 killed and wounded. The 3rd South Carolina lost in wounded and killed 117. Col. [James D.] Nance, Col. [William D.] Rutherford, Maj. [Robert C.] Maffett, Captains Gary, Todd, and [William W.] Hance were all wounded. Captains Summer and Foster killed. General Maxcy Gregg killed. We captured the aids of several Yankee Generals. Jackson's corps captured 600 prisoners; they broke through A. P. Hill's advance line and were taken prisoners. Gen. [Joseph] Hooker it is reported killed, [part of] his corps [wing] was opposed to Jackson, Sumner's was opposed to

McLaws' and Anderson and Ransom's Divisions suffered severely; none fought with more bravery; they occupied the top of the hill. The body of Capt. King of Gen. McLaws Division was found to-day; he had been sent to Gen. Cobb, and having tied his horse on top of Marye's Hill, ventured to descend the hill in front of the enemy and not more than two hundred yards from their sharpshooters. He was shot with four balls, one in the right hand, one in the ankle, one in the knee and one entering his left side and came out his right shoulder killing him instantly. He was a gallant officer, of fine talents and had distinguished himself on several occasions.

We are all well. Gen. McLaws is in fine health, depressed by the loss of Gen. Cobb and so many others of his best officers, but sanguine he can maintain his position. The Gamecock Kershaw has told his command that there is but one way for them to retreat, that is through the enemy's lines. 'Tis now nine o'clock and no engagement.

*** .

HARDAWAY'S BATTERY
LETTER FROM NEAR FREDERICKSBURG

10 MILES BELOW FREDERICKSBURG, VA., December 17, 1862 [12-30-62CS]

Knowing that your paper circulates among the friends of Hardaway's Battery, to relieve their anxiety, I respectfully request that you give place to this communication.

On the 4th inst., we drove the gunboats down the river at Port Royal, and in another fight with them on the 10th, disabled one which went off towards Rappahannock.

On the night of the 12th, we were ordered to move as rapidly as possible towards Fredericksburg, we, as usual, were on outpost duty six miles from our division.

A bitter cold march it was, and after making twenty-five miles through farms and by-ways, we reported to Gen. Jackson at 12 noon, the 13th, the battle then raging. The General ordered Captain [R. A.] Hardaway to place his guns to fire on the infantry as he thought they were wavering and would retire. We reported to Gen. Stuart, with whom we fought at Upperville, and were assigned position by his active and gallant Chief of Artillery, Major [John] Pelham, who is an Alabamian from Randolph county, and always greets us as old friends. The fire of artillery on both sides was most destructive, the batteries being near enough together for the Sharp shooters to use their rifles on men and horses.

The Whitworth [a breech-loading cannon imported from England], by order of Col. [Stapleton] Crutchfield, Jackson's Chief of Artillery, opened on the head of one of the pontoon bridges at Pratt's house, Gen. Franklin's headquarters, the other section firing on the infantry. The reserve was massed here, and we saw afterwards where the solid balls tore over the field and across the river, one passing through the mansion as if it were only an inch board. Some of the bolts we found in the ravine where the Yankees took shelter.

One Napoleon solid shot took off a man's hat in our battery, leaving him with a two days' headache.

One wheel of the Whitworth limber was shot off and furrows ploughed through the battery. The ambulances were constantly running, and the dead and wounded carried to the rear. All of Jackson's artillery was firing.

A loud shout from the wooded hills to the left of the railroad announced that we had driven the Yankees back, and then we let in on the quivering mass of humanity as it retired, like a blue wave to the river. Shell, shrapnel, and solid shot in a lethal shower poured upon them, and the cavalry videttes report that the supports to the batteries caught the panic, and were brought back at the point of the sword. The second line remained firm, and a rout was barely escaped. Jackson's corps sent off fifteen hundred prisoners afoot to Richmond.

The ground was covered at several places with the dead. Lt. [William B.] Hurt had charge of the Whitworth and Lt. [George A.] Ferrell of the 3-inch rifle. From the peculiarity of the projectiles we could recognize our shells, and in riding over the field subsequently we found they were put in the right place, and just where they were aimed. As we have fired two thousand, two hundred and thirty-three shots since the 25th of June last, at the enemy in ten battles, we might claim to be veterans, though most of us must "tarry at Jericho, to let our beard grow."

On the next day, the Whitworth was ordered by Gen. Lee to take a position to enfilade the enemy as they advanced across the field. Captain Hardaway, finding that a point south of Massaponax creek, on the old Spotswood estate, not only commanded the field, but also gave a fire on the flank of the Yankee artillery moved to it. The disadvantage was that twelve heavy rifles were just across the river; but he properly estimated that the bluff on the west bank would prevent them from getting range.

The rifles of Lt. Ferrell were ordered up in musket range, the gunners to lie down until the infantry came to canister range.

Every one dismounted, for the Sharp shooters were firing rapidly at easy range.

So soon as the pieces were in battery, Co. B, 4th U. S. artillery, opened upon them at two hundred and fifty yards with shrapnel from six Napoleons.

You know artillery is expected to withstand shelling that other troops cannot, but to lie down and take the fire of infantry and artillery without response, requires more courage than to storm the Malakoff, or even the gates of hell itself! (Speaking after the manner of men.)

Not a shot was fired in response. Very soon, Ben Brown, of Russell, had his leg badly cut by a fragment of shell, and the next shot Sergeant Augustus H. Saunders was killed instantly, having just sighted his piece. No one ever combined the gentleness of a maiden with the firmness and courage of a true man, in finer proportion than Sergeant Saunders. He always did his duty and never swerved from making others do theirs. No other man in the company was so universally loved and respected.

"Right in the jaws of death" we felt that we had rode, when with a sharp crack two miles on our right, and a whistling noise like the flittering of a swallow, came the Whitworth bolt. The Yankee battery fired a little wildly, then lost range and finally limbered up and went out under whip and spur with the sun flashing from their polished pieces. Confederate horses never could have made such time, for they are as Shakespeare describes the English cavalry at Agincourt.

The Whitworth gun retired every Yankee gun on their left wing in Franklin's corps [Grand Division]. No other piece was firing, and Gen. D. H. Hill congratulates the Captain on his success, as he had previously requested an account of our fight with the gunboats, at Port Royal, for publication.

Burnside has changed his base, leaving his dead unburied; and camp report says the dead bodies were set up as *dummy* pickets to conceal his retreat. His plans will be developed before my conjectures would reach you.

God raised up Lee greater than Washington, to carry us through this struggle. You and I may not live to see the end, but of its successful termination, I have never had a doubt.

We gird up our loins for the work before us, trusting in God and the right.

Yours, PROLONGE.

LETTER FROM V. A. S. P.

NEAR FREDERICKSBURG, December 19, 1862 [1-1-63 SR]

My indisposition, and consequent dullness, have rendered me totally unequal to the task of writing such letters as your readers expect, or such as the stirring events of this remarkable period demand. I will attempt this morning an imperfect account of the late conflict.

In viewing the battleground, one who had not participated would conclude that the carnage was truly terrible. The hill sides are dotted, even yet, with the enemy's slain. Before they accepted Gen. Lee's offer, or before permission was granted to them to bury their dead, they lay in heaps. Hundreds of dead horses can be seen in every direction.

From sources entirely trustworthy, as well as by their own confession, the enemy's loss in killed and wounded will not fall far short of twenty thousand! They were so badly cut up that they positively refused to advance against us a third time. There was a mutinous spirit in their camps which forced Gen. Burnside to withdraw his army to the North bank of the Rappahannock.

Only a small portion of Hood's Division was engaged, the 54th and 57th North Carolina, of Law's Brigade. A heavy force of the enemy had advanced in our immediate front and possessed a small copse of wood. A regiment of Law's Brigade [6th N. C.] was very near the point in a good position, and it was thought they would hold the ground against the superior numbers of the enemy; but to their shame and the astonishment of all beholders, they gave the Yankees one terrible volley, which staggered the advancing foe, and ran from the field! A few brave men remained, and keeping up such a brisk and deadly fire, the enemy were held in check until the 54th and 57th came up. These gallant regiments, led by brave officers, charged the Yankees with a yell, who fled in terror, leaving their numerous dead and wounded in our hands. Verily, if *some* North Carolinians will *run*, there are many noble, brave soldiers from the Old North State to redeem her honor. No troops have fought better than [Lawrence O.] Branch's Brigade. The North Carolina regiments in Hood's Division have always fought well. He would have none other than brave troops.

I regret to learn that the 31st Georgia, Lawton's Brigade, suffered very much in a gallant charge upon the enemy's batteries. Lieutenant Daniel McNair, a paroled prisoner, met some members of my company, and told them that his regiment charged the enemy several hundred yards, and that getting very near the battery, he discovered a very heavy force of infantry coming to its support. He said Lieut. Judson Butts was the only officer he saw at that time, whom he told that if they did succeed in taking the battery they would not be able to hold it. Whereupon Lieut. Butts ordered a retreat. Soon after he (Lieut. McNair) was struck by a fragment of a shell or something of the sort, which momentarily paralyzed him. He was captured, and after two days was paroled. He knew nothing of what become of the regiment after the retreat; and I have not seen any one belonging to the regiment or Brigade.

McLaws' division played a conspicuous part in the bloody drama. His post was a good one, but his list of casualties show that the men and officers of his command did their whole duty. The enemy's loss on that part of the line—Longstreet's left—is five to our one. Indeed, it must be, in killed and wounded alone, nearly or quite *ten to our one* on the whole line. Our casualties will not exceed eighteen hundred or two thousand. "Why this great difference?" you will naturally ask. I can give the noted instance which may serve to explain. When the Yankees advanced upon the centre with an object of breaking our lines, they came up in *columns—massed*, while our troops were in one column, and were protected by the railroad. They advanced for two miles over the broad level field without a shrub or tree to turn a bullet or protect a man. Our best batteries and bravest cannoneers poured a storm of iron hail into their dense ranks, each well directed shot killing numbers of men. When they came within rifle range, every shot which its object took effect upon those in the rear. In this way few shots were wasted and the mortality in the enemy's ranks was appalling.

Our pickets, until forbidden by Gen. Lee, held familiar conversations with the Yankees, who came over in little batteaus to trade coffee, bacon, &c., for tobacco. They acknowledged they were badly whipped. When asked if there was a mutiny in their camps on Monday, when ordered to renew the attack, they gave evasive answers, which confirmed the report.

The Medical Corps of Hood's division deserves favorable mention for the promptitude displayed in making ample arrangements for the wounded, and their kind treatment of the unfortunate sons of Mars, who were struck by balls or bombs.

An officer of Anderson's brigade which was stationed in the old field in advance of our line of defense and to the left, asked me if "that was not Toombs' [now Benning's] brigade which charged so beautifully across the field and made the Yankees run at the point of the bayonet, to the tune of a genuine Southern yell?" I replied that our brigade had not been engaged, although we were under fire. I supposed it was a portion of Law's brigade. "Well," said he, "it was done so pretty that I thought it was your brigade." I thanked him for his good opinion of our veteran brigade, and remarked that we always liked to close with the Yankees, who always "get further."

The army was absolutely disappointed when it was announced that Burnside had recrossed the river. But a small portion had engaged the enemy, and they felt slighted. So confident were they of totally routing the Yankees that they often said they could whip the whole Yankee nation if they would come up in front of our *impromptu* works. Gen. Hood remarked in my hearing that we could whip all the forces the enemy could bring against us.

On Tuesday morning [Dec. 16] when the whole army was alive with excitement consequent upon the enemy's retreat, a loud shout was heard away down upon our right. The shout swelled in volume and drew nearer and nearer. "What can be the cause?" was the anxious query. I strained my eyes in the direction, and soon saw a man in full gallop. I understood it then. "Jackson! Stonewall Jackson's coming! Hurrah for General Jackson!" His cap was off, and the old hero presented a fine spectacle as he galloped by with his noble, manly brow and slightly bald head exposed. In this way he rode the whole line, receiving the homage of an admiring soldiers; and, doubtless, was glad to see the road turn off from the men who loved so much to do him honor. He never appears before the army without exciting the liveliest enthusiasm. Whenever the boys begin to cheer he pulls off his cap and puts spurs to his horse as if anxious to get out of sight. None but a good man could receive the plaudits he does without becoming puffed up and vain.

The General had so completely metamorphased his *personel* by wearing an entirely new suit of Confederate grey that many failed to recognize him at first. He is really a fine looking man.

Gen. Lee is looking much better than he did last summer. He reminds one of Washington, whose virtues he possesses in an eminent degree. He is organized, quiet, kind, christian like, and is accessible to the humblest private in the ranks.

This morning we were in lines and started to take our position, supposing the enemy to be advancing again. The two signal guns were heard. Everybody heard them, but they were Yankees firing at one of our wagons going for forage. All quiet now as before.

V. A. S. P.

LETTER FROM TIVOLI, SCENES AFTER THE BATTLE, SACKING OF FREDERICKSBURG—FLAGS OF TRUCE

FREDERICKSBURG, December 21, 1862 [1-7-63ASC]

The weather remains fair and cool offering every opportunity for the enemy to renew their "on to Richmond," but as yet there are no signs of their intention to try their hand again at this point.

An alarm yesterday was given and our whole army was out under arms, but it proved false, and all contentedly returned to camp. For several days they have been busy, under a flag of truce, burying their dead. We visited one of their parties, thus engaged, on the extreme left of our line, and the officer in charge informed us that he had then buried one thousand and had a few more left to entomb—if entombing it could be called—a large pit four hundred feet wide was dug and the bodies were hurriedly and indecently thrown into the pit, one upon another until nearly full—a few shovels full of dirt are thrown on top, and this ends the ceremony—no shirt, no shroud, not even the martial cloak around them they are thus hid from sight and the pleasant valley that their presence renders hideous.

On a tombstone at Antietam is the following inscription made by the Yankees, "There lie the bodies of sixty Rebels. The way of the transgressor is hard." These Yankees here will need no epitaph to describe their deeds—for near them—ay! at their very feet, lies the city of Fredericksburg in ruins—yet with form erect lifting her fallen towers and desecrated temples up in the face of Heaven, a protest against tyranny, and the foe who have thus mercilessly ravished her. Many of her butchers sleep now within sight of the smoke of her burning dwellings—their only anthem shall be the curses of an oppressed people. Like thieves they came and like dogs are they buried, their epitaphs shall not be written nor marked their graves, for their deeds have proven them unfit for place in Heaven or on earth.

I speak warmly—but walk with me through the streets of the devoted city—houses shattered, pillars mark the place where in childhood and early youth, we worshipped our God. What shell and shot had spared the ruin and deliberate thieving of the Yankees had finished. Every house is broken open, every store is sacked and not a single moveable of any sort remains. What cannot be carried away is destroyed, pianos, bedsteads, bedding, and even the playthings of children are broken into fragments and hurled into the middle of the street. It seems as if there had been a carnival of madmen, a Pandemonium of destroyers. Even the plastering on the walls of the houses was scraped over by the brutal bayonets and all sorts of insulting and filthy deeds were performed in conspicuous places where they could not help but meet the eye and disgust the senses.

Yet at the end of the main street scarce a bow shot from town a thousand of the companions of those who committed these deeds lie in unhonored graves and through a just God, there is yet a prospect that the waters of the Rappahannock shall be black with the blood of thousands more.

As we strode along the town a child picked up from the ground a picture all shattered and torn. Holding it up the child exclaimed, "They call this crushing the rebellion—this crushing of pictures." We smiled with him but it was a bitter though interesting incident.

We conversed with many of the enemy engaged in this detail and find that all of them have a hope of the restoration of the Union. Yet all unite in wishing the war at an end—they are exclusively bitter against their officers and poured many an invective on the head of "Burney," as they call Burnside. The Yankees have a wonderful fondness for nicknames, they call McClellan, Mac; Lincoln, Abe; Hooker, Fighting Joe, and so on to the end of the list of their great men.

They boasted much of their superiority in number, and one of them said that there were 200,000 men in camps of instruction, who had not yet fired a gun.

An officer of high rank enquired of one of our men how it was possible we could so hate the old Stars and Stripes. His answer was that he cared for nothing in the shape of a flag—we might change ours every day and there would be little notice taken of it by our people. A flag meant nothing. A more appropriate answer would have been to have pointed to the ruins beneath us and have said, witnessing such scenes as these, should we not all swear eternal hostility to the banner under which you fight. Curses upon the flag. Palsied be the hands that maintain it.

We are much amused in camp at the Northern reports of the battles. At last accounts, Burnside had captured "*all but the* crest." He is not the first inexperienced navigator who, leaping at the crest, has been caught up by the under tow and dashed to pieces on the rocks beneath.

We are preparing for Christmas in camp. We expect to be able, by strict economy, to have full rations of hard bread and salt pork, at least on that day. In the clear water of the murmuring stream we will drink, health and a merry Christmas to you all.

Excuse the desultory character of this letter, having no news, you "must be content with gossip."

Yours,   TIVOLI.

LETTER FROM TOUT LE MONDE

FREDERICKSBURG, VA., December 27, 1862 [1-13-63SR]

There is little use to go back and rehearse what has already been written over and over again of the late battle, unless there were some lingering maliciousness to bore somebody. But let us try to bind up a letter from the rubbish and remains of what has not been told at all, or not so often as to become wearisome to the reader. The great battle has been fought on which the Federals had launched so many hopes, the result of which has sunk them, as their organs acknowledge, into national despair. Their folly, still persisted in, has made many a new grave and built another infamous and iniquitous chapter in history, for which, as sure as natural laws prevail, they will suffer. Besides the slaughter which has been occasioned, you have been told that the inhabitants—peaceful, inoffensive people—have been turned upon the world, rich and poor, equally homeless and destitute.

The number of forces engaged on our side has been ascertained to be less than 20,000—probably a fourth of our army present, but having no very accurate means of learning the enemy's force, we are left to conjecture. Prisoners noted for mendacity are not to be credited, but we can infer from the number of corps to which they belong, and from confessions through Northern journals, that not less than 50,000 assailed our right and left. This was probably half the force on this side of the river.

Gen. A. P. Hill, as you know, met them in the open field, and demonstrated that this army could defeat them fairly. The proof was incontestable there. On the left Gen. Cobb simply showed that they were not fools. Yesterday we rode over that ground. Unless one could see, there is no words to adequately portray the appearance of the field nor the marks still remaining, and destined to remain a long time, of the fight of these subtle messengers of death. A range of hills near the town rises suddenly from the plain on the Western suburbs. Just where the first acclivity begins a stone wall skirts along, affording line protection from bullets and shells. Upon this hill there was a strong earthwork to protect a battery of guns which commanded the town and much of the plain below it. This hill became a desirable spot to the enemy, because it also commanded many of our entrenchments and put their artillery on an equal footing which were perched upon the hills of the same range. Gen. T. R. R. Cobb was assigned to the stone wall and commanded to hold it. Never was a command more implicitly obeyed. In the evening, about the time of the advance on the right, a simultaneous advance was made to secure this much coveted position by the enemy's choicest *fools*, made drunk for the occasion. General Cobb looked upon the early home of his mother, and resolved to die or defend it; it was there nearby, to raise the sternest resolves in his heart. You have heard how the devils came up reeking and stinking in their loathsome inebriation, and the rain of death which fell suddenly, like a thunder bolt among them. It was truly awful. Confused and partly brought to their senses, they broke in confusion, to be replaced by the next line of hireling vagabonds, who, in turn, shared the same fate. On they came, and at every turn were heaped upon their miserable dead and wounded confreres. Our men, perfectly secure, dealt their fire with awful fatality. When their cartridges were spent, Gen. Kershaw's brigade poured in to their help, and our loss was sustained in reinforcing alone.

These were the troops that fought them, as well as we can ascertain. But look at the awful spectacle in front of this stone fence. Dead men fell upon the wounded, and poured out their blood, and the wounded were shot again and again, because they could not move from the withering fire. Houses, trees and fences were torn, riddled and pierced in ten thousand places. We looked upon the ground where the bodies lay, after they were removed, and a dull red carpet of clotted gore covered it everywhere.

Such was the scene of this slaughter. Has any one told you of the desolate little city? We rode along the streets, and only here and there we met a solitary, sorrowful citizen, returned to look upon his desolation, or saw the picket guard walking to and fro on his lonely post. The horses' steps echoed from the walls, or the flight of pigeons—stronger in home attachments than poor men—fell on the ear, the only sounds. Here and there shade trees or the houses showed signs where cannon shot had raged. As we progressed toward the river, these became more evident and plentiful. The great church spire, which rears itself near the centre of the city, was pierced with twenty cannon balls. The sacred sanctuary of God had not been spared.

Our camps in many places were not struck because Gen. Lee was confident of the result. Therefore, the boys just left the lines where the foe had fled, and again the even tenor of camp life began as smoothly as ever. Again the buskin was resumed and Ethiopian tragedy and farce stalked across the stage. "What," you ask, "Is't possible there is camp histrionics among the ragged rebels?" it is an existing reality. If you will come sometime and go with us to "Hood's Minstrels"—they show to-morrow night again—"Old Bob Ridley" will make your sides ache with fun. It is only a few hundred yards away just yonder in the woods. An enterprising number of young men from Gen. Hood's old Texas brigade formed a very fine company and have some very diverting amusement for camp. Their efforts to relieve the tediousness of the soldier's life has been kindly encouraged by the Generals, who are often seen mingling with the soldiers and laughing over the obsequious negro delineations. A few nights ago the Minstrels contributed by their performance over three hundred dollars to the sufferers in the city of Fredericksburg. There fun has been turned to charity, and Humor made mistress of Philanthropy.

Christmas is with us, but she comes clad in the dark weeds of death—the land wrapped in gloom—the grand Nativity in which all should give a free hand to fellowship and good will is welcome and rivulets of blood—the shout of victory is mingled with the wail of sorrow for those who have bought it with their lives. Such is the decree of fate for our land, and the directing of an inscrutible Providence.

TOUT LE MONDE.

Official casualties for the battle of Fredericksburg: Federals, 1,284 killed, 9,600 wounded and 1,769 missing for a total of 12,652; Confederates, 595 killed, 4,061 wounded and 653 missing for 5,309.

☆☆☆Winter 1863

After the victory at Fredericksburg the Army of Northern Virginia settled into winter camp and kept a watchful eye upon the Army of the Potomac (now commanded by Gen. Joseph Hooker) on the north bank of the Rappahannock. In February, two divisions of Longstreet's corps were detached and sent to Southside Virginia to protect the capital from Federal threats on the Peninsula.

LETTER FROM TIVOLI

CAMP NEAR FREDERICKSBURG, VA., January 9, 1863 [1-18-63ASC]

There has been a great dearth of news in the army of Northern Virginia since I last wrote you. We remain in *status quo*, facing the "nigger stealers," with nothing to vary the monotony of camp life, except the advent of the holidays. They came and swiftly passed away; brought with them but little merriment, but slight enjoyment, and left behind a pang of bitter remembrances in every breast. The pleasant memories of the past were all as "Dead Sea fruit." Let us all pray that the next advent of the New Year will find us all at home.

"Enjoying peace our valor won."

The army for the past few days have been much exercised on the subject of the news from the South-west. One day we learn from undoubted authority that [Braxton] Bragg has won a glorious victory, and that the Troy of the Mississippi is still untaken—the next day we hear Bragg is in full retreat and Vicksburg fallen. So frequent are the contradictory stories, that the soldier now denies the fact of a battle having been fought, and insists that there is no such place as Vicksburg on the maps. Come what may of these things the veteran army of Virginia will ever be found worthy of their brief yet glorious career.

The men are all in good health and spirits, and, thanks to the good folks at home, comfortably and neatly clad. Their discipline was effective and nearly perfect, and seldom have I seen soldiers bear themselves better. The performances of this Brigade [Anderson] in battle will claim a prominent position in the temple of Georgia's historic glory.

The health of the army is good. A few cases of small pox have appeared, but as yet it is not an epidemic among us. The troops have all been re-vaccinated, and we hope to escape this plague.

Fredericksburg still lies neglected and deserted. A few families have returned to their desecrated hearths, but the majority of the citizens remain away. The collections in the army for their relief reaches a very large sum—showing that the brave are always generous.

For the past week the weather has been fair but very cold, and the evidences are that the winter has set in in earnest. We have plenty of wood, and the camp fires that we light are equal to those that burned in Sherwood forest when Robin Hood was a blythe forester and wore his coat of green.

Yours, &c.,   TIVOLI.

LETTER FROM SOLDIER JIM

CAMP 8TH GA., NEAR FREDERICKSBURG, VA., January 11, 1863 [1-21-63ASC]

I drop you a line that you may be assured Soldier Jim is all right. We are encamped in the woods where the oak timber is immense and we can easily build good fires, though the weather has been mild and pleasant for this climate.

The army is in most excellent health and fine spirits; and were our ranks filled out by those who should be here, we would have the best army in the world. Many are away on furlough exerting themselves to be detached, and many citizens are giving their influence and doing what they can to reduce our ranks, instead of urging absent men to return to their commands.

It was rumored yesterday that the main body of the Yankees were falling back towards Washington. Such a movement on their part is advisable, for when our cavalry commissary becomes short, Gen. Stuart is informed of the fact, his force is soon in motion; and we know not which way his is gone, but he is soon heard of between the Yankee grand army and their capitol, relieving the Yankee commissaries and sutlers of their luxuries. He takes such horses as sent him, and as many bare backs as he cares to be bothered with, and returns to camp with a large supply of camp necessaries.

The Yankees may fight us till 1870, and we will not be conquered or coerced.

SOLDIER JIM.

OUR SPECIAL ARMY CORRESPONDENT TIVOLI
CAMP NEAR FREDERICKSBURG, VA., January 20, 1863 [1-28-63ASC]

The army for the past three days has been in a state of expectancy, as, by the orders issued by our commanders, as well as by the movements of the enemy, another fight throws its shadow before us.

For the past three days great activity has been noticed in the enemy across the river, and at a point ten miles below this, on the river, they have partially constructed causeways for the rapid movement of artillery to the river bank. Their pickets have also been strengthened, and mounted blue coats riding hastily up and down, betokens that "bustle" has become the order of the day with them. For what purpose these things are done, remains to be seen. Judging by the past tardy action of the enemy, we will all have a breathing time of several days ere we are called upon to hold bloody argument with them.

The spirit and the health of the army are good. The small pox has had but few victims. The disease, I am happy to state, does not take hold in the army, and the cases reported are those of men who have been absent from camp. On their return, the small pox has broken out upon them. They are at once sent to the Small Pox Hospital, near Fredericksburg. The whole army has been vaccinated, and by order of General Lee, every officer, private, attache and servant, have been revaccinated.

The troops of Longstreet's corps are healthily located, and for all I know, so are the rest of the army. The men have mostly built themselves comfortable quarters, and were never in better spirits for a fight. What Stonewall Jackson is to his men, Longstreet is to his veteran troops. Pointing to their blood-stained banners, they claim the first place among Generals for him. They style him "Lee's right bower," and take pride in singing songs to his praise. Truly, the hero of Bull Run, Williamsburg, Seven Pines, Richmond, Rappahannock, Thoroughfare Gap, Manassas, Boonesboro', Antietam, and Fredericksburg, can claim for himself and his hero soldiers, a first place in the chronicles of our nation. When the history of this war is written, no names will be more surrounded with the laurel of glorious deeds, than those of Longstreet and his veterans.

Yours, &c.   TIVOLI.

LAWTON'S BRIGADE
NEAR PORT ROYAL, VA., January 31, 1863 [2-7-63ASC]

This is the camp of Stonewall Jackson's corps d' armee. I have visited the several brigades composing it during the past two days, and find them in good health and spirits— ready, as they have ever been, to meet the insolent foe; and I but reiterate the opinion of both officers and men, when I say that this army, in its present position, is *invincible*. Whilst this army, generally speaking, is in excellent condition, it is my duty to inform the friends of Gen. Lawton's Ga. Brigade, composed of the 13th, 26th, 31st, 38th, 60th and 61st Ga. regiments, that many of the men in this Brigade are entirely barefooted, and many more are without socks, which are a necessary for a soldier's comfort in such a climate as this. In the 60th Ga. regiment 150 men did not participate in the battle of Fredericksburg, because they were without shoes; and this was to some extent the case with several other regiments. Some of the men in this brigade have been supplied since, but still, many are without any kind of a shoe.

Last Wednesday night [Jan. 25] a terrible snow storm prevailed, covering the ground with 10 inches of snow, and adding to the suffering of our men.

Whose fault it is, that these brave men are thus neglected, I shall not at this time understand to say, but will call the attention of our State authorities and their friends and relatives in Georgia to their condition. I trust that, in justice to our country's defenders, something will be done for their relief. I am informed that what I have said in reference to the condition of these regiments, is equally true of many others from Georgia. The men are bearing these hardships and sufferings without a murmur, which shows a devoted patriotism unequalled in the history of the world. In this connection, I desire to say to the benevolent and patriotic ladies of the Empire State of the South that thousands of their fathers, brothers and friends in this army are destitute of socks. I know that it is only necessary for them to be aware of the fact, and the soldiers will soon be supplied.

The roads here are all in horrible condition; in fact, many of them are impassable. The ground was quite rotten before this snow, and is becoming worse daily.

On the road from Guiney's Station to this place, I saw teams stalling with empty wagons, while every few hundred yards a wagon was mired in the mud to the axles, and abandoned; and in the road and roadside, at short intervals, lay numbers of dead mules and horses. At one place the road was literally blockaded by the bodies of three dead mules, lying stretched in the mud and water in one hedge.

From this you will see that an advance of the enemy soon is utterly impossible.

Of course it would not be prudent for me to say anything definite about the number of our men on the line of the Rappahannock, or the strength of their position, but it is enough to know that both are amply sufficient to repel any effort the enemy may make on our lines; and if Hooker should cross the river with his hordes of thieves and robbers, it will be only to meet with certain and inevitable defeat.

Our men now all have tents with chimneys, or log huts, and most of them are pretty well supplied with blankets.

It is amusing to see what a variety of crude huts are constructed. They may be seen in every shape and size imaginable. The chimneys are generally topped with an empty flour barrel—both heads being broken out. The rations now are flour and pickled pork, but they are rather short on account of the bad condition of the roads. In fact, I have no doubt that, unless great industry is used in "polling" the road from the railroad to the army, it will be impossible to supply them with commissary stores, and consequently the army will have to change its position.

CAMP.

LETTER FROM THE SECOND GEORGIA BATTALION
BIVOUAC NEAR U. S. FORD, VA., February 7, 1863 [2-16-63CS]

Judging that the friends of the 2nd Ga. Battalion would like to learn of their whereabouts and present occupation, I will try to inform them. We are encamped at present in the vicinity of United States Ford, about twelve or fourteen miles from Fredericksburg, up the Rappahannock. We have been here near three weeks, throwing up batteries and digging rifle pits, and have the place now in a fit condition to receive "Fighting Joe Hooker" and his vandals whenever they take the notion to find us, and that is very easily done, as we are not more than a mile distant.

We received orders last night at tattoo to clean up guns, etc., and be in readiness at a moment's notice, as the enemy were making demonstrations on the other side of the river, and we might expect an attack at any moment, but how they will manage to move while the roads are in the condition they are in is beyond my ken. It has been snowing, sleeting and raining here for the past several days and the mud in the roads is up to the hubs of the wagons. I have seen four mules stall with an empty wagon, and I suppose the roads are in the same condition on the other side of the river. Transportation is very difficult where we are, and we are thus kept on short rations, which causes a very general complaint. We have been getting only one quarter of a pound of bacon and a little sugar for some time past. Now, when the grease is fried out of a quarter pound of bacon and put in the biscuits there is none of the meat left. I hope something will be done, and that very soon, to remedy this evil, for if there is anything that a soldier needs and what he is right entitled to, it is full rations. If a man goes a mile from camps to buy him a little flour he is arrested by the provost guard and put to digging entrenchments, and still hundreds leave camp every day, for the gnawings of hunger, will make a soldier run every risk. I learn that Gen. [Ambrose R.] Wright has given the Commissaries five days to issue full rations to the men. I hope he will rigidly enforce the order.

The health of the battalion is very good at present, notwithstanding they have had to undergo pretty severe hardships for the past two weeks, laying out in the snow and rain, without shelter, digging rifle pits and batteries night and day, etc.

If anything of note transpires, I will keep you posted.

FURNITURE.

LETTER FROM TIVOLI

IN CAMP, NEAR FREDERICKSBURG, VA., February 8, 1863 [2-19-63ASC]

Everything seems quiet on the winter banks of the Rappahannock and "Fighting Joe Hooker" has not yet placed himself in a fighting attitude. The snow has melted from the ground, leaving the roads in a terrible condition.

We occasionally get the Richmond papers and our leisure moments are spent in a consideration of the prospects for an early peace, mediation, &c. All arrive at one very sound conclusion, and that is that the North is entirely disgusted with the war, and are very willing to quit, if they only knew how. Another battle here may show them.

Dr. North, of Georgia, has just joined Anderson's Georgia Brigade, as Ass't Surgeon. This gentleman has just returned from a compulsory visit to Washington, he having been captured at Warrenton, Va. He was carried to the Capitol prison, together with a negro boy belonging to him. On their arrival in the presence of the brute [William] Wood, keeper of the prison, the negro was informed by the scoundrel that he was free, and could do whatever he wished. He was his own man.

The negro positively refused to quit his master and continued his refusal until exasperated, the brute ordered Dr. North to make his negro quit him. On Dr. North's refusal, he and his boy were placed in a dark dungeon and kept there for nearly twenty-four hours. Wood expressed with many oaths his determination to keep them there for a month, but desisted when our captive officers threatened that when they arrived in Richmond they would lay this matter before President Davis, and have the *lex talionis* applied. The boy clung to his master's skirts and came back to Dixie well satisfied with having escaped the clutches of the Abolitionists. I mention this incident as it is not without its lesson.

The mails come very irregularly, and it is very seldom we get a paper from home, so that there is great scarcity of reading matter in the camps. Speaking of this, I notice with pleasure that Mr. [J. W.] Randolph, the Richmond publisher, announces as ready for publication a new novel entitled *Cosimir*, by Dr. C. E. L. Stuart, the author of many valuable works of fiction and lately the editor of the *New York Daily News*.

I am pleased to see that our Literature is thus extending and improving. Our arms will force a physical separation from the North and it is left for our Literature to create a moral and eternal separation. The bondage of Literature is, after all, the most disgraceful and abject servitude.

TIVOLI.

ANOTHER LETTER FROM TIVOLI

CAMP NEAR FREDERICKSBURG, VA., February 14, 1863 [2-19-63ASC]

To-day the sun shines brightly and the air is cool and pleasant. Yesterday we had rain all day and the roads still remain in bad condition. It will take at least two weeks continuance of the present weather before the roads will be ready to accommodate "Fighting Joe Hooker" and his ribald followers. Until then we can quietly smoke our pipes by the side of our merry camp fires.

On Wednesday last a tragedy occurred near camps that created much excitement. In the vicinity of camp there are many houses of ill-fame, and in one of these a man named Owens was concealed evading the Conscript Law. A young man named E. S. Lewis, a private in the Palmetto Sharp Shooters, with a comrade attempted to arrest him and in doing so he was struck by Owens over the head with a hatchet, and so seriously injured as to preclude any hopes of his recovery. The villain escaped and at last accounts had not been captured.

Speaking of conscripts, reminds me, that most all of the conscripts received here in the army are entirely worthless either in body or in mind and the class of substitutes received are very little better in quality. A few days ago, a man named Alfred Brooks, perfectly sound in mind was sent from your section to the 8th Georgia Regiment. He had in simplicity of his mind sold himself to a citizen of Oglethorpe county, who was cognizant of his condition, for $150—no part of which has he yet received. The Surgeon, who examined him in Georgia, passed him, but the Medical Officers here refused to receive him on account of his imbecility, and gave him a certificate for a discharge.

The health of the army is good, no more bare feet; no squalid rags; no poverty in equipment or in spirits, but "all is well," and those at home who have an interest in the welfare of the poor soldier can rest assured that we are comfortably clad and delightfully fixed against the inclemency of the weather. Our tents have all huge chimneys built to them, the hearths rivaling in size those of the old Baronial time, when oxen roasted whole at the turn of the spit. Our food is plain, yet wholesome, and the appetites with which the poor soldier sets down to his humble fare, more than repays for the absence of variety. Our feast is plenty; our sauce, content, and "good digestion waits upon the appetite."

I am sorry to close my letter by reference to a melancholy subject, but it pleases well the bent of my inclination to do honor to the memory of the martyred dead, no matter whether it be a martyr in the field of battle or in the nobler fields of Christian charity. Private W. H. H. Trammell, Co. D, 8th Ga. Regiment, a few weeks since left his company for the purpose of going to Richmond to nurse his brother, Lieut. Trammell, of the same company, who was there sick. He found the Lieutenant suffering with the worst form of confluent small pox, and, nothing daunted at the presence of this loathsome disease, he at once applied himself with an untiring energy and fidelity seldom equaled in the duties of a nurse. He continued in the infected room until his brother had recovered, and then, with the poison in his veins, laid down on the bed of sickness and of death. He suffered long, yet uncomplainingly, and took his place in the holy rank of Christian martyrs in Heaven without a sigh or complaint. This is a striking instance of Fraternal affection, and as such, let us all honor the memory of the quiet Christian boy of W. H. H. TRAMMELL, of Merriwether county, Ga.

TIVOLI.

LETTER FROM SOLDIER JIM

CAMP 8TH GA. REGIMENT, March 2, 1863 [3-8-63ASC]

We are all now encamped on a very dry oak ridge surrounded by springs and small streams. Our late camp was about two miles from this, located in a pine swamp, where we were almost up to our eyes in mud and water. A few nights ago, when on our march to this locality, we were filed out into the woods for camp. Soon we gathered pine tops and spread upon the ground, on which laid our wearied limbs, and covering with our blankets, slept soundly and dreamed sweetly, while a very heavy snow fell, which buried us all, and the weight of which awoke most of us about 3 A. M. A slight raising up of our heads, however, soon convinced us that the best policy was to be perfectly still till day, which we did.

The following day was a continuous rain, which brought an awful mud about our camp. I leave you to imagine its extent. Notwithstanding all this, our boys are quite healthy, and anxious to meet the foe again, if he must be met.

SOLDIER JIM.

LETTER FROM TOUT LE MONDE

RICHMOND, VA., March 10, 1863 [3-17-63SR]

Our last silence has been longer than was intended. It was *intended* to write as soon as we got here, but by accident—a very common accident in the army—a trunk, containing all the writing paper, wardrobe, household and kitchen furniture we possessed, went overboard in the mud, and has not been disinterred. The kindness of a friend furnished us with this parcel—just enough to be short—which, with most army correspondence, is desirable.

We left our winter quarters on the 17th of February, and then the snow was falling rapidly. It lay over four inches deep on the ground, and continued either to snow or rain for three days after, during which time the army struggled through everything—floundering in mud and rain—with most incredible suffering. One night will be ever memorable over all the others. The cold northeast wind, that brought on its icy wings incessant driving sleet to the outstretched army, which had nowhere to lay but on the cold, wet ground, and only drenched blankets and saturated clothes to depend on. Throughout the long weary night the log heaps were nursed with the most untiring affection, but the never wearying winds ceaselessly urged on the pitiless storm. Well, as P. W. A., your truthful correspondent, has enlarged upon this, we will desist. Suffice it to say, these invincible men shouted and laughed away their hardships, and are as happy and hearty, cheerful as if nothing had disturbed them.

On the morning of the 21st the sun rose clear, and the tall spires of our capital lay before us. Richmond, for which so much blood has flowed, was again before the old veteran—he who carried honorable scars that he obtained in its defense. 'Twas Richmond on which, for months of toil passed, eyes had not been laid—Richmond, swarming with vagabond officers, standing in grand positions, *a la militaire*, on the sidewalk, to see the soldiers pass—officers sporting every elegance of military attire and numerous evidences of a disposition to keep away from minnie balls and cannon shot   There were colonels, with huge whiskers, and captains, with huge whiskers and moustaches, mixed in with youthful lieutenants, with as much whiskers and moustaches as they could raise, sprinkled now and then with majors and lieutenant colonels—now and then a brig. general, carrying some tailor's establishment on their backs.

Richmond, teeming with an assemblage of the most villainous Shylocks probably ever got together—the city where a poor soldier who had put his whole life and energy forward to save, was requested by having his pittance of money extorted from him by a race of merciless wretches—the place where a hungry man can get a decent supper for twenty dollars, or buy a pound of coffee for $4.75!—the city where there is a Congress scrambling and kicking into a mire known as the financial question, into which it seems to get farther and farther—where sharpers and officials abound in Government Departments pilfering and robbing from day to day—the city where the women, as usual, are the best people in it, and love the soldiers—Richmond that has some good people in it, but not enough to quench that noxious germ whose future expansion will choke our young tree of Freedom as in the old Confederation.

On the 21st, General Hood led his division through with flying banners, and crossed over the James river. Here we rest six miles from the city, awaiting any movement of the enemy, which, it is supposed—for nobody knows—will determine our movements. The health of the troops is very good, and everything is very quiet except the little flurry about the news that comes to us through papers. It has afforded no little pleasure to see an account of the "grit" that handled the guns at Fort McAllister. Many a Yankee, from this example, is trembling now over the gloomy way to death which is so elegantly spread out before them in the "On to Charleston and Savannah." The day of scaring people with gunboats has entirely—in camp parlance—"played out." The dread reality that these places must fall by storming terrible earthworks (which Yankees have never yet accomplished) with rebels behind them, has bred a perfect harvest of horror about Yankee gizzards. We don't feel alarmed, and not at all conceited in the belief that this army of the South alone is invincible. We believe wherever southern blood is in arms, there are brave and earnest hearts there. When we see so many patriots hastening to the scene of danger, we cannot see cause for alarm. Nor will we believe that the new music that some of the monsters will make about the ears of the militia officers will cause any trepidation there. Doubtless they have gone to the front now to show other soldiers that when the fighting time comes they are ready for it. All eyes are now turned to the South and to Vicksburg. Many a prayer is said for your victories. Whether a simultaneous demonstration will be made here or not, none seem able to determine. Hooker we are told, still threatens from the opposite side of the Rappahannock, and may again attempt an insane advance on Richmond, but it is not apparent. Such as they got there the last time rather seemed to strike the final death blow to any hope of taking the Capital directly. However, there is no accounting for Northern insanity; more bloodshed may follow very soon after the weather is favorable.

How do you seem to view the prospects for peace now? The Yankee Congress has, we believe, voted just such power to Lincoln as will satisfy him; that, too, in the very teeth of all the threatened dissentions among the people. He has now absolute control of the militia force, with power to draw them out at his leisure and discretion; does this look like there was much of peace afloat there? Let not the people of the South permit one solitary energy to sleep over any delusive hope of peace. The war will not end soon, though it may have spent its direst efforts against us. It is left us to resist to the last—to the very last. Probably every one is satisfied that Napoleon is not on his way yet to mediate, and if any hope was cherished then, now it is abandoned. It should be our constant and unanimous ambition to assist in whatever we may to carry on the war, studying to be united, and to concentrate our energies. The unity of design and effort can not fail to carry us safely through.

It is a source of regret that we have no room to pay our compliment to the stay-home-boys. We intended to extol the ingenuity of some of that class in this letter—the ways and means resorted to, for resisting the polite requests of conscript and enrolling officers to "fall in". Maybe we can at some other time. Boys, we don't intend to neglect you, but excuse us this time.

Why, Miss D—, did you ask us if we would accept those socks? Gracious me! let me tell you. We had on hand a small piece of candle (wasn't saving it for "draw" by-the-by) say inch and a half long, which we on reception of them, immediately "combusticated" and having dorned said socks, elevated our feet *otium cum dinatate* on the tent pole and eyed the same with the utmost satisfaction for exactly (by town time) three-fourths of an hour. Then we took them off and put 'em away to keep till peace and low quartered shoes come again. Will it ever pass from our memory, that checked shirt, which was home made? Never. How delightful to have something that reminds us of our noble mothers and sisters at home, whose busy hands are showing contempt on every Yankee fabric. We almost hate a man now who wears broadcloth, because he reminds one of that most despicable race on earth—Yankees.

Our homespun is a sign of plenty and independence in the land, and that the dainty hand of fashion is not restraining our developing resources.

TOUT LE MONDE.

SECOND GEORGIA BATTALION

CAMP NEAR GUINEA'S STATION, VA., March 17, 1863 [3-27-63CS]

There is not much prospect of active service in this region for some time to come, as the roads are still in a condition almost impassible. The weather for the past week has been very disagreeable—hail, snow and rain every day, accompanied with very cold winds, making the soldier stick close to his log cabin and hug the fire.

Rumors float *ad libitum* in camp—"going to Georgia," taking the lead. "Gen. Lee has ordered the women and children out of Fredericksburg, and sent wagons to remove them," is the latest rumor, but it must be taken with many grains of allowance, as it is a stereotyped saying up this way. I think April will come and go, before we have any orders to leave our winter quarters and prepare for active service.

The health of the battalion, and especially Company A, is excellent at present. Since we arrived at our winter quarters, our company has considerably increased by the arrival from the hospital and from home of convalescent soldiers. The battalion has begun to resume its wonted appearance. May it never grow less.

FURNITURE.

ANDERSON'S BRIGADE

CAMP NEAR RICHMOND, VA., March 27, 1863 [4-4-63ASC]

We have been once again hurried out on one of those merciless tramps, burdened only with knapsacks and a total ignorance of destination, or the wherefore. At 4 o'clock, A. M., 21st inst., we were pushed into line with instructions to march towards Fredericksburg to play at "nucks" or "long taw" with the enemy, said to be crossing the Rappahannock at Kelly's Ford. At dark, same day, we bivouacked near Ashland, fourteen miles from Richmond. A courier came in from the front, accoutered cap a-pie, bringing intelligence of the utter rout of the enemy by Gen. Stuart [at Kelly's Ford on March 17]. Further advance being unnecessary, we remained the day, to rest the troops and dispose of the sick. On the third, we were on the backward march to old camps under cover of one of the severest snow storms of the winter. The men flung themselves into line, dancing the "snow reel"—laughing at distance and fatigue, or the unreasonableness of a return to camps through such snow—9 inches—and over such new made earth. The smile and good cheer that pervaded the mass, as its lengthy line moved on, was indeed encouraging, speaking louder than words, the tough and cartilaginous nature of men, now twenty-three months in the field. O! that some of those desponding ones who read only the fickle press of the country, could see these jolly fellows warming into life the stiff cool air, with their mirth and song. They would then confide in our physical ability, as well as determination, to conquer though all Lincolndom oppose. Every passer-by, every donkey, beast or object, are subjects of remark, such as "here's your iron-clad ginger cakes!" "Look here, stranger, come out o' that coat; I know you're there, for I see the tray of your trousers magotizing!" "I say, you slippery conscript, slide off them bones and take my luggage!" "Here's your tail supporters!"—(rear guard)

> "Here's your filthy Ninth, and dirty Seventh,
> The greasy Eighth and ragged Eleventh."

"Close up you Highlanders, and sing low—old 'Tige's' behind you. Can't give furloughs to service crabbs—don't deal in such path finders." "Hallo! I say, old cuss, got any whisky under that jacket? Know you have, because I see the stopper with the stuff oozing out between your eyes!"

On the morning of our march from Fredericksburg, Major R——, having his men in line, politely requested every one who felt himself unable to march to advance four paces in front. To his utter surprise, the whole column stepped out in triple-quick. The generous Major threw up his arms and exclaimed, "No! no! I did not mean all of you—only those who are sick—men, do you think me a resurrectionist! Sergeant, take your list to the Surgeon. Forward—march!"

Toward evening of the second day out, a most amusing incident occurred, having but one witness. A straggler, fatigued, wet to the skin, and burdened with extra baggage, plodded his way far in the rear, now up to his knees in mud, then to his middle in slush, suddenly struck his foot, when down went he, face-foremost into the unsightly mixture. Raising himself he attempted an outward, onward motion, when in two places, down he came a second time covered as before. Moving himself erect, cast his eyes about him, then looking up to heaven, he exclaimed in a plaintive voice: "Here's your mummy, already embalmed. Gabriel! Blow your horn, for now's your time." Then stepping to the wayside, seated himself on the trunk of a fallen tree, to strip and repent the day that made him a soldier and a slave.

Such scenes are of daily occurrence; many instructive, others amusing. But I fatigue you. Health of the troops in this old army is most excellent. Never better. Attributable to the short allowance of meat—four ounces—now issued. Sugar and rice supply the deficiency.

The 27th was observed with more than ordinary interest and solemnity by both officers and men. Gens. Hood and Anderson attended divine service in this brigade—the Rev. Mr. Crumley officiating. His text was from Mathew 41st chapter, 12th verse.

We leave tomorrow at 8 o'clock for parts unknown. The roads are barely passable. Look out for a stir.

                                                        CIRCUIT JUDGE.

LETTER FROM V. A. S. P.

CAMP NEAR PETERSBURG, VA., April 2, 1863 [4-8-63SR]

On the 28th ult., Gen. Benning arrived and assumed command of the brigade. This arrangement meets with general approbation, for Gen. Benning is regarded by all as a very able officer, and is known to be as brave as Caesar. He has the confidence of men and officers, who would follow him into battle with every assurance of success.

On Sunday, 29th, the brigade marched to Petersburg, and now occupies [James J.] Pettigrew's camps, three miles from the city. We started from our old camps at half past six, and reached this place by half past three—making a distance of eighteen miles in nine hours. This is about our usual speed. As we passed the camps of the Fifty-ninth Georgia (Col. Jack Brown), I heard several exclaim, "How fast they march! I wonder if they go this way all the time?" Some mischievous fellow replied: "We are not *Conscripts!*" Neither are they; but they know very little about "soldiering."

Gen. Lee issued an order recently preparing the army for the coming campaign. He exhorts officers and men to a faithful discharge of their duties, as tending to render the army efficient and invincible. All extra surplus baggage is to be stored in Richmond, and each officer is limited to the smallest amount of baggage possible. We are to have even less transportation this year than last. This arises from the difficulties of procuring animals, and the constantly increasing necessity for employing them to haul ordnance and subsistence.

During the Maryland campaign, which began the 1st September, to the time the army fell back to Gordonsville, about the 1st November—two months—the officers of the line did not have a change of clothes. I have spoken of their appearance before, which can be easily imagined by our friends at home. If it comes to that this summer, it will, indeed, be the most disagreeable portion of the campaign.

We may expect the most eventful as well as the most trying campaign of the war. Our armies are well appointed, healthy, buoyant, and eager for the shock of battle. We are, under God, more invincible than we have ever been; and the army will be deeply disappointed if victories do not follow in quick succession.

It is with feelings of shame that I chronicle the vandalism of *some* of Hood's division. A short time since a band of desperadoes (roughs, or plugs from our southern cities) entered a store on the pretence of searching for liquor, exhibiting a forged order to that effect. They *stole* a thousand dollars worth of goods; and then killed hogs of the same value from another peaceable citizen, and without so much as offering compensation, returned to camps to speculate upon their stolen property. Such vandalism should be punished with death. Any other punishment is too light.

Even this old brigade is not free from the charge of robbery and theft. A few bad men have brought odium upon this honored brigade. But a few days since, eight or ten bad characters belonging to company "F," 17th Georgia, from Columbus, got drunk, entered a house in Petersburg and destroyed a good deal of property. One, a man named Moon, was shot in the hip, I believe, for resisting the guard who were sent to arrest them. They were lodged in the city jail; and Moon, I understand has since died of his wounds.

A few garroters and thieves from the crowded cities are sufficient to give an entire brigade and division the name of thieves and robbers. Steps should be taken to arrest and bring to condign punishment these villains, to save good and true men the reproach. Gen. Benning has adopted a plan which I think will be efficient. On yesterday he addressed an order in the brigade, enumerating the enormities committed by bad men and the odium brought upon the whole command, thereby causing good men to suffer; and threatening that if any more depredations were committed, he would surround the brigade by a heavy guard, and allow no man to pass beyond the lines except through the guard quarters. Each man who thus passes out must be accompanied by a sentinel who will be held responsible for his return.

If it becomes necessary to enforce this order, it will impose a very heavy duty upon the men which they now escape. This will effectually stop depredations.

It is refreshing to turn from this unpleasant subject, when the painful duty of speaking of the faults of the army is imposed by a sense of duty, to the scenes I witnessed on Friday, 27th March—the day set apart by our God-fearing Chief Magistrate as "a day of fasting, humiliation and prayer." The day was very generally observed, and I was agreeably surprised to see many who make no professions of religion keeping the fast. The Chaplain of the 11th Georgia, the Rev. Mr. Simmons, assisted by Capt. [William M.] Verderee of the 59th, held services in our brigade. The turn out was respectable, and the sermon, or properly, the *address*, was fully equal to the occasion. After reading the 20th chapter of Chronicles, 9th Daniel, and other scripture appropriate to the occasion, he launched forth into the ocean of thought presented in the proclamation and delivered one of the best discourses I ever heard in the army. It was calculated to awaken thought and stir up the emotions of the soul.

The existence of a Supreme Being, the worship due Him from man, and the dealings of God towards His creatures, he presented in strong language, and vividly sketched the history of this revolution, in which the hand of God is plainly seen. By our own strength and prowess we could not have wrought the wonders and gained the victories which signalize the campaigns of 1862.

I wonder if the people at home observed that day as generally as they ought? Were the places of business and resorts of pleasure and amusement closed? Did the Christians fast?—not merely by abstaining from food, but in spirit—in deep humility of soul—in believing prayer? If they did, that day was a "day of deliverance" to the nation. Oh, how often I thought of and asked myself the question, are the Christians of the land, where no drums or marshaled hosts disturb the quiet of their peaceful homes, are they observing this day and interceding in behalf of our bleeding country? Something answered, yes. The assurance thrilled me with delight, for I believe in the omnipotence of prayer. If the grey haired warriors of the Cross, whose age forbids their participation in the bloody battles of the war, and the mothers, the pious wives and Christian sisters, will mightily besiege the Throne of Grace in behalf of our country and cause, our armies will be victorious in every battle, and very soon we will enjoy the blessings of peace, with the assurance of prosperity. Is not the glorious end to be gained sufficient to enlist all our energies? Surely it is. With you, then, grey haired sires and honored mothers, rests the issue! Your prayers can free us, or you; lukewarmness rivet the chains of slavery.

V. A. S. P.

LETTER FROM TIVOLI

CAMP NEAR RICHMOND, VA., March 26, 1863 [4-2-63ASC]

The weather continues dreadful—since my last there has been an hour or so, of sunshine stepping in as a short intermission between the snow, hail, rain, sleet, lightning, and thunder. We have been uncomfortable and are more weary to-day than at any time in the past long and weary twenty-four months. Our proximity to Richmond instead of being a source of plenty to us, is quite the contrary. Since our arrival here we receive but ¼ pound of bacon a day, with an occasional issue of rice, sugar and peas. These issues, however, are but occasional—say once a week. To be sure, we can visit Richmond and buy what we like, but one visit takes all the cash on hand, prices being so excessively high. Our horses are also short of forage. They are on half food and are likely to continue so at present. These things, although they make one feel uncomfortable and hungry at times, are not discouraging. No! we will continue in the war path long after our beef and flour have gone, living on the roots of the earth and the waters of the spring, even as our forefathers have done before us.

The health of our command is good, though not so good as at Fredericksburg. There are a few cases of intermittent Fever and Catarrh, but the scourge of the army at this season last year—the camp fever—has not made its appearance. The Small Pox has almost entirely disappeared—indeed I question whether there has ever been a case originating in the army. All the cases that I have heard reported were contracted out of camps—at hospitals and along the roads.

We expect to have a general review in a few days if the ground will get dry enough. Our industrious President is expected with a number of distinguished statesmen and soldiers who now fill the capitol. It will be a pleasing spectacle and both parties will be mutually pleased. The soldier will be delighted to see them who make their laws, and the statesmen will be gratified to see the men who carry these laws on the point of their bayonets. Sword and Pen—illustrious rivals in the race for fame.

A lot of court martial sentences has just been received. The last batch are more than usually severe. A number of men are to be shot, a few whipped, a large number to labor with a ball and chain, and some to be decorated with a flour barrel shirt. Have you ever witnessed the latter punishment? It is a severe one. The barrel is placed over the head of the defender, his arms being put through holes in each side. The barrel is marked in large letters, "Absent without leave,"—"I deserted my colors," and other sentences to describe the nature of the offence. The culprit feeling like a drowned rat, is then led up and down the line, or stationed in front of his regiment during dress parade. It is a punishment that is very much dreaded.

I am afraid, however, that as a general thing, court martials are too severe. I saw a man on a late terrific march of sixty miles, wearing all the way, a ball and chain, weighing about twenty-five pounds. His offence was a simple one, and knowing the man to be ordinarily a good soldier, my heart bled for him. I think that these new boards, for the trial of offences, will be advantageous to the soldier as well as to the service. I notice the President has selected for these boards the first men of the country, and men of sense are always charitable and kind. It is only men of narrow intellects and groveling natures that are cruel.

By the appointment of Col. L. M. Lamar, of the 8th Georgia, as a member of one of these boards, Lt. Col. J. R. Towers is promoted to the Colonelcy of that regiment.

Just this minute, as I crossed the "t" in the word "regiment," I hear a new order which would rejoice our animals mightily, had they reason and understanding. Their rations are raised to the old standard. This is a promise of better things in the future, and to-morrow, when I mount my gay Bucephalus, I shall have to be careful that he does not break the neck of

TIVOLI.

LETTER FROM V. A. S. P.

CAMP NEAR PETERSBURG, VA., May 5, 1863 [5-12-63SR]

At 9 o'clock, Friday, May 1st, Gen. Benning's command began a hurried march for Suffolk. We halted at sunset, making a distance of 20 miles. On the following day we reached our old camping ground on the South Quey Road (not South Key)—making a distance of 25 miles, after halting 2½ hours to rest in the heat of the day. On Sunday, May 3rd, we marched around to the north of Suffolk at quick time, to engage the enemy, or support Gen. [Evander] Law, who was engaging them. There was no general engagement. The enemy appeared in considerable force in front of Gen. Law, but did not stand long. Prisoners state that they were troops whose time expired in a day or so; that their General told them if they would charge the rebels they would be discharged and allowed to go home forthwith.

Passing around our line of earthworks, we were favorably impressed with their strength. Though crude, being made in most part of logs and dirt, they were as formidable as those around Fredericksburg. Our soldiers were in fine spirits, and very anxious to be led against the enemy. The Yankees were strongly fortified, and if reports be true, had a force scarcely inferior to our own. They had greatly the advantage in fortifications and heavy metal.

The question is asked, "Why did not Gen. Longstreet storm and take Suffolk?" There is at least one good reason why he or any good General would not sacrifice the lives of good soldiers, viz: the place is not of sufficient importance, unless we had Norfolk also. It would require a large force to hold it when taken; and our forces can accomplish more good almost anywhere else.

Gen. Longstreet did not fail in his enterprise. He succeeded most signally. For the time the enemy were unable to send reinforcements to North Carolina, and after [D. H.] Hill [on April 15] abandoned the siege of Washington, the enemy was constrained to send large forces to Suffolk to prevent its falling into our hands, thus weakening them at other and more important points. But he had another object in view. He secured immense quantities of bacon, a large lot of beef, cattle, horses, &c. An officer told me that there had been stored in Franklin by the wagon trains, first and last, 1,200,000 pounds of bacon! I do not think this is an exaggeration, for all the wagons at the disposal of the government, or that could be hired or pressed, were constantly engaged in hauling for three weeks.

Gen. Benning executed his commission in an able manner. He checked every effort of the enemy to cross the swamp or make incursions into eastern North Carolina as far as the Chowan. He captured many Buffaloes and among them the father of the notorious Jack Fairless, who has been acting as spy for the enemy. The proofs of guilt are strong, and the old sinner will surely hang.

IVOR STATION, May 6th.

While waiting to take the train I will finish my letter, which I began yesterday morning.

There was little else done by our troops than skirmishing and picketing. Some of our best men were killed or wounded, but I have been unable to learn their names. While the Eighth Georgia was on picket the enemy threw a shell into their breastworks, which went nearly through and exploded, covering Company E up with dirt. They describe the shelling as the most terrific they ever saw. Six companies of the 59th Georgia are now attached to Anderson's brigade, having taken the place of Major [John E.] Rylander's battalion. They were under terrific fire, and are said to have borne it heroically.

After Benning's brigade had halted, about 4 o'clock Sunday evening [May 3], a huge shell from the enemy's gunboats exploded on the left, killing Larkin Pearson, of Company I, 17th Georgia. A large fragment entered his left side, tearing his liver to pieces, from which he died in a few hours.

Between sundown, and dark the army began to retreat. Our brigade was already worn down by fatigue, and with them the night march was peculiarly hard. The brigade, or about half of it, reached the Black Water by 7 o'clock next morning, where we rested until 8 o'clock Tuesday morning [May 5]. The other half came in during the day. Never were men more wearied. The distance made that night was not far short of twenty-five miles. In the twenty-four hours we marched about forty miles! Has this been equaled during the war? I think not.

It is singular that the great retreat from Yorktown and from Suffolk, should have begun on the same day of the month, though a year apart. The first was, indeed, a trying march, but cannot equal the last. Unlike the first, the enemy did not pursue, except with a few cavalry.

At Franklin was heard of Lee's great victory on the Rappahannock [Chancellorsville]. It was complete. Our loss was heavy, and Gen. Jackson is reported as *severely* wounded. That is an ambiguous term. It is difficult to tell whether he is disabled for any length of time, or whether his life is in jeopardy. But let us hope for the best. The loss of "Stonewall" Jackson would injure us more than the loss of thousands of subalterns and soldiers.

We reached this point last night, after a tramp of twenty miles, and in the hardest rain of the season. The clouds seemed to have burst above us and let down their floods all at once. The fields were broad sheets of water, and the darkness was greatly intensified by the vivid flashes of lightning. Such peals of thunder as followed each flash! It seemed that all the elements were engaged in war, and the big artillery of Heaven was turned loose upon them to end the strife. In the intense darkness it was impossible to find a camping ground. We were called in a lane and ordered to burn rails and make ourselves *comfortable!* We obeyed the order. Near us was a large quantity of dry cord wood, of which we soon made blazing fires; and between nodding and napping spent the night as comfortably as possible.

All the brigades of Hood's division except Benning's have taken the train for Richmond, *en route* for Fredericksburg; and we will embark in a few hours. It is now a question whether we will be sent to Fredericksburg, since Gen. Lee's great victory. We may be stationed around Richmond until needed elsewhere. But these are matters of which we know nothing until they transpire.

What will become of poor Joe Hooker! He was the last hope of all Yankeedoodledom. He declared to the Yankee Congress that he had the *best army in the world!* If he lied not, he is deficient as a General—he is an imbecile; and like his predecessors, must pay the penalty of his blunder. What a host of heroes they have had! Winfield Scott, McDowell, McClellan, John Pope, Banks, (Stonewall's Commissary!) Burnside, and "fighting Joe" Hooker! Poor fools! Mere tools of a brainless tyrant, they deserved the treatment they have received at his hands. A few weeks at most will bring a new actor upon the Yankee stage of war and *strategy*.

I have another case of theft to report, and respectfully recommend to the consideration of his neighbors, Patrick McSwain, of Co. F, 17th Georgia. Charge: *Turkey stealing!* On Friday night, although we had plenty of meat, the aforesaid McSwain, impelled by a natural propensity to appropriate what does not belong to him, "took a turkey in out of the wet!" The owner identified him and the turkey too, whereupon McSwain was arrested, made to return the feathered animal, and march at the head of the column under guard.

V. A. S. P.

☆☆☆Battle of Chancellorsville

On April 27, three corps of the Army of the Potomac (38,000 strong) marched upriver, leaving behind the First and Sixth Corps to threaten Fredericksburg. Three days later the Federals crossed the Rappahannock at several shallow fords, and converged near Chancellorsville about ten miles in Lee's rear. Upon discovering this threat, Lee rushed westward and boldly took the initiative. On May 2, Lee sent Jackson's Corps on a 12-mile flank march to the lightly defended Federal right. At sunset, Jackson surprised the Federal Eleventh Corps, totally routing it.

For three more days, Lee attacked until the Army of the Potomac retreated across the Rappahannock.

SECOND GEORGIA BATTALION
[WRIGHT'S BRIGADE, ANDERSON'S DIVISION]
BATTLEFIELD AT BANKS' FORD, May 5, 1863 [5-13-63CS]

The "finest army the world ever saw," has been completely routed by "Lee's ragged rebels." The last of them crossed over at this ford last night, our batteries shelling them all the time. I learn from one of them that their officers had the pontoons broken up to prevent them from crossing over, but they waded it, plunging in in ever sort of confusion. A great many, I understand, were drowned, and a good many turned back and delivered themselves up prisoners.

The 2nd Battalion suffered severely in the past six days' fights, from the severe shellings of the enemy's batteries. We made our first charge yesterday evening across an open field, half-a-mile wide, the enemy pouring shot, shell, grape and canister into us from two batteries, and their sharpshooters blazing away at us. We drove them from their position without firing a gun and held it while [Carnot] Posey's Mississippi Brigade charged the battery on the flank and captured it. I send you a list of wounded of our company. There were none of them seriously wounded. The Battalion had only one killed, private Cleveland, of the Spaulding Greys. We had some 25 or 30 wounded. One of our company was shot through the brim of his hat, the piece of shell passing down in front of him and into his blankets. Another piece of shell struck one of our men's haversack, and fell inside.

I have not time to write any particulars, as I do not know when we will fall in, as the shelling continues.

FURNITURE.

PRIVATE LETTER, SECOND GEORGIA BATTALION, WRIGHT'S BRIGADE
CAMP NEAR GUINEA'S STATION, VA., May 8, 1863 [5-20-63ASC]

Dear Father and Mother: Through the mercies of a kind Providence I have been spared through the conflict and again have the privilege of writing home that I am safe. Thank God for my preservation.

I will endeavor to give you full details of the part our brigade acted in the recent conflicts.

On the morning of the 29th April we were aroused by the booming of distant cannon in the direction of Fredericksburg. The firing continued heavy and rapid until nine o'clock. It was supposed by all that the enemy were advancing. At eleven o'clock the long roll beat for us to fall in, and by half past eleven we were marching in the direction of Fredericksburg. While on the road I learned that the Federals had crossed in heavy force in front of Early's division four miles below the city. It was expected an immediate attack would be made upon Early's position, and our brigade was ordered to his support. We remained there until four o'clock p.m., when the enemy, not advancing, we were ordered to join our own division (Anderson's) which was six miles above us in the direction of United States Ford. We got to his headquarters and bivouacked for the night. It commenced raining about dark and we spent a miserable time, by our half burning fires until midnight, when orders came to fall in, being ordered to Chancellorsville.

Posey's and Mahone's brigades had been forced to fall back before superior numbers, and we were ordered to reinforce them. We trudged through the mud and darkness as well as we could. There was nothing to disturb the silence except the occasional clanking of some soldier's tin cup against his canteen, or perhaps a half muttered curse as some unfortunate fellow would slip and fall full length in the soft mire.

Daylight found us far advanced on the "plank road." It was a pleasant morning. The birds were warbling their sweetest notes in welcome of the bidding spring. The rain had ceased and the dark clouds had disappeared from the horizon—all was lovely and bright, and I asked myself if such a lovely day was soon to witness scenes of death and carnage. We advanced within a mile of Chancellorsville when the scouts brought in word that it was already occupied by a large force of the enemy, General Wright immediately determined to fall back and send for reinforcements; so we fell back three miles [to Zoan Church] and took position on both sides of the plank road, and concluded to await the enemy's advance. We waited until one o'clock but they did not come, when Gen. Wright sent a small squad of cavalry to the front to look for them.

The cavalry had not been gone more than forty minutes till they come dashing back as fast as their horses could run, and about twice their number of Yankee cavalry pursuing them, while at the same time a squadron of the Yankees were charging across a field to intercept their retreat. It was an exciting race, and I feared that our boys would be captured, but their horses were fast enough to save them. They passed where the body in the field would strike the road about the time the Yankees were a hundred yards from the road. As they were only two hundred yards from us, they halted and fired a volley into the Yankees, killing two of them. The Yankees left in a run without returning fire. There was heavy skirmishing on our right between Mahone's brigade and the dismounted cavalry.

We worked all night throwing up breastworks—ready for the enemy's advance next day, and were heavily reinforced during the night—both McLaws' and A. P. Hill's [R. H. Anderson's] divisions coming to our assistance. "Stonewall" Jackson arrived about an hour by sun and took command. He waited until nine o'clock for the Yankees, but as they showed no disposition to advance he determined to advance on them. Our brigade was in front and we did not go more than two miles before we found the enemy. Our company of the battalion and one of the 3rd Ga. regt. were sent to the front to bring on the engagement. In a few moments they were engaged with the enemy's skirmishers. Twelve pieces of artillery were brought up and were soon hurling their deadly missiles in the ranks of the foe. Our skirmishers were reinforced by the 3rd Georgia, and after a few rounds the enemy fell back.

Gen. Jackson ordered the artillery to advance and ordered Gen. Wright to endeavor to get in the Yankees rear and attack them vigorously. We filed off to the left and marched through the woods to conceal the movement from the enemy. As we were marching along we could hear the battle raging furiously to our right. We knew that Jackson was driving the enemy before him and we were all anxious to do the part which he had assigned us. After marching five miles we were getting close to the enemy and passing through a brigade of Stuart's cavalry when word came to hurry up, that the enemy was driving Stuart's cavalry pickets. We pushed forward as quickly as possible, soon checked their advance, and following them up drove them over a half a mile, when the artillery [E. P. Alexander's artillery battalion] was brought up and commenced throwing grape and canister into their retreating ranks. They soon returned to fire, however, from a battery of six pieces, firing shell, grape and canister at us. It was warm work certain. The firing lasted until dark. The battalion had four men wounded. The 22nd Georgia had two killed and fourteen wounded. The battery had three killed and five wounded, making twenty-eight in all.

After the shades of night had fallen around us, we moved up a road for two miles and bivouacked for the night. We had been without rations for two days, and the pang of hunger were giving us considerable pains. Next morning [May 2], we were permitted to rest and other troops were sent to the front. We were to wait until our rations were brought up from camp. While we were resting, twenty thousand [32,000] troops passed us under Jackson, going to the rear of the enemy.

About two o'clock our rations were brought to us. They consisted of biscuit, ham and sugar. We drew for three days. I got twenty biscuits, three-fourths of a pound of bacon, and one pound of sugar. I had to get two haversacks to hold my provisions. At three o'clock we were put in motion. There was heavy fighting in our front, and I supposed that we were ordered to the support of Posey's brigade. The 3rd Georgia was sent out to the right and were not engaged with the enemy, but we were held in reserve. The enemy advanced upon us where we were hid in a pine thicket, and ordered not to fire until they were within twenty feet of us. They advanced within two hundred yards of our position, fired a volley, and retired. We did not fire in return.

About four o'clock in the evening we heard Jackson when he commenced the attack in their rear. The firing was very rapid and continued without intermission until darkness put an end to the conflict. We had one man wounded in the battalion when the Yankees fired the volley into us. Soon after dark, the 3rd Georgia came in. They lost about thirty men that day.

A camp of soldiers at night is a sublime scene. I wish I could describe to you a camp at night, before a battle. That night is one that I shall never forget.

We were up next morning by daylight, and after a hastily swallowed breakfast, we were on the move. Jackson was already thundering in their rear. This was Sunday, the 3rd of May. We were formed in line of battle, and advanced upon a brigade of the enemy. We captured six hundred of them, however, who were not fast enough to get out of the way.

We advanced again, driving the enemy before us, until we came within three hundred yards of their breastworks, where we halted and waited for Posey's brigade. The firing was the heaviest I was ever in, and it is a mystery to me how any of us escaped with life. The men were dropping all around me, shot down. When the Mississippi brigade came up—they were flanking the right of the Yankees—the enemy fled in great disorder and we followed them, driving them into Rodes' brigade [division], who mowed them down by hundreds. We captured a large number of prisoners and several cannon, while the ground was literally covered with the dead.

In the battalion we had two killed and fifteen wounded—the killed being from our company. They were privates H. H. Cleveland and Lewis J. Maxwell. Henry Cleveland was a son of Dr. Allen Cleveland and a relative of ours. He was struck in the head by a grape shot and fell dead without a struggle. Lewis Maxwell lived twenty-four hours before he breathed his last. He met his fate calmly and resignedly; told the chaplain that he was ready to die, and hoped to meet his God in peace. It will be a severe blow to his mother, when she learns the news, for he was her only child. She is on the way somewhere now, bringing a substitute for her son. What a sad disappointment awaits her!

Although I was not hit, I was very near it. I believe I mentioned about having two haversacks on; a shell whistled by me, cutting them both off. It carried one of them at least forty feet behind me, while my biscuits, bacon and sugar was scattered around promiscuously. Several of the boys were struck by the biscuits, and more than one thought he was wounded. I had to rely on the generosity of my friends for the next two days for something to eat. The shell deadened my side for about two hours, and hurt me some for two or three days, but it does not pain me now. It was a narrow escape, and I felt thankful that my life was spared.

After the fight was over Gen. Lee rode up and down the lines. The boys greeted him wherever he went, and it must have been a proud moment for him. He had just routed the enemy and gained a glorious victory; and now to witness with what devotion his men loved him! It was inspiring beyond anything you can imagine. While here I learned that Gen. Jackson was wounded. His loss would be almost irreparable. It is to be hoped that his wounds will not deprive the army of his services after they have time to heal up.

About four o'clock in the evening we continued the pursuit of the Yankees. We got within two and a half miles of United States Ford and found them strongly entrenched. It was near sundown and an attack was postponed until morning and the battalion was sent on picket. We had some skirmishing through the night, but nothing else of interest transpired, except that about midnight, the Yankees fired a dwelling house in our front. The woods were illuminated for miles around. Why they perpetrated this act of incendiarism is unknown.

On the morning of the 4th we expected to commence the attack, when word come that Early's division had been driven from Fredericksburg and the enemy thirty thousand strong were coming in our rear. Our division (Anderson's) and McLaw's was sent to help Early. We got in position by five o'clock, and had the enemy nearly surrounded, and at a given signal the whole line was to advance simultaneously. The signal, three cannons discharged in quick succession, was given at a quarter past five, and we advanced at a double-quick. There were two batteries playing on our brigade, one in front of us and the other one on the right of our line of battle. Thus you see we had to face a front fire and at the same time was exposed to an enfilading one. The battery on our right was only six hundred yards distant. We could distinctly hear the commander of the battery halloo to his men, "Pour the grape into them; G—d d—m them; pour the grape into them;" and they did pour grape into us with severity.

We soon came upon their infantry, and Gen. Wright gave the order to charge them. We did so with a yell. They stood until we got in about fifty yards of them, when they broke and ran. Before they ran, they fired several shots at us hitting a great many of the brigade. We drove them out of their entrenchments, and drove them back into Wofford's brigade who got nearly all of them prisoners. We pursued the remainder of their army four miles when night put an end to the pursuit. What was left of them crossed the river that night at Banks' Ford.

We had eight wounded in the battalion.   I was struck twice, though both times was only grazed; one time on the wrist of the right arm, by a rifle ball barely breaking the skin. I saw the fellow when he shot at me. A small piece of shell struck me on the right arm near the shoulder, and went deep enough to lodge. I got one of the boys to cut it out with his knife while the fight was going on. Neither shot disabled me, and I have kept my place ever since. They wanted to put me on the list of wounded, but as the hurts were only scratches, I would not consent to it, lest you might see my name in the papers before I had an opportunity of writing, which of course, would have caused you a great deal of mental anxiety. My arm pains me at times but it will be all right in a day or two.

Next day the 5th, we started back to Chancellorsville to drive Hooker out of his entrenchments, but a thunder storm came up that evening and the attack was postponed until next morning. By sunrise we were advancing on their entrenchments, but we found them deserted. Hooker having crossed his entire force the night before. About five hundred stragglers remained behind, who were captured by our skirmishers. So ended the second battle of Fredericksburg.

The enemy advanced this time confident of victory, and outnumbered us two to one, but after a week's hard and desperate fighting we drove him back with terrible slaughter. The Yankee loss in my estimation will amount of twenty-five thousand killed and wounded, and about fifteen hundred captured.

I was very near not going into the fight; I had been sick so long; but when I got to thinking about it I could not stay behind. It is with pleasure that I am able to inform you that I am in better health now than I was before the battles. I think my health is fully restored.

If it had killed me I do not think I could have kept out of the fight, but I do not feel any bad results from the exposure and fatigue.

I am looking forward for a letter from home every day. Do not forget to send me the *Confederacy*. Write me often—write to brother Will and let him know that I am safe.

        Yours affectionately,   M. D. Martin.

Micajah D. Martin enlisted as a private in Company D, Second Georgia Battalion, on April 20, 1861. Appointed First Sergeant in early 1863, he was captured at Gettysburg on July 2, 1863, and sent to Fort Delaware on October 15, 1863. Martin was transferred to Fort Monroe, Va., on March 2, 1864 and took the oath of allegiance to the U. S. Government and forwarded to New York City on March 5, 1864.

PRIVATE LETTER, SECOND GEORGIA BATTALION

GUINEA'S STATION, VA., May 10, 1863 [5-19-63AWCS]

My Dear Father—To describe the battles of the 3rd and 4th insts. in all their terrific grandeur is beyond my power. To express in words the intense strain upon mind and body incident to so long a struggle—the hopes and fears, the exulting joy that victory and a fleeing foe give to the pursuing conqueror—is equally impossible. I shall attempt neither, but content myself with a simple narration of the incidents that occurred on that portion of the field over which I passed and where my brigade and division fought.

On Wednesday morning early, April 29th, Gen. Hooker, under cover of a dense fog, succeeded in throwing a large body of troops [Sedgwick's and Reynolds' corps] across the Rappahannock below Fredericksburg. Simultaneously, the major part of his army crossed at the different fords above the city, and at the same time a strong [cavalry] column from Washington City reached Culpeper C. H.   That day the enemy made every show of battle below, and Gen. Lee massed his troops round Hamilton's Crossing. That night, however, the Yankee General quietly withdrew most of his forces at this point and joined those already over the river above the city, leaving Sedgwick with 25,000 men behind. Our own immortal Lee at once comprehended the true designs of the adversary, and made ready to meet him in his flank movement.

Leaving Gen. Early's division to guard Sedgwick, he rapidly countermarched his whole line of battle, throwing Jackson on the left and the two divisions of Longstreet's command—McLaws and Anderson's divisions—on the right, and moved up the Plank Road towards the little village of Chancellorsville, 14 miles distant from Fredericksburg. In the meantime, however, the enemy meeting with no opposition in this quarter, had extended their line from below Culpeper C. H. far out into the country circling round Chancellorsville and reaching to Spotsylvania C. H., and bending sharply down to the river again. They occupied a long range of high hills running in a semi-circle, and on these they had rapidly erected the most formidable works.

On Friday some fighting and heavy skirmishing took place along and to the left of the plank road as far out as Spotsylvania C. H., and the enemy driven back some considerable distance. On Saturday they took the positions they intended to hold and would yield no more.

I had, as I believe I wrote you, made an attempt on Wednesday to find my brigade, but failed. Hearing from it on Friday [May 1], I determined to go up and wander along the lines until my search was successful. Early Saturday morning [May 2] I made hasty preparations, bade Mr. Potter good bye and started. A rapid walk of 18 or 20 miles brought me to McLaws' division on the plank road, about 2 o'clock. As I passed along the lines, the skirmishers in front were hotly engaged, and the artillery from both sides firing rapidly. It was evidently the design of Gen. Lee to avoid a battle until Jackson should reach a position far round on the enemy's right, for which he had been marching ever since daylight. I soon found Anderson's division to the left of the plank road, and Wright's brigade in a dense piece of wilderness right in front of the enemy. Just in the rear of the brigade I passed "our Ranse" [Wright] and staff on a little eminence, quietly watching the old 3rd Georgia skirmishing with a whole brigade of Yankees on a hill-side. I found the little battalion lying down in the woods, every man in his place. Officers and men all seemed glad to see me, and expressed great surprise that I should leave a safe place to join them now. The fact is, I loved the old company and battalion, and could not consent to see it endure and suffer without me, however, honorably I might have remained behind. Besides I thought our general needed every man he could get, and I saw enough of skulking to disgust me. I begged my officers to reserve compliments until the struggle was over and then they could decide my right to them.

By the time I had arrived and equipped myself, night closed over us. About sundown the great anxiety felt about Jackson was relieved by the sound of rapid and heavy firing on the enemy's right wing. All day McLaws and Anderson had held the foe at bay, and when their men knew that Jackson was ready to help them, it was with great difficulty we could be kept from giving three cheers. As the firing waxed warm under Jackson, we knew the old hero had secured his position, and was then only giving the invaders an earnest of what was in store for them the next day. Irregular firing continued all night between the pickets, but the main bodies of both armies rested for the death struggle on the morrow. Massed upon the hills behind strong entrenchments, the boasting and confident hosts of Hooker slept and dreamed, perchance, of a great and glorious victory on the coming day. Confronting them, the little army of our God-fearing chieftain, commending its fate to the God of battles, awaited with calm hearts and determined wills the momentous morning.

At last it broke—the clear, calm Sabbath. Before the sun rose, a cannon was fired far round on our left and over the hills and valleys the sound rose and swelled. Before it died away we caught the boom of another and another, and still another, and then in rapid succession battery after battery took up the fire—small arms joined in—it flew along the lines from division to division. McLaws and Anderson promptly answered Jackson's call to duty, and when the sun arose it struggled through the smoke of seven hundred cannon, and looked down upon 300,000 human beings in deadly conflict. I wish I could describe the incessant thunder of artillery—the hiss of shot and shell, and grape and canister—the whiz of the deadly minie balls that seemed to swarm in such numbers around us that the very air was hot with their breath—the wild yells of the contending armies—the short ejaculation which almost every moment greeted my ears coming from some one of our men as a shell or grape tore away an arm or shattered a leg—or as the fatal ball lodged with a dull *thug* in the body. It baffles description, and must be seen as we saw it to be appreciated.

At the very opening of the battle our army, on all sides, made a general advance. The enemy stood their ground and fought stubbornly, but so furious was the onset of our troops that nothing could stand before them. They yielded slowly, while their batteries poured incessant showers of grape and canister into our ranks as we advanced. In about an hour Anderson's division had pressed on for over a mile, when we came upon the enemy strongly posted behind a long line of breastworks, in front of which the trees had been cut down for some distance, and so arranged as to make it difficult for us to get through the tangled branches. While trying to dislodge the enemy from this position my brigade suffered its heaviest loss. One by one of the little battalion was wounded and taken to the rear—one of my company "D" was instantly killed—the gallant leader of the old 3rd Georgia lost an arm—Gen. Wright had his fine horse wounded under him. To add to the general tumult, the woods took fire, and the flames swept past us, burning many of the dead and wounded.

About 11 o'clock a general assault was made on the works by McLaws and Anderson, led by Gen. Lee in person, who rode, hat in hand, cheering us on. Right well you know with such a leader we could not fail. The charge in my brigade, owing to the nature of the ground, had to be made in column of regiments. The old 3rd Georgia led the way, my battalion just behind, while close on our heels came the 22nd and 48th. A wild shout went up from our two divisions—the enemy answered with a volley—while the cannon seemed to fire by broadsides. All to no purpose—over the works we went, and away flew the Yankees. The ground was literally carpeted with knapsacks, haversacks, oil cloths, blankets, &c., while their wounded and dead men were scattered thickly in every direction. They stopped no more until they reached another fortified position beyond Chancellorsville.

When we reached Chancellorsville the place was on fire, and we formed in line of battle right at the large hotel, which was burning rapidly. The Yankees had filled it with ammunition and fired it in their retreat. Right here, I felt, for the first time, anxiety about my safety. The shell and boxes of ammunition in the burning building were exploding continually, filling the air with brick and cinders. I expected every moment to be buried by falling walls. Besides this, a Yankee battery was playing on us up the road, in the very centre of which I stood. I could see the shells skipping over the ground and feel their rush as they passed just over my head. One passed between the legs of my left hand man and my own. Everything was in apparent confusion—Generals and aids and artillery were dashing hither and thither. The dead and wounded were lying thickly around the burning house, and as the flames rose higher, the poor wounded shrieked for aid; many were burned up, but none were our own men. The heat finally became so intense that my brigade had to move off to the right a short distance. I think I never obeyed an order with greater alacrity. Aid was soon given to the perishing wounded, and all saved who could be; many, however, must have perished, as I saw the clothes of at least fifty on fire. The shrieks of those who could not crawl away made my very blood curdle.

Other and more important matters soon engrossed my attention. We had scarcely formed before the skirmishers came in and reported the enemy advancing on us in large force. In our rear we had perhaps fifty pieces of artillery, and soon as their blue lines could be distinguished in the woods, we lay down and our batteries played over us. So deadly were the effects of the firing that the enemy broke in confusion and fled—repulsed by artillery. Prisoners afterwards taken said they never knew artillery to be served so well. This was the last fighting we did on Sunday, and is the part we took in the great battle and glorious victory of Chancellorsville.

During the morning my brigade took over 1,000 prisoners. At one time we took the entire surviving portion of the 27th Connecticut regiment, and made them march to the rear and stack guns. Little squads were coming through the woods all the morning, some calling out "don't shoot," and others with a white flag held up on a stick or ramrod.

The fighting soon ceased on Jackson's side, and we rested for the first time in six hours without having shells and balls whistling around us. Soon after Gen. Lee came riding down the lines. The sight of the old hero after such a victory was too much. We had never cheered him before, but now the pride we felt in him must have vent, and of all the cheering ever heard this was the most enthusiastic. He rode by with his head uncovered, and had to keep it so as long as he passed our men. The cheering finally died away far round on our left. Soon after this came the intelligence of Jackson's serious wound, and we felt that the victory was dearly bought. To-day [May 10] that great and good man breathed his last. But to proceed.

Sunday evening my division was marched down to the U. S. Ford and there spent the night, the Battalion doing the picket duty. Early Monday morning we took up the line of march for Fredericksburg. While the battle was being fought on Sunday, Sedgwick had driven out Early's division, taken the city and the heights as far out on the plank road as the toll gate.

Gen. Lee determined to attack him at once. We joined McLaws, who had gone down Sunday evening, passed round and formed a junction with Early, who had retaken the city and "Marye's Hill." Gen. Lee requested us to do the work up quickly, so we laid aside our blankets, &c., and prepared for work.

It fell to Wright's brigade to drive the enemy out of an old camp it used to occupy. To do so, we had to advance over a broad field for half a mile. About an hour and a half before sundown the attack began. We sprang at double-quick right across the field. The enemy's batteries opened on us as they did at Chancellorsville. The first line of Yankees broke before we fired a gun, and none of us had our bayonets on. We were told to dislodge the enemy from a fence ahead of us, and then stop for further orders. As we advanced on the fence, the minie balls and grape shot came like hail. In about 200 hundred yards of the fence, my gun was cut partly in two by a piece of shell, and a fragment passed through my coat sleeve. As we neared the enemy, they rose in a long blue line, gave us one volley, and fled. We took the fence and halted. General Lee says the charge of the troops was the grandest he ever witnessed. Had the enemy made any stand, they might have killed hundreds of us. In the charge, my brigade lost about seventy killed and wounded—the battalion about eight or ten. The enemy retreated on all sides, and by dark we had driven them over the river, taking 450 prisoners, and two batteries. If the Falmouth Heights had not bristled with cannon, we might have taken the last one of them.

[Harry] Hays' brigade was on my right in this battle, and fought desperately. I afterwards saw Uncle F., who was unhurt. At 2 o'clock that night we lay down to sleep, and the next morning Mr. Potter came to see how we were. Just before night we started again for Chancellorsville, and marched it through one of the hardest rains I ever saw fall. That night [May 5] we slept sweetly without fire, and wet as water could make us—rose early the next morning and went two miles beyond Chancellorsville—found the enemy all over the river—built large fires—hunted up Yankee rations, and ate the first meal in two days—collected as many Yankee tricks as we could carry—that evening marched back to Fredericksburg. Next day, I left for the Station, and the brigade went back to its old camps.

The brigade has about 400 men killed and wounded—some of the latter so slight that they never left the ranks and will not be reported. Three of the battalion were killed, one or two have since died, and two more are expected to die. Gen. Wright says we behaved like veterans—that the greatest difficulty was to keep us from getting ahead of the brigade.

Your affectionate son,   G.

PRIVATE LETTER, SIXTY-FIRST VIRGINIA VOLUNTEERS
[MAHONE'S BRIGADE, ANDERSON'S DIVISION]
HEADQR'S, 5 MILES FROM FREDERICKSBURG, VA., May 8, 1863 [5-21-63SR]

Dear Home Folks: Our inactive operations are at last over and quite a stirring Summer campaign has opened. I mailed a few lines to you at two separate times, assuring you of my safety during the past week, and stated that I would write more in detail as soon as we went into camp. On Wednesday, April 29th, we were ordered to fall back of the Rapidan and Rappahannock rivers, as the enemy had succeeded in crossing the river and was rapidly pushing his forces, about to flank us. We made the necessary preparations, tents were struck, rations cooked, baggage packed, and everything in readiness to move. We left camp about 12 o'clock Wednesday night, and marched until day through the muddiest road I think I ever traveled, and it being very dark, our progress was but slow and marked by many a laughable incident—men floundering and stumbling in the mud, officers giving their orders, men grumbling at their soldier's luck, having to march over a muddy road, over hill and down dale, on such a dark-gloomy night. When we halted the next morning we were on the turnpike, [near Zoan Church] within about five miles of Fredericksburg, and prepared to make a stand there against the Yankees, who were rapidly advancing.

Our brigade (Mahone's) had joined us at Chancellorsville, which is about fourteen miles from Fredericksburg, and situated at the junction of the turnpike and plank roads, and about four miles from the Rapidan river. This place is situated on quite an eminence, and the location is quite a fine one, commanding a view of the whole country around; it has only one house of any note, a large brick hotel and a few wooden houses, all of which have been consumed by fire. Our brigade was formed in line, arms stacked, and spades furnished the men with which to entrench themselves. The Yankee sharpshooters got up in range before our entrenchments were finished, and succeeded in picking off a few of our men, the artillery on our left keeping up a brisk fire with the enemy all the while at long range. We finished our entrenchments late Thursday night, April 30th, and of course slept but little.

The next morning, May 1st, bright and early, we were up and under arms, ready for the field. We expected that the Yanks would attack our fortifications, but they failing to do so, and their presence on this side being rather unpleasant to Gen. Lee, an advance of our line was ordered and promptly executed. [Cadmus M.] Wilcox on our right, and Wright on our left, the line moved up about 7 a. m. in splendid style. Our position (61st Virginia Regiment) in the line was in the centre and we were drawn up in an open field, whilst the remainder of the brigade was sheltered in the woods. We were exposed all the while to a murderous fire from the Yankee batteries immediately in our front; our skirmishers were thrown out, and pretty soon the sharp crack of the rifle was sufficient proof that the ball had opened and that the Yankee line was advancing. The old 61st was in a *ticklish* position, but she had to console herself with the reflection that the eyes of the brigade were on her, and remember her past good luck; not a man stirred or flinched, all seemed to take it for granted that they must remain there and hold their own.

We had been drawn up in line of battle about half an hour, when a solid column of Yankee regulars [Sykes' division] emerged from the woods in our front, and advanced to give us battle. As soon as our front was unmasked by the skirmishers, who were falling back, we opened on the advancing line; the Yanks quickly replied, several batteries on each side became engaged, balls whistled in every direction, the air resounded with the discharges of thousands of guns; but this was no time to think of dangers—the work to be done was before us, and the number of dead Yankees, who fell before our well aimed volleys, testify to how well that work was done. Our company was immediately under the guns of one of our batteries, and consequently we received the full benefit of the fire, directed against the battery, as well as that from the infantry; but not a man faltered, every one performed his duty. We fought them three hours and a half, from 11½ until 3 p. m., when the enemy's line, no longer able to stand this awful fire, gave way and retreated in great disorder, throwing away their guns, knapsacks and every thing that impeded their retrograde movement; our troops yelling and shouting in their peculiar style all the while, without lessening their fire on the retreating body. Col. [Virginius D.] Groner acted very well, encouraging his command by both words and actions; he sent to Gen. McLaws, who in Longstreet's absence commands the corps, requesting that we might be allowed to move our position, as we were so much exposed. McLaws returned a negative reply, saying, that as our position was quite an important one, we must hold it at all hazards, and the old 61st fought on until the Yankee line retreated.

Our company carried 20 men into the fight; 8 of this number were wounded, four it is thought mortally; one poor fellow had his thigh horribly crushed, another his left arm cut off by a shell, and the other badly mangled. Capt. V. O. Cassell was wounded in the knee, causing his leg to be amputated. I was struck and knocked down by a minie ball; which, luckily passing through my jacket, glanced on my hip, doing no damage save a sharp momentary pain. As soon as I fell, Captain [John G.] Wallace, thinking I was badly wounded, ordered some of the men to take me to the rear; they, regardless of my positive assertions that I was unhurt, seemed determined to carry out the order *nolens volens*, and it was some time before I could convince them that I was uninjured.

This fight took place on the turnpike which leads from Fredericksburg to Chancellorsville, at a point ten miles from the former and four from the latter place. In this fight our brigade was in advance, and our regiment held the most exposed position, being in an open field without shelter; the balance of the troops were entirely hid by the thick woods in which they were drawn up in line.

The Yankee troops who attacked our position were regulars. This was evident both from the regularity and quickness of their movements and from their stubborn fighting qualities; but they were fighting troops who, though they have not the military drill and air, nor are as well schooled in Hardee as the United States regulars, still the dear ties which bind our soldiery to home, their native land and its institutions, render them every inch soldiers superior to these regulars, who will always meet a stubborn and bloody resistance whenever they attack these ragged Rebels. The enemy fell back about 3 p. m., our brigade in pursuit, slowly pushing them towards the river. This was Friday, May 1st. We bivouacked that night in about two miles of Chancellorsville, at which commanding position the enemy had heavily entrenched himself, no doubt intending to make quite a stubborn fight.

Saturday, May 2. The next morning, Saturday, we were up, under arms and in line of battle before day. Just at day break the artillery from both sides opened quite a brisk fire, and our brigade moved in the woods a short distance, to get out of range of the enemy's shell. As soon as the artillery duel was over, which lasted about two hours, the brigade was moved back in the position they occupied the night before, and our regiment was sent in advance as skirmishers. We engaged the Yankee skirmishers' line all day without much damage to our side; and in the afternoon we were withdrawn and marched to our position on the extreme left of the general line, our brigade line resting on the [Fredericksburg] turnpike, commonly called Brock's [Orange Turnpike] road, which leads from Chancellorsville to Guinea Station, in about one mile of the former place. As our brigade moved off to their position in line, troops were seen moving in every direction; some had already reached their positions and were preparing entrenchments for the coming battle; others, like ourselves, were on their way to the general line. The whole country seemed alive with human forms, each man bearing a trusty musket. Everything indicated that the great struggle was near at hand, and all seemed in good spirits and confident of victory.

When we reached the left of the line, the heavy roll of musketry was heard, and soon afterwards we learned that it was Wright's brigade skirmishing with the enemy immediately in our front. Stretchers, borne on the shoulders of the ambulance corps, were passing with the wounded going to the rear, and some were returning empty to take some new victim to the hands of the doctor. In this skirmish Wright lost a great many men. I heard it remarked on all sides, "How well those Georgians fight—they don't know how to fall back." Such expressions as these were quite gratifying to me and made me feel proud of my adopted home. As soon as we reached our place in line, where a partial entrenchment of rails and clay was thrown up, we immediately went to work to strengthen our position and render ourselves as secure as possible.

About 5 o'clock in the afternoon, one of the batteries immediately in our rear opened upon the Chancellorsville entrenchments, and was quickly replied to by the Yankee batteries. Gen. Lee and staff rode by and took their position near our battery, and, regardless of the shot and shell which were falling all around them, seemed to be passive spectators of what was going on. Lee was on a splendid bay charger, looked every inch a General; but we all wished him safely at his headquarters in the rear, rather than see him expose his valuable life unnecessarily. The wounded and dying from Wright's brigade were constantly passing, testifying to how well merited was the reputation gained by the Georgians for their superior fighting qualities. Night coming on put a stop to the fight, and Wright's brigade filed past us, with thinned ranks, it is true but covered with glory.

Just before dark [Edward A.] Perry's Florida brigade passed us on their way to their position in line; they were apparently worn out, having been skirmishing all day with nothing to eat, but they were in fine spirits. This was the brigade that we routed so in the snow-ball battle last Winter, driving them into their tents; some such expressions as these proved that they recognized us: "Hallo, snow ballers;" "You beat us snow balling, but we will fight together to-morrow." Our men who had just received their three days rations, rushed into the road, and, unmindful of their own wants, emptied their haversacks and shared their last hard cracker with the hungry Floridians. If the Washington officials could be eye-witnesses of such disinterested acts of kindness of our troops to each other, which are by no means rare, they would soon see the utter hopelessness of their cause and determine to let us alone in future.

Sunday, May 3—We remained behind our breastworks that night, and the next morning, Sunday, the sun rose beautiful and bright—all nature seemed lit up with unusual brightness and splendor as if in mockery of the awful carnage which would soon ensue; not a gun was heard, there was a lull in the awful storm. I had almost began to think that the enemy had given up the fight and recrossed the river, and that we would be allowed to enjoy, in quiet and security this beautiful Sabbath day. But my hopes and expectations were not realized. About 8 a. m., the heavy rumbling of the enemy's guns at Chancellorsville was heard, and the whistling shell came whizzing over our heads, reminding us that the enemy were still on this side of the river, and that we would have hot work before this sacred day was brought to a close. Pretty soon the sharp clear voice of little Billy Mahone was heard: "Attention battalion, forward, guide centre, march." Right over our entrenchments we marched, the men grumbling at their luck, saying: "we build all the entrenchments but are never allowed to fight behind them." Right through the woods we go and deploy as skirmishers. As we advance towards the Chancellorsville entrenchments, "we are always in advance" is the cry of the whole brigade; still they march on without one coward heart, or faltering step among their numbers; the shell and canister come whizzing over and around them, still onward they go.

Pretty soon the Yankee skirmishers are seen, and the two lines are engaged in a deadly strife for the entire possession of the woods—all grumbling ceased, all thoughts of entrenchments and danger were forgotten, all were bent on the one purpose of clearing the woods of these Dutch invaders. Both sides fight on with a desperate determination for three or four hours without any marked change in their relative positions; at last, our ammunition getting scarce, and Mahone having determined not to retire until the Yanks were driven out, an advance of the skirmish line was ordered; with a yell, that resounded through the woods and drowned for the instant the heavy booming of the cannon, the brigade charged in splendid style; on, on goes this huge wave of Confederate souls, unmindful of all save their country's honor; on, over logs and ditches; on, through the tangled undergrowth, yelling and whooping at every stride. All thoughts of danger and defeat were swollowed up in the enthusiasm of the moment; all other feelings seemed to have left the breasts of these men save the consciousness that their country's cause was in peril; the Yankees pour a deadly volley into this devoted line, many fall, but this seems to heighten rather than depress the terrible enthusiasm of the moment—our line *halts!* "What, are we falling back?" No, a tremendous and murderous volley is returned upon the Yanks ranks, and with another scream and yell the charge is renewed. The Yanks fight well and stubbornly, but who can resist such an avalanche of Rebs? It would not be reasonable to suppose that human beings could stand such a charge. The Yankees seem to share this opinion, for they slowly give way. Now is our time, volley after volley from our brigade is poured into the ranks of the retreating skirmishers; *they* redouble their efforts to escape this terrible fire, *we* to complete more thoroughly the day's bloody work. Their retreat, which commenced in good order, terminated in a disgraceful stampede.

As soon as we succeeded in getting them pretty well under way in their hasty change of base towards Chancellorsville, we were relieved by another brigade, who gallantly sustained the advantage gained by us. We were filed out into the plank road, where a fine view of Chancellorsville was obtained. A white flag was floating over one of the batteries and the place was in flames; the enemy had been shelled out by Jackson's army in their rear; cheer after cheer rent the air at this great but sad victory. Many of our troops were advancing and taking possession of the evacuated entrenchments. We were allowed to lie down in the road, for we were entirely exhausted. A Yankee battery, over which the white flag was waving, had surrendered to Wright's brigade; but before his men could reach the guns, the cowardly scoundrels fired three shots at our line, cut their horses' throats, and deserting their guns, joined the retiring Yankee army. One of these shells passing over our heads buried itself in the body of an Orderly Sergeant, who was moving off with his regiment, killing him instantly. Poor fellow, as the shell struck him, how I pitied his hard lot—it is horrid to be shot down at any time even when victory is doubtful, but to be killed in the sight of victory and glory, with a cheer on his lips for the success of our arms, was peculiarly awful. The road was alive with Yankee prisoners being carried to the rear under guard. One of them told me that 70,000 of the grand army would go out of service on the 7th. They all seem to be heartily tired of the war, and thoroughly convinced that they can never force us back into the Union. Whether Chancellorsville was burned by our shell or by Yankee torches I have been unable to ascertain.

As soon as we were sufficiently rested, we were moved up to Chancellorsville. As we filed into the entrenchments, I think I looked upon the grandest sight I ever seen. There were seen on all sides Confederate troops drawn up in line, yelling and shouting in their peculiar style. There, over the entrenchments, instead of the hated banner of oppression and modern tyranny, waved the bright and rich banner of our infant Confederacy—its silken folds wafted to and fro by the pure breeze of old Virginia, seemed to lend a new charm to the scene and bless the memory of our departed dead. The evil fruits of war were discernable on all sides; the dead bodies of the Yankees could be seen all around. Some had fallen at their guns—others had been killed on their way to the rear; some were lying badly wounded, and the groans of the wounded and dying, though I hated the cause for which they fell, grated harshly on my ears, whilst I felt deep commiseration for the poor deluded victims of an abolition fanaticism. Everything that could be seen marked the footprints of war and the terrible battle field. Dead horses, dismounted guns, broken artillery carriages could be seen everywhere; knapsacks strewn in every direction, the ground ploughed up by shot and shell, the dead bodies of the enemy and the horrid stench of human gore were unmistakable signs of the bloody day's work; then, the large brick hotel, almost consumed, as the flames licked its massive sides, looked like the funeral pile of the dead and the dying. It was a horrid sight and not soon to be forgotten.

My cogitations were brought to a sudden close by a deafening shout. On looking to see what the cause of the new joy was, I discovered Gen. Lee and Gen. Stuart quietly riding down the line. The troops were congratulating the Generals on their successful plans, by which this signal victory had been gained. Stonewall Jackson and A. P. Hill had been wounded early in the fight by a North Carolina battalion. They were riding over the picket line, and were shot by our men under the impression that they were Yankees. Jackson, I understand has lost an arm. Hill was wounded in the thigh, and the command, consequently, devolved upon Gen. Stuart, who seems to have displayed good generalship and fought his men as well as if Jackson had been present.

We had been at Chancellorsville only about an hour when a courier came dashing in with news that the enemy had crossed at Fredericksburg, had gained Marye's Heights, and was rapidly pushing forward his force. This was a new dilemma; the enemy three miles this side of Fredericksburg, rapidly advancing, with only two brigades to oppose them; but Lee was equal to the emergency. He gave his commands with coolness and characteristic despatch. The troops moved off—Mahone's brigade in advance—in the direction of Fredericksburg. There was a particular position to be reached, about four and a half miles from the city, before the enemy should arrive. Our brigade, almost worn out by previous fatigue and exposure, knew what was expected of them and they redoubled their efforts; knapsacks and everything that impeded their progress were thrown away, the road was strewn with soldier chattels, and these brave men with blistered feet, hungry and worn out, but with their trusty musket and forty rounds of cartridges, *toiled on for nine long miles*, without one moment to rest. When in about two hundred yards of the position [Salem Church] we had hurried to occupy, I heard Mahone say to Groner, "Colonel, carry your regiment into that thicket and deploy as skirmishers, I will soon follow with the brigade." We had no time to lose; the Yanks were drawing near, half an hour later and *we would have been too late*. We had not the time to deploy by rote, but pushed into the thicket and deployed our line as best we could. There was considerable confusion incident to our being hurried into the woods without any definite orders, but soon every man was in his proper place and the line was formed.

We were not left long in waiting, for pretty soon the blue uniforms and Dutch faces of the Yankee skirmishers were seen through the thick undergrowth; several balls came whistling over our heads, but appeared to come from our rear; as soon as our troops had reached their position in rear of us, we poured a volley into the Yankee ranks and fell back. We had only advanced about one hundred yards in the woods to cover the front of our forces and keep the enemy back whilst they gained their respective position. Wilson and myself were on the extreme right and got out of the woods first. As we came out we saw a musket pointed at us and a man shouted, "a minute later and I would have shot you." As soon as we got over the fence, behind which our troops were in positions, horror of horrors! one whole brigade opened upon our skirmishers. I stood horror stricken for the instant, but as soon as I recovered my self-possession I ran along the line, begging the men for God's sake to cease firing, they were murdering our own men; but as the Yankees had gotten up and their balls came flying over, it was some time before we could convince the men that they were firing on our own skirmishers. It was a trying time for the poor fellows in there, and calculated to create a panic even among veterans, but they fell down behind an artificial bank, which partly protected them from the rear fire, and kept up a constant fire on the advancing Yankee line. It was [Paul] Semmes' Georgia brigade who in the hurry and bustle to reach their position, had not been notified of our being in front. It was a fatal mistake; several were killed and wounded; among the latter was Claude Murdaugh, shot through both thighs. As soon as we could be heard, the firing ceased and the regiment came out of the woods and promptly rallied around its colors; they all appeared indignant but not panic stricken.

We had but little time, however, to think over this adventure, for we were hurried to our position in line; the fight had already commenced, it was the most complete shower of shell, shot and minie balls ever seen; the Yankee column advanced in three lines, six ranks, closed *en massed*, one line would fire, fall down and load, the next would do the same thing, and so on to the third. It was an awfully grand sight, these two huge bodies engaged in deadly strife, balls whistling in all directions, men falling around; the groans of the wounded were horrible to hear; for two and a half hours the two armies fought, but it seemed like an eternity. The Yankees were fresh, not having been in the late fight. The battle seemed doubtful; at last the Yankees lose a little ground; *that* saved the day. Semmes and Wilcox with their host of Confederate hearts bear down on them, yelling all the while; the Yankee lines are broken; regardless of Hardee or Gilham's tactics, they rush headlong towards Fredericksburg, perfectly panic-stricken. It was the bloodiest battle of the war and a complete rout of the enemy. The woods are covered with their dead. Many prisoners have fallen into our hands, wagon loads of small arms have been taken and sent to Richmond. When you take into consideration that the forces of the enemy engaged in this fight were fresh troops, well disciplined and armed, and out-numbering three to one our force, which was worn out by three days hard fighting, marching and the fatigue incident thereto, and then remembering how complete the rout, you will agree with me in terming this one of the grandest victories of the war. Those of the brigade who have been in all the previous battles of the war, say that this was the most severe fire they ever experienced. Two battles in one day, and each a separate and distinct victory, is something to be proud of.

Gen. Early had gotten in their rear and retaken the Fredericksburg Heights, so the Yankees had to recross the river, leaving behind them many of their dead comrades, many prisoners and much ordnance; it was a total rout, and will tell fearfully upon the spirits of both the citizen and soldier at the North. We slept that night under arms, expecting the fight to be renewed the next day. It was an eventful Sunday through which we had passed, and I sincerely thanked the Giver of life that I had been spared to see it brought to a close. I then lay down to sleep and dream of my dear home and its loved inmates. All my dreams were pleasant, I thought that war, with its horrors had ceased, and that we were once more a happy, re-united family.

Monday, May 4—The next morning, May 4, we were up and under arms before day, expecting the fight to be renewed; but the news soon reached us that Early had retaken the Heights, that the enemy had recrossed the river, and consequently that the fight here was at an end. As our brigade had been in the hottest of the fight and had suffered severely, we were ordered into the trenches to rest ourselves. Firing could be heard all day in the direction of Chancellorsville, a sure sign that the Yanks had not recrossed the river there. Nothing of note occurred during the day, except we received a pretty heavy shelling from the Yankee batteries in the afternoon, doing, however, but little damage. We slept in the trenches that night.

Tuesday, May 5—The next morning, May 5, at about 12, m., we were ordered back to Chancellorsville to aid in driving the Yankees across the river, as they had heavily fortified their position, determined to make a bold and final stand. We joined the division on the plank road and started for Chancellorsville—the roads were dusty and the day quite warm. In about half an hour after we had joined the division, it commenced to rain in torrents; it was one of the heaviest thunder storms, I think, I ever saw. We were all soon drenched—the roads, which, a short time before, were dusty and disagreeable, were soon one mass of deep mud, large puddles of water, perfect ponds—had to be waded through; still we marched on, about a mile of Chancellorsville we halted for the night. Large rail fires were soon brightly burning all through the woods. We dry our clothes as best we can by the fire, and, with thoughts of home, catch a few moments repose on the wet ground, for there is bloody work before us in the morning.

Wednesday, May 6—The next day, May 6th, we started bright and early for Chancellorsville. On the road we heard that the previous days' rains had driven the Yanks across the river. As we filed through the enemy's entrenchments, which they had left the night before, I could not help feeling thankful to God for the heavy rains which had caused the Yankees to beat such a hasty retreat, for they had heavily entrenched themselves in quite a commanding position, and it would have required hot work to have dislodged them; but they had crossed the river, and the victory was ours. We were ordered into camp about five miles from Fredericksburg, where we are now quite comfortably quartered.

I saw yesterday's paper; it makes no mention of our brigade or division, but says that D. H. Hill's division opened the fight on Friday, and McLaws' on Sunday. This is an ungenerous mistake. Mahone's brigade led the advance in both fights, and on Sunday our regimental skirmishers fired the first gun, after Wilcox and Barksdale had been driven from Fredericksburg, and before McLaws' division got up from Chancellorsville. The mistake I suppose will be corrected—"honor to whom honor is due." These are a few of the many incidents connected with the late fights here, which, I think, as they were separate and distinct, should be termed the battles of Chancellorsville and Fredericksburg. Hooker, like all his predecessors, will, I suppose, have his official head cut off, and be superseded by some new Yankee aspirant for military distinction.

Sergt. John H. Bogart.

John H. Bogart enlisted on October 17, 1861 at Oak Grove, Norfolk County in Company C, 61st Virginia Infantry. He was promoted to First Sergeant on February 11, 1862, and reduced to Commissary Sergeant at his on request on August 1, 1863. While in hospital in Warrenton, Va., on November 3, 1863 Bogart was captured and sent to Old Capitol Prison in Washington D. C., later transferred to Point Lookout, Md., where he served in the prison hospital. After being exchanged on February 10, 1865, Bogart returned to duty and was captured at Sailor's Creek on April 6, and sent again to Point Lookout. Bogart was released on June 2, 1865.

PRIVATE LETTER, FIFTY-THIRD GEORGIA REGIMENT
[SEMMES' BRIGADE, McLAWS' DIVISION]
IN CAMP, May 7, 1863 [5-28-63ASC]

Dear Father and Mother: Our brigade was in three battles, one on the 1st instant and two on Sunday 3rd—one in the morning and the other in the evening. The loss in the brigade was 600 killed and wounded, 117 in our regiment. In our company 13 were wounded and none killed. The last battle was a fierce one and the bullets and shells flew thick around us, and we had no protection except a small ditch by the side of a brush fence. All of our boys stood up like men.

On the 28th of April the Yankees crossed the river in the night, three miles below Fredericksburg. The next day we went out but were not engaged. On the 30th the Yankees went back and moved up the river. We then went ten miles above Fredericksburg, leaving two divisions to hold our original position. On the first we met the Yankees near Raccoon ford, and fought them most of the day, driving them back two miles.

On the second, General Jackson came to our relief, and getting in their rear, the enemy was entirely routed, captured or killed. While we were resting here, General Lee received intelligence that the enemy had crossed at Fredericksburg, and was driving our two divisions before them up the river.

The divisions of McLaws and D. H. Hill [Richard Anderson] were ordered to meet them. We soon met our two divisions on the retreat, and glad enough they were to see us. Gen'ls McLaws and Hill told them to give way for their troops to take the front line, and they would soon show the Yankees the way to the river. The enemy charged us as soon as we were in line, but the charge was met firmly, and our forces then charged the enemy and turned the tide, and as he retreated we continued to charge him with impetuosity until night. In this action I shot 47 times, and my gun then was so hot and so much clogged up that I could not load it, so I threw it down and took another with which I shot 9 times.

Our Colonel [J. P. Simms] was close to our company all the time, and encouraged the men. He assisted me frequently in loading my gun, which enabled me to shoot much faster in a charge.

When the enemy came within about fifty yards of us, I saw their flag and told the Colonel to watch the color bearer, for I was going to take a fair crack at him. At the fire of my piece he fell, but I don't know who killed, for we were generally aiming at him. The next morning when we went out to look at him, we found him shot to pieces. We took their flag when we charged them. It had 32 stars on it.

On the 4th Gen. Hill [Early] flanked the enemy, we remaining in our position. Gen. McLaws then told us that the enemy was bagged, and we should soon tie the string—for Gen. Hill [Early], in their rear, would soon drive them on us, and we must not let them escape. At about an hour by sun, Hill [Early] opened on them with artillery in the rearm and we opened on them in front and poured a heavy fire into them till dark. Instead of coming towards us, they made for a ford on the river, where we poured the shot and shell into them as they crossed. We, however, could not approach the ford, as their batteries on the other side could have shelled us with impunity.

After the crossing we thought the battle was over, and rested until 2 o'clock the next day, when we received orders to go to the assistance of Jackson [J. E. B. Stuart]. A heavy rain fell on us all the way, and we were in line of battle at dark. We remained all night here, in 500 yards of the enemy's front, and were not allowed to speak above a whisper. During this night we suffered a great deal from cold. At daylight we went to building breastworks.

Our General again told us that we had them bagged, and we raised a shout which scared the Yankees so much that they began to fall back towards the river, and we commenced pouring shot into them from two sides. They left their works 12 o'clock that day—the 6th—[the night of the 5th] and were soon across.

We then started back for our old camp, which was 15 miles distant. It rained on us all the way. We found a desolated camp, for we had destroyed our tents before leaving, fearing that they might fall into the hands of the enemy; and such articles as we did not destroy were stolen by the cowards who staid behind under pretension of being sick.

I found a Yankee haversack with lots of ground coffee, sugar, salt, &c.; and many other tricks.

This victory is one of the most glorious we have gained.

When we returned to camp there were only 23 in our company, though we had started out with 43.

J. W. McGinnis.

John W. McGinnis enlisted as a private in Co. H, 6th Regiment, Georgia State Troops, on October 21, 1861, and was mustered out in April 1862. One month later, McGinnis was appointed Second Sergeant, of Co. E, 53rd Georgia Infantry, and was wounded at Sharpsburg, Md., on September 17, 1862. McGinnis was appointed First Sergeant June 1863, and was wounded and captured at Gettysburg on July 2, 1863. Sergeant McGinnis died of his wounds in a Field Hospital on August 27, 1863.

FIFTIETH GEORGIA VOLUNTEERS
[SEMMES' BRIGADE, McLAWS' DIVISION]
NEAR FREDERICKSBURG, VA., May 18, 1863 [5-29-63SR]

Perhaps a few lines from the "inevitable" 50th, respecting the share we bore in the late glorious campaign of the first week of May, along the banks of the now world-renowned Rappahannock, may not prove uninteresting to your readers from Southern Georgia, (where the regiment was raised) or unworthy a place in your columns.

On the 29th April the loud roar of our cannon heralding the advance of the "finest army on the planet," brought with it the order for Semmes' brigade, composed of the 10th, 50th, 51st and 53rd Georgia Regt's, to move to the front. The boys roused out of their comfortable winter quarters in short order, and in less than 20 minutes the brigade was *en route* for the river. We took position on the range of hills overlooking the river and town, resting on our arms during the night, raining heavily all night. Next morning it cleared off, and the misty river fog lifting. The scene on both sides of the river lay spread before us like a panoramic show. We saw at a glance the enemy had effected a crossing and lodgement on the southern bank, their long lines of infantry stretching away for miles and reaching to the river where they were crossing in three columns at Deep Run, could plainly be seen, and the loud huzzahs of their regiments heard, as their general officers galloped up and down their lines, huge trains of ordnance wagons and whole parks of artillery drawn up in readiness to cross, while here and there flying squadrons of cavalry dashing about, made up a scene to be seen and never forgotten; but high over all soared a huge balloon which ever and anon descended and rose again as it gained information of our position and movements. On the south bank their line crept cautiously along toward our right and Hamilton's Crossing, throwing out their skirmishers as they advanced, who coolly enough immediately pitched their shelter tents, and creeping out of the sun under them kept a quiet lookout on our picket line, who, almost crazy for the order to go at them and bag said shelter tents, could scarce be restrained within their lines. Along on the edge of the low hills lay our line of battle, grey, grim, and threatening, viewing the enemy's approach with almost a savage joy as they anticipated a certain triumph over their noisy, showy, advancing opponents. Soon the roar of cannon on our right showed where their advanced column had struck Jackson's line; toward evening a general retrograde movement was visible, and then came the news that the enemy in heavy force had crossed at Kelly's ford, was trying to gain a position in our rear to be supported by the column now amusing us in front.

As soon as night masked our movements, we were withdrawn from the river, and McLaws' Division, Semmes Brigade, in front, put off at railroad speed to meet and check their advance; that night at 11 p. m., we closed up with the enemy's lines at Wilderness [Zoan] church, who had been driving Mahone's Virginia Brigade before them, all the opposition they had. On the morning of May 1st, our extended lines showed the enemy our strength, and we quietly fell back on his main body, following him up closely. We formed line of battle at 9 a. m., and fiercely attacking, we drove in his skirmishers and forcing back his line steadily and surely in spite of their splendidly served batteries of light artillery, they finally broke, and throwing off their knapsacks and overcoats fled in the direction of Chancellorsville. The 50th suffered but little in this fight, having but two wounded; their front being covered with a low morass partially screened them from the enemy's fire. The 51st were not so fortunate, losing 47 killed and wounded, including their beloved Colonel Wm. M. Slaughter, of Albany, who was struck on the leg and arm by a portion of a shell, from which he died at 3 a. m. next morning. Capt. [Daniel A. J.] Sessions was also killed and Lt. Col. [Edward] Ball wounded in the head. In Colonel Slaughter the brigade lost one of its most efficient and able officers; ever present with his regiment, ever for duty, he was universally esteemed, throughout the brigade, and long will the gallant 51st feel and mourn his loss. That night we followed the rapidly retreating foe; such another litter of overcoats, arms, accoutrements, knapsacks and haversacks, bursting full with 8 days rations of crackers, it has never been my lot to witness before; the ground was literally strewn for miles with them. At night we approached Chancellorsville, where the enemy in huge masses were concentrating and strengthening their lines and throwing up entrenchments. Think of it, a vast attacking army who were to carry all before them, already drawing their terrified lines toward the river and covering themselves with earthworks. Where was their vaunted confidence in their men. But Lee and Jackson were on them, and terror and dismay was on them all.

So passed the night and morning of May 2nd, when, Jackson having gained their right and rear, the battle of Chancellorsville opened. Semmes' brigade formed part of the line on their left flank, cutting them off from Fredericksburg. The attack was on their front, right and rear, and raged fearfully during the night of Saturday until late, and commencing at before 5 a. m., May 3rd, until 9 a. m., ere the enemy's line finally gave way at all points, and they were hurled back in confusion and defeat on the river. Oh, for two hours of glorious Jackson then, and their retreat would have been finally cut off and the whole army captured; but God willed it otherwise, and our noble hero, wounded severely, by his own men, accidentally, on the previous night, lay on a bed of suffering, never more to lead the 2nd Army Corps of Lee's heroic army to victory; and the crushed foe lay in safety under the protection of their guns on the northern bank. Towards the last, Semmes' brigade received orders to advance on the enemy's works, when two regiments of the enemy surrendered to the 10th Georgia, who were in front as skirmishers.

Forming on the turnpike road we were suddenly ordered to the rear to confront and check Sedgwick's corps, who, having stormed Marye's Hill, was rapidly advancing on our rear, to the relief of "Fighting Joe" at Chancellorsville. We instantly started and met the enemy at Salem Church, some ten [five] miles from Fredericksburg, and commenced forming line (Semmes' brigade) on the left of the road, through an open field, fronting a pine grove, through which the enemy in three powerful lines were advancing. The 50th were on the left and had to form on the inner edge of the field over a cedar wattled fence in the woods beyond. Just as the regiments came up and received orders, on the right by file into line! the enemy suddenly rose 150 yards in front and poured a deadly fire in our ranks, killing Capt. R. J. McLean, Co. E, one private (D. McPherson) and wounding some ten or fifteen others. The regiment, however, under the gallant leadership of Lt. Col. [Francis] Kearse, dashed forward over the fence, and forming a kind of line, rushed cheering on to within sixty yards of the enemy, and taking position in a path leading through the woods, they poured a volley into the enemy's ranks that seemed to me to sweep their front rank entirely out of existence. The men then kneeling down in their places, fought there stubbornly and resolutely for over two hours, repulsing with great slaughter five successive efforts of the enemy to break our line. The coolness and firing of the men was superb, loading steadily and firing low. Every twig and bush for nearly three hundred yards in our front was cut off knee high, while the woods in front was covered with blue coats, lying dead in every conceivable form.

Night coming on, and the men having expended their cartridges (sixty rounds each), and having lost 180 in killed and wounded, the regiment was ordered to fall back to replenish ammunition, which was done in good order, some sixty yards, the enemy's fire having almost ceased.

The courage and spirit of the Fiftieth was undiminished by the terrible ordeal through which they had gone. The first thing they did on reforming line was to give three cheers for their officers, which was done with a will, making the woods ring and hastening the retreat of the baffled enemy. A Colonel of Mahone's brigade, on our left and rear, done us the honor to say he never saw a line formed more rapidly under fire, and never witnessed more dash and resolute fighting on the part of any regiment in Lee's army. That night the wounded were all gathered in and sent to hospital. Next morning our dead were buried, and then the task of burying the enemy's dead fell on us. Over one hundred lay dead in our front and fully a hundred more were buried by the enemy a short distance off. Our loss was 17 killed and 165 wounded, quite a number of which were slight wounds. On the 4th and 5th we lay in line, while Gen. Early and a portion of McLaws' division drove the enemy over the river. On the evening of the 5th we marched, in a heavy storm of rain, to United States Ford, but on the morning of the 6th the enemy fled again before our approach, and the last of the "finest army," &c., ingloriously recrossed the river, sans arms, sans coats, sans honors, sans everything. That day the army wearily retraced its steps back to their old camps, utterly worn out by the terrible labors of the seven preceding days, but cheered up by the reflection that they had done their duty thoroughly and well.

Our brigade has covered itself with glory, and our General declares no better fighting material exists anywhere; and the army, though mourning the loss of our Virginia Napoleon— the incomparable Jackson—is in better plight and fighting trim than ever before. I would enclose a list of our casualties, but understanding the Adjutant has already forwarded one for publication, have thought that sufficient.

P. M. G.

PRIVATE LETTER, FIFTIETH GEORGIA INFANTRY

[SEMMES' BRIGADE, McLAWS' DIVISION]
HEADQ'TS, 50TH REGIMENT, NEAR FREDERICKSBURG, VA., May 8, 1863 [5-18-63SR]

At length I am safe back in camp. After a terrible week of fighting and marching, I could scarce tell you where we have been, and at what places we fought. One thing is certain— Gen. Lee, with ----- men, has driven the enemy in rout and disgrace across the Rappahannock, although they numbered over 150,000. The 50th fought like heroes, to the great delight of Gen. Semmes; at the battle of Salem Church we lost in our regiment 181 killed and wounded, and it was there won the reputation of being one of the best fighting regiments in the army of Northern Virginia. The men, going into action under a heavy musketry fire formed and charged up to within sixty yards of the enemy's line, and taking position in an open road, fought there for over two hours against overwhelming odds, repulsed and drove off with great slaughter five successive regiments of Sedgwick's veteran corps, almost utterly destroying the 15th New Jersey and 93rd and 119th Pennsylvania. The 12th U. S. Regulars next charged us with better result; one of their Captains said it was the first time he ever had to order a retreat, but our fire was the most deadly he ever faced. The 43rd New York came next, but fared no better; we have their flag staff, presented to them by Gen. Simeon Draper. The men kneeled and took steady aim, firing, according to instructions, no higher than the knee; every sappling and twig in our front was cut off knee high by our balls, some of the men firing 110 rounds. The Colonel of the 41st Virginia said it was the most stubborn, resolute fight he ever witnessed. The remainder of Semmes' brigade fought splendidly; they were in position before the firing commenced, and were partially protected by a ditch. Capt. Richard J. McLean of my old company [B] was killed. The company losing 16 killed and wounded, it will be a sorrowful time in Thomas county.

I keep in good health; don't know how I escaped. Yankee prisoners say they tried to shoot me down for over an hour, but the terrible close shooting of my men saved me every time. We are back now at our old camp, wearied and worn out by eight days constant marching and fighting. We marched fifteen miles back through the most drenching rain storm I have ever been in; found everything in confusion and disorder, and nearly everything lost in the way of baggage. Thankful to God for my preservation, I have to mourn the loss of many brave officers and men. The 50th has, indeed, done well. But I must close, as other duties press me now.

***.

FROM OUR SPECIAL CORRESPONDENT "DIXIE."

HAMILTON'S CROSSING, VA., May 10, 1863 [6-4-63ASC]

Another great battle has been fought, and another great victory won upon the banks of the Rappahannock; a victory which adds brighter lustre to the fame of the troops under Gen. Lee, and is another proof of the justice of their claim to being the best army ever organized.

Gen. Hooker's plan was to make a feint in strong forces a little below Fredericksburg, as though he intended to give battle on the field of December 13th, while he moved his main force higher up, and crossed the river at points about opposite Chancellorsville, which is situated on the plank road leading from Fredericksburg to Orange Court House, twelve miles from the former place; and then by moving out from the river, towards Spottsylvania Court House and Guinea's Station, occupy a position on the flank in the rear of Gen. Lee.

Gen. Lee, either knowing or correctly anticipating a movement of this kind, withdrew the whole of his force (except Gen. Early's division and Barksdale's brigade, which were left to defend the crossings at and below Fredericksburg) and marched along the Orange C. House plank road to meet the enemy. As soon as Gen. Hooker became aware of this movement knowing that a battle in that neighborhood would be inevitable, he took position above and below Chancellorsville, and intrenched himself on both sides of the road, his works being at right angles to the road, and facing towards Fredericksburg. When within two or three miles of Chancellorsville, Gen. Lee came upon the enemy. Here he placed the divisions of Gens. McLaws and Anderson in position, while Gen. Jackson with his corps was ordered up the Catharpin road, leaving the plank road on his right. After passing up that road until he reached a point above the position of the enemy he turned to the right, and fell into the plank [Brock] road two miles above Chancellorsville, and immediately behind the enemy's entrenchments. This movement took the Yankees completely by surprise. McLaws and Anderson fought them in front and extended their line to the left, while Stonewall came down like a terrible tornado upon his rear, at the same time extending his right until the two wings of our army met upon the flank of the enemy, who were driven in wild confusion from their position on the road, and compelled to fall back between that and the river. Our right and left wings were then extended until our lines reached from the river below Chancellorsville, to the river above, thus occupying three sides of Hooker's position. Our line of battle then formed a V with the apex resting on the plank road at Chancellorsville, and the enemy between that and the river, a distance of five miles or thereabouts.

Never was a more daring movement attempted and so brilliantly carried out; never an enemy so completely out-generaled. From being the flanking party, he suddenly found himself not only flanked, but a strong and terrible force in the rear of his entrenchments. His prospects at this time were gloomy and desperate in the extreme, while ours were indeed glorious, and would doubtless have been realized to the satisfaction of the most sanguine, but that Gen. Early, by some (as yet) unexplained means, allowed the enemy to cross at Fredericksburg and force him from his strong position and to advance three miles up the plank road. In consequence of this it became necessary for Gen. Lee to withdraw Gen. McLaws' and a part of Gen. Anderson's division from the attack and send them down the road to drive the enemy back to Fredericksburg and across the river. The result was that the pursuit of the flying enemy had to be temporarily abandoned, and Hooker, taking advantage of this opportunity, so strengthened his position on the river, and on the hills beyond, as to enable him to make his escape. If Gen. Early had held his strong position, Gen. Lee would have completely destroyed Hooker's army. There is no telling what the grand results would have been.

But as it is, the victory is a great one, and fully justifies the confidence so long and implicitly placed in the army of Gen. Lee. Hooker, the fifth General sent forward for the reduction of Richmond and the overthrow of Lee, has been successfully met and signally defeated, with a loss in men of many thousands, and small arms beyond calculation. Never upon any battlefield have I seen so many muskets thrown down.

The part taken by Gen. E. L. Thomas' brigade in this battle reflects the highest credit upon the General, his officers and men. The brigade occupied a position on the extreme left of our lines of intrenchments and a third in the rear as a support. The enemy and our brigade were in a dense wood composed of scrubby, stiff, low, branching oaks, and large stubbed chinquepin bushes. In front of their breastworks the enemy had felled trees, thus forming kind of an abattis over which our men were compelled to pass. The character of the woods, together with the felled trees, necessarily made the approach to the enemy's breastworks, both slow and difficult. Added to this the brigade was exposed to an enfilading artillery fire.

The order to advance was given about six o'clock in the morning, when the whole line moved forward. Soon the enemy's skirmishers were driven in, and immediately in front lay the Yankees behind their works not more than forty steps ahead. Then there came forth one long, living line of fire from those works. But the brigade neither faltered or paused, but with a loud and terrible shout rushed forward and the next moment were on the works, while the enemy were flying in horror and confusion. They, however, did not stop here, but charged on the second line of breastworks with the same result, and then upon the line of supports which also gave way before the invincible pursuit of the routed enemy that it became necessary to recall it, because it had gotten in advance of our line of battle.

As an instance of the bravery and confidence of the men composing this brigade, I will state that the 14th regiment came in full view of the enemy's works sooner than Col. [Robert] Folsom supposed it would, on which account he had not ordered the men to fix bayonets. It would not then do to halt for that purpose, so the regiment rushed forward and was the first to break the Yankee lines, and that without fixing bayonets.

The brigade was actively engaged about six hours; and the advantages of the position held by the enemy, the difficulties presented by the dense woods, and the results taken into consideration, it may be said without vanity to have been one of the most heroic and glorious efforts made during the war. Such deeds need no words of praise, they need only to be told to speak for themselves. Suffice it to say that Gen. Thomas has received the highest and most gratifying testimonials of the conduct of himself and his brigade. Georgia may well be proud of a brigade which calls forth the praise of such men as A. P. Hill, Stuart and R. E. Lee.

Gen. Thomas' brigade met the famous [Daniel] Sickles' Excelsior brigade, who boasted they had never met a defeat. But they could not withstand the fury of Thomas' *wild Union diggers*, who rushed upon them without bayonets. The 14th Georgia [13th North Carolina] captured Brigadier Gen. [William] Hays and two Colonels of the Excelsior Brigade.

DIXIE.

WOFFORD'S BRIGADE

IN CAMP, NEAR FREDERICKSBURG, VA., May 10, 1863 [5-19-63ASC]

A brief account of the part performed by this brigade in the great battles of Chancellorsville, Brick [Salem] Church and Banks' Ford, may not prove uninteresting to the many friends of these gallant men. Hence I give the following, gathered from those who acted well their part in this bloody work.

We were aroused about day light Wednesday morning, the 29th ult., by heavy firing on the Rappahannock, about four miles below Fredericksburg, and same distance from our camp. We soon learned that the shrewd Yankees had surprised our Generals and men, (a fact not very creditable,) during a dark and foggy night and morning; laid their pontoons, effected a crossing, captured some of our troops, and massed a large force on our side of the river, which, under the protection of their heavy guns on the heights beyond, bade us defiance.

Orders came for our brigade to move about five, long before the usual breakfast time of the troops, and as they do not care to eat their scanty allowance too early lest hunger should make his stern demands before night, and not be supplied, many left for the battle-field without anything to eat; but cheerfully and quickly they were in line, all ready to meet the invader. It was gratifying to see these devoted men move off singing laughing, and shouting, but sad to know that so many of these heroes were leaving their "old camp," never to return.

Gen. [William] Wofford moved the command to the hills below the city, ready to move to any post of danger, when he should be needed, and Thursday morning took position behind breast works in the bottom, to the right of Gen. McLaws' division. Here he remained in line of battle until about twelve at night, the enemy evincing no disposition to advance against our position below town, and having crossed in heavy force at Kelly's Ford about 18 miles above the city were advancing on our left flank, and threatening our rear when we were marched away from our stronghold to meet him on a field of his own choosing. Leaving about twelve o'clock at night, the command marched up near Banks' Ford about four miles above the city, and remained for a short time in entrenchments, when the General ordered an advance, which was executed in gallant style but the cunning Yankees prudently withdrew before our troops.

We then took position on the Railroad where we remained until Saturday [May 2] about 3 o'clock p.m., when we moved by the left flank and took position across the turnpike road leading from Fredericksburg to Chancellorsville, and about one mile from the latter place, when we were subjected to a severe shelling, and one man was killed and several wounded. Our battalion of skirmishers made a charge on the enemy and a brisk engagement ensued in which the boys came near taking a battery. The enemy were so hard pressed that one of the caissons was blown up in the midst of the charge.

During the early part of the engagement Gen. Wofford led a charge of this battalion of sharpshooters on horseback, a thing very seldom done but often necessary to infuse the proper spirit into the soldiery.

Whilst the brigade was under the terrific shelling they marched slowly to the left as calmly and orderly as if on ordinary drill, until properly posted. No man was seen to cower or tremble in the presence of the foe and under his deadly fire. Commands were given quietly and firmly and obeyed quickly and correctly. Gen. Wofford and staff were in front of the brigade moving deliberately in the midst of danger and death, arranging for the awful conflict with as much composure and care as if attending to any ordinary business.

The line of battle—these officers and men standing as they were ready to enter the dread harvest of death presented a spectacle that would have moved the inmost soul of every patriotic Georgian could it have been beheld as it was by the writer. Here were our fathers, brothers and friends exposing their noble hearts to the last falling shafts of death, for the peace and happiness of our dear ones at home. Georgians look yonder at that dear boy who has been tenderly raised and ministered unto by the tender hand of a noble mother, not for rude and ruthless war, but for the delightful avocations of peace, all browned, ragged and dirty, and behold how serious, how resigned to die, how determined, how brave he appears. Not a muscle shakes, not a feature changes, as he looks far back to his happy home in Georgia, the brighter land of his birth, and then into the cannon's mouth, the greedy jaws of death and the soldier's shallow grave. Listen at the stately steppings of war; it vies with the awful tread of the earth-quake—the ancient hills of Old Virginia tremble, the volcanic thunders lay waste the blighted forest, but your noble warrior boy stands firm as Gibraltar's rocks. How varied, how grand, how terrible the scene—no tongue can tell it, no pencil can paint it.

The writer saw and greeted many bright faces this placid May evening who never saw another setting sun, but poured out their blood on the altar of their country in the holy cause of freedom.

Saturday night the brigade remained in line of battle until about sun up, when it advanced upon the foe to the right of the road about half a mile below Chancellorsville, when the gallant men encountered the terrible fire of the foe, well secured behind breast works constructed in rather a crooked line, through a very dense woods with large trees and undergrowth naturally so thick that it is difficult to get through. Besides the enemy have felled trees and small brush cross and pile so as to make it difficult to charge the works, or even to see things.

The enemy's line of works being irregular and our line of battle being nearly straight, brought some regiments and parts of regiments much nearer than others to the enemy, Phillips' Legion were not exposed so much. Cobb's Legion were greatly exposed and fought very near the works. The 16th was very near and greatly exposed. The 24th was equally near, but the ground occupied by the men was better, hence they did not suffer so much. The 18th fought at the angle of the enemies works and the line was subject to a terrible front and flank fire, and that part of the regiment suffered heavily. Here, under such great disadvantages, these brave men fought for hours, not a man nor an officer skulking nor shunning duty. The brigade was ordered merely to engage the enemy and press him, but not to charge him. If the order had been given to charge at first, the works would doubtless have been carried at once, for when the men were permitted to advance the enemy fled or surrendered at once. It is supposed that General Lee wished the attention of the foe engaged in front in order that Gen. Jackson's forces might accomplish something in the rear.

General Wofford and staff were constantly all over the field, when their presence were necessary. The Gen. seemed to set at defiance the skill of the best marksmen in the Yankee army—firing at him with good rest, proper range and partially concealed from danger. He seems to bear a charmed life and seems to be permitted to live to show friends how to fight and Yankees how to die. If we had plenty of such officers and men as compose this Georgia brigade, the war would soon close and peace would again plume her bright wings and fly to ten thousand happy homes, and joy's charming smile make radiant millions of glad faces.

Lieut. Col. [Capt. A. H.] Patton of the Sharp Shooters fell early in the action, whilst leading his command in a charge. He had passed safely through most of the bloody struggles in Virginia and Maryland, but here met a soldiers death and fills a warrior's grave under the sod of his native State. He visited his home in Georgia a short time since and on his return was heard to express some mortification at the want of appreciation, by some, of the defenders of the country, and to remark that some amateur warriors who made such fuss at the beginning of the war and before, and denounced every man as a traitor to his country who would not agree to drink at least a barrel of Yankee blood, were still enjoying a peaceful time at home, and seemed restless because the soldier's furlough was so long, and the only enquiry made was 'when are you going back.' Now he rests in his bloody soldier's garb under the soil of Virginia, and will never more be among those hot-headed and cold-hearted individuals. A soldier not filled with charity remarks that "he sleeps as a dead lion and his amateur acquaintances remain at home as living dogs."

About eleven o'clock the brigade advanced and most of the cowardly rascals surrendered. The brigade was not seriously engaged again that day.

Whilst this bloody tragedy was being enacted the enemy, under Gen. Sedgwick, crossed at Fredericksburg and those below town marched up, and a force variously estimated at from 15,000 to 25,000 strong attacked Gen. Barksdale's Mississippi brigade and captured the stone fence rendered immortal by our brigade on the 13th day of December, 1862, and captured six pieces of the celebrated Washington Artillery. This they did by overwhelming numbers, being enabled to attack in front and both flanks at once. This accomplished, this heavy force started to assist Hooker, by attacking our victorious army in the rear.

Fortunately they were too late, for he had got as much as Yankee nature could stand, and a little more, before this time; and Generals Anderson, McLaws and Early moved their divisions to meet this fresh army of vandals. Our brigade arrived just in time, near the brick church about 4 miles from Fredericksburg on the plank road, to sustain Generals Wilcox and Semmes, who were heavily pressed by greatly superior numbers, after fighting the great battle in the forenoon at Chancellorsville. The enemy were repulsed and held at bay Sunday night and Monday until our forces could be got into position. On Monday evening about three o'clock it was understood that we had the enemy in a semicircle, each end of this semicircle resting on the river above and below the ford. It was further understood that the attack would be made on the right, which would be the signal for the general advance of all our forces. Hours passed, the evening was passing, and the chances for the escape of the circumscribed foe were increasing, but no advance was made. General Wofford was chafing like a furious charger, so much was he impressed with the idea the enemy should be attacked at once, and so anxious was he to rush upon the cowards now at bay. But no order came until about six o'clock in the evening, when General Wofford received orders to move forward and take position on the plank road—the position then held by the enemy. This splendid brigade of tried veterans marched up with buoyant spirits, to the attack, but the enemy gave way and the General observing some evidence of disorder in his lines, ordered a charge, which was responded to with such a rush and such yells as only victorious Georgians can give, and the enemy fled. Coming to a house, we captured about 30 prisoners, amongst whom were a Lt. Colonel and several other officers. Learning from an old citizen at this house that the flight of the Yankees was an utter rout, the General took the citizen as a guide and pressed on in the charge through a terrible pine and cedar thicket so dense that a single individual could not pass through it in daylight without difficulty, until twelve at night, until we had got within half a mile of the enemy's pontoons on the river, where his frightened hordes were crossing. We had got nearly a mile in front of all other troops, when our own batteries were playing immediately in our front. Here the General halted and sent back requesting our gunners not to fire on us as we were friends. So great was the flight of the Yanks and so anxious to get "to hum," that they threw away guns, bayonets, knapsacks, coats, hats, breeches, socks, shirts, drawers, and almost everything a man eats, wears or uses, and they were so thick in places that scarcely we could ride over them. Our poor soldiers have more stuff that the cowards left than they can well carry. Every man has some trophy won from the vandals.

Many think this the greatest blunder of the whole war. We could have (as is supposed by some) reached our fortifications above the pontoons Monday evening or at night, and placed four guns in position that would have commanded the pontoons, river and bottom perfectly, so that no human being could have crossed, and by that means bagged the whole panic stricken army. Those holding this opinion say that our line of battle was not more than a mile from the gunpits, and that the left wing of our forces engaged, together with our artillery, could have forced its way to the gunpits commanding the crossing with much less difficulty and danger, and much quicker than Wofford's brigade could, force the enemy back near three miles, to within half mile of the crossing. If this opinion be correct, we have much to regret, and much reason to blame some one. It is very evident that the Yankee army was totally demoralized and panic stricken, for no men will or can fight after they throw away their guns, and everything impeding their progress. And as further proof of the fact that we might have bagged the whole concern, they are reported to have thrown obstructions across their pontoons to keep us from following them in their flight. The enemy seemed to be impressed with the idea of defeat, for he moved his pontoons up the river from Fredericksburg to Banks' ford, before he was passed on Monday, and got them to position before any charge was made, and on Monday night at 11 o'clock, began to cross, and succeeded in getting over and taking up his bridges early Tuesday morning. After Sedgwick got safely across, Hooker re-crossed above, and all retired toward Aquia Creek, supposing of course, we would follow them and ruin their cowardly army. So great was their fright, and so thorough was their demoralization that they are reported to have destroyed all their army stores in any way exposed to our supposed advance.

If this opinion be correct that we could have captured this body of twenty thousand men at Banks' ford, as a matter of course we should have got their bridges, over which our victorious army could have passed, cut off Hooker's retreat, captured or thoroughly dispersed the whole grand army of the Potomac, secured all his supplies, and had Washington City at our own disposal. This may seem somewhat extravagant, but those who entertain this belief say that a few brave, determined troops, led by a bold, dashing leader, can easily disperse any number of frightened, panic-stricken men, who have determined that they are whipped. How very important to the bleeding South is it that every favorable opportunity should be sought and well improved. How important that the dearly bought victories of our devoted soldiers, should be followed up and made complete! How important that such brave warriors should be led by a chief worthy such a soldiery.

Had this army been crushed, the spirit of the Yankee nation would have been broken, and in all probability our natural independence would have been acknowledged, the angel of peace would have flown in our shores, with prosperity and happiness in her wings and the stars and the bars waved like the wing of a God from Delaware to Mexico.

Notwithstanding these speculations and supposed failures, we congratulate ourselves, especially the men in the ranks, upon the achievements of a great victory. We have met and vanquished an army well supplied with all the appliances of war, conducted with admirable generalship and at least four times our number. We have driven him from our side of the river. We have never once failed to drive him from his fortifications and demonstrated to the fact that he will not stand and fight us in an open field.

Wofford's brigade has returned to its old camp, and the men are rested and ready for any emergency that may arise, and the officers seem confident that this veteran band can whip any number of the Potomac army on a fair field. We shall not be astonished to find ourselves promenading Pennsylvania avenue before November as conquerors. One of Gen. McLaws' staff remarked to Gen. Wofford next day after his brilliant charge, that they supposed he was going to Washington. The General says that with 30,000 Georgians he could have gone there easily.

J. R. PARROTT

TWENTY-SIXTH GEORGIA INFANTRY
[GORDON'S BRIGADE, EARLY'S DIVISION]
CAMP NEAR FREDERICKSBURG, May 10, 1863 [5-27-63SR]

At last we have had an opportunity of testing the prowess of the renowned "fighting Joe Hooker," and whether or not he can justly claim that reputation for military skill and invincibility for which northern journals have given him credit, I think may be determined by a glance at the history of these events occurring between the 28th April and 6th May. To give you some idea of these events, which have scarcely been mentioned, but which constitute no unimportant part in the embodiment of the entire series, is the object of this note, which I will make as brief as a truthful statement of the case will admit.

In the progress of events it came to pass that the Northmen gathered their armies to battle, and were gathered together between the Rappahannock river and Chancellorsville, both of which belong to Jeff. Davis, and pitched into the woods and forests thereof. And the men of Secesh were gathered together and pitched hard by the village of Chancellorsville, and set the battle in array against the Northmen. And the Northmen stood on a hill on one side, and the men of Secesh stood on a hill on the other side, and there was a wood between them. And there stood a forth champion out of the camp of the Northmen, named Joe Hooker of abolitiondom, whose height was (in his own estimation) much greater than considerable; he wore no helmet of brass upon his head, but his deportment gave evidence that he carried a goodly quantity of that material inside of his head. And he stood and cried unto the armies of Secesh and said unto them, why are ye come out to set your battle in array? am not I "fighting Joe Hooker," a Northman, and ye servants to Jeff. Davis? choose you a man for you, and let him come down, and if you be able to fight and to repulse us, then will we retire to the hill from whence we came, and recruit and re-organize, but if we prevail against you, then shall ye be our servants and serve us. And the Northman said, I defy the armies of Secesh this day, give me a trial that we may fight together.

When Jeff. Davis and all Secesh heard these words they were neither afraid nor dismayed, for, said they, behold! we have before us a son of Jesse, a Virginian, that is cunning in playing, and a mighty valiant man, and a man of war and prudent in matters, and a comely person, and the Lord is with him whose name is Robert E. Lee. And the men of Secesh arose and shouted, and pursued the Northmen until they came nigh to the Rappahannock, and fell into their rifle pits under the cover of their guns, while darkness hid them from the sight of the son of Jesse, the mighty warrior. And the wounded fell down by the way, and their slaughter was terrible. And the men of Secesh returned from chasing after the Northmen, and they spoiled their tents and gathered the trophies of their great victory.

While these things were occurring upon the left of our lines, I must tell you something of what was accomplished by a single division upon the right. On the evening of the 28th an order was issued to our regiment (26th Ga.) to be in readiness to march for our picket line along the Rappahannock at an early hour on the following morning, to take our regular tour in this kind of duty. The shadows of night had long fallen upon the earth, and the usual quiet pervaded our camps. When we lay down and consigned ourselves to the embraces of Morpheus, no thought of so early a conflict having a place in our minds. Sleep, balmy sleep, "tired, nature's sweet restorer," how welcome thy embraces to the weary, way worn soldier! The last thought of my waking moments being of home and absent loved ones, left the ground work for blissful, happy dreams; all of which were rudely dispelled, and this pleasing forgetfulness of realities broken by an unusual commotion in camp at daylight on the morning of the 29th.

I hurriedly arose and left my tent to discover, if possible, the cause of the excitement. Upon making inquiry of the first one I met, I learned that our pickets below Deep Run had been firing upon the enemy, who were laying a pontoon bridge below that point preparatory to crossing. Immediately every one in camp was astir, and there was hurrying to and fro, men gathering their arms and accoutrements, horsemen galloping in every direction. The actions of every man seeming to indicate his thoughts to be that the safety of his life depended upon the celerity and promptness of his movements, and orders were as quickly obeyed as they were hastily given. A few minutes only elapsed between the sound to arms, and the formation of the regiment prepared to move. The entire brigade was soon under arms and took up the line of march. A dense fog prevailed that morning and hung heavily over the earth, making it a most propitious time for the movements of the enemy. Our brigade having passed beyond Hamilton's Crossing, took its position almost upon the same ground upon which it fought on the 13th December last, the 26th Regiment again occupying the extreme left of the brigade. Gen. Early's whole division was extended along the line of the Richmond, Fredericksburg and Potomac R. R., a Louisiana [Hays'] brigade upon our right, and the others upon our left. Not long after taking position the 26th Regiment was thrown forward as skirmishers about 800 yards in front, the line stretching along the Port Royal and Fredericksburg road. By this time the enemy had completed the bridge and crossed over in considerable numbers, forcing the 13th Ga. to retire from our front line of pickets, where it had been on duty since Monday preceding. The entire number of the enemy which crossed during the day would not exceed 12,000 or 15,000. They seemed to manifest no desire for an immediate advance upon our line, but appeared contented with their possession of the south bank of the stream.

After our pickets retired from the immediate vicinity of the river, skirmishing between the opposing parties ended. An occasional shot from a battery on the opposite side of the river reminded us of their presence in that locality. Except this, and a shot now and then from one of our batteries, there was little firing during the day until late in the afternoon, when quite a lively exchange took place between their batteries and one which we had posted on a height near the crossing, resulting, as is often the case, in no immediate damage to either party. We lay in line of battle all that day (Wednesday) [April 29] and night; indeed, we remained in this position for eight consecutive days and nights. Thursday morning came, and the aspect of things remained the same. Saturday morning brought little change, except that during the previous night, or early that morning, the enemy brought over a battery and placed it in a position opposite the centre of our line, and directly in front of one of our batteries posted on a height to our left and rear. Each showed a knowledge of the presence of the other by the sending and the reception of an unlimited number of shot and shell from guns well and industriously worked. During the afternoon of Saturday the enemy recrossed the river at Pratt's place and disappeared from the south bank, both infantry and artillery. Sunday morning dawned on us, and with the earliest signs of its approach the distant sounds of rapid and incessant discharges of artillery, far to our left fell upon our ears, and we knew that the contest was waxing warm along that part of our lines. Early in the afternoon our division was moved out, and took a position behind some breastworks upon higher ground, and about three hundred yards in rear of our former position. Here we passed the remainder of the Sabbath day.

It is proper here to state that during our occupancy of the line stretching along the railroad, General Barksdale's brigade of Mississippians held Marye's Heights, assisted by a few pieces of artillery.

On Sunday morning the enemy, by bringing up an overwhelming force and precipitating it upon this brigade, (unsupported as it was,) drove it from its position and gained possession of the heights, besides capturing some five or six pieces of artillery. These heights are in rear of the town and completely command it, and their loss to us was no minor misfortune; it was therefore determined by our commanding General (who is always *Early* in his movements,) to retake that position cost what it might. With this view, about ten o'clock Sunday night we were roused from our slumbers by the command to fall in, preparatory to moving. We took up the line of march in the direction of the telegraph road, having reached which we turned to the right and lay in a ravine until daylight Monday morning, when we were again drawn up in line upon the open ground, the 26th Georgia having the extreme right of the line. The command, Forward! was given, and the long line moved as if by one impulse over the most unfavorable and uninviting ground that I ever passed in line of battle, rendered so from the fact that it had been a thick and heavily timbered wood, and this had all been cut down and the brush left upon the ground, which made our progress through it not only slow, but difficult and excessively fatiguing. An advance of a mile and a half brought us within view of the heights, as well as in view of a battery across the river, which greeted our coming with several shells, which fortunately did no damage. With a firm and steady front, and by a rapid and brilliant dash, our troops were soon in possession of the [Marye's] heights, encountering but little opposition, so sudden were our movements and so little were they expected by the enemy. After gaining possession of this point our forces occupied the rifle pits, (or as many of the troops as were required to fill them,) and we remained in this position until about three o'clock p. m., when we retired from these works, leaving Generals Smith's and Barksdale's brigades to hold them, and prevent the enemy from throwing a force in our rear.

Our division was formed in line of battle, our right resting upon the heights, our line being perpendicular to that made by the course of the river. While taking our position in line, and long after the commencement of a forward movement, we endured the fires from four different batteries, which were concentrated upon our line from as many different points; one across the river upon our right flank, a second upon the same side and in our rear, a third to our left and rear, and a fourth directly in front of the 26th Ga. Notwithstanding the heavy fire thus brought to bear upon us, or the bursting of shells, the plunging of heavy solid shot, or the whistling of grape, neither officer nor private seemed to waver or flinch from the post of duty. Colonel [E. N.] Atkinson commanding our regiment, (26th), Maj. [J. S.] Blain acting Lieut. Colonel, Capt. [B. F.] Grace acting Major, held their positions nobly, each and all of them evincing that coolness so necessary for the skillful and successful handling of troops upon the field of battle. As we stood in line previous to advancing, a loud and prolonged cheering was heard to our left which was taken up by one regiment after another along the entire line, and made those grand old hills echo again and again with the shout of defiance. Our skirmishers were thrown forward and were in a short time engaged with those of the enemy. We moved onward, our skirmishers continuing their progress, the enemy steadily yielding the ground as we swept the woods for a mile and a half beyond the heights from whence we started, darkness alone putting an end to the contest, and securing to Sedgwick (the Federal commander), the safety of many a man whom three hours more of daylight would have placed in our hands. It was a brilliant affair and handsomely executed, as any movement will be, led and conducted (as this was) by as gallant an officer as Gen. Gordon.

Under cover of the darkness the enemy recrossed the river, or the main body at least Tuesday morning came and found us still in line of battle; but all sounds of the conflict were hushed, and a deep and unbroken stillness prevailed. During the morning about three hundred prisoners were brought in, most of them belonging to the 49th New York regiment. The casualties in our regiment during this engagement amounted to three killed and twenty-one wounded, which I suppose is near the loss of each regiment in the brigade. Thus concluded active operations upon the right of our lines.

VERITAS.

Following his accidental wounding on the night of May 2, Stonewall Jackson had his left arm amputated. Pneumonia developed and on May 10, Gen. Thomas J. "Stonewall" Jackson died. It proved to be an irreparable loss for Lee and the Army of Northern Virginia.

DEATH OF "STONEWALL" JACKSON
May 12, 1863 [5-18-63ASC]

It is right that the heart of the nation should be moved by the death of one of her noblest sons. It is well and good for us all, that when we meet one another in the street and ask "what's the news," that the reply "Stonewall Jackson is dead," should bring a tear to the eye, a saddened tone to the voice, and sinking of the heart for a moment. I say it is well, because it shows how truly the people of the South appreciate real excellence, and how readily they acknowledge the worth of the man who has practically shown himself *willing to do his part* in the work before us.

I will not attempt an eulogy of the hero. Abler pens than mine will do him justice. In truth he needs no eulogy. It is already written in bloody characters on our battle flag. I simply desire to speak a word of encouragement to those of our people who are prone to take every mishap as an indication of coming evil, at least, if not of the speedy downfall of all our hopes; and I am sorry that there are so many such people.

First, I would say that we have many Generals left among us yet, quite equal to any the Yankees have, and fully able to meet the onset of whoever may be the unfortunate that will take the place of "fighting Joe" when he "goes up," as he certainly will, after the late engagement near Fredericksburg. Let all our despondents remember that ROBERT E. LEE is not dead, neither does he sleep; but with an unbroken front still keeps a "stonewall" between our capital and our foes. Let them remember that the gallant Longstreet—(Gen. Lee's "right arm,") is still a stumbling block in Hooker's path, and that Anderson and Hill, McLaws and Barksdale, and a host of stout-hearted Southrons are yet able to do duty; whilst "J. E. B." Stuart, (bless his bright cheery face,) has not yet forgotten how to dance an old fashioned reel with a pretty girl at 10 o'clock at night, nor to grab a Yankee thieving squad immediately thereafter—and without getting out of breath either.

Then, again, we have the leaders of our Western Army—Joe Johnston and Bragg, and M. L. Smith and [Simon B.] Buckner, and [Joseph] Wheeler and [Nathan B.] Forrest, to say nothing of "*le preux chevalier*" John Morgan, and beyond the Mississippi we have Price and Kirby Smith; and above all, we have the blessing of Almighty God on as righteous a cause as the sun ever shone upon. So let none despair. Reserves may come, doubtless they will; the Yankee nation is calling forth all its strength, but after all, what is it but a confession that we, too, are strong? strong—aye, invincible, so long as we keep our eye fixed upon the one goal— national independence and eternal separation from Yankees.

X.

STONEWALL JACKSON,
BY A CHAPLAIN
[*Soldier's Visitor*, Richmond, Va., February 1864]

Immediately before the battle of Chancellorsville, while the enemy were making a feint of crossing the Rappahannock, near Hamilton's Crossing, I was with my regiment in that neighborhood. Having heard that there was a fine battery on the hill near the Hamilton house, I thought I would go up and see it. On reaching the battery I found an officer standing there, with a cap drawn down over his forehead and an oil cloth over his shoulders. I took him for a captain of the battery, and addressed him as such, "What do you think the enemy is going to do?" said I, "will they attack us from that quarter?"

"No," replied the officer, "I think not; they tried at the battle of Fredericksburg and probably got enough of it that time."

After a little further conversation, the officer asked me to what regiment I belonged. I told him I was a chaplain of the ----regiment. "And to what church do you belong?" he asked. "The Presbyterian," said I. "Well," said he, "I'm a Protestant myself. Let us sit down here and talk awhile." So we sat down beside one of the guns, and the stranger gave me his views of the duties and responsibilities of a chaplain,—the kind of men they should be, and the vast opportunities of usefulness their positions offered them. I was much struck with his conversation; thought he showed an unusual interest in the religious welfare of his soldiers, and set him down as a remarkable pious man.

When the conversation had proceeded in this strain for some time, the officer arose, looked steadfastly across the river, and turning to me said, "You had better move away from here now, I think I shall have this gun fired directly." In a few minutes "bang" went the gun, and away sped the shot, ploughing through the enemy's ranks.

As I moved off, one of my acquaintances accosted me and said: "Well, Chaplain, what was the General saying?" "General?" said I, "I have not seen any general." "Why yes you have," said he, "you've been sitting down there talking ever so long with General Jackson."

Imagine my surprise when I found the unpretending man I had been talking with was the great hero of the war, whose name was on everybody's lips.

This little incident is striking illustrative of the character of Jackson. It shows notwithstanding his great achievement and world-wide fame, that his success has not puffed him up; that he assumed none of the airs of a superior, but was ready to enter into friendly conversation with anyone who might fall in his way.

It shows, too, how his religion was always uppermost in his mind. Here he was at that moment confronting the threatening enemy, on the eve of hurling the missiles of death amongst them, and yet deliberately sitting down with a chaplain, to talk with him as to his duties, and seizing the opportunity in that way to promote the spiritual welfare of the soldiers. Noble man! Such incidents are a eulogy louder than any words, however gifted or eloquent, could speak.

LETTER FROM V. A. S. P.

FREDERICK HALL, VA., May 11, 1863 [5-19-63SR]

At 4 P.M. on the 6th, the date of my last letter, the brigade took the train for Petersburg, where we arrived about sunset in a drenching rain. By the time we reached camps, two miles north of the city, it was dark and disagreeable enough, for the pitiless rain continued to pour down in torrents until 10 o'clock. The next day we marched to our old camps three and a half miles south of Richmond.

While at Ivor Station, Sidney C. Shivers of company K, was seized with several very severe fits or convulsions—epilepsy—which soon deprived him of consciousness, and lasted for hours. Our kind-hearted Assistant Surgeon, Dr. J. T. Palmer, did everything in his power to save his life, and succeeded in creating an artificial respiration. At Petersburg he took Shivers to the Ladies' Hospital, superintended by Mr. P. D. Woodhouse. The hospital is intended for officers. Dr. Palmer being a stranger, and unacquainted with the localities of the general hospitals asked Woodhouse to take Shivers in for the night, promising to remove him early next morning to some other hospital; but Woodhouse would not give him even this temporary shelter from the cruel rain! He said the hospital was intended only for officers, and that his orders would not allow him to take Shivers in even for one night. Dr. Palmer then asked permission to lay Sidney in the passage, but no, be could not do that even! "Well," said Dr. Palmer, "you prefer then to let a man dying with epilepsy lie out in this pitiless storm!" "I cannot help it," was his heartless reply, "it is against orders!"

Sidney C. Shivers, a noble young man, of good family connections, did die! Any common rake with gingerbread work on his sleeves, and bars on his collar, because he happens to hold a commission, would not have been turned away. Enlightened public opinion will condemn such *charity!*

Leaving Richmond at sunrise Friday morning, 8th instant, Gen. Hood's division reached Frederick Hall in Louisa county, yesterday by 1 p.m.—making a distance of fifty-five miles the way we came. The bridge across the South Anna being burned, we had to make a bridge detour to the left of Saturday. The country passed through is by far the prettiest of Virginia we have seen. The beautiful residences, the extensive plantations, capacious barns, and waving fields of grain argue a wealthy, prosperous and highly cultivated region.

To this division was assigned the duty of driving out Gen. Stoneman's formidable cavalry force, said to number ten thousand. But Stoneman was here, because he could not be elsewhere. Hooker's defeat and the possessions of the upper fords by Stuart's cavalry, forced him to remain for a short time in this region. He has found a way of escape, and ere we reached here, had gone. I hear something of a cavalry fight near Gordonsville, but the reports are so meagre and uncertain that I will not attempt a recital. Citizens report that the Yankees were in such a strait that they tried to swap their blue coats to negroes in order to facilitate their escape.

Gen. Lee's victory was complete. It was wanting in nothing. He has registered over seven thousand prisoners, and states that he captured more small arms than have been taken in any previous battle of the war. The disappointed Yankees have raised a howl of despair. Joe Hooker is an imbecile—a brainless braggadocia, and ought to be hung for his blunders! On the other hand, our papers give Hooker credit for fighting well, and say he has done better than any general who has fought us. His plan was a masterly one, but was not deep enough to overthrow our great Captain.

In the absence of interesting news your readers may be entertained by the relation of two or three rich anecdotes. I will make the venture at any rate.

Col. C****, commanding brigade upon a certain march in February, made his headquarters at a wealthy citizen's house, and ordered rooms, entertainment, &c., for himself and staff. The proprietor, his wife and daughters were all attention, doing everything in their power to entertain their honored guests, feeling flattered by the presence of such distinguished visitants. In the course of the evening the conversation turned exclusively upon literary subjects. The eldest daughter, cheered by the distinguished consideration shone her family, put on her best looks, her pretty face beaming with the sweetest smiles, assumed the pleasing task of entertaining the Colonel.

"Well, Colonel," asked his fair entertainer, "how do you like Shakespeare's plays?"

"Oh, delightful, delightful!" said the Colonel. "I think they are incomparable. I have read them all several times, and have had the double advantage and pleasure of seeing them enacted upon the stage by the best actors in America."

"Indeed!" ejaculated the lady, whose opinion of the Colonel's erudition was considerably raised; "Which piece do you like best?"

"Oh! Romeo and Pocahontas, Madame!" "Very beautiful, indeed!" (Exit lady in paroxysm of laughter.)

A good story is told upon Major [John E.] Rylander. When his battalion joined Gen. Anderson's brigade, he loved to show off their perfection in the drill, and had them out very often. Large crowds from the other regiments collected to witness the performance, and out of a spirit of mischief would tease the Major by hollowing "hurrah for Maj. Laplander! That's a good maneuver for Maj. Lowlander! Wheel 'em again, Maj. Greenlander!" The Major feeling himself aggrieved, made complaint to Gen. Anderson.

"General," said the Major, "I wish you would make your men quit calling me Laplander, Lowlander and Greenlander. It is very disagreeable."

"Look here, Major," said the General, and turning his grey eyes upon the Major like he was going to look clear through him, "Are you any better than I am?"

"No, no! of course not, General."

"They call me '*Old Tige*' and I don't get mad about it. I can't stop their fun, and don't mean to try!"

The Major went away looking like he wished he had not made the complaint.

Among other good camp jokes is one told on the band of the 20th Georgia. In Gatesville they serenaded several families, who gave them good things to eat and drink. At one place in lieu of brandy and wine, butter milk was sent out, and was drunk by the boys of the Seventeenth! They are now known as the "*Butter Milk Band!*" This new *sobriquet* teases them no little.

The army and nation are shrouded in deep mourning on account of the sad intelligence of Gen. "Stonewall" Jackson's death. How heavily has the hand of affliction been laid upon this infant Republic! How are the mighty fallen!

A great calamity has befallen us. But God's will be done! He will rise up another Gideon to do battle for us! The defeat of our army would not have cast a deeper gloom over our army and people, than the death of this incomparable leader and great Christian soldier. He was a host within himself. He was not less a Christian than a soldier.

Whilst we are bowed in mourning our infamous foe will soon send up a shout of fiendish delight! Their greatest terror is now removed by death! May the God of Battles, the God of Right and Justice succor us in this dark hour of affliction!

V. A. S. P.

LETTER FROM SOLDIER JIM

CAMP 8TH REGT. VOLS., NEAR RAPIDAN, May 18, 1863 [5-24-63ASC]

We have made an extensive jump since I last wrote, which was when we were facing the enemy near Suffolk, where we remained till the object of our expedition was accomplished. Our foragers were very busily engaged during our stay, and met with good success in the purchase of flour, bacon, corn, hay, &c.

We left the place about 10 o'clock p.m. [May 5], when the Yankees were pretty well quieted, excepting a few batteries that kept throwing an occasional shell across our lines. When we had gone off two or three miles, it was amusing to hear them still continue to shell the place we had left, but they continued to shell the place during the whole night. Next morning they made a vigorous assault on the place where our lines were, and gained a great victory, as they say. This assault was made when we were near 20 miles from them, and before they had discovered our movement.

Our Division is now back with Gen. Lee's army, where it has won fresh laurels. We are in splendid trim, and ready for the blue backs again. They were again badly butchered in the late fight. We suppose they will recruit and reorganize before they come at us again; but when they do, we will meet them and give them as pretty a fight as ever was put up in old Virginia.

Our camp is situated on one of the most beautiful little mountains I ever saw. We got fresh breezes, and are convenient to a spring that affords water for ten or twelve thousand men. We have nothing to fear but snakes, which are numerous, and often crowd into our beds. A few days ago I was lying in my blanket dozing, when I felt something moving on my body. I put out my hand and caught hold of a rattlesnake, which I dashed away without being bitten. Last night another one came to my shed, after I had lain down, but we gave him a scare, and he crawled away.

I remember that it has been exactly two years to-day since, we were mustered into the service of the Confederate States. One more year and our term will expire. By that time we expect the war to end, so that we may be relieved of the life as we have lived for two years. I don't know how many times we will whip Joe Hooker before he is satisfied, but it will be just as often as he will fight us.

SOLDIER JIM.

FROM OUR CORRESPONDENT "DIXIE."

GUINEA'S STATION, VA., May 17, 1863 [6-2-63ASC]

"All is quiet along the line of the Rappahannock." The army of Gen. Lee is quietly resting in its old camps, occupied before the recent battles. The rations have been increased, the weather is dry and pleasant, and the grass and clover afford excellent grazing for the horses and mules; so that if active operations are not commenced in a few weeks the army will be in a highly efficient condition. The duties required are of the lightest kind, and the leisure hours of officers and men are employed principally in writing letters and talking over the incidents of the late stirring scenes. Religious exercises also engage much of their time. There is scarcely a day that preaching is not had in every brigade, and every night the camps are vocal with songs of praise and worship to God. With such a cause as we struggle for, with the daily prayers, toils and encouragement of so many patriotic and Christian mothers, sisters and wives all over our land, and with such an army of brave, devoted veterans, among whom so many are God-fearing and God-worshiping men, led, too, by such men as Gen. Lee and his subordinates, who can, for a moment, doubt the final issue?

I see it stated by some of the correspondents of the press that it was Gen'l Rodes (formerly D. H. Hill's) division that performed Jackson's great flank movement upon the enemy at "the Wilderness;" and the Confederate Union says it was made by the brigades of General Rodes, Iverson and Doles. This is not only not strictly true, but unjust. The facts are, that the whole of General Jackson's corps were in the movement, except the division of General Early. In the march on Saturday General A. P. Hill's division was in the rear, and as the engagement was brought on later in the evening, none of his division, I believe, except General [Samuel] McGowan's, formerly Gen. Gregg's brigade, were actively engaged that night. During Saturday night, however, in arranging the line of battle for the next day, Gen. A. P. Hill's division was placed upon the extreme left, and Gen. Thomas' brigade, occupied Gen. Hill's extreme left, and in this position the division fought the next day.

It has been truly said that this battle was peculiarly fruitful of individual incidents. I will mention a few. Private Giles Mitchell, of Co. A, 14th Georgia regiment, captured a Colonel of the Excelsior brigade, and compelled him to dismount. In a moment Mitchell was wounded and rode the Colonel's horse to the hospital. Private Wm. Gardner, of the same company, took General [William] Hays, commanding Sickles' Brigade, a prisoner, and delivered him to General Thomas.

While in line of battle on Friday night, a Mississippi Regiment occupied a position in a thicket not more than fifty or sixty yards from the line of the enemy; and so reckless were they of danger, that they built up fires and went to cooking and eating while the enemy were firing at them, paying no other attention to it than occasionally calling out to the Yankees to know "what in the devil they meant."

On Sunday [May 3], while charging the enemy's breastworks, a big, rusty looking Irishman was observed advancing in line of battle, deliberately loading and firing, with a short stem pipe stuck in his mouth, puffing away, as if quietly taking "a bit of a smoke."

The Color Sergeant of the 49th Georgia Regiment is a very brave man. While the fight was going on, one of the officers of that Regiment attempted to take the colors for the purpose of forming a new line. The Sergeant positively refused to give them up, but said, "Show me the spot and I will plant them there." The officer compliments him very highly for the act.

Since writing my last, we have heard, with feelings of the deepest sorrow, of the death of Lt. Col. Jas. M. Fielder, who died in Richmond of his wound. No better neighbor, no kinder friend, more zealous patriot, honest citizen, or purer christian, has fallen a victim to the hand of the foe. His memory will be long cherished, and his loss mourned by the members of the 14th Georgia Regiment.

DIXIE.

LETTER FROM TIVOLI

CAMP 8TH GEORGIA, ON THE RAPIDAN, VA., May 20, 1863 [5-27-63ASC]

Again we of Hood's Division are on the Rapidan, and from the height on which we now are camped the eye can roam with pleasure over a panoramic view of Culpeper, Madison, Orange and those other counties that were the theatre of war last year.

We are glad to have left the Suffolk country and many are well satisfied to get back with Gen. Lee again. We all regret being absent from Chancellorsville as it is the first great battle we have missed, and the great roll of the achievements of this division will not be complete without the name of this great and glorious victory.

The army has not yet recovered from the severe shock produced by Gen. Jackson's death. It weighed upon all hearts with the weight of a personal calamity, and many and sincere are the expressions of veneration, respect and love for him, who was the rarest thing in history—a Christian soldier. Appropriately may his name be blended with that of Washington, and all ages will respect the dust of him who, with military abilities, judged by performances, equaled a Napoleon, and who in goodness and virtue equaled a Washington.

Our position is very healthy located, with plenty of substantial food, and the purest water springing from the mountain's side. There is very little sickness among the men; pneumonia, typhoid fever and ague being very rare.

We have divine service now daily at a brick church near camp, and it will interest many of our people to know that a deep religious feeling pervades the ranks, and many are joining the church. Gambling and drinking have almost entirely disappeared since Gen. Lee's order on the subject, and the improved moral condition of our army is a source of congratulations to every good Christian among us.

We drill for exercise now about four times each day, and the conscripts lately sent to fill our columns are being broke in gradually to the service. Out of every ten however sent here, not more than five are really of any service.

Every thing is dull in the way of news and excitement, and the probabilities are that matters will be here for some days.

TIVOLI.

LETTER FROM V. A. S. P.

CAMP NEAR RACCOON FORD, VA., May 16, 1863 [5-26-63SR]

Since my last nothing of very special interest has occurred with Gen. Hood's division. Leaving Frederick Hall Wednesday evening, we reached this point, near Raccoon Ford on the Rapidan, yesterday at noon. We march with such ease and rapidity that we make long distances in a very short time. Hence the name of "Foot Cavalry."

Yesterday evening and this morning were occupied in making out pay rolls and drawing money—an article we stood greatly in need of. But, with the present high prices, the money drawn will hardly keep us in tobacco and writing materials. As long as the money lasts chickens and eggs, butter and biscuits, and whatever can be bought, will be freely purchased by the soldiers regardless of price.

We will move somewhere this evening, but in what direction is not known except at headquarters. It is rumored that we will cross the Rapidan (Rapid Ann) and—and *what?* Nobody knows!

The Rapidan took its name from a fast young lady of the primitive time—the first days of Virginia aristocracy. Miss Ann, says the tradition, was pretty, nay beautiful, fascinating, captivating all hearts, and then cruelly rejecting them. The young men called her *rapid* Ann, because she could break hearts with such rapidity. One of the unfortunate swains who had come under her weird-like influence, worshipped at her shrine of beauty and was haughtily rejected by the beautiful Ann, wandered farther west to bury his sorrow in the wild forests on the upper Rappahannock. In crossing the southern tributary of that noble river, when it was slightly swollen, his horse was nearly washed from under him. The accident reminded him of his rejected loves, the unfortunate termination of his courtships; and he named the stream Rapid Ann. It appeared fordable, but came near unhorsing him; as the coquetting Ann seemed conquerable, but proved invincible.

I have not seen this recorded in the annuals of Virginia, or certified to by any of the old fathers. Therefore, you may take it for what it is worth.

We are in the most painful suspense about our friends engaged in the recent battles near Fredericksburg. We have not seen a list of casualties, or any other than the most general remark about the Georgians in the Richmond papers. Our State is so largely represented in Virginia, that a paper published in Richmond and devoted to the interests of Georgia troops would, in good hands, be a paying enterprise. I wish some one would start such a paper. The Virginia Press are strictly Virginian in their notices, articles and editorials. Soldiers from other States are barely mentioned. It should not be so.

I regret, exceedingly, to announce the resignation of Lieut. Jno. Sidney Hopson, of Company D, 17th Georgia. Ill-health was the cause of his resignation. Lieut. Hopson had the entire esteem and confidence of all the officers and men who knew him, and was especially endeared to us on account of his daring and skill upon the battle field. He was in every battle participated by the brigade, and passed through each bloody contest unscathed.

It is but justice to remark that the gentlemanly Captain of Company F, Phill. W. Gittinger, is using every effort to suppress the thieving of a few bad men, who unfortunately for him and the honor of the service, belong to his company. Such men cannot be managed but by the rigid enforcement of discipline.

Your correspondent has got himself into hot water by publishing the names of two or three hog thieves. Their parents cut out the slip and sent it to them. They denounce me for meddling in their affairs. Well, I can't help it. They must quit stealing, or I will publish their names. Parents should not quarrel with men. I am not supposed to know how they or their families stand at home. I deal with their actions *here*. A man should be weighed in the same balance here that he is at home. Theft is theft, no matter *where* committed. Being in the army does not mitigate the offence. Therefore, I would say to those offended parents: teach your sons better; awaken their pride; instill in them a high principle of honor, and when they are away, even in the army, they will be gentlemen.

Our regiment, brigade and division have suffered enough already. I am determined to use my humble efforts in putting a stop to the outrages and depredations of a few unprincipled men, who have brought all this odium upon us. I congratulate myself on being partially successful in my efforts. My letters upon this subject have had a salutary effect upon that class of men. I have not heard of a single case of hog stealing or depredation upon poultry yards since their publication.

V. A. S. P.

LETTER FROM TOUT LE MONDE
IN VIRGINIA, SOMEWHERE, May 24, 1863 [5-30-63SR]

This command is quiet, awaiting demonstrations from the enemy, who, from northern sources we are informed, intend to try the eighth "On to Richmond" very soon. It may be true that he is coming, for that people is just foolish enough to urge it; or it may be a lying trick to keep us still here and on the Rappahannock. The silly demonstration of the enemy below Richmond [a raid from Gloucester Point into Matthews County] had no effect in drawing off a man from Lee's army, and perceiving that we have not been materially weakened at Fredericksburg, it will be a sore trial to get Hooker's army again across the river there. He, however, if the dynasty will allow him, may attempt in desperation to retrieve his fortune in another advance. As it costs them only a few thousand Irish and Dutch, and gold declines under their disasters, the dynasty may allow it. It is generally believed he will advance soon— there is more arguments for than against it. As sure as he comes he is whipped—in fact the whole Yankee army confidently expect their usual thrashing and retrograde, after which "all hands" are allowed to have a good time, rations of whiskey—an Irishman will take a whipping for his whiskey, if he belongs to the Yankee army—and can read the pleasant things said by the *Herald* of "the last demonstration on the Rappahannock." Therefore you will understand that affairs have settled down into a calm again, when a few days ago things were stormy indeed. Our dead are resting gloriously now, and Jackson—the great and beloved Jackson—has gone out in a perfect sea of light with fame after fame, and honor upon honor crowding and thickening around his immortal name.

Our news from the West looks alternately cloudy and fair, and our greatest anxiety is for our success there. Not a fear is felt for the safety of the capital, but all eyes are turned on the gathering clouds that threaten the glorious and heroic city of Vicksburg. It is a very important point to us, and the whole South should be, if it is not, awake to the fact, and every effort thrown forward to save it. It is important as a thorn which goads the Northwest to perfect desperation, and has made more grey hairs in the dynasty's head than all his numerous troubles. Its importance may be observed in the immense force and gigantic preparation made to take it, and a failure on the dynasty's part to take it may—we won't say positively concerning any northern phenomenon—produce the very best results for us. Besides, no one can fail to see how important it is to have command of the Mississippi river, to better secure the protection of that State.

From the papers we learn that Burnside is vesting his spleen upon the defenseless captives who by misfortune have fallen into his hand. At Sharpsburg he took prisoners from this brigade (Gen. Toombs' then,) and treated them very kindly, even complimenting them for their heroic conduct in defending the Antietam bridge. We never thought that a thrashing at the Rappahannock would irritate him so much as to make him forget common magnanimity and wreak a contemptible vengeance on a defenseless prisoner, or that he would persecute the noble [Clement] Vallandigham. We hear now of retaliation, and that already lots are to be cast among some Federal prisoners (officers) now in Richmond, for the distinguished honor of dying because Gen. Burnside shot two of our recruiting officers taken in Kentucky. This awful course of war may lead those crazy wretches to inaugurate a war of extermination. It is deplorable, indeed, that this country, noted for its civilization once, has gone so rapidly into barbarism. We do not advocate the black flag, but we advocate justice and fight to the last, and if our enemies force the black flag upon us, then in the name of Heaven let us raise it until the whole world shall see the awful earnestness that actuates our determination to be free from these cut throats and vandals. It is a serious consideration, but one that concerns our welfare, and our government should not drink from it. It equally applies to every Southerner. There are none who can escape the black flag when it is raised, although some may talk grandly of its effect because they fancy themselves secure at home, and it should not have its gloomy folds flung to the breeze without the solemn conviction that it alone can secure our unfortunate from the enemy's wrath.

Solemn as it is, we cannot help recalling a funny incident connected with the black flag. On the morning after the night of the 18th September, the army crossed the Potomac with the enemy pressing upon our heels, but dared not cross after us. They cursed and swore at us from the opposite bank, threatening every minute to make a general advance. We happened to go into the little village of Shepardstown, which is just on the south bank, above the ford where the army had crossed the river, and in passing by the door of a small dwelling we stopped to get some water. A black flag hung in the portico, much to our astonishment, and we wondered whether the bold people of that dwelling had been wrought to such desperation by the enemy as compelled them to hang out that awful sign of resistance. An elderly lady appeared at the door as soon as our footsteps sounded on the doorway, and relieved our doubts. She was tall, stout, red-headed, with a firm look, and carried in her hand a bright barreled pocket revolver. She asked what we wanted and we answered water. "Very well," said she, "don't you see that," pointing to the revolver, "is to shoot the first man that goes into that yonder cabbage patch." It is most sincerely hoped that the Yankees will give us as little cause to exercise our firmness as we did that good Virginia lady the use of her small firearm.

From the Southern papers, and others that have taken it up, we notice with much regret the *adulation* which was heaped upon those worthless scoundrels taken by Forrest near Rome, on their passage through Atlanta and Augusta. [Col. Abel Streight and his raiders had surrendered to Gen. Forrest on May 3, near Galesville, Alabama.] Such liberties as were allowed them and such honors as were heaped upon them should be made criminal if there was not some palliative circumstances. The officer who wore our uniform and who jumped from his horse to shake hands with one expressing his delight at seeing him, in all probability, had not been where he could see many, and most favorably to him, the Yankee was *without arms*. Now in case of our ladies, we take a different view from most others. No doubt it was a purpose of showing southern generosity to a fallen foe, but the character of this foe was certainly not understood by them. The brave may be merciful to a dog, but there is little use of showing honors to such, because honors are lost on it. We cannot believe that our women—the women of the South—could neglect those who are in the field to cultivate the favor of such off-cast wretches as Forrest captured. If this army thought so, to-morrow hostilities would cease along the Rappahannock, and they most surely would be left to enjoy the favor of their choice. We could go to Yankeedom—no, any other place under the sun to find favor. We cannot and will not believe such; in fact it would be a southern negro degraded himself by noticing such ineffable types of wretchedness.

TOUT LE MONDE.

PRIVATE LETTER, A BRAVE BOY HAS FALLEN
—ALGERMORE T. W. BASS [5-28-63ASC]

Soon after getting home, in the summer of 1861, he volunteered in Capt. Jefferson Lamar's company, which was afterwards attached to Cobb's Legion. While at Yorktown, he had a severe spell of typhoid fever. After that he had but little sickness, and was always at his post, ready for duty. The Legion was under a heavy fire in the battles around Richmond but was not permitted to charge the enemy. He heroically endured the fatigues and hardships of the march into Maryland, and was always eager to encounter the foe. On the day of the battle at Crampton's Gap, in which the Legion suffered so terribly, and Lt. Col. Lamar was killed, he was ordered to guard commissary stores, and was deprived of the pleasure of going into the engagement with his company. After that battle he was transferred to Company B, 35th Ga., that he might be with his neighbors and many intimate friends. His transfer was regretted by his officers and the members of his company. The officers in the Lamar Infantry spoke highly of him as an excellent soldier. Many of the company said they never would forget Algie Bass for his kindness to them while sick; that he would rise at midnight to wait on them and minister to their wants, and would walk four or five miles at any time to obtain fruit for them. His kind and sympathizing heart was ever ready to relieve the suffering and promote their comfort. In the battle of Fredericksburg, on the 13th of December last, the 35th Ga., acted a gallant and conspicuous part. In a charge on the enemy, Algie advanced far ahead of his regiment, and his officers and company said there was no doubt that he killed a Yankee Colonel. When the battle was over, his Captain sent for him, and complimented him highly for his bravery and gallantry on the field, and remarked that he should consider him his right hand man. On Sunday morning, the 3rd inst., while charging the formidable fortifications of the enemy near Chancellorsville, which were captured by his regiment, he was shot through the head and died instantly. His Captain wrote that he fell at his post, nobly discharging his duty; that he was a brave boy and a good soldier, and his death was deeply regretted by all. His first Lieutenant, in writing of him, said, Algie had so distinguished himself that he was lamented, not only by his company, but by the whole regiment. He went into service about the first of August, 1861, and has never been home or had a furlough. Generous, brave, and always prompt to duty, he won the respect and admiration of his comrades and officers. It is a severe affliction to his parents to lose a son so young and noble hearted, so buoyant with hope and promise, and so brave and valiant. But it is consoling for them to think they have laid a noble sacrifice on the altar of freedom; that he fell valiantly contending for the rights of our country. His body quietly rests under the sod of Virginia, the native State of his parents, and his spirit, we trust, is in that happy land, "where the wicked cease from troubling and the weary are at rest."

W. A. B.

ANOTHER LETTER FROM SOLDIER JIM
CAMP RAPIDAN, May 25, 1863 [6-3-63ASC]

We are all quiet in camps at present. Drilling has become the order of the day which is very good for our health.

On Tuesday last we had a brigade meeting for the nomination of Governor in the State of Georgia, though very little excitement appeared to exist among the men. A few stump speeches were made and the nomination was postponed in consequence of a regiment being on picket. Yesterday the division was reviewed by Gen. J. B. Hood, the scene was said to be magnificent by all those who witnessed it. Many ladies were present which inspired a cheering feeling amongst the soldiers. After passing in review two batteries were run out in opposition to each other, after which the extensive lines were formed and ordered to charge, all proved successful in clearing out the way before them so the sham battle ended, and the different brigades marched back to their respective camps well pleased with the exercises of the day.

Our mail arrived from Richmond late in the evening and brought in more cheering news from Vicksburg, which was well calculated to make a soldier lay down on his blanket and sleep sweetly. We don't know how Mr. Hooker and his boys are getting on, but a few extracts from that side of the branch tell us bad enough. They are crying out for G. B. McClellan to come back to them, but little *George* don't reply. Then they say they must have Franklin, if not they are ruined and won't fight.

We believe that the poor fellows would sooner have peace on terms any than to cross the Rappahannock again under Hooker—don't blame them. I would not like to cross either and meet such an army as General Lee's, for he has so many rebels that don't care much where they shoot a yankee, and how many they kill. Orders are passing through camp to cook three days rations, and the boys are flocking to the commissary to fill their sacks with flour. Many of them cook their bread on boards, and sometimes sticks; besides, we notice them skinning the bark from the poplar trees to use as trays for working dough. Any way and every way we live— we are here to-day and to-morrow we may be somewhere else. So here we go.

SOLDIER JIM.

PRIVATE LETTER, TENTH GEORGIA REGIMENT
[SEMMES' BRIGADE, McLAWS' DIVISION]
NEAR FREDERICKSBURG, VA., Saturday Morning, May 23, 1863

Friend Jake: The general and private impression appears to be that we will move soon; but whether we are to fall on Washington or Richmond, the aforesaid impression does not appear to be quite so definite. When I speak of a general impression, be it distinctly understood that I do not by any hint or innuendo refer to General Lee's impressions, for in this army it is distinctly understood that the opinions of the last named General are of a very decided character, and everyone here will readily grant that he knows full well whether our invincibles will be precipitated on Washington, D. C., or Richmond, Dixie. At all events, a move appears to be on the tapis, and every indication is that it will commence soon, and very soon thereafter we expect to hear some of the big guns. I wish that we could put the same meaning to big guns that we used to when speaking of a fine speaker or lawyer, but alas! there is decidedly more thunder here than there.

There are some very interesting occurrences along our lines—some of them tender and melancholy, others ludicrous and amusing. A short time ago a Federal band came down to the river and played Yankee Doodle; when it had concluded the Yankees cheered loudly; they then played Dixie which caused our boys to cheer as loud; they then played Home Sweet Home, when a universal shout went up from both sides. A pleasant episode in a soldiers' life, and perfectly natural.

Two or three days ago two ladies from Augusta, Georgia, having heard of the fights came on to see their husbands. When they arrived one of them found her husband badly wounded, but the other received the sad news that her husband had been buried on the field. The sympathy of our regiment seemed to be aroused for her in her deep distress.

The other day a fine horse came down to the river of the Federal side, jumped into the river and swam to an island about half way across. The Federals called him by whistling, &c.; but our boys neighed like a horse, when the horse jumped in and swam to our side. Both sides seemed to enjoy it finely.

A. J. McBride.

Andrew Jackson McBride joined the 10th Georgia Volunteer Infantry on May 20, 1861 as First Lieutenant of Company E. He was elected Captain on October 16, 1861 and was wounded in the following battles: Crampton's Gap, Md., on September 14, 1862, Wilderness, Va., on May 6, 1864, and Cold Harbor, Va., on June 1, 1864. McBride was elected Colonel on March 2, 1865 and spent the final months of the war in hospital in Augusta, Ga.

INTERESTING LETTER FROM VIRGINIA
QUARTERS, GEORGIA RELIEF & HOSPITAL ASSOCIATION
GUINEA'S STATION, VA., May 27, 1863 [6-9-63AWCS]

Since the late battles the Government has had almost exclusive control of the Railroad from Richmond to the Army, so the Association has been able to do but little in forwarding boxes, &c., to the Georgia troops. Our soldiers generally appreciate the disadvantage under which we labor, and, although anxious to receive what their friends at home have sent them, wait patiently. I hope the Road will soon be opened daily for our use, when we can hurry forward the freight in our depot in Richmond before the army makes a move.

Requisitions for clothing are frequent and urgent since the battle. Many of the camps while the troops were fighting were robbed by negroes and skulkers. The dense wilderness through which the soldiers fought and charged not only tore the clothes they wore into rags but left its effects upon the face, hands and body, and the marching hither and thither through the mud and water after the hard rain of Tuesday, ruined shoes sadly.

With all these drawbacks, however, a livelier and more cheerful body than Gen. Lee's army does not exist. Most of the brigades are in their old camps. The fatigue of the marching and fighting is forgotten—daily drills go on as of old—reveille, tattoo and roll call come and go, and nothing reminds one of the late perils past and victories won, save the absence of familiar faces which lie, perchance, cold in death around Chancellorsville and along the Heights of Fredericksburg, or languish in the Hospitals of the Capitol.

The most pleasant intelligence to you will be that of the great religious revival now going on in almost every regiment in the army. I have had many accounts from Chaplains, and all agree in saying it seems to be genuine and powerful. Hundreds are joining the church every opportunity, and thousands crowd the anxious seats at night. An oath is seldom heard where volleys used to greet the ear. Card playing and gambling have almost entirely ceased, and many who used to indulge in these boldly avow their determination to do better. Jackson's daring and ardent patriotism were long since infused into the troops. Slowly, but I trust surely they are trying to imitate him in Christian zeal. But one thing I feel sure, could make our Lee a prouder man than he is to-day, and that would be to lead his army, all Christians, against the brutal and infidel foe.

You will also be pleased to hear that the troops are fed better than for several months past. I learn it is to be a permanent thing. The rations now, with economy, are sufficient, and I believe the troops are perfectly satisfied. The great need is vegetables, &c. Without them, I fear some sickness will be the result during the summer.

Arms, ammunition, and other spoils still come in from the battlefield. I hear from those who attended to the shipment of spoils that we have collected quite 50,000 muskets and rifles. Vast quantities of loose lead have also been saved. The battlefield around Chancellorsville is reported to be unbearable. The horses killed in the fight, and half buried bodies of the enemy have driven the citizens from their houses.

D.

LETTER FROM TIVOLI
CULPEPER C. H., June 6, 1863 [6-15-63ASC]

Once more we stand with the shattered walls of Culpeper, and again our line of operations points onward to the Potomac. Your correspondent entered Culpeper C. H. for the first time on the 27th of April, 1861. It was then a quiet, happy, tidy looking city, filled with the luxuries and comforts of life and abounding in the highest souled generosity. Every avenue was filled with bright eyed beauty, and content and happiness seemed to have made the old Court House their favorite seat. How sadly changed we find the place now! Shaken by the shock of twenty battles, mutilated by four barbaric invasions, her sanctuaries defiled, devastated by pestilence and famine and the citizens driven from their hearths depending upon God alone for food, that same just God that fed Elijah. The town has changed her features, and sack cloth and ashes fill the place of wine and scarlet.

When I reached Culpeper, I hastened to visit a friend to whose kindness I owe much for attention and care for when fever pressed upon my brow. I found the once happy home in ruins; the family scattered and the proprietor crazed in his trouble, sitting idiot-like, mumbling over some faint recollections of his former affluence. My heart ached over old Culpeper, and sad and sick, I wandered for a while gathering the flowers that grew in the wild neglected gardens, with that same luxury of color and perfume as when gentle hands planted, nurtured and culled them.

The antiquated Court House building still stands to amuse us with its quaint steeple, to which, by the by, there is a humorous history. When the house was in process of erection the commissioners offered a prize of $100 for the best design for a front and tower. A number of designs were examined and the present one selected. After its completion the scaffolding was removed and discovered to admiring eyes of the Culpeperarians, (pardon my coining such a name,) a *fac simile* of the Chinese Pagoda, so often found on the blue and white China ware, which was once in such high estimation by careful housewives. The cunning genius had made a literal copy of these Pagodas, and by the trick pocketed $100. This monument of his ingenuity—the town commissioners called it by another name—still stands, the admiration of all observers.

Yesterday we had a great review. Thousands of cavalry and infantry were upon the ground. The infantry rested on their arms and the cavalry pranced and maneuvered over the field to the delight of about 500 young and thoughtless beauties. The cavalry looked fine with the Prince [J. E. B. Stuart] of showy men at their head, dressed with gold and yellow trappings glistening on the plain grey surface like fire-flies on a darkening night. They were essentially a collection of pretty men, dressed in their best, while the poor, tattered, worn and tired infantry received not one smile from the light-hearted beauties who were out on that day. "The cavalry have more dash," said one of these beauties to me, and turned and waved her handkerchief at a figure bedecked with baubles like a Christmas tree with notions.

The cavalry parade was a beautiful sight, but I have no patience with such tom-fooleries. Better by far, had the men been spared the fatigue of an eight miles march through dust and sun to witness it, and better by far had the ladies remained at home to spin yarn and knit stockings for the soldiers.

At night a grand ball wound up the gala day, and at daylight this morning TIVOLI, having recovered from his Diogenes, like Homor, sprang a reel with one of the loveliest ladies of the Commonwealth, and ere the last murmurs of the music had ceased to ring in my ears, I sank to sleep to dream of a land of peace, peopled with kind and loving hearts, where war and rumors of wars could never come.

The roll sounds from camp to camp, and again we are about to march. A few hours perhaps will bathe the flowers of June in blood.

TIVOLI.

HOOD'S DIVISION, TWENTIETH GEORGIA REGIMENT
IN CAMP, CULPEPER C. H., June 9, 1863 [6-17-63SR]

A line from the army of Northern Virginia, may not be devoid of interest to yourself or readers. To premise with, allow me to say, that I feel a glowing pride in having my name associated with such gallant troops, as are now mustered under Gen. Lee. The army, that has lost in killed and wounded, from first to last, very nearly as many men as are now reported for duty, and has never during a period of two years, in numberless engagements, lost a battle, will, I hope, hold some place in this young nation's history. I speak, not to trumpet forth what I conceive to be our deeds of glory, or to institute comparisons with other troops, whom martial fortune has not favored as much as ourselves, but *gently*, to keep the public alive to the merits of the men, who have fought, toiled, and endured, so much to uphold (as McClellan would say of the Union cause,) the best interests of mankind.

Since the late battle, there has been but little doing in this department. Our time though, has been by no means thrown away. Gen. Lee is always at work. I heard an officer of Gen. Longstreet's staff say on yesterday, that he was the most *industrious* officer, by long odds, that he had ever seen in his life.

The army has within the last few days been reorganized. Stonewall Jackson let fall a sword, which it takes two brilliant Lieutenant Generals to raise. These are A. P. Hill and Ewell, who have been recently promoted. We have, therefore, three Lieutenant Generals, Longstreet, Ewell, and A. P. Hill, each of whom every inch a hero; each Lieutenant Gen. has three divisions. Longstreet has Hood's, McLaws' and [George] Pickett's—Ewell has Rodes', Early's and Ed. Johnson's—A. P. Hill has Anderson's, Pender's and [Henry] Heth's. I don't think it prudent to tell you what number of men this force comprises; but undoubtedly a goodly number, and I think an invincible one, whatever be the force of the enemy.

Our artillery, too, is in the finest condition. You would perhaps hardly credit it, were I to tell you I think it superior to the enemy's. *I think it is.*

My division, as the heading of my letter shows, is Hood's, and a grand one it is, I assure you. He knows more about the management of volunteers, than any officer I have ever seen; then, his regiments too, let me recount to you what glorious ones they are—the three Texas regiments, the third Arkansas, the fourth and fifteenth Alabama, the eighth, seventh, second and twentieth Georgia, and others. Are these not worthy regiments! I speak only from a conviction, when I say, that the column of United States forces which Hood meets, will come to grief.

I was a spectator some days ago [June 5], at a grand review of Gen. Stuart's cavalry, near this place. It was one of the grandest pageants on this continent. It would be telling too much to estimate the strength of the force reviewed. I was well satisfied with it, however. Nearly all middle Virginia was present at this brilliant display, and the horses of the mounted men were the finest ever collected in this country.

The news has, doubtless, long since reached you, that Hooker has retired to the front of Washington. We are making great preparations to move on him, and we are all ready once more to brave the "disastrous chances." Much as has been said and sung, of the profession that makes widows and orphans, I have never yet seen anything *grand* in battle. It is, I think, in the words of President Buchanan, a "*grave*" matter, and one in which, he who fights best, fights on principle. It is a glorious thing I know to die on paper, but my impression is, after witnessing very many, and of all descriptions, that a death upon the battle field transcends all others in horrid and grim reality. I do not wish to discourage or intimidate those who would try the field, I merely speak the words of truth and soberness. I say then that there is nothing inviting in the pounding of artillery, the rattle of musketry, the fierce yells of the engaged troops, the gasps of the wounded as they are struck, the horrid smell of human blood at night, or the long train of funeral ambulances; yet, this is battle that poets write of.

We have been very much concerned here of late, about our affairs at Vicksburg. We think all will be well there, but even if we were to lose Vicksburg, we need not lose courage. I think Mr. Micawber's creed applies as well to arms as to comedy—that no man ought to despond while he has a case of razors.

The weather with us is cool and delightful—never was weather more so to open a campaign. Then may it soon open and close. More anon.

H. C. M.

☆ ☆ ☆ Battle of Brandy Station

On June 9, three divisions of Union cavalry under Gen. Alfred Pleasonton crossed the Rappahannock River near Brandy Station, surprising and nearly routing Jeb Stuart's horsemen. At the close of the largest cavalry battle fought on the American continent, the previously underrated Federal cavalry emerged as a respected fighting force. Official casualties for the battle of Brandy Station: Federals, 81 killed, 403 wounded and 382 missing; Confederates casualties were totaled at 523.

LETTER FROM V. A. S. P.
CULPEPER, VA., June 10, 1863 [6-17-63SR]

Great activity has characterized army movements since my last. From the best information we have, the enemy is in very strong force on the Rappahannock, opposite Culpeper. Yesterday morning was ushered in by the heavy booming of cannon at Hays' [Beverly's] Ford, nine miles from the town. The firing was rapid, and betokened an early and desperate fight. Soon we were in line and drawn up in order of battle in the broad level plains east of Culpeper.

By ten o'clock, straggling cavalry men, as is usual, came "limbering to the rear" with various reports. Col. [Williams C.] Wickham's regiment of cavalry was surprised, completely flanked, but gallantly cut its way through the enemy. Gen. [William E.] Jones, says rumor, was also surprised, permitting the enemy to get into his rear. He, too, cut his way out, capturing some artillery in the meantime. I have this upon the authority of participants.

Our worthy and efficient Postmaster, Mr. A. McCardie, informs me that he saw three hundred prisoners brought into Culpeper, many of whom were wounded with *sabre cuts*. This substantiates the reports of the cavalry, and shows very plainly the desperate character of the fight. This was one of the *few* encounters in a hand-to-hand fight in which the sabre was the arm used. Our cavalry are too often satisfied with a few discharges of their pistols and carbines, and then "retire" to give the infantry a chance. An idea that cavalry are only fit for spying out the enemy's position, picketing, and opening the fight, seems to prevail. There seems to be good reason for this belief, for they rarely ever meet the enemy in a general arm of the service. In the ways of raids they have accomplished wonders. But where have they ever broken a column, or decided the fate of a battle? Forrest's, Van Dorn's and [John H.] Morgan's cavalry have perhaps imitated the brilliant exploits of Murat's horsemen; but they have not equaled their impetuous charges upon the enemy's massed columns.

Col. [Frank] Hampton is reported mortally wounded. I have no more reliable reports of the fight. It is not believed that the enemy's infantry are on this side of the river in any considerable force. Our friends may feel assured that Gen. Lee has a force here sufficient to meet any movement of Hooker. You may prepare to hear of the most stirring events of the campaign. Something grand is in pickle—whether an advance upon Washington or an invasion of the enemy's country, I will not venture to say; for it is impossible for one in a subordinate position, possessing limited means of information, to speak prospectively of our army movements. All may rest assured that whatever is done, will be done well, as long as our veteran Chief, Gen. Lee, is at the head of affairs. God will bless whatever he does.

The cavalry review of which I spoke, came off last Friday [June 5]. It was an imposing sight. One hundred and forty-four companies passed in review in the most splendid order. I counted twenty-six stands of colors, exclusive of those belonging to Stuart's horse artillery. After the review, there was a sham fight, in which the artillery fired over one hundred and sixty rounds, and the cavalry made several brilliant charges. The horses were generally good, and everything indicated a good degree of discipline. Many ladies, blooming in health and beauty, were present. Gen. Hood marched out his whole division to witness the review.

On the next evening we made a hasty march to Kelly's ford in a drenching rain, slept soundly and sweetly upon the wet ground, and retraced our steps the next morning. I have failed to ascertain the meaning of the movement.

I visited Gen. Semmes' veteran brigade Monday evening, and spent a most pleasant night with Capt. W. O. Flemming, and company, whom I found to be in excellent health. Gen. Semmes has one of the best commands in the army of Northern Virginia. At the battle of Salem Church they displayed a heroism and devotion to our holy cause not surpassed by any brigade in the army. In an open field, without protection other than the protecting arm of the Almighty, they met and repulsed four or five columns of Yankees, vastly superior in numbers, with terrible slaughter. In the heroic "Fiftieth," twenty-two brave Southrons sealed their lofty devotion to our cause by yielding their lives upon that bloody field. A hundred and sixty were wounded. I did not learn the casualties of the other regiments, though I learn they were proportionately heavy. Gen. Semmes set his men a noble example by leading in the sanguinary work. Lt. Col. Kearse, after his regiment had filed into line, waving his sword, called upon the men to follow, to which they responded with a yell which made the craven hearted vandals quake with fear. Prisoners and wounded report the fire of Semmes' men to have been the most terrible and destructive they had ever faced. Fine columns melted away before the sheet of flame and torrent of leaden hail which swept the field.

Evening before last all the Captains in Lee's army, from Decatur county, met at Maj. [Bolivar H.] Gee's quarters, and as you may imagine, had a pleasant chat. Will a favoring Providence ever permit them to meet again? God has signally favored them. Gordon's (Lawton's old) brigade had the honor of retaking Marye's Heights. Capt. Geo. W. Lewis tells a good anecdote in connection with the charge. A prisoner reports that one of the men said to the Yankee Colonel: "Do you hear that yell? We had just as well get away, for them d—d rebels will take this hill as sure as h—l." That "yell" had as much to do, perhaps, with the retaking of the Heights, as the musketry, for very few shots were fired.

On several occasions "that hyena yell of the rebels," at the "critical moment," has decided the fortunes of the day. It inspirits our men and strikes terror into the hearts of the enemy.

I hear a good joke in camps in this wise: A soldier of the Ninth Georgia, passing General Hood's quarters, said to him, "General, will you take a drink with me?" The General took the drink. The soldier, swinging the canteen over his shoulder, and feeling he had a right to be more intimate, thus addressed the General:

"General Hood, when you want a drink, 'here's your mule!'" Gen. H. thanked him for his kind offer. "General Hood, when you want any fighting done, 'here's your mule!'" The General, unable to control his risibles, laughed heartily, and assured the Georgian that he would call upon him.

I could amuse your readers with many jokes, but in times like these they want news.

AFTERNOON—But little is yet known of the fight. Two officers, participants, represent our loss as not exceeding two hundred; others estimate it as much larger. About four hundred and fifty prisoners have been brought in. It was a general battle, all of Stuart's and Stoneman's [Alfred Pleasonton] cavalry being engaged, and lasted from early dawn until near night. In the morning the Yankees repulsed our men at every point, but were in turn repulsed and driven across the river in the evening, with heavy loss. Some infantry were on this side near Waterloo bridge, and fired upon our cavalry. One of Cobb's Legion says there were numerous charges, hand-to-hand fights, in which the sabre was used. He says our men were outnumbered at all points, and crossed sabres with the enemy several times.

At one time General Stuart, says the report, was surrounded, and escaped by cutting his way through the enemy. One of his staff officers [Will Farley] lost a leg, and has since died. From all we can hear, it was a desperate fight. The enemy had five days' rations, and evidently intended to make a raid, but unexpectedly met Stuart.

V. A. S. P.

COBB'S GEORGIA LEGION
BRANDY STATION, VA., June 12, 1863 [6-23-63AWCS]

As we are at present indulging in the monotony of camp life, although being under orders to move at a moments notice, having four days rations cooked, I propose to give the readers of your valuable and interesting journal, a brief detail of the transactions of our "Legion" in the fight of the 9th instant, having the honor to be a participant. On the morning of the 9th instant, about five o'clock, we were aroused from our slumbers by the rattle of small arms and the booming of heavy guns. The sound of the bugle was soon echoing through our camps, warning us to prepare for coming events. We were not long getting ready, being soon in the saddle, and drawn up in line. Five minutes had not elapsed, before the command "forward, march," was given. Proceeding in the direction of Rappahannock river, we readily came in sight of the enemy's position, he having selected a thickly timbered piece of land for his operations, which prevented us from discovering his numbers. Skirmishers were immediately sent forward from Captains Rich's and King's companies, also a detachment from one of the South Carolina [1st S. C.] regiments, with instructions to dislodge the enemy if possible. Firing soon commenced between the opposing parties; our skirmishers succeeded in driving the enemy into the interior of the woods; when the Hessians were reinforced.

Their cavalry charged our brave little band of skirmishers; their number being much greater than ours compelled us to retire, which we did in perfect order, wheeling and firing upon the advancing foe. Our boys were discovered emerging from the woods, pursued by the Yanks. The "Jeff. Davis Legion," being nearest the enemy, were ordered to charge him, which they did successfully, routing the enemy completely. Our boys were again ordered to reoccupy their former position, which was in an expansive field. The vandals then sent forward a large body of infantry skirmishers [from Adelbert Ames' brigade]. Captain [W. B.] Young's company was ordered to dismount, together with a detachment from the "Jeff. Davis Legion," to encounter the advancing foe. It was not long, however, before the opposing parties became engaged in deadly conflict. While thus engaged, the enemy were reported in our rear.

Leaving our skirmishers supported by one regiment to hold the Yanks in check, our "Legion" was ordered to left about to meet the advancing column of the enemy which was threatening our rear. The move on our part was immediately executed, then the command of "gallop, march," was given with instructions from our brave and gallant general (Hampton) to charge them regardless of numbers. Proceeding through bogs, over ditches and fences for two miles, we came in sight of the advancing column of the enemy. There being one company already detached from our "Legion," besides a number wounded in skirmishing, reduced our command considerably, nevertheless, it did not weaken our determination or expectations. Onward our impetuous steeds dashed, until at length we came within pistol shot of the Hessians, who were pushing forward with alacrity in order to take possession of one of our batteries which was placed near Gen. Stuart's headquarters, and pouring destruction into the enemy's ranks. They had succeeded in getting within twenty paces of Gen. Stuart's headquarters when Cobb's Legion got into position. The command "charge" emanated from the lips of our gallant colonel ([Pierce M. B.] Young) who was in front; every countenance flashed with "victory or death," we dashed upon the infuriated Hessians with drawn sabres (while they used the pistol chiefly) with such impetuosity that led the Yanks to believe that the rebels intended to wound their feelings; there was weeping and wailing and cracking of

Yankee skulls. After ten minutes desperate fighting, the enemy's ranks became dismembered, then a general stampede followed. They left their dead and wounded in our hands (not very acceptable gifts, I assure you) to be cared for.

We captured five commissioned officers, among them a Lieutenant Colonel and Major. Their loss was fifteen killed and forty-five prisoners in this engagement, while that of ours did not exceed twelve.

There being a large body of the enemy in our front, our officers considered further pursuit imprudent. Soon, however, the rest of our brigade came to our assistance. The vandals discovering our force immediately wheeled about, and dashed off in the direction from which they came, our batteries at the same time hurling missiles of death among their demoralized ranks.

The repulse of the enemy at this critical junction changed the aspect of affairs wonderfully, having a tendency to turn the tide of battle; for which Cobb's Legion has the honor and credit extended to them.

Had they gained the position which they were aiming for, many true Southern patriots would have fallen in retaking it. The position [Fleetwood Heights] commanded our entire right wing, and would, beyond doubt, have proven a fatal stroke to us; but thanks be to God our little band was inspired with the love of liberty, they rushed up in the execrable foe with such violence that would have required men of iron hearts to withstand.

I will not speak of the gallantry displayed by any particular member of our command, because I would be doing others injustice. Too much cannot be said of the courage exhibited by those who were engaged.

I have only given your readers a detail of the fighting which came beneath my observation. Our line of battle must have been at least fifteen miles in length, Hampton's brigade occupying the right.

The boys are in excellent spirits, and express themselves ready and eager for another encounter with the Goths of the North.

I forebear mentioning the force we have at this point—at all events we drove three divisions of Yankee cavalry together with ten thousand infantry, across the Rappahannock. These statements are from prisoners captured during the engagement.

You may look for stirring news in a few days if reports be true, although the impression generally prevents that "somebody is going to be hurt" before many days elapse.

For fear of trespassing upon your valuable space I will close, hoping to see your interesting journal more often in camp, as it serves as a beacon light to many anxious hearts.

TYPO.

COBB'S LEGION, RICHMOND HUSSARS, IN THE BATTLE OF BRANDY STATION

CAMP NEAR STEVENSBURG, VA., Wednesday, June 10, 1863

Yesterday was truly a day of excitement. We were ordered out about seven o'clock in the morning for the purpose of meeting the enemy, who were reported to be advancing. We proceeded to a field about two miles from Brandy Station, which afterwards proved to be the battle field. As soon as we (our regiment) arrived on the field, a company of our regiment was dismounted and sent into a skirt of woods in our front to act as skirmishers. After skirmishing awhile, they were charged upon by a regiment of cavalry, and nearly all of them were captured before assistance could reach them. Our company was then dismounted and ordered forward, which order was promptly obeyed, and the ground lost by Capt. Rich's company was soon reoccupied, which we held until ordered to fall back to our horses. During our absence the regiment marched off to another part of the field, where they confronted the enemy and made as gallant charge as was ever made by any cavalry—routing the advancing foe and putting them to flight. Our company being separated from the regiment, we fell in with a squadron of the 1st S. C. Regiment, and started in pursuit of our regiments. We had not proceeded far before we came up with a regiment of Yankees, which we succeeded in driving back.

From this juncture of the fight the scales turned in our favor, and the enemy were driven back towards the river, and by sundown they were pushed to the north side of the Rappahannock.

Our Brigade occupied the centre, Gen. Jones on the left, and Gen. [Beverly] Robertson on the right. Gen. Stuart could be seen dashing along the whole line, maneuvering the different brigades, which he did as only he can, and in his characteristic style—our General figuring conspicuously in the operations of the day.

Our Brigade suffered pretty severely during the day; the other Brigades, I presume, suffered equally as bad. In regards to the casualties in the Brigade, I have not heard. Our regiment suffered heavily, the casualties summing up as follows: six killed, eighteen wounded, and twenty-eight missing. The fight was a severe one, lasting all day. It being very dry and dusty made it exceedingly oppressive. As the different regiments would move about, volumes of dust would rise from them like smoke from some half smothered conflagration, and at times whole regiments would be lost sight of for awhile, the dust being so intense.

Just as the sun was disappearing our brigade, or nearly all of it, were drawn up in line. Gens. Stuart and Hampton rode by. As they passed three cheers were given to each of them. Such cheering I never heard before. The day was ours, and every one seemed cheerful and enthusiastic. After the Generals had passed three cheers were given for our Colonels— Young and [W. G.] Delony—two as gallant men as ever commanded any regiment. Three cheers were sent up with a vim, and seemed to express the high regard and confidence of the men whom they so gallantly led.

There are several incidents that I should like to mention, and particularize the conduct of several individually, but where all did so well I think it useless. I cannot refrain, however, from mentioning the name of our company commander, Capt. W. B. Young, who is noted for his calmness and undaunted bravery in time of danger; and as for our Lieutenants, they are of the right material, and will reflect credit on any company.

SERGT. J. A. BRYAN, Co. B.

James A. Bryan, age 27, joined Cobb's Legion on Feb. 27, 1862, and was later captured in Stafford County, Va., on May 16, 1864. Bryan was exchanged on Feb. 13, 1865.

☆☆☆Pennsylvania Campaign

After the triumph at Chancellorsville, Lee decided once again to invade the North with the intention of taking the war out of the Confederacy. Repeatedly defeating Federal armies in Virginia for two years did not bring victory and independence for the Confederate States. Lee believed that only a battlefield success on the soil of Pennsylvania would earn the South its independence.

First the Army of Northern Virginia had to be reorganized after the death of Stonewall Jackson. Longstreet remained in command of the I Corps, Richard S. Ewell was given command of Jackson's old II Corps, and A. P. Hill was elevated to command the new III Corps, created from units from the I and II Corps.

On June 16, the vanguard of Lee's army once again crossed the Potomac River and headed north.

FROM THE TENTH GEORGIA REGIMENT
IN CAMP, NEAR CULPEPER, VA., June 14, 1863 [6-26-63AWCS]

Yesterday evening I was again the recipient of copies of the *Daily* and *Weekly Chronicle* for which I suppose I am indebted to you. I have nothing of interest to communicate at present, though lively times are anticipated at no distant day, if we are to judge from the different maneuvers through which we have recently passed. Since I last wrote to you our position has been changed, as you will readily observe from the caption above. It is rumored that Gen. Ewell, now in command of the gallant corps recently led through many victorious fields by the lamented Jackson, is now in possession of Winchester, the blue-bellies having fled at his approach, without the slightest resistance. If this be so, and there is no reason to doubt it, I should not be surprised to find myself in Maryland or Pennsylvania ere many weeks shall have elapsed, notwithstanding the insurmountable barrier that is to impede our way in the person of that world renowned and invincible individual known as "Fighting

Joseph Hooker," who is now in his own estimation (certainly not of any one else) the greatest living General upon the habitable globe.

We are at present encamped about twelve miles from Kelly's Ford, on the Rappahannock, on the opposite shore of which stream the enemy are said to be strongly fortified, in expectation of our crossing at this point. That our crossing will be effected, and successfully too, I entertain no doubt, but at what point I know not, nor would it be prudent in me to speak, were I in possession of particulars in reference to localities. Suffice it to say, that the Army of Northern Virginia, under the command of Gen. Lee, are invincible, hence no defeats in this section.

The health of the regiment is generally good, and the boys are as cheerful and gay as they possibly can be under the circumstances.

Having been on picket duty last night and a portion of to-day, and being somewhat fatigued, and news items very scarce, I will close, with my best wishes for your health and happiness.

Yours, &c.,   J. W. T.

LETTER FROM V. A. S. P.
[BENNING'S BRIGADE, HOOD'S DIVISION]
IN THE MOUNTAINS, VA., June 16, 1863 [6-25-63SR]

By a sudden transition we find ourselves in bivouac on a high hill, surrounded by a picturesque scenery. Leaving Culpeper yesterday morning, we made a distance of twenty miles, under the hottest sun we have ever yet sweltered. To give you an idea of the intense heat of the sun, I will state that we marched through old fields, almost entirely empty of timber, a cloudless, and it seemed brazen sky, by its convex form reflecting the concentrated rays of a burning sun. For hours not a breath of air stirring to cool our fevered brows, clouds of suffocating dust rising, blinding and stifling the men, and the scarcity of good water added greatly to the soldiers' suffering. Several men died from the intense heat—I do not know how many, but have heard the number variously estimated from five to fifteen.

Last night the soldier needed no rocking to put him to sleep, sweet, sound, oblivious sleep, in the open fields, with the rich, waving, luxuriant clover for his bed. The march was more moderate to-day. Gen. Longstreet is losing too many men by forced marches. We have not gone over six or eight miles to-day, halting at 1 p.m. to rest, or await orders, supposing that we will resume the march before night. We are in the western portion of Fauquier county. For those who love a broken, mountainous country, wild, picturesque scenery, the country passed through to-day has its charms. Often the soldier, rising a hill, carpeted with the beautiful clover in full bloom, suddenly comes upon a farmer's snug, comfortable residence, built in the deep, shady dell, as though he sought a hermit's life. His copious barns and numerous out-houses; the dark, shady path leading to a cool spring, and stone spring house, well filled with jars of milk and butter; and the fat cows and horses, browsing on the hill sides—these all speak eloquently of the comfort and ease enjoyed by the Virginia farmer.

Gen. Ewell has been at work. A citizen of respectable appearance met us to-day and says he witnessed a fight between Ewell and [Maj. Gen. Robert] Milroy, on Sunday last [June 15], at Winchester, in which the latter was badly used up. One report is that Milroy and his entire command, about 13,000, were prisoners, but that by some mischance or other, six thousand escaped! Of course we do not believe it. Several prisoners have passed us to-day, but they knew nothing of Ewell's actions. There is no doubt that Ewell has gained a decided victory, and punished the villainy of the miscreants who have so long and so mercilessly lorded it over the unfortunate people of the Valley.

The drum has beat to leave, and I must close. It is now 4:15 p.m.
—UPPERVILLE, June 17th.

A tramp of six or eight miles brought us to Markham Station on the Manassas Gap Railroad. The immortal Ashby residence is here. It was a situation, or location, fitted by nature to inspire in his breast the noble principles which made his name immortal. The whole region is incomparably beautiful. From the tall hills, waving in grain and grass and clover, the view is enchanting. The beauty of the deep shady dells and green hills is heightened by the rugged spurs of the Bull Run mountains on the one side, and the towering grandeur of the

Blue Ridge on the other. The region passed through yesterday and to-day is equal, in richness of scenery, to Western Maryland.

This has been another day of extreme heat. Not half of the division and perhaps of the corps, came up with their colors. In the 17th Georgia six men fainted under the burning heat of the sun. I have heard of no deaths to-day.

The defeat of Milroy seems to be more than confirmed. Citizens just from the Valley say positively that it is so. He had, however, a much smaller force than first stated—only 4,000 to 6,000. Ewell has done well if he has captured these. He did not halt a day, but started at once for Harper's Ferry, and the current report is that he is now closely besieging that place. Already one of his divisions is on the north side, pouring in shells by thousands upon the devoted garrison, from the Maryland Heights. Hope the report is true. Verily the mantle of Stonewall Jackson has fallen upon his chosen successor. A celerity of movement, not even surpassed by the illustrious hero whose place he fills, has thus far characterized the operations of Gen. Ewell.

We have various rumors of the enemy's movements. One is that Hooker is concentrating all his forces between Fairfax and Alexandria, to give us battle. Another is that a large force is ten miles in our front, occupying a gap through which he will have to pass to reach Fairfax. The 20th [Georgia] has gone out on picket. We are waiting rations to be cooked. A conflict cannot be long postponed. Stirring events are being developed. You may prepare to hear of the shock of battle, the crash and roar of big mounted cannon, the incessant rattle of murderous, death-dealing rifle, the wild, triumphant yells of victorious Southrons, and the cries and moans of bleeding, mangled patriots! What a scene to contemplate! Yet I expect to witness it before I am many hours older.

The citizens of the comely little town of Upperville opened their doors to the weary, way-worn soldiers to-day, and gave them all their bread, milk and butter. Servants with buckets of cool water stood at every gate, and furnished a cool, refreshing draught to hundreds of dusty soldiers. All honor to the true Virginians! They are a noble people.

V. A. S. P.

LETTER FROM TIVOLI
[ANDERSON'S BRIGADE, HOOD'S DIVISION]
SHENANDOAH RIVER, June 20, 1863 [6-30-63ASC]

The first moment of leisure after two weeks hard campaigning, I avail myself of, to write you of new triumphs that grace the Confederate service.

Rapidly moving from Fredericksburg across the Shenandoah at Front Royal, Lt. General Ewell in command of Jackson's old corps, passed around Winchester, occupied by Milroy, and perhaps 8,000 troops; and taking position on the heights that commanded the city, on last Sunday morning, opened fire upon the enemy, who were at once surprised and routed. The place was as completely invested as possible, and by successive charges, one line after another of the enemy's works were carried with slight loss to us, and they were driven into their citadel. Here they were requested to surrender, but refusing endeavored to make their escape in the best manner possible. Some few escaped to tell their story, but by far the larger portion fell into our hands.

The whole thing was carried out in real Stonewall style, evidencing that though Jackson be dead, his spirit still lives in the bosom of his ardent soldiers.

The capture of Martinsburg followed that of Winchester, and Ewell with his victorious troops passed on for Pennsylvania and Maryland.

The result of this splendid series of engagements, resulting to us in the loss of 250 killed and wounded, is summed up as follows:

> Killed and wounded (Yankees)......500
> Prisoners........6,700
> Wagons......300
> Horses and mules.....20,000
> Cattle.....300
> Pieces Field Artillery....28
> Siege guns 4

Oats (bushels).....15,000

Corn (bushels)....20,000

Large stores of Quartermaster and Medical Stores, and a moderate supply of Commissary store—the whole valued at between ten and twelve millions of dollars.

This is the most successful of all our operations in the Valley, and the people are much happier over the destruction of Milroy's band of licensed robbers than they were to be relieved from Pope and Banks. Milroy, when he came here, issued his proclamation, telling the people that,

> "Your places are mine; your sheep-specked pastures,
> Forests and yellow corn, land, grove and desert,
> Earth, water, wealth, all that you yesterday
> Were mountainously rich, and golden with,
> I, like an earthquake, this minute take."

The outrages perpetrated by him are too numerous to mention. He carried out his proclamation to the letter, and he has met with a just retribution.

During the time of Ewell's operations, you can well suppose we were not idle. We have since the 15th inst., marched 20 miles per day, through the hottest days of this summer, crossing the river three times, wading up to our shoulders. Many of the men fell out of the road and expired from extreme heat, and our sufferings have been intense. Many of our Georgia boys fell by the wayside, but I have not heard of any serious cases. They are doing well, and every hour rejoining their regiments.

It is not proper for me to give you the exact locality of our army, nor all our movements in detail; sufficient to say that we are in position to do much good and will accomplish our share in working out the scheme of victory, planned by Gen. Lee.

The cavalry under Gen. Stuart have also been active, and have, during the week, fought several successful combats [at Aldie and Middleburg], bringing in about 2,000 prisoners, with horses and equipments.

They have redeemed and brightened up the laurels lost at Brandy Station.

I have no time to write more, and add the following as appropriate to our position. In the life of M. Arago, the great French soldier and mathematician, it is stated that Carnot was reproved by a German Prince with the fact that the Republic does not wish to be recognized to which he made the following reply: "The French Republic does not wish to be recognized; it is in Europe, what the sun is in the horizon, and so much the worse for those who do not wish to see it and to profit by it."

Let us emulate the great soldier's spirit, and pointing to our past career and our present course of victory, it will not be long before the silver star on the Southern crown will shine out resplendant, honored and respected in every part of the civilized world.

TIVOLI.

SECOND GEORGIA BATTALION

[WRIGHT'S BRIGADE, ANDERSON'S DIVISION]

BERRYVILLE, VA., June 22, 1863 [6-30-63ASC]

After a tiresome march of eight days, Hill's corps camped at this place. Longstreet's corps has been encamped here for two days. Ewell's corps is in Maryland either at Hagerstown or Sharpsburg. Ewell's movements so far have been a complete success; captured at Winchester were four or five thousand prisoners, and an immense quantity of Commissary and Quartermaster's stores. It is reported that he has captured quite a large number of prisoners in Maryland.

We hear that there was a severe cavalry engagement at Upperville yesterday. I saw one of the wounded this morning, he said the enemy advanced with a strong force of cavalry and infantry and attempted to gain possession of Ashby's Gap, but were driven back by our cavalry.

There is a large train of pontoon boats with the army, and it is believed Gen. Lee intends crossing his whole force into Maryland. It is conjectured that Longstreet and Hill will cross at Point of Rocks and form a junction with Ewell at Frederick City, Maryland.

We leave Berryville to-day and I think the 25th of June will find us on the northern bank of the Potomac.

The army is in fine spirits and confident of victory. The men have stood the march better than expected, considering the oppressive heat and choking dust.

Although Gen. Lee has a large army, still success would be more certain if he had a larger one. There are thousands of soldiers away from this army who went home on sick furlough, who have fully recovered and ought to join their commands, but instead of doing so are enjoying the ease and luxury of home, while their comrades have to fight their battles with diminished ranks. It is hoped that the enrolling officers will send the laggards back to their duty.

When next I write I hope to be able to give you particulars of a glorious victory.

GEORGIAN.

LETTER FROM EWELL'S CORPS

WAYNESBORO', PENNSYLVANIA, June 25, 1863 [7-6-63SR]

I take the opportunity of the mail leaving this place, to drop a line, informing you of our whereabouts. On Wednesday [June 17], after the capture of Winchester, we took up the line of march for Martinsburg, where we were on provost guard duty for about two days; we were then relieved, and went to Shepardstown, remained there three days and then crossed the Potomac into Maryland again. We marched through Sharpsburg and over the Antietam bridge, which McClellan was so anxious to hold last year. There are no Yankees there now to guard it. On we went through Boonsboro' to Waynesboro', some three miles beyond the line of Pennsylvania and Maryland, and no Yankees yet. There is a report here that the Governor of Pennsylvania made a request on Lincoln for troops to defend the State from the Rebels, and Lincoln's reply was that Maryland and Pennsylvania must take care of themselves, as he had no troops to spare, as he had use for all to defend the Capitol. The Governor is calling for the militia to come out, he wants to get an army of one hundred thousand, and has tendered the command to Gen. McClellan. If the Southern boys have nothing worse than raw militia to contend with, I say good bye Harrisburg and Philadelphia.

The whole of Gen. Ewell's corps are now in Pennsylvania, and Gen. Longstreet's and A. P. Hill's will be in a few days. The men are in good plight and anxious to see the enemy. We passed through Waynesboro' this morning, and rumor says that we are on for Harrisburg. As we passed through Maryland to this place the people appeared to be civil, and nearly all that the men talked to claimed to be secesh, but say that their hands are tied. The people sell whatever eatables the men want, and will, in general, take Confederate money in pay; even in Pennsylvania the women, or at least part of them, that our men talked to, said they were secesh if they did live in Pennsylvania; at any rate they talk very kind to the "dear Rebels," and say they can't blame us. I suspect they are afraid we might disarrange their beautiful farms, as the Yankees did those of our people. So far our men have behaved themselves, taking nothing without paying for it, except in one instance, where some men broke into a woman's cellar and took some of her provisions—complaint was made and the men promptly put under arrest.

Everything in the eating line is very cheap. Butter at 10 to 15 cents apiece, and last, though not least among the soldiers, whiskey 25 cents per quart. One of the men having bought something of a Yankee lady, when going to pay he asked her if she would take Confederate money, she said, "Well, yes, I reckon I'd take it as a curiosity, as I have never seen any of it before." Others, if they did not like to take our money, would give the article.

How long this state of things will continue I cannot say, but I know our commander will set an example of forbearance on private property, which will teach the Yankees a lesson. If property is taken, let it be done by those in authority, or by orders from them. If I should get another opportunity of keeping you posted of our movements, depend on one.

U. T.

FORTY-FOURTH GEORGIA REGIMENT, THE ADVANCE INTO PENNSYLVANIA

[DOLES' BRIGADE, RODES' DIVISION]

GREENCASTLE, PENN., June 23, 1863 [7-7-63AWCS]

Mr. Editor: You request that we write two or three times a week—you will excuse us when you learn what we have had to do since our last. We barely have time this evening to catch a moment and write a short note, as we were informed a few minutes since that there would be an opportunity of sending off a mail to-night—the first since we left Virginia.

We would be delighted to give a full account of our trip from Fredericksburg to this place, but time will not allow, and perhaps this may not reach you. If we live to get through with the campaign we promise your readers a detailed account of all our movements.

We left Fredericksburg, Va., on the 4th inst. We marched to Culpeper C. H. on the 8th, on the 9th we supported Stuart's cavalry. The particulars of that fight (?) you have received, no doubt. On the 10th we started for the Valley of Virginia. We reached Berryville on the evening of the 13th and put the blue coats to flight. We captured eighty-seven prisoners and all the camp equipage at this place. We were left with our company in charge of the camp to destroy tents, &c., and parole the prisoners.

We started early next morning for Martinsburg. We had a hard march, but reached the town at sundown and again put the Yanks to flight. They set their stores on fire and welcomed us with their departing salute, firing only a few rounds at us. Our cavalry rushed into town and followed the retreating Hessians, and captured every piece of cannon, seven in number. We captured during the day and night some 200 prisoners. Thousands of dollars worth of commissary and ordnance stores were destroyed. We saved, besides, all that we could take care of.

We marched to Maryland, entering at Williamsport, on the 15th. The Confederate battle-flag was unfolded to the breeze over the dome of the U. S. Hotel, where cheer after cheer was given for the success of our cause—many a Marylander joining. We marched to Hagerstown on the 18th. Here we received such a welcome as we did not expect. The streets were crowded with ladies, who, with bright smiles and waving handkerchiefs, cheered us on. "Give me a rebel button," could be heard on every side. We had many private conversations with ladies and gentlemen, and we are satisfied that the intelligent and wealthy Marylanders are for the most part with us.

We remained here until the morning of the 23rd, (yesterday,) and then started for Pennsylvania. We are now in the United States—the Yankees have been trying to whip us into the Union for two years and more, but have signally failed. We have whipped them and marched into the Union.

We have an army flushed with victory. We have marched over two hundred miles, and are in just as good condition to-day as when we left our camp on the Rappahannock. Our company marched out of camp near Guinea's Station numbering sixty men. We are here in Pennsylvania with fifty-nine men. The "Greene County Volunteers" is the largest company in the 44th Georgia Regiment, and but one man has fallen out on a march of two hundred miles. We can not give brigades or divisions that are here, but ours you know and will again hear from. We are living finely among the Pennsylvania Dutch up here.

We are getting nice fat pork and beef, flour, molasses, butter and milk, coffee and sugar, &c., &c., with any quantity of brandy, whisky, wines and—but Gen.—has all such trash as the last named articles poured out upon the ground. Our time is out. We will write by the first mail that goes down to the white settlements.

J. W. B.

James W. Beck entered the Confederate service as a private in the Second Regiment Georgia Volunteers, and served for one year. He then raised Company K, 44th Georgia, and was mustered in as captain on March 17, 1862. Captain Beck was wounded at the battle of Malvern Hill on July 1, 1862, and was promoted to Major on May 5, 1863, and to Lieutenant Colonel on September 11, 1863. Colonel Beck served in all the battles until Hatcher's Run where he was prostrated with pneumonia. He was home in Georgia recovering when Lee surrendered. After the war, Colonel Beck was a minister and teacher in Milner, Georgia.

LETTER FROM V. A. S. P.

MARTINSBURG, VA., June 25, 1863 [7-11-63SR]

As our Postmaster, Mr. A. McCardle, leaves this evening or tomorrow, I will improve a short time allowed me for rest, by writing you a short letter.

Anderson's brigade did not meet the enemy at Snicker's Gap, nor did Benning's follow; but the next morning, Monday [June 22], we retraced our steps up the Shenandoah to the ford at Ashby's Gap; thence we went to Millwood, where A. P. Hill's corps was encamped. Here we rested until Wednesday morning, washed up and prepared rations.

Gen. Lee's recent order enjoining upon the troops non-interference with private property *in the enemy's country*, was published. Nothing is to be touched except by the proper officers designated for that purpose, who are to buy what the army needs, or take it, if the inhabitants will not sell; and in every case to furnish the parties from whom supplies are received or taken, with a certificate of the quantity and kind. How different is this from the way our foes treat us! They not only take what they want, promising to pay upon evidences of loyalty produced by the inhabitants, but give their brutal soldiery license to pillage and rob. The question whether we should not retaliate upon their citizens, by burning houses and laying waste the whole country of the enemy, is discussed with a great deal of earnestness. For one, I say we should not. We would degrade ourselves to the low, despicable character of the Yankee, as developed by this war, were we to retaliate in such a way. What! imitate the Yankees! God forbid that our fair national fame for chivalry and honor should be blurred by so foul, so brutal, so barbarous a mode of warfare as characterize our foes! Thank God, we have no Butlers, Milroys or McNeils! Our leaders are southern gentlemen—theirs are *Yankees!* I trust our government will never make war upon women and children, as the puritanical heathens of New England do.

We are within twelve miles of Williamsport, Md., where we will probably cross the Potomac to-morrow morning.

The whole of Gen. Lee's veteran army will have crossed the "Rubicon" in a few hours. Great events, vital interests to our beloved sunny South, hang tremblingly in the balance. "The wheeling sabre" of Ewell, like the sword which was suspended over Jerusalem, has already filled the hearts of our persecuting foe with dreadful apprehensions. Lee's victorious legions follow closely in his wake; and God blessing us, they will be made to feel the bitter curse of war. They will be enabled to form some idea of what we have suffered, though they will not be visited with the fire grand, the vindictive cruelty, the warfare upon women, the desecration of churches, the demolition of grave yards—in a word, the heartless barbarity which distinguishes their own soldiery.

We expect, of course, to fight bloody battles. By these, and those alone, do we expect to accomplish the great object of our mission—the bringing about a speedy peace. The army is in high hopes. God forbid that we should be disappointed. It is much stronger, by half, perhaps, than it was last summer. The men are healthier. Our excellent Surgeons, Drs. Hoyt and Palmer, assure me that sickness is rapidly decreasing. It is so in other brigades.

The Yankee army, on the contrary, is much weaker, and greatly demoralized. An invasion is meditated, and it is believed, will be successful.

Gen. Hood is reported to have said that if he were a betting man he would stake all he is worth that peace would be made by Christmas. Gen. Longstreet evidently entertains the same opinion, as one might infer from his recent order exhorting men and officers to a faithful and rigid discharge of their duties as tending to bring about a speedy peace. It is an eloquent, touching appeal, and found its way to every true soldier's heart of the *corps d' armee.*

This hope is strengthened by the reports we have from Vicksburg, that Grant has been killed and his army defeated. I have not seen this in the Richmond papers, but it is reliably reported by army officers who say they saw the statement in the Washington *Chronicle* and Baltimore *Sun.* I have not seen these journals, and therefore, give the report as I heard it. I hope that it is true.

I had the pleasure of seeing the "Prince of correspondents" "P.W.A." [Peter Wellington Alexander] on Tuesday. He is looking unusually well. Through his able letters, your readers will be well posted in the movements of the army.

More anon.   V. A. S. P.

LETTER FROM V. A. S. P., IN PENNSYLVANIA
CHAMBERSBURG, PA., June 26, 1863 [7-19-63SR]

Gen. Longstreet's corps crossed the Potomac Friday morning [June 26], and proceeded to within three miles of Greencastle, Pennsylvania. We ate breakfast in Virginia, dinner in Maryland, and supper in Pennsylvania. It is but a short distance across Maryland from Williamsport—say 11 miles.

At Williamsport, Gen. Hood halted his division an hour and issued a whiskey ration. While I believe a too free use of the "ardent" is injurious, particularly to the soldier, I believe the troops were benefited this time; for all the previous night and until 3 o'clock that evening they were exposed to a cold, drizzling rain. Furthermore, we had to wade the Potomac, and were not allowed to strip. In thirty minutes after the whiskey was issued, Hood's division presented the liveliest spectacle I ever saw. Good humor and wit ran high, and it was difficult even to hear one's self talk. But, as was to be expected, a few made "use and abuse" synonymous terms. Some men don't know when they had too much of a good thing. Cases of intoxication were, however, very rare.

We passed through Greencastle yesterday morning and Chambersburg at 6 o'clock in the evening—distant 11 miles. Greencastle is a considerable town, numbering about 4,000 inhabitants. The doors were all closed. They looked sad and down cast. A few, however, talked cheerfully and expressed a hope that peace would soon be made. The "Rebs" replied that "peace would certainly be made as the rebel army had *got back into the Union!*" We saw but one family that was really bitter against us, and they were renegade Virginians.

The Second Georgia band played "Dixie" as the long column with flying banners marched through Greencastle. The air was played so well that it called forth long, loud cheers from our boys. A young man standing on the sidewalk, remarked, "That's what we need to play going down South." The Rebs took fire at his taunt like a tinder box, and had not the fellow "dried up" quickly, he would have been handled roughly.

Chambersburg numbers about 8,000 inhabitants. It is decidedly a handsome town, and can boast a number of superb public and private buildings. The tower of the city hall was crowded with eager spectators, and many beautiful ladies, and handsomely dressed gentlemen, thronged the side-walks and balconies, gazing in wondering amazement at the host of rebels passing through.

Many old farmers expressed their surprise at our numbers, saying they did not think there were as many men in the entire South! When they ask our strength, the boys reply that we number about 300,000! One fellow in Chambersburg replied to the question, "Where is Milroy our commissary?" that he was at Harrisburg, and would feed us on powder and lead! He had no answer for the question, "Why are you not there to help him?" Some of the citizens are glad we are here, as the conscription law is suspended. Anything to avoid being drafted.

The country thus far is unsurpassed for fertility and beauty. The wheat, oat, barley and clover fields resemble the prairies of the West. The farmers have the most magnificent barns I ever saw. A Dutchman's pride is in his large well-filled barns. All the residences are neat, but substantial buildings of stone and brick, about one-fourth the size of their magnificent barns.

Our quartermasters and commissaries have impressed a great many fine horses, mules and beef cattle. Very little private property—that is, poultry, vegetables, bee hives, &c., and no household furniture, no pantries or milk houses have been disturbed by the soldiers. Orders are very strict in this respect.

The inhabitants say McClellan is in command at Harrisburg, and has a regular and militia force of 60,000. Gen. Ewell is at Carlisle, 15 miles this side of Harrisburg. We hear nothing of Hooker's whereabouts. By "grapevine" dispatch I learn that he is still hugging his breastworks around Washington and doing picket duty in the gaps of the Blue Ridge, momentarily expecting Gen. Lee to attack him! Poor tool of a crack-brained despotism, he is not less jeered and abused by his own kith and kin than by the impudent rebels. He is surely moving somewhere—perhaps towards Philadelphia. We are in the heart of their country with a large and formidable army. They must, of necessity, make some counter move or abandon their country to subjugation.

Much breath is spent in speculating about Gen. Lee's plans. It is different to fathom his designs; and it is well for us that it is so, as the enemy would soon check mate him if his plans were loosely laid or apparent to every body.   It is evident though, that one part of his grand programme, is to transfer the seat of the war to their own country, and let them feel for a while what war is. If successful, Washington will, of sheer necessity fall into our hands. But I will not speculate. It becomes me better to speak of accomplished facts.

5 p.m.—Our mail carrier has arrived with letters and Richmond papers, but no *Republicans*. He will return to Winchester to-morrow.

Since the preceding pages were written I have seen and heard enough to change materially the character of one paragraph therein contained. The 38th Virginia, on duty in town last night, entered the stores and took everything they wanted. Members of this brigade went to town this morning, and finding the stores open, took what they wanted. Chickens, bacon, vegetables, honey, butter, &c., are coming into camps in large quantities. Much of it was bought, the citizens readily taking Confederate money; while hundreds of soldiers are scouring the country, taking everything they can appropriate.   Virginians and North Alabamians are retaliating upon the Pennsylvanians for the depredations committed upon their homes. Report says that the citizens shut themselves up and the soldiers have everything their own way. A respectable young man in the 15th Georgia says the streets of Chambersburg are strewn with gloves and fragments of goods. General Lee should and will punish such vandalism, even against our enemies.

V. A. S. P.

THIRD ALABAMA INFANTRY, LETTER FROM PENNSYLVANIA
[O'NEAL'S BRIGADE, RODES' DIVISION]
ON PICKET ON BALTIMORE PIKE, NEAR CARLISLE, PA., June 28, 1863 [7-20-63MAR]

As the regiment is now in the enemy's country and expecting, at least, to remain here for a few days, I thought a note of the fact, together with a brief sketch of our trip thus far in the State, might be of some little interest to you.

On the morning of the 19th, instant, the regiment left its camp on the south bank of the Potomac, opposite Williamsport, Md., where we had rested for two or three days, and crossing the river again set foot upon the soil of Maryland. No enthusiastic crowd thronged the banks to welcome us to the good old State of the Howards, the Carlisles, Carrolls, and other great and good Southern spirits. Cold indeed was our reception—rendered still more so by wading that clear cold river so early in the morning.

But what cared we for the dark frowns that sat upon nearly every face; our course lay through that abolitionized portion of the State, and through it we were bound to go. We passed through the village without halting, and pushed on some eight miles on the Baltimore pike, passing through and going into camp about two miles beyond Hagerstown, on the banks of the bloody Antietam. Here we stopped for two or three days. The day following our entrance into the State was the Sabbath, and many of the men, accompanied by their company officers, were permitted to visit Hagerstown, to attend Divine service.

As the brigade marched through the main street of Hagerstown, many bright and beauteous faces attested the fact that some there are still left in that town, who have not bowed the knee to Baal or Abraham in whose breasts still burns the true Southern fire. The stars and bars—tiny things though they were, and waved by tiny white hands, handkerchiefs, bright smiles, on pretty faces; these, together with many kindly greetings, all gave an enlivening, cheering contrast to our reception at Williamsport.

After resting two days on the Antietam, the division again took up its line of march. Conjecture was rife as to where we were going. All doubt however was soon removed, for, returning to Hagerstown, the head of the column took the road leading to Chambersburg, Pa.

You might think that with the knowledge that we were about to invade the enemy's territory, would come a certain feeling of uncertainty as to our ability to carry out so grand an undertaking, in a style that should correspond with our former campaigns. Not so. When the fact became known that Pennsylvania was our destination, a shout of joy ran along the line, and when our troops crossed the line it was with a proud and defiant step, conscious that wherever Ewell leads, we can follow.

Our journey thus far in Pennsylvania has been uninterrupted by any Yankee force. I had thought they would dispute every inch of the ground, but here we are, within nineteen miles of the capital of the State, and yet no force has opposed our progress.

The first night in this State, we encamped on the outskirts of Greencastle, where we remained the next day and night, taking up the line of march on the morning of the 24th for Chambersburg, where we arrived at 12 o'clock, M. Our regiment was assigned Provost duty here—of which none of us were sorry—and the balance of the brigade passed through and encamped on the edge of town.

In Chambersburg we did not find a great amount of spoil. Most of the merchants had taken the alarm on the approach of our cavalry, and run their goods off by railroad, or secreted them. Shoes, hats and clothing, things that a few of our men needed, were not to be found, except in small, scattering lots. Flour, molasses, whiskey, medicines, stationery and hardware were more abundant, and the 2d mess availed themselves of the opportunity to fill, and sent to the rear sundry wagon loads.

Col. [Cullen A.] Battle was Commander of the Post, and became a general favorite with the citizens. No wonder; no one can become acquainted with him without entertaining for him the highest regard, as a soldier, scholar and Christian gentleman.

Leaving Chambersburg on the 26th, the regiment started on its march through mud and rain, but did not overtake the brigade—which had started early in the morning—until we got to Shippensburg, a small town of about 1,000 inhabitants, where we found the balance of our troops in camp, and ourselves bivouacked for the night.

We left Shippensburg on the morning of the 27th, and after a long and tedious march of nearly twenty-five miles halted on the roadside of the Baltimore pike, about one mile from Carlisle, where we now are, doing picket-duty, and living on the fat of the land. And now, where do we go? I cannot tell you to-day; perhaps to-morrow I might be able to do so. Some say Harrisburg, others think Baltimore. A few days will tell. There is a report that McClellan has command at Harrisburg, and has a force of considerable size, some say 60,000, others go as high as 100,000—mostly militia.

The people in this immediate section (Carlisle) seem to be opposed to the war; at any rate, they have given us quite a friendly reception, for I saw two or three ladies waving their handkerchiefs as we passed along the edge of Carlisle.

I have not time to write such a letter as I would like to, simply to give a hasty sketch of the trip; at some future time I'll write more in detail.

In haste, I close. ***.

LETTER FROM TOUT LE MONDE IN PENNSYLVANIA
[BENNING'S BRIGADE, HOOD'S DIVISION]
CHAMBERSBURG, PA., June 29, 1863 [7-14-63SR]

I'll take this chance to drop you these lines, but I can't say that they will ever reach you—our mail communication is now probably done for some time, I hope not forever. It is no longer a myth, we are among the Dutch of Pennsylvania. The country surpasses in improvement and evidence of comfort anything I ever saw in my life! Every spot of it almost is under the most thorough cultivation and plenty—even super-abundance—is everywhere. The class of people are rather of a low order, and, with all the appearance of progress are very far behind the age in intelligence. In fact they are nothing but simple farmers, whose greater aspiration is comfort. This is particularly evidenced in the character of the buildings, which are all plain and substantial, constructed of stone, without an exception devoid of architectural display. The barns are invariably the largest; and if anything, the most highly finished house on each farmer's premises. Every one has his wonderful big granary to contain the immense abundance of grain which annually flows in from the fruitful fields around it. Such splendid prospects for harvest I never saw, and if the resources for supply is as great throughout the north as it is here—and I suppose it is, there is little wonder that everything is so cheap.

Two days now that we have traveled into their country, we have passed one long succession of golden wheat fields, excepting where portions were devoted to hay making, which were the finest prospects of the kind I have yet seen. The people are circumscribed, as I have said, in their intelligence, and know little of the war or its ravages, being a simple minded set of dupes to the Washington dynasty. Their surprise and consternation knew no bounds when they found out that the "ragged rebels," were actually in their midst living and moving monsters among their granaries and fowl houses. "Mine Got" was on every tongue, expressing the hopeless despair which weighed down every Dutch heart. The old women went into fits and the old men racked themselves out of their wits in the old ancestral rocking chairs, despairing of another day of existence. They were ready to give up anything they had to the "devouring" creatures that presented themselves at the doors, respectfully asking if they had anything to sell. Their surprise was great when they were not hurt, nor any ferocious demonstrations of appetite made on their actual personages. They grew tame wonderfully fast, and in a short time professed that they were democrats, peace people and our friends.

This class we found in the country, but our reception in Chambersburg, which is quite a large and flourishing city, was very different indeed. There seemed to be a superabundance of venom, the offspring of an education from the miserable abolition sheets and anti-slavery speeches which had been ding-donged into them from time immemorial. Such long head men I never saw, and the features of the women would have made vinegar ashamed of itself for sourness. Some wreathed their pretty lips in ugly scorn and turned up their noses as if everything they saw before them was offensive to their olfactory organism. These expressions gave rise to much amusement in the ranks, and some of the sharpest cats were dealt to them by that inexhaustable source of fun—the soldiers wit. The town folks have promised us a good thrashing before we leave here. Their great wonder, they say, is that we were such fools as to undertake such a thing as an invasion—that we would be surrounded and cut off, and not one would get back to tell the tale. We replied that all that might be true, but when General Lee was surrounded and couldn't get out, there would be more Yankees hurt than ever were hurt before at any one time.

A victory for them will be so dear that the very name of victory brings a pang to their hearts. I am disposed to think, and I rather think they do also, that it will be an awful job to remove the stubborn Confederates from among them. But what he intends to do I am no more able to say than the stupidest darkey on any Southern plantation. He fools everybody, even our well-informed President Davis, I believe. Ewell has preceded us and got most of the good things that lay in the path of the conqueror—such as shoes and clothing generally, but an abundance of provisions is found everywhere. From the number of fowls that have made their appearance in camp to-day, I am disposed to think our men have been interfering with their roosts. This would be a just retaliation for the same thing committed by their troops in our country. However, there is something so disgraceful and low in this kind of robbery and vandalism over the helpless that I cannot but applaud Gen. Lee's strong efforts to suppress it. Only such things as are really necessary for our progress and supply is allowed to be taken and then our currency is offered at their market price for them to refuse or take as they think proper.

But many of the farmers have eluded our search for horses, having fled with them to the mountains to hide. Detachments will be sent after them. Some of the gentlefolks raise quite a storm about the Quartermasters ears when he comes with the news that, "I must have your horse, sir." Just about then the rebels are spoken of in very unpleasant Dutch terms. But the good humored Quartermaster takes the animal jocosely, hands him the Confederate money and gallops away; whereupon the enraged Dutchman in great wrath destroys the money, and just adds that much wealth to the Southern cause. Our resentment grows very strong when we think how much vandalism has been practiced in Virginia, but when it comes to practice it upon defenseless women, children and old men, a true Southern soldier can not find heart to do it. I fear there are some in our ranks who have been unmerciful, but it cannot be discovered who they are or they would be punished. Orders are very strict and read every day to the troops against vandalism. Gen. Lee is magnanimous towards the people. In our intercourse with the natives we have found only a few whom we might say are our friends and not practicing duplicity for protection. There is something about their cordiality that seem sincere, but the want of fidelity in those who are seared into friendship for us is apparent at first sight. If I had time I would detail incidents which might be interesting, but the only opportunity afforded for sending a letter is just at hand. A discharged soldier will attempt to-morrow to run through before our communication is entirely gone. These scraps of paper are all we now have at hand and if you can not decipher the hieroglyphics on them, consign the whole to that fatal *omnium gatherum* for all such trash, and be content to wait till it is possible to do better.

TOUT LE MONDE.

☆ ☆ ☆ Battle of Gettysburg

On the morning of July 1, advance elements of Gen. A. P. Hill's corps encountered Yankee cavalry on the outskirts of Gettysburg, Pa. A vicious fight ensued, with Hill's and Ewell's corps driving the First and Eleventh Corps of the Army of the Potomac (now under the command of Gen. George G. Meade) through the streets of Gettysburg to the heights south of town. On the morning of July 2, the two armies were drawn up on parallel ridges about a mile apart. Lee sent Longstreet to turn the Federal left and Ewell to turn the Federal right. Though somewhat successful, both attacks failed to drive the Federals from their position. On the afternoon of July 3, Lee had his artillery pound the Federal center for nearly two hours in an effort to soften up the position for an infantry assault. The attack was a failure; advancing across open fields, approximately 12,000 of Lee's veterans were shot to pieces with casualties approaching 50%.

On the night of July 4, the Army of Northern Virginia withdrew from Gettysburg and began its retreat to Virginia.

LETTER FROM TOUT LE MONDE

HAGERSTOWN, MD., July 7, 1863 [7-22-63SR]

The last letter we wrote you was from Chambersburg, Penn., which, in all probability, you have never received, for our communication has been cut off for the last eight or ten days by the enemy's cavalry hovering about the rear of Lee's army. However, from that point we will continue, as nothing of importance came before, unless it was the actual invasion.

Having rested well, General Lee turned his course towards Gettysburg, which lay in an easterly direction on the way to Baltimore. Near a little town called Fayetteville, a gap in a small range was passed, and on the night of the 2nd of July rested within a few miles of Gettysburg. News came to us that General Ewell had been fiercely engaged the same day, and that the enemy were in large force before us. Early next morning we passed on to our lines, which had already been formed just beyond the town, from which the enemy had been driven the day before; and our suspicions were correct, for the enemy's skirmishers were in full view. The dead of the battle which had been fought the day before lay in many places over the ground, and also a large number of the wounded of both armies were seen lying about the farm houses which we passed. These unmistakable signs of blood left us no longer in doubt of the path that was before us. Behind the position which the enemy held was a small range of mountains, which, it seem, was purposely selected to fall back into, in case our troops forced them from the low hills already occupied. The advantage lay largely in the enemy's favor, and the probabilities of forcing him beyond the range were very much questioned by many who thought anything of the coming battle. The morning was occupied in maneuvering and waiting for the enemy to advance. This, it seemed, he would not do, and Gen. Lee had come for the purpose of giving him battle. As soon as everything was adjusted the advance was ordered.

General Hood formed his line on the extreme right of the line of battle. At the command the line advanced to carry the right, at which point it seemed Gen. Lee had aimed as the weak point in the enemy's position. Every man had nerved himself for death; for as the skirt of woods, in which the line had been arranged previous to advancing, was passed, beyond lay a field a mile in width running to the foot of the range which contained 13 pieces of artillery, making a gradual ascent until the foot was reached. As soon as we came in sight a furious blast of cannon broke from the tops of the hills and mountains around and the terrific cry and screams of shells began. Slowly the line moved in order forward, such of it as we saw, and that was Gen. Benning's brigade, undismayed by the terrors that seemed to awake from the infernal regions. Our batteries now began to open in the rear, sending the hissing shot over, answering to the enemy's guns in front. They hardly attracted the fire of any of his, but all seemed concentrated on the advancing lines. Down the plunging shot came, bursting before and around and everywhere tearing up the ground in a terrific rain of Death. Still the old brigade moved on in its solid and beautiful line, the red star-gemmed cross floating defiantly in the midst. As it approached the guns, the rain of grape and canister began, mingling their sharp cries with the shrill whistle of the mad minie balls which seemed to come in showers. The ranks began to melt away, but springing forward with a shout the undismayed line steadily rushed on, determined this time to sacrifice every life or carry the cannon crowned hill before them.

The artillery raged with its fiercest fury, till now the very air seemed covered with the missiles of death. The storm of musketry that followed was the most terrific ever listened to by mortal man. The line reached the foot of the hill [Houck's Ridge]—that portion of it embraced by the 15th and 20th Georgia, the 2nd and 17th being forced into a gorge that lay between it and the mountain [Big Round Top] on the right. The 15th and 20th clambered over the rocks and pressed forward, and the 17th and 2nd plunged through the raking fire that now, more terrific than before, swept the gorge like a furious torrent. The enemy dismayed at such daring began to break before the fire which was now hurled through his ranks, and began a hurried flight to the mountain side which was lined with hundreds of minie rifles. The gunners [of the 4th New York Battery] fled from their guns, leaving the three splendid Parrot pieces which had been pouring death into the old brigade for one mile. The hill and its artillery was ours. The inaccessible mountains still lay before it, but its steep rocky sides were beyond the ability of our men to carry, under the awful hail storm that came like a torrent, from its summit. But secreting themselves behind the rocks, our men defied the plunging fires that vainly tried to drive them back. The enemy formed his lines and swept down the hill to recapture the guns, but the steady fore of the old brigade swept him away and broke his ranks in every futile effort. Again and again he formed and desperately stormed at the hill which contained his guns, but at each time his ranks were broken and hurled back on the mountain heights. All the while the summits were blazing with cannon. The shells and shrapnel shot descended, exploding in the earth and hurling the rocks to an amazing heighth, but in spite of all, our men held their places firmly. A part [the 1st Texas and 3rd Arkansas] of the Texas brigade were mingled in with the Georgians, and a braver lot of men never bit a cartridge. Coolly and deliberately every one waited till some favored one of the foe came within his range and sent the message of death to him. The attack commenced at near 3 o'clock, and raged until dark closed the horrors of that awful day. Then we stepped out from our hiding places to take away our dead and wounded. Silence reigned, except the wails of the maimed which rose dismally in the gloom and darkness. What an awful scene it was, there where everything was wrapt in night, with scarcely a thing visible, except the solemn mountains which rose darkly on the horizon, among the dead! The whole night was employed in removing the wounded for the next day's terrors. Those costly guns were rolled away, with the price of blood on them; the men placed in position to sleep away the hours which would bring on another grand day. So the day dawned.

But it seemed the idea which had infatuated our leaders to try these mountain passes had gone. The day before had taught a different lesson; for wherever General Lee had hurled his forces, they had driven the enemy until he reached the mountain passes. There he held his ground. Everywhere we had inflicted injury on the enemy, but our loss was terrific.

Gen. Hood was wounded, Barksdale killed, Semmes [mortally] wounded, [G. T.] Anderson, [Jerome] Robertson wounded; [Lewis A.] Armistead [mortally] wounded, Kemper [wounded] and [Richard B.] Garnett killed, all favorite generals of their commands, and perhaps others of whom we have not heard up to this moment. In our brigade Col. [John] Jones of the 20th Georgia, was killed, and also Lt. Col. [William] Harris, 2nd Georgia, besides numbers of other officers. Such mortality among officers was never known in the history of this war. So the day passed off with cannonading and some fighting on the right with cavalry, which resulted in capturing some two or three hundred. Our list of prisoners was swelled, so it was said, to 7,000. In the evening of the 4th the enemy came near flanking this brigade, but by a timely movement it barely escaped. The lines were drawn up behind and to the right of Gettysburg, where on the 4th Gen. Lee awaited the advance of the enemy. Except skirmishing he never came. At night Gen. Lee began to withdraw, and by the morning of the 5th was among the mountains on the turnpike towards Hagerstown. The enemy followed feebly, for it began now to be ascertained that he was withdrawing towards Washington. Now, this is written near Hagerstown, through which we passed last night. There was considerable cavalry fighting in the streets yesterday, hurting very few that we have learned. Everybody seemed frightened to death, for no lights were on the streets, and the city appeared like the residence of the dead. There is still some game and defiant residents who dare to maintain repugnance to Yankeeism. They report that after our army left last year no insult which their infamous enemies could heap upon them were spared them and some even arrested. But some are firm to the end.

It is much regret that our information would not allow us to give a more detailed account of the fighting of troops, but this will be excused when you learn we were busy all the while. But P. W. A. was on the ground. Your correspondent, V. A. S. P., was killed. He died nobly in the ranks, a brave and honorable soldier.

TOUT LE MONDE.

Captain Virgil A. S. Parks, of Company D, 17th Georgia, was killed leading his men into action on July 2 near Devil's Den. In the July 21 edition of the Savannah Republican, *the editors paid tribute to his memory:*

It was not our fortune to know Capt. Parks personally. He originally volunteered in the service of the *Republican*, and our acquaintance has been confined to his regular correspondence and a large number of private letters which he addressed to us from time to time. Others, who knew him better, represent him as a young man of noble character, fine talents and rising fortune. He was poor and friendless, but ambitious. In some way unknown to us he came under the notice of that excellent man and liberal benefactor, to whom so many are indebted for all they are in life, Hon. Alexander H. Stephens, now Vice-President of the Confederacy. The friendless youth became his protégé, was sent to school, to college, instructed in the Law, and sent forth in the struggle of life armed with the true weapons to conquer all its difficulties—a mind well stored with knowledge, and a character above reproach. His entrance upon a professional career was encouraging and full of promise, an honorable career awaited him. But the struggle for independence commenced, and he was among the first to rally around the standard of his oppressed country. He has served her faithfully and well, first as Lieutenant and then Captain, and for her has now offered up his life.

With his numerous and interesting letters all the readers of the *Republican* are familiar. He improved rapidly in his correspondence, was honest and truthful in all he wrote, and the high-toned morality that characterized his literary labors throughout, cannot have failed to strike the reader as one of their leading characteristics.

But the gallant soldier is no more.

"He sleeps his last sleep, he has fought his last battle,
And no sound can awake him to glory again."

LETTER FROM SOLDIER JIM

CAMP, 8TH REG'T GA., VOLS., NEAR HAGERSTOWN, MD., July 7, 1863 [7-27-63ASC]

Perhaps you have before this, heard of the great fight we had at Gettysburg on the Baltimore Pike, in Pennsylvania. It was probably the most desperate fighting that ever was known on this continent.

After we had entered the State of Pennsylvania and advanced some distance above Chambersburg, our column was halted for a few days rest, which time was consumed in washing, foraging, &c. The country is a beautiful one, and well supplied with the necessaries of life. The boys generally lived high. They paid for what they got when they would not take it, they pressed such things as they needed. In walking through the camps you might have found at the soldiers' table, such as chicken, butter, eggs, preserves, pies, &c. But we had not many days before we had orders to march.

Our column was turned and marched off on the Baltimore Pike. We had marched two days and nights, passing many sour looking faces, when our column began to move more slowly. We wanted no better evidence that Yankees were ahead, and very soon we could see the signs of battle, for the gallant Ewell was ahead of us, and had driven the Yankees two or three miles. Our lines were soon formed and we moved forward driving the cowardly fellows back to a small mountain [Houck's Ridge] where they had rock fences for breastworks, and their batteries planted on the mountain. Their batteries were soon charged and a number of their pieces, with about seven or eight thousand prisoners were captured. Their dead were left in heaps on the field. I suppose they sustained the greatest loss they have in any engagement during the war. Our loss was also heavy, but we drove them away from their position, and on the 4th we found that they were moving away towards the Capitol. Our army was very soon afterwards in motion. The wounded who were in a condition to be moved were sent across South Mountain, but those who were seriously wounded were left in charge of our Surgeons and nurses. Though they have doubtless ere this fallen into the enemy's hands.

The next day we moved off in a direct course for Hagerstown, our cavalry driving a force of Yankees before them. Since crossing the mountain we have captured about 300 prisoners and will probably take in a few more of the blue coats.

Before closing, I must say to you that the few "Grays" that are left are "good grit," and stand to the blue coats as long as there are any of them left. One of the Grays, viz: George Grambling, captured ten prisoners, and brought them out by himself.

This is a correct report from the "Grays."

SOLDIER JIM.

The collector of ten Yankee prisoners, George H. Grambling, Co. F, 8th Georgia Infantry, enlisted as private on May 22, 1861 and was appointed First Sergeant on July 4, 1861. Grambling was captured at First Manassas on July 21 and exchanged at Fort Monroe on November 13, 1861. Wounded at Deep Bottom, Va., on August 16, 1864, Grambling was listed: "Absent wounded for the rest of the war."

PRIVATE LETTER, ELEVENTH GEORGIA REGIMENT
[ANDERSON'S BRIGADE, HOOD'S DIVISION]
FUNKSTOWN, MD., July 8, 1863 [7-29-63ASC]

After much hard marching we reached Gettysburg, Pa. Gen. Hill had a fight the day before we arrived, and whipped the enemy badly, capturing about 6,000 prisoners. Our line the day afterwards was formed and commenced the fight about 3 o'clock. Hood's division fought in front of Woolf Mountain [Little Round Top], or as some call it "Devil's Den." Anderson's brigade fought in front of the mountain, and we met the enemy in the woods, at the greatest disadvantage troops ever had to contend with [on Stony Hill and in Rose's wheatfield]. The enemy were behind rocks and trees, and a stone fence, in which position our brigade charged them and drove them out. They then were reinforced and drove us back. A second time we rallied and charged them, driving back as before; but they reinforced and in turn drove us back. We now had only a handful of men left, but we rallied a third time and drove them to the mountain, where they took a position which we could not carry. Some think we killed five for every one we lost; though our loss was very heavy. Our regiment lost over 200 men. My company [H] lost 24 killed and wounded. Gen. Anderson was wounded. Gen. Hood and Col. [F. H.] Little were wounded. Captain [Mathew F.] Nunnally, of my company, was killed. The loss in the brigade was very severe.

J. W. Morrow.

THIRD ALABAMA VOLUNTEERS,
FROM A MEMBER OF THE GULF CITY GUARDS
[O'NEAL'S BRIGADE, RODES' DIVISION]
CAMP NEAR HAGERSTOWN, MD., July 9, 1863 [7-24-63MAR]

I last wrote you from "picket-post," near Carlisle, Pa. Since leaving that point, the regiment marched many a long and weary mile. In my diary I find that on the 30th ult. we received orders to "fall in." Having been warned the night before that we should move in the morning, I was up early, and before time had my Pennsylvania chicken fried and discussed, coffee made and drank, etc., etc.

I had anticipated, as did many others, that we would take the road to Harrisburg—the capital of Pennsylvania—and such was the expectation of our Dutch neighbors; but Gen. Lee fooled us all, by turning our faces toward Baltimore. You may rest assured that no little curiosity prevailed among the troops when we took up the line of march on the road leading direct to the metropolis of Maryland. Many were the *nice things* we would have—after taking the city; fine army boots; the best of clothing—Confed. grey, at that; elegant hats; coffee and sugar in abundance; molasses enough to swim in; everything, in fact, that a soldier's heart could wish or appetite crave; and finally, each man was to have a ration of good liquor—prescribed by the surgeon—every semi-occasionally, until he recovered from the fatigue and exposure that necessarily follow the performance of so grand an achievement as the capturing of Baltimore.

Disappointment, however, is common to all men, and especially so to soldiers. We did not go to Baltimore. After marching about thirteen miles the head of the column turned to the right, at a place of town called York Springs, taking the road to Gettysburg, Pa. About four miles brought us to a village named Heidlesburg [Heidlersburg], where the division went into camp.

Our journey to-day was not so tedious as many previous ones, owing to the fact that the road was quite good, the sun hid by clouds, with an occasional light shower of rain. Nothing of interest occurred during the day worthy of note.

HEIDLERSBURG, PA., *July 1, 1863.*

Left camp this morning at 6½ o'clock, taking the Chambersburg road. Reaching a small village called Middletown, five miles from Heidlersburg, the head of the column filed left into the Gettysburg [Carlisle] road. After a march of about three hours, our ears were greeted with the booming of cannon, and we soon found that, contrary to our expectations, a fight had been "fixed up" for that day. Rumor had told us that the enemy was near Gettysburg, but we did not anticipate meeting him before the next day. But here we were, in the suburbs of the town, and the enemy's cannon warning us not to approach any nearer. The surest method they could have adopted to draw our boys on. I have never yet seen a Yankee battery planted behind a town, or breastwork, or on a hill, or anywhere else, but that our Generals and men did not take a notion into their heads that they must see what was there; and the notion once in their heads, go they will, and go they do; though, to tell the truth, we sometimes do not get pay for the indulgence in this mania for seeing sights, or "sight seeing," as turned out to be the case at Gettysburg on the second day's fight. But I have digressed. Leaving the main road on our right, the division moved into line of battle, and then forward towards the town and enemy—the enemy's pickets (cavalry) falling back as we advanced. We did not move far before the brigade was ordered, with Iverson's and Daniels', to the support of our brave [W. P.] Carter, who opened his batteries upon the enemy. It was not a very pleasant place—lying behind those guns, at which the Yankees were hurling shell upon shell; but then we had it to do. Thanks to the enemy or somebody else, this suspense did not last long. Col. Carter, took his artillery to a better position [on Oak Hill], and our line formed again and moved forward, Daniels on our right and Ramseur on our left, until within musket range. The direction of our line brought our left into action earlier by some minutes than our right.

By some misunderstanding or mismanagement our regiment got cut off or separated from the balance of the brigade, when we were ordered to the support of Carter's battery, and so we went into the battle, I believe, between Gens. [Stephen D.] Ramseur's and [Junius] Daniels' brigades. At any rate, after some time spent in ineffectual efforts to get our regiment engaged in connection with our forces on our right, Col. Battle finally moved us by the left flank to another part of the field, where, placing us on the right under the command of Gen. Ramseur, the old 3d finally moved forward with a shout. The enemy was in our front, behind a stone fence; we could see them; they were "pegging away" at us, like good fellows, and Gen. Ramseur said they had to be driven from there. We did drive them from there. At the given time, Gen. R., riding to the front, clapped spurs to his horse, and waving his hat, cried out for us to follow him. Away dashed our leader—as fine a specimen of Southern chivalry as ever led a body of men into battle—and hard after came the line, their spirits fired with the enthusiasm and valor of the intrepid General before them. North Carolina and Alabama, side by side, vieing with each other in deeds of daring and endurance. Forward—forward; no halting; no measured trail; a charge, and the stone fence is gained, passed; the minions of a hated despot are flying in broken, confused masses, while the conquerors follow, pouring into their hated foe the messengers of death.

On our right the enemy had held their ground with more stubbornness or success than in our front; so that when we had driven them from the stone fence the line had to halt till the forces on our right could push them from a wood, from which they were enfilading us. It did not take long to accomplish this, and soon we had the satisfaction of seeing the whole Yankee line fleeing like frightened wild beasts toward town, followed closely by our boys. We run them into and through the town to the heights beyond; here they had previously fortified themselves and massed their artillery. It was late in the day; we had marched twelve or fourteen miles, driven them over more than a mile of ground, and our Generals—I suppose—thought it imprudent to push us further; so we were halted, and finally bivouacked in the streets and on the edge of town.

All glorious achievements seem to lose more or less of their brilliancy by some loss sustained in their accomplishment; at least so it seems in this. Our victory on this day was one only equaled by the first day [May 2] of Chancellorsville; and yet it is rendered a sad one to our little company by the death of Sergeant R. P. Sheffield, than whom a braver or better soldier never bared his bosom to the foe. Ever at his post in camp; faithful and impartial in the discharge of his duties as an officer, he won the respect of officers and men. In battle, bravest of the brave, he pushed forward, in the front, and was ever last to leave the field. He fell while the regiment was charging the enemy as they lay behind the stone fence I mentioned before, mortally wounded in the throat. Expiring in his brother's arms, his last words were, "Tell mother that I died in front, doing my duty." May he rest in peace; and may his stricken friends find some consolation in the thought that his companions in arms will ever honor his memory and tell with pride of his brave and chivalrous bearing.

Other members of our regiment were wounded in this day's engagement, but as you have doubtless received and published a list of them ere this, I will not attempt to enumerate.

So ended the first day's battle of Gettysburg. We had driven the enemy before us like chaff, and strewed the field with their dead and wounded; but we had driven them into their stronghold.

July 2, 1863.

To-day we lay behind a railroad embankment on the edge of the town, right under our batteries, which were planted on a hill in our rear some 75 or 100 yards. Nothing was done on our part of the line—the front—until late in the evening, when the whole line advanced about three-fourths of a mile. About 4 o'clock in the afternoon Generals Longstreet and A. P. Hill, on our right, and Generals Johnson on our left, opened a tremendous cannonading on the enemy's batteries on the heights in the rear of town, when our batteries in front took up the fire, and such another roar of artillery I have never heard since the war begun. During this engagement Longstreet and Hill drove the enemy some three miles on to the heights in the rear of the town, while Johnson on the left succeeded in driving them some distance; so that when night closed on the second day's fight the enemy had been compelled to fall back on either flank and on his centre to his mountain fastness behind the town. So closed the second day. Of the brilliant achievements of our men in Longstreet's, Hill's and Johnson's commands during this day, I cannot give you a *reliable full account*, as I did not witness them. I learn, however, that they several times charged up the mountain and drove the enemy from his breastworks, and on one occasion even captured a battery of some 30 or 40 pieces of artillery, but could not hold the place. In fact one of the Brigadier-Generals was killed while sitting on one of the pieces.

July 3, 1863.

At three o'clock this morning the division [brigade] moved from its position in front, around the left and behind the town, finally halting at the foot of the mountain [Culp's Hill] on which the enemy had fortified himself. Johnson's forces were already engaged, and had been for some time; in fact they had been there since the morning [evening] before; so, as soon as we moved forward we relieved them. It was a hot place, I assure you, and nothing but the numerous trees and rocks saved many a man's life. As it was many were wounded, the most slightly, I believe. Col. Battle and Major Sands were both struck on the leg below the knee, but neither sustained more than a slight injury. They are both with us, the Major limping very little.

We lay at the foot of the mountain blazing away at the enemy's breastworks (for we could seldom get a glimpse of a Yankee head,) and the rascals pouring a perfect sheet of fire at us for two or three hours, I should judge, when, through some wrong order or somebody's mistake, the regiment fell back, joining Johnson's command at the edge of the wood. We did not remain here long, for finding that we had got separated from the balance of the brigade we returned to the foot of the mountain again, where we lay until that night at 12 o'clock, when the whole line fell back to the side of the town from which we had driven the enemy on the first day's fight, and took our position on the hills where, on the morning of the 4th, we threw up breastworks and then took a rest. The enemy, during the 4th, showed no disposition to attack us. Not a shot was fired except by the pickets during the day, and we rested as well as we could in the rain and suspense.

Of our movements since the night of the 4th, at which time we fell back, it is not worth while I should write a full detail, suffice it that the entire army moved off in good order and without any loss worthy of note, reaching this point on the 7th instant about noon.

Doubtless Northern papers will claim the battle of Gettysburg as a victory for their army. Not so. They suffered most terribly, and nothing in the world but their strong position on the mountains in the rear of Gettysburg saved the Yankee army from being entirely routed. On the 3d day Longstreet and A. P. Hill opened on the enemy about 150 pieces of artillery, and a Yankee officer who was taken prisoner, told a surgeon in our division that so destructive was our fire that they were compelled to make details from their infantry every hour to work their artillery, and that the whole army was entirely demoralized. We have since learned that the enemy really commenced to fall back before we did by some hours.

I could write more, but to enter into minute details would consume too much space, which I fear I have already done. I cannot close, however, without speaking in the highest terms of our Colonel, Lieutenant Colonel and Major. More gallant and chivalrous gentlemen are not in the army, and I am proud to have such leaders. Thanks to the God of Battles they are all three safe. Our mutual friend, Sergeant S. behaved himself as usual, with the greatest gallantry. He is a brave and true soldier. In fact, nearly all the men acted nobly.

But here we are, the army of Northern Virginia encamped on the enemy's soil, a wide and now unfordable river between us and the fair land of our hope and pride. Think you our spirits are broken, or that we stand trembling least the enemy shall fall upon us and grind us to pieces? Dispel those fears. The army of Northern Virginia stands to-day upon the soil of Maryland, conscious of its ability to defeat at any time the menial hordes of Lincoln whenever they shall choose to attack us. I do not believe, and really hope it is not, the intention of our Generals to leave Maryland just now. We can subsist here, and so long as we can compel the Yankee Government to keep their large army here watching us instead of in Virginia threatening Richmond, why not stay here. I would not see another battle fought on the already bloody soil of the Old Dominion if there is any way to avoid it. We are strong enough to whip the rascals if they will either attack us in our position, or fight us on equal ground, but when they entrench themselves on mountains that it would puzzle a chamois hunter to climb, it is not to be expected that we will be able to rout them. I want this war to end with this summer's campaign, and I would prefer to do the remainder of the fighting here or north of here, but I fear the cowards will not favor us with any such chance at them.

C.

PRIVATE LETTER, THIRD ALABAMA REGIMENT
BIVOUAC NEAR HAGERSTOWN, MD., July 8, 1863 [7-23-63MAR]

Dear Wife: We received orders to march from Carlisle, Penn., on the 29th, and took the direction towards Gettysburg, which place we reached the second day. When within about five miles of the town, A. P. Hill's guns reminded us that the battle-ground was ahead of us, and as you have probably seen before this will reach you, the most bloody battle of the war was fought. About two o'clock our division became hotly engaged, and after three hour's hard fighting, succeeded in dislodging the enemy from a strong position on a series of hills, and from behind stone fences. Gen. Meade commanded the enemy, and, I think, showed great generalship in the disposition of his troops.

While the attack was being made they poured it into us, but to no purpose. Our turn soon came, and when they gave way we slayed them by the hundreds. According to their papers, two corps were nearly annihilated. In front of Gordon's Georgia brigade the ambulance corps counted 300 dead, and the rest of the field was in like proportion. We followed them through and to the other side of the city, but from some unaccountable reason the attack ceased, and what remained of the enemy took refuge on a tremendous hill, where very heavy reinforcements reached them during the night. This was on the 1st.

The next day Longstreet attacked on the right and drove them two miles back on the same hill [Cemetery Ridge], where they drew all their forces and concentrated them (together with a mountain on our left). Here they fortified, which, with the natural position made it almost impregnable.

Several attacks were made by us, and [Harry T.] Hays' Louisiana Brigade carried the heights at one time, but from want of concert of action; had to fall back again. About 7 o'clock P. M. our division was ordered forward again to make a night attack, but from some cause we were withdrawn. In this movement I got my foot in a hole and sprained my ankle very badly, and have been disabled ever since. The next morning two brigades from this division (Daniel's and ours) were sent three miles to the left to support Johnson's division in front of the mountain. Here another terrible encounter took place at 12 o'clock. One hundred and twenty pieces of artillery were placed in position, so as to obtain a concentric fire, and of all the unearthly noises it was the most terrific I ever listened to. That night another attack was made [Pickett's], and the next day the whole army rested.

During the night the enemy commenced to withdraw, and Gen. Lee fell back to this point to be nearer his base of ordnance supplies and to protect his trains. Our loss was of course heavy, and that of the enemy at least 30,000. We took 8,000 prisoners.

In withdrawing to this place, we had to leave all of our badly wounded. The Yankees played a very cute trick, when they found that Gen. Lee had retired after they commenced it, by following us with one brigade of infantry, to make it appear that they were driving us. They kept at a very respectful distance, and gave us no trouble. You must not consider me vain or egotistical if I put on paper that I was complimented by my brigade commander and a number of officers and men for the part I played in the fight. I would not write this but from a knowledge of the pleasure it would give those at home. Lieut. Ledyard lost his leg. He was doing well when we left, and will receive better attention than if he had been brought on with the army. I wanted to wait on him, but was so lame myself that I could not get about. There is a great deal of contraband news I would like to write you, but am afraid, lest my letter might fall into the enemy's hands. The head of our train was attacked coming over the mountains and about fifty teams captured.

*** .

LETTER FROM LEE'S ARMY
[WRIGHT'S BRIGADE, ANDERSON'S DIVISION]
WINCHESTER, VA., July 15, 1863 [8-4-63AWCS]

Duties which I need not mention kept me from entering Maryland and Pennsylvania with our army. On the 1st inst., however, I left this place and behind two good horses moved rapidly forward. Early in the evening forded the Potomac, a broad, beautiful stream, and entered Williamsport. There most of the stores were closed and the majority of the citizens closely shut up in their residences, giving a quiet, Sunday-like air to the place. The few I talked with insisted that the Confederacy had many friends in the town and State, who, to espouse our cause only needed the assurance that our army would permanently remain on that side of the river. 'Tis true that quite a number of ladies welcomed Gen. Lee on the stone bridge over the canal, and many along the road waved Southern flags and cheered on our troops; but the great majority of the men in that portion of the State are loyal to the old Union or want spirit to join us in resisting the tyrant at Washington. It is perhaps just to say that we were in the same section we visited last year—one avowedly Union in its interest and feeling. Had we reached Baltimore and the region round about, we *might* have met with a different reception.

Leaving Hagerstown to the right we took the direct road to Greencastle, Pa. The distance across the State by this route is not ten miles, and was the road over which a large part of our army passed. It led through a rich and highly cultivated region, thickly dotted with neat farm houses. Across the entire State I noticed that no property was injured. One could scarcely think a large army had but recently marched over the ground.

On the 2d we entered Pennsylvania. Soon after crossing the line I began to notice traces of the passage of our troops. Here and there fences were broken down, and a few fields of grain partially trampled under foot. Some of the less conscientious of the troops no doubt appropriated pigs, chickens and the like. Our Government took horses, cattle and forage of course, but *paid* for them. No private houses were burned, no agricultural implements destroyed, no wanton destruction of any kind indulged in, such as marks the march of the enemy through our land.

Never did an army leave a State with less real damage. Most of the misery and suffering brought upon our country were through the acts of soldiers from Pennsylvania, and it was hard for our troops to keep their hands off of property they felt they had so much right to destroy. Many at home censured Gen. Lee, we hear, for thus respecting private property. He expressly declared that he did not come to make war upon defenseless women and children, and requested his troops to refrain from the policy adopted by the foe in our own land. History, he said, would applaud the course, and the God of battles bless and sanction it.

The citizens of that portion of the State our army occupied are all Dutch—the men a milk and water looking set, who could not give us an honest gaze. Candor compels me to say that I did not see a passable looking female. All had a slovenly look, and shuffling gait, and I could imagine no position in which they would appear at all in their element, except over the kitchen fire and wash tub. Some were quiet, and some sullen; but some, boasting with rage, abused us in profane and vulgar language. No restraint was placed upon their tongues, and we only laughed at their raging. The country was the most beautiful I ever beheld. Everywhere fields of waving grain met the eye, while the vast numbers of dwellings and outhouses gave it the appearance of one vast village.

Before reaching Chambersburg, we turned to the right, in the direction of Gettysburg. At Greenwood, we first heard that a battle was going on. Urging on our horses, we rode to the top of a mountain, only eight miles from the battlefield. It perhaps falls to the lot of a few to have a grander view than the one we had from this elevated position. The lines of the two contending armies could be distinctly traced by the smoke of battle, while the roar of the cannon, as it rolled up the mountains, and reverberated from the peaks and cliffs, sounded like heavy thunder. Long lines of our cavalry stretched along the road beneath, while men on foot and single horsemen were moving to and from the scene of strife. Immense numbers of wagons dotted the fields on either side of the road, and horses were grazing quietly, as if nothing were going on.

As we neared our rear, the guns roared louder and louder, and the spiteful rattle of musketry mingled with the hiss of shot and shell. Leaving the conveyance, I made my way down to the lines, stopping here and there at the different hospitals, which were filled with wounded, who bore their pains like stoics.

The battle began on the 1st, about five miles from Gettysburg. Hill's corps was principally engaged on the first day, and drove the enemy beyond the town, killing, wounding and capturing great numbers. That night the enemy took position upon a high rocky hill—a perfect Gibraltar—and there awaited our advance.

The next day our lines were drawn—Longstreet on the right, Ewell on the left, and Hill in the centre. On the two wings Longstreet and Ewell drove back the foe with great slaughter, but the centre resisted every effort made to carry it. It appeared almost foolishness and a wanton waste of life to attempt it. Over an open field for over a half mile the hill sloped gradually from Hill's position to that of the enemy. It then rose abruptly to a narrow piece of level ground. On this the cannon were thickly planted. Immediately behind, the hill again rose, overlooking the cannon, and on it sides were three lines of battle, each arranged so the upper could shoot over the heads of the lower, and all protected by stone walls.

I cannot give you an account of the different attempts made to carry the position. The most desperate, however, and the only one which took the guns, was made by Gen. Anderson's division, or rather three brigades of it, Wilcox's, Perry's [Lang's] and Wright's. But very few of

Wilcox's or Perry's men reached the batteries. All those in Wright's who survived the fiery ordeal planted their colors there, but had to relinquish the hard-earned prize for the want of support, after fighting hand-to-hand with overwhelming numbers.

This charge is the theme of praise in the mouth of every one, and is considered the most reckless and daring of the war. In the advance over the open field Wright had no support on his left. As they pressed forward volley after volley greeted them, but led by the intrepid Wright, and assured by the presence of Adjutant General [Victor J. B.] Girardey, whom no danger can excite, they moved on, each step leaving the field strewn with dead and wounded. One after another fell, while the slaughter among the officers was terrible.

Col. [William] Gibson, Lt. Col. [R. W.] Carswell, and Adj. [Julian] Cummings of the Forty-eighth Georgia, Col. [Joseph] Wasden, and Adj. [J. D.] Daniels of the Twenty-second, with many other officers fell while leading on their commands. The Third Georgia also lost heavily in officers and only three out of the Second Battalion gained the hill. Undismayed by the heavy losses, the men pressed on, drove the enemy from the guns. Capt. Girardey planted the flag over them, and rallied the surviving portion of the brigade around him. Some began hitching up the horses to the cannon to lead them from the field. Maj. [G. W.] Ross, of the Second Battalion was wounded while thus engaged. The enemy seeing their weakness and that they had no support moved down upon them like an avalanche. In vain the little Spartan band looked back and called for aid to help secure the brilliant victory they had ruined their brigade to gain. None was at hand.

The enemy swarmed around them and the order was given to fall back. Sullenly and disappointed they fought their way, and back down the hill through the same awful fire in which they advanced they took their course. No rout or wild fleeing from danger characterized their move, but with blighted hopes they reformed and took their old position. Many shouldered their wounded friends and brought them off the field. The majority of the badly wounded who fell near the guns were left in the hands of the enemy. Without a doubt, if support had been sent General Wright, the battle would have soon ended in the complete rout of the Federal army.

Wright's Brigade took in about 1,000 men and lost in the neighborhood of 700. Scarcely a company had a commissioned officer left. In the Second Battalion three out of four of its companies were brought out by sergeants. Major Ross was seriously wounded in the thigh and left on the field. Gen. Wright was untouched and his Adjutant, Capt. Girardey also escaped. These two officers do well to go together. If possible, Girardey is the coolest man of the two. In the midst of the greatest danger he moves as if unconscious of the balls flying around him. As a gentleman, he is kind and polite. Has a word and smile for every one he meets. All love him and are never better pleased than when he leads them in battle.

On the third day the heaviest cannonading on record took place. On our side quite one hundred and fifty guns were in action, most of them playing on the centre. The enemy must have had over two hundred, for by their own accounts they used all their reserve.

For hours it was almost impossible to show your head, so thickly and incessantly flew the missiles of destruction. In a small grove near the position Wright's brigade occupied, the trees were literally cut to pieces. The loss on our side during the artillery battle was comparatively small. Our men had a slight hollow to protect them, and many dug holes with their bayonets large enough to hide their bodies. The enemy being massed upon a hillside had no protection, and from the testimony of prisoners, suffered greatly. The accuracy of our artillerists silenced many of the enemy's batteries, and their guns were frequently knocked out of position. In the evening Gen. Pickett's division made a charge on the heights, but failed, with heavy loss. Longstreet and Ewell continued to slaughter the enemy, and took many prisoners, massing up Meade's army until its lines were not over one-third the length it began the battle with.

Gen. Lee, unwilling to sacrifice more men in trying to carry the position, did not resume the battle on the 4th, and the enemy seemed to have no disposition to do it. In fact, during the entire battle we made all the charges, and nothing could draw them out of their stronghold.

That morning Gen. Meade began to withdraw his army. Gen. Lee, for reasons best known to himself, did not follow, but went south to Hagerstown and Boonsboro' Gap [Monterey Pass]. It is said by those who ought to know that our ammunition was nearly exhausted, and to pursue would have exposed our trains and left insecure the route to our base of supplies.

Of course the enemy immediately claimed a victory and filled all Yankeedom with boasting. When the truth is known—and it will leak out before long—it will be found that Meade left the battle field in our possession, and we voluntarily gave it up. Our army was not followed or molested. All the advantages are on our side. Our loss will not amount to 15,000; theirs by their own accounts, to 35,000. They did not capture a single gun. We took several. They only claim 6,000 prisoners. We certainly took 13,000. Our army is not seriously injured, and is to-day able to defeat the combined forces of the enemy in a fair fight.

Since our army left Fredericksburg, it has taken 25,000 prisoners, immense numbers of horses, mules, and wagons; exchanging everything old and worthless for new and strong; driven many thousands of cattle out of the rich pastures of Pennsylvania; been for over a month of no expense to our Government; and given the Commissary Department in Richmond an opportunity to collect up stores for the future use of the army. Some of the Northern papers are already fearing that the victory was not much of which to boast.

Our troops are in good condition and excellent spirits. They have heard of the fall of Vicksburg and Port Hudson; took one day to grieve over it; and now look at it as one of the reverses to be expected in a great war. They expect the people of the West, and all over the country to rise superior to calamities, and go to work to remedy them. Dark and gloomy days must and will come to all nations struggling for freedom against a large and powerful people, but they only test the materials of which the struggling power is made. If we deserve to be free, we will gain it in spite of difficulties. A thousand Vicksburgs are not the Southern Confederacy; and not until the last foot of ground is lost will we cease to claim a country, separate and distinct from the hated power of the oppressor.

Our wounded are having everything done for them that can be done here. Large numbers are in the city, and at Jordan Springs.

Dr. Claggett is in charge of the latter place, and manages things well. He is the highest style of gentleman, and an excellent surgeon. All his patients love him, and Georgia, with the whole Confederacy, owes him a debt of gratitude.

Rev. Mr. Gramley, of Georgia Relief and Hospital Association, was the first here from abroad, and, though innumerable difficulties, brought up supplies of clothing, medicines, bandages, &c., for the wounded. He is indefatigable in his efforts to relieve suffering, and has done great good. All who needed clothing have received it. The army is much in need of shoes and the Association hopes soon to be able to supply the Georgians.

My lengthy letter has been written while pressed with other engagements, and wants the care I should have preferred to have given it. Many interesting items are necessarily omitted. Take it for what 'tis worth, and with it, the best wishes of

Yours, truly,   D.

LETTER FROM LEE'S ARMY
[GORDON'S BRIGADE, EARLY'S DIVISION, EWELL'S CORPS]
IN CAMP NEAR MARTINSBURG, VA., July 18, 1863 [8-9-63MAR]

I presume that the fall of Vicksburg had such an effect on you all, and has so entirely absorbed your attention, that you have not taken much notice of Gen. Lee's invasion of Pennsylvania and Maryland. We have just recrossed into Virginia after that rather unfortunate invasion. I will trouble you with a short resume of it. You recollect that about the 4th of June Gen. Lee's army left the neighborhood of Fredericksburg and struck northward. Gen. Ewell's corps, to which my brigade is attached, marched immediately on Winchester, which was then occupied by the Federal army under the command of Gen. Milroy. After three days' fighting we captured the place, taking all the artillery, and all the wagons, as well as almost all the men of the enemy.

After that battle we crossed the Potomac river at Shepardstown, and proceeded without delay through the old battlefields of Sharpsburg and Boonsboro to the town of Waynesboro, Pennsylvania. We found the people of Pennsylvania dreadfully frightened. They expected they were to be the victims of the most atrocious barbarity. In Waynesboro we made the people hand over what boots and shoes they had, also other articles that we needed for the comfort of the soldiers. We marched a northeasterly direction from Waynesboro, passing through numerous towns and villages, without any adventure worth relating, and in two days arrived at the town of Greenwood. At this place the brigade to which I am attached was separated from the army and sent ahead on important duty.

We were ordered to press on to the Susquehanna river, and secure, if possible, the bridge which spans that river between the cities of Columbia and Wrightsville. I never enjoyed myself more than I did on this march. Our brigade was composed of a little over two thousand men, and we were not encumbered with wagons and ambulances. The day after we left Greenwood we approached the town of Gettysburg, which we took possession of after a bloodless skirmish with some militia who opposed our progress, in which we captured nearly all our assailants. We stayed in Gettysburg all night, and the next morning proceeded towards the city of York, through the most beautiful and highly cultivated country I ever beheld. Every thing that science could furnish had been applied to a soil already fertile. The houses were neat and well built. Every thing was in the most perfect order and every thing that man or beast could want abounded in great plenty. The inhabitants were all Dutch, and except in the management of their farms, were the most ignorant people I ever saw. They were intensely afraid of us. It seemed as if they felt that the Northern people deserved severe treatment at our hands, and expected, as a matter of course, to get their share of it. They brought out for us everything they had in the eating and drinking way, and I ensure you we fared well. I think those people make the most delicious bread I ever tasted. They have one day of the week which they devote entirely to baking—making on that day all the bread they expect to use during the ensuing week. We seemed to have reached every farm house just after baking day, for such oceans of bread I never laid eyes on before. They supplied us with milk, butter and cheese in the most extravagant abundance. They would take pay for none of these things from us. They seemed to be anxious to do everything to propitiate our good will. After we had left and the rest of the corps had come along, they recovered somewhat, finding that we possessed some humanities, and managed to trade with their customary sharpness. Two days after leaving the town of Gettysburg, we approached the city of York. The citizens of York were so badly frightened, that they sent out their Mayor to us to surrender the town when we had arrived within only nine miles of the place. York is a well built city, of fifteen thousand inhabitants, and of considerable commercial importance. We got a considerable number of pants, shoes, hats, &c., for the men at this place. When Major General Early arrived at this place, he levied a contribution, and raised $28,000 in greenbacks.

We staid in York but a short time, and then passed on towards the town of Wrightsville, on the Susquehanna, passing through the same kind of country as before. About 3 o'clock P. M. of the 28th of June we arrived within three miles of Wrightsville, and found the Yankees drawn up behind entrenchments to dispute our further progress. We formed as quick as possible and attacked them, and after a brisk battle of a half hour we routed them, taking nearly all of them prisoners. The few who did escape set fire to the bridge and completely destroyed it, thus foiling us in the main object of our expedition. Had we saved that bridge, the battle of Gettysburg, which took place some few days after, would never have been fought—the great fight would probably have taken place at the city of Harrisburg. It may be, however, that things have turned out for the best. The burning bridge came near consuming the town of Wrightsville, and it was only after the most strenuous efforts on the part of our soldiers that the town was saved. Those efforts I joined in, but I must say I did not fully approve of our exerting ourselves to any considerable extent, for I could not help thinking that in a similar case in our country a Yankee army would not exert themselves much to save our towns from burning. I was sorry for the poor women of Wrightsville. They were left almost alone. The men ran to the opposite side of the river on the approach of our troops, and left the women to shift for themselves. They were of course dreadfully frightened, and could not be consoled. We stayed in Wrightsville all night and part of the next day, and then retraced our steps to York, where we rejoined the rest of our division, and rested for a few hours.

During the whole of our journey from the State line to the Susquehanna, I was struck with the coarseness of the people. Except about farming, they are the most ignorant people I ever saw. I never saw the whole time while I was in Pennsylvania, a single woman who appeared delicate and refined. I saw a great many well-dressed ones in the cities and towns through which I passed, but they all showed unmistakable signs of lowness and vulgarity. Of course I lost no opportunities of speaking to them whenever I had the chance. I think I made quite an impression on one young lady. She was exceedingly obliging in the way of bread, butter, milk, and complimentary remarks, which later, I returned to the best of my ability. I have no doubt that I could have made a rebel of her if I had tried. She was altogether the best looking girl I saw, but I would not consider her good looking out of Pennsylvania. Like all Yankee girls she had a certain degree of sharpness and wit. She had great confidence in the ability of the Yankee army to drive us out of Pennsylvania; and when I told her "good bye," she very naively told me "to be sure and call and see her on my return if I was not in too big a hurry." I did not happen to come back by that road or I certainly should have accepted her invitation.

The men whom we met, who were almost all Dutch, were certainly the most cowardly wretches I ever saw. They all professed to be Democrats, or Copperheads, as they are now called, and said they were anxious for peace on any terms. I was impressed with the idea, that they desired to save their property from impressment on any terms; would tell any tale and act any part to effect that result. Lee's lenient policy caused their representations to be taken as truth, and except what was absolutely needed for the sustenance and transportation of the army, private property was carefully respected. A few wretches, who have no property to lose, and who saw from our actions that we did not molest unarmed men, proclaimed themselves Lincoln men, and as anxious for our subjugation, but there were but a few of them.

We were ordered from York to near Gettysburg to join the main army, which was making preparations to attack Gen. Meade's army, which was posted around that place. About nine o'clock on the morning of the first of July, we attacked the Yankees six miles from Gettysburg, and after a bloody battle drove them through the town to the heights beyond. In the first days' fight we captured about 10,000 prisoners, and killed and wounded at least 15,000 more. I acted with Gen. Gordon during the fight, and was fortunate enough to pass through safely. Had we pressed our advantage that night, I am convinced that we would have taken the heights and routed the Yankee army, but for some reason Gen. Lee would not allow us to advance, but made us lie upon our arms during the night and part of the next day following.

About four o'clock the next day our division was ordered to storm the heights. I have been under several pretty hot fires, but I never saw anything that was equal to this. We had to advance up a steep [Cemetery] hill, under the fire of between sixty and seventy pieces of artillery, and against the flower of the Federal infantry, behind entrenchments which they had thrown up the night before. The loss of life was terrific on both sides. We gained the entrenchments, but were so crippled that we could not hold them, and had to fall back. Our grand charge was made after dark, and it was truly magnificent. The tremendous roar, the shrieking of shells and the whistling of bullets, together with the glare and flashes of the guns, made up a scene that was splendid, were it only a little less dangerous. Generally speaking, in battles I have thought that every body but myself was in the most imminent danger—but on this night it seemed to me that I would be struck every minute—it did not seem possible for any one to escape. We fell back about five hundred yards from the Yankee entrenchments, and lay upon our arms all night. That night was one of the saddest I ever spent. It was the first time I had ever been engaged in a fight of any size, where we had not been completely successful. Added to that, our own wounded, and those of the enemy, lay on the battle-field in front of us, where neither party could get to them. All night long their shrieks and groans could be heard, and it seemed so hard to be unable to afford them any relief. On the same day one of Longstreet's divisions stormed the heights on the opposite side from us, with the same want of success.

On the 3rd of July, other divisions of the army attempted to take the heights but were unsuccessful. Gen. Lee then concluded to desist. On the 4th of July we quietly and slowly drew off, and fell back in good order, towards Hagerstown, Md. The enemy was so badly crippled that he did not follow us with much vigor—his cavalry keeping at a very respectful distance from our rear.

Our loss in the battles around Gettysburg, in killed, wounded and missing, I think will amount to about fifteen thousand. We lost ten Generals killed, wounded and captured. The *Yankee* loss I think, was about twenty-five thousand in killed and wounded, and they lost 12,000 prisoners. They lost no less that eighteen Generals in killed, wounded and captured.

Our army by no means consider that we were whipped, but we feel considerable mortification from the fact that it was the first time that we ever attempted to do a thing and failed. We have still a large and well disciplined army, and we feel that we can whip the Yankees yet. I believe, however, that our late reverses will lengthen the war considerably. We will have a great deal more of hard fighting, and will have to lose a great many more valuable lives. I believe, however, that we will ultimately succeed. We lay in line of battle three days at Hagerstown, waiting for the Yankees to attack us, but they would not gratify us. So we recrossed the Potomac at Williamsport, and passed through Martinsburg to this camp, where we have rested for the last two days. From present indications, I would not be surprised if we went into Maryland again this summer. If we do, look out for desperate fighting.

*** .

TWENTY-SIXTH GEORGIA INFANTRY
[GORDON'S BRIGADE, EARLY'S DIVISION]
CAMP NEAR BERRYVILLE, VA., July 20, 1863 [8-5-63SR]

On the 22nd day of June Gen. Early's division crossed the Potomac, near Shepardstown, the divisions of Generals Johnson and Rodes (with which Early's division constitutes the 2nd Army Corps) having proceeded the whole corps took up the line of march in the direction of the Pennsylvania line, passing through Sharpsburg, Boonesborough, Smithville and other villages in the State of Maryland. On the evening of the 24th we were camped at a small place scarcely deserving the name of a village, yet bearing the name of Greenwood, Franklin county, Pennsylvania. On the morning of the 26th Gordon's brigade was detached from the division and proceeded in the direction of Wrightsville, which is situated on the Susquehanna river at the point where the Baltimore & Ohio [Pennsylvania Central] Railroad crosses that stream. Our route lay through Gettysburg, Abbottstown, York and other unimportant villages and through fields of waving grain sufficiently ripened for the hand of the harvester. From the imperfect view which I had of the country and its inhabitants in thus passing through it, I know of nothing which I could name for which it is more noted than its fine grain, nice large cherries, Dutch farmers and ugly females. If the other portions of the State are to be judged by this, I should express it as my conviction that handsome females were much more scarce than Copperheads.

We met with no enemy to resist our progress, about one thousand of the Governor's militia were assembled in Gettysburg, but on the approach of our brigade, they took to their heels and probably did not stop until they hid behind their *curtin* [Pennsylvania Governor, Andrew G. Curtin] in Harrisburg. Not being as well trained and practiced in running as the soldiers of Hooker's army, some few of them could not make the time required for their escape and were consequently captured. On the afternoon of the 28th, the brigade arrived before Wrightsville, where we found fifteen hundred more of the militia, who had thrown breastworks across the road with the apparent function of disputing our passage. Four rifled pieces of artillery accompanied the brigade; these were divided and stationed at two different points, while the brigade was ordered into line of battle, not more than a dozen shots were fired by our artillery, when the line was ordered forward, our skirmishers who preceded us, found that the enemy had deserted his works and retreated towards the town; we immediately followed after, but arrived there too late to catch the game, for when a Yankee does run, he can outrun anybody, and there is no use in trying to catch him by a stern chase, you have either to head him off or give it up as a hopeless case. On reaching the town we found that the Yankees had crossed the stream, setting fire to the bridge on their retreat, which was totally destroyed. This was a costly structure, one and a fourth miles in length, and costing over one million of dollars.

On the 29th, the brigade continued towards York, at which place it rejoined the division. The evening of the 30th found us camped within seven miles of Gettysburg. At an early hour on the morning of the 1st, we moved in the direction of that place; our movements were slow and cautious, and seemed to indicate the close proximity of the enemy. We arrived in the vicinity of the town about eleven o'clock a. m.; the brigade was immediately formed in line of battle with the exception of the 26th regiment, which was taken to support a battery, but was relieved from this position in the course of half an hour and rejoined the remainder of the brigade which had been steadily driving the Yankees before them toward the town. By the time the 26th became reunited with the brigade, the heaviest of the fighting was over upon this part of the line. The brigade well sustained its hard-earned reputation for valor and courage as was attested by the lifeless bodies of between two and three hundred Yankees that marked a path over which the brigade swept in its onward course, besides numberless wounded whom the enemy could not secure in consequence of the rapid advance of our troops. Many prisoners also were taken. It was during the engagement that evening that Maj. [Peter Brennan] Bransen of the 61st, and Capt. [William L.] McLeod commanding the 38th, fell to rise no more, but they fell where the brave and the heroic ever fall upon the field of battle, at their posts. The Federals were forced to abandon their entire line, often retiring at a run; they were driven beyond the town, their left swung round, and in the movement, describing the arc of a circle, beginning at a point west of the town and extending southward in a regular curve.

At a point southeast of the town, are some heights which command every other position around, and was undoubtedly the most advantageous position that the enemy could have secured; their whole line was forced back to this point upon and near which they concentrated all their forces, both infantry and artillery. On the morning of the 2nd, the brigade was stationed upon the extreme left of our lines, but was removed from this point late in the evening, and ordered to hold a position between the town and the heights occupied by the army; we reached this position about twilight, while their batteries constantly threw shells across our pathway, and the flash of their guns lighted up the hilltop between us. The next morning a slight change was made by moving our brigade further to the right, thus placing a hilltop between us and the enemies batteries, the only protection that we had. We lay in this position until about three o'clock in the morning of the 4th, when the brigade was ordered to retire; passing through the town with the remainder of Gen. Early's division; we were placed in position upon a line crossing the National [Chambersburg] Turnpike at right angles, and distant from the town one and a half miles, the division of Gen. Rodes being in position half a mile to our front. The enemy had suffered too severely on the three preceding days, to cause them to desire a renewal of the conflict, and the day passed without any demonstration being made by them.

At two o'clock on Saturday night, the whole army was in motion, directing its course towards the South Mountain, Early's division bringing up the rear, Gordon's brigade forming the rear of the division, and the 26th Regiment the rear of the brigade.

Being thus in the rear, with long lines of artillery, trains of wagons, and heavy columns of troops in our front, of course our progress was necessarily slow. We did not make more than seven or eight miles that day, leaving the enemy an ample opportunity to press upon, annoy and harass us during the day. They seemed, however, to be quite wary in their approach, and our rear was undisturbed until late in the afternoon [of July 5], when their nearness made it necessary for the deployment of the Twenty-sixth, as skirmishers, which was promptly done, holding the two left companies in reserve. Our skirmishers advanced with rapidity and spirit, and were soon engaged with those of the enemy, driving them back for a considerable distance—their artillery at the same time throwing shells in goodly numbers at our retreating column, which, fortunately did no damage. In this skirmish some few of our men were wounded, among them Lt. [Charles S.] Walker, of Co. F, who fell into the hands of the enemy. The supposition is that Capt. [Ezekiel W.] Crocker and Lt. [J. T.] Hughes, of Co. I, were also captured. Some few of the enemy were killed and several wounded by our skirmishers, who were withdrawn half an hour after they were deployed. The enemy molested us no more during that day, and we camped at night at the foot of the mountain, which we crossed next day, arriving in the vicinity of Hagerstown on the 7th.

Saturday, the 11th, found us in line of battle near that place, and in such a position as to render an attack by the enemy rather desirable than otherwise, but he exhibited greater caution than courage, and the quiet along our line remained unbroken.

At twilight on the evening of the 13th, we abandoned this position and retired towards Williamsport, which place we reached about sunrise next morning, and crossed the Potomac.

Our present place of encampment near Darkeville, which would not have been inappropriately named if it had been called Darkville. It may be that I am writing from the shady side of this community. Be this as it may, I do not cherish any remarkable degree of affection for the spot; nor can I for any others, where the people (or a majority of them, perhaps) seem to believe that the world is kept in motion, and that all its internal machinery is governed, regulated and kept in proper working order through the agency of Abraham Lincoln and "greenback."

VERITAS.

Official casualty figures for the Battle of Gettysburg: Federals reported 3,155 killed, 14,529 wounded and 5,365 missing for a total of 23,049; Confederates reported 2,592 killed, 12,709 wounded, and 5,150 missing for 20,451, but their total losses may be as high as 28,000.

LETTER FROM TOUT LE MONDE

CAMP NEAR CHANCELLORSVILLE, VA., August 9, 1863 [8-17-63SR]

We are now partly on the great battle-field of Chancellorsville, where not many months ago our immortal men made the vandals "come out o' the wilderness." A part of Gen. Hood's division is guarding the U. S. Ford, or are in striking distance of it and also convenient to any point at which the enemy may aim on the favorite line of Gen. Lee along the Rappahannock. Everything is in readiness for the enemy's advance, let it be soon or late. Just such a disposition of our forces is made that he can not surprise any point on this line without having a serious matter of it before he can accomplish much. At the same time the inside line being shorter than the enemy's to Richmond, any sudden demonstration on that point would very soon be met by a counter demonstration by General Lee, no matter from what point he strikes. As it is, everything is said be quiet along the lines, including the noisy cavalry rows that are being enacted constantly with more "fuss" than blood by a great deal. It is said cannon were heard in the direction of Culpeper C. H. to-day, but the men go to sleep taking of it, saying, "Pshaw! that's nothing but cavalry." Any farmer can recall the ludicrous engagements that sometimes occur between two hostile Guinea fowls—in fact one may say every one has seen this excellent illustration of a cavalry battle, in which a combatant flees until the other stops and then pursues till time to flee again, and so on.

It is not necessary or interesting to say how many forces are near Fredericksburg, but it may be said some have traveled again over those grounds which history will hand down to every age to come. Yes, the sacred grounds of the gloomy "wilderness" were passed where the graves of the foe hold the dead quietly, and our own immortal patriots sleep sweetly on their glory. The enemy's works are still plainly visible facing in every direction, a plain exhibition of the trepidation which seized him when Jackson's cannon began to thunder behind his right flank. The works look north, south, east, west, in fact to every point of the compass, as though the approach of the terrible Rebel General was expected to be ubiquitous. Private holes in banks by the wayside and other steep places seemed designed to hold the carcass of some precious Yankee coward whose heart smote him when the Rebel shells began to fill the air with their awful screams. The knapsacks of the dead, fragments of cast off clothes, broken rammers of some murderous cannon, pieces of shells, whole Shrapnel shot and other indications of the once terrific battle-field still strew the wayside of the old plank road. The carcasses of the dead horses have not yet ceased to emit offensive odors, and the forest trees are marked where the cannon shot raged, by the dead branches, torn, shattered, and withered to an Autumn hue by the Summer's sun. But, standing by the red clay batteries on Marye's Hill, the scene is one of greater desolation. Everywhere the forests have disappeared, and the young, precocious shrubs of Spring and Summer have clothed the earth in a matted undergrowth. The numerous army of the South that once could be seen peopling every hill and dell are gone, except an occasional soldier, who, straggling from his distant camp, is observed plodding the dreary roads. The fields are bare of grain, the fencing all gone, and the rank weeds of neglect—a kind effort of nature to fill the void—supply the place of cultivation. Across the river the distant hills beyond the devoted little city stand out, and the bare untravelled roads of the enemy's make still checker the country in every direction. Grim fortifications frown along the line, but no cannon are there to make the frowns impressive. 'Tis not difficult, though, for one who has seen them as in days gone by, when they looked from a hundred embrazures, to imagine them looking fiercely over into our lines, even while gazing into their vacancies across the sultry fields. It was mid-day, and the August sun was pouring out his utmost effulgence, as the command wound around the formidable hills of the old line. One saw the former scenes through the clouds of dust that filled the air, and through the mist of heat that radiated from the ground, which made strange feelings of desolation and desertion come over us.

But the prospect was not improved by a visit alone to the city. What do you see? As you wind round the hill—under Marye's height—you come on the stone fence where Cobb fought the Irishmen. The field is there over grown with weeds, where the drunken hirelings came, and the Georgians slew them, looking very grave. Its glory is marred because its price was our beloved fellow-citizen and statesman Cobb, and the good Georgian who looks on it must turn away in sadness. Pass on to the town, through the lanes and streets half covered with weeds and grass. A few pigeons are seen fluttering before you, or sailing about the housetops, quite solitary. In the city, now and then, you see, maybe a group of citizens, maybe soldiers on duty, sitting leisurely under some shades discussing common topics. Up and down the dusty ways is the absence of every sign of animation or bustle—trade, commerce, industry, all gone. It was a grateful relief in passing out to hear the tinkling of the only blacksmith's solitary hammer in the city just on the suburbs. Closed doors look you blandly and sorrowfully in the face wherever you turn. A few of the inhabitants have come back in the hope that their cup of sorrow and suffering had passed. Has it?

Passing by a nice dwelling on Common street the merry melody of a piano was heard. The memories it brought were of home—of friends—of "days that are no more." Drawing near to listen, astonishment took the place of delight when it was discovered that the fair performer inside was rendering "Jim Crack Corn, Don't Care" in a style that denoted little regard for the pressing emergencies of the times. Besides a great hole was visible in one of the closed shutters, where the fragment of a bomb had torn its way through into the parlor. But that was common in every house, and, no doubt, to this the inhabitants, like the soldier to death, has grown indifferent and unmindful of it. The old church steeples still bear the marks of vandalism and Yankee meanness. Cannon balls have pierced them through and through in many places. On the banks of the river the crumbled houses show the signs of the fierce bombardment that was opened on the place before the famous crossing in December. Our pickets sit among the weeds and in the old deserted walls there now, watching across the water. With the help of your fancy, see how it stands.

The enemy are said to have no pickets lower than the United States Ford. Probably he is not going to advance for sometime yet. He will, doubtless, wait for the drafted fools. It was rumored in camp—yes, the report of a scout—that transports were seen on the 7th passing down the Potomac. Probably reinforcements for Charleston. Their hearts are set on that place, and may they never get it but in ashes—if at all. Probably before this reaches you the base of old Sumter will rock again under her thunder. If "a body" had anything, he'd take "something" to her good luck.

TOUT LE MONDE.

LETTER FROM LEE'S ARMY

NEAR SUMMERVILLE FORD, VA., August 10, 1863 [8-26-63AWCS]

We arrived at this camp on the 6th of this month. We do not know for what purpose we were ordered here, how long we will remain, nor when or where we go; neither do we care. Our confidence in our leaders assures us that "all is right." The encampment of McLaws' division is situated about eleven miles from Orange Court House, and about twenty-two miles from Fredericksburg.

There is a perfect news famine in the army. No incident worthy of note has transpired since we took up the line of march from Culpeper, on the morning of the 3rd, save the repulse of the enemy at Brandy Station, on the 7th, by a portion of Stuart's cavalry, in which we sustained a very trifling loss.

The health of the army is excellent. Many disabled by disease and wounds during our campaign into Maryland and Pennsylvania have recovered, and returned to duty. The Army of Northern Virginia is almost numerically as strong, and its spirits quite as buoyant and confident as before that campaign began.

Our reverse at Gettysburg, or more properly speaking, our failure to achieve such a complete and decided victory as has heretofore attended our arms, has in no wise depressed our hopes, nor abated one jot our confidence in our chieftain; nor created a doubt as to our future success, and the final triumph of our cause. If that spirit of determination which pervaded this army to endure any hardship and privation, to do all and dare all for our country's good, characterized in a corresponding degree the feelings and actions of the people at home, peace would soon overlay our land, as the "morning spreads upon the mountains."

But we find in almost every paper that reaches us, and they are few, murmuring and complaints against the President or some department of the government, or against some one of our Generals. Croakers of this character really appear to be almost as numerous as the frogs of Egypt. These evidences of disaffection and distrust are well calculated to depress our hopes, and to mar our anticipations of future success; but fortunately for the cause in which we are engaged, they have no influence upon the army, further than to excite our derision and even scorn for those who wanting either in patriotism or courage to defend their own rights and protect their own liberties, withhold counsel and encouragement from those who stand in the breach.

To those who have watched the progress of events, it is apparent that every reverse which we have sustained from the commencement of this war, was owing to the want of men. This want is not felt to a greater extent than of any previous period of our history. The enemy is marshaling his host of minions against us. Every effort has been put forth to increase his army. Conscious of our superior courage and skill upon the battle field, and of our capacity to endure the hardships of the service, he will never again fight us upon equal terms, but vainly hopes by overpowering numbers to consummate the work of our subjugation.

But our ranks still remain depleted. Some regiments have been reduced by actual casualties in battle to not more than two hundred effective men. In vain have they called for help. It seems that every effort that a man's ingenuity can invent has been resorted to by some to keep out of the service. Substitutes are obtained at most extravagant rates. Government contracts, however insignificant the profits, and appointments in commissary and quartermaster's departments are eagerly sought after. Every contemptible artifice and device is invoked to keep away from the battle field. When we consider what we are fighting for, it is amusing that any lukewarmness should be manifested; that any man with a spark of patriotism in his soul or courage in his heart can remain an idle spectator whilst battles are being fought involving such mighty issues. Base hankerings after money seem to have engrossed the minds and hearts of very many of our people, even whilst the country is bleeding at every pore.

How many men have become shoemakers, tanners, blacksmiths, wheelwright's, &c., who possess no skill in those trades, and who have assumed to follow them simply to evade the operation of the conscript law?

How many men long residing in our State, have sworn that it was not their residence and that they did not intend to remain in it? A very large proportion of our foreign population have the credentials of some European consulate in their pockets. Their liability to service seems to be a question free from all difficulty. Having resided amongst us for a long term of years, enjoying the benefits and protection of the government, and appealing to its courts whenever their rights of person or property have been assailed, they in turn are clearly subject to serve that government whenever the vindication of its rights or its honor demand their services. It is not necessary to refer to vague and rather undefined principles of international law to determine the liability of this class of our citizens to military service. The convention of the sovereign people of Georgia which adopted the ordinance of secession, also passed an ordinance declaring that all persons not born in that State would be held to be citizens, who did not within ninety days from the passage of the same, file an affidavit in a court of record that they did not intend to be citizens. This ordinance is as much a part of the organic law of our State as its Constitution. The power that made the one ordained the other. All persons, therefore, of foreign birth who resided in Georgia at that time and who failed to avail themselves of the exception contained in the ordinance referred to, are to all intents and purposes citizens as though they were to the manor born. They can vote or do any other act that any other citizens may do. The simple omission to file the required affidavit makes them citizens as perfectly and completely, as if they had been naturalized in conformity with laws heretofore existing. Why then are not these men enrolled for the service?

Will the patriotic and urgent appeal of the President go unheeded? Men we want, and men we must have. Fill up our regiments, and the sun of our independence will soon shine upon a redeemed and liberated people. I have thus hastily alluded to these grave subjects with the hope of directing attention to them. My apology is the want of something else to write about.

CORPORAL.

On August 1, in an effort to fill depleted ranks, President Jefferson Davis issued a proclamation granting amnesty to all deserters if they reported to their commands within twenty days.

A DESERTER'S CONFESSION [8-17-63SR]

Editor Republican: My conscience forces me to make public the following confession: I am a soldier in the Confederate service. I was a volunteer on the 4th of March, 1862, and received my bounty of $50. I should have been among the first volunteers without bounty, but that I had a large family and was a poor man. But I was anxious to be freed from the yoke of the Yankees as any one, so am I now. But I loved home and the dear wife and children, and the snug little farm which had always furnished us an ample support. I was sent to Virginia with my regiment soon after the battles around Richmond. We went with Gen. Lee (God bless the glorious old chief,) in the campaign in Northern Virginia and Maryland. My Captain always selected me as one for any important duty. This brought many hardships and perils, notwithstanding I was proud to be thus distinguished among my comrades, for I went to discharge my duty and help to gain our independence as far as I could. But in an evil hour I began to give way to dreams of home. The dear wife, six lovely children, the snug little home— were they all doing well? I feared not. I continued to dream and think of home. I had not heard from home in a long time. I asked for a furlough for 30 days. I thought it would and ought to be granted. The application failed. I was sadly disappointed, and yielding in an evil hour, deserted. Every man who looked me in the face seemed to say "*deserter*" to himself, as I was on my way home. I was never half so unhappy in my life, notwithstanding the near prospect of home. I went on, thinking the pleasures of home would quell the goadings of conscience. When I arrived, such a welcome greeting shone on the face of my wife and children! How happy for the moment! "My dear James," said my wife, seating herself upon my knee and putting her arm round my neck, "how glad we are to see you, we have such a good crop, and God has blessed us so while you have been the army. How long is your furlough?" I started as though stung with the fang of a serpent. "What's the matter James?" said my wife; "have you a wound?" I was obliged to confess the whole. "Oh! James! what shall we do? what will the neighbors say? what will General Lee think?" She did not know but General Lee knew me as well as my captain. When a neighbor came about he was sure to ask, "how long is your furlough?" I evaded in some way. I was almost mad.

I saw but a moment's happiness—when my wife first greeted me—until your paper reached me the other day with that glorious proclamation of our glorious President. I sat down and cried like a child. "God bless the President," welled up from my heart with my sobs. After all, he understands the trials and longings for home of the poor soldier, and does not attribute their absence to a desertion of the cause. May God bless him—he is right. My wife read it; we cried together. My arrangements were speedily made, and I am now in your city on my way to join my regiment in Virginia. I have never been reprimanded by an officer. Was in the second battle of Manassas, at Antietam, Fredericksburg and Chancellorsville. I go again to return no more, even if life is spared, until independence is gained.

A SOLDIER.

The amnesty had one condition: no amnesty for second offenders.

PRIVATE LETTER, FROM AN OFFICER OF THE FIFTH ALABAMA REGIMENT
[O'NEAL'S BRIGADE, RODES' DIVISION]
CAMP NEAR ORANGE C. H., VA., August 20, 1863

    Dear Father: Your letter came to hand to-day. There is nothing unusual going on. The company, and I believe the whole army, are in better health and spirits than they have been in the last twelve months. Every day brings down a car load of 1,500 or 2,000 men—many of those who were wounded at Chancellorsville and Gettysburg, many who have been lying off awaiting the blow-over of the big fight, which has been exploded by the Yankee change of base—and a great many who have been absent without leave, having availed themselves of the President's pardon to return unpunished to duty. My opinion as to the status of our present army, compared with 1862, would enlighten you but little. But as you have asked for it, I will try and give you a fair statement of facts in regard to our Pennsylvania campaign. As to the good or evil results, you can judge for yourself. I am inclined to think it was the greatest feat ever accomplished by any army.

    After the battle of Chancellorsville, in which we gained considerable advantages, the enemy were badly demoralized and called loudly for reinforcements, which were furnished by withdrawing troops from the Peninsula, thus relieving Longstreet, who came to our assistance, giving us, temporarily, a numerical advantage. This being a favorable moment for assuming the offensive, that course was determined upon, and on the morning of the 4th of June we moved off, leaving there a small force as a *feint guard.* We gained five days, the enemy not finding out what was going on until the 9th. We reached the Shenandoah Valley, and cut off Milroy with a very available portion of the Yankee troops, clearing the Valley and securing the crossing of the Potomac. We forced the enemy to go circuitously *via* Alexandria. The time thus gained enabled Ewell's corps to cross and march unmolested through Maryland and into Pennsylvania, threatening by the same move Cumberland on the west, Harrisburg on the north, and Washington and Baltimore to the southward.

    The enemy did not know which way to turn. We secured many horses, mules, wagons, cattle, &c., and drew supplies of provisions from the surrounding country. We marched to Carlisle, within fourteen miles of Harrisburg. The enemy concentrated all their outside forces at that place, expecting an attack. We then suddenly crossed the mountains to the right, and came down upon the right flank of Meade, marching twenty-five miles per day. We burst upon the forces who were advanced beyond Gettysburg like a storm, and scattered them like chaff, whipping and routing three of their heavy army corps, with two single divisions of ours. We followed him three miles to the heights in rear of Gettysburg, and certainly, had Longstreet and Hill come on in time to push our advantage gained by the first attack, we would have carried Gettysburg heights, annihilated Meade's army, and, I believe, have taken Washington and Baltimore. But they did not come until after dark. Ewell had attacked too soon; the evil could only be remedied by harder fighting on the morrow.

    During the night of the 1st, re-enforcements from Baltimore and New York with the militia from Harrisburg came in, formidable works were thrown up, and stared us in the face on the second morning. Our lines were completed and with one hundred and twelve guns bearing upon the short and massed ranks of the enemy, the fight opened they replying vigorously with at least two hundred heavy pieces. During the day of the second July, we charged them repeatedly, and gradually gained ground upon their left and centre. On the right Longstreet drove them out of their works for a mile and a half, but finding more formidable works and fresh troops upon a spur of the mountain [Little Round Top], he desisted and fell back, rendering our hard earned advantage worthless. We were withdrawn to our first position during the night. Ammunition and provision were distributed, our cannon positioned more securely, and disposition made for renewing the attack on the morrow. At the first flash of day on the third, the loud roar of three hundred guns burst forth. We again moved forward to the charge, victory wavering first on one side then the other until dark, when we again retired and knew that all our efforts had been fruitless, except to punish the enemy, whose loss was considerably greater than ours. A night attack was immediately determined upon. We again advanced, with empty muskets, to within three hundred yards of the enemy's works without being discovered, not a man faltering, though almost certain death stared him in the face. The order was countermanded, and we retired undiscovered. I believe that we would have carried the Heights had we gone on. I never saw such determination as was expressed by the men. Unless they were really impregnable, they would have been carried.

Our ammunition was exhausted, also our supplies; we had failed to eject the enemy as was intended. The rains of the four days previous had raised the Potomac so as to retard the crossing of our ammunition train. With an acknowledged advantage, we were compelled to fall back and leave the enemy in possession of the field. Our retreat was very leisurely executed, marching six or eight miles per day; and, with the exception of a cavalry raid upon our wagon train, almost unmolested. We halted in line on the 11th, and awaited the fall of the river. On the 14th the river rising, the enemy threatened our rear, our pontoons being up, we recrossed, just two weeks after the fight. Since the crossing we have not seen the Yankees, except in a mountain pass [Manassas Gap], which they got possession of, and for which they paid very dearly. Then, I lost one man from my company, T. D. Helton, killed. We settled down quietly here, offering battle, if the enemy should choose to accept, upon fair terms, no material advantage on either side. They have declined, and yesterday the news came in that they had retired to their entrenched camps. No prospect of a fight soon, unless we again go into Maryland, which I think very probable, this fall. Our armies are the best the world ever saw, and can never be disastrously defeated, whatever the odds may be.

Love to all at home.   G.

HURT'S—HARDAWAY BATTERY
[McINTOSH'S BATTALION, RESERVE ARTILLERY]
HEADQTR'S, ORANGE C. H. VA., August 26, 1863 [9-8-63CS]

Since the army returned to this side of the Potomac, I have often been asked by officers and soldiers from my State whether I did not lose one of my Whitworth guns in Pennsylvania. Not only I, but many of my men have been asked the same question, leaving me to infer that the impression is general that I *did* lose one of the said guns.

Now I deem it a duty due my company no less to my own feelings, to request you to give publicly through the columns of your issue to the following statement.

During the galling fire which was concentrated on my battery on the second day of the battle of Gettysburg the axle of the carriage of one of the Whitworth guns was struck by a fragment of shell and broken in twain. Being disabled, it was sent immediately to the field park for repair and returned to my position on the evening of the 3rd, when I immediately had occasion to commence firing it. After the sixth round the axle was discovered to have been broken again, this time by recoil. As in the other case, it was sent back to the field park under Sergeant Scarbrough, and his detachment followed by the gun's caisson.

When the orders of the 4th, causing the army to be moved off in the direction of Hagerstown were received, the gun in question had not been returned to my command. Leaving the battery under command of Lieut. Crenshaw, I went immediately in search and only found it on the morning of the 5th, on the Pittsburg and Baltimore pike, near the western base of South Mountain. By this time all of the wagon train and most of the ambulances had passed that point. The army—the troops—had moved off by another road. I learned that the repair train had moved off the evening previous before the gun could be repaired, that it was still in an unserviceable condition, and that it had been delayed on its march by continual stoppages, which were necessary in order to wedge the axle to prevent the two-ends from working out of the tree and the carriage from falling upon the ground.

Being *hors de combat* and apprehensive of an attack, I was naturally uneasy and hurried the march of the piece as much as possible without killing my horse. I followed the road that had been taken by Quartermasters, who had turned off the Pittsburg and Baltimore pike at Fayetteville on a mud road to Greencastle. Arrived within eight miles of that place I learned that an attack had been that (5th) day made on our wagon train in my front. This of course heightened my anxiety. But right here the carriages both of gun and caisson had stuck in the mud and my horses—none of which had had corn or other grain for twenty-four hours and some of which had been barefooted since the commencement of this march and were now lame—assisted by all the powers the cannoneers could exert at the wheels, were unable to extricate them. After trying in vain to procure horses from the adjacent farm houses and from the straggling squads of cavalry, I reinforced the moving power of the gun from that of the caisson, and left the rear part of the latter.

By these means only I could and did arrive at Williamsport, Maryland, on the evening of the 6th, just two hours before the enemy, advancing by the same road on which I had come from Greencastle made an attack on that place; during which two hours I succeeded in having the broken axle repaired. And the detachment received the flattery of General Imboden for its service in that action. So that I *did not lose a gun*, but only secured it at the sacrifice of the rear part of a caisson and a little horse flesh. The value of this gun can only be told by the enemy, who has *felt* its execution. I desire you to publish the foregoing communication in order to correct impressions which may have obtained to the effect that any exertion of mine was wanting to save from capture one of the best guns used in the field service of this army.

Respectfully yours,
WM. B. HURT, Capt. Artillery, Ala. Vol.

THIRTY-EIGHTH GEORGIA REGIMENT
[GORDON'S BRIGADE, EARLY'S DIVISION]
IN CAMP, August 28, 1863 [9-9-63AWCS]

A Christian spirit pervades the brigade to an unusual degree. The religious revivals are attended with flattering results—conversations and baptisms being of daily occurrence. Nightly meetings being held in the respective regimental camp grounds, and these contribute much towards the good work. Long may it continue.

What a pleasing contrast is there presented between the Federal and Confederate soldier. The one a foreign mercenary on an errand of plunder, with no higher idea of liberty than the license to satiate a vitiated appetite, and gratify a corrupt lustful nature. The other, called to the field by a sense of honor and the higher obligation of duty, leaves all he holds dear and bares the bosom to the dangers of the battle field willingly, rather than to see his home despoiled by a brutal foe without honor or mercy.

We have learned, with feelings of mortification, that there are those in Georgia who despair of the success of our cause. Shame upon all such. So base a weakness can only emanate from a cowardly nature. We, who have fought at the torn and bloody fields of Coal Harbor [Gaines' Mill], Malvern Hill, Second Manassas, Second Fairfax [Chantilly], Sharpsburg, Fredericksburg, Marye's Heights, Winchester, Gettysburg, and other minor engagements, and added to the galaxy of glorious names, [Marcellus] Douglas, McCreay, [William H.] Battey, [Alexander] Lawton, [Willis] Hawkins, [Peter] Brenan and hosts of others too numerous to mention, are unyielding that our efforts should be fruitless, and the blood of our heroes be spilt in vain. When first the tocsin of war vibrated throughout the borders of our young republic, we rallied beneath the banners that we have so often borne to victory, and beneath whose tattered folds we still intend to battle until that success which is inevitable, crowns our efforts with peace and liberty. "We are ever ready and faithful to the last," and rather than purchase peace at the price of bondage and chains, we are willing to make our beautiful land the grave of liberty.

I am glad to be able to say that the call of the President has been heeded. The roads leading to the different brigade encampments are daily thronged with convalescents returning to duty.

There are some speculations in camps concerning the furloughing of officers and men. It is a subject upon which there is much difference of opinion. If your correspondent is allowed to express his views on the matter, it is briefly this: Both armies are recruiting and marshalling their hosts for another conflict, which will occur between Culpeper and Fredericksburg, or at one of the two places named; for I cannot believe that Gen. Lee will attack them in their entrenchments. We can better afford to await the advance of Meade than do this.

Never was an army more buoyant in spirit or under better discipline than ours. The commissariat is well supplied. We are also being furnished with an excellent stock of clothing and shoes. The only trouble we now have to encounter, is want of forage for army horses. The rail road transportation is insufficient. Something must be done immediately in this connection or great losses will ensue to the Government during the winter. The poor stock cannot weather it, exposed as they necessarily will be to the rigors of this climate. I hope this matter will meet with the consideration due it from the proper authorities.

J. C. C.

☆☆☆Autumn 1863

In early September, Longstreet's corps was detached and sent to reinforce the Army of Tennessee, where it remained until mid-spring 1864. As a result, the Army of Northern Virginia lost most of its offensive punch and had to maintain a chessboard war of maneuver with only lessor known battles fought at Bristoe Station, Rappahannock Station and Mine Run.

SIXTEENTH MISSISSIPPI INFANTRY,
THE SCOFFER REBUKED
[POSEY'S BRIGADE, ANDERSON'S DIVISION]

Attached to Company "K", 16th Mississippi regiment, (Wilkinson Rifles) was an old negro man, familiarly known throughout the camp as "Uncle Dan." Uncle Dan, besides his good qualities as a body servant and faithful friend to his young master, to whom he was sincerely attached, was a devout Christian. He had been often heard to say, that when his "young marster went off to jine de wars, his ole marster and missus placed their son in *his* charge, with strict injunctions to stay with, and be a friend to him through sickness and health, and if it was his young marster's fate to be killed, to preserve the body and take it home." "And dis," said Uncle Dan, "I will do, de Lord permitting."

As was the custom, the Regimental Chaplain visited the street of Company "D" one evening for the purpose of holding prayer meeting; "Uncle Dan" was of course present, and the Chaplain could not have found among the boys a more attentive or devout hearer than the old negro. The service being ended, Dan was surrounded by a crowd, and was being eagerly questioned by the boys as to his intended conduct, (there being a fight expected.)

"Young marsters," said Dan, "You know not what a day may bring forth; to-morrow you 'spects to be in fight wid de Yankees, and none of you I dar say hab said your prayers. How does you know but dat you will be killed; am you prepared to meet the Great Judge and perhaps be sent to eternal damnation?"

Among the boys was one who was ever full of fun, ready for a frolic or fight, and withal an excellent young man, but one who, as Dan had said, was totally unprepared to enter Eternity. Young ---had been attempting to tease old Dan, and said:

"Well, old Methodist, as you are so much concerned about our after fate, supposing you pray for us. But if you do, I may certainly expect you to steal my last chicken to-night."

Dan said he would, and announced—"Let us pray."

The writer, who was a witness to the whole of the scene, had heard some of the most celebrated divines in the South, but never had he listened to a prayer offered to the Most High with such fervency, with so much emphasis, as was made by the old negro under the starry canopy of that October night, on Virginia soil. The old man prayed as only those thoroughly imbued with Christian zeal can pray. After his orisons for his young master and his natural protectors at home, with those present, had been offered, he prayed for our thoughtless young friend. That God might change and give him a better heart, and cultivate in him the true light of Christianity, so that when he was called from this earth, be it in battle or among his friends at home, he would be found ready.

A death-like stillness pervaded during the prayer, and when the old negro rose from his knees, young ----advanced, with tears in his eyes, grasped old Dan by the hand, saying: "My good old mother taught me when a child to pray to God; since growing up, she has admonished men, and always endeavored to instill in my mind the necessity of religion, and I have passed her counsel by. Boys, I am not naturally wicked, but heedless, thoughtless. To jest on religion again, I never shall. Uncle Dan, you have learned me a lesson, and shown me what I am; and by your prayer for me to-night, I am hereafter a changed man."

The shrill tattoo that instant separated us, but we were all visibly affected by the scene, and turned away to the soldier's duty, with old Dan's heartfelt prayer feeling its way down, down into our hearts.

The scoffer was rebuked, and never again was he heard to lightly speak of his Maker, or of religion, by those in camp, or by an old member of the 16th.

MISSISSIPPI.

A STRANGE STORY

CAMP PRICE, GREENBRIER CO., [West Virginia] VA., September 13, 1863 [9-24-63MAD]

To gratify the lovers of the curious and wonderful, I have concluded to give you a short and accurate description, as received from the witnesses themselves, of a strange phenomenon that made its appearance about ten miles west of Lewisburg, on the afternoon of the 1st inst.

Mr. Moses Dwyer, an honest and responsible farmer, whose veracity is unimpeachable; Mrs. Percy, who seems to have a very clear head and is a lady of respectability and character, as are the two other ladies who witnessed the phenomenon, were the persons from whom the following account was obtained. It was also witnessed by a youth, almost grown, and by a servant girl. They all testify, substantially, to the same facts, and are perfectly willing to be sworn to the truth of the statement made to me.

The day was bright, clear and warm. The locality a hill or mountain side, on which the sun was shining with full power. The first thing seen was something that the witnesses do not seem able to describe with clearness and accuracy. They say it was masses or bodies of vapor, mist, or something else, five or six feet high and two or three wide, floating in a perpendicular position, above the tree tops, moving on in a line with the utmost regularity and precision; then, passing through the tree tops, without having the line broken or disturbed. These bodies are described as being of a whitish, green color, and passed off in the distance. Then came a countless multitude of men, dressed in white, marching in column, on the ground, through an open field, up the mountain slope, at a rapid pace, quicker than double time, the columns only separated by a few feet. The witnesses state that they could see the men not only as a whole, but the individual parts—their heads, arms, legs and feet. Occasionally one would lag a little behind, and could be distinctly seen to quicken his pace to regain his position in the line. They were passing for an hour or more, and, it is thought, numbered thousands upon thousands. The field over which they passed is several hundred yards in length, and they covered the entire area in passing. Their general appearance was white, and they were without arms or knapsacks.

I have given the simple facts without coloring or exaggeration, as received from eye-witnesses of the strange sight. No person in this community doubts or questions the veracity of the witnesses, known as they are to be of highly respectable characters and entitled to credit. All agree that they saw something out of the ordinary course of nature.

X.

FIFTEENTH ALABAMA REGIMENT

[LAW'S BRIGADE, HOOD'S DIVISION]

NEAR FREDERICKSBURG, VA., September 7, 1863 [9-17-63CS]

Few regiments in the army of Northern Virginia have performed more arduous service than the 15th Alabama, now attached to Laws' Brigade, and commanded by that accomplished soldier and officer, Colonel Wm. C. Oates; and none are in a better condition for future services than that to which this gentleman has brought his command.

Leaving the walks of civic life at the breaking out of the war, without any previous military training, Col. Oates, by his natural talent and assiduous application, has become the equal of many who have made arms their profession; and I presume no officer could be found who possesses more fully the confidence of his superiors. This confidence has been created and justified by the capacity he has shown for the duties of every position he has been called to fill.

To form a correct estimate of Col. Oates as a tactician, one has only to witness the evolutions of his regiment, under his charge, on the field. The most difficult maneuvers are executed with a precision and rapidity that would not be discreditable to the veterans of a standing army. It is really a pleasure to see the performances of the 15th on the drill ground.

As an administrating officer, Col. Oates possesses rare qualities. A single fact places them in a clear light. For several months the duties of Quartermaster, and for part of the same time, those of commissary, besides those of a commanding officer, rested upon him; yet he sustained and discharged them all fully and sufficiently, aided only by officers detailed from the regiment, who had little acquaintance with those departments. Unlike many others, Col. Oates extends his personal supervision in every thing connected with the command; and the result is, an organization efficient in every respect.

As a disciplinarian, he is strict, but attentive to the wants and comforts of his men; and is severe to individuals only when the good of the service demands that he should be so. Like all faithful officers he has his seasons of unpopularity; but as a general rule he has the regard as well as respect of his men.

His courage and coolness has been evinced on nearly every battle-field in Virginia. At Gettysburg, as his regiment was retiring from the field, after the action, he fell, overpowered by heat and exhaustion, as did many other prominent officers on that day; but was no sooner recovered, than he hastened to resume his position at the head of his column.

Col. Oates has had, since entering the service, flattering opportunities for advancement in political life; but, he has turned away from them, preferring, while the war lasts, to serve his country in the field, and there to devote his energies to the establishment of our independence.

It is to be regretted that we have not in our midst more men like him; and the highest interests of our country demand that such should be, whenever and wherever found, allowed an ample field for the exercise of their talents and energies.

ORDNANCE.

PRIVATE LETTER FROM VIRGINIA,
THIRD ALABAMA REGIMENT

CAMP NEAR ORANGE COURT HOUSE, VA., September 10, 1863 [10-1-63MAR]

My Dear Mother: You may imagine that your letter was most welcome, being the first intelligence I have had from home since my return to my regiment, now two months since. Yesterday there was a grand review of the 2d "corps d'armee." Battle's brigade was formed at nine o'clock A. M., and we marched to General Rodes' headquarters, where the division was formed. We then marched to a vast open plain, a mile to the north of the town of Orange, where the whole corps of Ewell was assembled; the corps was then drawn up in three lines, Early's being first, Rodes' second, and Johnson's division the third line. I suppose the corps numbered fully thirty thousand men. After the whole corps was formed, the ranks were opened, and we were reviewed by Generals Lee and Ewell. This occupied several hours, as the Generals, accompanied by their staffs, had to ride down the ranks of each division, which was many miles of hard riding. After this was over, the whole corps wheeled into column of companies, and passed in review. The regiments of our brigade were divided into eight companies to a regiment; this took about five hours. After the corps had passed in review, and each division had reached its place in line, the ranks were again opened and ordered to present arms, and the review dismissed. It was really a grand sight to see the whole corps, thirty thousand men, drawn up in an open field. The three corps commanders were present, Gen. Stuart, and nearly all the division commanders of the army of Northern Virginia. It was a hard day's work, and it was quite dark when we reached camp, and the men were much fatigued. About fifteen brass bands were present, and when the corps was passing in review, every field and brass band struck up, making a considerable confusion of noises. Some of the brass bands of this corps are the finest I ever saw.

You have heard discouraging accounts from Lee's army you say—believe *nothing* of the kind. I never saw the army in better spirits, in better health, and more confident, than at the present time.

No desertions occur now, at all, the army is nearly as strong as it was before the battle of Gettysburg, and in order to show you the increasing condition of our army, our regiment carried out of Pennsylvania one hundred and fifty men, and at this time there are nearly four hundred men in camp. The same may be said of the other regiments. As for the boys being low spirited and *demoralized*, I declare, I have not heard *one word* of grumbling since I rejoined the army. The grumblers are all *at the home* of the men who are doing the fighting, and not among those who are under-going the danger and hardships. I have heard men say here that they would rather shoot "a croaker" than a Yankee.

This army will not accept peace on any terms, but the recognition of the Confederate States. It is true, there was a *great deal* of dissatisfaction among some of the North Carolina troops, whose homes, since the breaking out of the war, has been in the possession of the enemy, and that portion of the State is the most disloyal of the Confederacy. These men were among the first volunteers, and joined, as they supposed, the strongest side. The greater portion of the North Carolina troops are the best soldiers that we have in the field, and on every battle field in Virginia the blood of North Carolina has poured out more freely than that of any other State, there being more North Carolinians in this army than troops from any other State. This fact contributes largely towards rendering the army of Northern Virginia invincible.

It is truly gratifying to see the progress of religion in this army; revivals are going on at this time. We have a new Chaplain to our regiment, he is from Tuskegee, Ala. We have preaching and prayer meetings regularly every night. Nearly the whole brigade attends, and hundreds go up nightly to be prayed for, and many are being converted. A "Christian Association" has been formed, and Gen. Battle is President—a large number have already joined from our regiment. On Tuesday last I attended preaching at a country church, about five miles from camp; the church was crowded with soldiers and citizens, among them a number of ladies—a protracted meeting was going on. We had an excellent sermon, after which mourners were called up, and while the congregation were singing a good old hymn, nearly half of the soldiers who were present went up to be prayed for. It was a most affecting sight, and brought tears from the eyes of every woman in the house, (and there were not a few) to see those stout hearts touched, who never quailed in battle.

"All is quiet along the Potomac" at this time. We get along splendidly, and have plenty to eat and to wear.

Your affectionate son,   D. S. T.

SECOND GEORGIA BATTALION

[WRIGHT'S BRIGADE, ANDERSON'S DIVISION]

IN CAMP NEAR ORANGE C. H., VA., Saturday, September 12, 1863 [9-22-63CS]

There has nothing of interest occurred to break the dull monotony of camp life, since I last wrote. Every day the word is brought down, "all quiet in front." Our pickets on the Rappahannock are on very friendly terms with Meade's conscripts and substitutes; they exchange papers, and give tobacco for coffee, etc., etc. The army is still recruiting, and is now in fine fighting trim. We get full rations now, which is beef, flour and salt, and sometimes rice, sugar and peas. So you see we are living high, for it is not everybody that can eat beef and buy sugar these hard times. Our Quartermaster, also, has a good supply of clothing now on hand, and, while in camp here, we have determined to play the gentleman a while, and put on a *white* shirt at least *every two weeks*. The boys are in fine health and spirits. A. P. Hill's corps was reviewed yesterday by Gen. Lee. It was a grand sight; and while Uncle Bob was reviewing us, we were reviewing the fair damsels of Orange who came out to witness the grand sight.

Capt. Chas. J. Moffett, of our company, has been promoted to the Majorship of the Battalion, vice Geo. W. Ross, killed at Gettysburg. Lieut. H. M. Sapp has been promoted to the Captaincy, vice C. J. Moffett, promoted. Both promotions have given general satisfaction, and especially the latter. Too much cannot be said, in the praise of this gallant young officer, and were I to attempt to paint to you with my feeble pen, his many virtues, I feel assured that I would do him great injustice. Suffice it to say, he is every inch a soldier, and possesses all those noble qualities which go to make up the true soldier and gentleman. He is kind and courteous to all, and I believe he would willingly share his last morsel of bread, or his last dollar, with the lowest private in the ranks.

Below you will find a synopsis of his address to the company when he took command. It was received with three hearty cheers for Capt. Sapp:

My Friends: —In assuming the command of this company, of which I have been so long a member, a few words will not be inappropriate or unacceptable. Whilst I am not elevated to the Captaincy directly by your votes, I feel, nevertheless, that I am indebted to you for the promotion. More than a year ago you honored me with the position of a Lieutenant, and my rank has gradually increased, until I am entitled, by seniority, to the chief command. I make to you, therefore, my grateful acknowledgments, and assure you that the honor of having such a body of men under me as compose this company, fills me with a pride to which I cannot give suitable expression.

Long, long ago, we left home together to meet and repel the enemies and invaders of our country. I am proud of the reputation you have achieved. You have borne yourselves gallantly wherever you have encountered the foe, and entitled yourselves to the admiration and gratitude of your countrymen. Your trials and sufferings have been endured with that heroic fortitude which marks and distinguishes the true patriot and soldier. Heaven grant that you may all survive the bloody conflict in which we are engaged, and be permitted to enjoy the liberties for which you have struggled so long and so well.

When we look around us, we miss many familiar faces. Death has made sad havoc in our ranks since we first left our homes. Let us cherish the memory of our brave comrades who have fallen, and emulate the noble example they have left us; and let the remembrance of our mutual sacrifices and perils bind us together as brother soldiers, fighting for the same holy cause—the liberation of our country from the yoke of bondage which our hated foe is trying to place upon us.

For my part, I shall endeavor to be entirely impartial in my official intercourse with each one of you, and your conduct in the past leads me to expect on your part a prompt obedience of orders, a strict adherence to rules, and a faithful discharge of every duty.

I again thank you for the kindness you have ever shown me, and the manner in which you have honored me. Should a merciful providence permit me to survive the perils of the war, I hope to be able always to recur to my relations to you as your commander, with unalloyed pleasure and pride.

C. L. G.

SECOND GEORGIA BATTALION

CAMP ON RAPIDAN RIVER, NEAR ROBERTSON'S FORD, September 27, 1863 [10-6-63CS]

We still confront the enemy upon the banks of the Rapidan, and are making every preparation for an attack, which, however, I do not believe will be made at this point. We have the best natural position that I ever saw; the country is very mountainous here, and our batteries are stationed upon the hill tops which command the valley below for many miles up and down the river, while the hill sides are covered with rifle pits. I think Meade has too much sense to attack Lee in the position he now holds. At present all is quiet, and no prospect of a battle, but "we know not what a day may bring forth."

A member of the 48th Ga. Regiment, of this Brigade, deserted while on picket this morning at daybreak, and made his way into the enemy's lines. Our pickets fired at him, but without effect. Deserters from the enemy come over to us daily. One came over yesterday, who states that he is an English sailor, and was conscripted in Portland, Maine, and sent to the 19th Regiment from that State. He says that *three* [two] of Meade's corps have gone to reinforce [William S.] Rosecrans, and that the Yankee papers admit that Rosecrans has been badly whipped [at Chickamauga] upon ground of his own choosing. He also states that Meade's army is daily growing dissatisfied, and the conscripts are more trouble to them than they are worth, as the majority of them have to be kept under close guard while in camp, and are seldom sent out upon the picket line.

The weather is very cold in these mountains, considering it is only September, and with the scanty covering that we have, we find it almost impossible to sleep comfortably, especially in the latter part of the night; consequently we rise very early in the morning and start a fire to warm by. The health of our company, notwithstanding, is very good.

C. F. S.

OUTPOST, ARMY OF NORTHERN VIRGINIA
November 2, 1863 [11-10-63CS]

Meade still lingers in Fauquier, while Gen. Lee halts on the Rappahannock, and, Macawber like, is "waiting for something to turn up."

Meade has disclosed to the world the startling fact that he can conduct a retreat better than he can an advance. The little fame he won at Gettysburg is like foliage of the forest in autumn, descending rapidly to rise no more. He soon will have to walk the road that has already been trodden by McClellan, Hooker, Burnside, and others. It is evident that he is not equal to the work before him.

Gen. [Gouverneur K.] Warren has already been spoken of as his successor, and before the chill wind of December sweep over the earth he will be numbered among the things that were.

The destruction of the Orange and Alexandria railroad is so complete that the Yankees have been actively engaged in repairing it for ten days or more, and make but little progress in its reconstruction.

The country now occupied by Meade, once fertile, prosperous and happy, is now a vast territory of ruin and desolation. Dwellings prior to the war inhabited by happy souls with an abundance to subsist on, have been ruthlessly torn down to make quarters for a mean and insolent foe. There is not a house standing on the rail road from Manassas Junction to Rappahannock river, a distance of more than thirty miles. All enclosures upon the farms have been pulled down and destroyed; extensive fields, once yielding rich harvest, are cut to pieces by military roads. In lieu of valuable crops of corn may be seen bramble and high weeds waving triumphantly over land. A lone cavalier rides in vain in pursuit of a few ears of corn for his faithful and jaded steed, and returned in despair to his bivouac to brood over the evils of war.

This is the condition of the country now occupied by Meade. How long he will continue to make the upper Rappahannock his line for military operations I am not prepared to say. Should he remain where he is during the winter, he will receive some hard blows from Gen. Stuart, who never fails to harass the enemy when an opportunity presents itself.

John Minor Botts, a miserable traitor [living near Brandy Station], has been endeavoring to arouse the sympathy of some of the army in his behalf by telling them how much he has suffered by some of our troops stopping only one night on his farm.

This individual, during the occupation of Culpeper by the enemy, gave entertainments and invited the most prominent officers to his house; and from what I have heard I have not the slightest doubt that he communicated all he knew concerning our army and government. John Minor Botts should be imprisoned during the war by our authorities or banished. He is an enemy, and too dangerous a one to remain longer on the outpost.

Among the slaves captured by Major [John S.] Mosby, a few days since, there was one belonging to Gen. Wms. C. Wickham, of Hanover. He was stolen during Stoneman's raid, and carried to Washington. He seemed to be highly gratified at the idea of getting home.

DYKE.

ARMY OF NORTHERN VIRGINIA
CAMP NEAR BRANDY, VA., November 6, 1863 [11-13-63CS]

All quiet in the army of Northern Virginia. Our line is the Rappahannock river. The Yankees had put up block-houses at all the trestles and bridges on the Ohio and Atlantic railroad, with earthworks for artillery at the most important points. These precautions were taken against cavalry raids—and might be adopted by the C. S. Army with benefit in exposed positions. A square pen of logs is thrown up about six feet high and about thirty feet square. A ditch is put on the outside and the dirt thrown against the walls of the pen. A traverse of logs, stockaded, runs nearly across this pen, through the middle, to prevent a cross fire of musketry. The gorge, or entrance opening in the pen, and allowing only one man at a time to pass.

The block-house is composed of logs neatly fitted together. The lower story is about eighteen feet square. The upper story is set diagonally upon the lower story to give eight sides of fire, and the projection above allows a fire upon assailants attempting to burn the house. The lower story is eight feet high, and the upper seven feet. The block-house is portholed for muskets, and provided with a week's rations and water for about fifteen men. These structures were intended to dot almost every mile of the railroad. At Rappahannock river a heavy earthwork on each bank commands the approaches to the rail road bridge. We have changed the gorge and made the guns bear towards Washington instead of Richmond. And our guns now fill the embrasures.

It will be observed that the report of Gen. Lee of the movement that caused Meade's late retreat, carefully avoids attributing blame to any one. But with broad shoulders and a large heart he assumes all. It is this magnanimity that makes the army of Northern Virginia the army of the Confederacy, that keeps down heartburnings and jealousies, and makes each man resolve "to do better, next time." A little of this leaven would go farther than the Javert ingredient of another General's discipline, to secure unity and confidence, and to crown the heroic soldiers of the West with something more than laurels for their courage.

PROLONGE.

WRIGHT'S BRIGADE

RAPID ANN STATION, VA., December 23, 1863 [1-6-64AWCS]

Mr. Editor: You and your many readers of the *Chronicle & Sentinel* may like to hear from Wright's Brigade, which is stationed at present on the North side of the Rapidan River, to hold the position and protect the railroad bridge. The Brigade one might say is garrisoned here, for we are completely surrounded by cannon batteries, breastworks, redoubts, &c.; and if the Yankees should happen to run afoul of us here, they will meet with a warm reception.

Capt. Bell, who is on Gen. Wright's Staff, had his horse shot under him while out on a scout last Wednesday. The Captain was uninjured. The Brigade is at present under the command of Col. [E. J.] Walker.

Five men belonging to the 22nd Georgia, who attempted to desert, had their heads shaved, and were condemned to hard labor for the war in Richmond, and to each one of them wear a ball and chain.

A member of McIntosh's [Artillery] Battalion was shot for desertion on Friday, the 18th. He was struck by five balls, four in the right breast and one through the heart. His wife and sister witnessed the scene, which was truly heart rending. The men who shot him were detailed from this Brigade. He had nothing to say in defence of himself.

The duty of the Brigade at present is light, although we are on the front lines at this writing; but there is no danger of an attack just yet. There is a rumor that our Brigade will be relieved, but if we are we will have to rebuild winter quarters, for we have very comfortable ones, although we have to go something over a mile after fuel, which is getting to be scarce immediately around our division.

Lieut.-Col. [Reuben W.] Carswell has resigned, which the 48th Georgia very much regrets—and Major [Matthew R.] Hall becomes Lieut. Colonel, who is in every respect capable of filling the office. The Major has been with the regiment in all its hardships and trials, and proved himself to be a brave officer.

In the little affair that we had at the Wilderness [November 27], near the battle field of Chancellorsville, Lieut. J. K. Evans received a slight wound on the right side of his neck. He was sent to the front with orders to the picket line when he received the wound.

We receive our full compliment of rations, such as flour, beef, bacon, Irish and sweet potatoes, and soap.

The weather is very fine at present. We have had no snow and but little rain, but the Blue Ridge is in sight, and looks cold and dreary.

Gen. Lee is furloughing the army pretty rapidly—two out of every hundred; a very fair percentage; and as long as the enemy keeps his line where it is, Gen. L. will continue to grant furloughs.

A Yankee flag of truce came over a short time since, which had to be received by a general officer, and receipted for; and it was received by Gen. R. H. Anderson, who recognized the bearer of dispatches as an old acquaintance of his when he was connected with the U. S. Army. There was much speculation in regard to these dispatches—some avowing that they were asking for an armistice, others that it was about the exchange of prisoners. Gen. Lee went to Richmond on a special train on receipt of these dispatches; and when it was found out that he was in the city, he was invited to a seat on the floor of Congress, but declined, saying that he had important business to attend to.

As yet I have seen nothing in the proceedings of Congress concerning the three years troops—whether they intend to allow them to go home and there reorganize, or enroll them in the field and furlough them as they have been doing heretofore.

J. A.

ARMY OF NORTHERN VIRGINIA
[RICHMOND HUSSARS, COBB'S LEGION]
CAMP NEAR FREDERICKSBURG, VA., December 26, 1863 [1-6-64AWCS]

I have succeeded after the second attempt, in making my escape from the enemy. The sad news has probably reached you of the death of Lieuts. [N.] Pugh and [John W.] Cheeseborough. I remained with them until they both died, which I had them decently buried. Cobb's Legion has lost two gallant and brave officers by their decease. After their burial, I went to Gettysburg and reported to Gen. [Marsena] Patrick, provost marshal; told him I had a parole and wished to be sent on for exchange. He told me that my parole did not amount to anything; that there had been orders issued against it. He then sent me around to an old barn in Gettysburg where there were about four hundred of our men. We remained there some time and then sent out on our march.

We had for an escort Gen. Patrick and staff, and the 8th U. S. Regulars—I cannot call them soldiers or men, for they were more like brutes than either. They were certainly the meanest men that ever disgraced a uniform. I cannot go into detail of the horrible treatment we received at their hands—it would take more time and paper than I care to waste on them. In passing through towns especially they would manifest their brutality by hitting the prisoners with the butt of their guns—those who were sick and wounded, were forced in this manner to keep up with them, who had plenty to eat and plenty of rations in their haversacks. We had not eaten anything but six hard crackers for six days. Oh, how my blood did boil within me to see our men treated in this manner! But we were in their power and had to take it.

We at length reached Frederick City, Md., where we were to take the cars, and it was fortunate for me, for I do believe it would have been impossible for me to march any further. The next day my feet were so sore and I could hardly touch them to the ground. But I could not grumble at that, for the majority were in a worse fix than myself.

Nothing of interest occurred on our arriving at Baltimore. A lady was arrested for speaking to her husband, who was a prisoner, and she was taken off to some Yankee fort. We were then put on board a transport and sent to Fort Delaware, which is certainly one of the dirtiest places on the globe. There were a large number of prisoners there, and they were dying at the rate of thirty per day. The guard there was very little better than the 8th Regulars above mentioned, in firing at the men for disobeying orders. They have killed three or four men who were lying asleep in their bunks.

I will pass over the many acts of severe cruelty they have perpetrated, and try to tell you of my escape from there on the night of the 13th of August. I had four canteens tied to my breast to act as life-preservers and plunged into the Delaware River, three and a half miles wide at this point, with my clothes on; but I soon found that I could not swim with my coat and pants on, so I disencumbered myself of them, and after much exertion succeeded in reaching the opposite shore, in a state of complete exhaustion. After lying there about two hours I set out with a companion who escaped with me. I could not travel by daylight without coat or pants, so I had to take darkness for it. We traveled seven nights and at the end of that time I found myself exactly where I started from. This was somewhat discouraging. I told my companion (whose name was McCalthern) that I was going up to the first house I came to and tell them just who we were and ask for assistance. I accosted the farmer and told him my story, asking him if he would not give me a pair of pants. After some hesitation, he said he would, and gave me a pair. He gave us directions how to travel to reach Maryland. We set out in the day time, and reached Maryland without much difficulty, only that our feet were very sore from going barefoot so long. We lived on fruit, which was very abundant at that time. I will not mention any names, but I fell into good hands soon after reaching Maryland, where I got plenty of good clothing and plenty of Yankee money.

I found the people of Maryland as willing to assist a "Reb" as though he was one of their own children; and after I found friends once I assure you I did not want for anything.

After staying on the other side of the Chesapeake as long as I wished, I got on a boat and went to Baltimore where I tarried two weeks, and then took the cars on the Baltimore & Ohio Railroad, with the intention of getting off at the first station the other side of Harper's Ferry. When the cars stopped we jumped off and to our misfortune were halted by the Yankee guard. We could not give a very correct account of ourselves and the men were going to treat us as spies. We told them we were escaped prisoners, but they would not believe it until they telegraphed to Fort Delaware and found out the facts. After they found out who we were, they sent us back to Fort Delaware, when we were carried before Gen. [Albin F.] Schoepf. We were clad in citizens attire, and I suppose the general took a fancy to our clothes—any how, he ordered the Sergeant who had us in charge to take us down to the "dead house" and give us some dead "Reb's" clothes, and bring those good clothes to him.

The sergeant obeyed the order and we were both soon rigged out in old worn out uniforms which we were compelled to take or do without. He then ordered the sergeant to put me in the dungeon, where I was kept for a day or two, and then sent me back to the barracks. We had orders to go to Point Lookout. We were crowded on the transport with nearly two thousand more prisoners and all sent down into the hold. I know there was not half so much cruelty shown in the African slave trade in crowding slaves on vessels as the Yankees displayed here. Several men died from suffocation. One half had to sit down and the other half stand up, and relieve each other that way, for three days. They would not let us stay on deck for fear we would capture the boat.

We at length reached Point Lookout, where we fared a little better in the eating line. In the forenoon we got five hard crackers, and water called coffee; in the afternoon we had five crackers, a small piece of bacon or beef, and a cup of soup. I can say for the 2nd and 5th New Hampshire Volunteers, who were on guard there, that they treated us as prisoners should be treated; but we dreaded the 12th N. H. on guard. They never let the prisoners know their orders, and of course we were ignorant of doing wrong. They would soon let you know, however, by sending a ball after you. This regiment I think never came on guard but what some of them fired in the camp—and firing into a camp of nine thousand, they were very apt to kill some one. Ask some of the more civil of the men why they are so fond of firing at the prisoners, and they will tell you that they do it that they may have it to say after the war that they have killed a rebel.

If I was to attempt to give you an account of all the ill treatment received by the prisoners, I should certainly weary your patience. The Yankees have not given out 200 blankets to the men, who are almost starving with cold, and who have to carry their wood three miles on their backs. Only five out of a company of 100 men are allowed to carry wood—for the balance, 25 men are detailed for wood chopping for the Yankees, and sent out three miles beyond the picket every morning. There are always plenty of volunteers from the prisoners to go on this duty for the sake of the extra rations.

I thought I saw a very good chance to escape by going out on this detail, so I bought a fellow's place on it, dressed myself in a Yankee uniform, threw a blanket around me to hide it, and was marching along with the rest of the prisoners, part of the guard being at the head of the squad and part in the rear. After going two and a half miles beyond the picket, I handed a friend my blanket and turned right round and made out like I was a Yankee going back to camp. The guard did not halt me; they were marching one way and I the other. After passing the guard I ran through a field and got into the woods, and soon found the Yankee cavalry after me. I put as many fences as possible between us, reached a small creek and swam that, and then I was perfectly safe. I saw the Yanks on the other side of the creek, but they did not know I had swam it. There is no difficulty in finding good rebels when you get over there, and

I soon found friends to put me across the Potomac. After traveling through Virginia for three or four days, I appeared in our camp, taking the boys completely by surprise.

I have written you a longer letter than I expected, but I have shown you how the enemy treat their prisoners—but have only given you a few instances of their cruelty. Our prisoners I believe are treated well; all that I have ever seen were treated as well as we could treat them.

GEORGE C. TANNER.

George C. Tanner, age 17, enlisted in Cobb's Legion on April 3, 1862 and served as the bugler of Co. E. He is listed as "absent on Home Detail" on October 10, 1864. The two officers that Tanner buried at Gettysburg, Pugh and Cheeseborough, were among those disinterred and returned to Georgia in 1871. The following article is from the Savannah Morning News, *August 22, 1871:*

HONOR TO THE CONFEDERATE DEAD
**The Arrival of the Remains of Thirty-two Confederate Soldiers
From the Gettysburg Battlefield.**

The Steamer *America* arrived at her wharf yesterday morning and the committee appointed for the reception of the remains, with two hearses, met them at the wharf whence they escorted them to the Exchange, where they were placed in State in the council chamber during the day and looked with melancholy interest upon the three plain chests that contained all that remained of the thirty-two brave Southerners who fell on that memorable occasion.

At four o'clock the hour appointed for the ceremonies, the Committee accompanied by twenty-four pall-bearers who had been selected for the occasion met at the Exchange. The remains were carried down the street, and in the presence of a vast crowd of citizens, and a detachment of the Police force under command of Lieut. Howard, placed in two hearses preparatory to their transportation to the cemetery. The Policemen preceded by the Washington Coronet Band, marched on, followed by the carriage with the minister of the Episcopal church, Rev. Mr. Benedict and Col. J. F. Waring, formerly of the Jeff Davis Legion. Then came the two hearses with the remains of the dead soldiers, followed by those citizens, once soldiers, who desired to participate in the ceremonies and pay their last tribute of respect to the fallen comrades who's bones had rested on the battlefield for the past eight years. Among those present we noticed representatives of all the old volunteer companies of our city, as well as many others who participated in the struggles of the late Confederacy. As the procession moved through the streets, we marked the sad features of the crowds around. Every store and office along the line of their march was closed. Every respect was observed and the nature of the case demanded. Along the streets the ladies were observed standing at their doors and windows shedding tears as the melancholy cavalcade passed by. Never in the history of our city has a more quiet, melancholy, and sadly, appreciated occasion been before our people and never have they seemed to feel more seriously. Arriving at the cemetery, the pall bearers and entire procession advanced with uncovered heads in the presence of hundreds of ladies assembled for the purpose of paying a last tribute of respect to the dead heroes of the "Lost Cause". Three graves were prepared for the reception of the three caskets containing the remains and after the reading of the burial service by Rev. Benedict, the Police detachment fired a military salute. A hymn, "Rock of Ages" was sung during the interment.

After the graves were filled up and the last mortal remains of these thirty-two dead confederate soldiers were deposited in their final resting place, the ladies present numbering several hundred, came forward and strewed flowers upon their graves so that they were literally covered with floral offerings. This accomplished, the people turned sadly from the spot hollowed by the dust of the gallant men who gave their lives in defense of the Southern Cause.

Among the names of those interred yesterday are as follows: W. F. Brown, private, Co. B 15th Ga., W. F. Nash, private, Co. G 9th Ga., T. H. Lawrence, private, Co. G 24th Ga., W. L. Brewer, sergeant, Co. K 51st Ga., J. B. Forester, private 24th Ga., W. R. Bracewell, private, Co. G 49th Ga., James Corus, private, Co. H, 8th Ga., John B. Willoughby, private, Co. G 38th Ga., C. L. Walker, Lieutenant, Co. F 38th Ga., M. Lewis, private, Co. D 22nd Ga., E. M. Ballard, Captain, Co. C 8th Ga., R. W. Dyas, private, Co. A Cobb's Legion, E. F. Smith, Cobb's Legion, N. Pugh, Cobb's Legion, John Cheeseborough, Cobb's Legion, Noah C. Strickland, Cobb's Legion.

☆☆☆Winter 1864

The Army of Northern Virginia spent the third winter of the war in camps spread throughout Orange County. Depleted ranks had to be filled, for spring would bring the annual Federal "on to Richmond" campaign.

CAMP OF GORDON'S BRIGADE

ORANGE C. H., VA., February 4, 1864 [2-13-64CS]

The voluntary re-enlistment of our troops in this army will, doubtless, cheer the hearts of our friends at home. Ere this I suppose you have heard of the noble spirit which seems generally to animate the hearts of our undaunted soldiery. The little spark which first made its appearance in the army of Tennessee was soon fanned unto such a flame, throughout that army and Gen. Lee's, as to effectually destroy all the foundations upon which the faint hearts had heretofore rested their doubts in reference to the determination of our troops.

The soldiers of this army are to-day as sanguine of our final success as they were when the first tap of drum was heard calling them to arms. Tell our friends at home that our tattered and war worn flags are again floating in defiance of our enemies, and thousands of men whose souls are still burning with patriotic zeal, are rallying around them. As long as there remains one of these patriots they need not fear that our colors will trail in the dust, or that there will be any drawing back, on our part, until our last enemy shall be driven from our borders. There is no cause for despondency. We are yet determined to fight on and fight ever until the liberty shall be granted us, for which we have paid so much to purchase.

The following is a copy of a circular just issued to the troops of this Brigade by the Colonel commanding, who is one of Georgia's noblest sons, and on many fields of bloody strife he has illustrated his ability for command, and his devotion to our common cause:

HD'QTRS, GORDON'S BRIGADE, February 4, 1864.

The spirit of the Confederate troops exhibited at the opening stages of this war with our country's enemies, is again being displayed in her armies, by the voluntary re-enlistment of these brave men, for the war.

The mercenary hirelings of the Yankee army continue their inglorious, but merciless and barbarous warfare against ourselves, our homes, and our families, only for pay of hundreds of dollars in bounties and the sordid hope of future plunder. Such a degrading price of blood is scorned by men whose present reward is the delightful consciousness of doing right, and whose hopes rest unweariedly upon the independence of their country.

Soldiers of Gordon's Brigade—You who have never failed to win solid triumphs whenever you fought—your attention is called to this noble conduct of your comrades in arms. Will you not emulate this patriotic devotion? Will you not say to Georgia to hope on, though her foes desolate her borders, for her sons are undaunted? And to the Confederate Government, that it shall ever have your service cheerfully, without strict and without draft, conscription or bribe?

Faithfully relying on the Good Being, who, while permitting, through his infinite wisdom, many reverses to befall us, has still wonderfully shielded our Young Republic, we will meet the foe again with renewed energies and conquer a lasting peace, and preserve our liberty and honor.

Col. C. A. Evans

Since this circular was published the 26th, 31st and 61st Ga. Regiments have already enlisted; the others will, perhaps, do so to-morrow.

"RE-ENLSITED."

CAMP OF GORDAN'S BRIGADE

NEAR SUMMERVILLE FORD, VA., February 11, 1864 [2-24-64AWCS]

On the morning of the 6th, the hoarse rumbling tones of the "Long Roll" summoned all to arms. The continual booming of artillery had already warned us of the approach of the enemy. Gordon's Brigade, moving forward, found the enemy in some force on the south bank of the Rapidan River, hugging it closely, at and near Morton's ford. The Brigade was rapidly thrown forward into some entrenchments which fortunately had been thrown up at the right time and place.

The Yankees continued to shell our troops nearly all day, from batteries which they had in position on the North side of the river. This random shelling, however, inflicted upon us no material injury.

Late in the afternoon of the same day, our skirmishers were ordered forward to attack those of the enemy. Soon the reports of a hundred rifles and whistling minies announced the contest opened. Our lines continued to advance until they approached a house occupied by the enemy's sharpshooters. Here, each party claimed the other as prisoners, both calling out loudly at the same time "to surrender."

General Ewell followed closely the advancing lines. At one time it was reported to him that the Yankees in the house would not surrender, and our men were killing them—he quickly replied, "Let them kill them! Let them kill them!"

This exciting skirmish continued with unabating fury some time after dark. During the remainder of the night the enemy carried away all his wounded, but left seventeen dead on the field. It is somewhat remarkable that of these seventeen dead, all were shot in the left breast except one—and he was killed after dark.

The next morning found the enemy on the North side of the River. They may appropriately return thanks that the spirit moved them to recross so soon. For plans had been made for the effectual disposition of all Yankees found on the South bank of the River on the morning of the 8th. But they had moved far away before its earliest dawn.

None of the Brigade was regularly engaged except detachments from the Thirty-first, Thirteenth, and Sixty-first Regiments, and a few men from the Sixtieth. In the Thirty-first only one was wounded—Sergeant S. W. Corbett, Company A, severely in the right side. In the Thirteenth one wounded—Burkes George, Company K, mortally, in breast; he has since died. In Sixty-first one was killed and two wounded. P. Ryan, Company F, was killed; Riley Wilkes, Company E, was wounded in breast mortally, he has since died.

J. W. B.

LETTER FROM RICHMOND
RICHMOND, VA., February 13, 1864 [2-19-64CS]

The weather is beautiful—clear, warm and dry—the dust three inches deep in the streets, just as we see it in August. Add to the city excitements, the scarcity of food and the certainty (for now it seems to be) of every available man up to 50 to 55 being made to do some military service in the field or at home, and you have an idea of Richmond at this moment.

As I came up the street, just now, I saw gentlemen, official and unofficial, swarming in and out the doors of our manifold drinking shops, like so many bees at the holes of a hundred hives. Nor must you forget the chance of arrest, when you least expect it, by unauthorized parties.

"Are you over 45?" inquired a half drunken fellow, armed with a musket, of me, a few minutes ago. "No," said I, as I pulled out my exemption paper. "You needn't show no papers; you've got to come right along to camp." Surprised at this, I handed my certificate to a sergeant, who appeared to be as drunk as the man with the musket. While the sergeant was trying to read my paper, the private took me aside and said, with a drunken leer, "We are trying to fill up our regiment—the 8th Virginia—[Eppa] Hunton's old regiment—cut all to pieces at Gettysburg; but if you will get us a little something to eat or drink, specially to drink, we will"—I wheeled off before the rascal could finish his sentence, took my paper and hurried to my room. If I had not been compelled to finish this letter before the mail closed, I would have had these dogs arrested and punished. I recite the case just to show you how we get along at the capital in these days of military law and order.

PAN.

FIVE DAYS' EXPERIENCE IN A YANKEE BULL PEN

ARMY OF NORTHERN VIRGINIA, February 19, 1864 [3-4-64MAR]

The recent advance of the Yankee army upon our front was not altogether unproductive of good results. The whole move was characteristic of the vandal foe. The robbery of hen-roosts, the carrying off a few deluded slaves, and the capture of unoffending defenseless citizens, were the fruits of this "grand" advance. But of these I speak not. I propose to give you the experience of one of the victims to this advance, a gentleman of undoubted veracity, residing in Culpepper, in the enemy's lines. It was related to me in nearly the words that follow:

After my capture I was carried successively from brigade to division, corps and army headquarters; and each of their respective commanders expressed his regret at my detention but at the same time his inability to release me, saying he *"would have to send me up."* I thought I was high "up" already. However, I was soon transferred to the clutches of Provost Marshal General Patrick, and after some questioning by him, doomed to the celebrated "Yankee Bull Pen."

This pen, the summit of Yankee diabolical ingenuity, is about three-fourths of a mile from Brandy Station, and about 200 feet square. It is formed by logs twelve feet long, placed perpendicular in the ground. It is surrounded by an unfinished ditch six feet by five.

In it was collected a heterogeneous mass of poor humanity, mostly the off-scouring of earth, yet every grade and condition of society were represented. Here the Yankee and the rebel mixed upon equal terms, and each commiserated the other upon his hard fate.

There could be seen the Virginia gentleman, whose only crime was adherence to his native South, while close to him, and, in one instance, even chained to him, stood the hardened Yankee criminal. The old and young, rich and poor, soldier and citizen, the innocent and guilty, all alike stood huddled together; and last, though not least, there were sprinkled in the crowd many of the veritable "wooly-headed nigger." It seems that this is the grand receptacle of all prisoners of this prison. Prisoners of war, unless they have charges against them, are only kept here a short time; but others, such as deserters from our army, suspected citizens, &c., generally spend some time in this delightful "Pen."

On first being ushered in with *"you got dam rebel bushwacker"* from my Dutch guard, I was peculiarly struck with the animated scene that presented itself. In the middle of the enclosure was collected a motley group about fifty in number. Prominent in the crowd, stood a bare-headed man, dressed in the garb of a Confederate soldier, and from the taunts and jeers thrown at him, I soon learned he was the centre of attraction, and was kindly informed by some of the bystanders, that he was about to undergo *"initiation,"* which all had to do or pay a fine of fifty cents in greenbacks. As I was entirely destitute of that article I felt some interest in the proceedings. The poor fellow pleaded like a man. He admitted his inability to pay the fifty cents but offered any, even all his garments as a substitute, but it was in vain. To the sacrifice he must go. He was accordingly laid upon a blanket which was taken hold of at the four corners and elsewhere, by his Yankee friends, and in sailor language he was ho-heaved back and forward several times, and finally with a sudden heave, thrown some seven or eight feet in the air. You may imagine with what effect he fell upon the ground. This was repeated once or twice, when the poor fellow was left bleeding and almost senseless— while his tormentors turned to renew their torture upon some other luckless new comer. I afterwards met this man and recognized him as a deserter from our army. He told me a poor pitiful tale of regret. He had deserted his comrades in the hope of being welcomed with open arms by the Yankees; but he soon learned to his sorrow, first, that the authorities distrusted and incarcerated him; second, that even Yankees looked with little favor upon deserters. He had accumulated some clothes and tobacco, but had not been in the Pen long before all were gone; they had not even spared him his hat. There he stood, a perfect picture of despair, the past irrevocably gone, the future black with doubt and sorrow. Life to him, he said, was no pleasure, and he willingly welcomed death. There is a peculiarity in this feature of their treatment towards our deserters. I saw many instances of it. Indeed, it was the universal experience of all.

I found that the old settlers in the Bull Pen fared, in point of comfort, the best. They had built bunks, while those who came last had no covering but what they brought with them. Six or seven crackers and about half a pound of pickled pork was issued to us daily; and those who were fortunate enough to possess a canteen were allowed, accompanied by a guard, to visit the spring in the vicinity.

I met, while there, several acquaintances, and some whom I knew by reputation. I remember distinctly one, an old gentleman from Fauquier, Mr.---, whose hair was white with age, and yet it brought no palliation of his treatment. There were also two of the Black Horse chained together, and one of Mosby's men chained to a Yankee.

I overheard a conversation between an old negro man named Harry and some citizens who were captured a short time after I was. It seems that old Harry had left his comfortable home and kind master and sought freedom from his Northern friends; but even he, negro as he was, became the victim of their treachery and bad faith. He was told that he was too old to go North, and was kept there, well earning his pork and crackers by hard labor upon the unfinished ditch around the Pen. These citizens seemed to know old Harry well, and after some conversation with him about his prospects, one of them asked him why he left his good home, and if he was not happy when surrounded by his friends and protected by his master. The old man, in the most pathetic voice I ever heard, pointing upwards, exclaimed: "*Yes, master, as happy as the angels in Heaven!*" When asked if he was happy now, he only replied by shaking his head. I remained in this Pen five days, at the end of which time, there being no charges against me, I was released, and have made my way into our lines.

Such, Mr. Editor is the testimony of one in every sense reliable.

***

LETTER FROM VIRGINIA, EIGHTH ALABAMA INFANTRY
[PERRIN'S BRIGADE, ANDERSON'S DIVISION]
HEADQ'S. CRADLE OF INNOCENCE, CO. H, 8TH ALABAMA VOLS.
NEAR ORANGE C. H., VA., February 29, 1864 [3-18-64MAR]

After a series of beautiful days, preceded by the intense cold spell of a week before last, the weather has again changed. A host of dark clouds, pregnant with snow or rain, cover the sky. Whether they will have anything to do with retarding the opening of the spring campaign or not, remains to be seen. The enemy is again preparing for an advance, and is even now, as I am told, actually advancing by way of Madison Court House. For the last half hour heavy cannonading has been going on in that direction. Whenever or wherever Gen. Meade may think fit to try again the "on to Richmond," he will be opposed by an army of veteran volunteers that know how to hurl back with defiance the legions of Lincoln's mercenaries, the hired tools of a tyrant despot, who would, if he could, enslave a gallant people, so much superior in self-sacrificing devotion to their country and love of constitutional liberty, to the fanatics who have chosen him for their master. He will find a host of freemen arrayed to welcome the invader of their soil, "with bloody hands to hospitable graves," ready to obstruct the roads to the capital with their bleeding corpses and mangled limbs. No one here doubts the issue of the struggle in this quarter, whenever it shall take place. Would that all would have the same confidence in the armies of Generals [Leonidas] Polk and Johnston! But why doubt the gallant men composing those armies. Because they failed at Vicksburg and Missionary Ridge? It would be neither fair nor just. No doubt they will soon have an opportunity to show that they are not inferior either in fighting qualities or patriotism to the army of Northern Virginia, that glorious army, whose record is so brilliant, so glorious and so bright.

We are eagerly awaiting more news in regard to the enemy's movements against Mobile. That the good old city is to be attacked at last, seems to be evident. But one desire pervades the whole regiment; and that is to be transferred to the army of Mobile, that we may defend our own homes and protect our loved and dear ones from Yankee impudence and tyranny. A memorial has been sent to the Secretary of War, I believe, signed by the officers of the regiment, requesting him, if any troops should be transferred to Mobile, to send this regiment, or allow it to exchange with one of the Alabama regiments now near Mobile, which is willing to come to Virginia. The reasons given for the request are, I am told, that five companies of this regiment are from the city of Mobile, and the other five all from south Alabama, (the third Alabama has only four companies from Mobile, still Mobile claims that regiment as its own. Query: Why?) And if we were to be sent to Alabama we could no doubt recruit our fearfully thinned ranks a little. But few have an idea how terribly grim visaged war has reduced our numerical strength. Let me for instance cite as an example my own company, the Mobile Independent (?) Scouts. The company left Mobile numbering 88 men—officers, non-commissioned officers and privates. Since December 1862 there have been added at different times as many as 34 recruits. The casualties have been, since the commencement of the war, as follows:

By death from wounds and killed in battle—33.
By death from disease—11.
Discharged for disability—11.
Transferred to Ord. and Navy Departments—10.
Deserted—7.
Resigned—2.
Total—74.

Besides which three men are absent on detached or detailed service, which makes a grand total loss in the company of seventy-seven men, since its organization. Whether any company in the regiment has suffered more than this one I know not, the majority however have not lost quite as many. As a whole, I believe no regiment can show a more glorious record than the 8th Alabama. Its members have fought, bled and died at New Market, Wynne's Mill (Yorktown), Williamsburg, Seven Pines, Gaines' Mill, Frazier's Farm, Manassas No. 2, Sharpsburg, Fredericksburg, Salem Church (Chancellorsville), Gettysburg, July 2nd, and Gettysburg, July 3rd, St. James College, Md., Bristoe and Mine Run. No Alabamian need to blush for the behavior of this regiment at any of these glorious, blood stained, and to us sacred places. No troops, I am proud to say, have done more than Alabamians have; on every battle field from Virginia to Tennessee they have been foremost in the charge; but I grieve to say, no troops in this army have suffered more for want of clothing and shoes than those very heroes have. But a short while ago, at a time when this regiment was performing picket duty on the snow-covered hills on the Rapidan, no less than one-third of its members were barefooted. The State of Alabama had plenty of shoes. Its agent was offering them to all, *who could buy them*. Was it not shameful, that because the poor fellows could not save money enough of their scanty pittance to *pay* the State for the shoes, they had to go barefooted on the hard Frozen ground? Why can not Alabama supply its troops as well with shoes and clothing as North Carolina and Georgia do? Has it not the same facilities for importing and manufacturing as the other States have? If not, it ought to. I should not have referred to this subject, had not our wants been supplied by the Confederate Government; for, though soldiers, we are still sensitive, and glory in our independence. We have not forgotten that, when in December, 1862, the *Register and Advertiser* published a letter from "Scout," describing the sufferings of the Eighth Alabama, for want of shoes, on the icy hills of Fredericksburg, but one solitary offer to alleviate the suffering was made by a gentleman signing himself "W." But, look at the contrast: A few weeks ago the *Third* Alabama was presented to the people of Mobile, as being suffering for want of shoes, and behold, in a few days a sum of over seven thousand dollars was raised to alleviate *their* suffering. Whether the donors of the *patriotic* gift were really patriots, I shall leave to an impartial judgement.

March 4th, 1864—I was interrupted in my letter by an order to cook up two days' rations and get ready to move. On Monday night, the threatening clouds dissolved in rain, which poured down unceasingly till Tuesday night, when it changed into snow. At one o'clock, Monday night, we received orders to prepare to leave camp at two a. m., at which time we started on one of the most severe marches this regiment has ever had. We marched nineteen miles, to within a few miles of Madison Court House which is situated at the foot of the Blue Ridge Mountains, where we expected to catch the cavalry which cut the railroad between here and Richmond, but were not successful. The rain poured down incessantly; the roads were nothing but one mud hole, and the men were almost fatigued to death by the quick marching. Our regiment had again the *good* luck to go on picket on Tuesday night and return to camp on Wednesday. While on picket, it was necessary to relieve the men almost every hour; their wet and dripping clothes would freeze as stiff as sheet iron. When we arrived again in camp, we were almost broken down. The night of the battle of Williamsburg, the night we crossed the Shenanadoah, and the night we recrossed the Potomac, were nothing compared to this trip.

SCOUT.

On the night of February 29, a Federal cavalry force under Gen. Judson Kilpatrick crossed the Rapidan with the audacious intent on raiding Richmond and freeing the prisoners of war held there. After several days of bad weather along with the lack of surprise and poor execution, the ill-conceived raid ended in failure.

LETTER FROM HAMPTON'S CAVALRY [3-20-64ASC]

After a march of more than fifty miles, made in less than twenty hours, we came in sight of the enemy, or rather their camp fires; for it was about 12 o'clock at night. The command was then moved up with precision and caution to within a mile of the fires, and here we encountered their pickets. Then commenced the usual parley, which ended by the Yankees asking the direct question, "And who are you?" "Confederate soldiers," was the answer. Then followed a half dozen bang, bang, bangs, and off they went, as fast as horses could take them, to tell Mr. [Judson] Kilpatrick that somebody was on his road to Richmond. The prisoners say that the report brought in by these men did not receive credit, for Kilpatrick ordered them back to their posts, saying, "You have allowed yourselves to be run in by some citizens, so that you may warm yourselves," telling the men at the same time to lie down, that if there was anybody up there he would get up early in the morning and thrash them off. It appeared, though, that this thrashing idea existed in the minds of both Generals, for we immediately began to arrange a night attack.

One hundred men were dismounted and ordered with two pieces of artillery to the front. The two pieces were then taken to within 500 yards of the camp, but the officer in charge, finding the field so boggy from the rain and melting snow, would not trust his pieces upon it, and could maneuver only one piece on the road. The one piece was put in battery, and then the dismounted men were ordered to advance cautiously on the camp and await the bursting of the first shell—then to yell like demons and charge like devils. In a few minutes, the command "load" was given, then "ready"—a pause—then rang out clearly, "commence firing." Ye Gods! one piece of cannon made noise for five batteries—100 men yelled like thousands. No wonder that 4,000 [3,000] fled from 300. You were perfectly excusable, Mr. Kilpatrick, for the gates of hell seemed to have opened upon you, to one who did not know otherwise, and yet if you had known what a mere handful stampeded and really routed you, for you run five miles as fast as your horses could take you, wouldn't you have turned round and kindly taken us in, eh?

After the gun had thrown twelve shells in the camp, and the dismounted men had made their charge, a courier ran in to tell the General that the attack was gloriously successful. The enemy had fled, leaving about three hundred saddled horses, which they might have mounted as easy as not; carbines, sabres, pistols and cooking truck in abundance. About 125 prisoners were taken from the camp, representing five different regiments. Had Gen. Hampton taken a brigade, say his old one, on this old expedition, he would have ruined the Yankee cavalry. It was a capital affair, any way you look upon it, though, for a pitch dark night. It is a very easy matter for a man, when he has the light of day shining around him, to think and talk of what might have been done; but the dark, cold, rainy, snowy night, I thought you did a bold and fearless thing, General, and I thanked my stars, and you, that it was successful.

***.

SECOND GEORGIA BATTALION
[WRIGHT'S BRIGADE, ANDERSON'S DIVISION]
IN CAMP, MADISON STATION, VA., April 7, 1864 [4-16-64CS]

Stirring events are anticipated here in the course of the next few weeks, as the weather from being rainy and blustering, has become fair and pleasant, and the roads are drying rapidly and will soon resound with the rumble of the artillery and wagon trains.

We received orders yesterday to hold ourselves in readiness to march at a moments warning, and an order to send all surplus baggage to Richmond has been in camp several days.

The Battalion is stronger to-day than it has been for over a year, and such, I understand, is the standing of the whole army. Our corps numbers——thousand, more men than when it took the Pennsylvania campaign, which is owing to the large number of furlough recruits and the detailed men that have been returned to their commands. Everything appears favorable for an early campaign, which, it is to be hoped, will be the final one. I have no fears as to the result, as Mr. [Ulysses S.] Grant will almost assuredly "follow the footsteps of his illustrious (?) predecessors," if he attempts his "on to Richmond," *via* the Rapidan.

You will hear from me occasionally, if anything of interest transpires.

FURNITURE.

LETTER FROM "FURNITURE,"
SECOND GEORGIA BATTALION

CAMP, MADISON STATION, April 12, 1864 [4-22-64CS]

The officers of Hill's 3d Army corps held a Grand Tournament at our brigade camps yesterday, which was witnessed by many thousand spectators, including the beauty and elite of the surrounding country, as well as by several of the fair from the farther South. There were about fifty competitions for the prizes, five in number, and many splendid specimens of horsemanship were exhibited, as well as dexterous agility in cutting off heads and taking the ring. The first honor was awarded to Capt. [Lorenzo] Luckie, Co. H., 3rd Ga., after a close contest between him and Courier Cavett, of Gen. Hill's staff, who became the winner of the second. Capt. [M. F.] Taylor, of Gen. Hill's staff, and Major [H. S.] Hughes, our Brigade Commissary, were the successful competitors for the third and fourth honors. The first honor for horsemanship was accorded to Captain [J. F.] Cage, A. Q. M., Heth's Division, after several tie trials between him, Captain [Stockton] Heth, of Gen. Heth's staff, and Courier Cavett. The successful champion will crown his lady Queen of Love and Beauty, and the other successful Knights crown the Maids of Honor, at the Coronation Ball to-night. Gen. Wright was master of ceremonies, and was ably assisted by other officers. Among the Knights and spectators I noticed Generals Hill, Heth, Hampton, [Edward] Thomas, [J. R.] Cooke, [Joseph] Davis, [W. W.] Kirkland, and others.

All baggage and the sick have been sent to Richmond, and orders to move at a moment's notice are in camp.

FURNITURE.

The winner of the tournament's first honor—Lorenzo F. Luckie was mustered in as Second Lieutenant on April 25, 1861, and elected First Lieutenant May 12, 1861. Luckie was promoted to Captain and wounded at Malvern Hill on July 1, 1862 and again at the Battle of the Crater near Petersburg on July 30, 1864. Capt. Luckie died of his wounds on August 2, 1864.

☆☆☆The Overland Campaign

On May 4, the Army of the Potomac, 118,000 strong and now directed by Gen. Ulysses S. Grant, crossed the Rapidan and Rappahannock to seek out and destroy Lee's 61,000 man Army of Northern Virginia in the dense Wilderness. For the next two days the battle raged, ending in a tactical draw. Unlike his retreating predecessors, Grant pressed on towards Richmond. On May 8, at Spotsylvania Court House, the two armies met again, resulting in the bloodiest close-range fighting of the war.

PRIVATE LETTER, FROM A SOLDIER AT SPOTTSYLVANIA

SPOTTSYLVANIA C. H., VA., May 13, 1864 [5-26-64CS]

This is the eighth day of the battles around this point. The fighting has been almost continuous all the time. So far we have punished the enemy most terribly. I thought I had seen dead Yankees on other fields, but after the fight four days ago, I rode over the field and saw thousands of them laying stretched dead on the ground in every direction, and in every conceivable attitude and mutilation. The proportion of their dead is much, far much greater than I have ever noticed before on any field. We have killed, captured and disabled over 38,000 of them. Our own losses are in all 15 or 18,000 men. It is remarkable that there are so few serious and dangerous wounds among our men. The Yankees fought splendidly the first two days [May 5-6], but they are since greatly humiliated and yesterday were made drunk to revive their Dutch courage. They made several charges on different portions of our lines, but were invariably repulsed and with great slaughter. Last night, between midnight and day, they charged that portion of our lines occupied by Benning's brigade, but the boys had four guns each, (loaded and laying by them) awaiting and expecting the attack. They were not allowed to fire until the word was given. The order was issued to fire when the enemy had got to within fifty yards of our breastworks. The guns were so well aimed that but few of the Yankees ever got back to their line, to tell the tale. This morning the ground in front of the [brigade] is covered all over with dead and wounded. Prisoners we have taken, say their army is already whipt, and we know that things have all gone "our own way" from the beginning of this fight. We have ——— men, they have 160,000; yet we have advantage of them in position, and in fighting powers, in spirit and prestige. Gen. Grant said yesterday, that "if he failed in his efforts here he would have no use for pontoons with which to recross the river." Meaning that he would have *no men* left, or in other words that he didn't intend to fail as long as he had a man left to fire a gun. If he stays anywhere near here, his army will be cut to pieces, and he will go back to Washington with his finger in his mouth. Our troops occupy a line of 14 miles, running from "Shady Grove," 5 miles north of this point, to "Hamilton's Crossing," (on the Fredericksburg and Richmond R. R.) ten miles southwest of this point. The whole line is fortified, and so is every new position we take. The Yankees occupy a line of 10 miles, running from "Todd's Tavern" on the plank-[Brock] road from Orange C. H., down to Fredericksburg, southwest from the tavern. Lee is working like a beaver. Our army is all fire and enthusiasm. They can fight a month in their present position and whip the Yankees every time.

***.

PRIVATE LETTER, FROM LEE'S ARMY
WAGON TRAIN, NEAR MILFORD., VA., May 15, 1864 [6-9-64ASC]

It is some time since I wrote to you; since then a great many changes have taken place in our army. The Yankees crossed the river on the 3rd of this month, and have been fighting every day up to the present. Our army holds a position which the whole Yankee force and twice their number cannot drive us from. Grant has charged our breastworks every day; sometimes they come up in ten columns deep, but every time they have been repulsed with heavy slaughter. Our loss up to the present time is estimated at 15,000. The Yankees are said to have lost 45,000. If it had been any other than Gen. Grant, he would have recrossed the river before now; but he said that every man in his army would have to be slain, or we would go to Richmond. Well, I am glad he will lose every man he has got before he will get to Richmond. We had a very hard fight on Sunday [May 8]. I received a very severe wound in the left hand. I don't suppose I will have the use of it for two or three months.

Once the Yankees charged our breastworks and got possession of them. Old Bob Lee came up and told our men they would have to retake them. He raised the colors, and was about to lead the charge, but some of his aids seized the bridle of his horse, and would not let him go. The men told him if he stayed back they would take them in spite of h--l when he consented to remain. They charged and re-took the breastworks, capturing and killing the enemy in a terrible manner.

***.

FIFTEENTH ALABAMA INFANTRY
[LAW'S BRIGADE, FIELD'S DIVISION]
IN THE TRENCHES, SPOTTSYLVANIA C. H., VA., May 20, 1864 [5-31-64CS]

The past two have certainly been stirring weeks, prolific in events of momentous import. The whole Confederacy is taken by storm with good news. Rumors of fights and victories have floated about "as thick as leaves in Valambrosa."

Grant's grand movement commenced on Wednesday, May the 4th, when he crossed the Rapid Ann. By a sudden march he threw himself across the river and upon our right flank, but it appeared that Gen. Lee was awake to the maneuvering of this wily and self-reliant chieftain, as was sufficiently evidenced by the very warm reception extended him at Germanna and Ely fords. By forced marching Burnside [Sedgwick] came to his support on Thursday,

May 5th, and at Wilderness Tavern the struggle was renewed in terrible earnest. There has never, perhaps, been more desperate fighting upon any field than was performed here. For eight long hours this murderous work went on. The volleys were regular and steady, and to the uninitiated who heard it at a distance would readily have been mistaken for the echoing of a thunderstorm. All the evening long and far into the night the demon of destruction and woe held its carnival amidst the demoniac revelry of the bloody hours, and from cannon's mouth and musket's blazing throat another page in our country's history was traced in lines of flame and gore. Repulsed on all sides—at every point—the enemy gave back in wild disorder, leaving his dead and wounded, with an untold number of small arms neglected upon the field.

A light haze covered the ground on the morning of Friday the 6th, but soon disappeared before the sun as if God would allow the Angels of Heaven to look down and witness this awful spectacle of man's inhumanity to man. Again the pickets commenced a slow and straggling interchange of shots. At 6 o'clock the firing became general. The enemy now bent all his energies and summoned all his resources to the fearful arena where his fate and ours and the destiny of unborn millions vibrated amid the chances of war. The enemy had intrenched himself and a less formidable work was thrown up by our own troops. This interval of ground was very warmly contested. It was fought over in some places as many as four or five times, the combatants driving each other in turns from the opposite line of rifle pits. [Winfield S.] Hancock, on the plank road, was charged and driven back. Sedgwick's corps was thrown into confusion by a terrible charge from Longstreet's [Ewell's] veterans. Now our forces pierced the right centre of the enemy. The genius of our Generals and the invincible pluck of the Southrons again triumphed, and the enemy was hopelessly driven back. The fighting to-day was akin to sublimity. With unabated violence the battle had continued throughout the entire day. Never has the pen been called upon to record more brilliant exploits than our troops performed. Standing breast to breast against twice their number, seeking no reward, impelled by no hope of safety, guided and animated by no feeling but patriotism, and asking nothing but the privilege to die side by side with their countrymen upon a field baptized with liberty's grandest effort.

The enemy withdrew from the field in the night, and two days later [on May 8] the hostile hosts confronted each other on this classic spot, where our forces have accomplished a series of victories unparalleled in the annals of war. And made this modest little village famous henceforth as the scene of the fiercest and most obstinate battles of modern times. It is useless to disguise the fact. The enemy fought well, bravely, doggedly, and this army must certainly have fallen before the splendid efforts of Grant. Time and again would the combatants meet muzzle to muzzle, man to man, and as often would our hero band, with their peculiar battle cry, shake them off like dew drops from the lion's mane. How shall we account for these repeated victories? Is it not to be found in the spirit which actuates the respective combatants. Ours is a volunteer army; composed entirely of men who have willingly forsaken the comforts and security of home to do battle in the cause of liberty and right, not mere adventurers who have no ties to bind them to the land for which they are warring, and who are willing to take any chance of bettering their desperate fortunes, not paupers to whom the camp is a refuge from starvation, nor hardened miscreants, to whom war and butchery is a delight, but young men, for the most part educated and refined, who left peace, security, and plenty, for peril, privation and death.

It is not my purpose to go into the details of the battles. This is a task for the historian. Neither are we desirous of drawing any invidious distinction. Justice forbids this, when all have done so well. Gen. Law's Ala. Brigade, famous as one of the best in the army, has not only sustained its elevated character for chivalry, but won new laurels upon every field. Its modest little leader, who has won his spurs in the field, is the idol of his brigade and the pride of every Alabamian, and we predict a wreath entirely around his stars in a month, or two, or three. The friends of the 15th Ala., may well be proud of the gallant part it has performed. Under the lead of the accomplished, energetic and intrepid [William C.] Oates it has won a chaplet of glory as enduring as history. Noble fellows! Every one of them is a hero, and they delight to follow where their gallant Colonel leads, always in the hottest of the fray where the balls are thickest, and death surest. There was not room on the flag for the number of battles through which it had passed. There was the new—the work and gift of Glennville's fair daughters, and though the noble old patriot who has so gallantly upborn it is now prostrate on a wounded bed, its folds we are sure will never be allowed to trail before a foe.

S. D. L.

On May 21, Grant once again obliquely moved southeast towards Richmond and the old battlefields east of the city.

LETTER FROM TIVOLI
[ANDERSON'S BRIGADE, FIELD'S DIVISION]
MECHANICSVILLE ROAD, June 4, 1864 [6-16-64ASC]
My last contained minutes of operations up to the 25th ult. On that day we had skirmishing all along the lines and occasionally here and there a man killed. How facile these last words slip from my pencil—"A man killed." "Who is it?" "Jarvis of Company B, a good soldier." "Yes." This is the history and eulogium of the soldier who falls among us. In the excitement of the contest, we do not grieve over a comrade and when the casualties are enumerated, we have not the time to grieve particularly, and can only join in the general lament. You may be killed to-day, but your mess will be this day as merry without you.

In the afternoon, Gen. Mahone drove a column of the enemy over the [North Anna] river. Their resistance was not a positive one and clearly showed that Grant had no intention to assail our present position. It rained hard all night, making the roads in bad condition.

Towards evening, on the 26th, some slight appearance of an assault was made on our lines, but it was with the energy of the man who raises his arm to strike, but has not the courage to give the blow. When night came we had swept their line of skirmishers from our front, and with the rain falling heavily, we laid upon our arms to enjoy a quiet and uninterrupted sleep—a luxury for some time past denied us.

On the 27th, early in the morning, it was discovered that the enemy had left our front. Our pickets advanced to the [North Anna] river, picking up occasionally the stragglers and those anxious to fall into our hands. The following illustrative incident occurred:

Among the prisoners taken this morning I recognized a man who was very active, while I was a prisoner, in relieving the wants of soldiers. In one instance I had seen him divide his rations with a Confederate prisoner. I stated this to his guard, and in a few minutes the fellow was covered with donations. One man gave him a piece of fish, another bacon, and another bread. He thanked them, and said I thought you were all starved here. This is more than I have received in a week. One of our brave fellows asked him if he had a blanket. He replied in the negative, and as I turned off I saw the questioner throw a fine blanket to him.

On the 28th we took position near the Mechanicsville road, about eight miles from Richmond, where we threw up works of an extensive character. Here every day we had skirmishing with the enemy—the first serious meeting taking place between Ewell and Grant's right on the 1st of June. The result was encouraging to us, though attended with a heavy loss of valuable officers. On the 2nd things were unusually quiet, but on the 3rd [2nd] continued and fierce assaults were made on that portion of the line occupied by McLaws' [Kershaw] division of Longstreet's corps, covered by feint assaults all along the lines. They were [un] successful, owing to the Twentieth South Carolina Regiment breaking and giving way. Their gallant Colonel, L. M. Keitt, was seriously [mortally] wounded whilst attempting to rally his men. This was the first fight in which they were engaged, and they could not stand the fiery test to which the men of their brigade (Kershaw's) [J. W. Henagan] have so often been subjected. Never mind; the next time they will redeem themselves. The works were, after some severe fighting, recaptured. The night of the 3rd [2nd], [C. W.] Field's division were placed at work constructing new and stronger defenses along the line of the day's attack. After finishing them they occupied them, and the next morning had the honor of repeating their usual work and repelling the enemy seven distinct times.

Many of the Yankees laid down upon the ground during their last retreat, and are at present coming in over our works. Our boys are encouraging them with cries of "come on," whilst the Yankee pickets are throwing their bullets after them, and the screaming shell is bursting on their path. They present the perfect picture of fear, as I have seen it represented in an old painting by Raphael; and the smack of the lips appreciately over his wine by the jolly old friar, the smile of satisfaction that flits over the German's countenance at the taste of his lager bier, the ecstasy of the Englishman over his smoking sirloin of fresh beef, do not equal in any way the rich unctuousness of the sigh they give us as they get secure under the protection of our works, and our glorious heaven-like, defiant banner.

By the way, you can never appreciate the beauty of our ensign until you see it streaming in the sunlight over a victorious, proud and determined army. To us every shot we fire under it is the announcement to the world of our liberty and independence. They may not hear their echoes, but after a while *they shall.*

TIVOLI.

LETTER FROM TOUT LE MONDE

BATTLEFIELD, GAINES' FARM, VA., June 12, 1864 [6-23-64SR]

Having executed his right wing by means of his cavalry to the Pamunkey, and thrown the Totopotomy [Totopotomoy]—a small creek—along the front of his right, Grant has quietly gone into a fortified camp, his left and centre remaining pretty much as before. Here, no doubt, he will remain to await the arrival of such forces as he will be able to draw from various sources north and west. Besides, his men, who have, according to the strictest history, been badly handled in this last campaign, need rest and an opportunity to recuperate a badly shattered *morale.* However, during this oppressive quiet he has not been idle. His tendency is to strike out from this position like all the rest, by the left flank, in order to occupy the left bank of the James. No doubt he will eventually attempt this move, for, with all his dogged perseverance and hard-headed will, surely he will not attempt any further assaults on Gen. Lee's front. A move of any sort with him now is rather hazardous, and he feels it is so. He is aware that Gen. Lee is at the fighting point, and his eagle eye is on him day and night.

To move then with safety requires his utmost circumspection. It will require, to get away in safety to the James' a passage open across the Chickahominy, and that he is provided with ways and routes to put his whole army in motion at once. A division for the shortest time might prove very fatal. The armies are too close together to risk any great deal in order to change positions. He has the courage to venture, however, if there is the slightest prospect of success, and is cautious enough to guard well against exposure. But after all he may not design going across the James. The Northern journals speak of a permanent base at the White House, which may be only conjecturing, for Grant does not make confidants of many of *them,* and if appearances are true, is reticent even with the incumbents of the Executive Mansion at Washington. "He pulls up the pole after him," says Abe Lincoln, and all the telegrams are signed with [Edwin M.] Stanton's name instead of Grant's, when speaking of the army of the Potomac. He can alter his plan, however, of forcing Gen. Lee away from the Chickahominy so as to avoid direct assaults. He may under mine his field works as the fortifications at Vicksburg, and some morning when the rebellious fraternity are quietly sleeping, may suddenly find themselves taking an exalted flight in the "upper nether and surrounding air," while Grant is seen beneath the *debris* quietly marching into the long-looked-for and long *"fout for"* Richmond. This may be one of his "castles in the air" which the hard-headed butcher has been found building constantly in this last campaign.

He ought not to forget that a popular song says something about *heads* are broken or hearts are broken, or the like, &c., "wi' castles in the air." Grant may attempt further to effect a lodgment in some part of the Confederate lines by concentrating mortars at a certain point, and by dropping shells behind the works, force their evacuation. Both sides, it is said, are using them on our right, but this is not given as history, only as rumor, not having seen anything of the kind. The reports of the guns heard in that direction from this part of the line have a suppressed, under ground growl, characteristic of mortars, differing much from the clear ring of the rifle piece. Yesterday morning Longstreet's [Early's] skirmishers were driven in on the left, which corps now holds that position, and everything was inside ready for a fight; but the enemy, satisfying himself of our guarded front, retired again behind the fortified swamps of the Totopotomy, leaving everything as quiet as before. One of the prisoners taken in this feint said a brigade of negroes were supporting them. No negroes have ever confronted our men yet, but we hear of them very often.

The militia of Petersburg [on June 9] saved the city, and shows to the world that they can be made effective. The example set by the gallant citizens of Rome, Ga., on a former occasion [the Streight Raid in early May 1863], and this ought to have a good effect on our people. Gen. Johnston may find Gov. Brown's pets a valuable auxiliary in North Georgia. It is hoped, even if they are inexperienced, they will not disappoint their friends in the army.

TOUT LE MONDE.

LETTER FROM TIVOLI
IN THE TRENCHES, June 11, 1864 [6-18-64ASC]

Since my last my journal contains no matter of much importance. Our division [Field's] repulsed the enemy on the 3rd and 5th, whilst Early, in command of Ewell's corps, drove in their right and pressed it back for four miles. The enemy seems to have relinquished their plan of attacking our works. I see by one of Stanton's official gazettes that their loss in three days' fighting at Cold Harbor was some six thousand. Our loss will not in the same time amount to three hundred. This difference in loss will show you the advantage we have. I believe that it is utterly impossible for us to be driven from our works—at least by Yankees.

Our food is good. We are drawing one half pound meat, 1½ pounds of flour, onions, peas, coffee, sugar and rice every day. It reminds one of the first year of the war.

We have had bad luck with our Generals since this campaign opened. Besides a number killed and wounded, Gen. Longstreet was wounded on [May 6], Gen. A. P. Hill sick, Gen. Ewell so ill as to be forced to leave the field; Gen. [Charles] Field is now forced to leave his command, and it is as much as Gen. Lee can do to summon strength to get about. He is forced to ride to and fro in an ambulance, and has been in this condition ever since we left Spotsylvania.

Early commands Ewell's corps; Hill has resumed command of his; [John] Gregg has command of Field's division; but who can take the place of Lee. I dread to think of such a possibility for in the future of such a prospect looms up dark and threatening shadows of Bragg and Pemberton. There are but three men in our armies who command efficiently this army—they are Lee, Johnston and Beauregard. Bragg or [John C.] Pemberton would lead them only to a Lookout Mountain or a Vicksburg. God grant that no such necessity may occur.

TIVOLI.

PRIVATE LETTER, THE SPIRIT OF OUR TROOPS
TRENCHES AT COLD HARBOR, NEAR RICHMOND, VA. [7-1-64CS]

Amusing conversations are of constant occurrence. The other morning, one of our comic fellows, interrupted while eating by an unexpected volley, shouted angrily, "Why the devil can't you let a fellow eat his dinner in peace." "Why the devil," was the quick reply, "can't you fellows learn to stop this everlasting shooting during the day. If you come over this way," continued the Yank, "we will give you all furloughs." "If you will come this way," rejoined our spokesman, "we will give you all '*Final Discharges*.'" A friendly Yankee advised us, most earnestly, not to charge their breast-works, "for," said he, "if you do, you'll catch h—l." Another called out, "We are mighty tired of this thing; how do you feel Rebs?" "We haven't been better off since the war commenced," was the reply. During the short peace established by the flag of truce [June 7], the breast-works were crowded and much railery was interchanged. The Yankee bands came up and discoursed beautiful music, to the delight of our boys. Dixie was given in fine style, and was received by our men with cheers that made the welkin ring. Then commenced the Yankee Doodle, but our boys could not imitate the politeness with which the Yanks had listened to Dixie, and deep groaning ran along our line, interjected with cries of "That's played out," &c. Our rations have not, for two years, been as abundant and satisfactory. We get coffee, sugar, onions, peas or potatoes, bacon and flour, or corn meal. By regiments the men are unanimously setting one out of every three days' issue of rations to the destitute and suffering poor of Richmond. The noble, generous people of Virginia deserve this at the hands of the men of this army; but even in the consciousness of the simple justice of the preceding, is not the mere statement of the fact full of the loftiest eloquence?

☆☆☆Siege of Petersburg

After failing to dislodge Lee's army from the Cold Harbor defenses, Grant shifted his operations south across the James River and attacked Petersburg, a vital railroad center 23 miles south of Richmond. By the end of June, after failing to take the city by assault, Grant settled into a siege.

FROM WRIGHT'S BRIGADE

IN RIFLE PITS, NEAR PETERSBURG, VA., June 26, 1864 [7-20-64AWCS]

Since last writing you there has been more or less fighting on the left [right] wing of our line of battle, with an occasional artillery duel. In our immediate front everything is quiet.

On the 22nd inst., Wright's, Mahone's [Weisiger] and Wilcox's [Sander's] (old brigade) supported by others in the division, were sent to feel the enemy, which they found strongly intrenched. We captured nearly the whole picket line, and then charged the remainder out of their rifle pits. There was some 2,000 or 2,500 prisoners captured, besides artillery, small arms, shovels and axes, and accoutrements [in the Battle of Jerusalem Plank Road]. It was a hotly contested fight for a while, the enemy holding their own until our support came up and flanked them.

While forming the line of battle, General Wright and staff rode up on a small hill, in plain view of the enemy, and not very far from them, for we heard the enemy say, "Shoot them — officers," and just then a shower if bullets saluted the ears of the party; but that did not last long, for Gen. Wright as coolly as ever rode up and gave the command "forward!" which was done, and our skirmishers soon had the skirmishers of the enemy going. We then drove the enemy out of their rifle pits and held them until we got off all of our wounded.

I do not know the loss in the brigade, or in our regiment, (the 48th) but it is not light. Company C had three wounded—Lieut. C. A. Robbe in the arm; Sergt. J. H. Read, in thigh, bone broken; Corp. [Patrick] Carroll, hand, finger shot off.

On the 23rd we again went down to where the enemy had destroyed the Petersburg and Weldon Road, and on arriving there, and while forming our line of battle, we could see the enemy commit their depredations on the road. We formed in line of battle, the 3rd Georgia thrown out as skirmishers, who succeeded in driving the enemy's skirmishers in, the remainder of the brigade following by the right flank. We marched on in this way until we came to an open field, when the line of battle was again formed, there being a space of several hundred yards between the 22nd Georgia, and the 2nd battalion and 48th. We moved in line across the field until we struck the woods, halted, sent out videttes, and continued for two or three hundred yards further, when the enemy commenced pouring it into us from behind their hastily thrown up breastworks.

In this little affair, Col. M. R. Hall was in command of the 48th and 2nd Georgia, and a more cool and gallant officer never led troops.

Capt. L. G. Doughty, who was on our right flank and in command of the 22nd Georgia, was killed in this charge, while leading this regiment. Capt. Doughty proved himself to be a brave and gallant officer, and where his duty called him, there was he always to be found. His company and regiment deeply regret his loss, and the field and company officers, as well as his old company, tender their sympathies to his bereaved parents. Dr. Swinney has charge of his remains. Capt. Doughty was struck in the left cheek bone, the ball ranging upwards; he did not live but ten minutes after he was shot.

The weather is almost suffocating, and especially to the soldier, who has to carry his rations and blankets, water, gun, accoutrements, &c. On some of the marches, men are often seen lying fainted by the roadside. There is quite a number of sick, who are being sent back to the brigade hospital, where they will receive every possible attention.

Dr. Swinney is with us, and when he is about the boys are satisfied. A more skillful surgeon is not in the service. He is always ready and willing to give a helping hand to wounded and sick men. As a proof that he is a man of good feelings and a kind heart, I would state, that he always attends to the wants of the sick and wounded before thinking of his own.

Dr. E. T. Parker, our Assistant Surgeon, is always with us in rifle pits, and everywhere else, to dress the slightly wounded.

Col. [William] Gibson is still suffering from the wound he received at Gettysburg.

This warm weather is causing a great deal of sickness.

J. A.

LETTER FROM TOUT LE MONDE
PETERSBURG, VA., June 24, 1864 [7-17-64SR]

Grant has at last accomplished his design of crossing to the south side of the James, and inaugurating a new campaign, despite the assertion that he made at Spottsylvania, of "fighting it out at this line, if it takes the whole summer." But to change a base or tell a lie is as common with one Yankee General as another, from the urbane and gentlemanly McClellan down to the Beast, the Butcher or the Brute. About the 15th of June he crossed and prepared to advance on Petersburg. Gen. Lee sent Pickett forward to occupy the works confronting Butler, that General Beauregard might withdraw and concentrate at Petersburg. The rapidity and energy of Grant's movements necessitated the withdrawal before Pickett occupied the works. A small line of skirmishers which alone held them were driven out by the enemy, and those formidable lines which Gen. Beauregard had wrested from Butler were again in his possession. But it was extremely necessary to abandon them, and no blame falls on Gen. Beauregard.

Crossing the pontoons above Drewry's Bluff on the 16th June, Pickett pushed forward to find the works [the Howlett Line] just occupied. Field followed with his division, and a line of battle was at once formed—Field occupying the right and Pickett the left. Two lines were easily taken by the skirmishers, but the last and most important remained in his possession. On the 17th Pickett ordered a charge with a heavy line of skirmishers, but the eagerness of the men in the works could not be restrained, and the whole line sprang over and went forward. The ardor of the moment spread along the whole line, and Field's men, who had no orders, went forward almost pell-mell with the line of the left, and the works, not strongly guarded, were taken in less time than it takes to describe it. The enemy fled in considerable rout, excepting some who had not the courage to fly, remained and were taken. It is said over two hundred prisoners fell into the hands of those two divisions, the majority of them taken by Pickett. The singular alacrity of this attack called forth a very pleasant little compliment to Gen. Anderson (R. H.), commanding Longstreet's corps, which has been published in the Richmond papers and copied elsewhere, but which, from its very tone—so unlike Gen. Lee's official despatches—was not intended for publication. However, before this had been accomplished and the works recovered, the enemy succeeded on the evening of the 16th in reaching the Richmond & Petersburg Railroad, and partly destroying about one mile above Walthall's Station. The damage done consisted mainly in turning over the track and burning about fifty cross ties. About night of the 17th news reached General Lee that the enemy had massed in front of Petersburg, and succeeded in forcing, after a tremendous struggle, the outer works east of the city by overpowering, the heroic little army under General Beauregard.

Before reinforcements came up, Wise's brigade [on June 15] stood like a wall of fire before the devoted city. Its lines were too contracted and flanked, but they stubbornly yielded to numbers and gave back. Capt. [Nathaniel] Sturdivant and his men stood to their guns, dealing death when the enemy were at the very mouths of their fierce pieces. Only a few of them escaped, if any, and news comes in that Capt. Sturdivant, after being captured, was brutally murdered by the negro troops. Before the enemy could again attack, reinforcements, as well as we can learn in the confusion which follows the whole affair, were hastened forward to the second line barely in time to meet the enemy, who now under cover of night moved on it. Assaults after assault followed, but were fearfully repulsed. The enemy drew off. Fearing the overpowering numbers which would assail him on the next day, Gen. Beauregard sent to Gen. Lee for reinforcements, and at midnight of the 17th McLaws' old division, under Gen. Kershaw, was sent from near Fort Drewry to his aid with all possible haste. In the meantime Gen. Beauregard, after night, deemed it expedient to attack the enemy and recover the ground lost. With [R. F.] Hoke's and Bushrod Johnson's commands—two small divisions—he undertook this bold design. Moving forward rapidly, in the pale light of a new moon, the first works were again seized after a short struggle. The enemy gathered and came again, and in turn our men were driven out. A second assault placed them once more in our grasp, and now, for two hours, an awful struggle, seen writhing in the lurid flashes of the cannon and small arms took place for these works between the undaunted little Confederate army and Grant's overwhelming legions. Again, we lost them and the enemy hold them yet.

McLaws' [Kershaw's] division came up, and the city was safe until the rest of Longstreet's [Anderson's] corps arrived on the 18th. The citizens greeted those time honored veterans, one would imagine almost with tears in their eyes. They marched through the streets with shouts and huzzahs, while banners and handkerchiefs waved from every side to welcome them in this trying moment. The excitement quieted down at once, and night found the trembling non-combatants again able to lie down with a feeling of security. Grant having failed by a *coup de main* to take the city, contented himself with strengthening his works, sharpshooting on the lines and slowly moving his left towards the Weldon and Petersburg Railroad. In these struggles our loss was great in killed, wounded and missing, besides about ten guns. The enemy's loss was as great in prisoners, killed and wounded, but as they had no guns exposed, they lost none. The advantages to the enemy in gaining position was something, as he is enabled from one point to shell the city, but otherwise his prospects for taking it are as bad as ever. It is unfortunate for the poor women and children of the eastern part of the city, known as Blandford, to be molested in their quiet homes when there is no home or shelter for them elsewhere. Many of them have gardens, on which they mainly depend for a living, which, if abandoned, would throw them on the world, more deserved of charity than ever. The enemy is base enough to elevate long ranged guns and send their cowardly messengers of destruction among them. Some thought at first they were random shots, intended for our works, passing by accident in the city; but observations this evening produced another impression. Innocent children playing before the doors, and their mothers sitting quietly inside, not dreaming at twilight that the day would be disturbed by these visitations, were suddenly compelled to fly for life and hide among the gullies and ravines, the only safe place left them. The sputtering fuse marked the curved line of each villainous shell as it left the gun and the fact was apparent at once, that it was aimed at the city. Its fiery streak, like a mad comet, flew high, and the missile burst above the house tops, scattering its fragments among the buildings. One flew lower and burst in a gable, tearing off part of the roof. Those that, by defective fuses, failed to burst, crashing through the building first entered, not sparing furniture or anything in their way; then, perhaps, into another, and finally into the earth. Woe to the poor woman or child crouching in its path. They are pitiless monsters whose hearts smell as if they had come from the devil. Civilization implores, but the Trans-Atlantic crocodiles weep and the Pharisee prays, while the gloomy clock of Horror pushes by the days.

[David B.] Birney on the night of the 21st, moved his [2nd] corps towards our right, as if to reach the Weldon & Petersburg R. R. Gen. Lee knew his position as soon as it was taken. Gens. Mahone, with Gen. R. H. Anderson's division, was ordered to move against him with Mahone's [Weisiger's], [John C. C.] Sanders' and Wright's brigades on the following day [June 22]. Towards evening, when all was apparently quiet, a sudden outburst of musketry in front of our right commenced an engagement, which, as few knew anything of it, was startling on account of its suddenness. It quickly died out, and to our astonishment an entire brigade of the enemy came marching up under guard from the firing, who said that they had been surprised and completely flanked. It appeared that this corps, 2nd A. C., commanded by Hancock, who is sick, had built temporary works to repel an attack, expecting an advance from the front. General Mahone indulged this fancy by ordering General Wright with his Georgians to demonstrate heavily in their front, and at the same time with the other brigades, one of Virginians, the other Alabamians, moved rapidly in Birney's rear. Falling suddenly on them in reverse, it is difficult to imagine a greater panic than was produced. An entire brigade, with the Colonel [Brig. Gen. Joseph Hayes] commanding it, and ten stands of colors, surrendered. Sending these to the rear, Gen. Mahone quickly placed his men in the works and prepared to hold them. The enemy with fresh lines came to the attack, determined to recover the lost works. Now the musketry became perfectly terrific. Again they were beaten, and again came back, but at each time to suffer defeat. After four heavy assaults the night came on and found our arms holding the works. The position gave us no advantage, and after moving out the wounded, four guns which were captured, and 1,500 small arms, it was abandoned. Yesterday

Mahone again attacked the enemy at Ream's Station, drove him three miles and captured 486 prisoners, making two thousand two hundred and twenty-eight in all, with a very slight loss to his own command.

The railroad is in our possession, and Grant holds himself before the Eastern part of the city.

TOUT LE MONDE.

LETTER FROM TOUT LE MONDE

PETERSBURG, VA., July 6, 1864 [7-20-64SR]

Our letters only get through now by private conveyance. The Post Office Department in this new Confederacy, is best known as a "slow team." Where interest does not lend a spur to energy, all offices tend to make themselves sinecures. The Southern Express has been little hindered by cutting the Railroad twenty-five miles, and Richmond editors constantly acknowledge indebtedness for favors from this enterprising company. The soldier languishing in the trenches from day to day, by the supineness of the postal officials, must miss the infinite solace of getting those dear treasured letters from home, for, Heaven knows, how long. With the slender protection afforded to our southern communication by our cavalry, and the dignified inertia of the Department, we affectionately bid you all farewell till Providence sees fit to provide a means of communicating with you.

[U. S. Gen. James H.] Wilson in his last raid [on the Weldon, Richmond & Danville, and Southside Railroads] suffered severely, in fact nearly lost his command, besides 700 negroes abducted from their owners, but owes his debt of vengeance to Mahone, who put himself in Wilson's path and tore him up in the rudest kind of manner. The cavalry of ours followed him very well after he was whipped, and dogged the poor fellow most woefully—in so much that he was scattered to the four winds, losing fifteen pieces of artillery, and a stream of prisoners that haven't ceased to come in yet—blue villains that overstrained mercy, has spared to eat up bread and meat in Georgia—scoundrels that God has forsaken, and whom we treat as civilized prisoners of war. It is a noble triumph of civilization to spare the vanquished brave foe, and to him honor for his valor, but what question is there about the destruction of these ravishing, stealing, devastating villians that disregard humanity in raiding through our land. Could we not, as a brave people, say that no mercy should be left to our own men, if they so unhumanly conducted themselves in the enemy's country? Our blood runs cold at some recitals that come to our ears since the advent and exit of these Huns, but we must follow the example of our patient government, which, it seems, cherishes endurance that has long lost its virtue.

Watch a train of wagons from the mountain top moving through the far off valley, and the eye can scarcely discern that it moves; so the train of events drags along here since Birney and [Philip] Sheridan and Wilson have met with disasters. The weather is exceedingly dry, no rain having fallen on our army since June 3d, and, with the eternal and ubiquitous dust, the beaming sultry sun, the doleful sight of the parched and wilted vegetation, one feels like inviting the somnolency of Rip Van Winkle to escape it all. On some parts of the lines a few sharpshooters peer above the works, and manifest a little energy by popping an occasional ball over at an adventurous head, but the potent rays of the ardent Phoebus above us, forbid activity. Even the sound of cannon comes lazily to the ears across the radiant fields, and the only lively things, the shell, kicks up a cloud of dust that slowly floats away in the languishing zephyr. The "Mortles" as the "tar heel boys" insist on naming those surly visitors from the enemy's mortars, are growing less frequent in the enervating summer days. In the cool breezes of night, which happily relieve the oppressive heat of the sun, they become quite active, at times marking the dark sky with tracks of curved fire, and dropping behind, or in, or on the works, scattering fragments of death around. Our batteries reply—mortar batteries— and we see scampering occasionally in the fire light reflecting from behind the enemy's works, and then a volley from our rifles follow these refugees from the unceremonious visitor who "hopes he don't intrude." The lines are close together in some places; in others a distance of five hundred yards separate them. Wherever they are close the place is kept warm by the sharpshooters; and a head, nor even a part of a head, is not safe above the earthwork. A good soldier was sitting, a day or two ago, just after sunrise, a few steps behind the works, and thought himself hid, but a lynx-eyed sharpshooter saw his head exposed above the supposed protection. As poor Tom raised a cup of coffee to his lips, the bullet aimed at him crashed through his brain, and he was dead. No word of farewell to comrades, no cry of pain, not a whisper escaped him as he slowly sank down to sleep. Friends straightened out the lifeless form, covered him over with his faithful blanket till night, then laid him away with prayer by the side of comrades who bravely fell as he did.

Day and night, with little intermission, the enemy continues to throw shells into the city. Nothing is effected by it, save an occasional murder of a woman or child. These have now been frightened away, and the sacrificing non-combatants have gone out of the reach into the country, some crowding in with friends, others sojourning in tents by the dusty wayside. The usually gay thoroughfares are solemnly quiet when the shriek of the Parrot missiles are not heard in the air or lumbering through the dwellings. One looks down the deserted vistas and about the gloomy, tenantless buildings, and imagines some powerful spirit has laid an enchanted hand upon the devoted city. Here and there great holes are seen through the walls, or windows smashed, colonades crushed, pavements torn up, or other marks of the raging cannon shot. If the city is not burned, for many years the signs of this infamous vandalism will remain to instruct the future historian.

A word, and we will close abruptly. It is below the real figures that Grant has lost 14,000 men and 19 pieces of artillery since arriving before Petersburg.

TOUT LE MONDE.

LETTER FROM TOUT LE MONDE

CHAFFIN'S FARM, August 1, 1864 [8-20-64SR]

So little of importance has transpired in the vicinity of Richmond since our last, the body of a letter could not be raked nor scraped from the dull monotony. But the morning of the 30th July somewhat changed the aspect of affairs, for "something turned up," leaving a hole in the ground, all so suddenly in the early morning light that the sleepy nations and careless Confederates were amazingly astonished. For a long time our eyes have been steadily turned on the last northern prodigy of military ability—United States Grant—to discover what he was really up to, holding himself so silently hid away behind his formidable works east of Petersburg. It was generally conceded that he was going to attempt something at some day before the close of summer, gathering our intelligence from the vague hints of Yankee army correspondence alluding to future movements of their idol, which was to "electrify the whole nation." But no satisfactory clue to what the movement would really be, could ever be obtained. Prisoners, long distinguished for mendacity, warned us of the truth that Grant was mining our works in front of Petersburg, but with the usual want of reliance in these unmitigated liars, no attention was paid to their statements. It turned out that their accounts were true for once. Having completed a mine which formed its way under Pegram's battery, near the Baxter road, which leads out from the city due east, Grant prepared a plan (which would have been credible, if it had fooled Gen. Lee) intended to leave Petersburg as little defended as possible, and, by the breach which his mine when sprung would make, force a way into the city. A heavy force [led by Gen. Hancock] threatened Richmond from the north side of the James, which was crossed about the 27th. This force made a feint to secure a strong position near Deep Bottom, and in fact appeared in so much strength that Gen. Lee sent forces adequate to meet it if it should prove a serious attempt on Richmond. Some inattention on the part of our pickets allowed their reconnoitering force to surprise a battery of 4 Parrott guns, which fell into their hands. But this terminated the demonstration from the north side.

Believing that he had sufficiently drawn away Gen. Lee from Petersburg, and that our lines were weak there, Grant, on the morning of 30th, blew up the battery above mentioned, and assaulted the lines while our men were in confusion from the unexpected event. Two divisions from Burnside's corps, led [supported] by the negroes, (now the most respectable and valiant soldiers in Grant's army) succeeded in gaining the breach, and effecting a lodgement in our works. What our casualties really were by the explosion is not yet ascertained; one hundred and fifty, including 20 of the battery, it is thought, will cover the loss. The main loss was in recovering the works. Gen. Mahone was quickly apprised of our disaster, and hurried his command from the right to the support of Gen. [Bushrod] Johnson, who was holding the line across the Baxter road. With two brigades, Wright's Georgia and Mahone's [Weisiger's] Virginia troops, a part of the lost lines were recovered, but a part remained in the hands of the enemy until Sanders' Alabama brigade arrived, and then a second assault took the works from the enemy and all the troops that held them, together with the artillery which had been placed along them by the enemy.

A short duration of confusion, a few of our men lost, a temporary possession of our lines, and the grand "electric" movement recoiled on Grant in a most miserable failure. He leaves the ground that he gains in a stampede, save the slaughtered Africans and Dutchmen which covered it, and who will never stampede any more battlefields. Over a thousand prisoners crouched shivering behind the works they had rushed up to the confusion caused in our lines by the explosion, who surrendered most joyfully when our lines again hurled themselves back on them. The crater of the home-made volcano, which was about thirty feet deep and as many wide, was filled with a crowd of dastardly refugees from Confederate bullets, consisting of a general [William F. Bartlett], his staff, some Dutchmen, many negroes in Yankee attire, all in wonderful *olla podrida*, the general constituting a sort of centre ingredient. Thus were the lines re-established, and thus was the immortal fool and little concern, Grant, forced to witness a month's preparation blown into folly and discomfiture. Instead of drawing Gen. Lee away, the place was more strongly guarded and more closely watched than ever. Gen. Lee, no doubt, was disappointed about the mining operation. He never, probably, supposes that Grant was reduced to the puerile folly of mining out an army that can defeat him in an open field. This was the grand maneuver that was to "electrify" the northern people. There is not a ten year old darkey in the South but could not be induced to shake his sides with mirth if one would explain to him the ludicrous condition in which Grant and Lincoln find themselves now. As the *Examiner* says, it is too serious with death for us to laugh; but, indeed, the outside world must be grandly amused at the miserable farce of taking Richmond and leaving the "sacred" soil of Yankeedom open to be trampled over by [Early's] Rebel invaders, who knock at the very door of their own capital. He sends a force [the Sixth Corps] to save Washington from this army. Early quietly withdraws, with everything he wants, into the Valley of Virginia. Back goes Grant's veterans to shell Petersburg, and back goes——, [Early] falls on the sagacious traveler, [David] Hunter, and sets him fleeing in squads across the Potomac. Again Yankeedom is in consternation over a storm that they had supposed passed, and again Grant's veterans, twenty thousand strong, are flying towards their capital, to beat the Rebel invader to that point. The whole picture could be drawn at once by making a pleasant, active little man, calmly hold a great fat booby off at arm's length, in spite of his struggles, and "whaling" him for amusement over the cranium with a "good hickory."

The removal of Gen. Johnston from the command of the army in Georgia, occasioned great surprise in this army, and a general feeling of regret was manifested by all. To speculate on the expediency of such a change at this juncture after the step already taken by the President, if any editor and correspondent in the South should inveigh against it, and history must determine for us all if it was just and proper to take it. Probably it is right, no doubt it is better for us if Gen. Hood can get the earnest support of the Administration, which it is complained was not extended to Gen. Johnston. It is difficult to believe that our President, with all the noble patriotism that has characterized him in this great struggle, could descend to little personalities or spites when such momentous questions and interests are involved as these which effect us now. Rather let us judge that it was not in the power of the President to throw any aid in Gen. Johnston's favor, and that Gen. J's. removal arose simply out of an honest difference between two great patriots.

If Grant, who would doubtless have been an especial favorite of Macawber, causes anything else of interest to "turn up," our delight will be to keep you, in our poor way, informed.

TOUT LE MONDE.

LETTER FROM VIRGINIA, A GHASTLY SCENE
PETERSBURG, VA. [8-11-64CS]

I have visited the chasm caused by the enemy's explosion. It appears to be about 40 feet depth and some 200 feet in circumference, and resembled more what one would imagine to have been the effects of a terrible earthquake than anything else to which we could liken it. Immense boulders of earth were piled up rudely, one above the other, and great fragments of bomb-proofs, gun-carriages, limbers, &c., were lying promiscuously in every direction. One man was caught between two boulders, near the surface of the ground, and literally crushed between them. He still remained in this painful position with only his head and neck visible, our men not having had time to extricate him. Life had long been extinct, but the ghastly-looking face was unmarked by a scratch, and the head perfect, but slightly reclining on the shoulder.

The sides and bottoms of the chasm were literally lined with Yankee dead, and the bodies lay in every conceivable position. In one spot we noticed a corporal of infantry, a sergeant of artillery, and a big, burly negro, piled one upon top of the other. Some had evidently been killed with the butts of muskets as their crushed skulls and badly mashed faces too plainly indicated, while the greater portion were shot, great pools of blood having flowed from their wounds and stained the ground.

Between our breastworks and the enemy's large numbers of dead and wounded were still lying, the latter begging piteously for water and praying to be cared for. Our men could not relieve them, as they were in full range of the enemy's sharpshooters, who had not ceased their firing, even under such appalling circumstances as we have described.

The length of the "sap" made by the enemy is supposed to have been about 600 feet, but the work is not so great as many unacquainted with the appliances used for such purposes would suppose. Immense augers, made specially for such occasions, are brought into requisition, and by this means, we are informed, a vast deal of work can be accomplished in a short space of time. Just where the mine was sprung and the explosion occurred, the earth is formed of hard substance, such as is generally known as "pipe clay," and this accounts for the great boulders of earth which were rent asunder and upturned by the force of the explosion.

The labors of the enemy in this operation have been poorly repaid. The very timely arrival of Gen. Mahone, and the quick perception of his military mind soon placed our gallant boys in position and retrieved the disaster.

The enemy's losses from all causes are estimated at 3,500 men. We have over 1,000 prisoners in our possession, 14 battle flags, and upwards of 2,000 stands of small arms. We took no cannon, because the enemy brought none with them. The four pieces captured by the explosion, attached to Pegram's battery, were afterwards dug up from the rubbish uninjured.

Our entire loss is ascertained to be about 800. Among the killed, I regret to state, are some of our very best men.

***.

LETTER FROM "BOHEMIA."
FORTY-THIRD ALABAMA INFANTRY
[GRACIE'S BRIGADE, JOHNSON'S DIVISION]
PETERSBURG, VA., August 17, 1864 [9-1-64MAR]

If my letters reach you as seldom as Alabama papers arrive at this point, the news contained in them is stale indeed. Montgomery papers of the 1st of July only reached us on the 10th of this month, and Mobile papers never find their way to our camp at all. Is this the fault of the Post office Department, or do the sundry officials, through whose hands they pass, appropriate all "printed matter" that is intended for us who are on the front? It is a crying evil, and I sincerely hope that the press and the "army correspondents" will call the attention of the Department to it, and, if possible, have it remedied.

Long ago I wrote you that the siege of Petersburg was fast becoming a farce; that it would soon cease to be of any interest even to our own people, and that the outside world would laugh at it, as the most ludicrous exhibition of human folly on record. I did not anticipate the explosion and assault of the 30th, but that has had no effect in changing the result, which everybody saw was inevitable. Neither our people nor the Southern press seem to have fully appreciated the depressing influence that the defeat of the 30th has created in the North. Their papers call it a great calamity—a terrible blow to the Federal cause, and a grand triumph for the rebels. Never before has a defeat been so distinctly and clearly acknowledged. The opposition papers all say Grant's campaign has ended; that the work of subjugation has to be commenced anew, and that ruin and bankruptcy are staring the North in the face. The Republican organs charge Burnside and Meade with mismanagement, and a court of inquiry was called to investigate the matter. But the court is suddenly dissolved, under the pretence that it had been illegally convened, but in reality because facts and figures would come to light that would be of infinite service to the Chicago [Democratic] Convention. In the meantime, corps after corps is withdrawn from before the city; and the siege becomes as uninteresting as that of Troy while Achilles was keeping his tent and shunning the battlefield. The Yankee lines have been contracted, and now are not more than three miles in length, on the south side of the Appomattox. It is said Burnside's corps are the only troops in our front. Where are all the balance of the "Grand Army of the Potomac"? The policy of concentrating and massing their army has been abandoned, and the "Army of the Potomac" is now at Washington, in the Valley, before Petersburg, at Bermuda Hundreds, and across the James, fighting mosquitoes, sand flies, and the malaria fevers of Deep Bottom. As far as regards aggressive warfare, the army which last May, "in the pride, pomp and circumstance of glorious war," crossed the Rapidan on its mission of conquest, has ceased to exist. One portion of it is at this time engaged in a singular piece of work. Having failed in every attempt, and being moved by some strange desire to re-enact the siege of Vicksburg over again, Gen. Grant [Butler] has undertaken to cut a canal across Dutch Gap and turn the channel of the James river. What he expects to accomplish by this, I cannot conceive. Even if successful in turning the river, the upper end of the canal would be below Chaffin's and Drewry's Bluff, and if he should carry his transports and gunboats through, he would have these fortifications, the only thing that opposes his advance, still before him. But as there was a canal at Vicksburg, the strategy of Gen. Grant makes one at Richmond imperatively necessary. The Yankee papers say "Gen. Grant looks confident and hopeful," and that "he thoroughly understands the work before him, and knows exactly what he is doing." Possibly, he may be carrying out some well matured plan, but if there is any mortal man who does fully understand the situation, and can see reasons why Gen. Grant should be "confident and hopeful," he is gifted beyond all the rest of the world, and ought certainly to revise "Jomini's Art of War," and show that the tactics of all the great captains, since Marlborough's Line, were a mistake, and Napoleon's maxims the idle speculations of a foolish theorist.

We Alabamians felt ourselves humiliated at the surrender of Fort Gaines, but we still have faith in the bravery and patriotism of the people of Mobile. "Brave men are the best wall," was the saying of the Spartan King, and history proves its correctness. Look at Charleston, that is still free and defiant—at Petersburg, that for sixty-six days has been exposed to the shot and shell of the enemy, and yet has been neither burned, knocked to pieces nor greatly injured. On the 15th of June the Yankees took Battery No. 5, and their guns commanded every part of the city. Since that time an entire new line has been built, and the troops of Beauregard and Lee have fortified the place stronger than it was before the outside works were taken. Let not the people be demoralized by shell. Let those non-combatants who cannot leave, dig "bomb-proofs" in their yards; let the fire companies be vigilant and active; let every man who can shoot a gun or handle a spade take his place in the trenches, and Mobile can safely bid defiance to Yankee fleets and armies.

BOHEMIA.

August 18, 1864

My letter of yesterday was not sent off, being too late for the regimental mail carrier. I will, therefore, add a few more lines. The fight near Deep Bottom on the 16th was a very unexpected affair. No one thought Grant would be so foolish as to divide his forces and attempt to take Richmond with only half of his defeated army by the same route that McClellan had failed on. But his fortunes are growing desperate, and desperate men have nothing to lose by trying every chance. He has met with another defeat. The "ubiquitous Mahone" again met him, and as at Ream's station and the result of the 30th, victory again perched on his banners. In this division is Wilcox's old brigade of Alabama troops. They have been engaged in almost every battle in Virginia, and have never yet met with a repulse. Alabama may well be proud of this gallant brigade. Having come to grief on the north side of the James, Grant will be compelled to concentrate again. He will have to abandon his canal, or else withdraw from Petersburg. To-day he threw a portion of his force round to the left [initiating the Battle of Weldon Railroad (Aug. 18-21)], and there has been some sharp fighting in that direction. The result is not yet ascertained, but from the fact that the firing has ceased and no troops have been moved from the line, and no unusual excitement created at headquarters, it is reasonable to conclude the Yankees have had their usual luck.

At two o'clock this morning the artillery all along our front opened on the Yankees. Till daylight the firing was rapid and continuous; mortar shell were bursting, howitzers, Napoleons and Parrott guns filled the air with all the horrid thunder of modern warfare. The object was to try the strength of the Yankees. They replied very feebly. From the front of [Archibald] Gracie's only four guns could be seen, and only seven mortars were used. This shows that they have removed many of their heavy mortars and guns. They have quit shelling the city, sharpshooting has comparatively speaking, ceased and sometimes two or three days pass without a mortar shell being thrown at the brigade. Gen. Gracie is at present commanding the division, during the temporary absence of Gen. Johnson. There is no more watchful or more energetic and accomplished officer than Gen. Gracie. He deserves promotion, and I hope will not be long before he may be made Major General.

After a long dry spell, the rain fell in perfect torrents day before yesterday. The ditches were turned into small creeks, and all our "bomb-proof" hiding places flooded. Through one part of our line a small branch passes. The Yankees had dammed this up on their picket line, and behind this a large pond was quickly formed. The Yankee cut their line and let off the water, and it rushed down like a mill-race, sweeping away ditches and salients, traverses and sand bags, and completely routing two companies, that had to seek higher ground. The water annoyed the Yankees greatly—nearly all their works, in our front, are on lower ground than ours, and their ditches seem to have filled up. All that evening they were busy bailing them out. Our sharpshooters took advantage of this, and poured a heavy and continuous fire into them. They must have suffered pretty heavily. If the wet weather continues, it will necessarily cause a great deal of sickness, but as the Yankees are confined to swamps of the James and Appomattox, if they can stand it we can.

BOHEMIA.

LETTER FROM TOUT LE MONDE

NEAR RICHMOND, VA., August 20, 1864 [9-1-64SR]

It is possible that our communications south [Weldon Railroad] is again cut, and some days may elapse before it is open again. Indeed, the enemy, who day before yesterday occupied a position on the Weldon and Petersburg Railroad are still on it, and up to the hour of writing have not been driven from it. Yesterday he was attacked and driven down it two times, losing many killed and wounded and two thousand prisoners, but another battle is necessary to force him from it entirely, which will most likely be delivered to-day. This railroad has been a sore place to Grant, having alone cost him 6,000 prisoners, to say nothing of his killed and wounded. We are not informed that any artillery has been taken this time, but in previous times he has lost nineteen pieces. Baffled and beaten at every point, enraged over his disappointed hopes and ambition, the whole North crying out against his failures, he now begins to feel really desperate. He flies from one point of his lines to another, trying vainly to force a way here; then flying back, vainly tries to force a way yonder, only to howl under a succession of failures and add again and again to his hecatomb of dead already sacrificed to the malice of his master at Washington. What they will not do in the name of the Lord is yet to be seen. His last advance from the north side of the James [Second Deep Bottom] was a repetition of his usual ludicrous failures, resulting in some painful losses to us, but in his utter and disgraceful defeat.

On the night of the 13th his prisoners tell us he crossed over two corps to the north side to carry by a *coup de main* our works there and force a passage suddenly to the capital. He found by experimenting with skirmishers on the 14th that our lines were guarded. The plan of forcing his way suddenly was in consequence abandoned, and he employed the day maneuvering towards our extreme left, as if intending to march entirely around our flank. This was found again impracticable, and it seemed on the 15th he was so at a loss to decide that the day passed off without any further effort to harm us than a little sharpshooting. Grant was present himself, with Hancock and the Monkey in Chief [Edward] Ferrero, dancing master, tight rope performer, and commander of the *corps de darkies*.

On the 16th, it was generally thought that from what Grant had seen he had common sense enough to go back to his den at Bermuda Hundreds and around Petersburg, but to our astonishment and the gratification of the troops generally he decided on an assault. This was commenced on our extreme left opposite Gen. Mahone's troops, about 12 m. in the day, near Fussell mill, on the Darbytown road. From the manner in which the attack was made, and the large force thrown against the lines, both of negroes and whites, our lines were temporarily broken. It happened in this way: In front of Gen. [V. J. B.] Girardey's brigade, distance 100 yards or more, there was a ravine which screened the maneuvers of the enemy, and allowed them to mass in large numbers while they were advancing or demonstrating at other points. Our line was far from being a heavy one, and having arranged an assaulting column in column of regiments, negroes in front, the enemy advanced suddenly on this small brigade, striking the front of the 10th Georgia battalion. These overwhelming numbers of the enemy were met with the usual heroism of those determined men, but pushed on one column on another, they were virtually shoved upon Girardey's men, who, overpowered, were driven out in confusion. The brave and undaunted Girardey was, unfortunately, shot while exhorting his men to deeds of heroism, which was to surpass their past brilliant name. A ball entered his forehead and he died at his post—a braver and brighter spirit never passed away. The enemy then poured over in large numbers, turning our flank and forcing back the other troops—happily in order—which found themselves flanked by the break in the lines. A part of Law's and Anderson's brigades were hastened forward by Gen. Field, who quickly confronting the horde that were advancing up the Darbytown road, received them so warmly that they were checked at once. [James H.] Lane's North Carolina troops and [Samuel] McGowan's South Carolina brigades soon reinforced Anderson's and Law's men, who were bearing the brunt of a heavy fight, and the enemy were partly forced back to the works. Benning's Georgia brigade was hastened forward from the right, under Col. D. M. DuBose, and arrived while the fight was raging very severely. The day was excessively warm, and the trial of bringing up men under such a sun at the double-quick step was no ordinary one, but no men ever came up better than this last brigade. They were scarcely on the spot before being fronted and joined on to the right of Lane's troop, they were thrown in. A charge was made along the whole line and the works carried instantly. The enemy were shot down in heaps at the entrenchments, in some places the negroes falling on the corpses of the whiter Yankees. Three or four hundred prisoners were secured, of which, strange to say, only two of the misguided negroes remained among them to reach the Libby. Col. [Alexander A.] Lowther, of the 15th Alabama, was wounded badly; and Major [William] Oates lost an arm; Major [George W.] Cary, of the 44th Alabama, was painfully, but we are happy to say, not mortally wounded. Still further to our left, which was guarded by cavalry, the enemy made an advance and drove back these forces a short distance, in which Gen. [John R.] Chambliss was killed and left in the hands of the enemy. Subsequently the enemy were forced back in disorder, and two or three hundred prisoners were captured. The *Washington Chronicle*, of the 15th, taken since, says this movement was to capture Chaffin's Bluff and destroy the pontoons there, that General Lee might be cut off from the forces on the north side of the James, and of course Richmond would fall easily. Fine programe—part of "my plan"—no doubt, and the awful Richmond is to fall now. What has become of that serviceable gentleman known as the fool-killer?

This paper contains a long dissertation on peace, manifesting considerable concern about the probable plans of certain peace factions among the northern population. Of course, as an exponent of the Gorilla [President Lincoln], it is alarmed at any symptoms of the decline of his power, and these unmistakable signs of resistance are ominous to the *Washington Chronicle*. Its daily bread depending on Lincoln and the war; its pockets growing heavy with the iniquity of the Ape King—all the north is crazy to even dream of peace. Such is the opinion of the *Chronicle* and the rhinoceros hided *New York Herald*; hail fellows well met.

As soon as information of the operations around Petersburg can be obtained we will write again; at present our command is north of the James.

TOUT LE MONDE.

LETTER FROM TOUT LE MONDE

NEAR RICHMOND, VA., August 31, 1864 [9-6-64SR]

This day closes the eventful summer of 1864, which to-morrow will drop into the eternal past, but whose fame of blood will go on till history forgets all that lays behind it. May it be the last of its kind forever. May those hopes of peace, which now come as a bright light through surrounding darkness prove not *ignis fatuus*, whose delusions shall plunge us into deeper darkness hereafter.

The concourse of events in this department of our war has fled towards the Weldon Railroad. Only a small force now occupy the strong fortifications across Dutch Gap, north side of the James, among which Ferrero's "braves" are seen along the picket lines, tacitly acknowledging that negro soldiers are only fit to be placed under cover of the gunboats. Among them are seen a sufficient number of whites to "guard the guard," all purporting to be under the command of [Robert S.] Foster, who is a considerable favorite with his troops, for a very quaint reason, when we recollect the South is to be whipped back into the Union. They like him because he holds a quiet place and a strong one in Dutch Bend. Across the river, Butler still holds his line near Bermuda Hundreds, and the gunboats which are ever ready to gather him and his horde "as a hen gathereth her brood" when danger threatens. His canal, which is to cut off enough James river to put him seven miles nearer Richmond, progresses, so the Yankee papers say, very finely, but we venture to assert never was any canal pushed ahead "very finely" under more difficulties. On a high hill southwest of this progressive work is what is known as Howlett's battery, erected by Confederate engineers, and containing some distressing heavy guns that are manned by Confederate artillerists, who take a very wanton delight in constantly, day and night, casting from these guns heavy explosive bodies of iron into this very work. What is worse, the very spot where workmen are seen, becomes a mark for their malicious practice. A few words will describe how the work is conducted. One man watches all the while, and when the cloud of white smoke rises from Howlett's battery, he jumps into his hole with a cry to "look out." This cry is generally disobeyed to the letter, as everyone, to the man, looks in, which he hardly does before down comes the crashing shell directly into the very excavation he vacates. The explosion over, back the working party goes to the picks and spades and the man to the lookout. The number of dodges requisite to complete a day's work and the time occupied in so doing, raises the question whether the working party earn their rations for the work or for the dodging that is done. When Butler's canal strikes the James at its north end (not the north end of the river,) where will he find himself? We heard an anecdote which will, perhaps, illustrate his position. A mischievous sow found the trunk of a hollow tree that opened into a prosperous corn field which hollow tunneled a fence that had defied her greatest efforts to penetrate. She made use of it to the annoyance of the owner, who chasing her out through her entrance, turned the log so that both ends opened outside the field. When Mad. Pork came the next time she entered as usual, but to her surprise came out on the outside. Thinking there was some mistake, she entered again, but the same result followed. The darkey, who was watching, relates that this time her surprise knew no bounds, and uncurling her tail, left with it sticking out straight behind, so hasty was her flight.

The news before Petersburg is more important at this time than anything else, as it seems the stirring times on the banks of the Potomac have subsided or drifted southward. Grant had so far gained possession of the Weldon Railroad that it was necessary to make an attempt of some magnitude to drive him back from it. To anticipate a little, the result so far has been a failure, but the fruits have been substantial and glorious. Over five thousand prisoners are recorded, nine pieces of artillery and seven stands of colors in our hands. Grant's losses are certainly fifteen thousand, including all, while our own will not reach five thousand, including everything. The battle of the 25th [Ream's Station] was important for many reasons, but particularly for our cavalry [Hampton's] fighting as dismounted men. They have now shown a distinguished ability for charging and taking earthworks, which has been denied to them before.

On the morning of the 25th Gen. A. P. Hill brought up forces at Reams' Station, by way of Boydton plank road, from near Petersburg. Gen. Hampton's cavalry, which was already there, engaged the enemy's cavalry about four miles below the station, and pressed him back across the railroad as far as Malone's crossing. About 4 p. m. Gen. Hill [Heth] determined to assault the works which crossed the road. To accomplish this, four brigades of dismounted cavalry were to form an assaulting column on the east of the road, and five of infantry to make another, west of it. Anderson's Georgia Brigade and [Alfred M.] Scales' North Carolina troops were first thrown forward, but these were repulsed in confusion without effecting a lodgment. Then Gen. Heth, with [J. R.] Cooke's, [William] MacRae's and Lane's North Carolina brigades, moving a little to the right and advancing with the cavalry, marched through every obstacle of earth and abattis and the hail storm of bullets and grape shot, up to the works, from which the enemy, seeing such determination in the assailants, fled precipitately, leaving the cannon in our hands. The cavalry did not falter, but vied with the infantry, as we are told, in being the first to reach the enemy's lines. The cavalry line secured six hundred prisoners; in all twenty-five hundred are reported from this single charge. The infantry had a most desperate fight hand to hand, at the works, but the enemy soon fled, and some of the infantry sprang to the artillery, which were turned against the fugitives with great effect. Driving them across the road, they were forced off in a southeasterly direction, who, but for the night, that now came on, would have been terribly destroyed. During the battle, Pegram's celebrated battery was engaged, and with its enfilade fire on a part of the enemy's line did most fearful execution. After the fight, in the track of the shot from guns, men were seen torn to pieces—heads, arms and legs scattered around, and bodies horribly mangled.

We cannot refrain from mentioning the distinguished cavalry brigades that were engaged with so much effect, and which will not be forgotten in the future history of these battles. They were [M. C.] Butler's, Rosser's, [Rufus] Barringer's and [John R.] Chambliss'—he who was killed on the north side of the James on the 16th of this month.

Night closed on our victorious men too soon, and so much remained for them to do next day, that no further effort has been made to drive the enemy further. During the night the enemy had so strengthened his new lines and got up so many fresh troops, Gen. Hill did not deem it advisable to continue the battle. As they stand, the enemy still command the road in such a manner that it is not of any use to us. It has been destroyed about 2½ miles below Reams' Station, but the loss of it is far from capturing Richmond.

Whether General Lee intends that they shall continue to hold it, *nous verons*. Rations have not grown any shorter since Grant's possession of it.

TOUT LE MONDE.

This was the last known letter penned by "Tout le Monde." With no additional information provided by the editors of the Savannah Republican, *his identity and fate remain a mystery.*

HURT'S—HARDAWAY'S ALABAMA BATTERY
NEAR PETERSBURG, VA., September 8, 1864 [9-17-64CS]

September brings with it chilly mornings, and we find our Summer equipment of blankets insufficient for comfort, just before day. We are in hopes however that we may add to this on the next battle field which may be fought soon, and if on the right, we are sure to be there. In the meantime as long as wood can be had, we can make ourselves comfortable by means of fires.

Yesterday the Yankees were discovered to have constructed a railroad running from City Point to some point to the right of this city. The Whitworth gun of the battery was immediately placed in position to command it, and opened fire on the first train that passed up. The first shot was at random, the engineers having neglected to triangulate the distance; it however had the effect of increasing the speed of the train from ten to thirty miles an hour. The second shot, fired while the train was moving at the latter rate and three miles distant, struck a little beyond the track and would have struck the train, if it had not passed out of range during the flight of the shot. Watch was kept for the next train or return of the same, but not one made its appearance before dark. Lieut. [George] Ferrell now has a fine opportunity of practicing, and the firing will be resumed whenever a train makes its appearance.

The section of 3 inch rifled guns is still in park off the line and the men are pleasantly encamped in an apple orchard, the trees of which answer good purpose in the heat of the day by affording shade. At no time during the campaign has there been such inactivity as has characterized the conduct of the army during the last week. There has been no movement or shifting of the troops whatever; at least on this (south) side of the Appomattox river. You may form your own conclusion from our facts.

HAUSSE.

LETTER FROM HURT'S BATTERY

NEAR PETERSBURG, VA., September 10, 1864 [9-18-64CS]

There has been heavy firing of artillery along the line in front of [Joseph] Finegan, and about forty of our men were captured last night. It was however retaken with the same number of prisoners this morning. At about eleven o'clock the enemy opened fire on the Whitworth guns. One of the shells struck and exploding, killed Sergeant John P. Borom, the last of the three noble sons of Mr. Benj. Borom, of Macon county, who enlisted in the Battery.

Ever thus it has been that the best and bravest are the first to fall.

In haste,   HAUSSE.

PRIVATE LETTER, INICIDENTS OF PICKET LIFE [9-15-64MAR]

Some time ago an order was issued by our commanding general prohibiting deserters from the enemy entering our lines, and the pickets were instructed to waive them back, and if they did not go to fire upon them. For a week after the promulgation of this order, many attempts were made by deserters to enter our lines, and it was amusing to see their signals and signs, that they were "all right," while our boys would not understand them. The consequence was, that in a little while the stream of deserters ceased to flow, and we thought ourselves rid of such troublesome customers forever.

We hold a line in close proximity to the enemy, the rifle pits occupied by the pickets being in some place only fifty yards apart; but an arrangement existed preventing firing by either party upon the other. During the "armistice," frequent attempts were made by the Yanks to exchange papers and swap coffee for tobacco; but orders were strict, and officers alert, so that no opportunity was allowed, had the inclination prevailed, to trade with the enemy. Among the tricks resorted to by the enemy to hold communication was this: They would write anything they desired to communicate upon a small piece of paper and roll it around a Minie or a grape shot and throw it across the line. One of these missiles brought over the following:

"Johnny—Will you trade papers with us? We have all about the capture of the *Alabama*, the raid upon Harper's Ferry, &c. Meet me half way; you need not be afraid of our shooting you. We can have a friendly game of euchre, and wind up with whiskey."

"Johnny Reb—Is the Fifty-third Virginia still on this line? I have two friends in that regiment—got acquainted with them while exchanging papers, and think they are nice fellows, from appearances. Toss your reply over as I do this."

No notice was paid to these communications, and after the deserters were stopped for some time, our General became desirous to learn something of the enemy's motions, and issued an order offering a fifteen days' furlough for a captured Yankee. Now, as soon as this order was made known along our picket lines, everybody wanted the furlough, and all sorts of tricks were practiced to entrap a Yankee.

Our boys commenced shaking papers and beckoning, but blue bel—breast "smelt a mice" at so much fondness expressed in a moment, and failed to come out of his hole.

Some good stories are told upon some of the boys, two of which I remember just here.

A reb starts out with a paper, and a pistol concealed, to meet a Yankee who showed himself in the woods fifty yards from our pits. Getting within five steps of Yank, he presents his pistol and cries out, "Surrender," but just then another Yank, close at hand, poked his gun around a tree and says, "Swap papers, damn you, and get you gone." Which reb did in *fast* time.

A good one is told on two young officers who wanted a furlough. One goes out unarmed with a paper, and waived it for some time to entice Yank to come over, while the other stood ready to rush to his assistance.

After a while a burly, Irishman came up, and the captain at once grappled him and endeavored to lead him in. But Irishman was too stout; and shouldering our spunky little captain, was walking off with him, when up ran the lieutenant with a pistol, and Irishman "caved in" and was brought over a prisoner; but Gen. Pickett said he couldn't give a furlough upon any such capture as that, and sent the Irishman back, as he wasn't taken with arms in his hands.

Then came General Order No. 65, and we teased them over the lines. In a day or two the order worked like a charm, and they came rolling in by the dozen. We sometimes got fifteen deserters in one night; all claiming protection under General Order No. 65.

***.

SIGHTS ON A BATTLE FIELD [11-2-64SR]

A friend of mine who has just returned from an engineering tour in the vicinity of Fredericksburg tells me that he saw in the Yankee trenches at Spottsylvania C. H. a dead Yankee taking aim with his musket. He had been there for five months. He was sitting bolt upright, with the top of his head blown off, and his gun still capped was ready to fire. Our ordnance officer, who had been gathering the engines of war dropped on this bloody field, permitted the dead man to retain his musket for the novelty of the spectacle. Owing to the long continued drought this Yankee, in common with many others who had been left unburied, did not petrify, but dried up like jerked beef. His form was almost perfect, except about the intestines, which had disappeared, and there is no telling how long he would have sat there if the ordnance officer had not pulled his musket out of his hand. The corpse at once sunk into a little heap of dust. My friend wrenched off the skull, stuck it on a pole, as a monument to mark the spot where this strange spectacle had so long been visible.

***.

PRIVATE LETTER FROM LEE'S ARMY
AT THE FRONT, October 10, 1864 [11-11-64MAR]

Dear Mother: We are under marching orders, but I may have time to answer your letter. You say that outsiders know more than we at the front. Allow me to state that outsiders know nothing to what we do. We get the Richmond and New York papers every morning. We know by experience the bearing of every move, the influence of every battle. More than all, we know ourselves. Were the spirit and determination of this army known, there would be less croaking. Were the exertions, the talent, the self-denial of our noble President known, there would be less grumbling. He is not the Governor of a State, but the President of the Southern Confederacy; knows the vital parts and how to best defend them with his limited means. If you knew Virginia as well as I do, you would not call Early's campaign a fool's errand. The Valley was open to the enemy. Had they taken Lynchburg, they could have held it and Richmond would have been lost to us forever. In that same Valley the immense wheat crop was just ready to harvest. Early went up there, drove Hunter out, sent the wheat to Lee, and then what was to keep him from entering Maryland and Pennsylvania, driving off their fat beeves, hogs and horses, scaring the Yankees, drawing off a large part of Grant's army, from here, and playing the dickens generally. He couldn't have been spared to go anywhere else, and his campaign was a complete success. Sheridan being heavily reinforced by Grant, compelled him to fall back, and Early, reinforced by Lee, is racing Sheridan back towards Washington. He will run him out of Virginia; probably follow him into Yankeedom, and give the Valley farmers time to put in another wheat crop. Never mention Joe Johnston as a *General* again. If any one say that he *was* careful of the lives of his men, refer them to the useless slaughters at Seven Pines. That he was a good "retreater," refer them to the sacrifice of Government stores on the Potomac in 1862, the wasted ammunition, the deserted cannon at Yorktown, the piles of burning bacon, flour and clothing at Williamsburg, the railroad and tunnel left in perfect order by him for Sherman's use in Georgia. A *good retreater*. Well, I wish he may continue his retreat out of the country. He promised that if Jeff Davis would let him bring Sherman to the Chattahoochee, he, Sherman, should never again water his horse in the Cumberland. Davis warned him that he had no reinforcements to send him, and then, in the face of all the hue and cry of the country, he let Johnston bring Sherman to the Chattahoochee, where he was about to comply with his promise by continuing his retreat and allowing Sherman to water his horse where he pleased. And still Jeff Davis treated him badly. "No more of that an' you love me." As for Mobile, it is safe. I remember that you wrote me "once upon a time," that Charleston had fallen. It is possible that Mobile may fall, but not at all probable.

My fears for the safety of Richmond and Petersburg are all gone. They may be taken, but I doubt it. You speak of their being "surrounded." I will just say that they are twenty-two miles apart, connected by an impregnable line of forts and earthworks, and that it would require more than 3,000,000 men to form around it a very weak line. The idea that this army—the Army of Northern Virginia—will ever "surrender." Well, I'll merely say that I wish you could be in some safe place and see and hear it go into one fight. No matter, Jeff. Davis is the right man in the right place, has done and will do all that man can do, and history will hand him down to posterity as the greatest man of this or any other age. "A prophet is not without honor save in his own country," &c. Take Jeff. Davis abroad. The deep, undying hatred of our enemies towards him is the greatest compliment that can be paid him, and I have often seen in Northern papers comparisons drawn between him and Lincoln that reflected anything but credit to the latter. Jeff. Davis never wrote a "State paper" but that it was copied, quoted from, and held up as a model of modest manliness, truth and statesmanlike ability, all over the world. Without bombast, arrogance, foolish boasting or the sounding of trumpets before him, he has gone on, heedless of the hue and cry of disappointed politicians, the barking of very small dogs, and has done what he thought best, silently and thoroughly, leaving it to future ages to do him justice. You can judge of his shrewdness in minor concerns, when I tell you that his agents bought greenbacks, sent them North, purchased bacon and pork, and run them through the blockade at such a rate that a vessel can't leave New York without first giving bond that the cargo shall not come South. I know this to be true.

Mississippians, some of them, are wroth because Mississippi is not defended better. Well, show me a point within fifty miles of that river where a large army would do any good, and where it couldn't be flanked out by half its numbers, and I'll then give you good reasons for its not being there. No, cavalry is your means of defense, and if they won't fight, Jeff Davis can't help it. Now, let me tell you where lies the trouble. In his speech at Augusta on the 4th ult., President Davis made public the melancholy truth that two-thirds of the Confederate States Army were absent from their posts, besides thousands of skulkers who have never belonged to it. Oh! women of the Sunny South—our mothers, sisters—you for whom we are suffering and fighting; for hunger, starvation, nakedness, will you help us? You, and you alone, can do it. Drive out every deserter and skulker. Don't let them sit by your fireside, eat at your table, while we are baring our breasts to the storm for your sakes. Sister, when you see a deserter or cowardly skulker enter your house, think, oh! think of your older brother, whose bones lie bleaching on the field of battle—think of your husband, who has rallied again and again to the flag of his country, who has done his whole duty, for he has done all he could. Think, Sis, of your poor "Buddy Tom," who sits here, crouching over the fire, (for it is cold here) cold and hungry, but cheerful and resolute, ready to grasp his rifle and "forward" at any moment, think of all this and don't envy him his entertainment. Ask him, "Sis," when the war is over, when peace and independence crown our efforts, and the soldiers come home, where will you hide your coward head. Drive them out, send them here, and if they wont fight, why we'll make them build our breastworks and cut wood. The women can do this. Will they? I have promised that as long as they want me to, I will stand between the women of the South and the accursed Yankees. Whenever they withdraw their sympathy and support, their approving smiles and sympathizing tears, and say by their actions "quit fighting, we are willing to give up," then I'll lay down arms and quit the country.

***.

☆☆☆Valley Campaign Autumn 1864

Throughout the war, the fertile Shenandoah Valley served as the breadbasket of the Confederacy and was now vital to Lee's army. The Federals finally realized this, and from May through October 1864 continuously fought for control of the Valley.

Partly in effort to relieve pressure on Richmond, and partly to continue receiving supplies from the Valley, Lee ordered Jubal Early's command to drive the Federals out of the Valley and perhaps even to threaten Washington, D. C. Grant responded by placing his most trusted subordinate, Gen. Phil Sheridan, in command of the Army of the Shenandoah, with orders to destroy Early's army.

SKETCH OF GENERAL EARLY

Old Jubal Early, or, as Gen. Lee calls him, his "bad old man," has won a name, during his sojourn in the Valley of Virginia, of which he is well worthy. Did you ever see him? If not you have missed one of the greatest curiosities of the war. He is a man of considerable corporosity, with a full face, which has the appearance of the full moon, when it is at its height in redness. He is about six feet high, and of immense structure. His voice sounds like a cracked Chinese fiddle, and comes from his mouth somewhat in the style of a hardshell Baptist, with a long drawl, accomplished with an interpolation of oaths. In the winter his head is encased in a net striped woolen skull cap drawn down over his ears, while his body is contained within the embraces of a Virginia cloth overcoat striking his heels. His legs are covered by leggins of the same material, wrapped from the feet upwards as high as the knee with white tape. He is as brave as he is homely as any man you saw, except Parson Brownlow, who is said to rival his Satanic Majesty in his personal appearance. There are many anecdotes related of old Jubal, but I cannot at present call to memory but one. During the battle in the Wilderness, on one occasion a regiment from South Carolina was ordered to charge the enemy. For some reason they faltered. Old Jubal hearing of it rode up to the head of the column, and in that peculiarity of tone for which he is noted, cried out a the top of his voice, "Boys, you got us into this d—d scrape, and by G—d you shall help us out. Charge!" The regiment were so cut by the remark that they rushed upon the foe, driving him from every position.

*** .

PRIVATE LETTER FROM THE VALLEY,
COMPANY A, THIRD ALABAMA INFANTRY
[BATTLE'S BRIGADE, RODES' DIVISION]
IN LINE OF BATTLE, NEAR STRASBURG, VA., September 20, 1864

Yesterday (the 19th) we fought the enemy near Winchester, and during the early part of the engagement we whipped them badly, driving them at all points, but about two o'clock unfortunately our cavalry, holding our left flank, gave way, and the enemy came pouring down upon us, and our whole line gave way, on some portion of the line in considerable disorder. We fought them as we fell back, and I can assure you I never have seen so many dead Yankees. The fight opened about eleven o'clock, at least our division became engaged about that time. We were marching by the flank, coming from Bunker Hill, when the command was given to "load, front, forward, guide centre." So you can see how quick we became engaged. The Yanks were driving our cavalry and Gordon's old brigade, now commanded by Gen. Evans, but we soon drove them and completely routed them. Had our cavalry held their own the battle would have turned out differently; but as it was, they compelled us to retire before them. Unfortunately for us and the Confederacy, Gen. Rodes was killed when the fight first opened. Could he have been spared, we all believe the day would have ended in our favor. He was killed by a piece of shell, striking him in the back of the head. Our brigade was highly complimented on the field by Gen. Gordon and Gen. Early—in fact, Gen. Early rode up to Gen. Battle and told him that he had saved the day. Gen. Early and Gen. Gordon were conspicuous on the field, especially the latter. He was in the line of battle on horseback all day.

The Yanks no doubt will claim a great victory, but it is the dearest bought victory they have gained during this war. Our regiment lost about seventy-five men in all, mostly wounded.

I am so tired and broken down that you must excuse this letter and its composition. We fought all day yesterday and marched all night.

H. C. M.
MOBILE CADETS

LETTER FROM THE FIELD

NEAR NEW MARKET, VA., October 10, 1864 [10-26-64MAR]

Letters received in the army from home indicate a feeling of despondency about the situation, which I do not think the true condition of affairs warrants. To judge properly of our prospects, and what has been gained and lost, we must look at the campaign of the year as a whole, and not take isolated cases of failure and misfortune as the criterion. The Confederacy covers an immense area, and the capture of a single point, or a number of places, while it entails suffering and want in their particular localities, does not result in the defeat of the cause. General Johnston is reported to have said, when asked about defending Atlanta, that he was fighting not to defend Atlanta, or any given point, but to defeat Sherman's army, and if let alone he was confident of his ability to accomplish that end. So it is with all the armies of the Confederacy. It would of course be more pleasant if we could hold every place, but as this has been found impossible in the history of all wars, we cannot expect to be made exceptions. Looking over the whole field I cannot see grounds for despondency—but rather an inducement for those who are hiding behind details of favoritism and contracts, to swell the ranks and give the final blow to abolition hopes of subjugation, confiscation and emancipation.

The people of Mobile and the interior of Alabama have less to complain about than any section of the Confederacy. They have never felt the war. It is true the enemy have reduced the forts on the lower bay, but they are mere picket posts, and affect the defence of the city proper very little. From this quarter no apprehension need be felt. By the almost superhuman efforts of the dauntless Forrest and his men Mississippi has been almost entirely cleared of the enemy, and in Louisiana, Texas and Arkansas, with the exception of a few small garrisons, these States are in our undisputed control. Gen. Price is knocking loudly at the gates of St. Louis. Tennessee's hills are ringing with the victorious shouts of Confederate troops. Kentucky is quailing before the orator General, and Hood is reported in the rear of the armies of Tennessee, Cumberland and Ohio, and with the aid of our cavalry and people, with a splendid prospect of ruining them. Ten months ago all of these places were at the mercy of Yankee rule. There can be but one conclusion drawn from these facts. *The enemy have not the troops to hold them.*

When Grant was made Lieutenant General he acted upon the idea that Atlanta and Richmond were the vitals of the Confederacy, and with these reduced our cause was hopeless. To accomplish this he concentrated the available force of the United States, and commenced his work. From the most reliable information he crossed the Rapidan river last May with 240,000 [120,000] men, and by the casualties of battle and disease alone lost over 100,000 [60,000]. Of his remained 140,000 nearly one-half have left him. Many by desertion and more by expiration of time of enlistment. It's estimated now that his effective force is about 80,000. To reduce Richmond he must invest it, and to do this properly will require three times the number he is believed to have now. At Atlanta his Lieutenant has been more fortunate, but Georgia has not been subjugated, and if our people are determined to be free and will only give their services for two months to Gen. Hood, Sherman will find that in the capture of Atlanta he has caught a tartar.

There never has been such an opportunity since the war commenced to utterly ruin an army as presents itself in this case. His line of communications is hazarded if not destroyed. He is in a hostile country, surrounded by people who have the strongest reasons for hatred of him and his army, and turn which way he will, he must fight his way for 200 miles before his position can be considered a safe one.

In the Valley of Virginia, although the heretofore victorious Jackson's corps has met with two reverses [Third Winchester and Fisher's Hill], from causes which I do not feel at liberty to state, Sheridan is unable to carry out the programme laid down for him—the capture of Lynchburg, and the destruction of the Central, South-side and the Danville Railroads, and there are already indications that he will abandon "this line," and commence a new campaign, via Orange Courthouse and Gordonsville. He advanced boastingly to Harrisonburg after the battle of Strasburg and Fisher's Hill, but has been obliged to fall back to that place again. From citizens we learn that, despairing of holding the Valley by prowess of arms, Grant has ordered him to destroy all articles of subsistence for man or beast, and well has he obeyed the order of his brutal master. For forty miles the country is a barren waste, and over one hundred families have been forced to go North to get articles of actual want. Houses, barns, grain, forage, horses, cattle and poultry have been swept away. Yet with all this constancy of these noble Virginians has not been shaken. If the discontented and croakers at home really want consolation, let them contrast their condition with that of these unfortunate people. It is with the cruel and contemptible scoundrels who have reduced this and other districts to poverty and want that Abraham Lincoln says we shall return to him. At first he invited us to bonds of fellowship and reconstruction, but he now demands our property and rights, and returning as a conquered people. Supposing for an instant that there are any who are willing to stop the war and attach themselves to the hated Union, can it be possible that they would go back as slaves? No other course is left them. Lincoln has declared that these are the only terms he will accept. Life, liberty and property at the mercy of a vulgar rail splitter. Think of that! As certain as we are subjugated so certain will this be our lot. It is a question for the South to decide. She has it in her power to determine it in her favor. There are the means and material in the country, and with a vigorous and proper effort on the part of the people this war can be ended with our independence before the expiration of this year.

ALABAMA.

At dawn on October 19, Jubal Early's Confederates surprised and routed two Federal corps encamped along Cedar Creek, four miles north of Strasburg.

BATTLE OF STRASBURG [CEDAR CREEK]
CAMP NEAR NEW MARKET, VA., October 20, 1864 [11-4-64CS]

Since I wrote to you last from this camp, many and important movements have been made by this army. My last letter was written just after our little fight of last Sunday [Tom's Brook, Oct. 9]. After that affair, we lay in the front of the enemy offering battle for three days; but as they refused to attack us, we then made an attack upon them [at Hupp's Hill on Oct. 13], as I shall state directly, which proved a perfect success.

I understand that Gen. Early gives General Gordon all the credit for the movement, and his action on the field pronounces him one of our first Generals, both in planning and in executing.

About sunset on Wednesday, the 18th, orders were issued to all the army to be in readiness to move at twilight—soldiers leaving their cups and canteens, and officers their swords, behind, so that the movement might be as secret as possible. Early in the night we were on the way, crossing rivers and winding around the foot of the mountains, along unfrequented roads and by paths, until four o'clock, a. m. Thursday morning brought us in full view of the enemy's picket fires, a short distance in our front. Here we halted until our cavalry [Col. William H. F. Payne's] came up in beautiful order and passed on to the front. At half past four o'clock we waded the river [North Fork of the Shenandoah] and pressed on toward the enemy's camp, which was strongly fortified.

No pickets were encountered until within about two miles of camp, when they fired on our cavalry.

It was a complete surprise. Just at break of day a part of Kershaw's division charged upon their strongest position and took it at the first onset, capturing sixteen pieces of artillery in the first charge. We continued to drive them through their whole camp, some two or three miles in extent. They made three stands to save their camp—at one time behind a stone fence—but were driven from every position they then held into the woods beyond Middletown.

As our troops had become much scattered and mixed up in the pursuit, General Early here ordered a halt, to reorganize and to collect the straggling men.

Their tents were left standing, and in many places their bed clothing just as they had jumped from bed. Their camps were filled with all kinds of plunder from the adjacent country. Chickens, turkeys and cows were tied to stakes, waiting to add delicacies to their tables. All kinds of plunder was strewn upon the field. Coffee and sugar were especially sought for by our men, who felt the need of them after the night's march.

This plunder proved the loss of the day afterward. Although strict orders were issued that no one should stop to plunder, a great many did so, and did not afterwards join their command; so that when our line of battle was afterwards formed on the road running through Middletown perpendicular to the pike, about one-third of the army was in the rear. About half-past three or four o'clock, the enemy, having received reinforcements from Winchester, made a simultaneous attack along our lines, at the same time flanking us with a force perpendicular to the left of our lines. Very soon the left was compelled to give way; and as the enemy continued to advance perpendicular to our line, the whole gave way, and the enemy pressed on and drove us across the river [Cedar Creek]. In the confusion, the enemy's cavalry dashed upon our train just after it had crossed the creek and captured a number of wagons and some eighteen or twenty pieces of artillery. It is useless to disguise the fact that our army was completely stampeded. All attempts to rally the men proved utterly useless, and they crowded down the river like droves of cattle. Five hundred resolute men formed on the hill this side of Cedar creek, could have easily prevented the loss of our train, but unfortunately, each man was pressing to the rear so fast that he had no time to stop.

Upon the whole, this fight proved much more disastrous to the enemy than to us. We lost many guns and wagons in the evening, but not so many as we had captured in the morning. The whole field for miles was covered with the enemy's dead. I suppose, from my own observation, that at least a thousand of the enemy were killed and left on the field, whilst our men I saw very few. I was across the whole field, and saw certainly not over forty dead Confederates. Our loss was small compared to that of the enemy. We captured about two thousand of the enemy in the morning, and I am certain that we did not lose one half so many in the evening.

Our army was organized again at Fisher's Hill and moved back to this point last night.

Many deeds of gallantry were, no doubt, performed on different parts of the field. I will only mention two which have come to my knowledge. Early in the morning, Gen. [John] Pegram, seeing a single Yankee about to carry off a piece of artillery, dashed upon him and cut him down with his sword. Gen. [William] Terry, commanding the First, Second and Third brigades of Jackson's old division, deserves great praise for the several attempts he made to check the enemy advancing on the flank after [C. A.] Evans' brigade had broken on his left. He rallied some two or three hundred men behind a stone fence, some half a mile behind the original line, and fought until the enemy again flanked his left, when he called for a few men from this number and formed a skirmish line in front of their advancing column. This he did a second time, until the enemy drove them back to the field, and the remnant that he had rallied were compelled to retreat.

The disaster was caused by the lack of troops. The enemy's line extending some half a mile to the left of ours, we were easily flanked, and compelled to fall back. It is said that ten thousand fresh troops from Winchester joined the enemy in the interval between the two fights. We brought off all our prisoners and many of the wagons in the morning.

General Ramseur was severely wounded through the body, and fell in the hands of the enemy.

Of officers we lost very few; but this loss falls very heavy upon the division, which had so lately lost their beloved Gen. Rodes.

A. T.

Official casualties at the battle of Cedar Creek were: Federals, 644 killed, 3,420 wounded and 1,591 missing for 5,665; Confederate estimates, 320 killed, 1,540 wounded and 1,050 missing for 2,910.

FROM THE 7TH C. S. CAVALRY REGIMENT

[DEARING'S CAVALRY BRIGADE]

CAMP 7TH C. S. CAVALRY,. A. N. V., NEAR PETERSBURG, October 30, 1864 [11-8-64CS]

As our brigade was engaged in the fight on the [Boydton] Plank Road, October 27th, and suffered severely, especially in officers, I concluded I would make known a few facts of the engagement through the medium of your column.

Col. [V. H.] Taliaferro commanding the regiment was struck by a ball in the right breast, producing a painful though, not serious contused wound. He had aligned his regiment as soon as they had crossed the bridge [across Hatcher's Run] in the face of the enemy, amid a perfect storm of balls, and ordered the advance. I could but admire his gallant bearing and his men as they charged in unbroken line up the steep hill, driving as chaff before the wind the Yankee minions who confronted them. Through the orchard and field they swept and took the house of Mr. Burgess, the lower story being quickly vacated by the enemy, but the upper one was still full. Two heavy lines of Yankees were now advancing and being about to be flanked the order to retire was given. Sullenly and slowly the regiment fell back, contesting every inch of ground until it crossed the bridge.

It was in a short distance of the Burgess house that Col. Taliafero was wounded. Poor little Ben Edwards fell a corpse near by. Here Lieut. Bryant was severely wounded in both legs. Lt. Johnson fell to rise no more; and Capt. Clements, Adj. Haden and Lieut. Welsh, were stricken down wounded beside their comrades. In the charge every man moved forward without disorder, firing as they went.

Dearing's brigade won that day golden opinions from Heth's division of Infantry, who arrived just in time to see the charge made, and I learn Gen. Mahone said he had never seen cavalry fight before as they did.

In the early part of the day Lt. Mathews was ordered up with one of his howitzers and fought it manfully, though four pieces of the enemy's were opposed to us, and the infantry fire was withering. Left with only one man, Billy sponged, rammed, pricked the cartridge and sighted the gun himself; afterwards one of Gen. Hampton's aids served the vent for him, using the thumb of his gauntlets for a thumb-stall.

From the beginning of the engagement to the close every man of the command seemed as if he applied Longfellow's line to himself,

"Be not like dumb driven cattle,
Be a hero in the strife."

The next morning, the regiment followed the enemy, who commenced retrograding in the night, leaving all their dead and wounded, which will outnumber ours ten to one, on the field.

ALEX.

LETTER FROM BONAUD'S BATTALION

CAMP NEAR PETERSBURG, VA., December 23, 1864 [1-8-65CS]

We are now stationed about four miles from the city, snugly ensconced in our winter quarters, log cabins daubed with mud, listening with impunity to the keen and sharp winds of Virginia, as they howl around us unmolested. The weather in this region is very cold; no comparison with the good old States of Georgia or Alabama. Snow storms and heavy sleets are of frequent occurrence, rendering the faithful sentinel very uncomfortable, and the life of the soldier very disagreeable, but all this we must bear with great fortitude and without murmuring, when we take into consideration that our lives, our fortunes, our property, and in fact our all depends upon the acts of our brave soldiers, who have so long confronted the enemy, and I must say in this army successfully, but how could it be otherwise than victorious, when we have the gallant and intrepid Lee for a leader. He stands as a living monument acknowledging no superior—knowing no defeat. His presence is sufficient to inspire new zeal and fresh courage into his army, and when he gives that old and familiar command so well known to soldiers, "Forward, Guide Centre," woe be unto the Blue Coats. Without detracting or plucking a single laurel from the brow of other Generals, would that we had a Lee to command all our armies, Liberty would soon perch upon our Banner and we once more be free, but while I am willing to ascribe all the praise that is due our much beloved commander,

I must not forget the gallant men that compose this mighty army, noble old veterans who have followed him nearly four long years through all the toils, hardships and vicissitudes of the bloodiest war that was ever known to man, without complaint and without flinching, and who now stand to-day as they have ever stood ready to meet and drive back the vandal foe who would pollute and inhabit our soil. Gallant warrior long may you live and be permitted to reap the just reward now in store for you.

Now that the wild and dashing Yankee General [Sherman] has traveled the entire circuit through Georgia, burning and pillaging as they went, characteristic of their race, have arrived safe to the "Happy Land of Canan," all Yankeedom is jubilant, and Father Abraham ready to exclaim— return then good and faithful servant you have accomplished this much with so few men, I will now place you supreme commander of the Grand army of the Potomac. And Grant, oh, shame, to his name! The great Federal Tycoon, who publicly made his boasts "that Richmond, the doomed city, must fall," will be led up to the altar, only to be sacrificed. Then the spring campaign of 1865 will be inaugurated, with Sherman at the head of the Grand army, if largely recruited with new levies, hirelings and Bounty Jumpers, will be hurled against the invincible Lee, only to be defeated; and he, Sherman, then will follow in the same wake of his illustrious predecessor. So wags the world and the Rebellion still lives.

The good people of old Virginia and North Carolina, are preparing a magnificent dinner for General Lee's army, to be given on Christmas day, we anticipate a merry time to see the many thousands of veterans hovering around the festal board enjoying all the luxuries and dainties that heart could wish; and then hear them exclaim with one united voice, *"Dum vivimus vivamus;"* behold them farther pledging themselves, to each other, to stand by and strike for their country's flag until the last armed foe expires, and her independence is acknowledged.

> T. J. KEY,
> CAPTAIN COM'G. CO. "H."
> BONAUD'S BATT.

Captain Thomas J. Key was from Muscogee, Alabama. His company was formerly Co. C, 20th Battalion Alabama Artillery.

LETTER FROM BOHEMIA

IN THE TRENCHES BEFORE PETERSBURG, December 29, 1864 [1-8-65MAR]

Both parties seem to be resting preparatory to the coming campaign—both retain their old position, and though sharpshooting has in a great measure ceased, it is still not safe for a man on either side to show his head above the works. The Yankees seem to have been satisfied with the late expedition of Gen. Warren. Grant fired one hundred guns for the surrender of Savannah, and the Yankees all along the lines appeared to be greatly delighted. They probably believe that Mr. [John] Farnsworth spoke the truth the other day, when, in Congress, he declared that "the rebellion was crushed, and the supremacy of the Union would soon be restored. The defeat of Butler and his armada at Wilmington will probably make them understand that there is life in the land yet, and gold will bounce up again on Wall street.

Among a small class of little men, both in the army and at home, it has become fashionable to decry the people and to talk about the excellence of a strong government. It is enough to say that these men belong to either one or two classes—ignorant and conceited young men, who have been unexpectedly elevated above their level, and are an apt illustration of "the beggar on horseback;" and stay-at-homes, who are frightened out of their wits at the events of the war. Nothing so fully illustrates the intelligence of our people as the choice made by the army in their officers, when every vacancy was filled by election. Look for a moment at the roll of distinguished officers who owed their first promotion to the choice of the men. Compare with these the appointments of the government. Is there any comparison between Rodes, [Lunsford L.] Lomax and Law, who were colonels by election, and the men who now hold that position by virtue of executive appointment or by accidental promotion? No soldier who makes the comparison will ever blush for the choice of his comrades. Congress is considering the propriety of consolidating the old regiments. It ought by all means to be done;

but when two regiments are to be united the men ought to elect their officers anew, and the commissions of the present officers vacated.

It has been cold, wet and snowy weather during the past week. Life in the trenches is by no means, injurious. Our quarters are very much cramped, the ditches are muddy, and the wood issued is base in quality and not sufficient in quantity. The men have generally good brick chimneys and manage to keep warm by great economy of fuel. Clothing is greatly needed, and if the Quartermaster of Alabama could manage to send on a supply, he would win the gratitude of many cold, ragged and shivering men. Socks, pants and jackets are greatly needed. I have seen in the last few days men on guard in the snow and rain with clothing on that was nothing but shreds and patches. It would be useless, however, to send clothing here and expect the men to pay for it. They have not been paid in six months and not one in ten has any money. Alabama might afford to give clothing to the men who for four years have maintained her honor on a hundred battlefields, and have never yet sustained a defeat. The soldiers knew that the State has clothing, but they fear it will be issued to the "Bomb Proofs," the stragglers and the pets at the post throughout the State. Can you not call attention to this matter?

BOHEMIA.

FROM MOSBY'S COMMAND
EDGE HILL, NEAR UPPERVILLE, VA., December 29, 1864 [1-6-65MAR]

The Yankees, after having destroyed everything in the Valley accessible, made a *detour* into (Mosby's Confederacy) Fauquier and Loudoun. This expedition was commanded by the notorious Gen. "Fannie" [George A.] Custer. He crossed the Shenandoah on the 27th of November, with five thousand men. As soon as across the river, they commenced applying the torch to every barn, stable, hay and wheat stack found, likewise driving off the stock of all description. Mosby, of course, was not idle, but watched them closely, and pounded upon them whenever an opportunity presented itself, killing and capturing upwards of seventy of the cruel, inhuman vandals during their stay. The citizens, represent them as being the most inhuman, barbarous, hardened wretches which have ever passed through that country. The wails, tears and entreaties of women (as they saw the last wretches,) were answered only with a savage oath and scornful laugh. Virginia! It is a beautiful name and well appropriated to what was once the fairest spot upon which the sun has ever shone; her sunny skies and balmy climate, where the ocean breeze meets and blends with the invigorating air which sweeps over mountain, and forest, and prairie; her bays, lakes and glorious rivers; her magnificent mountain ranges, sublime forests and widely spread and luxuriant plains, present a realm to be cultivated by man such as few spots on earth can rival, and none surpass. Nature, with a prodigal hand, has lavished upon Virginia a concentration of her choicest gifts. Virginia was once the ornament of the world; but now, since its sacred soil has been polluted by the presence of the hordes of the North, it is but little better than a barren waste; the property stolen, the houses burned, and many of the citizens murdered. Sons of Virginia, our Virginia, thus polluted? Echo answers, no. We will fight them as long as there is a man left; we will feed upon the acorns of the forest and fight them.

Mosby having become so intolerably annoying to the enemy in the Valley, Gen. Sheridan sent daily a large body of cavalry to patrol the Shenandoah, to prevent Mosby from crossing. He at first sent from five hundred to a thousand; but meeting with no resistance for more than a week, reduced his patrol to from one hundred and fifty to two hundred and fifty. Having allowed them to come sufficiently often to become a little careless, Captain W. H. Chapman, (commanding the battalion during Col. Mosby's visit to your city,) on the 17th of December, with one hundred and twenty-five men, crossed the river at Berry's Ferry, and awaited in ambush the usual visit of the Yanks. Soon a body of about a hundred and fifty made their appearance. Our prudent and gallant officers waited until they were as near as they wanted them, when they gave the order to charge. At the first yell of Mosby's boys the Yankees broke in utter confusion. Captain Chapman pursued them several miles, killing and wounding forty, and capturing fifty-one. Among the killed was Captain [William W.] Miles, who was commanding the 14th Pennsylvania.

ALPHA.

☆☆☆1865 Forlorn Hope

By January 1865, little hope was left for the Army of Northern Virginia. This was an army that was not built to sustain siege warfare; its greatest victories were usually the result of swift movement and decisive attack. Capitulation was now only a matter of time. After ten miserable months in the trenches defending Richmond and Petersburg, the grim end would come faster than anyone expected.

LETTER FROM BOHEMIA

IN THE TRENCHES BEFORE PETERSBURG, VA., January 19, 1865 [2-3-65MAR]

The fall of Fort Fisher took everybody by surprise. The *Examiner* makes it the occasion of a bitter article against Gen. Bragg and the President. The army generally look upon the capture only as an end of blockade running, and do not anticipate any great advantage to the enemy from it. Blockade goods went up higher than ever before and Confederate money depreciated in full proportion. It matters but little if the supply of fancy goods could be entirely exhausted. This is no time for the display of European fashions and Yankee ingenuity, and the end of the blockade running, which has had a demoralizing effect on all engaged in the trade, may prove beneficial. We have had no Western mails this year, and are completely in the dark in regard to both Hood and Sherman. The Yankees say Hood, with a few thousand ragged, demoralized and half-starved rebels, is at Tuscaloosa, and that Sherman will soon be at Branchville. But we place little confidence in such reports.

Congress, I fear, has killed the Consolidation Bill. Some measure of the kind is absolutely necessary, but the bill when passed the House was very unpopular with the army, and unless something more equitable can be devised the whole thing had better be indefinitely postponed. We have too many officers and too few soldiers. If nothing better can be done, would it not be well to require all subalterns to carry a gun? Several thousand effective men might, in this way, be added to the army.

Mr. [Henry S.] Foote has been arrested on his way to the United States, and Congress has recommended that he be released. Mr. [William R.] Smith, of Ala., withdraws from the House, on account of a newspaper article that appeared in the *Sentinel*. Did his constituents send him here to attend to their interest, and will he go back to them and say, "I abandon your cause, because somebody in the *Sentinel* newspaper said ugly things about me"? The cause of his withdrawal was not the *Sentinel*; but like hundreds have ever done and will always do in times of peril, he grew faint-hearted, and his object is to propitiate the friendship of the enemy.

No candid and sensible man can for a moment doubt the final triumph of the South. The army well knows that Grant's ranks are filled with negroes and European paupers. But 18,000 votes were given in the whole of the army around Petersburg and Richmond for President. Every legal vote was polled. This shows the proportion of Americans that we have to contend with. The army of the Potomac, with which General Grant began the campaign last May, has disappeared. The army of Northern Virginia is as strong, as well officered, as formidable and as determined on victory as they were on the banks of the Rapidan. However unpropitious things may appear in the West, there is no reason for despondency. January, February and March have been our *unlucky* months, while the opening spring has ever witnessed success and glorious victory. This year will not prove an exception.

The past ten days have been clear and cold, but the men in the trenches have not suffered any. They all have good brick chimneys and are very well supplied with wood and coal. No one is sick. But two men of my company have been sent to the hospital since the 15th of November, and not more than eight or ten from the regiment. No one has died from disease. I have not heard of a single case of pneumonia, usually so fatal to troops during the winter months.

The enemy are perfectly quiet. Sharpshooting and picket firing has ceased in our immediate front, though still kept up on our left, near the Appomattox. Gracie's brigade are the only Alabamians in the trenches. The others are in winter quarters. We have never been relieved since the 17th of last June. I send you this by a furloughed soldier and hope it will reach you.

BOHEMIA.

LETTER FROM BOHEMIA
PETERSBURG, VA., January 12, 1865 [2-8-65MAR]

A flag of truce to pass some ladies through the lines gave me a good opportunity of seeing the Yankee works from the Baxter Road, round towards the Appomattox; being the front of the right [left] of our lines, so long held by [Robert] Hoke's and [Bushrod] Johnson's divisions. They have apparently three lines, the picket line, main line, and back this still other breastworks, in some places completed, and in others seemingly in a half finished condition. On almost every elevation they have strong batteries, with from two to six guns mounted. These batteries all protected by abattis, deep ditches and every other contrivance to defeat an assault. The mortar batteries, being generally under a hill, cannot be seen. The amount of work done by them is surprising great, and everything seems to have been done without the view of taking Petersburg, but to prevent the "Johnny Rebs" from storming and carrying the lines of the besiegers. The [military] railroad from City Point passes about half a mile in rear of their last line, and we can see the trains passing, at the place it crosses the Baxter Road, about three-quarters of a mile distant. No siege in history can compare with this in the amount of labor expended, and nowhere has labor been so unprofitable. In spite of trenches and parallels, forts and batteries, and in spite of their grand railroad, the enemy are no nearer Petersburg than they were the 17th of June. In fact, on the Baxter Road they occupy the identical position from which the 43rd Alabama Regiment drove them on that memorable night, and which they reoccupied after our troops withdrew.

Everything is perfectly quiet all along the lines. The Dutch Gap Canal has so far failed. The *bulkhead* was not blown out, and if completed it must now be done *under the fire* of our guns, by manual labor. In this as in everything else, save insulting women and Ministers of the Gospel, Beast Butler has proven a miserable failure.

On the 9th and 10th it rained a perfect flood. Ditches were filled with water, breastworks gave way, "bomb proofs" tumbled in, and in one or two instances buried the inmates beneath the timber and mud. Three men, I have been told, were killed in Johnson's division in this way. One of them belonged to the 59th Alabama regiment, one was a North and the other a South Carolinian.

The heavy rains have effectually stopped all military movements. The campaign has doubtless ended in this department.

Everybody is interested in the new consolidation bill, and the army generally are in favor of it. The men, however, cannot see how it is that the troops who elected Lomax, Rodes, Battle, [H. D.] Clayton, Law and Gordon, are no longer qualified to choose their own officers. But they care very little about the matter, and would not defeat the bill for that cause. It will probably be passed in some shape before this reaches you.

BOHEMIA.

LETTER FROM BOHEMIA
TRENCHES BEFORE PETERSBURG, VA., January 25, 1865 [2-15-65MAR]

It is almost impossible to obtain any information of affairs that are transpiring almost in our immediate neighborhood. On Sunday night [22nd] heavy firing was heard on the lines, apparently near Howlett's House, on the James. Up to this date no one knows the cause. Some say that Pickett's division carried a part of the enemy's lines; others that Ft. Harrison has been retaken; others that it was a gunboat fight, and that the heavy explosion which shook houses in Petersburg was caused by the accidental explosion of a tender to one of the iron-clads. The town is full of rumors. In the trenches it is worse. Here every idle story finds some credulous listener, and nothing is too absurd to find advocates, not only among the privates, but the officers of the army. This want of information, these hundred flying rumors, make letter-writing difficult. No one can tell what is true, what is *contraband of war*, and what is mere exaggeration. I make it a rule only to state what I know to be facts, and generally only

those that come under my own observation, and if on this account my letters contain less of interest than those of my brother scribblers, I cannot help it. [Francis P.] Blair has returned to Richmond. Why, no one can tell. It is whispered about that he is authorized to propose an armistice for 90 days. Strange to say, many believe this true. It must be that
"The wish, is father to the thought;"
for the Yankee Government has not given the slightest intimation of anything of the kind. Our Government is showing too much anxiety about peace, and is thereby in danger of encouraging the war party of the North. It would be well for Mr. Davis to remember the sound advice given by Old John Allen, of Holland House notoriety, to a young diplomatist:
"Don't ever appear anxious about any point, either in arguing to convince those you are treating with , or in trying to obtain a concession from them. It often happens that your indifference will gain a much readier access to their minds. Earnestness and anxiety are necessary for one addressing a public meeting; *not so for a negotiator.*" There is good sense in this. Peace is certainly the object for which we are fighting and the whole people pray for it; but better continual war than "a peace of Utrecht," which "everybody was glad of, but nobody proud of." A few days will probably develop old Blair's purpose—until then we must wait patiently.

Unusual quiet has prevailed along the lines south of the Appomattox during the past two weeks. Sharpshooting has almost ceased. Yesterday three or four mortar shells were thrown at Wise's brigade, and a few at the "Pocahontas" part of Petersburg. The Yankees seem to have brought a new kind of shell into use, at least it is *new* to me—I am not an expert in ordnance matters. The shells thrown yesterday exploded twice with an interval of several seconds between the explosions. The men call them "double-barrels." No damage whatever was done by them.

Congress has passed the Consolidation Bill, and every good soldier will approve of its being put immediately in force. Some of its provisions are very objectionable, but any change of the present system must be an improvement. Some few officers will lose their commissions, but they will be no loss. No really valuable officer will be dropped.

After several days of terrible weather, we again have bright sunshine, but it is still very cold. Ice hangs on the sides of the ditches, the ground is frozen hard, and a keen north wind is blowing. Any kind of weather is preferable to rain. Against snow and sleet, against the bitterest cold, the soldier can protect himself, but against slow, steady, *soaking* rain, that keeps his blanket wet and puts out his fire, and renders his picket post a mud puddle, he is powerless, and consequently in a bad humor with everybody, and ready to quarrel on a straw.
BOHEMIA.

LETTER FROM BOHEMIA
PETERSBURG, VA., February 19, 1865 [3-10-65MAR]
I avail myself of the kindness of Lieut. [John H.] Snyder, who will start for Mobile to-day, to write you a brief letter.

Richmond and Petersburg have ceased to be the points of interest and all eyes are now turned anxiously toward the South, and are watching with deep anxiety the progress of Gen. Sherman. No one, unless it be those in authority, has any idea of his destination, of his strength, or of the force opposed to him; but all hope that Gen. Lee will throw every obstacle in his way, and that Sherman's march will result as Cornwallis' did seventy-five years ago. In the meantime this army is calmly waiting the issue; confident in their own resources, and trusting to the skill of their great chieftain, the soldiers look hopefully to the future. Never has the Army of Northern Virginia been in better fighting trim, and never was the spirit of the troops more resolute and determined. Before the departure of the Commissioners, and while Blair was in Richmond, there was much dissatisfaction in the ranks; but the treatment of Messrs. [Alexander H.] Stephens, [John A.] Campbell and [Robert M. T.] Hunter, and the express declaration of Lincoln that we must submit to Yankee rule, caused a feeling of defiance to spring up, not only in the army but among the whole people of Virginia, and now no one dreams of compromise, concession or peace, but all are determined to fight as even this army never fought before.

There is reason to believe that the Peace Commission has had a contrary effect on Gen. Grant's army. Deserters are frequent, and all of these say that the Army of the Potomac is badly demoralized. One man, an orderly sergeant, came to our regiment last night. He says that his company is the largest in his regiment, and that there are only 21 men for duty; that Grant's army is weaker than it has ever been, and the men are running away by hundreds, and that no recruits are coming in; that his is the 9th corps, and that it is not much larger than a good division. I am inclined from my own careful observation to believe his statements, which certainly corroborate the views of Mr. [Henry R.] Pollard in the *Examiner* of week before last.

Congress will probably pass a law for putting negroes in the field. There are hundreds in our army in favor of it. But is it not incipient abolitionism? Is it not giving up one of the very principles for which we contend? Will it not be humiliating for us, the white men of the South, to admit that we owe our freedom to negro slaves? If every able-bodied man in the South would do his duty, if the cowards and skulkers in the rear could be brought to the front, there would be no necessity for arming the negro. If, however, the experiment is to be tried, let us give it a fair test, and let the "Corps d'Afrique" be put in the field as quickly as possible.

BOHEMIA.

On March 25, Gen. John B. Gordon led a forlorn hope in breaking the Federal stranglehold on Petersburg. The attack at Fort Stedman was the final offensive operation of the Army of Northern Virginia and ended in disaster with nearly 4,000 Confederates taken prisoner.

PRIVATE LETTER FROM THE TRENCHES, FORTY-FIFTH GEORGIA INFANTRY
[THOMAS' BRIGADE, WILCOX'S DIVISION]
NEAR PETERSBURG, VA., March 28, 1865 [4-15-65CS]

Dear Captain: Before this letter reaches you, you will no doubt have heard of the bloody ordeal your old regiment passed through on the 25th inst. And knowing that you feel a deep interest in our welfare, I will give you a short history of the part taken by the 45th Georgia on that day.

On the evening of the 24th, we received orders to be ready to move at a moment's warning. At 10 o'clock p. m., Lane's and Thomas' Brigades were on the [Jerusalem] plank road leading towards the leadworks. We arrived in rear of Gordon's command about 2 o'clock that night. We were then placed in a ravine, and remained there as reserve until Gordon captured the works, and returned to his old lines. I don't think this move paid, as our loss was very heavy in falling back, which was about 9 o'clock a. m. We then received orders to come back to our quarters, and arrived there about 10 o'clock. The men had hardly taken off their accoutrements, before we were ordered to fall in, and march to the right where the enemy were making some demonstrations. We marched half a mile, halted, and were ordered back to camps; and arrived just in time to get on our housetops and witness a fight that was going on in our immediate front. Col. [Thomas J.] Simmons who had stopped a moment to see Gen. Thomas, came dashing up and ordered us to fall in immediately.

We were soon in line and marching at a doublequick to join in the conflict. The 45th and 49th Georgia regiments being nearer the works than the 35th and 14th, were the first upon the field. The enemy [the soldiers of Maj. Gen. H. G. Wright's Sixth Corps] had captured the works occupied by our pickets, in a ravine about three quarters of a mile in advance of our main works. We were ordered by Gen. Lane to take them with our two regiments, Col. Simmons commanding the two. Lt. Col. [Charles A.] Conn commanding the 45th. We found our line of battle on the brow of a hill, about two hundred and fifty yards from our rifle pits, now occupied by the enemy. The skirmishers were soon sent forward and we commenced the advance. As we passed the crest of the hill, we saw the hateful foe on forbidden ground. With a yell from one end of our line to the other that made the "skies ring," we were up and at them like a "thousand bricks." Our line was good, our yell frightful, our fire murderous, and our victory complete. The enemy in confusion fled, falling at every step. The gallant Lt. Col. Conn fell here, his last words were, "Forward boys, forward." On our extreme left, far in advance of our lines, there was a regiment of Yankees about two hundred and fifty in number, doing some execution for us, and eight of our sharpshooters charged and drove them back to their old line.

Col. Simmons, Lt. Colonel Conn, and Major [Aurelius W.] Gibson, acted most gallantly. I am unable to state the loss of the enemy, but their loss in killed and wounded was far greater than ours. Thus far all things worked well; but now comes the unpleasant part of the story. In going into a fight, we should always have one way to go in, and two to come out—but this was not our fortune. We had none to go in and none to come out. General Thomas and Col. Simmons were both opposed to the move, but the order was given, and their duty was to obey.

After we held the lines two hours or more, the army formed a line of battle, consisting of four brigades and two regiments of another. The hill was blue as far as we could see, both to the right and left. Our two regiments, numbering in all about four hundred guns, fought them until they were within fifty yards of our front or works, they had nearly surrounded us, they having five thousand, we four hundred! Our ammunition was about this time completely expended, and Col. Simmons gave us orders to fall back. We had a hill of two hundred and fifty yards to run up, the enemy firing into us both right and left. We knew if we escaped it would be a miracle, but we thought we would try it. Some did not hear the command, and remained in the pit and gave the Yankees the benefit of the butts of their guns. We fell back re-formed in our main works—having ninety-eight all told in the 45th Ga., and about one hundred in the 49th. Those that remained behind were captured. Our gallant brigade commander, was struck by a spent ball, but did not leave the field. On Sunday and Sunday night we remained quiet.

On Monday morning [March 27] Lane's brigade, with sharpshooters of Thomas' and Scales' brigades, attacked the enemy's picket line, drove them in, and we established our lines on the hill in our front, where it should have been placed at first. We sent in a flag of truce then to recover the bodies of our men, which was granted. Major [Arthur] McClellan, who is on Gen. [H. G.] Wright's staff of the U. S. A., was bearer of the flag of truce. He said he never saw men fight as we did on Saturday. He gave us the credit of being the most gallant, if not the most desperate fighters he ever saw, or rather that ever fought his command.

When we were ordered to the right, Capt. [Warren] Bush was on picket from our regiment with thirty-seven men, and the Yankees charged the pickets of our entire brigade, and were repulsed three different times by our picket force alone. The fourth charge was with two lines of battle, and our men were compelled to surrender. I send you a list of the casualties in our regiment. Ensign [Nathan] Bodie has been dropped from the roll, and is now waiting for the report to carry to Georgia. I have written in great haste, he is waiting only on me.

Yours truly,   Jno. Hardeman

John T. Hardeman was mustered in as Junior Second Lieutenant in the 45th Georgia on March 4, 1862 and elected Captain on August 23, 1862. Five days after writing the above letter, April 2, 1865, Hardeman was wounded in the thumb during the last battle for Petersburg and was admitted to Stuart Hospital at Richmond for amputation. Captain Hardeman returned to duty the same day in time for the final campaign of the war.

☆ ☆ ☆ Surrender at Appomattox

The overwhelmed Army of Northern Virginia finally abandoned the Petersburg and Richmond defences on the evening of April 2, and attempted to rally farther west, possibly to link up with other Confederate armies and fight on.

Bled white at the battles of Five Forks and Saylor's Creek and nearly surrounded on April 8, Lee realized further resistance was futile and requested a meeting with Grant to discuss a cessation of hostilities. The following day, April 9, the two generals met at Appomattox Court House and the Army of Northern Virginia ceased to be and took its place in history. Upon returning to his survivors, Lee said: "I have done for you all that it was in my power to do. You have done all your duty. Leave the result to God. Go to your homes and resume your occupations. Obey the laws and become as good citizens as you were soldiers."

GENERAL LEE'S ARMY PAROLED AND DISBANDED
[*Richmond Whig*, April 25, 1865]

The paroling of the Army of Northern Virginia at Appomattox Court House, was concluded on Friday the 14th inst. The men, as they were paroled left in squads, except Anderson's Georgia Brigade, which went away in a body. General Grant has been officially informed that the army has been paroled and disbanded and the property turned over to the United States. According to the official report, Gen. Lee surrendered 26,115 men, 159 pieces of cannon, 71 stand of colors and 15,918 stand of small arms. The number of wagons, caissons, etc., is estimated at 1,100, and of horses and mules at 4,000.